Privatization in Rural Eastern Europe

STUDIES OF COMMUNISM IN TRANSITION
General Editor: Ronald J. Hill
*Professor of Comparative Government
and Fellow of Trinity College
Dublin, Ireland*

Studies of Communism in Transition is an important series which applies academic analysis and clarity of thought to the recent traumatic events in Eastern and Central Europe. As many of the preconceptions of the past half century are cast aside, newly independent and autonomous sovereign states are being forced to address long-term, organic problems which had been suppressed by, or appeased within, the Communist system of rule.

The series is edited under the sponsorship of Lorton House, an independent charitable association which exists to promote the academic study of communism and related concepts.

Privatization in Rural Eastern Europe

The Process of Restitution and Restructuring

Edited by

David Turnock

Reader in Geography, University of Leicester, UK

STUDIES OF COMMUNISM IN TRANSITION

Edward Elgar
Cheltenham, UK • Northampton, MA, USA

© David Turnock 1998

All rights reserved. No part of this publication may be reproduced, stored in a retrieval system or transmitted in any form or by any means, electronic, mechanical or photocopying, recording, or otherwise without the prior permission of the publisher.

Published by
Edward Elgar Publishing Limited
8 Lansdown Place
Cheltenham
Glos GL50 2HU
UK

Edward Elgar Publishing, Inc.
6 Market Street
Northampton
Massachusetts 01060
USA

A catalogue record for this book
is available from the British Library

Library of Congress Cataloguing in Publication Data

Privatization in rural Eastern Europe: the process of restitution and
    restructuring / edited by David Turnock.
        (Studies of communism in transition series)
        Includes bibliographical references.
        1. Land reform—Europe, Eastern—Case studies. 2. Land reform—
    Europe, Central—Case studies. 3. Agriculture—Economic aspects—
    Europe, Eastern—Case studies. 4. Agriculture—Economic aspects—
    Europe, Central—Case studies. 5. Privatization—Europe, Eastern—
    Case studies. 6. Privatization—Europe, Central—Case studies.
    I. Turnock, David. II. Series: Studies of communism in transition.
    HD1333.E852P75 1998
    338.1'847—dc21   97–35281
                                                                      CIP

ISBN 1 85898 203 0

Electronic typesetting by Lorton Hall
Printed and bound in Great Britain by
Biddles Ltd, Guildford and King's Lynn

Contents

List of Figures	vii
List of Tables	ix
List of Abbreviations	xiii
List of Contributors	xv
Preface	xvii

1	Introduction David Turnock	1
2	Albania Derek Hall	49
3	Bulgaria Frank W. Carter	69
4	Czech Republic Ivan Bičík and Antonin Gőtz	93
5	East Germany Olivia Wilson	120
6	Hungary Zsuzsanna Varga	145
7	Poland Bronisław Górz and Włodzimierz Kurek	169
8	Romania David Turnock	200
9	Slovakia Vladimír Drgoňa, Alena Dubcová and Hilda Kramáreková	251
10	Slovenia Igor Vrišer	274

11 Aspects of Farm Diversification   301
    *Floarea Bordanc, Stanisław Grykień, Nicolae Muică and
    David Turnock*

12 Conclusion   356
    David Turnock

Index   401

Figures

1.1	States of Eastern Europe	2
1.2	Resources of Communist Eastern Europe	4
1.3	Rural population in the mountains of Eastern Europe	29
4.1	Czech Republic: aspects of privatization of agriculture, 1994	96
4.2	Czech Republic: aspects of agricultural production, 1994	100
4.3	Czech Republic: aspects of agricultural land and employment	106
5.1	East Germany: the New *Länder* of reunified Germany	121
5.2	East Germany: reprivatization of rural land	127
5.3	East Germany: agricultural land leased from the *Treuhandanstalt*	129
5.4	East Germany: farm businesses	132
5.5	East Germany: conceptual model of emerging rural areas	139
6.1	Hungary: regional assistance	161
7.1	Poland: state sector share of agricultural land, 1994	170
7.2	Poland: privatization of state enterprises	174
7.3	Poland: private sector employment, 1993	176
7.4	Poland: rural unemployment, 1994	179
7.5	Poland: investment in agriculture, 1992	184
7.6	Poland: rural dwellings with piped water, 1992	186
7.7	Poland: rural telephones	187
7.8	Poland: shops in rural areas	188
7.9	Poland: fallow and temporary setaside	192

7.10	Poland: decline in cereal yields between 1988–1990 and 1992–1994	194
7.11	Poland: decline in cattle, 1992–1994	195
8.1	Romania: the Carpathians and Agency/Commission for Mountainous Regions	234
8.2	Romania: landslides in Vrancea	238
8.3	Romania: natural potential of the environment in the Pătârlagele area of the Buzău Subcarpathians	240
8.4	Romania: economic and settlement planning for Bihor county	242
9.1	Slovakia: aspects of agriculture, 1994	252
9.2	Slovakia: cooperatives and rural settlement in the Nitra area	270
10.1	Slovenia: systems of agricultural land use, 1985	289
10.2	Slovenia: agricultural population, 1991	293
10.3	Slovenia: types of farm by income source in the villages of Plužna and Polje pri Vodicah	294
11.1	Ecofarms in Poland	304
11.2	Aspects of organic farming in Poland	306
11.3	Markets for ecofarms in Poland	308
11.4	Fruit-growing areas of Romania	323
11.5	The distilling process for the production of plum brandy	327
11.6	Rural tourism in the Romanian Carpathians	336

Tables

1.1	The land of Eastern Europe	3
1.2	Agricultural population of Eastern Europe, 1985–1994	5
1.3	Socialist agriculture in Eastern Europe, 1950–1980	12
1.4	Agricultural output, employment and investment in Eastern Europe, 1960–1980	13
1.5	Rural population of Eastern Europe, 1900–1990	28
2.1	Albania: selected agricultural production and livestock numbers, 1990–1994	53
3.1	Bulgaria: regional distribution of land restitution applications, August 1992	71
3.2	Bulgaria: urban and rural population, 1946–1994	73
3.3	Bulgaria: population by regions, 1992	73
3.4	Bulgaria: agricultural production, 1991–1994	75
3.5	Bulgaria: livestock production, 1992–1995	77
3.6	Bulgaria: agricultural production by region, 1994	80
3.7	Bulgaria: livestock in the Varna region, 1990–1995	82
3.8	Bulgaria: grape production, 1991–1994	83
4.1	Czech Republic: agricultural holdings, January 1990	94
4.2	Czech Republic: use of agricultural land, September 1995	99
4.3	Czech Republic: potential fertility and production intensity	104
4.4	Czech Republic: legally protected areas and protected landscape areas	112
7.1	Poland: private sector workers, 1989–1994	175

7.2	Poland: private sector employment by economic branches, 1989–1994	175
7.3	Poland: macroregions with the highest levels of hidden unemployment in agriculture	180
7.4	Poland: investment in agriculture, 1985–1992	183
7.5	Poland: rural infrastructure, 1980–1994	185
7.6	Poland: agricultural production, 1989–1994	191
8.1	Romania: role of the private sector in agriculture, 1990–1995	206
8.2	Romania: individual farms and associations, 1994–2000	207
8.3	Romania: analysis of households, 1992	208
8.4	Romania: land-use change, 1989–1994	211
8.5	Romania: agricultural production by regions, 1989–1992	212
8.6	Romania: agricultural activity, 1985–1994	214
8.7	Romania: market prices for agricultural produce in county centres	224
9.1	Slovakia: value of agricultural land, 1994	259
9.2	Slovakia: regional distribution of agricultural enterprises, 1994	260
9.3	Slovakia: organizational structure of agriculture, 1992–1994	261
9.4	Slovakia: profitability of agricultural enterprises, 1993–1994	262
9.5	Slovakia: agricultural production, 1991–1994	263
9.6	Slovakia: land use, 1950–1993	264
9.7	Slovakia: agricultural production in the Nitra district, 1991–1994	265
10.1	Slovenia: number and types of farms by source of income, 1960–1991	277
10.2	Slovenia: farm structure, 1902–1991	278

List of Tables xi

10.3	Slovenia: the role of private farms in crop production, 1955–1996	281
10.4	Slovenia: the role of private farms in pastoral farming, 1955–1997	282
10.5	Slovenia: privatization programme	283
10.6	Slovenia: categories of land and land ownership, 1950–1996	284
10.7	Slovenia: production by state social enterprises, 1960–1996	287
11.1	Typology of tourist villages in Romania	337
11.2	Households joining the agrotourism project in Romania	344
12.1	Percentage change in agricultural production in Eastern Europe, at constant prices, 1990–1996	369
12.2	Cereal production and trade in Eastern Europe, 1980–1993	370
12.3	Yield and production of major crops in Eastern Europe, 1961–1993	372
12.4	Agricultural population, 1985–1994	377
12.5	Distribution of settlements in Croatia, 1948–1991	383
12.6	Net trade in agricultural products in Eastern Europe, 1988–1994	390

Abbreviations

AIC	agricultural-industrial complex
bn	billion
CAP	Common Agricultural Policy
cm	centimetre(s)
CPEs	centrally planned economies
cu.m	cubic metres
CzK	Czech crown
DM	Deutsche Mark
EBRD	European Bank for Reconstruction and Development
ECU	European Currency Unit
EU	European Union
FAO	Food and Agriculture Organization
FCS	Former Czechoslovakia
FFRY	Former Federative Republic of Yugoslavia
FGDR	Former German Democratic Republic
FSU	Former Soviet Union
Ft	forint
g	gram(s)
ha	hectare(s)
hl	hectolitre(s)
IFOAM	International Federation of Organic Agricultural Movements
IMF	International Monetary Fund
kg	kilogram(s)
km	kilometre(s)
kWh	kilowatt hour(s)
m	metre(s)
m.	million
mg	milligram(s)
mm	millimetre(s)
n.a.	not available
NGO	non-governmental organization

NZl	new zloty
OECD	Organization for Economic Cooperation and Development
PHARE	Pologne–Hongrie: Assistance à la Réconstruction Économique
qu	quintal
SkK	Slovak crown
SME	small and medium-sized enterprise
SOE	state-owned enterprise
sq.km	square kilometre(s)
sq.m	square metre(s)
t	tonne(s)
th.	thousand
UN	United Nations

Contributors

Dr Ivan Bičík, Department of Social Geography and Regional Development, Faculty of Science, Charles University, Albertov 6, 128 43 Prague, CZECH REPUBLIC.
bicik@prfdec.natur.cuni.cz

Dr Floarea Bordanc, Institute of Agrarian Economy, Romanian Academy, Calea 13 Septembrie 13, CP1-7789 Sec V, Bucharest, ROMANIA.

Dr Frank W. Carter, School of Slavonic and East European Studies, University of London, Senate House, Malet Street, London WC1E 7HU, UK.
f.carter@ssees.ac.uk

Professor Vladimír Drgoňa, Katedra geografie, Fakulta prírodných vied, Univerzita Konštantína Filozofa. Tr.A. Hlinku 1, 949 74 Nitra, SLOVAKIA.
geograph@unitra.sk

Dr Alena Dubcová, Katedra geografie, Fakulta prírodných vied, Univerzita Konštantína Filozofa. Tr.A. Hlinku 1, 949 74 Nitra, SLOVAKIA.
geograph@unitra.sk

Professor Bronisław Górz, Wyzsza Szkola Pedagogiczna, Instytut Geografii, ul. Podchorazych 2, 30-084 Kraków, POLAND.

Dr Antonín Götz, Department of Social Geography and Regional Development, Faculty of Science, Charles University, Albertov 6, 128 43 Prague, CZECH REPUBLIC.
bicik@prfdec.natur.cuni.cz

Stanisław Grykień, Instytut Geograficzny, Uniwersytet Wrocławski, Plac Uniwersytecki 1, 50-137 Wrocław, POLAND.
grykien@geogr.uni.wroc.pl

Dr Derek Hall, Leisure and Tourism Department, Scottish Agricultural College, Auchincruive, Ayr KA6 5HW, UK.
D.Hall@au.sac.ac.uk

Dr Hilda Kramáreková, Katedra geografie, Fakulta prírodných vied, Univerzita Konšantína Filozofa, Tr.A. Hlinku 1, 949 74 Nitra, SLOVAKIA.
geograph@unitra.sk

Dr Włodzimierz Kurek, Instytut Geografii, Uniwersytet Jagiellonski, 31-44 Kraków, Ul. Grodzka 64, POLAND.

Dr Nicolae Muică, Institut de Geografie, Str Dimitrie Racovita 12, 70307 Bucharest 20, ROMANIA. Also Facultatea de Geografie, Universitatea, Str Cuza Vodă 31, 1100 Craiova, ROMANIA.

Dr David Turnock, Geography Department, University of Leicester, Leicester LE1 7RH, UK.
dt8@le.ac.uk

Dr Zsuzsanna Varga, Budapest University of Economic Sciences, Department of Economic History, 8 Fővám tér, Budapest 1093, HUNGARY. Also Kossuth Lajos University, Institute for History, 1 Egyetem tér, Debrecen 4010, HUNGARY.
zsuzsanna.varga@econhist.bke.hu

Professor Igor Vrišer, Univerza v Ljubljani, Oddelek za geografijo, Filozofska fakulteta, Aškerčeva 2, 61000 Ljubljana, SLOVENIA.

Dr Olivia Wilson, Lecturer in Geography, De Montfort University, 37 Lansdowne Road, Bedford MK40 2BZ, UK.
ojwilson@helios.dmu.ac.uk

Preface

This project has grown out of the Economic and Social Research Council's 'East-West Programme' and the development of a research cluster dealing with rural matters. It has been possible to extend collaboration with specialists in Britain and in the various East European countries to the point where a well-rounded review could be made of the general issues of rural change and the specific nature of these problems in the different countries. These matters have not been widely debated in the Western literature, yet they are very important for the region where a considerable proportion of the population is still living in the countryside and where the provisions for land restitution have comprised a major component of the privatization programme. Agriculture is critical for the wellbeing of the rural population, since the secondary and tertiary sectors are relatively poorly developed and levels of commuting to urban-based employment are low by Western standards. Therefore, while acting in accord with the claims of 'natural justice', governments must be mindful of the need to build an efficient agricultural sector that can generate employment and compete on international markets. The maintenance of raw material deliveries to the food-processing industry is another important issue which has relevance for jobs in manufacturing, the supply of urban food markets and an acceptable trade balance. But the problems are not only those of today, for all experts are agreed that East European agriculture will require fewer workers in future and therefore if unemployment is to be kept under control more non-agricultural work will be needed to compensate for jobs lost through the inevitable consolidation of farm businesses. Furthermore, if massive rural-urban migration is to be prevented, many of these new jobs must be provided in the countryside, particularly in key villages and small market centres.

I am grateful for all the encouragement received from Edward Elgar and from colleagues on the East-West Programme who helped in gaining a place for this work in the Studies of Communism in

Transition series. I am also much obliged for the cooperation of authors in both Britain and Eastern Europe who accepted a demanding schedule and coped with a barrage of editorial queries. Ruth Pollington of the University of Leicester Geography Department produced most of the maps. There are, however, two principal regrets. First, it proved impossible to attract contributions from the Yugoslav successor states, with the exception of Slovenia. To an extent this was due to the problems of civil war, economic sanctions and blockade, which affected all these countries for much of the time the book was under preparation. It may be suggested that the weight of these problems detracted from the significant rural reform that this book is concerned with. Nevertheless, the gaps are unfortunate, even though the available English language literature has been used as fully as possible in the general chapters. Second, it has not been possible to deal fully with the privatization of all aspects of the rural scene. The authors have understandably placed agriculture at the centre of their work and although each contribution does, in its own way, look into such matters as food processing, tourism and light industry, as well as transport and other rural services, these topics are not dealt with consistently. However, the introductory and concluding chapters attempt to place agriculture in context, and a penultimate chapter has been drafted to consider several important facets of rural diversification.

Finally, I wish to acknowledge the skilful help of the editorial staff at Edward Elgar in turning a complex manuscript into a handsome book. The production also benefited enormously from the assistance of Professor Ronald Hill and Ethna Frayne, particularly with regard to the production of camera-ready copy complete with diacritical markings.

David Turnock
Leicester, January 1998

1. Introduction

David Turnock

This book deals with the countries recognized in 1989 as the eight communist states of Eastern Europe. This area may be divided into a northern (Central European) group comprising Czechoslovakia, Eastern Germany (the German Democratic Republic), Hungary and Poland; and a southern (Balkan) group consisting of Albania, Bulgaria, Romania and Yugoslavia. However, Romania would argue for inclusion in Central Europe and following the break-up of Yugoslavia in 1991, Croatia and Slovenia would make a similar claim. But, leaving this problem aside, the reality is that today there are thirteen states in the region, allowing for Czechoslovakia's demise in 1993 while retaining an interest in East Germany even though it is now part of a unified German state (Figure 1.1). The individual country studies will of course follow the present political arrangements, but this introductory chapter, which discusses the situation prior to the present phase of economic transition, will work primarily in terms of the earlier structure of eight states with the abbreviations FCS, FGDR and FFRY to refer to the former Czechoslovakia, former German Democratic Republic and former Federative Republic of Yugoslavia.

There are substantial potentials for agriculture throughout the region, but the situation varies from country to country as the land-use profile indicates (Table 1.1). The continental extremes of climate and the fluctuations from year to year impose constraints which can be partially alleviated by irrigation, while soil fertility varies between the chernozems of the southern steppelands and the podzolized soils of the northern plain where glacial activity has resulted in much local variation (Dawson 1982). Fertilizers can improve yields, but intensification requires heavy investment. The mountainous regions have considerable value, especially in the south, because the scope for summer grazing

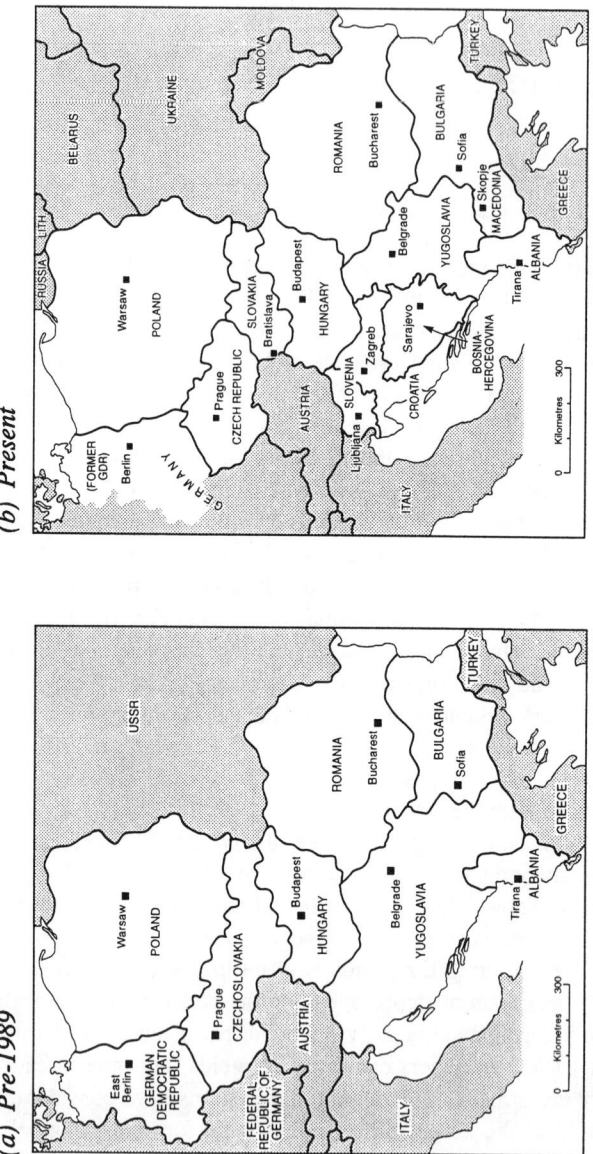

Source: D. Turnock, *Eastern Europe: Notes on the Geography of Transition*, Leicester: University of Leicester Geography Department, 1997, p.5.

Figure 1.1 States of Eastern Europe

Table 1.1 The land of Eastern Europe

Country	Area distributed according to altitudinal zones (th.ha)						Land use (th.ha)				
	Below 200	200-499m	500-999m	1,000-1,499m	1,500-1,999m	2,000 plus	Total	Arable	Pasture	Forest	Other
Albania	7.2	6.2	7.5	5.6	1.9	0.4	28.7	6.0	6.2	13.5	3.0
Bulgaria	35.2	38.5	23.2	9.6	3.5	1.2	110.9	43.8	18.1	38.4	10.6
FCS	15.1	68.4	40.9	3.0	0.4	-	127.9	51.7	16.9	45.4	13.9
FGDR	74.6	22.8	10.8	0.0	0.0	0.0	108.2	50.2	12.3	29.4	16.3
Hungary	77.6	14.8	0.6	-	0.0	0.0	93.0	53.3	12.9	15.9	10.9
Poland	234.2	69.1	9.1	0.3	0.0	0.0	312.7	149.2	40.3	86.9	36.3
Romania	103.8	63.9	45.9	17.8	5.1	1.0	237.5	105.0	44.6	63.4	24.5
FFRY	71.8	72.0	70.1	34.0	6.9	1.0	255.8	78.8	63.4	92.6	21.0

provides a useful complement to the arable enterprises on the adjacent low ground. The four northern countries have 62.6 per cent of the land below 200 metres and only 0.6 per cent above 1000 metres while the four southern countries have only 34.4 per cent below 200 metres and 13.9 per cent over 1000 metres. The northern countries have 47.4 per cent of their land arable compared with 36.9 per cent in the south. The mild contradiction between these figures is resolved by the fact that the southern countries have lower latitudes and higher temperature and sunshine levels, so much of the mountain zone has a significant agricultural potential. The four southern countries and the southern half of Hungary have mean July temperatures in excess of 20 degrees Celsius, and with the exception of Bărăgan, Dobrogea and Moldavia (Stefănescu 1977) rainfall exceeds 50 centimetres (Figure 1.2). Only limited areas in the northern group, such as Hungary's Great Plain, offer both good soils and a warm climate during the growing season (Ando 1980).

On the other hand, where the agricultural population is concerned (Table 1.2), the southern countries have a slightly higher agriculturally active population: 15.8 persons per hectare of agricultural land compared with 15.4 persons per hectare in the north in 1991. But the difference would be far greater if the low figures for Hungary (8.5), FCS (10.9) and

4   *Privatization in Rural Eastern Europe*

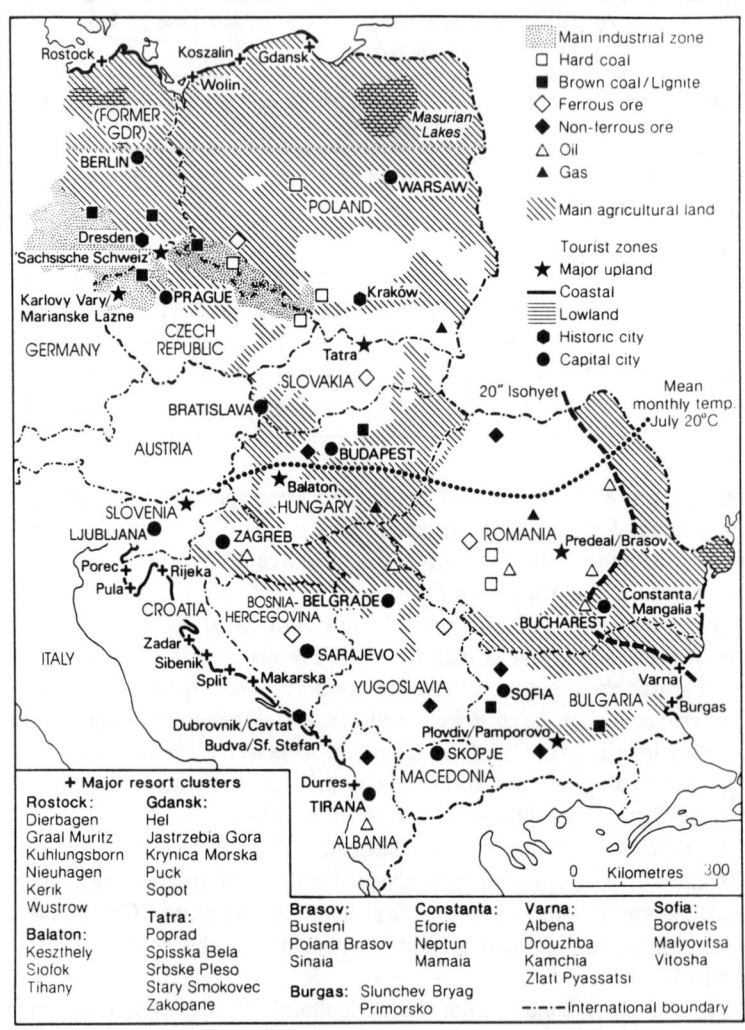

Source: D. Turnock, *Industrial Geography: Eastern Europe*, Folkestone: Dawson, 1978, p.14.

Figure 1.2   Resources of communist Eastern Europe

Table 1.2 Agricultural population of Eastern Europe, 1985–1994

Country	Population active in agriculture (thousands) and percentage of the total active population											
	1985		1990		1991		1992		1993		1994	
	N	%	N	%	N	%	N	%	N	%	N	%
Albania	715	52.0	762	48.5	756	47.7	764	47.1	762	46.4	758	45.7
Bulgaria	670	14.9	539	12.2	519	11.8	504	11.4	486	11.0	464	10.6
FCS	906	11.1	772	9.3	747	9.0	727	8.7	n.a.	n.a.	n.a.	n.a.
FGDR	873	9.3	758	8.1	736	7.9	n.a.	n.a.	n.a.	n.a.	n.a.	n.a.
Hungary	752	14.5	590	11.5	565	11.0	541	10.5	517	10.0	496	9.5
Poland	4,676	24.4	4,030	20.8	3,914	20.1	3,806	19.5	3,713	18.9	3,613	18.2
Romania	2,839	25.0	2,356	20.2	2,265	19.4	2,154	18.6	2,078	17.9	1,997	17.1
FFYR	2,679	26.7	2,254	21.7	2,237	20.8	n.a.	n.a.	n.a.	n.a.	n.a.	n.a.

FGDR (11.8) were not overshadowed by the high figure for Poland (20.7) which greatly exceeds those for FFRY (15.7), Romania (15.1) and Bulgaria (8.4) – but not Albania, where labour intensity reached the remarkable figure of 62 persons per hectare. These figures cannot sensibly be correlated with the physical resources for they reflect the farm structure (especially the maintenance of private farms under communism in Poland and FFRY) and the availability of non-agricultural employment (especially high in FCS and FGDR) and the strong support given to rural areas in Albania, underpinned by strict migration controls. Table 1.2 also indicates the scale of the shake-out of agricultural labour that may be expected for all countries to reach the level of Bulgaria, FCS, FGDR and Hungary (9.9). The other four countries would have to reduce their agricultural population by 46.7 per cent from 9.17 to 4.89 million. While this will not happen overnight, it is an indication of the scale of the problem for the medium term and indicates that rural problems are potentially as problematic as those of the towns where unemployment is a major social issue.

HISTORICAL BACKGROUND

It is worth considering how East European agriculture has reached the present stage in its development. The region played an important role in transmitting prehistoric technology to Western Europe, and the base for subsistence was clearly demonstrated in the Dark Ages when the region proved to be highly congenial for settlement by groups migrating from the Eurasian heartlands. By the Medieval period, grain surpluses were moving westwards from Poland's Baltic ports while livestock were being driven in the same direction overland. However, the east was peripheral to the centre of innovation and wealth creation in Western Europe, where rival commercial centres were developing their maritime trade. The Habsburg and Prussian empires took action to stimulate their respective economies at the turn of the eighteenth century and considerable industrial success was achieved (Verdery 1991). But the Ottoman Empire failed to modernize in the era of factory industry and growth was stifled as intermediaries intercepted the flow of wealth heading for Istanbul. The Ottoman administration had little to offer the Christian peoples of the Balkans at a time of increasing national awareness (Sugar 1977). It was only after the Treaty of Adrianople (1828) that the Danubian Principalities of Moldavia and Wallachia could begin to trade with Western Europe through the ports of Braila, Galaţi and (after 1878) Constanţa. Then the Balkan states started to gain their independence from the Ottoman Empire in the late nineteenth century and the process was completed by the creation of Albania in 1912 (Augustinos 1991). Romania became one of the world's leading cereal exporters as the large estates of the steppelands were opened up by the railways and placed in close touch with the Black Sea and Danubian ports.

The abolition of feudalism was accompanied by land reform sufficient for the peasants to support themselves; nor was there enough non-agricultural employment to break the link with the land, so country families were dependent on work offered by the estates and managed under neo-feudal principles. In Slovenia, a class of private farmers emerged out of the abolition of the feudal social order in the Habsburg Monarchy in 1849–50. But although the former serfs became landowners, one-third of each estate (by value) remained in the hands of the lords, because feudal landed property was preserved by law in cases where the lords had been

Introduction

farming land themselves (Berend and Ranki 1974). Moreover, the law assigned most of the woodland to the lords as compensation for the loss of the feudal services they had previously enjoyed. Thus, two social classes arose out of the reforms: a class of landed proprietors and a class of small peasant farmers. In Romania, feudal obligations were swept away in 1864, but the peasants remained dependent on the large landowners, who paid only low wages while imposing burdensome labour contracts (Chirot 1989). Violence was not widespread, but the Romanian peasant revolt of 1907 showed that there was stress in the countryside and deep-seated problems for the reformers to address.

The demands of the agrarian proletariat for a division of the estates intensified with the collapse of the Habsburg Empire after the First World War. Under land reform legislation in FCS, FFRY and other countries, large holdings of arable land (and very large estates in general) were confiscated to create a reserve for allocation to state farms, communities and individual households. The result was a colourful mosaic of small parcels and strips which converted most landless peasants into smallholding proprietors. Medium-sized farms in Slovakia generated considerable rural prosperity and accelerated the transition towards a capitalist economy. However, the disappearance of large estates was sometimes injurious to food-processing industries, while some areas that remained overpopulated in relation to the agricultural potential suffered from a lack of capital investment (especially during the crisis years of the 1930s) and stimulative market prices until close economic links were forged with Germany (Basch 1944). Most farms were very small and minifundia was even more evident in 1949 than in 1930: 65.4 per cent of holdings were no larger than 5ha in 1930 (71 per cent in 1949), while 20.8 per cent were of 5–10ha in size (19.5ha in 1949). Only 13.8 per cent were larger than 10ha in 1930 (9.5ha in 1949). Labour-intensive methods reflected the limited employment opportunities outside agriculture where the peasant character of farming was enhanced by share-cropping arrangements to supplement the produce from the peasants' own land. Thus the agricultural emphasis persisted (Zagoroff et al. 1955) amidst acute problems of rural overpopulation (Moore 1945). Then, after the Second World War there was further expropriation to transfer land from the remaining estate owners to landless peasants and smallholders. But this further effort in support of peasant proprietorship was overtaken by the consolidation of the communist collectivization programme.

THE COMMUNIST SYSTEM

This highly variable resource base was exploited under communism to gain unprecedentedly high levels of output through a combination of (i) reorganization to create a large socialist agricultural sector and transform social relations in village life (Allcock 1980; Ellman 1982); and (ii) capital investment to modernize the infrastructure (Jackson 1971; Wädekin 1977, 1982). In the process, distribution was improved and closer links were forged with the food processors (Bencze 1971). Communist industrialization rested on an assured supply of cheap food and raw materials. Thus agriculture was reorganized in order to proletarianize the peasantry and control production at prices determined by the state (Francisco et al. 1980). The ethos of revolution prevailed, supported by economic arguments concerned with the overall planning of investment and production over large areas without the complications of individual peasant decision-making. With state control of prices and capital investment (including the supply of farm machinery through special depots) there could be effective coordination and development. State farms comprised former experimental units and crown domains while cooperatives (or collectives as they were usually labelled in the early days) arose through coercion to pool peasant land, livestock and equipment without compensation apart from a right to work for the new organization and retain a small private plot (Francisco et al. 1979). This enabled the state, through the party hierarchy, to secure food deliveries from communally-farmed land, while leaving each peasant with the option of additional work to secure a measure of self-sufficiency for the family and to create small surpluses for sale on local markets. Agriculture was always relatively undercapitalized, given the priority for industry, and hence a formula had to be found that would combine control with incentives for efficient use of labour.

The former monocultural aspect of Balkan agriculture was removed. Thus bread grains occupied 48.3 per cent of Albania's sown area in 1990 compared to 84.5 per cent in 1938. Industrial crops became important in diversifying and raising the level of agricultural production. Of course, Eastern European farming retained considerable diversity under socialism, with many variations on the basic logic of combining cereal farming with stock rearing and fattening. The mountain districts certainly specialized most heavily in stock rearing (cattle, sheep and pigs) and much of the remaining cereal production (especially rye and maize) was undertaken in the interest of local self-sufficiency. But the main arable zones in the lowlands also expanded their herds and raised whole complexes of buildings for the purpose. The arable sector provided the fodder and the finished animals were conveniently situated in relation to the domestic food market and the international trading system. There was, however, a danger that such a strategy pursued by the state farms and cooperatives would ignore the full potential of the mountain grazings and that the individual farmers prominent in such areas would lack the incentives to maximize output. In Romania, the state farms began to show more interest in the mountain grazings during the 1980s, in some cases as a result of permission to clear woodland. Meanwhile, industrial crops (flax, hemp, sugar beet and sunflowers) appeared in the most suitable areas, as did orchards, vegetable gardens and vineyards.

Crops were allocated to zones with appropriate physical conditions so that comparative advantages could be exploited. Hence the cultivation of cotton in the central Albanian coastal districts of Fier, Lushnjë and Durrës, sugar beet in the Korçë Basin, and vegetables in the districts around the main urban centres of Tirana, Durrës, Shkodër and Vlorë. Intense specialization was discouraged by the inefficiency of interregional trade, which perpetuated traditional emphasis on self-sufficiency. But there were some outstanding specialities (some of long standing). Bulgaria retained its reputation for tobacco and also for oleaginous roses yielding rose oil or attar of roses for the manufacture of perfumes (the latter specialism prominent in the Kazanlik Valley). Specialization was also noticeable in connection with local market demand, sometimes providing a base from which successful entry into longer-distance commerce has been possible. Horticulturists at Turany near Brno in FCS enjoyed a strong local market for flowers, and then started trading with Western Europe. Other centres of horticulture arose in the vicinity of the northern cities of Eastern Europe since flowers are widely appreciated as presents when there may be few obvious alternatives. There was (and still is) a massive output of carnations in the immediate surroundings of Warsaw and especially Jablonna, where many families successfully changed from mixed farming to the production of flowers under glass, benefiting from a pure water supply underground and carefully prepared manure. A good local organization was created for an industry that could employ one person full time for every 250sq.m of glass (Morgan 1985).

Communist agriculture achieved significant intensification (Dohrs 1971). Irrigation was quite successful despite some cases of salt accumulation through poor water management. Bulgaria's irrigated area increased from 0.13m.ha in 1950 to 0.72m.ha in 1960 and almost 1m.ha in 1968 (however, well short of the 2m.ha target which a 1959 decree had set for 1965). Romania eventually exceeded this level as the steppelands of Bărăgan and Dobrogea were transformed. But costs were high when artificial water storage and distribution systems were taken into account. Two harvests each year were necessary to justify the investment, yet output rarely met this target despite cooperation between Bulgaria and the FSU to establish optimum watering rates for different crops and to establish computerized control systems. River floodplains were protected by the construction of dykes so that former permanent grasslands could be drained and converted for arable farming. Much of the Lower Danube was improved in this way, although the artificial confining of a river could be dangerous without large storage in the mountains (geared perhaps to hydro-electricity generation or navigation facilities) to prevent a sudden rise in river levels after heavy rain or snow melt.

Bulgarian sheep were crossed with the Soviet 'Romanov' breed and Soviet 'Bezostaya 1' was widely used in Bulgaria as a basis for new lowstalk varieties of wheat such as 'Ogosta', 'Trakia' and 'Vratsa'. Fertilizer applications were increased in step with output from the chemical industry but some heavy dressings proved counterproductive. More effort went into the improvement of farm machinery (including machines suitable for use on small farms) and storage facilities. There was some success in terracing eroded hill slopes, a strategy that was often combined with the establishment of orchards and vineyards linked with enhanced capacity in the food-processing industry. In Albania, a dense network of drainage channels extended over 0.20m.ha of land. Expansion of cultivable land entailed an improvement in desalination methods, reclamation from coastal and lakeside lagoons, and an extension of cultivation in upland areas, often through extensive terracing (Hall 1987). Increases were achieved in per capita production over the years 1952–82 in the range of 1.7 per cent (Romania) to 2.7 per cent (Bulgaria), and Hungary succeeded not only in meeting home market demand but in boosting exports (Held 1980). But such were the increases in home demand for food, fodder and agricultural raw materials that in Eastern Europe as a whole a net surplus was converted into a deficit. In 1934–38, net exports from Eastern Europe were equivalent to the production from 3.74m.ha

Introduction   11

(6.4 per cent of a total area of 58.30m.ha). By 1962–66, however, there was a net import equivalent to the output from 2.97m.ha (5.9 per cent of the total land area of 50.56m.ha) (Borgström and Annegers 1971).

Communist agriculture was riddled with contradictions, as befitted an economic sector that was critical for central planning yet was always a low priority for investment in view of the labour that remained on the land. There was sufficient commitment to generate some 60,000 victims of forced collectivization, yet 'peasant structures resisted the ways of socialist transformation' (Buruiana 1996, p.45). In theory, agriculture should have been organized into large state-owned enterprises (SOEs) comparable with the industries that were nationalized and restructured. But the state lacked the means to direct agriculture in this way and state farms therefore comprised only one facet of the socialist sector. Most countries quickly settled for the pragmatism of this two-legged approach (state farms and cooperatives) (Pryor 1992; Sokolovsky 1990). However, an ultimate (although unattained) goal of Albanian rural collectivization remained the full state ownership of agricultural activity through the transformation of cooperatives into state farms and the abolition of private plots and herds. State farms were preferred in areas where labour was scarce because of deportation, and farming had therefore to be more capital intensive. Thus in FCS, state farms played a dominant role in border regions, especially in the west where they were responsible for maintaining the 7-metre 'ploughed strip' which was part of the elaborate system of frontier security along the 'Iron Curtain'. On the other hand, small private farms were retained in Poland and FFRY (Szurek 1987; Tomasevich 1955) where they were valued as an alternative to collectivization (Korbonski 1965) (Table 1.3). On the whole, however, performance was constrained by the imperative of party control and the emphasis on scale, rather than by the initiative and innovation of dedicated workers. Few workers had good qualifications, and there was little interest in agriculture as a worthwhile career: peasant parents felt ashamed if their children chose to work on the land in preference to following a professional career.

There were exaggerated expectations of productivity gains to follow simply from the abolition of private ownership, overlooking the problem of dependence of agriculture on the residual labour force which lacked the ability or motivation to migrate to the towns. It may well have been a mistake to disturb the peasantry by collectivization in countries that lacked the means to carry out a comprehensive agricultural revolution.

Table 1.3 Socialist agriculture in Eastern Europe, 1950–1980

Country	Year	State farms		Cooperatives		Percentage of farm land in socialist agriculture
		A	B	A	B	
Bulgaria	1950	90	0.77	2,501	0.23	11.4
	1970	156	6.00	744	5.50	99.6
FCS	1950*	182	0.49	3,138	0.31	27.1
	1980	200	10.50	1,722	2.50	92.7
FGDR	1950*	559	0.32	1,906	0.11	5.7
	1980	469	0.87	3,946	1.28	94.5
Hungary	1950*	454	1.48	2,185	0.20	30.6
	1980	131	7.59	1,338	3.48	n.a.
Poland	1950	5,679	0.25	635	0.30	10.4
	1980	2,096	1.67	2,286	0.37	25.1
Romania	1950	363	2.07	1,027	0.28	23.6
	1980	407	5.00	4,011	2.26	90.6
FFRY	1950	858	0.43	15,605	0.13	31.6
	1970	270	1.32	1.102	0.56	30.1

Notes: A Number of units; B Average area (th.ha).
* Nearest available figures have been used.

Sources: Miller et al. 1973; Trend 1974; and FAO Yearbooks.

Wädekin argues (1990, p.326) that, notwithstanding the rationale of extracting capital from agriculture tied (indirectly) to the idea of collective production, discrimination against private farms arose from 'ideological prejudice and a preference for directive planning'. Thus in Romania, cheap food and cheap labour were extracted while capital inputs remained low and collectivization extended to all areas except those with severe administrative and infrastructure problems where a quota system was retained. But in FCS and FGDR, there was less labour in agriculture (Lazarcik 1967) and so 'remuneration of labour and capital inputs on socialist large-scale farms could not be kept much below that in other sectors of the economy' (Wädekin 1990, p.325). Table 1.4 examines the changing relationships between labour and capital and shows some evidence of a split between the north, where capital investment was maintained, and the south, where the size of the residual labour force allowed a degree of substitution.

Table 1.4 *Agricultural output, employment and investment in Eastern Europe, 1960–1980*

	1960				1970				1980			
Country	A	B	C	D	A	B	C	D	A	B	C	D
Albania	44.4	71.3	1.6	0.3	34.5	62.0	1.8	0.5	n.a.	55.9	n.a.	n.a.
Bulgaria	32.2	55.5	1.7	1.2	22.6	35.7	1.6	0.9	16.5	18.1	1.1	0.9
FCS	14.7	25.9	1.8	1.5	10.1	18.3	1.8	1.5	7.3	13.1	1.8	1.6
FGDR	16.4	17.3	1.1	0.9	11.6	13.0	1.1	1.3	8.5	10.6	1.2	1.1
Hungary	30.8	38.9	1.1	0.6	17.7	26.4	1.5	1.5	15.8	18.2	1.2	0.5
Poland	30.3	44.2	1.5	0.6	17.5	34.7	2.0	1.3	15.3	28.5	1.9	1.1
Romania	34.9	65.6	1.9	0.7	19.1	49.3	2.6	1.1	14.5	30.5	2.1	0.7
FFRY	25.0	56.2	2.2	0.9	18.3	49.8	2.7	0.7	14.8	32.3	2.2	0.4

Notes: A Contribution of agriculture and forestry to national income (percentages).
B Contribution of agriculture and forestry to employment.
C B divided by A.
D Agriculture and forestry's share of state investment divided by A.

Sources: Wädekin 1977 and Statistical Yearbooks.

At the same time, some land was underused; although the urban fringe lands were highly valued (Daroczi 1984), 'a dramatic decrease in agricultural land, especially of arable land [complemented by] the expansion of forests, occurred in peripheral areas like Sudetenland' after the Germans were expelled (Bičík and Štěpanek 1994, p.259). As farms in the mountain and karst regions were abandoned (some during the Second World War), woodland has increased from 838.4th.ha in 1900 (41.3 per cent of the total area) to 1,020.1th.ha in 1993 (50.4 per cent). In the Alps of Slovenia, the declining use of the high pastures (reflecting the general devaluation of agricultural land under socialism) created ecological problems and so the local authorities tried to protect the better land from development and fragmentation. Land close to the towns was especially vulnerable to 'social fallowing' and a replacement of agricultural uses with recreation and tourism. Because of a labour shortage, the state/social agricultural enterprises began to hire workers from other parts of FFRY.

Stones were cleared to create small square fields and vineyards after the Second World War near Primosten in Dalmatia, but with poor transport these are now abandoned in an era of machine cultivation (Gams 1991). By the end of the 1970s, it was reported that the terraced fields of the Adriatic coast were reverting to juniper scrub (Thomas 1978).

REFORMING THE COMMUNIST SYSTEM

Throughout Eastern Europe there was pressure to produce more food to compensate for the inadequate supply of consumer goods (Deutsch 1986). Administrators and industrial workers had to be given incentives, even though there were too many of them in employment. Therefore, a higher agricultural output was needed to provide for salaried workers whose incomes rose faster than their production. 'Under these circumstances the excess purchasing power turns to foods to an overproportionate degree, while the regimes hesitate to raise the official retail food prices'; thus there is increasing food production 'but at high and growing subsidy cost, and still lagging behind the rise in demand' (Wädekin 1990, p.327). 'The explicit or implicit return, although to varying degrees, to the small, mainly family unit of production under the constraints of natural endowment and low economic development level is the common denominator of recent agrarian policies' (ibid. p.330). But little was seen of this trend in FCS and FGDR, where there were better conditions for large-scale modernized farming. The FGDR was perhaps the most successful in expanding output within the confines of the socialist system. Farm workers were better integrated into the collective and state farms than even their Soviet counterparts. They purchased most of their food and spent relatively little time tending private plots. Specialization was very evident (Bajaja 1980) as the collectives and state farms combined effectively within specific areas of specialized production (Freeman 1983; Sinclair 1979).

The other countries also tried to increase cereal production to avoid the burden of imports which came increasingly from outside the member states of the Council for Mutual Economic Assistance (Comecon) (Dando 1974). The crisis was deepened by the need for livestock feed (given consumer demand for more meat) and by transfers of cereal lands to other arable enterprises such as industrial crops (Turnock 1989, pp.239–53). The high cost of cereal imports (much of it from hard-currency countries) brought great efforts to increase self-sufficiency during the 1980s. In 1985, cereal imports were only 1.8m.t (on top of domestic production of 108.9m.t) whereas in 1980 the figures were 18.1 and 97.4m.t, respectively. However, the picture varied considerably in different countries: in 1985 there were net exports in Hungary (2.1m.t), FFRY (0.8) and Romania (0.1) and net imports in Bulgaria and FCS (both 0.4), FGDR (1.7) and Poland (2.4). The cereal question is complex and should be seen in the context of demands from the pastoral sector; the reduction in cereal land through allocation to other crops; and inefficiency in production, harvesting and storage. On the other hand, the fisheries help to reduce pressure on agriculture. Higher yields were obtained during the 1980s, while the sown area was broadly maintained. There was better storage and increased efficiency in irrigation. Investment included World Bank assistance to FFRY in the mid-1980s. Efforts in plant breeding to produce new varieties were adjusted to prevailing climatic conditions and disease hazards. As domestic cereal production increased from 97.38m.t in 1980 to 108.95m.t in 1985 imports fell dramatically from 16.12 to 1.85m.t.

Over the years, the Stalinist model was subjected to overhaul. Mere organizational changes did not secure the increased output that was expected and higher investments have been needed to secure the fertilizers, machines and irrigation waters required to boost output from a dwindling workforce (becoming more elderly and more highly feminized as the young male population opted for work in the towns). Regular wages and improved welfare benefits were introduced, and the importance of economic rather than ideological incentives led to the allocation of specific tasks to individuals and groups in return for payment by results. There was a further element of welfare because, although the profits of the more successful cooperatives were checked by loan repayments and the charges levied by the machine and tractor stations, the weaker farms could usually generate some income for their members through the periodic writing-off of debts. However, the strong peasant links with the land through private ownership were broken and many young people left for careers in industry. Agriculture was not attractive to young people with good educational qualifications and so the farming population grew older, while many of the menfolk commuted to factories in the towns and left the agricultural work to be increasingly feminized (First-Dilic 1978).

Meanwhile, farms became larger, in keeping with keeping with communist notions of gigantism (Brezinski 1990). Until 1962, the aim in FCS was to establish a cooperative in each village. This meant that each farm covered 200–300ha divided into fields of 8–15ha. But during the 1960s there was amalgamation, internal specialization and larger fields (15–30ha) created by the destruction of 'biocorridors'. These trends continued after 1970, when the largest cooperatives farmed up to 6,000ha with individual fields of 30–60ha. There were larger machinery parks and greater fertilizer stocks; also some modernization of farm buildings. The average size of a cooperative farm in FCS increased from 490ha in 1950 to 2,500ha in 1980. At the same time, the average size of a state farm in FCS increased from 490ha in 1950 to 10,500ha in 1980, while socialist agriculture as a whole increased its share of the land from 27.1 to 92.7 per cent. In the 1970s, the FGDR state launched an agricultural productivity drive. Both cooperatives (*Landwirtschaftliche Produktiongenossenschaften*: LPGs) and state farms (*Volkseigene Güter*: VEGs) were reorganized into specialist arable or livestock enterprises (Bergmann 1992). By 1989, the average arable LPG covered 4,600ha and employed about 240 workers (although many of these were working in service, administrative or maintenance/construction jobs rather than agricultural jobs). Livestock farms were smaller in area but were organized on a highly intensive basis. In the 1980s, formal cooperation between arable and livestock farms was encouraged with the establishment of 'cooperative associations'. Typically, a cooperative association consisted of one arable and two or three livestock farms. However, despite policies to industrialize agriculture, productivity levels remained well below those of West Germany – although there were variations between farms depending on soil quality but also on social relations between cooperative members. Labour productivity was poor, with more than 800,000 workers employed on cooperatives and state farms in 1989 (11 per cent of the total labour force compared to 4 per cent in West Germany).

Some very large organizations emerged as groups of state farms (Kostrowicki 1975). An *Agrokompleks* (agricultural complex) of eight large enterprises based on Nitra in Slovakia managed 45,000ha and enjoyed the backing of a local agricultural college. In Poland, one such organization was set up in the Masurian Lakeland, providing a model for a similar approach to the development of agriculture in the Sudeten Mountains. However, *Agrokompleks Sudety* was a failure because of overcentralization. The livestock herds failed to expand as expected and frustrated local managers were forced to 'borrow' animals from private farms to impress visitors from Warsaw (a not uncommon strategy in all countries affected by central planning). Large-scale organization including efforts to integrate farmers and food processors more efficiently was certainly attempted, notably through the cooperation councils in the FGDR (Schinke 1990) and agricultural–industrial complexes (AICs) in Bulgaria (Wiedermann 1980, 1982). The latter were first approved in 1970 and by the end of the year 170 were in existence, each with 28,000ha of land and 6,200 workers on average (Entwistle 1972). The AICs then integrated with industry to create industrial–agricultural complexes – the first ('Dimitur Blahoev' at Ruse, 1973) combined the local sugar refinery with two AICs working a total of 40,000ha (Wyzan 1989). This made for efficiency in the use of transport and helped to overcome anomalies evident in Poland, where potato processors sometimes drew supplies from distant parts of the country (Stryakiewicz 1985). These large units gained considerable political clout because they were represented by people with expertise and local knowledge, often subsidized local councils and became responsible for some industrialization in the villages. Thus, 'it has been exceptional for local councils to seek to limit the activities of large scale farms and their associated industries even if they are environmentally hazardous' (Persanyi 1990, p.42). But some investment was illogical because pig-rearing required imported protein and domestically produced feed sustained by artificial fertilizers while meadow land and cattle pasture were left underused and the environment was damaged by disposal of slurry from the pig farms (ibid., p.43).

Reform also sought to release peasant energies (Bell 1984; Cochrane 1986). Arguably, small-scale organization is not preferable *per se* but it is attractive in the context of surplus unskilled rural labour and deficient linkages (upstream and downstream), which constrain the efficiency of large organizations. Thus the household plots that were originally intended to provide subsistence to farmworkers were now to be geared to small-scale production for the market, a change that altered not only the function of the plots but also the social status of the producers themselves, especially when additional land was taken on. There was some emphasis on small enterprises in most countries (MacIntyre 1988), but the best examples can be seen through the change of emphasis in Hungary as the government stimulated a business culture among the peasantry

(Szelenyi 1988; Szelenyi and Manchin 1986) and strengthened the viability of cooperatives in the process (Swain 1985, 1987). There was a significant subsistence element in peasant activity and some local food stores were forced to close. But peasant farming generated modest incomes and was especially significant in marginal areas (away from the plains) where large-scale farming required high subsidies (Elek 1980; Enyedi 1990). As Hungary's 'New Economic Mechanism' allowed unprecedented autonomy, the primary sector attracted investment, maintained a good food supply and so ensured political stability (Swain 1992). The silent revolution was effective in producing more food, boosting rural incomes and promoting *embourgeoisement* 'of great masses of people' (Kovach 1993, p.175). Importance attached to marketing (Benet 1988, 1990) and agricultural exports to Comecon countries were buoyant (Jaehne 1980). However, the investment costs led to high market prices which many could not afford, and because the farms were overstaffed and insufficiently committed to innovation and efficiency, they made little profit.

The Hungarian system encouraged individuals to expand output from their gardens and plots through various forms of collaboration with the state sector (Hollos and Maday 1983). Improved coordination measures brought together cooperatives, state farms and private plotholders so as to make the fullest use of land and labour. In Hungary, where the New Economic Mechanism reduced the role of the state in price fixing in favour of free market forces, competition could develop between different farming systems (Vasary 1990). Small farms gained both economic and social significance as suitable machinery became available, with the option of loaning additional equipment from the state farms, where there was spare capacity (Volgyes et al., 1980). The cooperative at Ócsa near Budapest allocated private plots according to the number of cows each member agreed to look after (0.75ha for each animal), while at Pastzo (Nógrád County), vineyards were leased to responsible individuals in units of 1,500sq.m. In some villages in northeastern Hungary (Szabolcs-Szatmar county, for example) cooperative farms planted orchards and arranged for periodic spraying while contracting out the other routine work (including the harvesting) to individuals who knew there was a guaranteed market at the end of the day. Another cooperative near Sopron collaborated with several hundred individual gardeners and smallholders to produce grapes, vegetables and poultry for sale in Austria under 'small border traffic' arrangements. Many of Hungary's rural dwellers were keen to accumulate property and cooperate in new forms of organization, following these successes. Whereas in 1981, the large enterprises rented out a total of 9,100ha of arable land, the figure grew to 47,100ha in 1987 and 310,100ha in 1991 – a 35-fold increase in 10 years (Harcsa 1993). This meant that the percentage of land held by large enterprises but worked by small-scale producers increased from 4.2 per cent in 1981 to 5.9 per cent in 1988 and 11.2 per cent in 1991. Thus the traditional large-scale production system was starting to break down by the late 1980s. Where mechanization was most effective (with cereals and other field crops), the large enterprises continued to dominate, but when much manual labour was needed (in orchards, vineyards and vegetable gardens) the small-scale producers moved to the fore.

By the end of the 1980s, Hungary's cooperatives were transferring not only land and livestock to the small producers, but buildings and machines as well. Instead of contracting to undertake one phase or element in a production cycle, the small producer could now take responsibility for the entire process. In the transfer of buildings, greenhouses (24.7 per cent), sheep pens (17.3 per cent) and poultry houses (13.9 per cent) were most significant because the enterprises involved were precisely those which could be carried out by the labour resources of the family unit. The cooperatives even tried to introduce entrepreneurial forms within their own organizations, despite the difficulties that arose from direct regulation through a breakdown of the fundamental ownership relations. Although commanding the status of co-ownership, the members found themselves under the control of what was, in effect, a wage labour-based organization. Excluded from decision-making, they had no effective control over matters relating to prices, state subsidies and credit agreements. Thus even within the confines of the communist system, the cooperatives changed out of all recognition in the course of the 1980s, with radical changes in land management and decision-making related to the challenging economic environment of the time. Elsewhere, Wyzan (1990) relates the success in Bulgarian agriculture to the encouragement of individual peasant farmers under Bulgaria's economic reforms of 1973, which allowed peasants to own unlimited numbers of animals and required the AICs to provide pasture and veterinary assistance under a contracting system established in 1977. Meanwhile in Poland, General Wojciech Jaruzelski wanted improved food deliveries to help normalization and the peasants' increased output (Korbonski 1990). Intensive enterprises on the edge of cities became very prominent, such as the production of flowers in the Warsaw area already noted, and productivity gains were achieved elsewhere (Morgan 1989, 1990).

COMMUNIST AGRICULTURE AT THE END OF THE 1980s

The reforms in agriculture solved immediate problems but arguably contributed to the upsurge of more radical change which overthrew the communist system at the end of the 1980s. Szmatka (1993, pp.4–5) refers to the notion of a threshold situation when the system is poised to transform itself. To operate smoothly the system must be 'finished', but in such a state it cannot easily change without the risk of dissolution. The inefficient state–socialist economy could not fulfil rising expectations and so agriculture played a significant role in bringing about the transition to a market economy (Elek 1991) because the resumption of 'bourgeoisification' among farmers, even on a small scale, became a special form of 'a silent revolution from below' (referred to by Manchin and Szelenyi 1985, p.266). Of course, there were misgivings at the time the reforms were introduced and, despite the disappearance of the old Stalinist prejudice against private-plot farming, ambivalence persisted. While the urban population was pleased with the improved food supply, there was a supposition that smallholdings were becoming 'gold mines' when the high prices paid on urban markets appeared to be financing new houses and consumer goods for the villagers. Education was needed to legitimize the materialist ambitions of the rural dwellers and encourage the latter to direct their affluence along socially acceptable channels. Higher taxes on the peasants, like those imposed in 1974, could easily sap initiative and result in a reduced output of fruit, vegetables and meat. As it was, the reforms boosted individual activity and initiative. People worked for their own benefit and ultimately for the benefit of a new system (Ziolkowski 1993).

However, despite some flexibility under the command economy, private peasant farming was heavily constrained. Individual farms were retained in small areas (usually the mountain districts) where settlement patterns and field systems made cooperation very difficult logistically. But there were usually restrictions on amalgamation and the use of non-family labour, and in any case, state control of distribution and prices gave little encouragement to private enterprise. There were many small farms in Poland (Korbonski 1967) and FFRY (Halpern 1967; Stipetic 1982) where there was no political will to persist with coercive policies. But private peasant farming needed a stimulative regime to increase production, and this was not always in place. Although the Polish reforms were significant (Cook 1984; Galeski 1982), there was no interest in structural change to boost efficiency in private farming (Tomczak 1988). Peasant farming was deemed acceptable in a transitional situation, but the industry remained weak and a generation of Polish youth left the land. Ideology had a destructive influence in terms of feeding the population: it was 'not adjusted to our present-day reality and problems' (Tomczak 1990, p.288). In FFRY, farms remained small, with curbs against amalgamation, although people were keen to retain land for reasons of sentiment and security. In recent years, Croatian farms have decreased more slowly than production (Stambuk 1991).

But in the mountain areas especially, the infrastructure needed attention, in addition to the regimes of subsidies and tax concessions recommended in Slovenia (Meze 1984); and diversification was often crucial in maintaining family incomes (Stasiak 1977). In some cases the peasants could take significant initiatives. Pine and Bogdanowicz (1982) have shown how Carpathian farming communities in southern Poland were able to diversify on the basis of pluriactivity extending to light industry, tourism and even temporary migration to the United States, taking advantage of family ties with migrants who left the area at the beginning of the century. In the case of the remote community of Tymova in the Novy Targ area, once slated for evacuation and resettlement in Silesia, villagers were able to use their connections with the administration to undertake a number of communal projects which cumulatively had a great effect on developing the infrastructure. In 1954 the villagers built a railway station with their own funds and labour. Improved communications helped to stimulate a growth of tourism, while links with industrial enterprises brought in finance for a new school in return for summer holiday camp facilities. Moreover, the village found ways of maintaining control of its own farm equipment when the government tried to enlarge the 'agricultural circles' intended to secure machine services for small farmers. Thus by operating in a politically correct way, the villagers took action which the authorities did not intend but could not prevent. As a result, the village community was safeguarded and living standards improved as large modern houses were built to accommodate both tourists and extended families. Romania's private peasant farmers were tightly controlled during the 1980s by the reimposition of production plans (quotas) and the setting of maximum prices which often made it unattractive to sell additional produce on the free markets. Agroindustrial Councils for State and Cooperative Farms were integrated with the work of land survey institutes concerned with irrigation and fertilizer use, and also with a rural planning system that designated the council seats as new towns and envisaged the destruction of outlying villages that were considered to have no place in the new order.

Economic problems were mounting on account of the rising cost of government intervention to keep food prices low. There was massive support for agriculture and although the work was deliberately maintained on a labour-intensive basis, socialist agricultural enterprises usually received inputs at prices below the actual home price or world market price. Generous credit facilities also led to many non-viable projects with the repaying ability of the enterprise insufficiently taken into account. However, Hungary's food production sector encountered difficulty in the early 1980s when the communist government had to reduce indebtedness and control the balance of payments. Agriculture played its part and the state used all possible means to increase agricultural exports in order to earn convertible currency. But at the same time, changes in the world economy led to a fall in prices for the major agricultural products. There was pressure to keep domestic food prices low, but the growing discrepancy between agricultural and industrial prices, along with the growth in the tax burden and a reduction in subsidies, greatly reduced the profitability of the cooperatives. They had to sell some of their assets (buildings, livestock or machinery) in order to stay in business.

Environmental degradation was also a problem due to soil and water pollution and soil compaction from use of heavy farm machinery. Problems were evident in Hungary, where pesticides and fertilizers are applied at high levels by international standards. Agricultural areas also suffered from serious soil erosion (Churska 1976) although some use was made of conservation measures such as ploughing across the slope and establishing small plantations (Skrodzki 1972). But measures were also needed to cope with wind erosion which was a significant cause of soil degradation in those parts of the Sudeten Mountains that have only a thin layer of good soil (Jahn 1972). As a result of copper smelting at Głogów in Poland, several villages (including Biechów, Bogomice, Wroblin and Zukowice) had to be evacuated because of contaminated soil, although some farm production continued to come from land polluted in this way (Rosenbladt 1991). There was also acidification (by 1pH on average across Hungary) while waterlogging and salination have resulted from irrigation, including 125th.ha from the first Tisza barrage (which was poorly planned). Farmyard manure became less widely used and this created further pollution problems, especially in the case of the large quantities of liquid manure generated by intensive livestock-rearing units. Large monocultures (for wheat and maize) also have environmental disadvantages. Many hedges and spinneys were removed and streams canalized so that natural habitats were eroded while protected areas were far too limited; indeed, the protected areas in Hungary were mostly cultivated by agroindustries, leading to conflict between conservationists and farm managers. On the positive side, the closed borderlands of FCS, often devoted to military training areas, did offer ecological advantages with high natural and environmental values, in contrast to the Jablonec/Liberec area and other parts of the northern border (with FGDR) where there were fewer restrictions.

The decline of woodlands has been taking place over the long term and there are cartographic and statistical sources that trace the process through the nineteenth and twentieth centuries (Szymanski 1978). However, during the socialist period there was damage through the spruce monoculture and restructuring to emphasize other fast-growing species. Meanwhile, the effects of pollution were very evident in the forests exposed to emissions from power stations not only in Poland (Turoszów) but also in FGDR (Cottbus). On exposed sections of the higher ground, defoliation became very evident, as at Sklarska Poręba (south of Jelenia Góra) in the Sudeten Mountains. Some of the damage to forests arose from insect attacks (also from drought, frost and strong winds), but the consequences were all the more serious because the trees were already in a poor condition. Between 1981 and 1987, 11th.ha of pine forest were damaged in the Sudeten Mountains, mostly in the west (Gory Izerskie and Karkonosze) and overall only 65 per cent of the Sudeten forests were still in a healthy state in 1983). There was a significant fall in the density of woodland (wood mass per unit of area) and the amount of wood produced.

Further rural problems arose from the mismatch between piped water supplies and sewerage. Because of the greater priority given to piped water supplies, 88 per cent of rural dwellings in Hungary had piped water in 1987 but only 49 per cent had sewerage (in 1945 the percentages were

25 and 18). The dwellings with running water but no sewerage (which increased fourfold between 1972 and 1987) generated almost 150m.cu.m of sewage per annum, but only a sixth of this was collected by tank trucks, leaving the rest to seep into the soil. Drinking water became so polluted that more than 700 villages had to be supplied by tanks, bottles and plastic bags. The situation was also bad regarding solid waste, because garbage collection was provided only for the towns and the more urbanized villages. Thus, 'throughout the countryside the margins of villages and the edges of towns and watercourses are strewn with rubbish' (Persanyi 1990, p.46). Recycling schemes made an appearance, but up to 1989 there were insufficient collection points.

Environment problems generated considerable public protest at the end of the communist era. The most sensitive issues were largely rooted in urban problems, but there were some actions by articulate and highly-motivated city dwellers in defence of scenic features in the countryside against both the threat of mining or industrial development and the perceived ambivalence of country folk. But rural people also became more environmentally aware during the 1980s and started to protest about the large-scale dumping of hazardous waste. They might accept their own contribution to environmental degradation but were sensitive to the damage when additional waste was imposed on them (Persanyi 1990, pp.50–51). In Poland's flysch Carpathians there were calls for more effective prediction of environmental change and clarification of the nature of water circulation and soil denudation under different types of land use (Czeppe 1976). In eroded areas of the Polish Carpathians it was recommended that cultivation should be reduced in preference for woodland, grassland and orchards (Gerlach 1976). It was argued that forest should be established on all slopes of more than 30 degrees and parts of the interfluves as well as zones adjacent to river channels. Arable was acceptable only on slopes of up to 15 degrees (Gil and Starkel 1976). The scheduling of protected areas and national parks became more common (Singleton 1987) and there was much more emphasis on environmental management generally, as indicated by the literature on FCS (Carter 1985), Hungary (Compton and Pecsi 1984; Pecsi and Probald 1974) and FFRY (Jancar 1987).

COMMUNISM AND RURAL SETTLEMENT

Rural society and the rural economy in Eastern Europe tended to be dominated by socialist agricultural enterprises. Although the villages retained their traditional agricultural functions, there was considerable social change because of socialist farms which eliminated the differences between rich and poor peasants (Szelenyi and Manchin 1986; Vasary 1987). However, it has been pointed out that in the poorer countries, the relatively low level of mechanization and continued dependence on carts (driven by the *conductori* of Romanian villages, in contrast to the working peasants' *maistri*) gave the remnants of the *kulaks* a grip on the cooperatives' affairs (Kideckel 1993). There were some radical changes, most notably through resettlement in Poland's 'Recovered Territories' where Germans were expelled to make way for Poles displaced further east (Hamilton 1975). There was some immediate post-war rebuilding after war damage, as in the case of Lucimia in the Góra Puławska area of Poland (Harris 1948), and gradually, houses were replaced by new structures in more modern styles. Some small apartment blocks were provided for state employees, but most rural housing remained owner occupied with the emphasis on single-storey cottages. There were some new functions, for investment occurred not through the development programmes of cooperative and state farms, but through the plans of silvicultural and woodcutting enterprises.

As well as being the main source of rural employment, the cooperatives and state farms provided key rural services (retail, leisure and culture, welfare, repair and construction) for members, their families and other rural inhabitants. Moreover, the highly formalized cooperative system (going far beyond traditional forms of mutual assistance) generated a small corps of salaried officials who, as party members as well as farm managers, became part of the village élite, while the scope for security police activity among this group (and other sections of rural leadership concerned with commerce, education and even the church) effectively neutralized the villages politically. Important modifications to the basic cooperative farm model were made in Hungary and elsewhere in the late 1960s when many 'supplementary establishments' were created to provide non-agricultural employment for rural dwellers. They helped to correct for the structural imbalances in the economy which left the rural areas without small- and medium-sized state factories, and because they operated at low cost compared with state industry they boosted the income of the large agricultural production units. Klekner (1992) has referred to the role of agriculture in developing fringe areas through non-agricultural activities linked with cooperatives; such activity increased four times between 1970 and 1987 while the value of agricultural output doubled.

There were also state mining and manufacturing companies (particularly those with interests in light engineering, food processing and textiles). Rural industries multiplied in the 1970s at a time of labour shortage in the towns (Barta 1986). It was often a spontaneous process, not driven too formally by regional planning but owing much to the initiative of local government in maximizing the benefit of contacts with large state enterprises through arrangements for subcontracting. Many units were badly equipped with obsolete machinery, but some rural growth areas emerged and improved rural living conditions often resulted. There was some rural development through tourism, with 'resort villages' attracting investment from the state (road building; hydro-electrification); cooperatives (camp sites; motels); and the individual household (second homes; bed and breakfast accommodation). In the Slovenian Alps, craft workshops were prominent, and by the 1980s increasing use was made of the mountain pastures (compared with the situation in the 1960s and 1970s) as livestock numbers started to grow again (Thomas and Vojvoda 1973). This was because of improved accessibility, as the number of second homes increased, and the less-favourable situation in non-agricultural activities. Pollution from Jesenice and other industrial centres made only a slight impact (Senegacnik et al. 1983).

Services improved as the budgets of education and health ministries impinged on rural services, but rural education was often deficient (Ciechocinska 1989). Public transport was particularly sensitive to the needs of the commuter because falling employment in agriculture gained some compensation from commuting to work in the cities, particularly the regional centres where light industry was promoted. Small commercial developments provided additional shopping and catering facilities. Yet there were clear deficiencies compared with standards of the towns. Investment in buildings and infrastructure was generally low, with the result that much rural housing was of substandard quality, the rural road network was poorly maintained, and water supply and drainage supplies were inadequate, as noted above. In Thüringen only 67 per cent of rural households were connected to sewage treatment plants, and much sewage was disposed of untreated. In Poland, the rural population (and particularly the farming population) is much less well educated than the urban population. This is partly due to the weakness of the education system in rural areas and the large distances that children must travel to get to school; but as a result, agricultural advancement is constrained. In FGDR an average telephone provision of ten phones per 100 of the population (compared with 50 in West Germany) worked out at one phone per two apartments in East Berlin compared with one in ten in Dresden and Rostock, while at the other extreme 2,000 villages had no connection with the telephone network at all.

Thus, by the mid-1980s the cooperative peasantry included a significant working-class element because of the relocation of industry in favour of the provinces and the growth of daily commuting from rural areas to industrial centres (Beck 1976). Those who combined farmwork with non-agricultural activity were very numerous in southeastern Poland and in other areas close to the large urban centres. Because of the tradition of pluriactivity, the numbers working in agriculture on each 100ha of utilized farmland fell only moderately in Poland from 26.8 in 1950 to 19.7 in 1993. However, the effect of the large rise in numbers employed outside agriculture meant a decline in the proportion employed in agriculture from 53.6 per cent to 25.5 per cent over the same period, although even this percentage is high by European standards. The net result across Eastern Europe was a growth in rural prosperity as supplementary incomes derived from small-scale production financed housing improvements, including much new construction. Furthermore, people became used to making their own economic decisions, based on flows of information about the situation in the markets and business generally. In this way, small-scale production helped in the development of an entrepreneurial culture in the villages and small towns. In much the same way, Polish farmers were members of a 'dual occupational class', enjoying a salary and a 'social net' from their employment with the state while having the time and energy to work intensively on their own farm (Giordano 1993, p.14).

But the depopulation was now becoming an almost universal feature of rural change (Enyedi 1976; Stasiak 1992), except in Albania where internal migration controls were maintained (Sjoberg 1991). The rural share of the population has fallen steadily across the six countries as a whole, from 73.3 per cent around 1900 to 39.8 per cent in the late 1980s, while the maximum absolute level was reached by the 1960s and in some countries twenty years earlier (see Table 1.5). After increasing by 0.62

Table 1.5   Rural population of Eastern Europe, 1900–1990

	Rural population (m.) and percentage of the total in:									
	1897–1900		1939–41		1961		1980		1988–90	
	N	%	N	%	N	%	N	%	N	%
Bulgaria	3.00	80.9	4.08	83.3	4.95	62.7	3.35	37.7	3.06	34.1
FCS	7.05	58.0	7.15	49.5	5.84	42.8	4.18	27.3	3.81	24.4
Hungary	4.25	62.0	5.00	53.6	5.23	52.5	4.66	43.5	4.33	40.8
Poland	17.21	73.5	20.25	63.2	15.25	51.3	14.76	41.3	14.62	38.4
Romania	9.18	82.0	13.06	78.0	12.49	67.9	11.19	50.4	10.48	45.7
FFYR	9.12	86.0	12.67	79.2	13.30	71.7	12.09	53.9	11.24	48.0
Total	49.81	73.3	62.21	66.6	57.06	58.1	50.23	43.6	47.54	39.8

Source: Eberhardt 1994.

per cent per annum during the first four decades of this century there was a decline of 0.58 per cent per annum during the 1960s, 1970s and 1980s. Regional trends can be clarified with some difficulty from statistical yearbooks although strict comparability across the whole region is not attainable. In the 1980s, rural growth continued in some mountain regions of Albania and FFRY although the prevailing trend was clearly negative (Figure 1.3). As in Slovenia, the rural population has aged through selective out-migration and many private farms now lack successors; while 11.0 per cent of Slovenia's population is aged over 65, the proportion in the rural areas is 12.1 per cent, compared with 21.5 per cent for the active population. In Poland, people of post-productive age amount to 15 per cent of the rural population across the country as a whole, but in the east the figure is 20–30 per cent. Migration to the towns has also affected the gender balance because of the high level of movement by females in some regions – for people aged 20–34, there are 88 women for every 100 men. Hence there are problems in transferring farms to younger people and a shortage of women for young farmers to marry. These difficulties are most evident

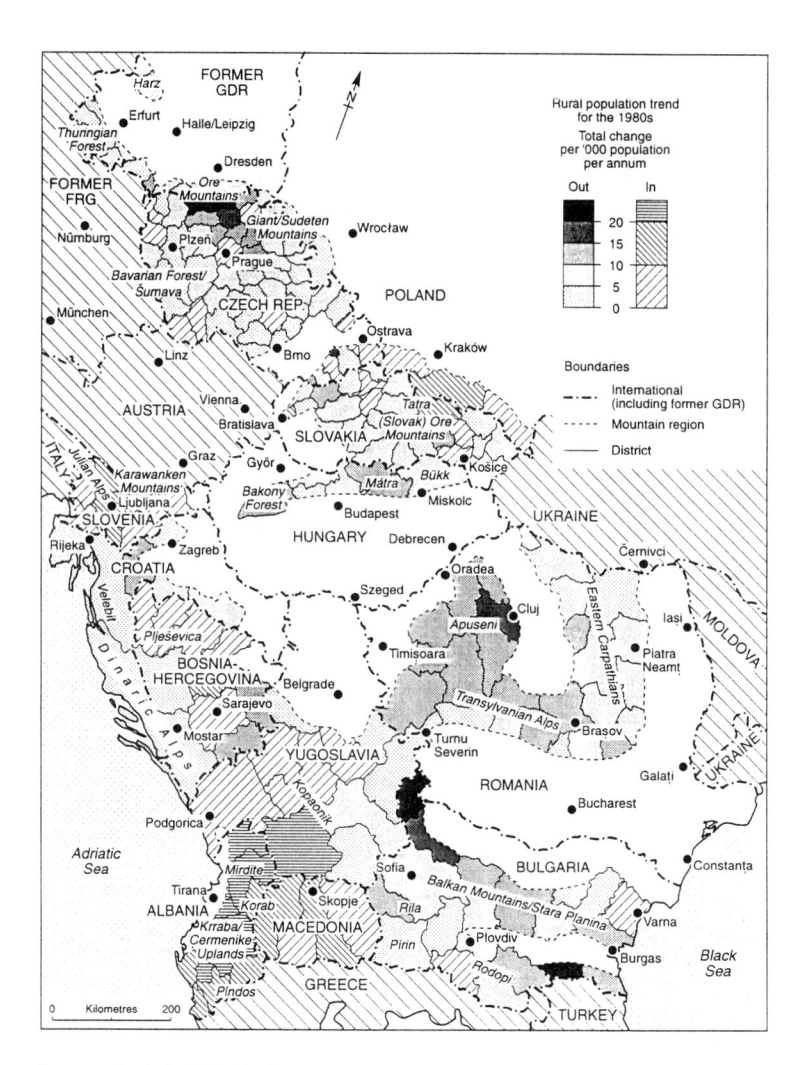

Source: Statistical Yearbooks.

Figure 1.3 Rural population in the mountains of Eastern Europe

in areas which are most heavily dependent on agriculture and they may be linked with the feminization of farmwork. Apart from their normal family duties, women are heavily involved in the fields and in tending animals. This is clearly unsatisfactory because it increases the attractiveness of an urban lifestyle and, at the same time, discourages the introduction of modern farming methods.

Slovenia's urbanization is fairly typical for Eastern Europe. In 1900, the urban population consisted of almost 191,500 people or 15.1 per cent. Meanwhile the agrarian population accounted for 73.2 per cent, because apart from a few industrial and mining settlements the rural areas were entirely dependent on agriculture. There were few large towns, apart from Trieste, to which the surplus rural population could migrate, and so there was much emigration to America and Western Europe at this time. However, using several indicators (population growth and density, migration, commuting and the proportion of the agrarian population), Ravbar (1992) calculated that 50.2 per cent of the population is now urban (covering 4.4 per cent of the territory), while 30.3 per cent is 'rural-urbanized' (17.4) and 19.5 per cent is 'rural–agrarian' (78.2). This distinction between two sections of the rural population arises from the polycentric plan carried out by the communist authorities between 1970 and 1985, when many industrial plants were built in rural areas. Out of a total of 424 settlements with industrial plants, 226 started in this way. As part of the programme to expand industry and create socialist agricultural enterprises, there was an attempt to build cooperative centres in each large village, providing a seat for local self-government. These centres of socialization were inspired by the Soviet *agrogorod* and they included shops and a hall which could also be used as a cinema. However, this initiative was abandoned with the collapse of the collectivization drive, although it helped to widen the network of rural centres with local administration, primary school, post-office, shops and a medical service. Thus there is an 'urban–rural continuum', involving a gradual transition, and areas in the vicinity of large towns that have experienced a suburbanizing process and a growth of holiday homes are in a very different situation compared with those in the remote countryside.

Thus two demographic situations now occur in rural Slovenia as a result of the transformation of the last half century – areas of transition and areas of depopulation – complementing the urban areas of concentration. Demographic stagnation and prominence of the urban way of life are typical of the transitional areas, which comprise 52.2 per cent of the population and 29.9 per cent of the state territory. Areas of depopulation (characterized by underdevelopment, limited employment possibilities and an ageing population) involve 10.3 per cent of the total population and 32.2 per cent of the territory – mainly border areas, with mountain or karst terrain, remote from the main lines of communication and mostly agrarian in character. The communist authorities tried to overcome these differences through a series of regional development measures between 1971 and 1986. The differences between the most developed (urban-industrial) areas and the least developed (agrarian) regions narrowed from 1:2.5–3 in the 1950s to 1:1.5 in the 1980s. But the market economy signals the danger of widening disparities and independent Slovenia is continuing with a regional policy through a 'Development Stimulation of the Demographically Endangered Areas Act' passed in 1990. The state offers financial and expert assistance to the affected areas for various projects to stimulate small private enterprises and improve the local infrastructure. Credits are available under favourable terms, along with grants and income tax concessions.

These distinctions can be picked up in other parts of Eastern Europe through the contrasts between 'key villages' and the outlying settlements with relatively few facilities – such as the *tanya* and dwarf villages of the Great Hungarian Plain which now face an uncertain future (Enyedi 1980). The dispersed pattern of settlement appropriate under a system of small, largely self-sufficient peasant farms is not so satisfactory in the context of large commercial farms with labour deployed from central points (Timar 1989). A population of some 2,000 is considered to mark the threshold for key village characteristics (Lacko 1986). Socialist agriculture may therefore have had an important bearing on growth trends (Held 1980), as studies in FGDR have shown (Berentsen 1982; Freeman 1979). In Poland, the state farms and agricultural schools played an important role in the expansion of villages (Kwiatkowska 1976). In Pomerania (northwest Poland), state farms took over manorial farms in some villages and absorbed many of the peasant farms. The whole village was sometimes taken over where the settlement was small, remote and constrained by poor soil conditions. Enlargement of state farms may effectively amalgamate several villages and create a viable consolidated unit in contrast to the more fragmented settlement patterns associated with peasant holdings and the early dissolution of cooperative farms (Szulc 1978).

Key villages have been favoured by investment in light engineering, food processing and textiles, services and an intensified agriculture.

However, rural industry was initially discouraged through nationalization and the concentration of capacity in large urban-based units. Small-scale enterprises tend to be more prominent in the larger villages (Kovach 1991), although diversification was common throughout the mountain regions (Stasiak 1977). Also, the larger villages usually have much better services, while at the beginning of the 1970s, electrification had still to reach some of the hamlets and medium-size settlements on the Hungarian Plain (Sarfalvi 1971). Variations in the employment structure also related to population size (Enyedi 1980) and levels of educational attainment were similarly structured with respect to settlement groups, with particularly poor kindergarten/nursery facilities in the smaller settlements (Sarfalvi 1980).

Some efforts were made by the planners to bring the town closer to the remoter rural areas (Hajnal 1989). This could be done by creating new towns through a change in the administrative status of villages enjoying some nodality of location and established market functions. In some cases, large-scale industrial development led to the emergence of a completely new industrial centre, for example, at Dimitrovgrad in Bulgaria and Gh. Gheorghiu-Dej (now Oneşti) in Romania. Alternatively, new assembly points might arise for manufacturing, as at Eisenhüttenstadt in FGDR and Leninváros (now Tiszaujváros) in Hungary; and again at decongestion points on the edge of conurbations, as at Tychy in Poland. However, gradual urbanization based on well-situated villages offered the best way forward, although with no prospect of absolute equality (Leszczycki 1976) since the range of services required depended on the local environmental profile (Werwicki 1982). On this basis, some radical programmes evolved to consolidate rural settlement, notably in Hungary in the 1950s (when there was a plan to eliminate *tanyak* and consolidate population in *agrogorods* on the Soviet model) and Romania in the 1980s, through the late President Nicolae Ceauşescu's plan for agroindustrial towns and the destruction of 'non-viable' villages (Ronnas 1987, 1989). However, the Hungarian project was not pressed too strongly and consolidation was often frustrated when people from small settlements chose to migrate directly to the towns (Csatari and Enyedi 1986). The Romanian plan seemed more likely to succeed (Sampson 1984) given Ceauşescu's ideological commitment: he claimed the building of socialism as a personal hobby, recalling Stalin's boast that there was no fortress the Bolsheviks could not storm. More generally, however, the 'unbridled voluntarism' of the rural programme has been linked with a personal inferiority complex and a wider perception of communism's inferiority in Romania in the inter-war years (Tismaneanu n.d.). But the plan was overtaken by the revolution in 1989 and so it transpires that, at the end of the communist era, most cases of village abandonment have resulted not from comprehensive settlement projects but from the piecemeal extension of lignite quarries in FCS and FGDR and soil contamination in the Głogów 'Copper Basin' of Poland. In Bohemia, 65 villages were destroyed to make way for the expansion of huge lignite quarries: eventually five separate complexes, each covering some 25sq.km, required the resettlement of 180,000 people. This was a far greater upheaval than the much-publicized programme of *sistematizare* in Romania in the late 1980s, where only a handful of villages were destroyed before the revolution.

REGIONAL PLANNING

Under the central planning system, investments were arranged spatially through a system of administrative regions (Fisher 1966). Regions were therefore important for economic management (Hajdu 1987; Horváth 1987). Major changes to the regional administrative system were normally undertaken by communist governments at the outset (Berentsen 1981) and each national system was overhauled from time to time, as the Romanian experience demonstrates (Helin 1967). However, it was at the centre that decisions were made and the regions were largely passive recipients of plan directives (Berentsen et al. 1989; Bachtler 1992; Mihailovic 1972). Regional authorities exercised a limited influence (Bennett 1989) and although Poland's planning organizations were abolished in 1949, their influence remained apparent in the first medium-term plans of the communist regime, and a law on spatial planning was passed in 1961 to ensure 'adequate development for particular parts of the country' (Stasiak 1993, p.9). Equalization was a goal frequently mentioned in policy statements (Koropeckyj 1972) and each country had its own particular strategy as suggested by studies of Hungary (Sillince 1987) and Poland (Hamilton 1982).

There was also some increase in local independence through administrative reforms in the 1980s (Palne Kovacs 1988). Local authorities could now exercise greater initiative and they became more accessible to lobbying by local societies. In FCS, the administrative reform of 1983 gave more power to 'basic-level national committees that are closest to the citizen and are in the best position to judge the legitimacy of citizens' needs and interests' (Vidlakova and Zarecky 1989, p.179). The 1978 reform in Bulgaria provided for an elected mayor (*kmet*) with the duty to manage public services and organize social and cultural activities, although with inadequate finance and administrative power until 1988. Provision was made for merging of municipalities to create 'associated municipalities' to find more efficient solutions to local problems concerned with infrastructure and the assimilation of new economic activities. There was probably most substance in the reforms in Hungary, where there was an attempt to revive local democracy by providing a new administrative body (*eloljaroszag*) in villages that did not have their own administrative functions because of the merging of councils. Their role was to defend local interests and mobilize local initiatives (Maurel 1989, p.121). This measure was one of several important changes in the administrative reform of 1984 (Hajdu 1989). There was also local economic management by councils in 1986 and the responsibilities of local government were expected to increase further, even under the communist system. Finance was always a sticking point, however, and it is significant that in the FGDR after 1980, some plan targets were handled by local authorities resourced by lump-sum payments. This gave them 'direct access to the financial resources derived from the economic enterprises in their localities' (Brauniger 1989, p.201) and, with it, the stimulus to use the money as efficiently as possible, perhaps carrying out more building work (such as dwelling units) than the sum was notionally geared to. In Poland there was a new regime of regional autonomy through the subordination of some 1,800 enterprises to voivodship administration and a wider reintegration of society at the individual settlement level as well as the voivodship (Ciechocinska 1989). There was more finance for small towns and villages in the 1980s, but the budget was tight everywhere. Hence, thinking moved towards tax-raising powers for local government (Nagy 1993).

There were considerable contrasts between regions. Broadly, a distinction can be made between 'urban regions', where the regional centre was a large city with half a million population or more and where the urban population in the region as a whole was relatively large, and 'rural regions' where urbanization was more restrained and where population was lost by migration to stronger regions. In the case of Poland, there was a net loss of population to Warsaw from the surrounding regions of Lomza, Płock, Siedlce and Radom; also to Poznań from Gniezno, Konin and Piła (Zurek 1975; Zurkowa and Księzak 1980). Regional policies tended to seek 'equality' through promoting industry in the administrative centres, which impacted on rural areas through increased commuting and permanent migration. But the trend towards convergence was always slowed by the built-in advantages of the advanced regions, expressed in high places through political clout (Ianos 1988). Low productivity and inefficiency in some backward areas also made for caution (Palairet 1992), although the importance of international trade gave some advantage to the use of coastal locations and sites on the Soviet frontier (Ghenovici 1985).

Regional contrasts were very much related to urbanization and industrialization levels, and were not rural problems directly. The literature made considerable mention of the problems of backward areas (Farago and Hrubi 1988). Regional disparities narrowed to some extent, although problems remained (Demko 1984; Szelenyi 1978). Studies of regional inequality became quite numerous in the late 1970s and 1980s (Fuchs and Demko 1979; Kende and Strmiska 1987; Nelson 1983). In the case of Poland, insufficient attention was given to the problem during the quarter century from 1950 to 1975 (Kuklinski 1976). The country seemed to split into two halves (Gorzelak and Szuk 1989) with polarization between the urbanized areas (Kowalski 1986) and the more backward rural regions (Zimon 1979). Kortus and Adamus (1989) have explained how the Polish state experienced problems in trying to industrialize the Carpathian region of the country, long neglected under the Habsburgs (with the exception of Bielsko's weaving traditions and the oil of Krosno, Jaslo and Gorlice) and only modestly favoured by factories which were built between the wars (as at Jaslo and Sanok). Hydropower projects built after 1945 were successful, but factories were too large, creating oppressive commuting and environmental problems and generating conflicts with the region's tourist industry. It was particularly difficult for the Podhale peasants to come to terms with the shoe factory at Novy Targ and there was a heavy turnover of workers as a result. The carbon-electrode plant at Novy Sącz infringed planning principles and caused pollution which again conflicted with local tourism. Small, clean industries were much to be preferred and a broad-based strategy was needed instead of the fetishizing of industry.

In the case of FFRY, there was regional autonomy for both administrative and economic organizations. Indeed, 'the spheres of authority granted to the regional level made it possible for the administrative agencies in each of the republics to become the major redistributional centres' (Perger 1989, p.105). But regional development was of great political importance in a multinational situation (Milanovic 1987; Pleskovic and Dolenc 1982) and reference should be made to the special fund of 1965 for 'Insufficiently-Developed Areas'. This involved the allocation of up to 2 per cent of the social sector economy's gross material product to the less-developed regions as well as an interregional reallocation of resources. However, the power of local authorities and effectiveness of specific regional measures should not be exaggerated. There was much rural neglect, which probably reached its highest levels in border regions where security considerations were dominant (Kovacs 1989). Reference has already been made to the depopulated state of Bohemia's western borderlands where a broad 'green belt' was maintained through the expansion of forests and a decrease in both agriculture and settlement. In Hungary, it has been noted that collectivization had a negative effect, because large-scale agricultural enterprises often disregarded farming systems that would have maximized local income and employment. Enlargement of cooperatives by amalgamation then led to the setting up of the headquarters within the most prosperous community, leaving the weaker villages to be further marginalized when new investments were allocated. In 1980, the population density in these border communities stood below the rates to 1900, due to pronounced out-migration followed by natural decrease, which has played the primary role in recent decades.

In FGDR, a very elaborate control system was introduced at the time the Berlin Wall was built in 1961 (Shears 1971). It was not possible for FGDR citizens to enter a strip of territory extending back for several kilometres from the frontier with West Germany. Many villages were cut off from normal circulation and some sensitive areas were cleared altogether with the exception of 'reliable' families. Consequently, the frontier areas had to be supported with their own closed economies and light industries were extended at this time, including a textile factory at Tanne which employed a hundred workers. Some modifications to the regime allowed a revival of the tourist industry in such Harz Mountain villages as Schierke and Tanne, but after 1989 free circulation has been possible. This has been good for tourism but disastrous for many of the protected manufacturing industries. Hungary took particular interest in the development of border regions where there were large cities isolated from much of their historic hinterlands (Tóth 1993). Szeged's growth was impeded by the proximity of the frontier but the city benefited through the policy of establishing counter-poles for Budapest (Krajko 1980). Some local cross-border arrangements were made: Hungarian agricultural products were processed at Beli Monastir in Croatia and a customs-free area was established at Sopron to encourage Austrian enterprise. Hungary also became involved in the Alps–Adria Working Community (Horvath 1993).

CONCLUSION

East European agriculture had to attempt a rapid transition from feudalism to capitalism in the course of the nineteenth century, yet within the context of a well-populated countryside where a personal stake in the land was an important political priority. Democratic governments have had to recognize the need for land reform while also recognizing that there has never been enough land to go round and seeking to safeguard food production for the home market and for export. Urban-based employment was certainly appreciated as a solution to land hunger and a prerequisite for the acceptance of large farms, yet the level of growth was quite insufficient in most countries for any transformation to be achieved before the communist period. Indeed, under communism there continued to be a rural population in the Balkan countries and also in Poland, to justify a labour-intensive approach to agriculture, although with sharply-contrasting forms of organization. Communist agriculture was widely perceived in the West as a disaster area, but with hindsight it is evident that failure to meet production targets was usually the result of 'tight' planning that made insufficient allowance for the weather. Broadly speaking, unprecedentedly high output levels were achieved thanks to heavy state support, through the central planning system, to deliver the necessary inputs and to keep food prices for the consumer low. After all, boosting the food supply (especially for meat) was of critical importance for raising urban living standards in general and rewarding the party faithful in particular. The farm workers were hardly pampered, but they usually gained enough to rebuild their houses even if it was industrial salaries that had the greatest effect on rural family budgets.

Eastern Europe now has to cope with the political challenge of land restitution and the economic problem of regulating an inevitable decline in intensification so that agriculture can become profitable for both work and investment. There will certainly have to be a further substantial shake-out of labour which makes the rural problem today as much an exercise in generating non-agricultural employment as it is one of stabilising the farming business. Once again, Eastern Europe is faced with the task of reconstruction and, with the existence of relatively open frontiers and free trade, it is possible to see the scope of regional specialization in a range of industries concerned with the processing of food, timber, ores and other raw materials, and also in tourism, given the climatic profile of the Balkans and a cultural landscape appropriate to many specific recreational themes. Many of these activities could impact very considerably on rural areas, and, in realizing these potentials, Eastern Europe can take advantage of easy lines of communication such as the Black Sea and Mediterranean route to the Middle East, and the railways and waterways linking the region with Western Europe. Eastern Europe also has a growing population which can provide a cheap and adaptable workforce, although one that will have to gear up to productivity levels closer to those in the West and accept a new work ethic in which individuals identify fully with the enterprise (agricultural or otherwise) and contribute to its success. Each country will have to find its own way through the minefields, balancing the potentials with the uncertain mood of domestic voters and global business interests.

REFERENCES

Allcock, J.B. (1980), 'The socialist transformation of the village: Yugoslav agricultural policy since 1945', in R.A. Francisco et al. (eds), *Agricultural Policies in the USSR and Eastern Europe*, Boulder, CO: Westview, pp.199–216.

Ando, M. (1980), 'Natural resources and economic development in the South Hungarian Plain', in G. Enyedi and J. Meszaros (eds), *Development of Settlement Systems*, Budapest: Hungarian Academy of Sciences, pp.151–7.

Augustinos, G. (1991), *Diverse Paths to Modernity in Southeastern Europe*, Oxford: Blackwell.

Bachtler, J. (1992), 'Regional problems and policies in Central and Eastern Europe', *Regional Studies*, **26**, 665–71.

Bajaja, V. (1980), 'Concentration and specialization in Czechoslovak and East German farming', in R.A. Francisco et al. (eds), *Agricultural Policies in*

the USSR and Eastern Europe, Boulder, CO: Westview, pp.263-94.
Barta, G. (1986), 'Rural industry in Hungary', in G. Enyedi and J. Veldman (eds), *Rural Development Issues in Industrialized Countries*, Pecs: Hungarian Academy of Sciences, Centre for Regional Studies, pp.34-44.
Basch, A. (1944), *The Danube Basin and the German Economic Sphere*, London: Kegan Paul Trench Trubner.
Beck, S. (1976), 'The emergence of the peasant worker in an upland Transylvanian mountain community', *Dialectical Anthropology*, 1, 365-75.
Bell, D.P. (1984), *Peasants in Socialist Transition: Life in a Collectivized Hungarian Village*, Berkeley, CA: University of California Press.
Bencze, I. (1971), 'Fruit and vegetable canning in the Great Hungarian Plain', in B. Sarfalvi (ed.), *The Changing Face of the Great Hungarian Plain*, Budapest: Hungarian Academy of Sciences, pp.89-105.
Benet, I. (1988), 'Hungarian agriculture in the 1970s and 1980s', in J.C. Brada and K.-E. Wädekin (eds), *Socialist Agriculture in Transition*, Boulder, CO: Westview, pp.183-95.
—— (1990), 'Hungarian agricutural policy in an international perspective', in K.-E. Wädekin (ed.), *Communist Agriculture: Farming in the Soviet Union and Eastern Europe*, London: Routledge, pp.307-20.
Bennett, R.J. (ed.) (1989), *Territory and Administration in Europe*, London: Pinter.
Berend, I. and G. Ranki (1974), *Economic Development in East Central Europe in the Nineteenth and Twentieth Centuries*, New York: Columbia University Press.
Berentsen, W.H. (1981), 'Regional change in the GDR', *Annals of the Association of American Geographers*, 71, 50-66.
—— (1982), 'Changing settlement patterns in the GDR 1945-1976', *Geoforum*, 3, 327-37.
—— et al. (eds) (1989), *Regional Development: Processes and Policies*, Budapest: Hungarian Academy of Sciences.
Bergmann, T. (1992), 'The reprivatization of farming in Eastern Germany', *Sociologia Ruralis*, 32, 305-16.
Bicik, I. and V. Stepanek (1994), 'Post-war changes of the land-use structure in Bohemia and Moravia: case study Sudetenland', *GeoJournal*, 32, 253-9.
Borgström, G. and F. Annegers (1971), 'Eastern Europe: an appraisal of food and agriculture in the thirties compared with the sixties', *Tijdschrift voor Economische en Sociale Geografie*, 62, 114-25.
Brauniger, J. (1989), 'The German Democratic Republic', in R. Bennett (ed.), *Territory and Administration in Europe*, London: Pinter, pp.191-202.
Brezinski, H. (1990), 'Private agriculture in the GDR: limitations of orthodox socialist agricultural policy', *Soviet Studies*, 42, 535-53.
Buruiana, C. (1996), 'Rural communities from Romania 1945-1989: resistance and change', in A. Barbic et al., *Rural Potentials for a Global Tomorrow*, Bucharest: International Rural Sociology Association with Bucharest University and the Romanian Academy, p.45.
Carter, F.W. (1985), 'Pollution problems in postwar Czechoslovakia', *Transactions of the Institute of British Geographers*, 10, 17-44.

Chirot, D. (ed.) (1989), *The Origin of Backwardness in Eastern Europe: Economics and Politics from the Middle Ages until the Early Twentieth Century*, Berkeley, CA: University of California Press.

Churska, Z. (1976), 'Tentative evaluation of the intensity of soil erosion as determined by natural conditions and type of land use: a case study of the valleys of the Drweca and Lower Vistula', *Geographia Polonica*, **34**, 176-93.

Ciechocinska, M. (1989), 'The level of educational achievement in Poland: a town-countryside comparison', *Geographia Polonica*, **56**, 213-25.

Cochrane, N.J. (1986), *The New Economic Mechanism in Bulgarian Agriculture*, Washington, DC: US Department of Agriculture, Economic Research Service.

Compton, P.A. and M. Pecsi (eds) (1984), *Environmental Management: British and Hungarian Case Studies*, Budapest: Hungarian Academy of Sciences.

Cook, E. (1984), 'Agricultural reform in Poland: background prospects', *Soviet Studies*, **36**, 406-26.

Csatari, B. and G. Enyedi (1986), 'The formation of new clustered rural settlements in Hungary', in G. Enyedi and J. Veldman (eds), *Rural Development Issues in Industrialized Countries*, Pecs: Hungarian Academy of Sciences Centre for Regional Studies, pp.96-105.

Czeppe, Z. (1976), 'Mapping of the geographical environment in the West Carpathians', *Geographia Polonica*, **34**, 69-71.

Dando, W.A. (1974), 'Wheat in Romania', *Annals of the Association of American Geographers*, **64**, 241-57.

Daroczi, E. (1984), 'The protection of agricultural land on the urban fringes: the case of Veszprem city', in P.A. Compton and M. Pecsi (eds), *Environmental Management: British and Hungarian Case Studies*, Budapest: Hungarian Academy of Sciences, pp.51-74.

Dawson, A.H. (1982), 'An assessment of Poland's agricultural resources', *Geography*, **67**, 297-309.

Demko, G. (ed.) (1984), *Regional Development: Problems and Policies in Eastern and Western Europe*, London: Croom Helm.

Deutsch, R. (1986), *The Food Revolution in the Soviet Union and Eastern Europe*, Boulder, CO: Westview.

Dohrs, F.E. (1971), 'Nature versus ideology in Hungarian agriculture: problems of intensification', in G.W. Hoffman (ed.), *Eastern Europe: Essays in Geographical Problems*, London: Methuen, pp.271-97.

Eberhardt, P. (1994), 'Distribution and dynamics of rural population in Central and Eastern Europe', *Geographia Polonica*, **63**, 75-94.

Elek, P.S. (1980), 'The Hungarian experiment in search of profitability', in R.A. Francisco et al. (eds), *Agricultural Policies in the USSR and Eastern Europe*, Boulder, CO: Westview, pp.165-84.

—— (1991), 'Part-time farming in Hungary: an instrument of tacit decollectivization?', *Sociologia Ruralis*, **31**, 82-8.

Ellman, M. (1982), 'Agricultural productivity under socialism', in C.K. Wilber

and K.P. Jameson (eds), *Socialist Models of Development*, Oxford: Pergamon, pp.979-89.
Entwistle, E.W. (1972), 'Agrarian-industrial complexes in Bulgaria', *Geography*, **57**, 246-8.
Enyedi, G. (ed.) (1976), *Rural Transformation in Hungary*, Budapest: Hungarian Academy of Sciences.
—— (1980), 'Regional types of living conditions in Hungary', in G. Enyedi and J. Meszaros (eds), *Development of Settlement Systems*, Budapest: Hungarian Academy of Sciences, pp.205-17.
—— (1990), 'Private economic activity and regional development in Hungary', *Geographia Polonica*, **57**, 53-62.
Farago, L. and L. Hrubi (1988), *Development Possibilities of Backward Areas in Hungary*, Pecs: Hungarian Academy of Sciences, Centre for Regional Studies.
First-Dilic, R. (1978), 'The production roles of farm women in Yugoslavia', *Sociologia Ruralis*, **18**, 125-39.
Fisher, J.C. (ed.) (1966), *City and Regional Planning in Poland*, Ithaca, NY: Cornell University Press.
Francisco, R.A. et al. (eds) (1980), *Agricultural Policies in the USSR and Eastern Europe*, Boulder, CO: Westview.
—— et al. (eds) (1979), *The Political Economy of Collectivized Agriculture*, New York: Pergamon.
Freeman, V.D. (1979), 'Agricultural development and rural change in the GDR', *Sheffield City Polytechnic Department of Geography and Environmental Studies Occasional Paper No.1*.
—— (1983), 'Agricultural reorganization in the GDR 1965-1980', *GeoJournal*, **7**, 59-66.
Fuchs, R.J. and G.J. Demko (1979), 'Geographic inequality under socialism', *Annals of the Association of American Geographers*, **69**, 301-18.
Galeski, B. (1982), 'The solving of the agrarian question in Poland', *Sociologia Ruralis*, **22**, 149-66.
Gams, I. (1991), 'Systems of adapting the littoral Dinaric karst to agrarian land use', *Geografski zbornik*, **31**, 5-106.
Gerlach, T. (1976), 'Present-day slope development in the Polish flysch Carpathians', *Geographical Studies, Polish Academy of Sciences, No.122*.
Ghenovici, A. (1985), 'Seashore location of industry: a new phenomenon in the Romanian industry distribution', *Revue Roumaine: Géographie*, **29**, 39-45.
Gil, E. and L. Starkel (1976), 'Physico-geographical investigations and their importance for the economic development of the flysch Carpathian area', *Geographia Polonica*, **34**, 47-61.
Giordano, C. (1993), 'Not all roads lead to Rome', *Eastern European Countryside*, **1**, 5-16.
Gorzelak, G. and R. Szuk (1989), 'Spatial order and Polish disorder: problems in the Polish space economy', *Geoforum*, **20**, 175-85.
Hajdu, Z. (1987), *Administrative Division and Administrative Geography in*

Hungary, Pecs: Hungarian Academy of Sciences, Centre for Regional Studies.
—— (1989), 'Hungary: developments in local administration', in R. Bennett (ed.), *Territory and Administration in Europe*, London: Pinter, pp.154-67.
Hajnal, B. (1989), 'The role of small towns in the development of an underdeveloped region: the case of Szabolcs-Szatmar county', in P.A. Compton and M. Pecsi (eds), *Theory and Practice in British and Hungarian Geography*, Budapest: Hungarian Academy of Sciences, pp.257-72.
Hall, D.R. (1987), 'Albania', in A.H. Dawson (ed.), *Planning in Eastern Europe*, London: Croom Helm, pp.35-65.
Halpern, J. (1967), 'Farming as a way of life: Yugoslav peasant attitudes', in J.F. Karcz (ed.), *Soviet and East European Agriculture*, Berkeley, CA: University of California Press, pp.356-84.
Hamilton, F.E.I. (1975), *Poland's Western and Northern Territories*, Oxford: Oxford University Press.
—— (1982), 'Regional policy for Poland: a search for equity', *Geoforum*, **13**, 121-32.
Harcsa, I. (1993), 'Small scale farming informal cooperation and the household economy in Hungary', *Sociologia Ruralis*, **33**, 105-8.
Harris, L. (1948), 'Lucimia restituta: rebuilding a Polish village', *Geographical Magazine*, **20**, 438-43.
Held, J. (ed.) (1980), *The Modernization of Agriculture: Rural Transformation in Hungary*, Boulder, CO: Westview.
Helin, R. (1967), 'The volatile administrative map of Rumania', *Annals of the Association of American Geographers*, **57**, 481-502.
Hollos, M. and B.C. Maday (eds) (1983), *New Hungarian Peasants: An East Central European Experience with Collectivization*, Boulder, CO: East European Monographs.
Horvath, G. (1987), *Development of the Regional Management of the Economy in East Central Europe*, Pecs: Hungarian Academy of Sciences Centre for Regional Studies.
—— (ed.) (1993), *Development Strategies for the Alpine–Adriatic Region*, Pecs: Centre for Regional Studies, Hungarian Academy of Sciences.
Ianos (1988), 'Geographical mutations in the territorial distribution of industry in Romania in the second half of the twentieth century', *Revue Roumaine: Géographie*, **32**, 85-9.
Jackson, W.A.D. (1971), *Agrarian Policies and Problems in Communist and Non-communist Countries*, Seattle, WA: Univerity of Washington Press.
Jaehne, G. (1980), 'Problems of agricultural integration within the CMEA', in R.A. Francisco et al. (eds), *Agricultural Policies in the USSR and Eastern Europe*, Boulder, CO: Westview, pp.221-35.
Jahn, A. (1972), 'Niveo-eolian processes in the Sudetes Mountains', *Geographia Polonica*, **23**, 93-110.
Jancar, B. (1987), *Environmental Management in the Soviet Union and Yugoslavia*, Durham, NC: Duke University Press.
Kende, P. and Z. Strmiska (1987), *Equality and Inequality in Eastern Europe*, Leamington Spa: Berg.

Kideckel, D. (1993), *The Solitude of Collectivism: Romanian Villagers to Revolution and Beyond*, Ithaca, NY: Cornell University Press.

Klekner, P. (1992), 'The role of agriculture in the development of fringe areas', in M. Tikkylainen (ed.), *Development Issues and Strategies in the New Europe*, Aldershot: Gower, pp.121-30.

Korbonski, A. (1965), *The Politics of Socialist Agriculture in Poland 1945-1960*, New York: Columbia University Press.

—— (1967), 'Peasant agriculture in socialist Poland since 1956: an alternative to collectivization', in J.F. Karcz (ed.), *Soviet and East European Agriculture*, Berkeley, CA: University of California Press, pp.417-36.

—— (1990), 'Soldiers and peasants: Polish agriculture after martial law', in K.-E. Wädekin (ed.), *Communist Agriculture: Farming in the Soviet Union and Eastern Europe*, London: Routledge, pp.263-78.

Koropeckyj, I.S. (1972), 'Equalization of regional development in socialist countries: an empirical study', *Economic Development and Cultural Change*, **21**, 68-86.

Kortus, B. and J. Adamus (1989), 'Characteristic traits of industry in the Polish Carpathians', *Zeszyty Naukowe Uniwersytetu Jagiellonskiego: Prace Geograficzne*, **76**, 95-100.

Kostrowicki, J. (1975), 'Transformation trends in the spatial organization of agriculture in Poland 1960-1990', *Geographia Polonica*, **32**, 27-41.

Kovach, I. (1991), 'Rediscovering small-scale enterprise in rural Hungary', in S. Whatmore et al. (eds), *Regional Policy Perspectives on Small-scale Production*, London: Fulton, pp.78-96.

—— (1993), 'Part-time small-scale farming as a major form of economic pluriactivity in Hungary', in J. Szmatka et al. (eds), *Eastern European Societies on the Threshold of Change*, Lampeter: Edwin Mellen Press, pp.175-92.

Kovacs, Z. (1989), 'The effects of a national border: human geographical approaches', in P.A. Compton and M. Pecsi (eds), *Theory and Practice in British and Hungarian Geography*, Budapest: Hungarian Academy of Sciences, pp.75-91.

Kowalski, J.S. (1986), 'Regional conflicts in Poland: spatial polarisation in a centrally planned economy', *Environment and Planning A*, **18**, 599-617.

Krajko, G. (1980), 'Main tendencies in the development of Szeged', in G. Enyedi and J. Meszaros (eds), *Development of Settlement Systems*, Budapest: Hungarian Academy of Sciences, pp.131-9.

Kuklinski, A. (1976), 'Strong and weak regions in socio-economic policies', *Przegląd Geograficzny*, **48**, 389-400 (in Polish with an English summary).

Kwiatkowska, E. (1976), 'New forms of rural settlement in the voivodship of Torun in the 30 years of People's Poland', *Przegląd Geograficzny*, **48**, 635-48 (in Polish with an English summary).

Lacko, L. (1986), 'The place of village development in the settlement development policy of Hungary', in G. Enyedi and J. Veldman (eds), *Rural Development Issues in Industrialized Countries*, Pecs: Hungarian Academy of Sciences Centre for Regional Studies, pp.29-33.

Lazarcik, G. (1967), 'The performance of Czechoslovak agriculture since

World War Two', in J.F. Karcz (ed.), *Soviet and East European Agriculture*, Berkeley, CA: University of California Press, pp.385-410.

Leszczycki, S. (1976), 'Methods to activate less developed areas', *Przegląd Geograficzny*, **48**, 379-88 (in Polish with an English summary).

MacIntyre, R.J. (1988), 'The small enterprise and agricultural initiatives in Bulgaria: institutional innovation without reform', *Soviet Studies*, **40**, 602-15.

Manchin, R. and I. Szelenyi (1985), 'Theories of family agricultural production in collectivised economies', *Sociologia Ruralis*, **25**, 248-68.

Maurel, M.-C. (1989), 'Administrative reforms in Eastern Europe: an overview', in R. Bennett (ed.), *Territory and Administration in Europe*, London: Pinter, pp.111-23.

Meze, D. (1984), 'Mountain farms in Slovenia', *Geographica Iugoslavica*, **5**, 47-54.

Mihailovic, K. (1972), *Regional Development: Experiences and Prospects in Eastern Europe*, The Hague: Mouton.

Milanovic, B. (1987), 'Patterns of regional growth in Yugoslavia 1952-1983', *Journal of Development Economics*, **15**, 1-19.

Miller, C.E. et al. (1973), *Agricultural Statistics of the Soviet Union and Eastern Europe*, Washington, DC: US Department of Agriculture.

Moore, W.E. (1945), *Economic Demography of Eastern and Southern Europe*, Geneva: League of Nations.

Morgan, W.B. (1985), 'Cut flowers in Warsaw', *GeoJournal*, **11**, 339-48.

—— (1989), 'Recent government policy and private agriculture in Poland', *Resource Management and Optimization*, **6**, 291-305.

—— (1990), 'Some aspects of recent improvements in the productivity of private agriculture in Poland', *Geographia Polonica*, **57**, 99-110.

Nagy, C.K. (1993), 'Local development strategies', in A. Duro (ed.), *Spatial Research and the Social-political Changes*, Pecs: Hungarian Academy of Sciences Centre for Regional Studies, pp.103-7.

Nelson, D.N. (ed.) (1983), *Communism and the Politics of Inequalities*, Lexington, KY: Heath & Co.

Palairet, M. (1992), 'Ramiz Sadiku: a case study in the industrialisation of Kosovo', *Soviet Studies*, **44**, 897-912.

Palne Kovacs, I. (1988), *Chance of Local Independence in Hungary*, Pecs: Hungarian Academy of Sciences Centre for Regional Studies.

Pecsi, M. and F. Probald (eds) (1974), *Man and Environment*, Budapest: Hungarian Academy of Sciences.

Perger, E. (1989), 'An overview of East European developments', in R. Bennett (ed.), *Territory and Administration in Europe*, London: Pinter, pp.93-110.

Persanyi, M. (1990), 'The rural environment in a post-socialist economy: the case of Hungary', in T. Marsden et al. (eds), *Technological Change and the Rural Environment*, London: Fulton, pp.33-52.

Pine, F.T. and P.T. Bogdanowicz (1982), 'Policy response and alternative strategy: the process of change in Polish highland village', *Dialectical Anthropology*, **7** (2), pp.67-80.

Pleskovic, B. and M. Dolenc (1982), 'Regional development and multinational country: the case of Yugoslavia', *International Regional Science Review*, **7**, 1-24.
Pryor, F.L. (1992), *The Red and the Green: The Rise and Fall of Collectivized Agriculture in Marxist Regimes*, Princeton, NJ: Princeton University Press.
Ravbar, M. (1992), *Suburbanizacija v Sloveniji*, Ljubljana: Univerza v Ljubljani Oddelek za geografijo.
Ronnas, P. (1987), 'Agrarian change and economic development in rural Romania: a case study of the Oas region', *Geografiska Annaler*, **69b**, 51-63.
—— (1989), 'Turning the Romanian peasant into a new socialist man: an assessment of rural development policy in Romania', *Soviet Studies*, **41**, 543-59.
Rosenbladt, S. (1991), 'Environmental concerns in Poland', in G. Stokes (ed.), *From Stalinism to Pluralism: A Documentary History of Eastern Europe Since 1945*, Oxford: Oxford University Press, pp.188-92.
Sampson, S. (1984), *National Integration Through Socialist Planning: An Anthropological Study of a Romanian New Town*, Boulder, CO: Westview.
Sarfalvi, B. (ed.) (1971), *The Changing Face of the Great Hungarian Plain*, Budapest: Hungarian Academy of Sciences.
—— (1980), 'Regional divergence in the educational level of rural settlements', in G. Enyedi and J. Meszaros (eds), *Development of Settlement Systems*, Budapest: Hungarian Academy of Sciences, pp.219-24.
Schinke, E. (1990), 'New forms of farm organisation in the GDR as compared to the USSR and East European states', in K.-E. Wädekin (ed.), *Communist Agriculture: Farming in the Soviet Union and Eastern Europe*, London: Routledge, pp.251-62.
Senegacnik, J. et al. (1983), *The Direction of Regional Development of Slovenia: Slovene Alps Northeast Slovenia Bela Krajina*, Ljubljana: Institute of Geography/*Geographica Slovenica* **14**.
Shears, D. (1971), *The Ugly Frontier*, London: Chatto & Windus.
Sillince, J.A.A. (1987), 'Regional policy in Hungary: objectives and achievements', *Transactions of the Institute of British Geographers*, **12**, 451-64.
Sinclair, R.P. (1979), 'Bureaucratic agriculture: planned social change in the GDR', *Sociologia Ruralis*, **19**, 211-26.
Singleton, F. (1987), 'National Parks and the conservation of nature in Yugoslavia', in F. Singleton (ed.), *Environmental Problems in the Soviet Union and Eastern Europe*, London: Lynne Rienner, pp.183-98.
Sjoberg, O. (1991), *Rural Change and Development in Albania*, Boulder, CO: Westview.
Skrodzki, M. (1972), 'Present day water and wind erosion of soils in northeast Poland', *Geographia Polonica*, **23**, 77-91.
Sokolovsky, J. (1990), *Peasants and Power: State Autonomy and the Collectivization of Agriculture in Eastern Europe*, Boulder, CO: Westview.
Stambuk, M. (1991), 'Agricultural depopulation in Croatia', *Sociologia Ruralis*, **31**, 281-9.

Stasiak, A. (1977), 'Changes in the professional structure of the rural population of Poland', *Przegląd Geograficzny*, **49**, 677-88 (in Polish with an English summary).

—— (1992), 'Problems of depopulation of rural areas of Poland after 1950', *Landscape and Urban Planning*, **22**, 161-76.

—— (1993), 'Development of spatial planning in Poland on a regional and countrywide scale', in A. Duro (ed.), *Spatial Research and the Sociopolitical Changes*, Pecs: Centre for Regional Studies, 7-14.

Stefănescu, I. (1977), 'Changes occurring in the agriculture of Dobrogea during the last hundred years', *Revue Roumaine de Géographie*, **21**, 87-101.

Stipetic, V. (1982), 'The development of the peasant economy in socialist Yugoslavia', in R. Stojanovic (ed.), *The Functioning of the Yugoslav Economy*, White Plains, NY: M.E. Sharpe, pp.167-200.

Stryakiewicz, T. (1985), 'The relationships between the location of the agricultural processing industry and the produce base of the Poznan region', *Geographia Polonica*, **51**, 189-98.

Sugar, P.F. (1977), *Southeastern Europe under Ottoman Rule 1354-1804*, Seattle, WA: University of Washington Press.

Swain, N. (1985), *Collective Farms Which Work?*, Cambridge: Cambridge University Press.

—— (1987), 'Hungarian agriculture in the early 1980s: retrenchment followed by reform', *Soviet Studies*, **39**, 24-39.

—— (1992), *Collectivization in Hungary: Background Notes*, Liverpool: University of Liverpool Centre for Central and Eastern European Studies.

Szelenyi, I. (1978), 'Spatial inequalities in state socialist redistributive economies', *International Journal of Comparative Sociology*, **19**, 63-87.

—— (1988), *Socialist Entrepreneurs: Embourgeoisement in Rural Hungary*, Madison, WI: University of Wisconsin Press.

—— and R. Manchin (1986), *Peasants, Proletarians, Entrepreneurs: Transformation of Rural Social Structures under State Socialism*, Madison, WI: University of Wisconsin Press.

Szmatka, J. et al. (1993), 'In search of the syndrome of threshold situation', in J. Szmatka et al. (eds), *Eastern European Societies on the Threshold of Change*, Lampeter: Edwin Mellen Press, pp.1-14.

Szulc, H. (1978), 'Property structure and types of transformation in the layouts of West Pomeranian villages in the period from 1945 to 1975', *Przegląd Geograficzny*, **50**, 87-99 (in Polish with an English summary).

Szurek, J.-C. (1987), 'Family farms in Polish agricultural policy 1945-1985', *East European Politics and Societies*, **1**, 225-54.

Szymanski, B. (1978), 'The initial results of investigations concerning the degree of afforestation in the Kielce region', *Przegląd Geograficzny*, **50**, 603-19 (in Polish with an English summary).

Thomas, C. (1978), 'Decay and development in Mediterranean Yugoslavia', *Geography*, **63**, 179-87.

—— and M. Vojvoda (1973), 'Alpine communities in transition, in Bohinj, Yugoslavia', *Geography*, **58**, 217-26.

Timar, J. (1989), 'New features of the linkages between tanyas (farmstead settlements) and towns in the Great Hungarian Plain', in P.A. Compton and M. Pecsi (eds), *Theory and Practice in British and Hungarian Geography*, Budapest: Hungarian Academy of Sciences, pp.273-94.

Tismaneanu, V. (n.d.), 'Understanding National Socialism: A Comparative Approach to the History of Romanian Communism', Wilson Center Smithsonian Institution East European Program Occasional Paper, No. 25.

Tomasevich, J. (1955), *Peasants Politics and Economic Change in Yugoslavia*, Stanford, CA: Stanford University Press.

Tomczak, F. (1988), 'The development strategy of agriculture in Poland', in J.C. Brada and K.-E. Wädekin (eds), *Socialist Agriculture in Transition*, Boulder, CO: Westview, pp.159-69.

—— (1990), 'Farming and socialism in Poland: towards a new understanding of the peasant question', in K.-E. Wädekin (ed.), *Communist Agriculture: Farming in the Soviet Union and Eastern Europe*, London: Routledge, pp.279-89.

Tóth. J. (1993), 'Historical and today's socio-economic conditions of regionalism in Hungary', in A. Duro (ed.), *Spatial Research and the Sociopolitical Changes*, Pecs: Centre for Regional Studies, pp.15-28.

Trend, H. (1974), *Agriculture in Eastern Europe: A Comparative Study*, Munich: Radio Free Europe.

Turnock, D. (1989), *Eastern Europe: An Economic and Political Geography*, London: Routledge.

Vasary, I. (1987), *Beyond the Plain: Social Change in a Hungarian Village*, Boulder, CO: Westview.

—— (1990), 'Competing paradigms: peasant farming and collectivization in a Balaton community', *Journal of Communist Studies*, **6** (2), 163-82.

Verdery, K. (1991), *Transylvanian Villagers: Three Centuries of Political Economic and Ethnic Change*, Berkeley, CA: University of California Press.

Vidlakova, O. and P. Zarecky (1989), 'Czechoslovakia: the development of public administration', in R. Bennett (ed.), *Territory and Administration in Europe*, London: Pinter, pp.168-79.

Volgyes, I. et al. (1980), *The Modernization of Hungarian Agriculture*, Boulder, CO: Westview.

Wädekin, K.-E. (1977), 'The place of agriculture in the European communist countries', *Soviet Studies*, **29**, 238-54.

—— (1982), *Agrarian Policies in Communist Europe: A Critical Introduction*, The Hague: Nijhoff.

—— (1990), 'Determinants and trends of reform in communst agriculture: a concluding essay', in K.-E. Wädekin (ed.), *Communist Agriculture: Farming in the Soviet Union and Eastern Europe*, London: Routledge, pp.321-31.

Werwicki, A. (1982), 'Problems of small towns in Maria Kielczewska-Zaleska's research', *Przegląd Geograficzny*, **53**, 263-8 (in Polish with an English summary).

Wiedermann, P. (1980), 'The origins and development of agro-industrial development in Bulgaria', in R.A. Francisco et al. (eds), *Agricultural*

Policies in the USSR and Eastern Europe, Boulder, CO: Westview, pp.97–135.

—— (1982), 'Agricultural development in Bulgaria 1976–1985', in K.-E. Wädekin (ed.), *Current Trends in the Soviet and East European Economy*, Berlin: Duncker & Humblot, pp.273–302.

Wyzan, M.L. (1989), 'The Bulgarian experience with centrally-planned agriculture: lessons for social reformers', in K.R. Gray (ed.), *Contemporary Soviet Agriculture: Comparative Perspectives*, Ames, IA: Iowa State University Press.

—— (1990), 'Bulgarian agriculture: sweeping reform mediocre performance', in K.-E. Wädekin (ed.), *Communist Agriculture: Farming in the Soviet Union and Eastern Europe*, London: Routledge, pp.290–306.

Zagoroff, S.D. et al. (1955), *The Agricultural Economy of the Danubian Countries 1935–1945*, Stanford, CA: Stanford University Press.

Ziolkowski, M. (1993), 'Individuals and the social system: the types of individuality and varieties of its contribution to society', in J. Szmatka et al. (eds), *Eastern European Societies on the Threshold of Change*, Lampeter: Edwin Mellen Press, pp.207–24.

Zimon, H. (1979), 'Regional inequalities in Poland', *Economic Geography*, **55**, 242–52.

Zurek, A. (1975), 'Spatial structure of urban migrations in the Kielce voivodship', *Polish Academy of Sciences Geographical Studies*, No.113 (in Polish with an English summary).

Zurkowa, A. and J. Księzak (1980), 'Elements of spatial structure of internal migrations in Poland', *Przegląd Geograficzny*, **52**, 81–102 (in Polish with an English summary).

2. Albania

Derek Hall

This chapter aims to evaluate briefly the context, nature and consequences of Albanian rural structural adjustment which has taken place since the early 1990s. The domestic political, economic and social context for such processes of change remains fluid, and original empirical research and documentation is still relatively fragmentary. None the less, in terms of the comprehensive structural shift which the country, and especially the countryside, has undergone in recent years, and the considerable upheaval which has accompanied it, the Albanian experience represents an instructive model of rural transformation. Some observers would argue that the transition should have been easier in Albania than elsewhere in the region because of the poverty of the economy and small scale of the country (Åslund and Sjöberg 1992). While such domestic processes have been proceeding, the sense of potential external threat from an overspill of the wars of Yugoslav succession, not least arising from the position of Kosovar Albanians in a greater Serbia, has added a further layer of uncertainty. Despite the plight of Kosovo not being included in the Dayton accord, the Bosnian peace process and its implications for the rest of the former Yugoslavia appear to have brought some stability to the region.

CONSEQUENCES OF STATE SOCIALISM

A distinctive ultimate goal of Albanian rural collectivization, although not attained, was the full state ownership of agricultural activity in the transformation of cooperatives into state farms and the abolition of private plots and private herds (Baci 1981; Bollano and Dari 1984; Wildermuth 1993). Aside from questions of scale and infrastructure, agricultural collectivization had several major consequences. First, the former monocultural aspect of Albanian agriculture was removed. Thus bread grains occupied 48.3 per cent of the country's sown area in 1990 compared to 84.5 per cent in 1938 (DeS 1991, p.183). Industrial crops became important in diversifying and raising the level of agricultural production. Second, an emergence of regional specialization exploited the comparative advantages of physical conditions. Hence the cultivation of cotton in the central coastal districts of Fier, Lushnjë and Durrës, sugar beet in the Korçë Basin, and vegetables in the districts around the main urban centres of Tirana, Durrës, Shkodër and Vlorë.

There was also a considerable development of land reclamation and irrigation programmes, permitting a much greater area of cultivated land to be used for both food and industrial crops. By 1990, 423th.ha out of a total of 700th.ha of arable land were under irrigation, representing 60 per cent of the total cultivated area. A dense network of drainage channels extended over 200th.ha of land. Expansion of cultivable land entailed an improvement in desalination methods, reclamation from coastal and lakeside lagoons, and an extension of cultivation in upland areas, often through extensive terracing (Hall 1987; Kusse and Winkels 1990). Although by the end of the 1980s cultivable land had increased by about 240 per cent since the end of the Second World War, population growth had been even greater, such that the amount of arable land per person had decreased by 10 per cent, a process which had accelerated during the 1980s.

Unprecedented social unrest following urban food shortages led to experiments in decentralizing economic and administrative control during 1988. In a few selected districts, brigades of 30-60 peasants, corresponding to one or two extended families, were given the right to 'own' small herds. In just over a year this semi-privatization of livestock led to a fivefold increase in the number of cattle held. As a result, cooperatives were permitted to sell their surplus at local markets, and were encouraged to market their farm and livestock products in major urban areas. To stimulate meat and vegetable production and raise rural incomes, an encouragement of private agricultural plots followed. Peasants were allowed to rear cattle on their own plots, and cooperatives were asked to transfer stock to their members for this purpose: in hilly and mountainous areas 2,000sq.m to each member, in addition to their private plots, and in lowland areas peasants were given up to 2,000sq.m (EIU 1990, p.36). Although persistent drought tended to limit the programme's effectiveness, the domesticated animal population again increased dramatically.

AGRICULTURE SINCE 1991

Political change in 1991 brought new, albeit confused, land and private property laws. These dissolved all cooperatives but forbade the purchase or sale of land. Anarchy in the countryside ensued as cooperative land (230th.ha out of a total of 531th.ha) was distributed among the peasants, some of whom also seized land and livestock. In the rush to regain lands held before 1944, former rural landowning families unilaterally fenced off territory, in some cases destroying economic installations and buildings such as schools (Zanga 1991) in the process. Essential foodstuffs were rationed and the country became almost totally dependent on imported supplies. Looting of warehouses followed.

Whole areas of upland agriculture, particularly the hillside terracing which had received substantial investment of financial and labour resources in the 1960s and 1970s, were abandoned, as rural to urban and upland and lowland migration gained pace (Hall 1996a). Collectivized agriculture had absorbed a rapidly growing workforce during the 1970s and early 1980s, but following privatization the agrarian sector would no longer be able to accommodate annually up to 70,000 young people entering the national job market. Nor, with new freedoms and priorities, did young people look to the sector as a first-choice 'career'. While a shedding of surplus rural labour might have appeared to present an ideal opportunity for agricultural mechanization, difficult topography, the emergence of small family holdings and capital shortages severely constrained such developments. The new Democratic Party government urgently needed to focus its attention on completing and consolidating land reform so that external aid could be switched away from food and on to the transfer of skills and appropriate technology and information (Hall 1992b).

Fragmentation

Redistribution of cooperative land produced more than 379,000 family holdings of 0.8–2ha, with an average size of 1.85ha (Deslondes and Sivignon 1995), covering 75 per cent of the country's arable land. In a series of interviews with 542 farm families undertaken during 1992, IFDC (1993) found the average age of farmers to be 46 years and the average cultivated area 0.7ha; mean distance of travel to cultivated fields was 0.8km, to markets for agricultural inputs 6km and to markets to sell produce 17.4km. Ninety-eight per cent of farm households reported owning animals: 90 per cent owned cows (on average 1.5 per family) and 63 per cent sheep (6.1 per family). Less than one per cent of farmers hired labour for agricultural work, emphasizing the small-scale and essentially family-based nature of post-socialist farm operations.

The problems confronted by such family farms, and reflected in some of the above findings included: (a) a lack of capital and space to improve production techniques; (b) uncertainty of input supplies; (c) exposure to competition and risk; (d) primitive marketing and unstable markets; (e) poor access to information and technical assistance; (f) lack of forward planning; (g) high rates of interest for credit and unpredictable rates of inflation; and (h) an inadequate legal system to permit the buying and selling of land (Leiby and Marra 1993).

These problems raised questions such as the extent to which market mechanisms could establish a sectoral balance of production within the country. During 1992, annual agricultural output increased in volume by 17 per cent. Large increases were recorded in the production of green vegetables, pulses, potatoes, water melons and dairy produce. A dramatic decrease in the output of industrial crops such as cotton reflected the preferences of new private peasant farmers to grow crops intended for consumption and for domestic markets, from which they could derive larger profits than from industrial crops, the processing of which had been disrupted. Such trends have continued (Table 2.1).

'Capitalist' farmers' cooperative associations began to emerge after the April 1992 electoral defeat of the communists. About a hundred associations, each made up of 15–20 families joining voluntarily and electing a management board, were established, mostly in lowland arable areas, with total landholdings averaging 40ha, although ranging from 25 to 300ha. Their formation helped to stimulate market awareness, an increase in productivity and a greater use of machinery, and assisted a move away

Table 2.1 Albania: selected agricultural production (th.t) and livestock numbers (th.), 1990–1994

Commodity	1990	1991	1992	1993	1994
Grains	621	299	253	467	508
Vegetables	393	362	565	580	585
Sunflower seed	16	5	3	2	2
Cotton	12	4	1	0	0
Sugar beet	169	58	46	27	60
Soya beans	7	3	2	1	1
Fodder	11	3	4	18	20
Forage	2,300	2,148	2,991	3,237	3,500
Meat	92	84	91	96	106
Wool	3	3	3	3	3
Cattle	633	640	566	655	670
Sheep	1,143	1,180	1,232	1,415	1,480
Goats	776	816	858	948	1,020
Poultry	5,259	3,704	2,538	3,359	3,600

Source: EIU 1996a, pp.56–7, after Albanian Ministry of Agriculture.

from the subsistence agriculture and use of female and child labour which was characterizing the new family farms. For example, land sown with grain was shown to be three times greater per family within the associations than in non-associated farms, while land devoted to water melons, which had experienced significant market price reductions, was ten times less (Anon 1993). The more advanced farms and members of the farming community were more likely to join cooperative associations so that their membership tended to reinforce differences between farms. Since 1992, a number of trade centres have been set up by agricultural training centres to assist the newly private farmers.

Land Rights Complications

The lack of incentive for Albania's private farmers to produce cash crops for the domestic market needed to be seriously addressed. The problem arose out of the combination of small size of holdings and the legal inability to trade in land due to the absence of a proper record of land ownership. The government came under mounting pressure from former property owners to abrogate the July 1991 land law which redistributed land formerly held by agricultural cooperatives to their former members rather than to the prior owners who lost their land during the communist era. An organization representing these former owners, the Property with Justice National Association, heightened its campaign for the full restitution of confiscated property. The government responded by presenting a draft compensation law which provided for full compensation for those with land of no more than 15ha and a graduated compensation scheme for others: between 15 and 100ha compensation was fixed at 10 per cent, and above 100ha at 2 per cent. This would be paid in state bonds, but delays have been experienced, and the government has attempted to mollify criticism by promising former landowners the provision of land in tourist development zones along the coast (EIU 1996a, pp.55–6).

Certainly in the early years of privatization and redistribution farmers appeared to receive only vague legal status as tenants. The law forbade the further purchase of agricultural land in order to prevent these 'tenants' from causing additional confusion by selling the pre-1946 owners' land before compensation arrangements could be secured. Two problems followed from this: (a) the tenant farmers would feel insecure until they knew for certain that they legally owned the land they tilled, thereby inhibiting investment in it; and (b) the (presumably temporary) prohibition on land purchases prevented good farmers from expanding their activities. One possible way out of this dilemma surrounded the position of the 150th.ha of former state-farm land. This was now partially or wholly farmed by its former employees who lived in hope that they would receive full title to the land within three years. However, some of the former state-farm land could be given to tenants of former landowners so that the latter could be given some of their land back if they wanted it, and some of the poor aspiring highland farmers could be offered lowland land.

Only in August 1995, after persistent delay, was legislation passed entitling owners to sell and buy agricultural land (Anon 1996d). By this time, more than 506th.ha or 94 per cent of all farmland had been transferred to private ownership, creating 420,000 private farms (EIU 1996a, p.55). At the time of writing, land rights issues had still not been fully resolved. Indeed, in a number of cases they had been complicated by migration, the development of spontaneous settlements, and the dispossession of some former communists. Administrative and political uncertainty continued, with a national referendum rejecting the draft constitution promulgated by president Sali Berisha in November 1994 (Schmidt 1995) and a cross-party committee being given the task of preparing a new constitutional framework. Parliamentary elections were due in May 1996 and presidential elections in March 1997. Political, economic and social hang-overs from the communist period also continued to arise on a regular basis. For example, in May 1994, 113 peasants began a hunger strike in the northeastern town of Kukës, demanding US$1,600 compensation per person for houses and arable land lost when the communist authorities flooded their village in conjunction with the building of a hydro-electric power dam on the Drin river. Although called off when the government agreed to compensation payments, the hunger strike was reinstated in December 1994 as the money had not been disbursed (ibid., pp.11–12).

External Assistance

Foreign agricultural missions, notably of German, Italian and Dutch specialists, visited Albania in the waning months of communist power to provide advice and technical know-how for agricultural recovery. Fiatagri became involved in pilot projects in the north of the country for mechanizing the sowing and harvesting of 300ha each of maize and rice, employing machinery previously untried within the country. The Italian company later provided laser technology to aid soil levelling. Albanian reports of these projects were optimistic, quoting a 50 per cent increase in maize yields with a 50 per cent reduction in cost after the first year (Anon 1990), and a doubled yield with costs reduced by 58 per cent (and in the case of rice by 75 per cent) at the end of the two-year trial period. A joint venture with the French Ducros company, based in Durrës, secured a monopoly on processing all cultivated oleaginous crops and indigenous flora, allowing the company to operate tax free for at least three years (Anon 1991).

One problem confronting Albanian farming was the degree to which the huge amount of food aid being supplied to the country represented serious competition for, and an inhibiting influence on, domestic food production. At the same time, farm animals were being smuggled across the border into Greece to pay for the increasing flow of consumer goods moving in the opposite direction (Dizdari 1992). By the end of 1992, the Albanian government was arguing that it would be another three years before the country could reattain 1989 living standards, and that wheat production in 1993 would be 700th.t short of the amount needed to provide the population with a daily loaf of bread. Following an international conference of funding institutions held in Tirana late in 1992, five priorities were established for the Albanian agricultural sector (PHARE 1993): (a) the transformation of state farms; (b) development of rural credit and input-output marketing; (c) rebuilding and extension of irrigation and transport infrastructure; (d) the issue of formal land titles; and (e) development of agroindustry. The extension of farm credit to farmers with small and medium-sized holdings, and to farm associations, coupled with training schemes to enable a rational use of mechanical and non-chemical agrarian aids, was now of prime importance.

It was agreed to make available not less that US$100 million to support Albanian agriculture. The World Bank-EU PHARE Programme drew up a development strategy emphasizing the role of rural businesses, with an investment sum of US$30 million. The International Development Agency established a rural development fund to grant loans of US$20–1,000 to enable small farmers to buy implements, processing equipment and livestock in order to help establish small rural businesses. By 1996, some 4,000 loans had been made. Communes in the country's ten poorest districts were to receive between US$11,000 and US$25,000 to improve rural infrastructures and aid employment generation (EIU 1993, p.47). Germany, Italy and Greece would provide US$20 million to renovate agricultural equipment and tractors, and irrigation would receive US$40 million from a variety of sources including the World Bank. Investment support would also be provided for animal husbandry, forestry, the privatization of the food industry and upland development.

Joint ventures
With foreign support, in 1992 the Ministry of Agriculture established an agency for restructuring and privatizing the country's 225 state farms, which covered 23 per cent of the country's cultivable land. A three-stage programme was developed: (a) provision of credit guarantees to cover immediate investment requirements; (b) dissolution of some state farms, which was particularly necessary in upland areas to distribute land and implements among former workers; and (c) a

reorganization of other state farms into joint-stock companies with joint participation of workers, managers and the state.

In the latter case, the lowland district of Kavajë became a model. The fruit-growing farms of Kavajë and Rrogozhinë, with a total land area of 864ha, established joint ventures (Albitalia and Agrifoods) with Italian-Romanian Adventure East Service SRI to employ 600 workers. The nearby Gosa state farm joined with the Italian company Manfredonia FG to employ 650 (Anon 1993). The Italian-Romanian group later set up a joint venture with the Spitalle Frutore Durrës agricultural enterprise with the intention of improving agricultural processing and of stimulating tourism. The project also envisaged the development of 300ha of heated glasshouses, not just for the improvement and diversification of agricultural production, but also to supply hot water for Durrës residents (ATA, 15 June 1993). In addition to a total of 13 joint ventures in agriculture, representing an investment of US$28 million and employment for 4,500, by 1996 some 32 joint ventures, worth US$22.5 million, had been established in food processing. Although representing mostly Italian and Greek capital, such developments have also seen the Egyptian-based Kato Aromatik investing US$14 million in nine factories for the production of children's food and pharmaceutical products from aromatic plants in a complex at Vorë, on the Tirana-Durrës road (Anon 1996b).

Privatization of agricultural mechanization enterprises (formerly known as machine and tractor stations), begun in 1992, entailed the redistribution of some 5,500 tractors. Thirty repair centres were also sold off. The import of equipment, purchased on credit by new private firms and through Albanian *émigrés* working abroad, was also inaugurated at this time.

INFRASTRUCTURE AND RURAL DEVELOPMENT

Rural training and support is still required. Of US$25 million aid for Albanian agriculture, US$6 million was allocated for restructuring the Tirana Agricultural University at Kamëz (Leiby and Marra 1993). The EU TEMPUS and PHARE programmes and a range of charities have attempted to reinvigorate agricultural education, although the sector has lost the status it held under the communists. One area for exploration has been the extent to which farm credit could be extended to farmers with small and medium-sized holdings, and farm associations, and be coupled with training schemes to enable a rational use of mechanical and non-chemical agrarian aids. Through the better availability of credit, together with clearer legislation on the buying and selling of agricultural land, the government aims to assist the consolidation of landholdings into larger, more viable units (EIU 1996a, p.55).

A shortage of good-quality water has continued to pose problems for a number of rural areas. Most agricultural land used to be supplied with good water from the mountains via irrigation canals. These have been seriously neglected and underfunded in recent years, resulting in collapse, disrepair and clogging through the deposition of waste debris. Some farmers are able to water their crops from wells, but ground water is often saline, notably along the coastal plain. Many farmers rely solely on rain-water which, given the unreliability of recent years, can result in repeated crop failure and indebtedness. Water supply enterprises are to be privatized.

Many distant villages are still only accessible by foot or mule. Farmers may travel up to three kilometres to their fields and 20km to the nearest market. Hitching lifts and bicycling remain common practices. The privatization of public transport has seen interurban links improved with fast coach services employing second-hand vehicles imported from Greece and Italy. But local rural public transport has deteriorated with the loss of the availability of cooperative and state farm buses. Further, little investment is being put into the country's rail network as fast interurban roads and the international east–west highway link are receiving priority funding (Hall 1996b, 1996c; Rugg 1996). Although a rural telecommunications strategy has been under review, the country's overall provision, at 16 lines per thousand population, is the lowest in the region, going down to a figure of only seven per thousand in the rural areas (EIU 1996a, p.66).

Only slowly is a reliable power supply being made available in the countryside. A number of aid schemes have often exerted only a local impact, although an ECU90 million EU, EBRD and World Bank aid package to improve electricity distribution should see results during the latter part of the 1990s. Regional migration and the development of spontaneous settlements in some parts of the country has again only served to exacerbate such infrastructural shortcomings. Meanwhile, the level of chemical use on the country's land has been relatively limited, with, for example only 13 per cent of farmers reporting such use for their 1992 crop, while more than half of all farmers applied animal manure as fertilizer (IFDC 1993). Albania could thus be well placed to respond to the growing Western niche market demand for organically grown food. Although perhaps presenting short-term problems of organization and marketing, a significant segment of Albanian agriculture devoted to organic farming could provide an appropriate sustainable future for the rural population, complemented by small-scale green tourism.

Rural Tourism

As a key sector for Albania's rural development, tourism has been identified as perhaps best meeting the objectives for assisting the country's medium-term regeneration in terms of: (a) being able to develop a sustainable, environmentally sound industry; (b) generating employment opportunities; (c) encouraging appropriate investment; thereby (d) contributing to a refurbishment and enhancement of infrastructure; and (e) optimizing foreign exchange earnings and generating economic benefits for all regions of the country (Touche Ross and EuroPrincipals Ltd 1992, p.2).

As a country of great diversity within an area no larger than Wales or Belgium, Albania possesses a wealth of natural and cultural heritage: long stretches of sandy beaches, high, unexplored mountain ranges, large lakes with abundant fish life; wide expanses of forests, varied wildlife and a variety of climatic regimes from Mediterranean to Alpine; colourful folklore, customs and crafts; and well-preserved and restored archaeological and architectural assemblages. All suggest opportunities for developing small-scale niche specialist tourism opportunities for individuals and small groups in the remoter interior of the country to help spread the economic benefits of tourism and extend tourism seasons. Such heritage resources are, however, vulnerable (Hall 1992a, 1993, 1994). On paper, Albania's post-communist decision-makers have appeared to be among the more committed in the region to sustainable forms of tourism development (Atkinson and Fisher 1992; Spaho 1992, 1993). But the previous prescriptive nature and low level of international and domestic tourism development – numbers of foreign visitors peaking in 1990 at 30,000 (EIU 1991, p.44; Hall 1991) – was no reliable indicator of the country's potential for mass tourism and its destructive consequences. An economy of shortage looking for a short-cut route to economic growth can easily underestimate the negative impacts and be overoptimistic in assessing the rewards that such development might bring, and the political appeal of hard currency generation and job creation is strong when a country's economic fortunes are low.

Living through an economy of shortage for several decades has forced upon the Albanian population an innate sense of innovation and the ingenious use of available materials. But large-scale rural to urban migration and emigration, after decades of enforced rural living for up to two-thirds of the population, and a much wider and greater availability of material goods, will inevitably result in a loss and diminution of traditional rural craft skills. Tourism development needs to avoid imposing on Albania an international set of standards of tourism architecture, furnishing, and service which, while objectively raising standards of comfort and efficiency, would reflect mass production, international anonymity and blandness, and further reduce the requirement for local craft skills. Governmental emphasis on national cultural pride, while not being overtly nationalistic in this region of nationalistic poisons, will need to be maintained and supported by funds for the promotion of national culture in vernacular architecture and building conservation, museums, artisan workshops and artistic performances: 200–250 thousand Albanians could be employed in this way in response to the demands of tourism.

As part of a somewhat faltering four-year tourism development plan (five-year plans now appear to be anathema) which has attracted US$150 million of investment, Italian and Kuwaiti interests are involved in developing a number of projects along the hitherto largely untouched Ionian coast, including three tourist villages at Ksamil, a US$2 million tourist harbour at Orikum, and a hotel on the superb Llogara pass. Austrian interest involves a further tourist village of 700–800 beds at the beautiful Porto Palermo as well as plans for a centre in the northern mountains. Along the more developed Adriatic coast, tourist village and hotel developments are planned for Golem near Durrës (Misha 1996).

Numbers of visitors to the country in 1995 were said to have increased to 70,000 plus 35,000 day trippers from Corfu (ibid. 1996), although there were only 57,000 in total (an increase of 28 per cent over 1994) according to EIU (1996b, p.45). But the position of minister for tourism was abolished in the December 1994 political reshuffle. While the need to integrate tourism with other – particularly rural – aspects of economic development may now be enhanced, the importance of cultural and environmental considerations may not be uppermost in the priorities of the subsequently created post of deputy prime minister and minister of construction and tourism, one of two deputy prime-ministerial positions established.

MIGRATORY COMPLICATIONS

When the tight border controls separating Albania and Greece were lifted at the end of 1990, large numbers of Albanians took the first opportunity in half a century to leave the country. In January 1991 alone more than 10,000 Albanian citizens, many of them ethnic Greek, crossed the border. While pull factors were the attractions of lifestyles and access to income unimaginable at home, immediate push factors included a lack of faith in domestic reform and the sense of insecurity as the communists lost their grip on power. Much of the emigration took place from the south of the country, where some of the most impressive hillside terracing schemes had been undertaken. The fact that they were often put in place by mass 'voluntary' labour schemes (Lani 1984), projects which now symbolized in the eyes of the population, and particularly the ethnic Greek minority, the excesses of the former regime, helped to explain their early post-communist neglect.

Between 1990 and 1993, some 300,000 people – almost 10 per cent of Albania's total population – succeeded in leaving the country, 150,000 of whom travelled to Greece to seek work. Many were forced to return, notably from Italy and Greece, often more than once. However, together with an Albanian diaspora which now had easier access to kith and kin within the country itself, emigrants in work outside the country have been returning remittances estimated to be worth between US$300 million and US$1 billion per annum: the country's major source of external income after aid, and equivalent to up to a third of GDP and several times the value of Albania's exports. One symbol of this new source of income and its conversion to conspicuous consumption, although even more an indication of the pent-up desire to reach out to the rest of the world, has been the rapid growth of satellite dishes, which now cling to many rural and urban dwellings. Tirana alone is said to have 20 satellite dish wholesale importers. By the spring of 1994 sales had reached 25,000 in less than two years (Koleka 1995).

Albanian border villages and southern towns have been depopulated by 60 per cent or more. In some hillside Ionian coastal villages, for example, plans have been developed for houses abandoned by emigrants to be refurbished in vernacular style using indigenous materials and run by local people to accommodate small numbers of ecotourists (Fisher et al. 1994; Farrow 1995), thereby assisting local economic, cultural and social regeneration. The Albanian government has been confronted with claims, some originating from Greece, that it has encouraged northern Albanians to settle in such areas both to meet the demand for good agricultural land and to dilute what is left of the minority population. With improving relations between Tirana and Athens, however, tensions over the treatment of Albania's ethnic Greeks, and indeed over Greece's ethnic Albanians, have subsided in comparison with the region's other hot spots (Hall and Danta 1996).

An in-migration of more than 300,000 Kosovar Albanians (Anon 1994; Smith 1994), responding to Serb pressures, has acted both to exacerbate rural conditions in those parts of the country adjacent to Kosovo which are some of the most impoverished in Albania, and to exert further pressures on rural to urban and interregional migratory movement within the country. Further, it stimulated the development of local grey economies along the border involved in overcoming UN sanctions against Serbia for the benefit of ethnic Albanians in Kosovo and Montenegro. The availability of such potentially lucrative activities may have acted to deflect local effort away from agriculture.

Although birth control measures are now widely available, Albania's natural growth rate stands at 2 per cent per annum (compared to a European average of 0.4 per cent) (ATA, 8 January 1994), even though infant mortality, at 27–32 per thousand, is four or five times that for Western Europe (Schmidt 1995 p.12; EIU 1996a, p.49). Albania thus still has Europe's fastest-growing population, although this has been tempered by the large-scale emigration of the early 1990s which saw the removal of ten per cent of young men of working age from the country between 1990 and 1992. While some upland agricultural schemes have been abandoned through lack of capital resources, there is keen competition for farmland on the fertile coastal lowlands and in accessible upland basins, fuelled by natural and migratory population pressures.

Under the communists, administrative, environmental and economic policies were pursued to contain the rural population and to eliminate as far as possible unplanned rural to urban migration. As a consequence, at the end of the 1980s, Albania was unique in Europe in terms of: (a) two-thirds of the country's total population living in rural areas; (b) having a rural population which was still growing in absolute terms; and (c) experiencing most of its urban population growth through natural increase rather than because of in-migration. It was inevitable that once such policies and constraints on rural mobility were replaced, along with their communist sponsors, hitherto suppressed migratory tendencies would be realized. As a consequence, many spontaneous migrants, notably from the country's harsh northeastern districts of Kukës and Dibër, have moved southwards in search of better land, access to major urban areas, or both, preferring the middle coastal lowlands and access to the commercial centres of Tirana and Durrës. Some 350,000 have migrated in this way in just three or four years (EIU 1996b, p.41). It has been argued that the ruling Democratic Party, whose president Sali Berisha hails from the northeast, did not prevent these large-scale movements because the people involved came from the districts associated with the party's leadership, and because it was viewed as electorally opportune that they should settle in the opposition parties' urban strongholds (Anon 1996c).

The resulting growth of spontaneous settlements, additional unemployment pressures and social tensions have heightened the country's rural and urban social problems. Estimates of the number of illegal homes erected on the outskirts of the capital, for example, indicated that more than 3,000 had been put up by mid-1994 (Marrett 1994), suggesting an additional population of at least 15,000. During 1993, Tirana's population rose from 286,000 to 300,000, an increase of about 5 per cent (ATA, 21 February 1994). Estimates of the city's population in 1996 ranged from 250,000 (EIU 1996a) to 450,000 (Standish 1996), with the more alarmist predictions suggesting some 1.2 million people might be living in the capital by the turn of the millennium – a figure approaching a third of the country's likely total population. The spontaneous settlement of Bathore, near Kamëz, is of particular concern. Attracting some 30,000 settlers, the 'town' has little by way of infrastructure: no drinkable water or sewerage system, electricity or roads. Many children do not attend school and one estimate suggests that 90 per cent of young children and many adults suffer from disease, including rickets and skin infections. In August 1995 an attempt to evict Bathore's residents failed and the authorities subsequently legalized the settlement, promising a two-kilometre asphalted link to the main road and several drinking water fountains (Anon 1996c).

The Albanian authorities lack experience in coping with migration pressures and possess inadequate means of containing spontaneous settlement development. Several problems have therefore arisen (Hall 1996a). First, by occupying land adjacent to main roads, rural migrants have disrupted the functioning of some utility services, impeded traffic flow and have posed potential accident problems. Traffic is a general problem, with large numbers of untrained and inexperienced drivers at the wheels of dubious second-hand cars (Keay 1993), 10,000 of which were imported in 1994 alone. Second, the large numbers of people involved and the buildings being erected pose health problems within the sites themselves and present potential threats to neighbouring settlements, as witnessed by a cholera outbreak in 1994. Third, the unplanned increase in population and built-up areas, such as the rapidly growing district of Babru in the capital, has implications for physical planning strategies and has placed additional burdens and social pressures on existing urban populations already experiencing high levels of unemployment. Fourth, spontaneous movement to relatively fertile areas has hampered redistribution of agrarian land. Fifth, the process is also compromising tourism development: by 1996, for example, there were 2,800 spontaneous dwellings established on Durrës beach, hitherto the country's major tourism focus (Anon 1996c).

CONCLUSION

Agriculture now accounts for more than half of the country's gross domestic product, rising to 55.5 per cent in 1994 from 40.2 per cent in 1990 (EIU 1996a, p.50). Its contribution increased by 14.4 per cent in 1993 and 6.8 per cent in 1994, and although projections levelled this growth out at 7 per cent for 1995, 5 per cent for 1996 and 6 per cent for 1997 (EIU 1996b, p.35), early reports (in the newspaper *Lajmi i dites*) suggested a 13 per cent increase for 1995. Even so, the food, drinks and tobacco sector accounted for 30 per cent of all imports for the first nine months of the year, although the agriculture ministry was expecting that this level would begin to decline during 1996 as new private enterprises in the food sector began production. This would be particularly significant for dairy and poultry products, honey, fruit and vegetables (Anon 1996a). Further improvements will follow when a land market develops to permit structural consolidation; with between a half and two-thirds of the country's population still living in the countryside (Sjöberg 1991, 1992, 1994), the consequential spatial readjustments will have major social ramifications. The changing circumstances of Albanian agriculture demand policies for stimulating alternative rural employment opportunities and appropriate urban occupations. Overall, unemployment in 1994 was 18 per cent of the workforce. Average monthly salaries for the country as a whole were US$50–60, with significant rural–urban differences: the average monthly pension level in urban areas was US$25 and in rural areas just US$7 (EIU 1996a, p.51).

While domestic and international capital investment remains relatively limited (Hall 1994), most new employment will continue to be generated by the kiosk economy: the buying and selling of consumer goods and household items usually imported from neighbouring countries and fuelled by expatriate remissions. A growth in services (restaurants, taxis, repairs and construction) has been largely the result of small-scale entrepreneurial endeavour, but such activities are more effective and profitable in urban areas. The villages remain generally poorly provisioned, and the status of rural work remains low. In the wholesale food sector, however, despite serious flaws in quality, profitability has been increasing by almost 200 per cent per annum (Anon 1995), although this will subside as the effects of price liberalization level out (Misha and Vinton 1995). Western niche markets, such as those for the provision of organically grown fruit and vegetables, should be addressed as a means of stimulating cash crop production and boosting exports. However, such development does require technical assistance and training and injections of capital. According to the OECD (1995), Albania should reinforce its long-held position as one of the world's leading producers and exporters of medicinal and aromatic plants. The country contains some 3,500 species of flora, with several hundred being endemic and sub-endemic (Demiri 1983; Piperi and Kajno 1990), of which 865 are claimed to have curative properties. Annual exports of medicinal herbs have totalled 20th.t with a value of about US$20 million. As part of an increasing interest in the country from the Arab world, the Egyptian company Kato Aromatik is investing in the growing of aromatic herbs for its pharmaceuticals developments noted above.

More dependent upon the rural economy than other countries in the region, Albania has experienced substantial domestic upheaval in the transition from the communist period. Despite comprehensive landholding fragmentation, a disorganized internal market and disrupted irrigation systems (Deslondes and Sivignon 1995), an upturn in the country's agricultural fortunes has been sustained. As a model of comprehensive structural adjustment programmes (Christensen 1994), Albania's far-reaching agrarian change has been notable. Nonetheless, foreign assistance is being maintained: a three-year US$33.6 million loan for rural road construction from the World Bank and a US$47 million EU PHARE programme emphasizing infrastructural investments were just two elements of the assistance announced during 1995. Given continuing domestic and external pressures and strains exerting themselves on the rural Albanian population, internal migration and emigration, and the growth of spontaneous settlement in relatively less-impoverished areas of the country are likely to continue for some time to come.

REFERENCES

Anon (1990), 'Fruitful collaboration', *New Albania*, No. 6, pp.6–7.
—— (1991), 'Albania: open for business', *East European Markets*, **11** (16), 14–15.
—— (1993), 'The hope for Albania's economic salvation', *Albanian Economic Tribune*, **1** (13), 30–31.
—— (1994), 'Keeping out', *The Economist*, 21 May.
—— (1995), 'Albanian food industry recording high profits', *East Europe Agriculture and Food*, No.149, 30.
—— (1996a), 'Albania', *East Europe Agriculture and Food*, No.160, 31.
—— (1996b), 'Albania', *East Europe Agriculture and Food*, No.162, 30.
—— (1996c), 'Albania', *East Europe Newsletter*, **10** (2), 7.
—— (1996d), 'Albania: country survey', *East Europe Newsletter*, **10** (7), 1–6.
Åslund, A. and Ö. Sjöberg (1992), 'Privatization and transition to a market economy in Albania', *Communist Economics and Economic Transformation*, **4** (1), 135–50.
Albanian Telegraph Agency (ATA) (1993), *Buletin*, Tirana: ATA.
Atkinson, R. and D. Fisher (1992), *Tourism Investment in Central and Eastern Europe: Structure, Trends and Enviromental Implications*, London: East West Environment Ltd.
Baci, I. (1981), *Agriculture in the PSR of Albania*, Tirana: 8 Nëntori.
Bollano, P. and F. Dari (1984), 'The transition to state farming', *Albanian Life*, No. 28, 15–17.
Christensen, G. (1994), 'When structural adjustment proceeds as prescribed – agricultural sector reforms in Albania', *Food Policy*, **19** (6), 557–60.
Demiri, M. (1983), *Flora ekskursioniste e Shqiperise*, Tirana: Shtëpia Botuese e Librit Shkollor.
DeS (Drejtoria e Statistikës) (1991), *Vjetari statistikor i Shqiperise*, Tirana: DeS.

Deslondes, O. and M. Sivignon (1995), 'Albanian agriculture – from the cooperative to subsistence farming', *Revue d'Etudes Comparatives Est–Ouest*, **26** (3), 143.
Dizdari, P. (1992), 'Pendimi është gjeja më vlerë në botë', *Tribuna Ekonomike Shqiptare*, **1** (5), 34.
EIU (Economist Intelligence Unit) (1990), *Romania, Albania, Bulgaria: Country Report No. 3*, London: EIU.
—— (1991), *Romania, Albania, Bulgaria: Country Profile 1991–1992*, London: EIU.
—— (1993), *Romania, Albania, Bulgaria: Country Report No. 2*, London: EIU.
—— (1996a), *Bulgaria, Albania: Country Profile 1995–1996*, London: EIU.
—— (1996b), *Bulgaria, Albania: Country Report 1st quarter 1996*, London: EIU.
Farrow, C. (1995), 'Qeparo – bringing people together', *Focus*, No.16, 9–10.
Fisher, D., I. Mati and G. Whyles (1994), *Ecotourism Development in Albania*, St. Albans: Ecotourism Ltd/Aulona Sub Tour/Worldwide Fund for Nature.
Hall, D.R. (1987), 'Albania', in A.H. Dawson (ed.), *Planning in Eastern Europe*, London: Croom Helm, pp.35–65.
—— (ed.) (1991), *Tourism and Economic Development in Eastern Europe and the Soviet Union*, London: Belhaven.
—— (1992a), 'Albania's changing tourism environment', *Journal of Cultural Geography*, **12** (2), 33–41.
—— (1992b), 'Skills transfer for appropriate development', *Town and Country Planning*, **61** (3), 87–9.
—— (1993), 'Albania', in F.W. Carter and D. Turnock (eds), *Environmental Problems in Eastern Europe*, London: Routledge, pp.7–37.
—— (1994), *Albania and the Albanians*, London: Pinter.
—— (1996a), 'Albania: rural development, migration and uncertainty', *GeoJournal*, **38** (2), 185–9.
—— (1996b), 'Albanian identity and Balkan roles' in D.R. Hall and D. Danta (eds), *Reconstructing the Balkans*, Chichester and New York: Wiley, pp.119–33.
—— (1996c), 'Balkan transport and cityport development in an era of uncertainty', in B.S. Hoyle (ed.), *Cityports, Coastal Zones and Regional Change*, Chichester and New York: Wiley, pp.105–19.
—— and D. Danta (eds) (1966), *Reconstructing the Balkans*, Chichester and New York: Wiley.
IFDC (International Fertilizer Development Center) (1993), *Agriculture in Albania*, Birmingham, AL: IFDC.
Keay, J. (1993), 'Fast and loose on the roads', *The Guardian*, 13 July.
Koleka, B. (1995), 'Satellite dishes bring viewing revolution in Albania', *Albanian Life*, **57** (1), 28.
Kusse, P.J. and H.J. Winkels (1990), *Remarks on Desalinisation and Land Reclamation in the Coastal Area of the People's Socialist Republic of Albania*, The Hague: Netherlands Ministry of Agriculture, Nature

Management and Fisheries.
Lani, R. (1984), 'The youth are a great revolutionary progressive force', *Albania Today*, No. 77, 14-8.
Leiby, J.D. and M.C. Marra (1993), 'Albanian agriculture: perspectives on the future', *Albanian Economic Tribune*, 1 (13), 24-5.
Marrett, M. (1994), 'Can Albania put its house in order?', *The European*, 12 August.
Misha, G. (1996), 'Albania: on the beach', *Business Eastern Europe*, 25 (14), 6.
—— and L. Vinton (1995), 'Big problems, small progress', *Business Eastern Europe*, 24 (18), 7.
OECD (1995), *The Albanian Agro-food System in Economic Transition*, Paris: OECD.
PHARE (1993), *Albania: Orientation Paper*, Brussels: EC PHARE Office.
Piperi, R. and K. Kajno (1990), *Flora mjekesore e Korçës*, Tirana: Drejtoria e Arsimit Shëndetësor.
Rugg, D.S. (1996), 'Albania as a gateway', in D.R. Hall and D. Danta (eds), *Reconstructing the Balkans*, Chichester and New York: Wiley, pp.135-48.
Schmidt, F. (1995), 'Between political strife and a developing economy', *Transition*, 1 (1), 8-13.
Sjöberg, Ö. (1991), *Rural Change and Development in Albania*, Oxford: Westview.
—— (1992), 'Underurbanization and the zero growth hypothesis: diverted migration in Albania', *Geografiska Annaler*, 74B (1), 3-19.
—— (1994), 'Rural retention in Albania: administrative restrictions on urban-bound migration', *East European Quarterly*, 28 (2), 205-33.
Smith, H. (1994), 'Serb grip tightens on "holy" Kosovo', *The Guardian*, 26 July.
Spaho, E. (1992), 'Tourism: promising contracts', *Albanian Economic Tribune*, 6 (10), 17-19.
—— (1993), *Personal Interview, Deputy Minister of Tourism*, Tirana, 26 March.
Standish, A. (1996), 'Albania stumbles on road to democracy', *The European*, 4 April.
Touche Ross and EuroPrincipals Limited (1992), *Albania Tourism Guidelines*, Tirana and London: Ministry of Tourism, Government of Albania and the European Bank for Reconstruction and Development.
Wildermuth, A. (1993), 'Land- und Forstwirtschaft', in K.-D. Grothusen (ed.), *Albanien*, Göttingen: Vandenhoeck & Ruprecht, pp.343-75.
Zanga, L. (1991), 'Albania: the woeful state of schools', *Report on Eastern Europe*, 2 (41), 1-3.

3. Bulgaria

Frank W. Carter

Bulgaria began its transition to a market economy in 1990, following the demise of the former communist government led by Todor Zhivkov in 1989 (Bristow 1996; Jones and Miller 1996; Zloch-Christy 1996). This transition has had considerable influence on the various regions of the country and particularly the countryside. Four and a half decades of collectivization have been followed by a de-collectivization process which carries risks of a further rural dislocation, although it is hoped that change will occur without the coercion and violence which accompanied the destruction of private (including peasant) systems of farming in the 1950s. However, while the complexity of de-collectivization and the shifting economic and political context make generalizations difficult, it is already apparent that Bulgaria's countryside is changing. This chapter will highlight the relevant factors, including those legal and socio-economic components crucial for the transformation process. There is also an analysis of spatial (especially regional) differences which have become evident over the last five years.

THE LAND LAW OF 1991

Bulgaria's National Assembly passed the Law for Agricultural Land Ownership and Land Use in February 1991 (Nikolaev 1991). Unfortunately, because of numerous weaknesses it was soon realized that it would not achieve its desired purpose. An amended law on farmland was passed in March 1992 and the Ownership and Use of Farm Land Act became law in the following month (*Drzhaven Vestnik*, Sofia 1992, Nos 28 and 34). The main objective was to restore private property rights to the landowners (or their heirs) in possession before the creation of the collectives and in accordance with the land area determined by the Law for Land Ownership passed in 1946 (Kopeva et al. 1994). The amended 1992 law was concerned with five main issues: agricultural land restitution; land settlement; transferability of property rights; liquidation of collective farms and distribution of their non-land assets; and finally, institutions dealing with land ownership (Davidova 1994).

Ownership certificates were easily granted where old land boundaries (roads, fences, woodlands, reservoirs and rivers, including ravines and dry river beds) had remained undisturbed by collectivization. Similarly, certificates were also issued providing that, prior to collectivization, bygone estate boundaries could be traced from cadastral surveys of settlements; the main proviso here was that the estate's area, location, borders and neighbouring properties should be clearly designated, along with any changes in the boundaries. Greater difficulties exist where there is a lack of boundary evidence. In such cases, land ownership was recognized in principle, providing it was established that former owners, or their families, were entitled to land restitution. The idea behind this is that restituted landholdings should be so designed as to aid both cultivation and transport access. Wherever possible, small reclaimed estates were situated close to present-day settlements. However, all cases had to await land surveys and the production of a plan for farmland division. The aim here was to avoid problems of land fragmentation by awarding consolidated holdings. Normally, owners would receive the equivalent quantity and quality of land they had previously possessed in some part of the original pre-war estate.

Initial reaction to this offer revealed that more than half a million of an estimated two million former owners had submitted applications for nearly 2m.ha out of a possible 4.6m.ha of arable land. Nearly a fifth of the applicants (18.2 per cent) were previous owners and more than three-fifths (62.5 per cent) were heirs; the remainder (19.3 per cent) made land claims on other grounds (Nikolaev 1992). Extension of the deadline for a further three months up to February 1992 brought the level of submissions to 700,000: 35 per cent of the potential candidates (*Duma*, Sofia, 28 February 1992). By the final closing date of 4 August 1992, some 1.7 million applications, nearly all of whom were Bulgarian residents, had been lodged for the 5.6m.ha of land available for restitution (Izvorski 1993). Responsibility for implementing the restitution process lay with the country's 301 municipal land commissions,

Bulgaria

accountable for the 4,811 territories attached to settlements. A regional breakdown of these applications is seen in Table 3.1.

Table 3.1 Bulgaria: regional distribution of land restitution applications, August 1992

Region	Settlement territories	Number of applications	Area claimed*	Number of persons
Burgas	491	165,930	752.3	687.4
Haskovo	919	175,299	662.9	606.9
Lovech	502	300,577	890	804.8
Montana	401	227,212	720.6	670
Plovdiv	495	214,246	512.3	459
Ruse	508	195,112	678.9	614
Sofia city	70	27,413	59.9	53.7
Sofia region	888	234,108	612.7	574.3
Varna	537	165,834	774.3	694.9
Total	4,811	1,705,731	5,663	5,165

Note: * Units of 10,000ha.

Source: Kopeva et al. 1994, p.206.

The Lovech region appears to be one of the most attractive areas for restitution. As part of the Danubian Plain it contains a mantle of fertile *löess* soil, which lends itself to the cultivation of cereals and market-gardening crops. Prior to collectivization, it contained numerous peasant smallholdings and during the communist period it was one of the country's main agricultural regions (Donchev 1994). Another appealing area for land restitution appears to be in and around the capital Sofia. While land within the city is limited, the surrounding Sofia region is primarily agricultural. Its major commercial crop is tobacco, while other crops include barley, rye and sugar beet, along with grapes and vegetables. There is also an abundance of rich grazing land, especially for sheep (Levinson 1995). Perhaps the least attractive areas for restitution purposes are the regions of Haskovo and Plovdiv. The former is a hilly region on the Greek frontier, subjected to heavy mineral exploitation (lead and zinc) and metallurgical production during the communist period. The population is ethnically mixed and there have been tensions between the Turkish and Bulgarian inhabitants in some towns such as K'rdzhali. The latter comprises the Marica valley, subjected to intensive agricultural production by the communists, but also with much industrialization which has resulted in some pollution of agricultural land.

Clearly the amended agricultural land law has effected a transfer of ownership of all agricultural land back to the previous owners (or their heirs). However, there are limiting provisions. First, any owner who does not use agricultural land for a period of three years will be required to pay a municipality tax assessed on the value of the potential yield related to size and geographical conditions. Second, no household shall acquire more than 600 decares under the land law (one decar is 1,000sq.m) and in specific areas of intensive production the limit is 200 decares. Third, no persons may own agricultural land unless they reside permanently in Bulgaria. Finally, the land must only be used for agricultural purposes (Touche Ross et al. 1993). Five years on, the return of land is still bogged down as major political parties fail to finalize the programme. Everyone in Bulgaria is alarmed at the state of the nation's agriculture and the far-too-passive policy of the government in speeding up the land reform (Brachkov 1996; Pandov 1996).

THE RURAL POPULATION

The rural population accounts for just under a third of the total but the years 1989–91 witnessed a rise in the country's urban residents, while the rural population declined (Table 3.2). Then during 1992–94, both categories declined, although the share of rural population initially increased above the 1989 level, in spite of the absolute decline, but only to fall again in subsequent years. The 1992 census helps to clarify differences in urban and rural population shares at the regional (*oblast*) level (Table 3.3).

There is a clear regional divide in rural population shares. Four regions have two-fifths or more of their inhabitants in this category and are well above the national average. These include Ruse and Montana in the fertile Danubian Plain, the Sofia region and the more backward

Table 3.2 Bulgaria: urban and rural population, 1946–1994

Year	Total	Urban	Rural	Rural (%)
1946	7,029.3	1,735.2	5,294.1	75.3
1956	7,613.7	2,556.1	5,057.6	66.4
1965	8,230.8	3,828.4	4,402.4	53.5
1973	8,647.4	4,917.2	3,730.2	43.1
1989	8,992.3	6,079.8	2,912.5	32.4
1990	8,989.2	6,114.3	2,874.9	32
1991	8,974.9	6,122.3	2,852.6	31.8
1992	8,484.9	5,704.8	2,780	32.8
1993	8,459.9	5,720.5	2,739.3	32.4
1994	8,427.4	5,715.9	2,711.5	32.2

Sources: *Naselenie*, Tsentralno Statistichesko Upravlenie, Sofia, p.18; *Statisticheski Godishnik na R.B'lgariya 1987–1992*, Sofia; *Statisticheski Spravochnik 1995*, Sofia, pp.28–9.

Table 3.3 Bulgaria: population by regions, 1992

Region	Total	Urban	Rural	Rural %
Burgas	851,669	575,622	276,047	32.41
Haskovo	906,275	539,169	367,106	40.50
Lovech	1,016,391	653,112	363,279	35.74
Montana	630,313	356,983	273,330	43.36
Plovdiv	1,220,402	786,584	433,818	35.54
Ruse	768,271	419,466	348,805	45.40
Sofia city	1,189,641	1,138,421	51,220	4.30
Sofia region	985,952	588,741	397,211	40.28
Varna	915,949	646,725	269,224	29.39
Total	8,484,863	5,704,823	2,780,040	32.76

Source: *Naselenie 1992*, Natsionalen Statisticheski Institut, Sofia, 1994, pp.8–12.

area of Haskovo. Of those with a rural population below two-fifths, only Lovech (in the Danubian Plain) and Plovdiv (Marica valley) are above the national average. Three regions are below the norm: Sofia city is understandably among them, while the regions of Varna and Burgas, bordering on the Black Sea, are strongly urbanized through the growth of tourism, which has utilized former agricultural land, and the legacy of heavy communist industrialization, especially around the ports. Comparison with Table 3.1 suggests there is only a weak relationship between land restitution applications and percentage of rural population. Lovech region proved popular for applications, yet was among the lower group for numbers of rural inhabitants. Meanwhile, the Sofia region fared better on both counts. The relatively small number of applications from Haskovo and Plovdiv are not reflected in the former region's total rural figures, but the latter had inferior results on both reckonings.

THE AGRICULTURAL ECONOMY

Pre-war Bulgaria was a predominantly agricultural country with more than four-fifths of its labour force employed on the land. The last pre-war farm survey of 1934 revealed that the country had 884,869 private farms covering 4.37m.ha – an average farm size of 4.94ha. More than two-thirds were located on owner-operated land (Davidova 1994, pp.42–3). After the communist takeover, there was forced collectivization of private farms, together with the industrialization of agriculture. Field boundaries were eliminated and the creation of very large socialist farms meant that land ownership was almost totally superseded. During the period up to 1989, agriculture's importance in the national economy diminished in terms of employment, income, capital stock and investment. Indeed, agriculture in Bulgaria fell to a position of importance below the average for European CMEA countries. Growth rates fell steadily from very high levels in the early post-war years to virtual stagnation in the 1980s. After 1975 in particular, arable farming did very badly in comparison with livestock production, with an absolute decline in performance levels as well as a worsening record in comparison with CMEA averages. Agricultural production suffered increasingly from inefficiency which, in turn, affected input intensity and combined factor productivity growth (Wallden 1991).

Post-1989 agricultural debate was dominated by proposals for privatization (Kapitanski 1990; Risina 1990). Fifty-five per cent of the country's total land area was farmed (some 61,000sq.km), but in 1990 less than 5 per cent was worked on a small 'private plot' basis; mainly for the production of potatoes, meat, eggs and milk. By 1993, these plots had increased to occupy 34 per cent of the land, following the privatization programme that began early in 1991. In that year, agricultural land covered 6.16m.ha. Some three-quarters (4.64m.ha) consisted of arable land, of which three-fifths was sown (3.76m.ha) with less than 5 per cent (0.29m.ha) used as meadowland. The other quarter (1.52m.ha) comprised commonland and pastureland. Despite the start of decollectivization, there were still 2,073 collectives and state farms in existence in 1992.

The significance of private farms for agricultural production in 1991 can be seen in Table 3.4. In no category did the private sector register a

Table 3.4 Bulgaria: agricultural production (th.t), 1991–1994

Crop	State		Private		Private (%)	
	1991	1994	1991	1994	1991	1995
Wheat	4,497	3,788	522	1,275	10.4	25.1
Maize	2,775	1,362	1,725	952	38.3	41.1
Barley	1,502	1,146	307	442	16.9	27.8
Sugar beet	856	112	44	42	4.9	27.3
Sunflower seed	434	596	4	141	0.9	19.1
Seed cotton	18	6	0	0	–	–
Tobacco	57	25	5	23	8.6	47.9
Tomatoes	616	443	361	382	36.9	46.3
Potatoes	498	476	404	465	44.8	49.4
Grapes	748	498	386	324	34	39.4

Source: Statisticheski Spravochnik 1995, Sofia, pp.154–5.

higher percentage share than the state sector, although the margins were small in the cases of grapes, maize, potatoes and tomatoes – labour-intensive crops, often well suited to small private farmers. Cereals, such as wheat and barley, were still grown predominantly by the state sector, while sugar beet, sunflower seed, cotton seed and tobacco were also well suited to the highly mechanized production systems of the state sector. However, the private sector was much more prominent in respect of some other commodities: 85.2 per cent for honey, 57.3 per cent for meat, 53.5 per cent for eggs, although only 40.9 per cent for wool and 38.7 per cent for milk. Less than 2 per cent of the 51,171 tractors in use in 1991 were in private hands. However, between 1991 and 1994, private sector shares increased in all categories, most dramatically in sugar beet, sunflower seed and tobacco. Fundamental to this change was the increased use of tractors in the private sector, which accounted for 38,008 machines in 1994 (about half the national total). The private sector made less progress in respect of the four crops where performance was already high in 1991. But there was a big improvement in wool (89.8 per cent) and milk (83.7 per cent), where the private sector role was weak in 1991, while shares of eggs, meat and honey advanced to 60.9, 80.2 and 96.1 per cent, respectively.

A very important aspect of Bulgaria's post-1989 agriculture has been the decline in state livestock production (Table 3.5), which has not been compensated for by growth in the private sector. In 1992, the two sectors together maintained some 1.7 million head of cattle, 3.9 million pigs, 9.9 million sheep and 32.3 million poultry. But by 1995 the number of cattle had declined by almost 0.6 million, pigs by 0.9 million and sheep by 3.4 million. By contrast, poultry showed a slight increase of 0.33 million but, on the whole, livestock accounted for a smaller share of farm production than in neighbouring countries.

Forest and woodland in Bulgaria covers more than 35 per cent of the territory, a proportion which has changed little in total area in recent years thanks to afforestation during the 1980s. There are both deciduous trees (55.9 per cent), including oak and beech, and coniferous species (30.6 per cent), but only about 15 per cent of the forested area has any relevance for industry through cellulose/paper and furniture production. The period 1991–94 has seen some growth in commons and pastures entering the private sector (an increase from 94 to 793 decares) but this is still only 2.5 per cent of the total. Inland

Table 3.5 Bulgaria: Livestock production, 1992–1995 (th.)

	1992		1993		1994		1995	
Type	State	Private	State	Private	State	Private	State	Private
Cattle	1,310	418	974	488	750	507	638	509
Buffalo	25	18	22	18	17	14	14	12
Pigs	3,141	820	2,680	838	2,071	747	1,986	1,062
Sheep	6,703	3,261	4,814	3,582	3,763	3,293	3,398	3,136
Poultry	21,707	10,682	19,872	12,001	18,211	12,497	19,126	13,595
Bee farms	494	435	429	376	338	296	248	232

Source: Statisticheski Spravochnik 1995, Sofia, p.160.

water fishing appears to have a low priority, particularly on the Danube river where hydro-electric schemes are held responsible for reduced catches.

At present, the greatest agricultural crisis facing the country concerns cereal production. The wheat shortage has meant that Bulgaria will have to import 800th.t of wheat together with 400th.t of maize and 200–300th.t of barley to provide sufficient bread and fodder for 1996–97, according to preliminary assessments by the Ministry of Agriculture. For reasons that remain unclear, the Ministry has only agreed to import 400th.t of wheat, only a quarter of what is necessary to provide sufficient bread for the population. Bread is already rationed (330g per person) in the northern district of Veliko Turnovo, and has also been reported in other areas: Silistra on the Danube, Kyustendil in the west, Smolyan and several districts in Pazardjik region in the south as well as villages around Plovdiv. All the signs point to a 'winter of discontent' (Penkova 1996).

THE VILLAGE

Of all the changes in the Bulgarian countryside, perhaps the demise of the villages has been the most obvious. Prior to the Second World War, four-fifths of the population depended on agriculture and the villages accommodated communities of peasant proprietors. The average size of

800,000 small individual farms (comprising 85 per cent of all holdings) was less than 10ha, thanks to the patriarchal system of land ownership whereby a deceased father's lands were divided up between his sons. In addition, the holdings were usually fragmented (Beaver 1940). The size of the average plot was less than one hectare.

Certain aspects in village layout and architectural style date from the feudal period and in particular the Ottoman occupation, although many have been radically altered by the modernization of the communist era. Kovachevitsa, on the River Kanina in the Rhodope Mountains in the southwestern part of the country (20km north of Gotse Delchev), is well known for its characteristic local architecture. White-painted stone and wooden houses, roofed with slabs, are embellished by bow windows, decorative chimneys and spacious porches overlooking backyards and narrow, winding cobblestone lanes. The first settlers were Bulgarian fugitives escaping from mass Islamization of the Rhodope region by the Ottomans in the mid-fifteenth century. The villagers worked in stock breeding and lumbering, along with carpentry and construction work. The village flourished in the nineteenth century when there were about 250 households. In 1848, a large church was built and six years later its first secular school was founded. A community social club (*Svetlina*) was established in 1861. However, the population declined in the 1950s from some 1,500 inhabitants to 200, through mass migration associated with collectivization. By the early 1990s, Kovachevitsa had about 110 houses, mostly built in the nineteenth century and by now desperately in need of repair (Hadjiev 1991). Perhaps Kovachevitsa is indicative of a general decline in village life, because Bulgaria's villages have seen their population halved from 5.3 million in 1946 (when three-quarters of the Bulgarian people lived in rural areas) to 2.7 million in 1994 (32 per cent of the total) distributed among 4,444 villages and 636 hamlets (Table 3.2) (Carter and Žagar 1976; Donchev 1994, p.186; Ninov 1994; Philipov 1978; Tsekov 1992).

Paradoxically, the remaining rural population perceives the city less as a place of prosperity, offering good prospects for the young, and more as a difficult and dangerous environment (Garnizov 1995). As a result, villagers are reappraising their own situation *vis-à-vis* their urban counterparts and raising their own sense of esteem after years of self-condemnation. The lifestyle has improved, while living costs remain relatively low. Country people have more opportunity to satisfy their elementary needs and have immediate access to good-quality foodstuffs. The lower crime rate is appreciated, as is the greater sense of security, familiarity and warmth in personal relations. Nevertheless, the population of the villages is old and it is decreasing because of the low birth-rate and high mortality over the last decade.

THE REGIONAL DIMENSION

During the 1980s, variations in agricultural production existed between Bulgaria's nine administrative regions (Wallden 1991, pp.26-7). For example, there was a high concentration of sugar-beet production in the Lovech and Ruse regions of the fertile Danubian Plain; tobacco came mainly from the warmer Haskovo and Sofia regions; while sunflower seeds and maize were largely produced in the Montana and Varna regions, as well as in the Ruse region (around Razgrad). Nearly half the apple production was centred on the Plovdiv region, while potatoes were prominent in Plovdiv and Sofia, as were melons in Haskovo. The coastal regions of Burgas and Varna were prominent in cereal production (for example, barley) and viticulture. By contrast, there was relatively little concentration in respect of livestock, fodder production (lucerne, maize and silage) and apiculture. The 1980s witnessed only small regional shifts in the production of wheat, maize and fruit, but more significant spatial changes took place in the production of sunflower seeds and the raising of sheep and cattle. The declining tobacco crop experienced greater convergence (Haskovo region), as did such high-demand products as meat (pigs and poultry) and vegetables. During the 1980s, the Burgas, Plovdiv and Sofia regions suffered a general decline in their agricultural significance because of an increasing emphasis on industry. By contrast, the more rural Lovech region performed outstandingly well in livestock raising and in the production of sunflowers and vegetables by comparison with Haskovo, Montana, Ruse and Varna. In general, these agricultural production trends have continued during the early years of the 1990s (Table 3.6). Clearly, the coastal and Danubian Plain regions of Burgas, Lovech, Montana and Varna have retained their significance in cereal production. Ruse region is important for maize, while Ruse and Varna together dominate the production of sunflower seed. The decline in tobacco production is

Table 3.6   Bulgaria: agricultural production by region 1994 (th.t)

Region	Cereals	Maize	Sunflower seeds	Tobacco	Vegetables	Fruit
Burgas	446	46	78	1	186	165
Varna	963	326	166	1	91	131
Lovech	486	163	94	–	99	99
Montana	467	211	65	–	45	48
Plovdiv	222	59	59	3	220	139
Ruse	665	485	128	2	106	91
Sofia city	26	5	–	–	25	12
Sofia region	145	42	–	7	84	113
Haskovo	368	25	56	11	120	73
Total	3,788	1,362	596	25	976	871

Source: Statisticheski Spravochnik 1995, Sofia, p.156.

evident, but Haskovo retains a clear lead. Burgas and Plovdiv are clearly prominent in fruit and vegetable production: Burgas produces a quarter of the country's grapes and Plovdiv nearly two-fifths of the apples. The general decline in livestock production is evident everywhere.

THE IMPACT OF THE TRANSITION ON THE COUNTRYSIDE

In contrast to the cities, there have been few changes in Bulgaria's villages. There appears to be a minimum of investment either in construction or in the restoration of existing buildings. But an immediate effect of the transition has been a shift from large farming units to private farms. There has been a near-total disappearance of the old cooperative farms, especially those concerned with livestock production. However, the process of returning agriculture to private hands has disrupted production rather than the reverse. So far, there has not been a revival in the critical domestic sector, which still accounts for about a fifth of both GDP and employment. The privatization of state-owned agricultural enterprises is now moving ahead slowly (Buckwell et al.

1994; Yarnal 1994a). The Bulgarian Ministry of Agriculture began the process with 90 units, but by October 1994 only 30 transactions were complete; these included pig and poultry farms, flour mills, machine repair workshops and inland fisheries (Troev 1994a).

Agriculture Ministry experts rightly predicted that output decline in 1994 would be less than in the previous three years. Meanwhile, specialists, including Western experts, maintain that a considerable recovery will only occur when prospective landowners receive their full legal titles. This will then enable those with smaller plots to sell and thus facilitate consolidation into more economically viable farms. This suggests that free market forces, not government attempts to reform old cooperatives, will act as the main driving force in evolving agricultural structures. But it may still take some time before land restitution is complete. Early in 1993, government officials predicted that the land reform programme would be accomplished by the end of 1993. However, by the end of September 1994, according to agricultural ministry sources, only half of Bulgaria's farmland had been returned to new owners with full legal title rights by the end of September 1994. The proportion advanced to 60 per cent by December 1994, but the process was still not finished a year later. It is widely accepted that private ownership of land is a positive move in the long term, but many of the immediate effects have been negative. There has in fact been some reaction to the initial emphasis on privatization and it seems that if mistakes are to be avoided in future, there must be some form of rural cooperation.

Initially, there was chaos with the dismantling of the old cooperatives by government committees after 1991. The committees managed to obliterate a considerable part of Bulgarian agriculture, especially stock breeding. Mistakes were made by some committees because farm output overall fell by almost 15 per cent in 1992. Lacking agricultural experience, committees sold off fodder belonging to the cooperatives before animals were allocated to individual farmers, while some animals were given back before the redistribution of land had taken place and the peasants had the wherewithal to feed and breed them. As a result, many pigs, sheep and cattle were disposed of unnecessarily. In the Sofia region, thousands of sheep were sold alive to Italy and Greece, while a large number were slaughtered. As a result, sheep flocks often contain less than 100 head and they will continue to be small until grazing land can be consolidated into larger areas. One effect of this is that fewer and much younger sheep are sent to market, often at six months rather than the normal 12 (Levinson 1995, p.146). Similarly in the Varna region, livestock breeding witnessed massive decline over the period 1990-95: cattle declined by 70 per cent, cows by 75 per cent, sheep by 55 per cent, pigs by 51 per cent and poultry by 41 per cent (Table 3.7). Cows as a percentage of all cattle shifted violently from 40 per cent in 1990 to 50 per cent in 1994 before falling back to 46 per cent in 1995 (42 per cent in the private sector).

Table 3.7 Bulgaria: livestock in the Varna region, 1990–1995

Type	1990 total	1994 total	1995* total	1995* Private
Cattle	49,173	21,927	14,563	9,779
of which cows	19,635	11,088	6,773	4,101
Pigs	208,659	93,386	101,712	56,010
Sheep	316,743	169,061	141,433	134,864
Poultry	1,223,269	650,992	721,244	568,134

Note: * 1 January

Source: Statisticheski Baromet'r 1995 (5 November), Sofia, p.2.

Some agricultural products have also suffered (Buckwell et al. 1993). Vegetable production has declined in the Sofia region, despite an increase in the land available. The problem has arisen in part from the loss of former Comecon markets and the trade barriers erected by the EU. Land restitution has meant that some market-gardening units are too small to be cultivated efficiently, while the costs of using irrigation water have proved prohibitive (Knight et al. 1995). All this has led to increased prices on local markets, together with limited quantities of vegetables now being supplied from abroad (Levinson 1995, p.146). There are also problems for tobacco growing because the whole industry will face serious difficulties if production from the new private farms cannot be stimulated. In the early 1980s, Bulgaria was the largest tobacco producer in Europe (with a fifth of the total output) and held seventh place in world production. But by 1993, Bulgaria was producing only a tenth of Europe's tobacco and had dropped to fourteenth in the world rankings (Troev 1993).

Bulgaria's vineyards are also undergoing change. Already in the mid-1980s Mikhail Gorbachev's anti-alcohol campaign was affecting Bulgarian sales to the FSU, which absorbed more than two-thirds of all the country's wine exports. This combined with a mid-1980s crisis in Bulgarian agriculture, leading to a decrease in vineyard planting. Then, further adversity for viticulturists came in the late 1980s, resulting from damaging climatic conditions in the form of increased drought and frost (Fartzov et al. 1992). The net effect was a decrease in output from 4.5m.hl in 1985 to 1.8m.hl in 1990. Fears are now growing about the break-up of the country's state wine monopoly with the drive for privatization. The large state vineyards which covered some 80th.ha in 1990, compared with some 15-20th.ha of local vineyards linked with the villages. As these large vineyards are broken into small cooperative units, the loss of scale economies is having adverse effects on wine production (Table 3.8). Moreover, the erosion of the old forms of cooperation between the former state enterprises (which previously solved technical problems and production shortfalls) is also proving detrimental. An even worse scenario may emerge with a large increase in small private individual plots (no larger than 30ha) whose owners lack resources for long-term planning (since the first wine crop is only obtained after five years of cultivation). So private owners will opt for quick profits, although Bulgarian agronomists believe that current yields of between 300-350kg/decare could be increased to 800 kg/decare with improved husbandry methods (Dempsey 1991).

Table 3.8   Bulgaria: grape production 1991-1994 (kg/decare)

Type	1991	1992	1993	1994
Table	540.2	501.2	380.4	338.5
Wine	459.1	494.3	367.4	374.1

Source: Statisticheski Spravochnik 1995, Sofia, p.157.

Clearly, some of the problems associated with crop decline may be related to the 1991 land law which provided restitution for all those who owned land prior to the forced communist collectivization. But, half a century later, about three-fifths of these owners (or their heirs) live in urban centres and many are either unable or unwilling to return to agricultural work. Some cultivate their newly acquired plots only at weekends, using primitive equipment (spades and wooden ploughs) because financial hardship, combined with small plot size (merely 1.6ha), usually precludes the use of machines. There seem to be three options for these new landowners: they can try to sell the land, or lease it out, or else form a cooperative with other owners. Unfortunately, no real land market has yet been developed and, because of the lack of proper legislation, land leasing is not widespread. Thus the option of forming new cooperatives appears the most attractive. There are certainly ample precedents, for the Souhindol cooperative, north of Gabrovo, was set up in 1909 and shows how such endeavours can prosper under market conditions (Billaut 1988). As a result of the new restitution law, property belonging to Souhindol has reverted back to its pre-communist owners, but the reorganized cooperative is working efficiently and is investing in bakeries, meat-processing plant, vineyards and additional livestock. Such success stories suggest that Bulgaria's agricultural sector can recover. Inadvertently, the decline in stock breeding has gradually led to higher meat-purchasing prices, which in turn have instilled greater optimism among stock breeders and fodder producers. Foreign companies are realizing the potential in modernizing Bulgaria's once flourishing food and agroprocessing industries. For example, the privatization programme quickly led to a Belgian–American–British consortium buying a maize products plant at Razgrad in the northeast. This move has been copied by other multinational food-processing groups from Denmark, France, Greece, the Netherlands and Switzerland. Furthermore, aid from Western governments and credits from international institutions have also been forthcoming for Bulgaria's agricultural sector. Early in 1994, the World Bank's first agricultural credit (a US$50 million loan) was negotiated with Bulgaria's Ministry of Agriculture for improving the private sector's access to medium- and long-term credit (Troev 1994b).

POLLUTION AND THE BULGARIAN COUNTRYSIDE

One of the greatest legacies inherited by the Bulgarian countryside from the communist period is that of pollution (Carter 1993). Under the communist system, the aim of agricultural operations was to achieve maximum yields at the minimum of cost, using very extensive fields worked by large agricultural enterprises. But there was a loss of soil fertility because maximum output was maintained by the application of chemical fertilizers, which encouraged soil compaction and erosion leading to a loss of biodiversity and other long-term factors detrimental for cultivation (Yarnal 1995). The countryside also suffered from the effects of industrialization through air and water pollution. The Bulgarian ecological movement 'Ekoglasnost' warned the public in 1989 that all fruit and vegetables were contaminated by both chemicals and atmospheric pollutants (Radio Sofia, 12 December 1989). As if this were not enough, the radiation fallout from the Chernobyl disaster of April 1986 added to the country's long-term pollution problems. But only after the fall of communism did the full extent of pollution in the countryside emerge. In 1990, it was disclosed that some 54th.ha of farmland were polluted with heavy metals and cultivation on the 900ha worst affected had to be prohibited (Gavrilov 1990; Georgiev 1994; Radio Sofia, 27 April 1990).

Thus by the early 1990s it was evident that many parts of the country suffered from soil pollution. Extensive soil contamination occurred in three main areas. First, on the northern slopes of the central Stara Planina Mountains, around Veliko Turnovo and the headwaters of the Jantra affected by industrial pollution emanating from places like Elena and Gorna Or'ahovitsa (Markov 1994). Second, an elongated tract to the south stretched along the southern slopes of the Sredna Gora Mountains from the Topolnica Valley eastward towards the industrial centres of Stara Zagora and Jambol. Third, a major region was located farther south in the eastern Rhodope Mountain region, spreading from the industrial towns of Haskovo (in the lower Maritsa Valley) and Topolovgrad towards the Turkish frontier (Iordanova and Ilieva 1994). Other less-extensive areas were located, especially in the more industrialized western half of the country: the Sofia conurbation, the Botevgrad and Slivnica areas and the Ogosta and upper Maritsa Valleys. In the east, concentrations of pollutants were found in the

Ludogorsko Plateau, the Varna hinterland and the Fakijska Valley near the Turkish frontier.

Clearly, industrialization has added its impact to the problem of soil pollution. In 1990 Ekoglasnost reported that 4.7m.ha of arable land, (about 44 per cent of the national territory), was eroded, polluted or totally destroyed because of the annual emission of 68m.t of dust and toxic gases. The agricultural environment was also damaged by the extraction industry. For example, more than 300sq.km of arable land were considered unfit for cultivation following zinc extraction at Plovdiv mines, southeast of Sofia (Dempsey 1990). The village of Kouklen in the Plovdiv region, located near to a non-ferrous metal works and a chemical plant, was testament to this degradation. Tests on villagers' dead cattle revealed that death was due to lead, cadmium and zinc poisoning. Lead concentrations in straw and fodder samples reached 100–400mg/kg (10mg/kg being the acceptable limit). Cow's blood registered 400–500mg of lead (against the norm of 350mg), while milk yields contained twice the permitted lead level. About 100ha of strawberry fields and 200ha of apple orchards had to be uprooted by local farmers as a result of withering branches.

Kouklen is one of 13 villages located within a 20km radius of these enterprises, which cover 120ha of the Upper Maritsa Valley's most fertile land. Around these works, some 4th.ha of land have been affected by pollution, 1,200ha of which result from heavy metal poisoning. Lead concentration in sunflowers has been recorded at 590 times above the safety level and grapes 330 times. Similar concentration quantities of cadmium, zinc and nickel were also found. In order to reduce further disasters, short-term measures for crop changes were adopted. Cereals and beans were only grown for seed purposes; tomatoes and peppers have been replaced by fibre and ethereal oil crops, while vegetable growing was prohibited. Local cows were given regular blood tests prior to their eventual evacuation from the area (Gencheva 1990).

Another area to suffer badly from soil contamination, mainly through the release of heavy metals from industrial units and refineries, is the Black Sea coast and its hinterland (Marinova 1994). Both the Varna and Burgas regions suffer severe soil degradation from heavy metal pollutants (Carter, 1996). Moreover, recent research in the Burgas region has revealed serious problems with soil erosion, calculated at 43.1t/ha each year (twice the national average and the highest rate recorded anywhere in the country). Much of this is due to excessive application of fertilizer during the communist period, together with poor animal waste disposal methods. This resulted in inadmissibly high nutrient levels in the water supply which suffered further contamination from unsafe levels of agricultural pesticides (Yarnal 1994b). Forests in the Black Sea area were also subjected to the pollution onslaught. Research on replanting and forest management needs in the countryside around the Varna–Devnja industrial complex indicates the need for improved phytofilter proportions to achieve higher levels of resistance to local air and soil pollution, thereby improving the region's microclimate (Gorunova and Mourgova 1988). All these examples lead on to the question of how environmental problems in the Bulgarian countryside can be resolved in the future. The younger generation of rural dwellers believes that, regardless of cost, action must be taken quickly if the countryside and its resources are not to be damaged permanently. It is clear that following privatization, the rural landscape will be controlled by small-scale private farmers, large commercial agribusinesses or cooperatives. One way of solving the pollution problem may be through application of the 'polluter pays principle' (PPP), which should encourage the rational use of scarce environmental resources and stimulate the careful use of chemical fertilizers and liquid manure. If properly enforced, this principle would avert leaching of nitrates and phosphates into the ground and surface waters. It could encourage Bulgarian farmers to reduce the application of such chemicals, benefiting not only water supplies but also other environmental factors. A reduction in the overapplication of pesticides would be desirable not only for agriculture, but also for wild life (for example, Bulgaria lies on important bird migration routes between Eurasia and Africa). Stricter adherence to an ethical code of practice could be enforced through an environmental inspectorate or as part of an eco-police organization's duties. Finally, improvement of the Bulgarian countryside may rest with the question of attitude on the part of Bulgaria's planners as well as the farming community. Together, their participation would help not only in reducing pollution through technical and economic measures, but would also involve changes in outlook and ideas.

Unfortunately, this may take some time to achieve. In reality, the country's new private farmers generally lack the financial means, the horticultural knowledge and the inducement to embrace environmentally friendly practices. But they are unlikely to employ massive pieces of machinery, apply artificial chemical fertilizers or burn dangerous materials. More critical will be the environmental attitudes of cooperative farmers and agribusiness managers; many of them will be more interested in the profit motive than in sound ecological practice. If they are not adequately controlled, their application of large-scale farming methods will encourage greater use of environmentally dangerous chemicals, pesticides and heavy machinery. Moreover, among such economic operators the idea of a PPP would be unacceptable, creating much apprehension about any future possibility of a more environmentally friendly countryside.

CONCLUSION

This chapter has highlighted certain elements of change in the Bulgarian countryside since the fall of communism. It is an area of great significance for the languishing national economy in the short term. This is because Bulgarian agriculture is potentially rich; it is capable of feeding the nation, absorbing some of the unemployed and helping to overcome the foreign exchange crisis. In the early 1990s, attempts were made to secure these benefits by laying the foundations for a private agricultural sector. Critical in these aspirations was a law which returned land to its former private owners or their successors, which it was hoped would lead to some emancipation of the market square. But in spite of such reform efforts, Bulgaria failed to create a rational agricultural policy to provide the essential information and inducement needed by aspiring private farmers.

The new land law only strove to recreate the pre-communist agricultural sector when two-thirds of Bulgaria's active employment was bound up with the working of small farms. Under the communist regime, this profitable private agricultural sector more or less vanished; by the early 1990s, only 12 per cent of arable land was held by private farmers. The privatization process has not progressed as rapidly as envisaged, mainly because of the unwieldy and prolonged nature of the legal process, together with the inadequacy of training and finance on the part of the new owners. Early attempts by cooperatives to obtain access to commercial credit from banks were hampered by ill-advised loans and doubts over their economic viability. This situation improved in 1993 when state-owned banks became legally obliged to grant agricultural loans, including the provision of indirect subsidies (Panov 1994).

During the second half of the 1990s, the Bulgarian government's main concern will be to accelerate the privatization process. Agriculture, as one of the country's major economic sectors, should be given high priority in this respect (Koltchakova 1995). Fortunately by the autumn of 1994, the privatization process was beginning to overcome earlier weaknesses arising from a lack of political will on the part of some elements in Bulgarian society (Novkirichki and Paneff 1995). There was procrastination through internal political feuding, combined with a succession of three general elections within a five-year period; it was common for economic policy-making to be overshadowed by political expediency. Moreover, until the end of 1994, other factors such as inflation, recession and rising interest rates also had a negative effect on Bulgarian agriculture. In turn, production was jeopardized because low incomes constrained development (Mileva 1994). Inevitably this took its toll on the Bulgarian countryside, which was subjected to many fluctuations created by the ups and downs of the democratization process (Terzieva-Karayaneva 1995).

Many of Bulgaria's contemporary problems in the countryside, including a declining rural population, mismanagement in the agricultural sector, regional decline in the production of some profitable crops and failure to combat pollution, have been closely related to political factors. Old-style communists still influence official thinking on agricultural matters. This makes it very difficult to predict future developments in the countryside, given the constantly changing pattern of events in the country. It is possible that the prospects of mass privatization will encourage those more reluctant former state managers to become more enthusiastic about involvement in the private sector. Certainly Bulgaria has great natural resource potential for agriculture and tourism where analysts expect to see faster economic growth in the future. Thus Bulgaria's countryside may well flourish, given the country's agricultural traditions and a willingness on the part of the new landowners to rise to the demands of independent farm work. Even if the majority of landowners agree, as most probably will, to consolidate their land into production cooperatives, they are likely to retain small parcels which can be used for both subsistence and local market sales

(Keliyan 1993). This should ensure that some traditional aspects of the Bulgarian countryside will persist for the benefit of future generations.

REFERENCES

Beaver, S.H. (1940), 'Bulgaria: a summary', *Geography*, **25**, 159-69.
Billaut, M. (1988), 'Le mouvement coopératif en Bulgarie', *Revue d'études slaves*, **60** (2), 481-91.
Brachkov, I. (1996), 'Land reform mine field', *The Insider: Business and Current Affairs* (Sofia), **6** (5), 8.
Bristow, John A. (1996), *The Bulgarian Economy in Transition*, Aldershot: Edward Elgar.
Buckwell, A. et al. (eds) (1994), *The Transformation of Agriculture: A Case Study of Bulgaria*, Boulder, CO: Westview.
Buckwell, A., A. Davidova and S. Davidova (1993), 'Potential implications for productivity of land reform in Bulgaria', *Food Policy*, **18** (4), 493-506.
Carter, F.W. (1993), 'Bulgaria' in F.W. Carter and D. Turnock (eds), *Environmental Problems in Eastern Europe*, London: Routledge, pp.38-62.
—— (1996), 'Bulgaria's Black Sea coastal region: geographical problems and perspectives', *Problemi na Geografiyata* (Sofia), No. 1, 43-56.
—— and M.M. Žagar (1976), 'Postwar internal migration in southeastern Europe', in L.A. Kosinski (ed.), *Demographic Developments in Eastern Europe*, New York: Praeger, pp.260-86.
Davidova, S. (1994), 'Changes in agricultural policies and restructuring of Bulgarian agriculture: an overview', in J.F.M. Swinnen (ed.), *Policy and Institutional Reform in Central European Agriculture*, Aldershot: Avebury, pp.31-75.
Dempsey, J. (1990), 'Bulgaria's ecologists hope to clean up in poll', *Financial Times*, 6 June, p.4.
—— (1991), 'The sweet and dry tastes of competition', *Financial Times* (Supplement on Bulgaria), 17 May, p.17.
Donchev, D. (1994), *Fizicheska i Sotsialno-Ikonomicheska Geografiya na B'lgariya*, Veliko Trnovo: Slovo, pp.564-89.
Fartzov, K., S. Dimov and T. Arsova (1992), 'Characteristics of the 1990 grape harvest and vintage in Bulgaria', *Journal of Wine Research*, **3** (1), 63-5.
Garnizov, V. (1995), 'The changing map of popular attitudes to the reform process in Bulgaria', in E. Dainov and V. Garnizov, *Politics Reform and Daily Life*, Sofia: Centre of Social Practices, New Bulgarian University Centre for Liberal Strategies, pp.7-23.
Gavrilov, V. (1990), 'Environmental damage creates serious problem for government', *Radio Free Europe/Radio Liberty Research*, **1** (21), 4-12.
Gencheva, I, (1990), 'The Kouklen children still have a chance', *Bulgaria* (Sofia), July-August, 22-3.

Georgiev, B. (1994), 'Metod za izchislyavane na korektsionni koefitsienti pri otsenka na selskostopanski zemi,zam'rseni s tezhki metali', *Problemi na Geografiyata* (Sofia), No. 3, pp.61-7.
Gorunova, D. and M. Mourgova (1988), 'S'stoyanie i dinamika na gorskite ekosistemi i promishlenya kompleks Varna-Devnya', *Problemi na Geografiyata* (Sofia), No. 1, 22-32.
Hadjiev, K. (1991), 'Kovachevitsa', *The Insider: Bulgarian Digest Monthly*, No. 11, 21.
Iordanova, M. and M. Ilieva (1994), 'Otsenka na agroproizvodstveniya potentsial na teritoriyata na uzhnite kraigranichni obshtini', *Problemi na Geografiyata* (Sofia), No. 2, 62-74.
Izvorski, I. (1993), 'Economic Reform in Bulgaria 1989-1993', *Communist Economies and Economic Transformation*, **5** (4), 519-31.
Jones, D.C. and J. Miller (1996), *The Bulgarian Economy: Lessons from Reform during Early Transition*, Aldershot: Avebury.
Kapitanski, I. (1990), 'Sotsialno-ikonomicheski problemi na preodolyavane krizata v selskoto-stopanstvo', *Selskosopanska Nauk* (Sofia), **28** (5), 9-13.
Keliyan, M. (1993), 'Auxiliary work in the household run farm in the period of changes in Bulgaria', *Eastern European Countryside*, **1**, 73-8.
Knight, G.C., S.B. Velev and M.P. Staneva (1995), 'The emerging water crisis in Bulgaria', *GeoJournal*, **35** (4), 415-23.
Koltchakova, E. (1995), 'Bulgarie et privatization', *Les Enjeux de l'Europe* (Paris), No. 15, 56-7.
Kopeva, D., P. Mishev and K. Howe (1994), 'Land reform and liquidation of collective farm assets in Bulgarian agriculture: progress and prospects', *Communist Economies and Economic Transformation*, **6** (2), 203-17.
Levinson, A. (1995), 'The impact of privatization on settlement patterns in southwestern Bulgaria', in M. Tykkyläinen (ed.), *Local and Regional Development During the 1990s Transition in Eastern Europe*, Aldershot: Avebury, pp.137-48.
Marinova, M. (1994), 'Industrie, Natur und Sozialismus in Bulgarien', in P. Jordan and E. Tomasi (eds), *Zustand und Perspektiven der Umwelt im östlichen Europa*, Frankfurt am Main: P. Lang, pp.12-24.
Markov, I. (1994), 'Zonalnost v geografskoto razprostranenie na selskoto stopanstvo v Yantrenskiya raion', *Problemu na Geografiyata* (Sofia), No. 4, 22-9.
Mathijs, E. and J. Swinnen (1996), 'Agricultural privatization and decollectivization in Central and Eastern Europe', *Transition* (Prague), **2** (15), 12-16.
Mileva, N. (1994), 'Bulgarian agriculture in the period of transition', in R. Avramov and V. Antonov, *Economic Transition in Bulgaria*, Sofia: Sofia Press, pp.169-94.
Nikolaev, R. (1991), 'The new law on farmland', *Report on Eastern Europe*, **2** (18), 9-10.
—— (1992), 'Bulgarian farmland law seeks to hasten privatization', *Radio Free Europe/Radio Liberty Research*, **1** (21), 30-33.

Ninov, Z. (1994), 'Raioni v B'lgariya, dominirani ot golemi sela s neblagopriyatna demografska situatsiya', *Problemi na Geografiyata* (Sofia), No. 3, 3-8.
Novkirichki, A. and S. Paneff (1995), 'La privatisation enfin en cours en Bulgarie', *Les Enjeux de l'Europe* (Paris), No. 15, 58-60.
Pandov, T. (1996), 'Private agriculture: the socialist approach', *The Insider: Business and Current Affairs* (Sofia), **6** (5), 9.
Panov, O. (1994), 'Delayed privatization and financial development in Bulgaria', in M. Jackson and V. Bilsen (eds), *Company Management and Capital Market Development in the Transition*, Aldershot: Avebury, pp.185-226.
Penkova, R. (1996), 'Government impotent on wheat crisis', *The Insider: Business and Current Affairs* (Sofia), **6** (7-8), 3.
Philipov, D. (1978), 'Migration and settlement in Bulgaria', *Environnment and Planning A*, **10**, 593-617.
Risina, M. (1990), 'Privatizatsiyata v selskoto stopanstvo - podkhodi i problemi', *Ikonomika i Upravlenie na Selskoto Stopanstvo* (Sofia), **35** (4), 308.
Terzieva-Karayaneva, P. (1995), 'Bulgaria: slowly, but steadily on the road to democracy', in B. Góralczyk, W. Kostecki and K. Żukrowska (eds), *In Pursuit of Europe: Transformations of Post-communist States 1989-1994*, Warsaw: PAN, pp.27-39.
Touche Ross, Sinclair Roche and Temperley (1993), *British Gas: Doing Business in Bulgaria - CBI Initiative Eastern Europe*, London: Kogan Page.
Troev, T. (1993), 'Tobacco industry seeks greater incentives', *Financial Times* (Supplement on Bulgaria), 5 May, p.32.
—— (1994a), 'Agriculture: reason for optimism', *Financial Times* (Supplement on Bulgaria), 13 October, p.14.
—— (1994b), 'Agriculture: potential spotted by foreigners', *Financial Times* (Supplement on Bulgaria), 13 October, p.14.
Tsekov, T. (1992), 'Regional policy for rural settlements in Bulgaria', *Tijdschrift voor Economische en Sociale Geografie*, **83** (5), 402-8.
Wallden, S. (1991), *Bulgaria's Agriculture: Situation, Trends and Prospects - Final Report*, Athens, Brussels and Luxembourg: DMP Development Monitoring and Planning Ltd and European Communities Commission.
Yarnal, B. (1994a), 'Decollectivization of Bulgarian agriculture', *Land Use Policy*, **11** (1), 67-70.
—— (1994b), 'Agricultural decollectivization and vulnerability to environmental change: A Bulgarian case study', *Global Environmental Change*, **4** (3), 229-43.
—— (1995), 'Bulgaria at a crossroads: environmental impacts of socioeconomic change', *Environment*, **37** (10), 6-15, 29-33.
Zloch-Christy, I. (ed.) (1996), *Bulgaria in a Time of Change: Economic and Political Dimensions*, Aldershot: Avebury.

4. Czech Republic

Ivan Bičík and Antonín Gőtz

In December 1989, Czechoslovakia launched a series of changes to create a free democratic society with a market economy. Differences of opinion about the aims and objectives, combined with historical differences between the Czech Lands and Slovakia, helped to bring about a division of the federal state at the beginning of 1993. This chapter therefore deals with the rural aspects of the Czech Republic's social, economic and political evolution towards a higher stage of development and organization. There have been major structural changes in both economy and society, linked with new patterns of regional differentiation. Following the experience of West European countries in the 1960s and 1970s, the secondary sector has declined, especially in the case of heavy industries favoured under totalitarian rule but less acceptable today than manufactures with a high labour and research input. But the service sector, which remained underdeveloped during the communist period, has seen rapid growth. In addition to restructuring and the creation of new branches, there has been an absorption of labour released from both the industrial and agricultural spheres. Services now account for about 55 per cent of the economically active population and further growth is expected. However, the main emphasis in this chapter will lie with the re-evaluation of the country's agriculture through changes in ownership and production. There will also be discussion of rural settlement patterns and functions, and the regional dimensions of change will be taken into account.

CHANGES IN FARM OWNERSHIP AND PRODUCTION

Until 1989, agriculture was very highly socialized, through a wide range of 'centrally guided' enterprises which included seed-dealing enterprises, military farms, breeding companies, school farms and other units controlled almost exclusively by the state (sometimes by organizations other than the Ministry of Agriculture itself). But cooperative and state farms were predominant, being responsible for 61.3 and 25.4 per cent, respectively, of all agricultural land (see Table 4.1). The former included the 'private plots' used by the members for their own needs and subsistence, but they covered only some 14th.ha of agricultural land (0.3 per cent of all land under cooperative management) and 3th.ha of arable land (0.1 per cent). Thus they never had the importance of their Soviet *kolkhozy* counterparts. Meanwhile, the state farms were dominant in border regions, because they managed most of the land confiscated from the Sudeten Germans after 1945. State control over Czech agriculture was virtually complete and private farmers retained only 1.3 per cent of the arable land. About a quarter of their small plots were situated in the foothills of the Beskids near the Polish border, and it is possible that the Polish practice of retaining a high level of private ownership exerted an influence in this area. Half of the

Table 4.1   Czech Republic: agricultural holdings, January 1990

	Land (th.ha)	%	Arable (th.ha)	%
Centrally guided enterprises[a]	349	8.0	230	6.0
State farms	1,089	25.4	801	25.9
Cooperatives	2,637	61.3	2,152	66.5
Private farms	168	3.9	44	1.3
Others	53	1.4	5	0.3
Total	4,296	100.0	2,232	100.0

Note: [a] Including seed farms, military farms, breeding companies, school farms and other units controlled almost exclusively by the state (sometimes by organizations other than the Ministry of Agriculture itself).

Source: Statistická ročenka o pôdnom fonde v ČSFR (Bratislava, 1990), p.324.

land that continued in private ownership was situated in Moravia, a traditional family-farming region with a high level of religious observance.

The more durable link with the land in the eastern half of the country is reflected in the restitution process which was started after 1991 (Figure 4.1a). Under the land law various legal entities, cooperatives and state farms in particular, had to give back the land to the previous owners or their heirs. The duty to return the land which was confiscated from its owners, mostly real farmers, after the 1948 communist coup, has not yet finished because some claims remain unclear, not only in respect of land, but also with regard to buildings, machinery and livestock. The value of restituted holdings amounted to CzK29.5 billion at the beginning of 1994. Privatization is 80 per cent complete as regards the primary agricultural property. Eighty-two per cent of all restitution claims were settled by the beginning of 1996, with particularly good progress in all regions except Prague and the borderlands where there have been difficulties in justifying claims. At the same time, 94.5 per cent of the food industry had been privatized. Meanwhile, the cooperatives had to transform themselves into 'cooperatives of landholders' with the consent of all those involved at a general meeting. Management is now in the hands of democratically elected bodies representing both the pre-1949 landowners (or their heirs) and the present farm employees. However, some farming companies have purchased land from the beneficiaries of restitution to the extent of CzK9 billion, or 30.5 per cent of the total value of restituted property. Naturally, the new owners had to borrow money to finance their purchases and they will probably need 20 years to pay off all their debts.

Meanwhile, privatization of 316 state farms (with an average area of 6,225ha) has meant a further radical change in the organization of agriculture. Thirty-one state farms were privatized through the 'coupon method', which results in highly dispersed ownership in the first instance, while the great majority (261) were sold to individual persons or groups of people, often technicians, drawn from the middle and upper echelons of the communist management, having both a good knowledge of each holding and sufficient skills to draw up sound privatization plans. Another 19 state farms were disposed of through restitution to private farmers and five farms (including one in Prague) were liquidated. Altogether, the state farms were transformed into 1,800 private holdings with an average area of some 700ha. Most of

(a) Restitution of agricultural land

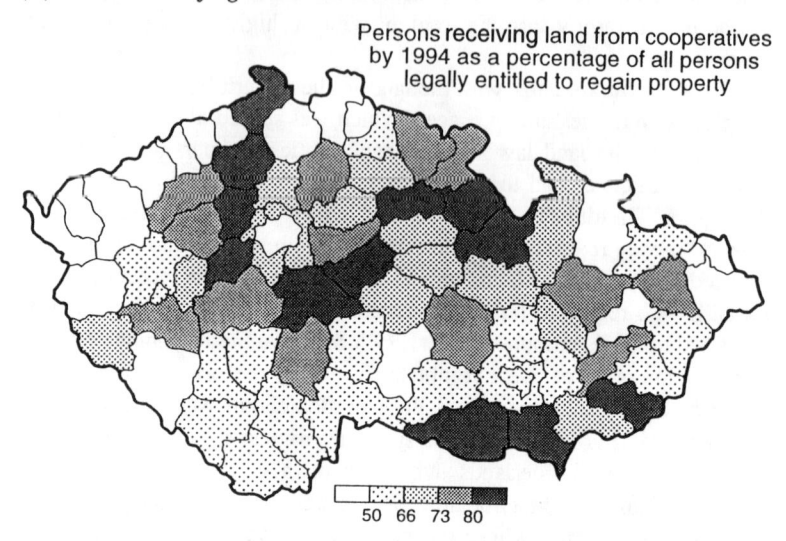

Persons receiving land from cooperatives by 1994 as a percentage of all persons legally entitled to regain property

50 66 73 80

(b) Predominant size of private farms

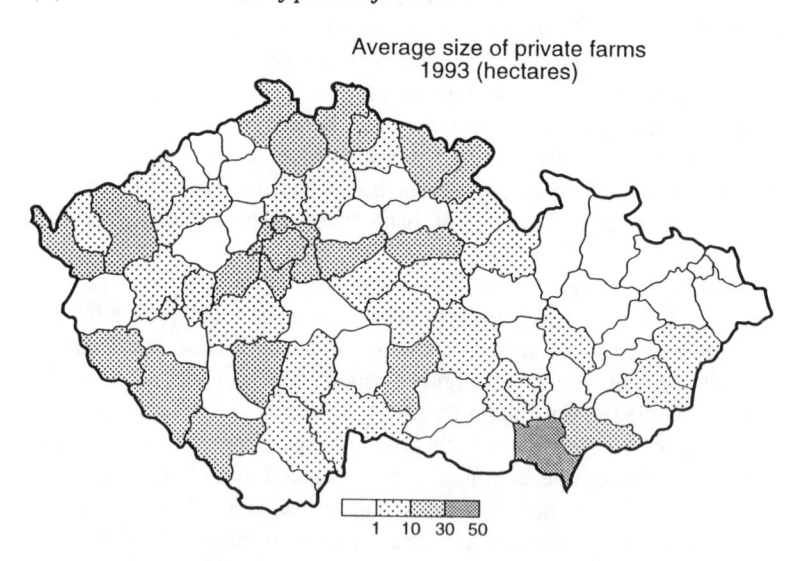

Average size of private farms 1993 (hectares)

1 10 30 50

Note: For names of districts, see Figure 4.2.

Source: Götz 1994.

(c) Agricultural land belonging to private farmers

Agricultural land belonging to private farmers 1994 (percent)

10 15 20 35

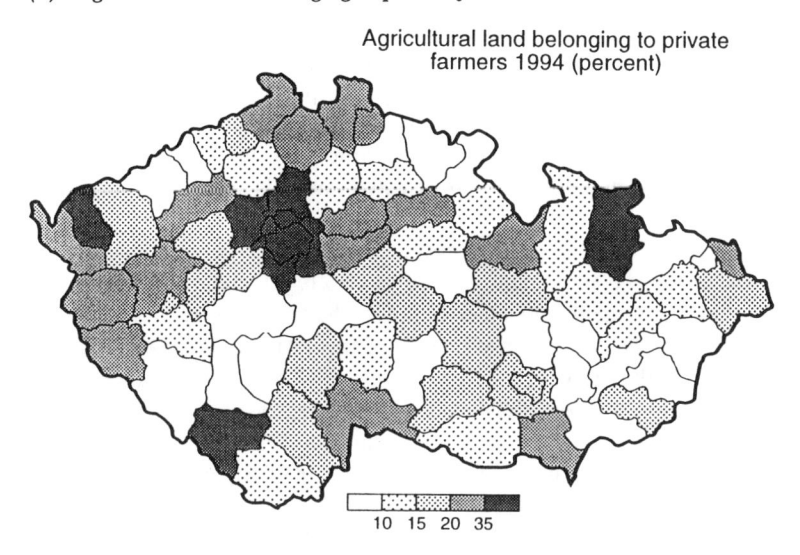

(d) Transformation of agriculture

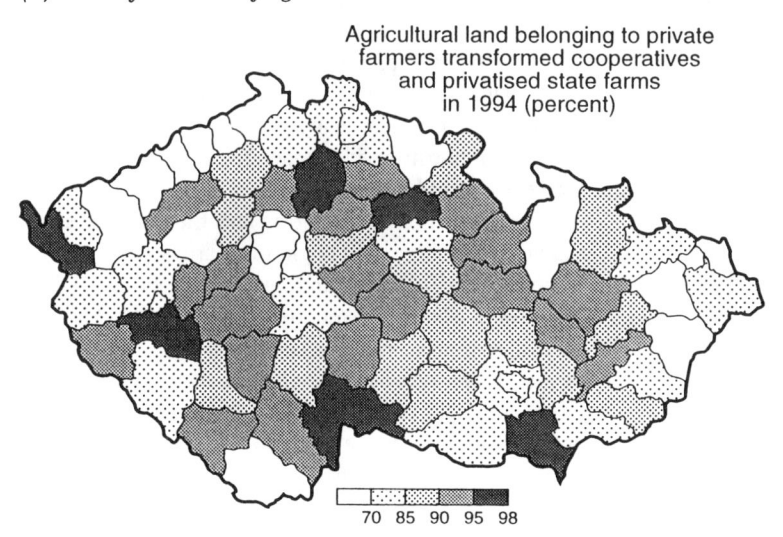

Agricultural land belonging to private farmers transformed cooperatives and privatised state farms in 1994 (percent)

70 85 90 95 98

Figure 4.1 Czech Republic: aspects of privatization of agriculture, 1994

them are run as companies with up to eight individuals sharing ownership. The 1995 value of the privatized state farmland amounted to some CzK15 billion. The new owners had to take over part of the debts of state farms (CzK4.1 billion), although the purchase price was lowered by the same amount. Two-thirds of the state farm area has now been privatized, but because it is mainly farms with limited equipment and relatively few buildings that are affected, the outstanding area (approximately 0.5m.ha) is very substantial in value terms: CzK17-20 billion. So far there has been little interest in farms with large buildings and the most expensive equipment, valued at CzK17-20 billion. It seems that the large cowsheds and other buildings have been greatly overvalued and it is probable that only a tenth of this estimate will eventually be realized on the market.

According to the official data of the Agriculture Ministry's 'Green Report on the State of Czech Agriculture in 1996', privatized and de-collectivized agricultural holdings account for 98.3 per cent of the total area of agricultural land (Table 4.2). The average farm business covers 132ha (1996) but there are important spatial variations because private farmers are predominant around Prague, reflecting the good marketing opportunities, especially for eggs, milk and vegetables (Figure 4.1b). The number of private farmers is both significant and stable along the Polish border where there are many small private farm businesses, but numbers are small in Central Moravia despite fertile soil and the proximity of the Ostrava agglomeration. In other words, many owners retain only a token area and lease the rest to transformed cooperatives (as in the Hana Lowland and the northern part of South Bohemia).

The larger holdings of privatized state farms and transformed cooperatives are prominent everywhere, although they are somewhat less dominant in the North Bohemian borderland and around Prague where the pace of transformation is somewhat retarded (Figure 4.1c). Many of the claims made in this area have not yet been settled because of the complicated tenure and property relations. Owning land near Prague, where the land is fertile and the demand for food is high, is a most attractive prospect and the economic incentive tends to result in sharp ownership disputes. Over the country as a whole, two-thirds of all property claims have been settled, but there is a higher figure in East Bohemia where, significantly, only a slight decline in agricultural production has taken place, and also in the southernmost districts of Moravia and in some Central Bohemian districts. By contrast, a low rate of settlement (less than

Table 4.2 Czech Republic: use of agricultural land, September 1995

Type of agricultural business	Number	Average size (ha)	Land area (ha)			
			Total		Arable	
			Ha	%	Ha	%
Individual farmers	22,443	34.2	768,304	23.3	585,141	20.6
Entrepreneurs[a]	951	55.5	52,779	1.5	40,701	1.4
Other private persons[b]	789	6.4	5,032	0.1	3,465	0.1
Trading companies[c]	1,463	680.0	995,682	28.0	797,696	28.1
Cooperatives	1,151	1,447.2	1,665,727	47.0	1,367,239	48.1
State farms	80	660.0	52,797	1.5	41,715	1.5
Other	27	272.7	7,363	0.2	6,157	0.2
Total	26,904	131.9	3,547,684	100.0	2,842,114	100.0

Notes:
[a] Food industry or trade enterprises where agricultural production is not the main activity.
[b] Owners of small farms who are not registered as farmers but who use part of their land for subsistence while renting most of it to others.
[c] Limited liability companies which are mostly 'using' former state farm land with payment spread over 20 years. Legislation sanctioning the sale of such land has not yet been approved. Hence the observation in the text that 0.5m.ha of state-farm land has still to be sold while the area still 'used' by state farms is only 52.8th.ha.

Source: Ministerstvo zemědělství (1996).

one half) appears in West Bohemia and in the industrial regions of North Bohemia, both of them being regions extensively resettled after 1945 and heavily affected by open-cast coal-mining. Both demographic upheaval and the environmental damage have complicated restitution claims because there are many cases where ownership is uncertain (Figure 4.1d). Over much of the country only residual state farms, school farms and military farms are outstanding (Ptáček 1996).

AGRICULTURAL PRODUCTION

In the late 1980s, agricultural output was very high because of planned exports to other communist countries (especially FSU) and the Middle

100 *Privatization in Rural Eastern Europe*

(a) *Agricultural production types*

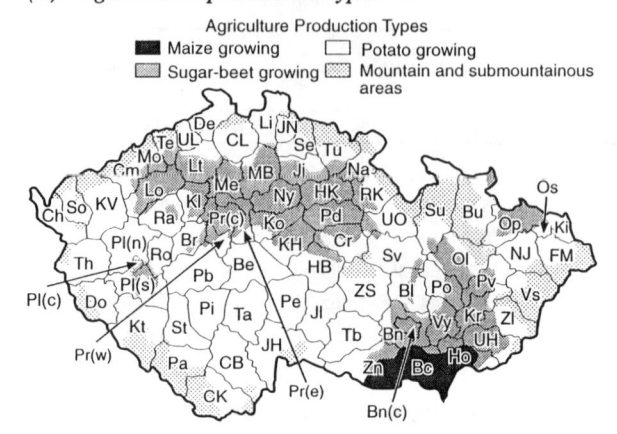

Agriculture Production Types
- ■ Maize growing
- □ Potato growing
- ▨ Sugar-beet growing
- ▦ Mountain and submountainous areas

(b) *Gross agricultural production*

Agricultural production 1994 in thousands CzK/ha

4 12 16 19 21 24 28

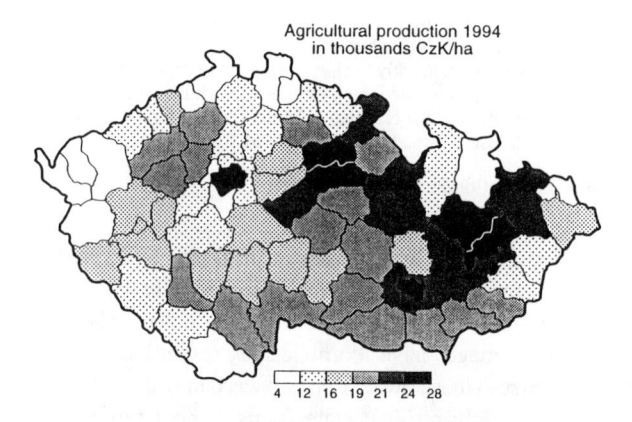

Names of districts: Bc Břeclav; Be Benešov; Bl Blansko; Bn Brno; Bn(c) Brno City; Br Beroun; Bu Bruntál; CB České Budějovice; Ch Cheb; CK Český Krumlov; CL Česká Lípa; Ch Chomutov; Cr Chrudim; De Děčín; Do Domažlice; FM Frýdek Místek; HB Havlíčkův Brod; HK Hradec Králové; Ho Hodonín; JH Jindřichův Hradec; Ji Jičín; Jl Jihlava; JN Jablonec nad Nisou; Ki Karviná; KH Kutná Hora; Kl Kladno; Ko Kolín; Kr Kroměříž; Kt Klatovy; KV Karlovy Vary; Li Liberec; Lo Louny; Lt Litoměřice; MB Mladá Boleslav Me Mělník; Mo Most; Na Náchod; NJ Nový Jičín; Ny Nymburk; Ol Olomouc; Op Opava; Os Ostrava; Pa Prachatice; Pb Příbram; Pd Pardubice; Pe Pelhřimov; Pi Písek; Pl(c) Plzeň City; Pl(n) Plzeň (north); Pl(s) Plzeň (south);

Czech Republic 101

(c) Agricultural production per capita

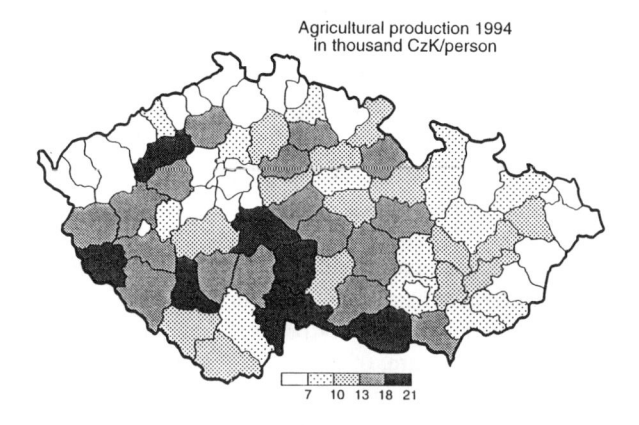

Agricultural production 1994
in thousand CzK/person

7 10 13 18 21

(d) Average production potential for agricultural land as percentage of the best land available 1984 (the basis of the system of subsidy payments used in the communist period)

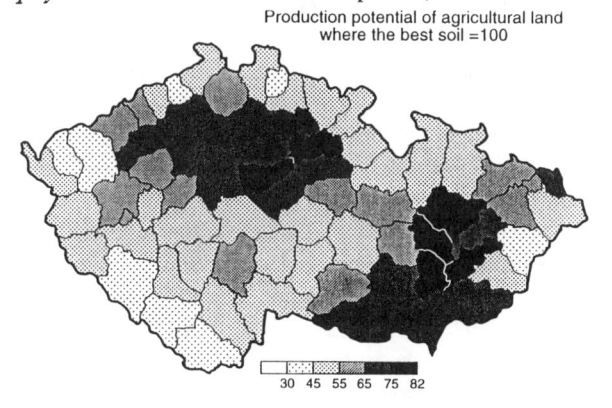

Production potential of agricultural land
where the best soil =100

30 45 55 65 75 82

Po Prostějov; Pr(c) Prague City; Pr(e) Prague (east); Pr(w) Prague (west); Pv Přerov; Ra Rakovník; Ro Rokycany; RK Rychnov nad Kněžnou; Se Semily; So Sokolov; St Strakonice; Su Šumperk; Sv Svitavy; Ta Tábor; Tb Třebíč; Te Teplice; Th Tachov; Tr Trutnov; UH Uherské Hradiště; UL Ústí nad Labem; UO Ústí nad Orlicí; Vs Vsetín; Vy Vyškov; Zl Zlín; Zn Znojmo; ZS Žďár nad Sázavou.

Sources: Atlas ČSSR, 1966 (a); Czech Statistical Office (b); Gőtz 1994 (c); Výzkumný ústav zemědělské ekonomiky (VÚZE) (d).

Figure 4.2 Czech Republic: aspects of agricultural production, 1994

East. The potential was maximized according to a system of basic agricultural areas researched in 1960, reflecting land fertility and labelled according to the characteristic crop (which was not necessarily the one most widespread) (Figure 4.2a). Only in southern Moravia is there enough warmth for maize to ripen, but the sugar-beet region is also warm and fertile. Potato growing is typical in the uplands but there are some elevated areas, especially along the borders, where fodder and forage are most characteristic. However, a policy of intensive production was not economically rational because the country had clear natural advantages in only a few commodities. With the collapse of Comecon, Czech agriculture is now geared to the domestic market, apart from the export of some high-quality products such as hops and malting barley. Meanwhile, there are, of course, some imports of commodities which cannot be produced under Central European conditions. A high level of crop and animal production is desirable in the run-up to EU membership, but during the early 1990s measures have been taken to limit output, following the experience of EU members in the 1970s. Thus, between 1989 and 1994, agricultural output decreased by about a quarter and intensity is now about 20–30 per cent below the most advanced European countries. The decrease has arisen through lower yields and reduced profitability in animal husbandry. Meanwhile, with the cancellation of the differentials used in the communist period, the location rent is playing a more prominent role through maintenance of intensive agriculture in the lowlands, where farming is profitable, while arable enterprises have been gradually eliminated in the foothills. This latter trend is also desirable in the context of environmental conservation, where more careful management is needed after the years of large-scale production in the 1980s.

In the new situation, the state is revising the inherited policy of substantial financial support for both agriculture and the food industry. Until 1990, intensive farming was encouraged by a high level of support for agriculture as a whole. Moreover, to encourage production in the less attractive foothill zones, higher subsidies ('differential bonuses') were paid to cooperatives and state farms, although not to private farmers. Cooperatives and state farms were divided into 48 categories according to soil quality. Those with the poorer soils received subsidies, whereas farms with average conditions were given only modest subsidies and the richer farms were subjected to a land tax on their production so that, to some extent, the more successful farms subsidized the rest. When a cooperative operating under the most difficult conditions sold to the state agricultural products worth CzK1 million, the state gave another CzK0.92 million in subsidies.

However, the Ministry of Agriculture retains a regime of subsidies over what is approximately the poorest 25 per cent of agricultural land. The aim is to encourage the transfer of arable land to meadows and pastures. Money is also available to subsidize the maintenance of meadows and pastures under the most difficult conditions. Meanwhile, the transfer from arable land to forestry is being supported on steeply sloping land. In 1996 subsidies were also made available to stimulate the transfer of arable land to meadows, pastures and forests in those regions where the average price of agricultural land stock in the given land registry unit was lower than CzK31,000 per hectare on the Ministry's own list. However, only 26 per cent of the value of agricultural production in 1994 arose from subsidies (Ministerstvo zemědělství 1995). This is well below the EU level of 50 per cent and far less than Finland (67 per cent), Japan (74 per cent) and Switzerland (82 per cent). Figure 4.2b shows the impact of these spatial policies over the past five years. It seems that a close correlation between agricultural production and natural conditions has not yet been achieved because the Labe Basin registers a lower agricultural output per hectare than the Bohemian–Moravian Uplands, where there is high potential erosion and natural conditions for farming are generally poor. The anomaly may arise from the transfer of farmworkers in the fertile Labe Basin to other employment, both in the region itself and in the environs of the Prague agglomeration (Figure 4.2c).

The regions around the Prague and Brno agglomerations distinguish themselves with a relatively high intensity of agricultural effort because of a 'suburban' or even 'gardening' type of land management. In Moravia, farming is now well adjusted to the natural conditions, with the Haná Lowlands as the most fertile region, although there is the exception of the Moravian part of the Bohemian–Moravian Uplands, mentioned above. Meanwhile, East Bohemia, with both lowland and mountain environments, is the most intensively farmed region. This can be attributed to the tradition of good husbandry and high intensity of agriculture. Finally, the limited agricultural potential of the West Bohemian borderland does not have negative social consequences because there are work opportunities in Germany to compensate for the steep decline in production in the border areas. In summary, Table 4.3 ranks the (former) regions

Table 4.3 Czech Republic: potential fertility and production intensity

Order	Potential fertility	Production intensity/ha 1994
1	Central Bohemia	East Bohemia
2	South Moravia	South Moravia
3	North Moravia	North Moravia
4	East Bohemia	South Bohemia
5	North Bohemia	Central Bohemia
6	West Bohemia	North Bohemia
7	South Bohemia	West Bohemia

Source: Gőtz and Bičík 1996, p.211.

of the country according to theoretical assumptions of natural fertility and levels of intensity actually achieved in production in 1994 (in CzK/ha of agricultural land stock) (Figures 4.2d and 4.3a).

The area of arable land has been decreasing in line with production, but in most districts the area has remained stable, even in the Bohemian-Moravian Uplands (Figure 4.3b). Yet while there is stability in the hilly Ždár region, the agricultural land stock has decreased by 4 per cent in the most fertile part of Moravia: Olomouc, in the Haná Lowland. The largest decrease in arable land has occurred in the regions bordering Germany because of the disintegration of state farms, some of which were working whole districts such as Cheb and Tachov. Another factor has been the very small scale of land restitution in these regions. Meanwhile, the area of meadows and pastures has increased significantly over 1990–95, by about one-sixth, mostly due to the transfer of arable land. The largest increase was recorded in the mountainous borderland with Germany: a 135 per cent increase in the Tachov district. But some lowland districts (such as Kutná Hora and Olomouc) have also seen a high increase, for which no clear explanation has been found (Bičík and Gőtz 1996; Gőtz 1994) (Figure 4.3c).

EMPLOYMENT IN AGRICULTURE

In 1996, agriculture employed 222,000 of the economically active population, compared with about 600,000 at the time of the 1991 census. Thus there has been a decline of about 60 per cent, meaning that only 5 per cent of the economically active population was employed in agriculture in 1996. This is a larger proportion than Germany (4 per cent) and the United States (2 per cent), but similar to France and lower than neighbouring countries experiencing transition: 8 per cent in Slovakia, 10 per cent in Hungary and 26 per cent in Poland. The rapid decrease in manpower arises in part from the loss of jobs on state farms, where employment levels were previously excessive, and partly from the closure of non-agricultural activities on former cooperative and state farms (such as construction, repairs, transport and even manufacturing). Until 1989, the taxation system encouraged cooperatives which tried to diversify their economic profile. But the additional employment was returned as agricultural because farming was the main business of the enterprises concerned. Only this anomaly can explain the fact that despite a substantial decline in output and a loss of more than half its manpower, agriculture did not collapse completely within four years. A similar situation occurred when the German population was deported and the number of employees fell by a half: in 1936 there were 2,233 thousand farmers in the Czech part of pre-war Czechoslovakia (out of a total of 3 million) but only 996 thousand in 1953 (out of a total of 1.5 million) (Houska et al. 1971). However, there are significant variations in the ratio of agricultural jobs to land (Figure 4.3d).

The ratio of farmworkers to the population as a whole has fallen from 1:16 in the late 1980s to 1:40 today. However, there are regional variations which correlate with the extent of the decline in agricultural production; for example, there has been a steep decline in the western borderland in comparison with Moravia and the upland region close to Slovakia. The decrease in employment has also resulted in an increase in labour productivity in agriculture (about 7 per cent each year) greater than the improvement in industry (5 per cent), although it is not reflected in any change in agricultural practices and arises simply from the loss of employment in the non-agricultural work previously associated with the socialist enterprises. However, paradoxically in view of employment trends, the highest labour productivity is achieved by the districts of East

106   *Privatization in Rural Eastern Europe*

(a) Price of land 1992 (Ministry of Agriculture)

Mean price of agricultural land 1992 in thousands of CzK/ha

18 37 47 60 75 80 86

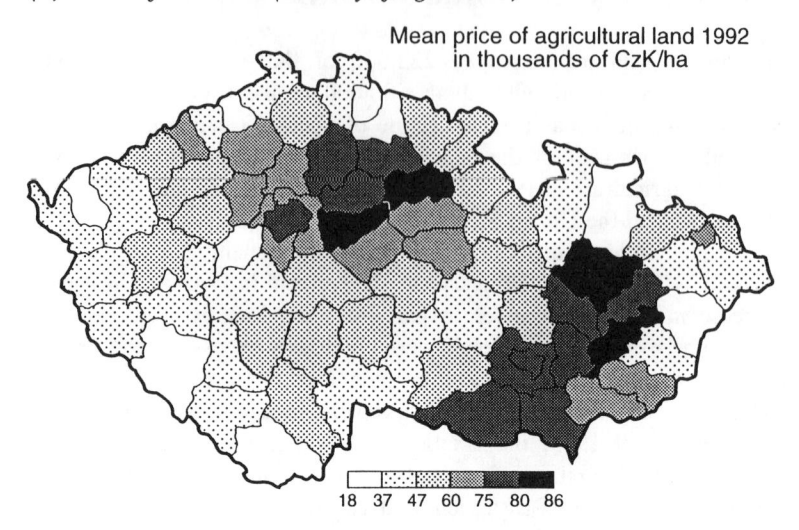

(b) Changes in the area of agricultural land 1990–1995

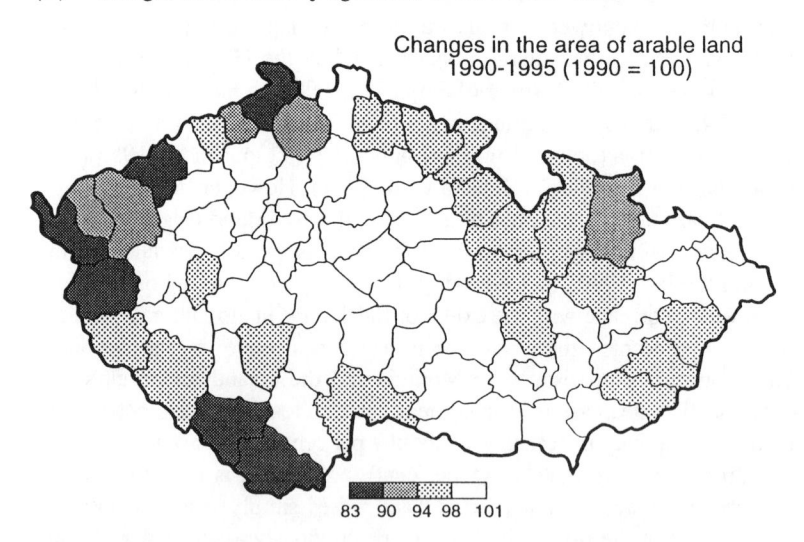

Changes in the area of arable land 1990-1995 (1990 = 100)

83 90 94 98 101

Note: For names of districts, see Figure 4.2.

Sources: Ministry of Agriculture (a); Český úřad katastrální (b and c); Výzkumný ústav zemědělské ekonomiky (VÚZE) (d).

(c) Changes in the area of permanent grassland 1990–1995

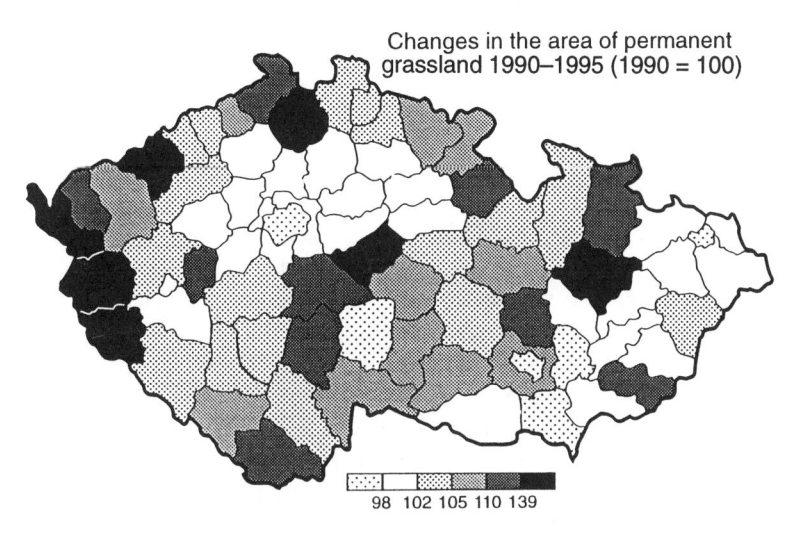

(d) Agricultural land per person employed 1995

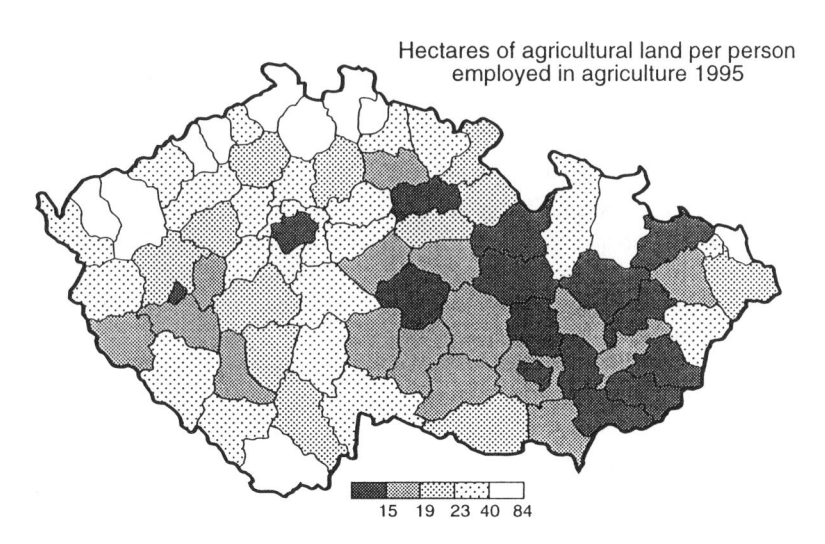

Figure 4.3 Czech Republic: aspects of agricultural land and employment

Bohemia and Haná in Moravia, whereas productivity remains low in West Bohemia. Unemployment generally is low, about 3 per cent, and only 9 per cent of the unemployed are farmworkers. In the Labe Basin, which has a developed industry, people can find other jobs, but opportunities are limited in the Bohemian–Moravian Uplands.

CONSERVATION

Socialist agriculture achieved some successes, including a sufficient output of food and raw materials through modern and relatively efficient methods. Farm managers were highly educated and rural living standards were relatively good, especially for cooperative members. But these successes were based on the exploitation of past investments in rural infrastructure, without adequate renewal, and what can only be described as plundering of the natural resources. The land has been permanently damaged by soil compression and changes to its chemical composition, while the quality of both surface and underground water has deteriorated. The creation of large fields was irrational in the context of the country's natural conditions; water management was complicated and recreation functions were compromised, not least by the loss of aesthetic quality in the landscape. Thus agricultural production must be stabilized at a lower level, not only to reflect the fall in demand but also to facilitate a measure of environmental recovery.

A greater concern for conservation is also very necessary in view of the country's characteristic hilly terrain. About a third of all the agricultural land is threatened by water erosion and the danger was increased by large-scale land management. Large fields extending to tens of hectares were created on terrain that was quite unsuitable, while soil was compressed by heavy machinery and further damage arose from the application of fertilizer in the form of liquid sewage delivered from large stock-rearing units that did not use bedding material. In the 1980s, the waste material generated by large cattle, pig and poultry farms equalled the sewage output of a town of 40–80 thousand inhabitants. There was little interest in building cesspools or purification facilities and therefore the present decline in farming intensity may be seen as positive in environmental terms through a reduced burden on the landscape. However, although the government would like to encourage sustainable agriculture (ecofarming) there is only a limited demand for high-priced foodstuffs at the present time. Consequently organic farming is very much in its infancy.

New programmes are now being drafted to secure the conversion of arable land to pasture through methods adopted by the Research Institute of Agriculture and Environment. A decline of 5–7 per cent in the arable area (which currently comprises 31,580sq.km: 73 per cent of all agricultural land and 40 per cent of the total area of the country) may now be expected, with particular emphasis on the foothills and mountains. To a lesser extent, the area of forest is expected to grow in these same areas. The rate of ploughed land is extremely high in the lowlands. In the lowlands, too, some reduction in arable will occur in the interest of the environment because the proportion of arable land is very high at the moment. Geographers in Prague are monitoring these trends at the level of land registry units of which there are a total of some 13,000 in the country as a whole. The land-use situation for the years 1845, 1948, 1990 and 1995 is being compared and some results have already been published (Bičík et al. 1996). Figures 4.3c and 4.3d summarize the principal trends evident between 1990 and 1995.

CHANGES IN RURAL SETTLEMENT

In the communist period, the central places system was integrated into the planning process in order to maximize efficiency in the provision of services, including transport and housing construction. The settlements were initially classified into two categories: central settlements (*střediskové sídlo*) and non-central communities (*nestřediskové sídlo*). But in the early 1980s there was further conceptualization through recognition of two types of central settlements: metropolitan areas of regional importance (*sídelně-regionální aglomerace*, SRA), and urban regions of more local importance (*městské regiony*, MR). The non-central communities were also divided into various categories in order to recognize those with recreational functions or with other potential offering the prospects of long-term stability. In such cases, state subsidies were available for family housing whereas the 'non-preferred' settlements did not have this benefit. Such selectivity certainly speeded up the process of spatial concentration and transformation of the whole settlement structure, with positive and lasting results in many areas. But in the late 1980s, this approach was criticized by some experts because its was culturally damaging in the more peripheral areas where an ageing of the population, a decline in the housing stock and a general deterioration was evident in many localities. Although the proportion of the rural population may not change significantly in the near future, further changes in distribution seem likely.

According to their position in relation to the urbanization cores, two basic categories of rural settlement can be distinguished (Ryšavý et al. 1989): Category A covers the central and non-central communities located outside the SRAs and MRs. Thanks to their location, some have good, or at least average, development potential, while settlements located in backward regions will have fewer possibilities. Category B, then, relates central and non-central communities lying within the SRAs and MRs, and usually creating their outer zone. Development trends have been quite different in the two groups. Between 1869 and 1985, the population of Category A settlements fell by 1.53 million, with a decline from 49 to 21 per cent in proportionate terms relative to the total population. But in Category B settlements, the population increased by 238,000, although there was a proportionate decline from 23 to 19 per cent. At the same time, Category B settlements have seen a big change in social and professional structure with reduction in the percentage fully employed in agriculture from more than 75 per cent in 1869 to 8–10 per cent today. Category A settlements have not seen such radical change: 30–60 per cent of the active population has been employed in agriculture until recently. At present, regions with clusters of Category B settlements pose the most acute problems in unemployment, economic restructuring and the development of private business.

The Functions of Rural Areas

In keeping with the country's thousand-year-old traditions associated with its rural space, agricultural and silvicultural functions remain basic, as does the residential role, along with water management, recreation, transport and other services associated with the industrial revolution. Today, landscape and environmental functions connected with the conservation of nature are becoming more prominent. Between 1948 and 1989, major changes occurred as a result of socialist management of rural landscape by the totalitarian society. New functions, when added to the historic significance of the Czech countryside and the additional roles acquired through industrial development (with differing levels of intensity in the interaction between rural and urban areas) provide the context for regional diversity in rural landscapes today. Thus, in the western border areas, the Iron Curtain syndrome involved a special regime of agricultural management which radically influenced the area 'behind the barbed wire' – not least through the preservation of genetic stock irretrievably lost in other places. Now that the Iron Curtain had been lifted, the ecological value of the border environment can be more widely appreciated.

By contrast, rural regions with high exposure included the densely populated regions of the North Bohemian brown coal basin. Since the 1950s, fertile farmland in this mining and industrial region was transformed into gigantic open-cast pits for brown coal production. A total of 140 communities, with a combined population of some 50,000, disappeared in the face of the advancing quarries and spoil heaps. This process of devastation came to a head in the period 1960–85 through an extraordinary concentration of population, active in a wide range of economic activities in the towns and villages on the fringes of this once-rural area affected by deep mining of brown coal and subsequently by the opencast workings. Between 1973 and 1990, the agricultural area 'temporarily out of use' in former Czechoslovakia on account of mining and other economic activities, increased from 9,301ha to 15,891ha (of which 12,730ha lay in the Czech Lands in the latter year) (Bičík 1995; Bičík et al. 1996). It is significant that such land was deemed to be only 'temporarily out of use', because this designation meant that the state enterprises did not have to pay the fees normally payable for non-agricultural use of agricultural land under the land stock protection laws of 1966 and 1975. As a result, the state mining companies made no payment whatsoever for the land resources which they exploited. To this day, only a small portion of the exempted land stock has been restored to agricultural use, and given the surplus of agricultural production there is no economic imperative to undertake reclamation. Therefore the area remains quite devastated, with the mining function responsible for the heaps of overburden now moderated only by the growing volume of material directed to the open pits by the country's waste managers.

Both regions, in their different ways, point to the need for more effective environmental planning. Fortunately, the country has considerable experience because the first reservation (Žofín Virgin Forest) was designated in 1839 and in 1858 another natural, conserved area known as the Boubín Virgin Forest was exempted from the normal regime of forest management. This tradition of environmental conservation generated regimes of management and protection which can be used on a larger scale today. In total, about one-fifth of the country comprises national parks, natural reserves and other areas protected as ground-water storage (Table 4.4). Such land cannot be used for agriculture, or may be so used

Table 4.4 Czech Republic: legally protected areas and protected landscape areas

	Area (sq.km)	
Category	1990 (1.1)	1996 (31.12)
Legally protected areas		
national parks	385.0	1,111.2
(nature reserves)*	(481.4)	(823.5)
Protected landscape areas	10,244.4	10,423.7
Total protected areas	10,629.4	11,534.9
Total area of state	78,864.0	78,886.0

Note: * Nature reserves are located partly in national parks, partly in protected landscape areas, and partly outside protected areas; therefore, this area is not included in the total protected area.

Source: Ministerstvo zemědělství 1995, p.154.

only in conjunction with appropriate (that is, more expensive) farming methods. The draft proposal of the Czech coordination centre of the World Conservation Union (IUCN) has identified about 28 per cent of the national territory as being deserving of care under a national programme for both natural and cultural heritage. At a conference in June 1995 in Sofia, the Council of Europe document on a 'European Strategy of Biological and Landscape Diversity' was adopted. This prospect of internationalizing the environment conservation effort is very much in line with the activities of some Czech institutions. In 1995, work was completed on a 'Supraregional System of Environmental Stability', the Czech name for the international supraregional environment network. This methodology proved to be more workable than the three schemes which had been formulated previously. At the same time, the concept of EECONET was adopted, taking advantage of the results of an IUCN review of the country's natural resources. Following legislation it is to be hoped that environmental functions of the rural areas will be enhanced (Míchal and Kopecká 1996).

But an effective environmental policy will require reeducation for all users of the landscape and adequate land-use documentation, for business intentions must be harmonized with the potentials of the landscape, including their limitations, and the developments needed for the efficient discharge of the various functions associated with each territory. Land-use documentation needed to profile the quality of each area, including interaction with society, is being based on detailed field mapping at a scale of up to 1:10,000 to show the present state of local, regional and supraregional systems of environmental stability. These systems constitute a basic network of natural systems which should not be violated, although many enterprises and individuals do not, as yet, pay adequate respect to the law. The survey work started in 1988, and virtually all parts of the country had been covered by 1996. As a result of this work, some violations have now been stopped.

Recreation
The recreation function is also of great importance, having emerged gradually since the Middle Ages to gain great impetus at the end of the nineteenth and the beginning of the twentieth centuries when the first summer villas were built on the edge of Prague and other large cities. Such development was first tied to the railway, but it was later car travel that guided the most affluent families to second homes in a wider range of suburban settlements. However, it was very significant for public health that the socially weaker classes of society soon began to enjoy excursions to the urban–rural fringe areas, including overnight stays, even if the limited provision of visitor services in the rural areas and the general condition of the economy made camping essential. Such activity was common in Prague's southern environs in the 1920s and 1930s, when many simple timber chalets (sometimes in joint ownership) were built close to streams in areas of scenic interest accessible by railway. Hence the appearance of cottage settlements, a new element of the rural landscape, in forests as well as in some marginal (that is, steeply sloping) agricultural land. Such settlements expanded while traditional rural communities were stagnating, and

under communism, when certain activities generally available to free societies were constrained, there was an unprecedented boom in the construction of cottages around Prague and the provincial cities. By the end of the 1980s, this trend was characteristic even of small towns where there were no major environmental problems in the urban cores.

It is also worth noting that, with the expulsion of the German population in the late 1940s and the subsequent imposition of the Iron Curtain, much of the rural housing stock was destroyed in the western border areas and whole villages disappeared. However, in some parts of North Bohemia (the foothills of the Giant Mountains and the Lusatian Mountains), the houses abandoned by the departing Germans were preserved because of the growth of cottage activities which had started in the pre-war period. Now, there were larger, better equipped agricultural properties available and the local authorities were only too glad to get rid of them, especially in the 1950s when they could be purchased for less than one month's salary. Then the subsequent depopulation of other rural areas, starting in the early 1960s, provided further opportunity for urban dwellers to gain property on very advantageous terms in some very attractive locations, in addition to other places that were less well known and relatively inaccessible, including some intensively farmed areas and even wasteland where the development of second homes was not always appropriate. Cottage activities became central to the lifestyle of the totalitarian period and interest is still maintained today even though other options are now available.

Tens of thousands of families move out of town every weekend in the summer season to second homes where they enjoy gardening and sporting activities as well as a different set of personal relations to those experienced in large, anonymous, high-rise apartment buildings. The 1991 census enumerates some 396,000 second homes, including 214,000 recreational cottages and small houses, 54,000 recreational chalets (largely created from the original agricultural homesteads) and another 128,000 flats used for recreational purposes. Such properties may be grouped into 'inner communities' where families enjoy close relations with neighbours, often combining for sporting or social arrangements such as musical evenings and bonfires. Overall there are now five recreational properties per one square kilometre of national territory and 11 recreational properties per 100 permanently occupied apartments. In every hundred residential buildings a total of 18.5 are used only as recreational properties.

Second homes are a distinctive form of tourism in the hinterland of large towns. Three-quarters of all rural communities are affected to some extent (and substantially in the case of those communes – about one-third of the total affected – where there are concentrations of second homes). Such development represents a spread of the urban way of life and a modification of rural values, given the great care lavished on the houses to maintain an attractive appearance, an increased concern for the appearance of the village as a whole of settlement and the establishment of personal contacts between the rural and urban populations. But recent geographical surveys of second homes close to Prague have revealed much about the condition of these properties and possible changes in their use in the future. Given the relatively ample size and good condition of most properties it can be assumed that at least some of them will be used (possibly after reconstruction) for permanent residences and so relieve the growing housing shortage. As was the case when the cottage movement first started, transformation into permanent accommodation will probably occur in areas with good transport services affording easy journeys to the workplace in less than 45 minutes.

The decline in commuting and the growth of new rural employment

The rural areas already have important residential functions linked with travel to work in the towns. In the past, this function was tied primarily with employment within rural communities, but commuting is now well established. In 1991, a total of 1.76 million residents commuted to work in locations lying outside their place of residence. In 1980 the figure was 1.70 million, so there has been an absolute increase and a growth in proportion (relating to the economically active population) as well. Commuting also affected another 633,000 students travelling to school every day. However, at present there is a decline in the number of commuters, partly because of the run-down in public transport in the past five years and significant increases in fares. Also, a section of the rural population is now able to pursue business at home in areas that were effectively closed in the past: small farms and workshops, shops, public houses and boarding houses. This trend has been reinforced by the loss of many urban jobs and the transfer of several thousand town dwellers to new homes and occupations in the countryside where houses have been purchased (or obtained through restitution) as a base for work in computer programming, translating or painting.

The search for new functions in rural areas today is seeing a return of some traditional activities that were curtailed under socialist planning - notably the small businesses referred to above. In the rural areas, both old and new houses provide space for such new functions at relatively low cost (to both owners and tenants) compared with the urban situation. There are also new jobs connected with wholesale trade and cottage industry; environmental protection; landscape and water management; agrotourism; and sewage treatment. The transport function is also creating new jobs in road maintenance, including the building of new highways of national and international importance; and reconstruction and construction of new roads of long-distance and supraregional importance, including bypasses through urban-rural fringe areas. Rural roads attract a lower priority but there is much work to be done to make up for past neglect, given the higher standards in neighbouring countries. Meanwhile, agricultural policy includes support for non-productive (that is, service) functions and for specific regional programmes. Services are particularly important at this time because of neglect in the communist period when industrial development and the wellbeing of the working class were of primary importance. Emphasis is being placed on ancillary activities concerned with agrotourism, biogas and the use of renewable energy sources. Meanwhile, services must be maintained and infrastructure overhauled (Hrabánková et al. 1994).

While farm production must be reduced to eliminate surpluses, there must also be an attempt to stabilize the settlement pattern and ensure continued use of pastureland where landscape quality would be damaged by further neglect (Valašsko, Pošumaví, Kaplicko and other regions). Regional programmes are being carried out in a number of districts with the aid of experts from the Institute of Agricultural Economics (VÚZE) and the Ministry of Agriculture. Such programmes, submitted through the regional offices of the Agriculture Ministry, are trying to achieve objectives appropriate to each district: restructuring agricultural production, coping with high unemployment and lack of opportunity outside agriculture by creating new jobs in the service sector and renewing energy sources. Measures have also been taken to stabilize settlements suffering from low incomes and heavy out-migration through improvement in the housing stock, support of small businesses and investment in technical infrastructure. Other programmes have enhanced landscape quality through changes in agricultural production, better management of pastureland and formulation of environmental policies. Support has come from abroad through bilateral and multilateral assistance projects and there has been a considerable input by PHARE. Such funding has gone directly to the regions eligible for assistance or has been allocated from the centre.

CONCLUSION

The present rural transition has meant radical change for the cooperative and state farms that were central to the socialist system. But a difficult situation, involving hardship for many families, has been complicated by a general surplus of agricultural production. Individual farmers and the revamped cooperatives are under pressure because per capita food consumption is down by a quarter on 1989. The prices paid to farmers are low while the cost of fertilizers and building materials has increased in relative terms. Meanwhile, food processors (mainly in private hands) keep their retail prices high. Most farmers do not process their own output and so are dependent on the processors. In contrast to the situation between the two world wars, there is no system of long-term contracts and risk-sharing: instead the farmers bear all the risks and uncertainties. However, the Minister of Agriculture declared in October 1996 that agriculture was at the crossroads. Subsidies would be cut or (in the event of accepting the EU system) extended. Prices of land and rural property are low and many large buildings (including modern equipment) built over the last twenty years to support a system of mass production for meat and milk are effectively redundant. Individual farmers will smallholdings face severe competition from the cooperatives and large private farms derived from the sale and subdivision of state farms. An agricultural lobby consists of highly trained managers running these larger enterprises.

The transition in Czech agriculture has been very uneven from the regional point of view. The hilly regions are supported by indirect subsidies which contribute to stability. But conditions in the lowlands are variable, depending on the ease with which surplus labour can be transferred to other employment. It is also significant that the accessibility of farms to the food processors and urban markets varies considerably. However, there is government support for rural programmes helping farmers to engage in non-agricultural activities such as farm tourism and restoration of ponds. Moreover, ecological programmes are being implemented to accelerate the transfer of arable land to grassland in the hill country. A land market has developed and rural properties no longer required for agricultural purposes are being acquired as second homes for urban dwellers, which means that dereliction is minimized. However, the rural communities are now less stable. Most rural dwellers have only a minimal interest in agriculture and they also lack a commitment to live and work permanently in the rural areas.

As for the future prospects for rural settlement, some general trends can be identified even though the 1991 census data predates the major transitional changes. First, it is clear that the fastest growth is occurring in and around Prague, where there is a low unemployment rate of below one per cent and an intensive rhythm of construction activity. Second, it can be assumed that the present high proportion of families owning a second home (currently over 12 per cent) will decline, given the prevailing housing shortage and the opportunity to convert second homes into permanent homes, especially in the hinterland of large cities. In some districts of Central Bohemia, more than a third of all residential buildings are linked with recreational use and if these are rural properties, originally providing permanent accommodation for farming, it may be assumed that many can again be used on a permanent basis after refurbishment and possible conversion into flats. Already 11 per cent of the owners of recreational properties in Prague's hinterland are using renovated accommodation for other purposes, and another 30 per cent are considering doing so.

Third, the development of rural business is mainly concerned with services, including tourism. However, the opportunities are largely confined to border areas, especially the areas close to Austria and Germany, and other places near the main lines of communication or with fine scenery, or both. These activities will doubtlessly contribute to a certain revitalization of rural settlement and regional development, but progress will depend on state assistance and, perhaps, some help from abroad, at least in the initial stages. Fourth, the transfer of the rural population to towns will no longer be an important process but interaction between urban centres and surrounding rural areas will intensify. Fifth, the problems of the 'inner borderland' will continue to be manifest through a declining and ageing population, and a dilapidated housing stock with only limited opportunities for recreational use. These regions will constitute the major problem areas of rural settlement, with only limited development opportunities. Public transport has deteriorated in these areas as many unprofitable bus services have been withdrawn and hence the process of social decay seems set to continue.

REFERENCES

Bičík, I. (1995), 'Possibilities of the long-term human nature intereaction analysis: the case of land use changes in the Czech Republic', in I.G. Simmons and A.M. Manion (eds.), *The Changing Nature of the People–Environment Relationship: Evidence from a Variety of Archives*, Prague: Univerzity Karlov (Proceedings of the Žďár u Mnichova Hradiště meeting of the IGU Commission on Historical Monitoring of Environmental Changes 1994), pp.79-91.

—— and A. Gőtz (1996), 'Regionální aspekty transformace českého zemědělství', in M. Hampl et al., *Geografická organizace společnosti*, Prague: Charles University Faculty of Science, pp.239-54.

—— and V. Štěpanek (1994), 'Post-war changes of the land use structure in Bohemia and Moravia', *GeoJournal*, **32** (3), 253-9.

—— et al. (1996), 'Land use/land use cover changes in the Czech Republic 1845-1995', *Geografie-Sborník České geografické společnosti*, **101** (18), 92-109.

Gőtz, A. (1994), 'Regional differences in transformation of Czech agriculture after 1989', *Geografie-Sborník České geografické společnosti*, **99**, 93-100.

—— and I. Bičík (1996), 'Main regional changes in agriculture of the Czech Republic after 1989', *Acta Facultatis Rerum Naturalium Universitatis Comenianae: Geographica*, **37**, 207-13.

Houska, V. et al. (1971), *Vývoj zemědělství a výživy v Československu*, Prague: SEVT.

Hrabánková, M. et al. (1994), *Regionální politika v zemědělství*, Prague: Výzkumný ústav zemědělské ekonomiky (VUZE).

Michal, I. and V. Kopecká (1995), 'Evropska ekologická síť: vize a realita'. *Veronica: Časopis ochránců přírody*, **9** (4), 1-4.

Ministerstvo zemědělství (1995), *Zelená zpráva: zpráva o stavu českého zemědělství*, Prague: Ministerstvo zemědělstvi.

—— (1996), *Zelená zpráva: zpráva o stavu českého zemědělství*, Prague: Ministerstvo zemědělství.

Ptáček, J. (1996), 'Czech agriculture in transition', *Geografie-Sborník České geografické společnosti*, **101**, 110-27.

Ryšavý, Z. et al. (1989), *Dlouhodobé tendence vývoje osídlení v Československu*, Prague: Výzkumný ústav výstavby a architektury (Vstupni studie 37 stran).

5. East Germany

Olivia Wilson

The fall of the socialist regime in 1989 and reunification with West Germany in October 1990 marked a dramatic and fundamental change in the lives of the population of Former German Democratic Republic (FGDR). Reunification initiated a political, economic, social and geographical restructuring process without precedent in Western Europe (Wild and Jones 1994). The agricultural sector has been one of the worst affected industries in terms of job losses (Tissen 1994), and this has severely affected the wider rural economy and society. The aim of this chapter is to analyse patterns and processes of agricultural and rural restructuring (hereafter 'rural restructuring') since reunification, with particular emphasis on the emerging geography of rural areas.

Reunification was followed by administrative reform through the substitution of 14 *Bezirke*, the main administrative units during the GDR period, with five *Länder* plus Berlin as a city state (Schmidt and Scholz 1991) (Figure 5.1). Each *Land* has an elected government, responsible for administering and implementing federal policies but also for formulating its own laws and policies (Jones 1994). It is, therefore, important to analyse the role of both the Federal government and the *Länder* governments in the restructuring process. The total land area of 9.5m.ha (compared with 23m.ha in West Germany) contains some of both the poorest and the most fertile soils in Germany. Large areas of present-day Brandenburg and Mecklenburg-Vorpommern have marginal sandy soils, while the upland areas of Sachsen and Thüringen are suitable only for extensive farming. The most fertile farmland is a band of loess soils running from Magdeburg in Sachsen-Anhalt to Dresden in Sachsen (Gerbaud 1994). Reunified Germany has the third largest agricultural area in the European Union (EU) after France and Spain, and is the main producer of rape, potatoes, beef, veal, pork and milk (BML 1994).

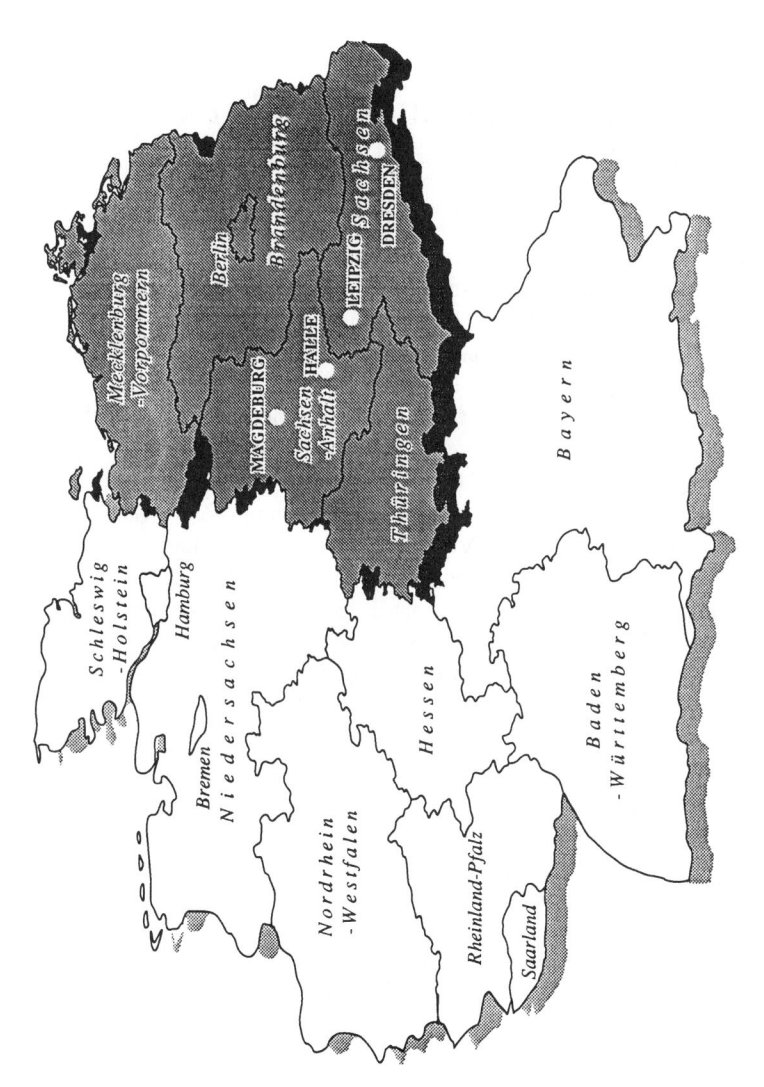

Figure 5.1 East Germany: the New Länder of reunified Germany

The chapter is divided into three sections. First, the context of rural restructuring will be outlined, with an analysis of rural economy and society of the FGDR, and the main problems facing a reunified rural East Germany will be identified. Second, national and regional policies and laws to guide the rural restructuring process will be identified and discussed. Third, the emerging geography will be examined, and the future outlook for rural areas considered.

THE CONTEXT OF RESTRUCTURING: RURAL ECONOMY AND SOCIETY DURING THE GDR PERIOD

In order to understand rural restructuring in reunified FGDR, it is important to have some understanding of how rural areas developed in the post-Second World War period, as the current problems are legacies of this period, and past land ownership patterns have direct relevance for the present development of land ownership and farm business patterns. In 1939, at the outbreak of the Second World War, today's East Germany had an inequitable distribution of land ownership with 28 per cent of the agricultural area owned by estates of 100ha or more (Thöne 1993). Large *Junker* estates were concentrated in present-day Mecklenburg–Vorpommern and Brandenburg. Between 1945 and 1949, a sweeping land reform in the then Soviet Occupation Zone resulted in the expropriation of 3.3m.ha of agricultural and forested land. All estates of more than 100ha were expropriated without compensation, as were many smaller estates. Of these lands, 2.1m.ha were redistributed to more than 500,000 beneficiaries including landless farm workers, refugees from former German territories to the east and smallholders. Most of the 210,000 farmholdings that were created were far too small to be economically viable (average size 8ha) and many were abandoned (BMIB 1979). The remaining 2.2m.ha of expropriated land was retained by the Soviet occupiers (and later taken over by the GDR state).

The expansion of private land ownership proved short-lived. Following the creation of the GDR in October 1949, a collectivization policy was initiated (Bergmann 1992). Farmers were encouraged (and later pressurized) to form farm cooperatives (*Landwirtschaftliche*

Produktionsgenossenschaften or LPGs). By 1960, LPGs covered over 80 per cent of the agricultural land area (Thöne 1993). The majority of LPGs were so-called 'Type III' cooperatives, where farmers surrendered user rights to all their land, livestock, machinery and farm buildings (Thöne 1993). Although farmers retained ownership of their land in theory, in practice they had no control over the management of their property or profits from it, and over time the importance attached to ownership of private property declined (Hagedorn 1992).

Of the expropriated land withheld by the state, 450 th.ha went to form state farms (*Volkseigene Güter* or VEGs) while the rest was distributed to LPGs, although it remained in state ownership. The amount of state-owned agricultural land increased by 900th.ha during the 1950s because of further land expropriations and the appropriation of farms abandoned by their owners who fled to the West (BMIB 1979). Only 5.4 per cent of the agricultural land area, mainly horticultural smallholdings and Church lands, remained in private ownership and control throughout the GDR period (Neander 1992).

In the 1970s, the state launched an agricultural productivity drive. LPGs and VEGs were reorganized into specialist arable or livestock enterprises, and many small LPGs were merged (Bergmann 1992). By 1989, the average arable LPG was 4,600ha in size and employed about 240 workers (although many of these were employed in service, administrative or maintenance and construction jobs rather than in agricultural jobs) (Anon 1990). Livestock farms were smaller in area but organized on a highly intensive basis. In the 1980s, formal cooperation between arable and livestock farms was encouraged with the establishment of 'cooperative associations'. Typically, a cooperative association consisted of one arable and two or three livestock LPGs (Gerbaud 1994). However, despite policies to industrialize agriculture, productivity levels remained well below West German levels although there were variations between farms depending on soil quality but also on social relations between LPG members (ibid.). Labour productivity was poor, with more than 800,000 workers employed on LPGs and VEGs in 1989 (11 per cent of the total labour force compared to 4 per cent in West Germany).

Rural society and economy in the GDR were dominated by the LPGs and VEGs. As well as being the main source of rural employment, the cooperatives and state farms provided key rural services (retail, leisure and culture, welfare, repair and construction) for members, their families and other rural inhabitants. However, although social welfare provision was comprehensive, investment in buildings and infrastructure was low, with the result that much rural housing was of substandard quality, the rural road network was poorly maintained (MLN 1995), and water supply and drainage supplies were inadequate. For instance, in Thüringen only 67 per cent of rural households were connected to sewage treatment plants, and much sewage was disposed of untreated (TMLNU 1995). Environmental degradation was also a problem due to soil and water pollution from overuse of fertilizers and pesticides, inadequate disposal of slurry and soil compaction from use of heavy farm machinery (Anon 1990). Abandoned military training bases and mining and quarrying activities have also left a legacy of contaminated land (the latter particularly in Sachsen).

RURAL RESTRUCTURING SINCE REUNIFICATION: THE NATIONAL FRAMEWORK

The rural restructuring process differs from other East European countries in that the former state has no autonomy over the process. Although the *Länder* governments have a high degree of regional autonomy, the key policies and laws that provide a framework for restructuring have been decided by the Federal government and the European Commission (EC), and inevitably are influenced by wider political and ideological considerations such as the impact of reunification on the farm sector of Former West Germany and the EU (Wilson 1996). Thus, it is necessary to recognize the contrasting farm structures and traditions of the two parts of Germany. The farm structure of former West Germany is characterized by small family farms (average size 19ha). Although post-war agricultural policy increased the efficiency of farming, it also protected family farming (Jones et al. 1993). The large-scale, cooperative organization of farming in the east therefore represented a challenge to the farm lobby and agricultural policy-makers in the west.

The Federal government, backed by the EU, has taken an active and regulatory role in the rural restructuring process in East Germany. This role has focused on achieving four goals: the reintroduction of private property rights in land; the establishment of commercially viable farm-holdings; the maintenance of the rural population and improvement in living standards; and the protection and enhancement of the rural environment. Laws and policies to achieve each of these goals will be considered in turn in this section, while in the next section the emerging geographical outcomes of these policies at regional and local levels will be considered.

Reintroduction of Private Property Rights in Land

This was seen as a priority by the Federal government for two reasons, both practical and political. Privatization and clarification of property rights were recognized to be essential prerequisites for the establishment of viable farm businesses. It was also recognized that claims for restitution of land from former owners whose lands had been expropriated by the Soviet occupiers or, later, the GDR state, must be addressed, as well as the needs and demands of agricultural workers and managers in the LPGs and VEGs.

In June 1990, before reunification, an Agricultural Adjustment Act (hereafter 'the 1990 act') was passed by the Federal government which set out the legal framework for restructuring of agricultural land and property. The stated aims of the act were: to reinstate private property rights in agricultural and forested land; to treat all ownership and business forms equally; and to enable the development of a diverse agricultural business structure and a viable and competitive farm sector (Jones 1994). The act laid down clear guidelines for the restructuring of LPGs, which were to be reformed into western-style businesses (limited liability companies or registered cooperatives) or liquidated by the end of 1991 when the LPG ceased to exist as a legal form. Procedures were set out to regulate the return of property to former LPG members and to rationalize often highly fragmented properties through voluntary land exchange or formal land consolidation schemes (*Flurneuordnung*). A further problem that the act addressed was the separation of ownership of land and buildings that occurred during the GDR period when buildings were built without reference to land ownership. Measures were set out to enable consolidation of ownership of land and buildings as part of the process of *Flurneuordnung*.

The commitment to treat all ownership and business forms equally, although probably politically necessary, was an ambitious goal, given the number of ownership and business forms with an interest or stake in the restitution/privatization of land and property. The groups with claims to land ownership are shown in Figure 5.2. The property-owning members of the LPGs (Group 4) formed the largest group with a direct interest in the reintroduction of private property in land, and had the right to reclaim and withdraw their land and property from the LPG. Group 1 includes so-called land reform victims of 1945–49 who lost estates of 100ha or more. Under the terms of the unification treaty, however, they were not given the right to restitution of their former lands. Farmers whose lands (up to 100ha) were expropriated after 1949 (Group 2), many of whom fled to the west, are entitled to restitution, providing they can prove their claim. The land reform beneficiaries (Group 3) who brought their lands into LPGs in the 1950s were given the right to reclaim their lands, but only if they or their heirs were still working in the agricultural industry (Watzek 1995). Finally, Group 5 includes the small group of owners who retained ownership of their lands throughout and hence are not directly affected by the restitution and privatization process. In addition to those shown in Figure 5.2, three other groups can be identified which have an interest in the reintroduction of private property rights: farm workers in LPGs or VEGs who have no direct claims to land but wish to purchase or rent farmland; LPG members (owners and non-owners) who wish to remain within a 'reformed' LPG; and West German farmers who wish to acquire land in the east.

According to the framework of the 1990 act, two-thirds of East Germany's agricultural area is eligible to be reclaimed by owners, former owners or their heirs, but the remaining third is to be privatized by the state. The VEGs are being sold on the open market by the *Treuhandanstalt* (THA) which was set up to oversee the privatization of all the industrial assets (Wild and Jones 1994). The remaining state land from the 1945–49 land reform and other state land that has not been reclaimed by groups 2 and 3 is to be privatized in stages by the Land Settlement and Administration Company (*Bodenverwertungs- und Verwaltungsgesellschaft* or BVVG), an agency of the THA, in order to give all landowning and business groups an equal chance to acquire land. In 1994, the Compensation and Indemnity Act ('the 1994 act') was passed to regulate this sale. Land has initially been leased on 12-year terms to applicants, but from October 1996 until 2003 the lessees will be given the option to purchase land (up to a certain amount) at subsidized rates. Privatization will, therefore, not be completed before 2003 (Klages and Klare 1995). It can be seen in

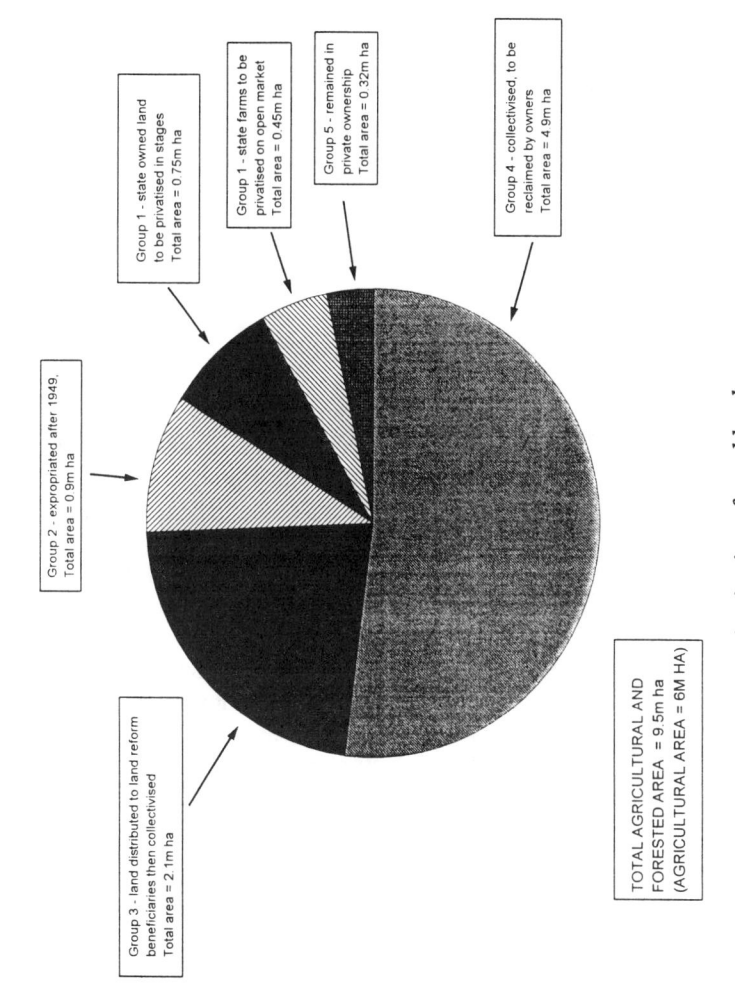

Figure 5.2 East Germany: reprivatization of rural land

Figure 5.3 that the majority of state land has been leased to farm cooperatives and companies, followed by returning occupiers (Groups 2–4). Assuming that the majority of land will be purchased by the lessees, it appears that 'non-family farm' businesses will be the major beneficiaries of the 1994 act. Only a small proportion of land has been leased to non-resident new occupiers, indicating that the majority of land has been leased to East German farm groups.

The 1994 act also deals with the thorny issue of how to compensate victims of the 1945–49 land reform. Two alternatives are proposed. First, they are entitled to receive compensation based on the rateable value of their properties in 1935 (generally compensation will be calculated as being three times this value). Second, instead of compensation, they may apply to purchase state land on favourable terms, as it is anticipated that not all of the leased land will be bought by lessees (ibid.). Although this latter decision has been controversial (Watzek 1995), the amount of land sold to land reform victims at subsidized rates will be small, and they are unable to purchase their former lands under this scheme.

The Establishment of Commercially Viable Farmholdings

The integration of the East German farm sector into the Common Agricultural Policy (CAP) following reunification in 1990 had severe financial implications for farm businesses. Higher production costs than West German producers, loss of markets and a fall in demand for agricultural produce resulted in a fall in farm incomes for all East German producers (König and Isermeyer 1993). In addition, many LPGs were saddled with large debts inherited from the GDR period (estimated at DM7.6bn).

To prevent a large-scale financial crisis, and to help new farming businesses to become established, the Federal government introduced a number of special policy measures in 1991 (Jones 1994). First, agricultural adjustment aid was offered (until 1995) to all farm businesses, except small part-time holdings, to compensate for loss of income. Second, a debt restructuring package was introduced to alleviate the debt burden on reformed LPGs. Third, special grants and loans for investment in buildings, machinery and livestock were offered as part of a joint Federal–*Land* 'Improvement of Agricultural Structures and Coastal Protection' programme. Three schemes in particular have been targeted at

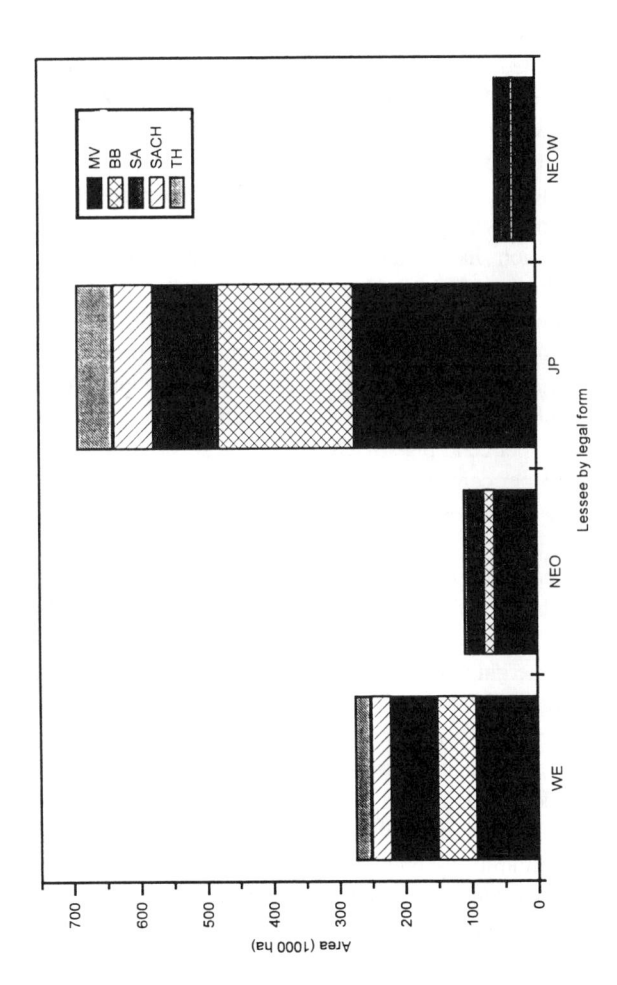

Notes: The following abbreviations are used for the New *Länder*: BB Brandenburg; MV Mecklenburg-Vorpommern; SACH Sachsen; SA Sachsen-Anhalt; TH Thüringen; WE Wiedereinrichter (reinstated occupier); NEO Neueinrichter, ortsansässig (locally resident new occupier); JP Juristische Personen (corporate or cooperative businesses); NEOW neueinrichter, die ortsansässig werden (new occupier from outside the local area).

Source: BVVG 1994.

Figure 5.3 East Germany: agricultural land leased from the Treuhandanstalt

East German farm businesses: a scheme to help (re)establish family farm businesses; an Agricultural Credit Programme for investment in farm buildings, machinery and livestock for all farm business types; and a scheme to help the restructuring of LPG successor businesses.

The Federal government undertook to act as guarantor for up to 80 per cent of the value of loans taken out under these schemes to encourage investment confidence (BML 1995). In addition, about half of East Germany's land area has been designated Less Favoured Area (LFA) under the CAP. Farmers in LFAs are eligible for additional deficiency payments as compensation for farming in marginal areas (BML 1994). Meanwhile, Federal subsidies to agriculture in the New *Länder* between 1991 and 1995 amounted to a total of DM17.25bn (Anon 1995). In addition, FEG received DM2.6bn from EU structural funds between 1991 and 1993, and will receive another DM6.3bn between 1994 and 1999 for agricultural structural change and rural development under the Objective 1 programme (Schrader 1994). The *Länder* governments also contribute financially to agricultural programmes.

Agricultural production has fallen significantly since reunification because of a decline in the level of protection for agriculture and CAP measures to curb production. In 1994, 17 per cent of the arable land area was in 'setaside', resulting in a significant drop in arable production, although yields per hectare have increased since reunification (Anon 1995). Livestock numbers have dropped dramatically since 1990: beef and dairy cattle by 47.5 per cent; pigs by 68.9 per cent; sheep by 64.4 per cent and poultry by 13 per cent (ibid.). The farm labour force has fallen equally dramatically as farm businesses of all types have reduced labour costs. In 1994 there were only 173,500 people employed in agriculture, a fall of almost 80 per cent since 1989 (ibid.).

Figure 5.4 shows the emerging farm business structure of FGDR by legal ownership form. It shows clearly that non-family farm business forms dominate the emerging farm business structure in terms of land area, although more than 18,000 family farms have been established. In 1994, 78 per cent of beef cattle, 75 per cent of dairy cows and 83 per cent of pigs were being raised on cooperative and corporate farms (Kruse 1995). Although numbers of registered cooperatives are declining, limited liability farm companies and farm partnerships are successfully adapting to the new economic conditions (König 1994).

There are a number of reasons to explain why family farming has not become more dominant in East Germany. First, many of the reestablished properties are too small to form viable farmholdings without renting additional land, and the owners lack capital to undertake necessary investment. Second, attitudes to family farming are ambivalent after 40 years of collective farming. Many owners are unwilling to start a farm business and prefer to remain within a farm cooperative or limited company as they lack necessary experience to farm alone, and prefer the security and social benefits of working in a large farm business (Bergmann 1992). Family farming is mainly becoming reestablished in areas with a tradition of family farming such as Sachsen-Anhalt (full-time farms) and Thüringen (part-time farming), although this is dependent on the presence of non-farm employment (Neander 1992). In much of the north there is no tradition of family farming, although this is where most of the land available for privatization is located. These obstacles to the wider establishment of family farming, together with the initial leasing of state land, mean that the majority (90 per cent) of land is rented, with some farm businesses renting land from several different owners (Abel 1995).

Despite the Federal government's ideological preference for family farming, and claims that its policies have favoured family farming (Bergmann, 1992; Watzek 1995), the farm structure of East Germany remains in stark contrast to that in West Germany with much larger average farm sizes and a much stronger corporate and cooperative farm business presence. It seems unlikely that family farming will ever become the dominant type of farm business in the east. Many of the family farms that have become established are, however, much larger and more efficient than their western counterparts.

In addition to changes in the farm sector, restructuring has also occurred in the farm input, processing and marketing sectors of the food chain which were also state controlled during the GDR period (Anon 1990). Restructuring has led to closure of many firms and a decline in employment. For instance, the number of dairies declined from 246 in 1989 to 48 in 1995 (Anon 1995).

(a) By number of businesses

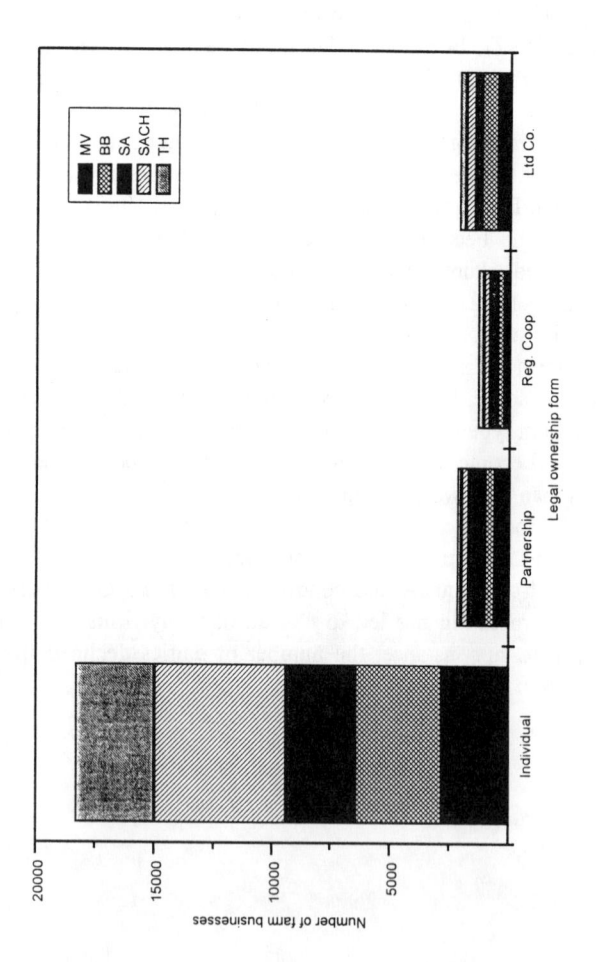

(b) By agricultural area

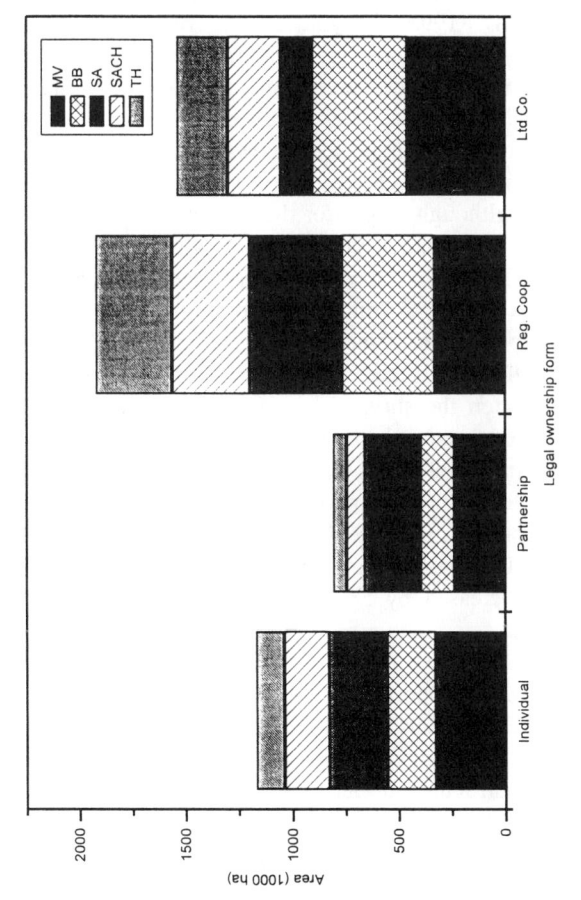

Notes: Abbreviations for New *Länder* as in Figure 5.3.

Source: Kruse 1995.

Figure 5.4 East Germany: farm businesses

THE MAINTENANCE OF THE RURAL POPULATION, IMPROVEMENT IN LIVING STANDARDS AND THE PROTECTION AND ENHANCEMENT OF THE RURAL ENVIRONMENT

Rural restructuring in East Germany has been accompanied by fundamental social and economic upheavals in rural society almost as great as those caused by land reform and collectivization in the 1940s and 1950s. The impact of restructuring has been socially and geographically uneven, however. Elderly workers and women have been most affected by unemployment or enforced early retirement, and are least likely to be reemployed (MLN 1995). They have been effectively marginalized. Other redundant workers have greater opportunities of finding new employment in non-agricultural employment or even self-employment, but retraining and support services are essential. Even those workers who remain in agriculture must learn new farming and management skills. In many rural households one or both adult members are unemployed, and although wages for those employed have inc-reased, so too have costs of living, so that for many households real earnings have fallen (Fink 1994). One widely adopted response to rural restructuring has been to migrate, and most rural areas have experienced depopulation since reunification. In Mecklenburg-Vorpommern, falling birth-rates magnify the effects of out-migration, and together threaten the survival of essential rural services such as primary schools. Birth-rates there fell by 30 per cent between 1989 and 1994 (ibid.). Many rural shops have also closed since reunification, unable to compete in the new market economy, which has disadvantaged those without cars in particular (MLN 1995). Car ownership has risen, however, since unification. For instance, in Sachsen-Anhalt the number of cars increased by 58.8 per cent between 1989 and 1992 (MRSWSA 1993).

Peripheral rural areas with low agricultural potential and lack of alternative employment opportunities have experienced the worst impacts of restructuring (Tissen 1994). Reunification has caused a geographical shift in core–periphery relations as the former border with West Germany is now central within reunified Germany, while the border with Poland and the Czech Republic is more peripheral. Most commercial investment in rural areas is targeted at rural–urban fringe areas surrounding the major urban centres, particularly Berlin, and along the major east–west transport corridors.

A central goal set out in the German constitution and Federal planning law is to achieve and protect equal standards of living in all parts of Germany (Wild and Jones 1994). Responsibility for achieving this goal is shared between the Federal and *Länder* governments. While differing in policy details, all the *Länder* recognize the need to diversify the rural economy in a sustainable manner in order to maintain population, improve standards of living and enhance landscape. They also recognize that the only way to achieve these goals is through developing an integrated rural development strategy.

Policies to improve the efficiency and viability of agriculture have been discussed above. The role of the *Länder* is to implement Federal policies, and to supplement these with additional policies, especially relating to 'greening' agriculture, promoting locally grown produce and also providing training and advice for farmers. The development of new industrial and energy uses for renewable resources is identified as important to provide markets for alternative crops. However, it is recognized that much marginal land will be taken out of production (to be afforested, turned over to extensive pasture, or managed for conservation or recreation purposes). In Sachsen, for instance, the *Land* plans to increase the forested area from 27 to 30 per cent of the total land area (SSUL 1994).

Job creation outside agriculture and forestry is seen as the main priority by the *Länder* governments, as they recognize that there is no prospect of any growth in agricultural employment. Financial support for job creation is provided through a joint Federal-*Land* programme for the 'improvement of regional economic structures' (BML 1994). This programme is aimed at improving industrial infrastructure and enabling the establishment and expansion of firms. Small- and medium-sized firms are identified as being most suited to rural locations. In Mecklenburg-Vorpommern, rural unemployment in 1994 stood at 13 per cent, but the *Land* government admits that without subsidized public work schemes it would be twice as high (MLN 1995). A key area identified as having potential for job creation is recreation and tourism, especially in more peripheral rural areas. The strategy pursued by all the new *Länder* is to encourage growth of 'green' tourism and recreation through preserving and improving the landscape and improving provision of amenities and facilities (for example, accommodation but also walking, cycling and horse-riding routes) (SSUL 1994). All the *Länder* offer subsidies to farmers to diversify into farm tourism and help in marketing rural tourism enterprises. For rural areas closer to urban centres, an improvement in transport links is identified as a priority to enable commuting. In particular, better public transport links are to be developed. Training schemes are identified as essential to accompany and stimulate job creation. In some cases training schemes are targeted, such as Sachsen's training scheme for rural women (SSLEF 1995). Mecklenburg-Vorpommern offers financial support for child care to both men and women who wish to attend training courses (MLN 1995).

Dorferneuerung

Improvements in village housing, infrastructure, environment and social and cultural amenities are also identified as important goals to maintain the present population, particularly young people, and to attract new people into rural areas. One scheme that aims to contribute towards achieving these goals is *Dorferneuerung* or village re-generation. The scheme was developed in West Germany in the 1960s and it is a method of integrated rural development, in that through village regeneration many interrelated goals can be achieved. For instance, Sachsen-Anhalt identifies nine objectives to be achieved through *Dorferneuerung*: a competitive, varied and environmentally friendly agriculture; reinstatement of family farm businesses; renovation and reuse of former agricultural and forestry buildings; protection and renovation of historical buildings; improvement of living and working conditions; development and strengthening of the village centre; improvement in infrastructure; promotion of community involvement and responsibility; and encouragement for further community initiatives for economic, cultural and social developments (MELFSA 1991).

Funding for the scheme comes from the EU structural funds and Federal government (under the programme for agricultural structural improvement and coastal protection) as well as from the *Länder*. Villages participating in the scheme receive subsidies to cover 80 per cent of costs of community works (for example, replanning the village centre; improving transport, communications and utilities) and up to half the cost of private works (for example, external housing renovation and repairs).

Each *Dorferneuerung* scheme takes five years to complete and requires subsidies of one million DM on average (TMLNU 1995). In Sachsen-Anhalt, more than a thousand villages participated between 1992 and 1995, and the *Land* aims to include all the remaining 800 villages of fewer than 2,000 inhabitants in the scheme by the year 2000 (Architektenkammer Sachsen-Anhalt 1996).

The scheme has been most successful so far in achieving physical regeneration in villages, for instance resurfacing village streets, constructing new water and drainage systems, laying underground electricity and telephone cables and installing new street lighting. Less success has been achieved in creating new jobs or safeguarding services. Regeneration is also hampered by unresolved ownership questions over village housing, much of which stands empty in a poor state of repair, and by the presence of LPG farm buildings in some villages which detract from the village environment and may be unsuitable for alternative uses because of asbestos used in construction (Grube and Rost 1995).

Environmental Protection

All these schemes for rural development are formulated to protect and enhance the rural landscape and protect ecological habitats. In addition, specific environmental protection schemes have been formulated. Despite a legacy of environmental degradation, East Germany has many important semi-natural woodland, grassland, heath, bog and water habitats (Reichhoff and Böhnert 1991). Five new National Parks, six Biosphere Reserves and several regional Nature Parks have been designated since reunification (ibid.). The new National Parks are located in Mecklenburg-Vorpommern (Vorpommersche Boddenlandschaft, Jasmund and Müritz); Sachsen-Anhalt (Hochharz) and Sachsen (Sächsische Schweiz), and bring the total number of National Parks in Germany to ten. Once all the planned Nature Parks are designated, a quarter of East Germany's land area will be protected. Measures to combat the effects of acid rain and restore the health of forests have also been launched, as well as policies to restore derelict and contaminated land from abandoned military bases and mines and quarries.

THE EMERGING GEOGRAPHY OF A REUNIFIED RURAL EAST GERMANY

The high level of centralized state control during the GDR period led to uniform farm business structures and production patterns which masked regional differences. Today, while all the new *Länder* face similar problems and challenges, regional and local differences are reappearing. The influence of past land ownership structures, rural social relations and cultural traditions, as well as variations in soil quality and geographical accessibility, are all evident in an increasingly differentiated countryside. *Länder* governments act as 'regional filters' in the policy-making process, by interpreting Federal policy and initiating their own policies, thereby further adding to the contingent nature of restructuring. Brandenburg has most openly stated its own vision for rural development. In 1992 it published its own policy proposal for agriculture entitled *Der Brandenburger Weg* (the way forward for Brandenburg) in which it stated that EU and Federal agricultural policies had led agriculture into a dead end, and were in need of fundamental reform (MELFB 1992). All the *Länder* stress the need to protect and enhance the cultural landscape, partly to promote recreation and tourism but also perhaps to reassert local rural identities.

Figure 5.5 presents a model of rural restructuring by showing the key factors influencing change at different spatial scales and possible outcomes. Three emerging types of rural area are identified:

1. *Development areas experiencing pressures for non-agricultural development.* These areas may be characterized by: a high demand for return of land from former owners for development or intensive agriculture (for example, market gardening); high levels of investment in infrastructure by Federal or *Länder* governments; relatively high land values; relatively low unemployment; stable or rising populations (possibly boosted by 'newcomers'). Examples of these areas include the urban fringes of Berlin, Magdeburg, Halle, Leipzig, Dresden and Erfurt, and rural areas bordering key transport corridors.
2. *Agricultural development areas.* These are areas of high soil quality which may be characterized by: a high demand for land to reestablish or start private agricultural businesses (family farms or

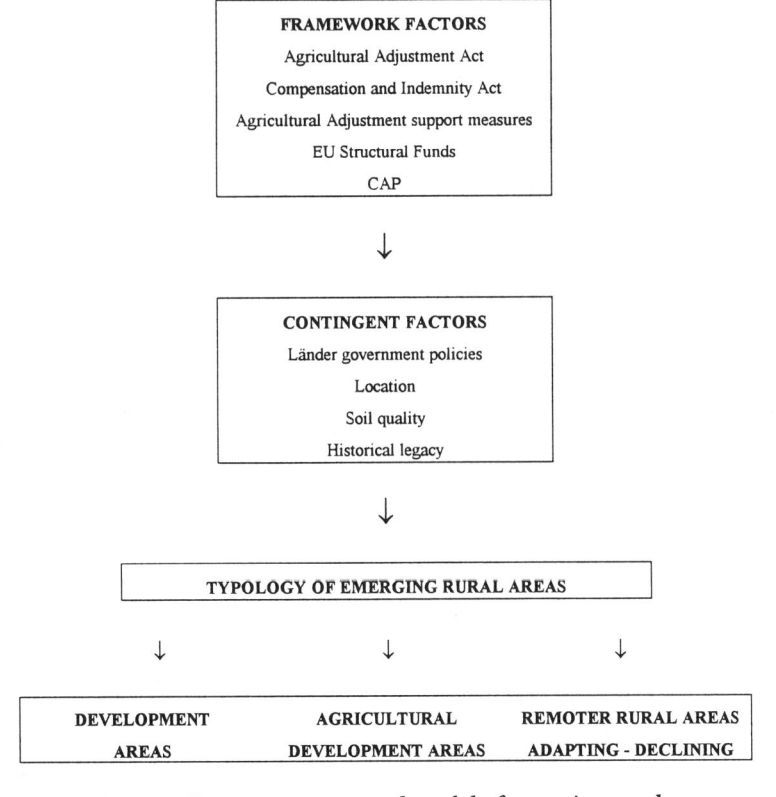

```
              ┌─────────────────────────────────────────┐
              │         FRAMEWORK FACTORS               │
              │      Agricultural Adjustment Act        │
              │    Compensation and Indemnity Act       │
              │ Agricultural Adjustment support measures│
              │          EU Structural Funds            │
              │                 CAP                     │
              └─────────────────────────────────────────┘
                              ↓

              ┌─────────────────────────────────────────┐
              │         CONTINGENT FACTORS              │
              │       Länder government policies        │
              │                Location                 │
              │              Soil quality               │
              │            Historical legacy            │
              └─────────────────────────────────────────┘
                              ↓

              ┌─────────────────────────────────────────┐
              │    TYPOLOGY OF EMERGING RURAL AREAS     │
              └─────────────────────────────────────────┘
                    ↓            ↓              ↓
              ┌──────────────────────────────────────────────┐
              │  DEVELOPMENT    AGRICULTURAL   REMOTER RURAL AREAS │
              │    AREAS      DEVELOPMENT AREAS  ADAPTING - DECLINING │
              └──────────────────────────────────────────────┘
```

Figure 5.5 East Germany: conceptual model of emerging rural areas

partnerships); high levels of investment in agricultural buildings, equipment and livestock; a stabilizing population after initial decline; relatively high land values. This category refers mainly to the band of loess soils stretching from Magdeburg in Sachsen-Anhalt to Dresden in Sachsen.
3. *Remoter rural areas*. These are isolated from urban centres and with marginal soil quality (designated LFA). These can be subdivided into two types: either *adapting*, which may be characterized by: diversification of the economy (for example, growth of tourism); reestablishment of individual farms, many part-time; a stabilising population; high but falling unemployment; low land values; for example, southern Thüringen, southwest Sachsen, southern Brandenburg and the coast of Mecklenburg-Vorpommern; or *declining*, which may be characterized by: high unemployment; lack of demand for reestablishment of farms; many reformed LPGs but facing financial difficulties; population decline; lack of local control over restructuring (much state land administered by the BVVG); lack of investment; low land values; for example, eastern Sachsen, northern Brandenburg and much of inland Mecklenburg-Vorpommern.

The types identified here are not necessarily exclusive, in that agricultural development areas may overlap with development areas, giving rise to conflicts. Furthermore, although the model shows a one-way process (top down), in practice restructuring in any locality is a contested process with interactions between agencies at different spatial scales. In addition, the model does not include the pockets of highly degraded land in rural areas which face their own particular problems (such as the coal and uranium mining areas of Sachsen). It should thus be seen as a preliminary working model to illustrate the range of possible outcomes of restructuring and to highlight the differing problems facing different areas.

CONCLUSION: FUTURE PROSPECTS

The aim of this chapter has been to give an overview and analysis of the process and pattern of restructuring since reunification. It has outlined the problems arising as a legacy of the GDR period and has examined the main policies and laws drawn up and implemented by the

Federal and *Länder* governments to stimulate rural development. It has highlighted some of the factors leading to geographical variations in the restructuring process at local levels.

The whole process of rural restructuring has been highly regulated by the Federal government. As stated earlier, in contrast to other East European countries, East Germany has had little autonomy over the transition process. The key laws and policies have been drawn up by the Federal government to reflect western ideologies and interests. But again, in contrast to its eastern neighbours, East Germany has benefited from the financial resources of West Germany and the EU. A primary goal of the Federal government has been to restructure the rural economy as rapidly as possible and to integrate it into the CAP, but at the same time to attempt to be 'fair' to all interest groups and to achieve sustainable development. Although aiming to be a neutral arbiter between different interest groups, inevitably, given the contrasting structure of agriculture in West Germany and the EU, the Federal government has tended to favour family farms over large, corporate and cooperative businesses. Despite preferential treatment, however, it appears that non-family farms will be a dominant part of the new agricultural structure in East Germany, and will acquire most of the privatized state land.

The ideological influence of West Germany can also be seen in the rural development strategies being pursued by the *Länder*, with their clear emphasis on appropriate (small-scale) development and environmental protection and enhancement. However, the high commitment on the part of the Federal government and the EC to achieving a diversified and sustainable countryside is also clear from the level of financial resources provided. For instance, *Dorferneuerung* schemes are lengthy and costly undertakings but promise to achieve lasting improvements in rural society. The establishment of viable farm businesses and the provision of non-farm employment are both crucial to maintaining the rural population and must remain policy priorities. In addition, the maintenance of rural services and improvements in rural housing will be crucial to support rural living standards.

Many contingent factors acting at regional and local level are causing geographical variations in the process and outcome of restructuring. Although all rural areas have experienced the dramatic reduction in agricultural employment, the socio-economic impact on localities and individuals is uneven. Some localities are adjusting while others are lagging behind. Adjustment itself may cause problems; for instance, in pressured rural-urban fringe locations, conflicts are likely to centre upon the environmental impacts of commercial and residential developments. The social and economic challenges are greatest, however, in remoter rural areas which may need additional help to adjust to the new economic and political situation. Furthermore, support must also be given to those marginalized by restructuring – in particular women and the elderly.

The first stage of restructuring (clarification and restitution or privatization of property rights and establishment of competitive farm businesses) may be coming to a close, but the long-term viability of rural communities will still take a long time to secure. Many uncertainties remain over which Germany has only partial control. For instance, the future of the CAP after the year 2000 is uncertain, as is the future development of the EU itself. An expansion of the EU eastwards to include other former socialist states would increase East Germany's geographical and political centrality within Europe, but would inevitably reduce the level of financial support currently enjoyed.

REFERENCES

Abel, C. (1995), 'Prospects rise in the East', *Farmers Weekly*, No. 27, 77–9.
Anon (1990), 'East German agriculture overview', *Agra Europe East Europe and China Agriculture and Food*, No. 90.
—— (1995), 'Die Agrarwirtschaft in den neuen Ländern', *Agra Europe*, No. 36.
Architektenkammer Sachsen-Anhalt (1996), *Dorfentwicklungsplanung in Sachsen-Anhalt*, Magdeburg: Architektenkammer Sachsen-Anhalt.
Bergmann, T. (1992), 'The reprivatisation of farming in Eastern Germany', *Sociologia Ruralis*, 32, 305–16.
Bodenverwertungs- und -verwaltungs GmbH (BVVG) (1994), *Verpachtung landwirtschaftlicher Fläche*, Berlin: BVVG.
Bundesministerium für Ernährung, Landwirtschaft und Forsten (BML) (1994), *Agrarbericht der Bundesregierung*, Bonn: BML.
—— (1995), *Für unsere landwirtschaftliche Unternehmen*, Bonn: BML.
Bundesministerium für innerdeutsche Beziehungen (BMIB) (1979), *DDR Handbuch*, Bonn: BMIB.
Fink, M. (1994), 'Entwicklung der Lebens- und Arbeitssituation in ländlichenhaushalten', *Landbauforschung Völkenrode*, 152, 11–22.
Gerbaud, F. (1994), *La transition agricole dans les nouveaux Bundesländer: une transition sous tutelle? Une réponse géographique? Rapport pour le Ministre de la Recherche et de la Technologie*, Berlin: Centre Franco-Allemand de Recherche en Sciences Sociales de Berlin.

Grube, J. and D. Rost (1995), *Dorferneuerung in Sachsen-Anhalt: alternative Siedlungsentwicklung*, Magdeburg: MELFSA.

Hagedorn, H. (1992), 'Die Bauernfrage in Deutschland-Ost', *Berichte über Landwirtschaft*, **70**, 396-409.

Jones, A. (1994), *The New Germany: A Human Geography*, Chichester: Wiley.

——, F. Fasterding and R. Plankl (1993), 'Farm household adjustments to the European Community's set-aside policy: Evidence from Rheinland-Pfalz', *Journal of Rural Studies*, **9**, 65-80.

Klages, B. and K. Klare (1995), 'So werden Alteigentümer jetzt entschädigt', *Top Agrar*, No. 5, 44-7.

König, W. (1994), 'Umstrukturierung und Neugrundung landwirtschaftlicher Unternehmen', *Landbauforschung Völkenrode*, No. 152, 63-80.

—— and F. Isermeyer (1993), *The Restructuring of East German Agriculture in the Course of the Unification of Germany*, Braunschweig-Völkenrode: Institut für Betriebwirtschaft, Bundesforschungsanstalt für Landwirtschaft.

Kruse, S. (1995), 'Entwicklung der Struktur der landwirtschaftlichen Betriebe in den neuen Ländern', *Informationen für die Agrarberatung*, **3** (6), 2-24.

Ministerium für Ernährung, Landwirtschaft und Forsten des Landes Brandenburg (MLB) (1992), *Der Brandenburger Weg*, Potsdam: MELFB.

Ministerium für Ernährung, Landwirtschaft und Forsten des Landes Sachsen-Anhalt (MELFSA) (1991), *Richtlinien über die Gewährung von Zuwendungen zur Dorferneuerung im Rahmen der Gemeinschaftsaufgabe: Verbesserung der Agrarstruktur und des Küstenschutzes*, Magdeburg: MELFSA.

—— (1995), *Land- und Forstwirtschaft in Zahlen*, Magdeburg: MELFSA.

Ministerium für Landwirtschaft und Naturschutz des Landes Mecklenburg-Vorpommern (MLN) (1995), *Interministerielle Arbeitsgruppe zur Entwicklung ländlichen Räume: Erhaltung und Entwicklung der ländlichen Räume in Mecklenburg-Vorpommern*, Schwerin: MLN.

Ministerium für Raumordnung, Städtbau und Wohnungswesen des Landes Sachsen-Anhalt (MRSWSA) (1993), *Landesentwicklungsbericht*, Magdeburg: MRSWSA.

Neander, E. (1992), 'Nebenerwerbslandwirtschaft in den neuen Bundesländern - Informationen und Mutmassungen', *Landbauforschung Völkenrode*, **43**, 169-75.

Reichhoff, L. and W. Böhnert (1991), 'Das Nationalparkprogramm der ehemaligen DDR', *Natur und Landschaft*, **66**, 195-203.

Sächsisches Staatsministerium für Landwirtschaft, Ernährung und Forsten (SSLEF) (1995), *Ländlicher Raum: ein Programm stellt sich vor*, Dresden: SSLEF.

Sächsisches Staatsministerium für Umwelt und Landesentwicklung (SSUL) (1994), *Landesentwicklungsplan Sachsen*, Dresden: SSUL.

Schmidt, H. and D. Scholz (1991), 'Die neuen deutschen Länder: Chancen und Probleme aus geographischer Sicht', *Berichte zur deutschen Landeskunde*, **65**, 65-82.

Schrader, H. (1994), 'EU-Strukturpolitik zur Entwicklung der ländlichenhaushalten', *Landbauforschung Völkenrode*, **152**, 23-38.

Thöne, K.F. (1993), *Die agrarstrukturelle Entwicklung in den neuen Bundesländern*, Cologne: Verlag Kommunikationsforum GmbH.

Thüringer Ministerium für Landwirtschaft, Naturschutz und Umwelt (TML) (1995), *Die Entwicklung ländlicher Räume im Freistaat Thüringen*, Erfurt: TML.

Tissen, G. (1994), 'Sozioökonomische Entwicklung in ländlichen Räumen', *Landbauforschung Völkenrode*, **152**, 3–10.

Watzek, H. (1995), 'Zu problemen der Landwirtschaft in Ostdeutschland', *ICARUS – Zeitschrift für Soziale Theorie und Menschenrechte*, **3**, 9–13.

Wild, T. and P. Jones (1994), 'Spatial impacts of German Unification', *Geographical Journal*, **160**, 1–16.

Wilson, O. (1996), 'Emerging patterns of restructured farm businesses in Eastern Germany', *GeoJournal*, **38**, 157–60.

6. Hungary

Zsuzsanna Varga

Since 1989, Hungarian agriculture and food processing has undergone significant ownership and organizational changes. There has also been a severe crisis related to a drastic fall in output and a sharp contraction in exports. Many agricultural cooperatives and food-processing enterprises went bankrupt in the process, while agricultural unemployment increased and a general shortage of capital led to very low investment and a deterioration in the stock of machinery. Depression was particularly severe in areas with relatively unfavourable natural conditions. Hence economic, social and environmental issues are intertwined. Therefore it is critical for the future of rural areas and for the sustainable exploitation of natural resources that the problems should be solved.

The first part of this chapter will consider the legacy of the socialist system as far as the situation of the agrarian sector is concerned. This is an essential context for the study of the present restructuring process. The second part will describe the changes which have occurred in the economic and social structures of rural areas following 1989. An examination of the situation at national level will be followed by discussion of regional issues. A mix of political, economic and social processes underpins the present crisis and policy changes will be needed to find a way forward.

THE INHERITANCE FROM SOCIALISM

Hungary's food production sector encountered difficulty in the early 1980s when the communist government had to reduce indebtedness and control the balance of payments (Földes 1995). Agriculture played its part and the state used all possible means to increase agricultural exports in order to earn convertible currency. But at the same time, changes in the world economy led to a fall in prices for the major agricultural products (Juhász and Mohácsi 1994). Meanwhile, there was pressure to keep domestic food prices low, but the growing discrepancy between agricultural and industrial prices, along with the growth in the tax burden and at a reduction in subsidies, greatly reduced the profitability of the cooperatives (Szakács 1989). They had to sell some of the assets necessary for the maintenance of production (buildings, livestock or machinery) in order to stay in business (Sipos and Halmai 1988). By the middle of the 1980s, one-third of the large establishments had already sold assets essential for growth and most were therefore unable to contemplate expansion. Thus the system of large-scale, capital-intensive, medium-quality production was seriously undermined.

Important modifications to the basic *kolkhoz* model were made in Hungary in the late 1960s. Many 'supplementary establishments' were created to provide non-agricultural employment for many rural dwellers. These not only helped rural areas but corrected a more general problem in the economy – namely the lack of small- and medium-sized industrial enterprises. Because these units operated at low cost compared with state industry, they boosted the income of the large agricultural production units (Pető and Szakács 1985). At the same time, household plots were integrated into mainstream agricultural activity as complementary forms of production (Tóth 1970). While originally the system functioned to supplement the income of agricultural workers earned through work on the cooperative farm, they came increasingly to be geared to small-scale production for the market, a change that altered not only the function of the plots but also the social position of the producers themselves. By the mid-1980s, the largest group of small-scale producers were not members of the cooperative peasantry, but consisted of those who belonged to the industrial working class, because the relocation of industry in favour of the provinces meant a working-class majority in the countryside. The net result was a growth in rural prosperity as supplementary incomes derived from small-scale production played an important role in sustained housing improvements, including much new construction (Enyedi 1994). Furthermore, people became used to making their own economic decisions, based on flows of information about the situation in the markets and business generally. In this way, small-scale production helped in the development of an entrepreneurial culture in the villages and small towns.

However, such positive trends only concealed the true nature of the impending crisis in large-scale production arising from the external environment in the late 1980s. In this dangerous situation it seemed desirable to reward initiative by giving more responsibility to individuals with the skill and commitment to deliver produce at low cost. This approach was fully reciprocated by elements in the rural population keen to accumulate property and participate in new forms of organization, following the success of the earlier experiments (Tóth 1989). Even at the beginning of the 1980s, the agricultural cooperatives were starting to rent out their arable land to private individuals, but whereas in 1981 the large-scale agricultural production units rented out a total of 9,100ha of arable land, the figure grew to 47,100ha in 1987 and 310,100ha in 1991: a 35-fold increase in 10 years (Harcsa 1993). This meant that the percentage of land held by large enterprises but worked by small-scale producers increased from 4.2 per cent in 1981 to 5.9 per cent in 1988 and 11.2 per cent in 1991. Thus the traditional large-scale production system was clearly breaking down in the late 1980s. Where mechanization was most effective (with cereals and other field crops) the large enterprises continued to dominate, but where much manual labour was needed (in orchards, vineyards and vegetable gardens) the small-scale producers moved to the fore.

By the end of the 1980s, the cooperatives were transferring not only land and livestock to the small producers, but buildings and machines as well. A particular private producer did not merely undertake entrepreneurial activity on the basis of one contract made for a particular phase or element of production, but could now organize the necessary farm buildings and in some cases handle the machinery to carry out the whole production process him- or herself. Among the farm buildings it was the transfer of the greenhouses (24.7 per cent), sheep pens (17.3 per cent) and poultry houses (13.9 per cent) that made the biggest contribution to this process. It was most often the case that small-scale producers were able to achieve the greatest predominance in those sectors where one family could, through the labour of its own members, fully stock the buildings it had acquired with animals or utilize the land available for market gardening. The cooperatives even tried to introduce entrepreneurial forms within their own organizations, despite the difficulties that arose from direct regulation through a breakdown of the fundamental ownership relations. Although commanding the status of common ownership, the members found themselves under the control of what was, in effect, a wage labour-based organization. Excluded from decision making, they had no effective control over matters relating to prices, state subsidies and credit agreements. Thus even within the confines of the communist system, the cooperatives changed out of all recognition in the course of the 1980s through land management decisions related to the challenging economic environment of the time.

NEW ECONOMIC AND SOCIAL STRUCTURES

The new centre-right government which came to power in the aftermath of the 1990 elections found itself confronted with a wide range of intractable problems in agriculture. Legislation was needed to transform the cooperatives and provide for restitution (Juhász and Mohácsi 1994). But unfortunately there was no overall agricultural strategy to deal with all the problems consistently. Under pressure from small parties within the governing coalition, especially the Smallholders' Party, agrarian policy was approached through the principle of historical justice. No fewer than four property restitution laws were passed by parliament in 1991–92, each designed to give land back to different groups affected by the land seizures undertaken by the communist authorities. At the same time, they tried to create the necessary economic conditions for the restoration of peasant farming (Juhász and Mohácsi 1993).

However, the beneficiaries of restitution were not committed to small-scale agriculture even though their social origins lay among the pre-communist peasantry. Between 60 and 70 per cent of them had no connection with agricultural production, while the majority of the people actually working in agriculture at the time had no connection with the peasant landowners of the pre-socialist period. Thus, instead of strengthening the link between landownership and agricultural entrepreneurship, the legislation tended to separate the two interests. Political considerations also impinged on legislation to regulate the transformation of the cooperatives, which parliament accepted after some delay in

January 1992. The government's antagonism towards cooperatives was quite clear, because immediately after the fall of communism, ideologically-based opposition was manifested in analogies between Hungarian cooperatives and the Soviet *kolhozy*, despite all the reforms implemented since the 1960s. Even the cooperative manager became effectively a *persona non grata* in the eyes of the new authorities. The attacks on cooperatives (including their leaders and technical staff) did not merely take place at the ideological level, but also in the framing of measures which restricted their room for manoeuvre (Domokos 1992). There was a big reduction in subsidies for the cooperatives and the general thrust of legislation (referred to below) was to encourage private farming as opposed to common forms of land management (Prugberger 1995). Thus, the government imposed economic and political constraints which made it difficult for the cooperatives to evolve new organizational forms and thereby complicated the process of agricultural reform.

The politically inspired reevaluation of the farming system affected the small-scale producers and other private enterprises as well as the cooperatives. Indeed it further complicated what was already a poor economic environment for agricultural development. The new economic policy overestimated agriculture's capacity to cope with the problem of high inflation, compounded by the loss of important markets. Subsidies were drastically reduced from 22 per cent in 1989 to 8 per cent in 1992, while taxation increased. The government's policy of reducing real incomes led in turn to a fall in domestic food consumption, while failing to control the growing gap between agricultural and industrial prices. The liberalization of tariff policy, which had previously protected the domestic food-processing industry, further reduced demand for agricultural products. Moreover, the bulk of the income generated by the privatization of the food processing industry was absorbed by the state treasury when it could have been used very effectively for the modernization of the sector as a whole (Keserű 1993). In view of these circumstances it is hardly surprising that agricultural production declined: it was not only a case of changing the system through a complicated privatization process, but of altering the whole business environment in which agricultural and food-processing enterprises operated. The price 'scissors' – which meant that increasing amounts of agricultural products were needed to secure manufactured goods – and the diversion of resources from agriculture seriously hindered the development of a new entrepreneurial approach on cooperative and private farms alike. A comprehensive rural development strategy was needed, but between 1990 and 1994 such a long-term approach was lacking. On the other hand, the socialist–liberal coalition, which came to power in 1994, is now trying to strengthen the cooperative movement through economic and social policy measures (Hovanyecz 1996).

THE IMPACT OF PRIVATIZATION

In the case of state farms, the privatization process may proceed in two ways. The first option is complete privatization through a transfer to domestic ownership. Each former state property will be farmed by a private individual or by a number of separate companies: limited liability companies (*Korlátozott Felelősségű Társaság*, Kft), or public limited companies (*Részvény Társaság*, Rt). The other possibility is partial privatization, with state management continuing in the context of a joint venture involving a substantial injection of foreign or domestic private capital (Zsarnóczai 1995). However, little progress has been made with the privatization of the state farms, mainly because there is insufficient purchasing power to buy the properties. For this reason it is very difficult to forecast how much land will remain in state ownership and how such farms will be able to survive in the new climate. It is also unclear to what extent those benefiting from land restitution will be prepared to make their land available for the state farms to use. This is a problem because the state has explicitly refused to transfer state-owned land to privatized state farms, thus forcing the newly privatized farms to negotiate with the state to farm the land for which it was once responsible. This represents a further burden on the new company and indeed on the sector as a whole. The difficult market also complicates the privatization process. The explicit ban on foreign ownership of agricultural land acts as a deterrent to outside investment. Meanwhile, the lack of external resources further hinders the situation of those plants which are struggling with financial problems (Juhász and Mohácsi 1993).

There has been some progress in privatizing the food-processing industry. The external (mainly foreign) investors have been attracted to factories producing standardized and branded goods: industries concerned with tobacco, soft drinks, sugar, spirits, and confectionery production, along with brewing and the manufacture of vegetable oils. Such enterprises usually have a relatively good financial and marketing position (Alvincz and Mohácsi 1993). However, in the absence of a comprehensive privatization strategy for the food-processing sector, progress in enterprises concerned with cereals, dairying and meat processing (including poultry) and canning has been slower than expected and relatively limited. The market is limited and there are serious financial and structural problems, because privatization has weakened rather than strengthened the vertical integration of the various subsectors in the food-processing industry (Juhász and Mohácsi 1994). It was unfortunate that the way the restitution laws were implemented hindered the participation of agricultural enterprises in the privatization of the food-processing industry. Nevertheless, the change in ownership in the industry (reducing the proportion of state ownership to 45 per cent) has brought many positive results. There has been a general process of de-monopolization; as a result competition has intensified and, thanks to foreign investment, subsectors such as confectionery, tobacco and spirits have seen an improvement in quality and a widening in the product range in addition to an increase in overall enterprise stability. Privatization has also had good results in terms of closer integration between food processors and farmers.

In the case of the cooperatives the idea of privatization is, strictly speaking, inappropriate, because the peasants retained their ownership rights. However, these rights could not be freely exercised under communism (Szakács 1989) because, although the law stated that any members leaving a cooperative could retrieve their land, in practice this meant they received land of equivalent value from the state reserve. Such land was generally of low quality and not actually in use. Legislation governing the reorganization of cooperatives was accepted by parliament in January 1992. A transitional law covered the transformation process whereby the cooperative property was divided among its members in the form of business shares. Distribution was to take place on the basis of accounts at the end of 1991. Meanwhile, a law on cooperatives set out the procedures under which 'collectively functioning, real, free cooperatives would come into being on the basis of the individual property of their members'. Each cooperative was required to convene at least three meetings for its members during 1992: the first would define the property available for allocation, the second would decide on the question of division and the third would deal with the transformation of the organization and the application of new basic regulations.

The cooperatives had a free hand in deciding how property with a total value of Ft247 billion at 1992 prices would be distributed. But as a general principle it was stated that at least 40 per cent should be allocated according to 'the time content of the membership relation'; that is to say that property would be allocated according to the years of membership on the part of the individual concerned; another 20 per cent was to be allocated according to the original contribution of land, livestock and machinery; the remaining 40 per cent was not covered by the law and much discussion took place within the cooperatives as to how it should be disposed of. Most decided to recognize the amount of work done by each member, on the basis of the incomes that had been received. Thus the members who had commanded the highest incomes received the largest number of business shares (Rab 1994). But the situation which arose from this procedure was highly complex because distribution was complicated by the need to consider both active and retired members as well as former members and their heirs (Laczó 1994). The process was made still more difficult by the lack of statistical information dealing with the total property at the disposal of each cooperative.

However, the value of the business shares received by each member was well below the level required to secure a small farm. Indeed, in the great majority of cases those who wished to secure the necessary capital for entrepreneurial activity through the sale of their shares could realize only 5–30 per cent of the nominal value. Nevertheless, many people did try to realize the value of their business shares because of several pressures imposed on them. Furthermore, under the cooperative basic law, many unemployed cooperative workers were obliged to realize the value of their business shares in order to obtain an income, due to the fact that the law abolished the obligation on the cooperatives to employ all its members. A major problem lay in the liabilities of business shareholders with regard to taxation, loans and delivery obligations. Other problems arose from the removal of obligations on cooperatives to employ members on a regular basis and to offer light work that would generate supplementary income for older and retired members. The result was a laying-off of labour on a scale previously unknown. Given the uncertainties over the extent of potential liabilities, many shareholders have renounced their interests because any unrealistic hope of profitable farming activity seems to be ruled out. Such action has been particularly common in the northeastern crisis regions of Borsod-Abaúj-Zemplén, Nógrád and Szabolcs-Szatmár-Bereg (Magda and Helgertné Szabó 1993).

The Research and Informational Institute for Agricultural Economics (AKII), the Ministry of Agriculture (FM) and the Cooperative Research Institute (SZKI) carried out surveys of different types of agricultural cooperative, largely selected on the basis of their size, in order to obtain a general picture of the transformation process. Some 40 per cent of the property is owned by active cooperative members and their property has the highest per capita value. Retired members also acquired about 40 per cent, while the remaining one-fifth fell into the hands of the former members and their heirs. However, since the initial allocation, the number of external owners (that is, non-member shareholders) has increased because of the inheritance of business shares from retired cooperative members who are deceased (Tóth and Varga 1995). Furthermore, restitution led to an increasing number of business shareowners not involved in farming. It also emerges that the active members may be in a minority, although the cooperative law states that the owners of each company should carry out the agricultural work themselves. This is a contradiction which has caused much uncertainty in the exercise of property rights, for the fragmentation of both land and business share ownership has hindered the cooperation necessary to plan production and secure credit.

It is important to recognize the interests of these different shareholder categories, although all of them are looking to worthwhile dividends on their business shares. First, there are the cooperative members whose ownership is based on their work within the cooperative; second, there are shareholders who are unemployed or who have work outside the cooperative; the third group consists of retired people; and there is a fourth category of external business shareholders who are not cooperative members. These groups are strongly differentiated from each other as regards both their business interests and their representation possibilities (Herczeg 1995). The first group is actively involved in the work of the cooperative and has a primary interest in maintaining this activity and maximizing income from this source. Although their business shareholding entitles them to a dividend, their income from work within the organization makes a much greater contribution to the family budget.

Unemployed members are entitled to all the benefits of membership as laid down in the law and so, in addition to dividends, they are keen to ensure that wages are linked with good performance in order to improve their prospects for regaining employment.

Meanwhile, the retired cooperative members are interested in the welfare functions of the cooperative, although these obligations complicate the management of the cooperatives because, with reduced government support, they can only administer their social programmes with great difficulty and in some cases not at all (Rab 1994). Of course, unemployed and retired members enjoy the same rights as the economically active members, but their interest is to maximize dividends and various forms of financial support whereas those in employment will try to secure increased pay at the expense of higher dividends. Both groups may attend members' meeting and exercise full voting rights, whereas non-member shareholders are admitted to meetings as non-voting witnesses only. Finally, the external business shareholders are also interested only in dividends: they will tend to oppose higher wages for the workers and support for other categories of the membership, although their lack of voting rights means that they cannot organize opposition to measures which threaten their interests. For this reason, their questions and proposals are generally pushed aside. While there is a possibility of conflict between any two or more shareholding categories, the division of interests between these categories and between cooperative members as a whole and the external owners, emerging through the restitution process and connected to the definition of property, is particularly sharp and calls for delicate compromises.

A legally sanctioned process of defining landownership rights was implemented in parallel with the definition of property rights. The intention of the politicians was that land should not remain in the hands of the cooperatives. Under the restitution laws the cooperatives had to set up four land funds: the first for all the land to be redistributed through restitution; the second for the land covered by the business shares; the third for between 30 and 40 *aranykorona* (a Hungarian measurement of land value, loosely translated as 'golden crowns') of members' and employees' land; and the fourth for state property. As a result of the implementation of the restitution and the cooperative laws, more than two million landowners appeared, and individual ownership was dominant among this group. But the use of land and its ownership became strongly divorced from each other because of the large proportions of non-rural and non-active owners. Efficiency and entrepreneurship was constrained by the necessity to rent land, thereby introducing a new production cost which served to draw resources away from agriculture. However, the land act did not allow foreign ownership and an upper limit was imposed, although both stipulations were subject to negotiation (ibid.). Nevertheless, the regulations were widely seen as discouraging to capitalists who, with the agreement of local farmers safeguarding their own interests, might otherwise have been prepared to invest in agricultural production.

In the conditions existing in Hungary today, it is possible to recognize different groups of landowners according to their agricultural interests and aspirations. The first group, consisting of the beneficiaries of restitution and including many pensioners and urban dwellers, will offer their land for rent and thereby gain a source of income. The second group is made up of former cooperative members and employees who exercise their ownership rights through a continuation of the cooperative system. They may wish to continue a kind of private plot farming on part of their property, while using the rest for 'common farming' which secures both a job and the services needed to support their private agricultural activities. A fairly high proportion wish to maintain their small-scale production activity as a supplementary source of work, existing in symbiosis with the large enterprise with which they associate simply as labourers. In this way they seek to preserve the established duality of large- and small-scale production.

The third group are those cooperative members and employees who simply wish to maintain secure employment for themselves through landownership. They place the whole of their land into a cooperative which, to a greater or a lesser extent, guarantees them a job. This kind of ownership strategy is a special case when efficient household production is impossible, and for this reason they attach their land to a larger production unit. One can find examples among producers of tobacco, onions, and red paprika, who can earn as much by producing such crops on a household farm as from farming the larger land area independently. The fourth group of landowners, made up of newly independent agronomists or traders, wish to farm their own land. It is among this group that there are real attempts to create a private farm-based economy. However, this predominantly 'middle peasant' system of private farming is possible only if larger areas of land can be acquired, through either renting or purchase, to justify long-term investment and a viable production plan. The fifth group is made up of those who seek the *tanya* (homestead) 'middle peasant' ideal (Juhász and Mohácsi 1995). This system combines a home in a small agricultural town or large village (*mezőváros*) with periodic visits to work a small farm situated some distance away. During these absences, schoolchildren will usually stay with grandparents. Most of the farms require part-time labour only and cooperation is not well developed. However, although the *tanya* farms are functionally no different from smallholdings on which the family reside permanently, the traditional migratory pattern and the scope for intensive production of fruit and vegetables is still attractive to many families.

On the whole, the links between landownership, agricultural entrepreneurship and work performance have weakened and the restitution law has complicated, rather than eased, the earlier problems relating to property relations in agriculture. The transformation of the cooperatives and the state farms has only partially moderated the oversized large-scale agricultural enterprises economically, and improved the conditions for real membership and entrepreneurship. But because of the former dominance of large enterprises over the smaller ones and because the partners did not operate on a level playing field, many enterprises which were probably basically viable but undermined by the unfavourable economic environment, have either survived or have been reborn as large enterprises in new forms.

THE NEW COOPERATIVES

According to data for 1995, 94 per cent of the cooperatives remained in existence in a new form and only 6 per cent were transformed into private companies (Herczeg 1995). Even so, change involved considerable risk, while the value of the business shares remained low because of a low level of trading in the stock. However, there are advantages through the level of mechanization of production in the large units and connections with other economic sectors such as the food-processing industry. Also, there is the notion of mutual assistance which no other organization can provide. Above all, there are few alternatives because most cooperative members do not have access to capital or business knowledge. Thus combining small properties within a cooperative appears to be a necessity, defending its members from the cold force of the market (Karalyos 1992).

The new cooperatives, with only a few exceptions, will be production based. However, they are developing their service and commercial functions, even though this process is slow. Meanwhile, the property-owning members are, in a complementary way, undertaking private production which is integrated into the work of the cooperative. Some of the reconstituted cooperatives embrace internal entrepreneurial forms which involve the renewal of the decentralization process started at the end of the 1980s (Rab 1994). Under cooperative law, such activity is deemed to be 'entrepreneurship of the member based on property ownership' (Karalyos 1992); in particular cases it can appear as a form of internal entrepreneurship. Cooperative headquarters then restricts itself to the management of property, cooperative services to the members and coordination of the entrepreneurial activities of the members. This is essentially the basis of the holding company form of cooperative model (ibid.).

Decisions to retain cooperative systems were usually reached by very large majorities. Surveys show that 91 per cent of members decided in favour of the retention and the modernization of their cooperatives. Those who wanted to break away and become individual farmers were much smaller in number than the architects of the legislation had supposed. Nevertheless, today, the majority of the economically active working and retired members, as well as a significant part of the technical staff and management, are keen to retain the cooperative system. The retired members have a source of income to supplement their pensions because of dividends obtained through their business shares and rents for the land they own. In addition, they may expect that social support will continue to be available. Meanwhile, the majority of the economically active workers are content to go on working for the cooperative (Magda and Helgertné Szabó 1993). They can see very clearly the difficulties of starting up their own farms, because even during the 'golden age' of private plot farming in the 1960s and 1970s, cooperative members were unable to accumulate the necessary capital from small-scale production to set up as independent private farmers. Moreover, the lack of a credit and financial organization to help independent private farms is a very serious drawback.

Another constraining factor is that the agricultural infrastructure is built on the premise of large-scale production. Within the cooperatives, agricultural work has become so specialized that the average skilled agricultural worker is only a specialist in his or her own particular part of the production process, and this is to say nothing of the problems of marketing, finance, taxation and bookkeeping. There is also an overriding problem of market uncertainty, which is compounded by the lack of a real processing industry (Juhász and Mohácsi 1995). The cooperative peasants therefore lack the necessary finance, equipment, land and management experience to move into the insecure world of private, individual production at a time when agriculture's income-generation capacity is so uncertain. All that usually develops is a new form of private plot production which threatens to undermine the capacity of the large establishment to provide services to its members (Varga 1993), while a vicious circle is created where the consequent weakening of the cooperative erodes the infrastructure on which the private plot system depends. The vast majority of those who have left the cooperatives, either individually or in groups, no longer wish to engage in agricultural activity. Independent farmers in the *tanya* areas are already getting most of their income from 'supplementary' farm occupation (Rab 1994). This is because in such areas work for large production units, which is the major occupation, has fallen to a minimum, and so working the *tanya* (initially a legal supplementary activity) now accounts for most of the agricultural activity (ibid.). The majority have tried to orientate themselves towards various kinds of service-based entrepreneurial activities in the service sector, dealing with agricultural machinery or commerce. It is common for people to leave the cooperatives in groups and for new partnerships to emerge because this way it is easier to raise the finance to secure former cooperative properties, such as mills, workshops and commercial premises. While many in this category will retain livestock and some farm equipment, others may prefer to sell all their property to secure the maximum return in the short term.

Some of those inclined towards entrepreneurship may well have been independent farmers in the past, but it will be impossible to build a new private agricultural system on the basis of this elderly group. Others are economically active and wish to farm their restituted land as a hedge against unemployment and impoverishment, or they may already be unemployed and seek to maintain a small amount of land that can provide their food and generate a little income. But because of capital shortage and limited knowledge and business experience, the future of these small farms is highly problematic. Much will depend on agricultural policy and the ability of these groups to represent their interests through the political process. Of course, where the cooperative has become bankrupt or has been dissolved, there is little alternative for the members but to take up private farming. But the future is highly uncertain because they are forced into private farming on just two or three hectares of land with the benefit of whatever equipment they have been able to salvage from the former cooperative. They will not be able to call on the help of larger agricultural enterprises. Many private farmers will be people with no other option, although the economically active group may succeed if they can cope with the pressures and bring sufficient capital and resourcefulness to bear on their holdings of land, buildings and machinery. When groups of people break away from the cooperatives with entrepreneurial intentions, they may well combine with non-cooperative members and use external land and business contacts to establish some kind of private company, often combining their business shares with those of relatives (ibid.).

It is not uncommon for the management of a dissolved cooperative, along with close business shareholder relatives and friends in the village, to purchase restitution coupons at low prices and so obtain land and machinery defined as the property of the membership. In this way, the capital resources of a family or partnership can secure a viable farm business (Prugberger 1992). If more businessmen and women are going to enter farming there will have to be a better credit system and incentives to provide good prospects for profitability, but at present it seems that of the million people currently employed in agriculture and food processing, only about 10,000 can be expected to become entrepreneurs. The number directly employed can be expected to fall, while those with supplementary income from agriculture can be expected to increase. There is insufficient 'attachment to the land' to achieve a renaissance in the agricultural sector in the absence of all the economic preconditions already referred to. Yet the social aspects are important because many rural dwellers are existing on very low incomes because the social functions of the cooperatives have been eroded. It is important that local or national government, or both, should accept responsibility for these welfare functions, which are no longer being discharged adequately in many cases (Keserű 1993). Even if industry can eventually absorb the unemployed, further rural depopulation will leave the villages impoverished. Hence the need for a conscious programme of job creation in rural areas. Such attempts will be discussed in the concluding part of this chapter.

RURAL REGIONS

The impact of changes in agriculture varies from one region to another. The breakdown of the uniform economic structure built up under communism will mean increasing differentiation in terms of enterprise size and ownership, as well as the structure of production and technology. Existing differences are exacerbated by the relative success of some regions in adapting to new challenges, while others have become seriously burdened with severe employment difficulties. Figure 6.1 (top) shows the regions that were already identified as underdeveloped at the beginning of the 1980s (using data for the 1970s on levels and economic development and living standards), while Figure 6.1 (bottom) shows the underdeveloped areas at the beginning of the present decade. Many of the underdeveloped regions are located in frontier areas because the revision of the borders after the First World War weakened the existing economic structures in these areas, especially when the expulsion of part of the population resulted in a lower intensity of land use. Collectivization, then, had a negative effect, because large-scale agricultural enterprises often disregarded farming systems that would have maximized local income and employment. Enlargement of cooperatives by amalgamation then led to the setting up of the headquarters within the most prosperous community, leaving the weaker villages to be further marginalised when new investments were allocated. The 1980 population density in these border communities stood below the rates to 1900, because of pronounced out-migration followed by natural decrease, which has played the primary role in recent decades (Hoóz 1992).

The environmental conditions (climate, soil, relief and drainage) tend to be relatively unfavourable in the underdeveloped areas. The value of the arable land belonging to the large agricultural enterprises was about 30 per cent below the average because of difficult terrain in hilly and mountainous areas (Nógrád, Borsod-Abaúj-Zemplén, Vas and Somogy counties), poor sandy soil (Nyírség) or flooding hazards (Békés county). The cooperatives generated only low incomes from their farm sales and were often unable to cover the bulk of their expenses with income from sales. In the early 1980s, 40 per cent of the large-scale agricultural enterprises in these regions were working at a loss (Dorgai and Varga 1989; Fazekas 1994). The

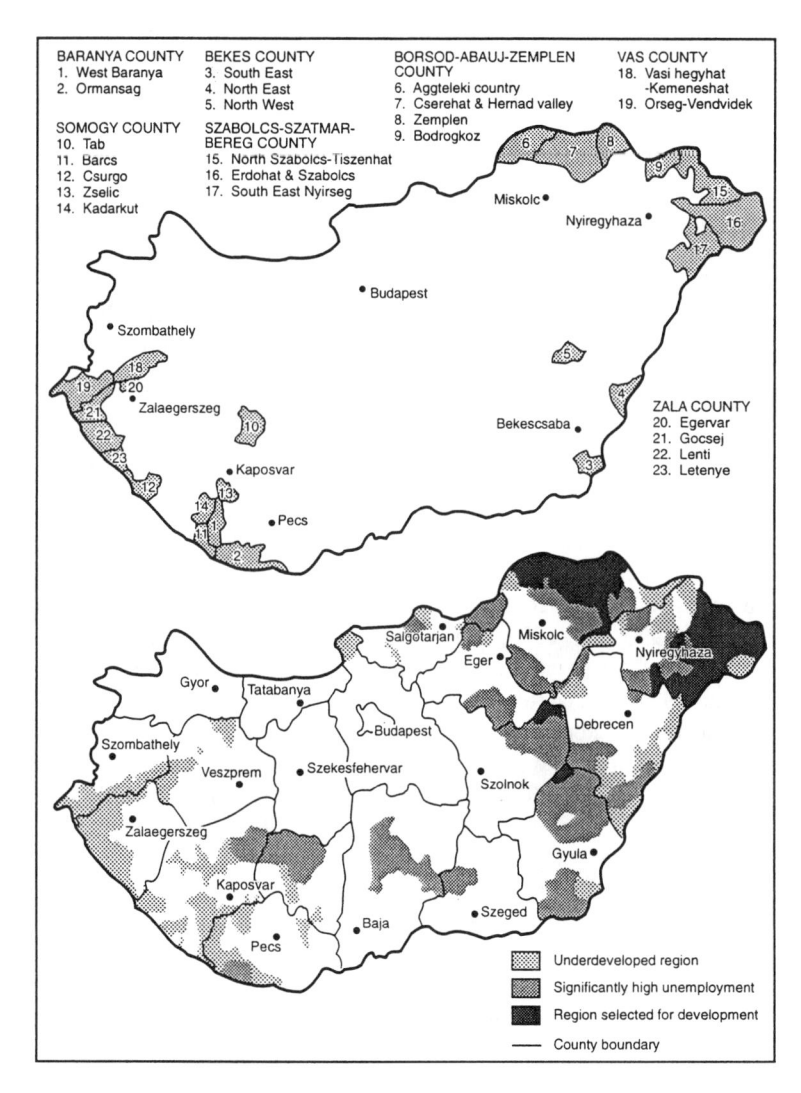

Figure 6.1 Hungary: regional assistance: (top) underdevelopment regions, 1980; (bottom) underdeveloped regions, 1990s

situation was complicated by an inadequate supply of equipment. The small number of agricultural workers in relation to the area of land, caused by a growth of commuting and migration, further hampered the development of these regions. But there were additional complications arising from the absence (or very limited development) of local industry. Because of the lack of alternative sources of employment, the section of the population that was not prepared to commute or move away from the area in search of work (generally the women became dependent on the large agricultural plants and integrated small-scale production), even though the potential was limited by the poor natural resources discouraging to both the large enterprises and the small producers. In spite of this, the development of supplementary industrial production units by the local cooperatives did confer a large benefit by expanding employment opportunities (Teknős 1987). Meanwhile, many of the people living in settlements without any basic infrastructure (post office, school and so on) migrated from the district or commuted some distance to work, despite the poor infrastructure and low educational qualifications.

The transition has exacerbated the employment problems in these underdeveloped regions because industrial and agricultural production fell by about 30 per cent as a result of the major economic recession between 1990 and 1994, partly due to the disappearance or transformation of the large state-owned enterprises and agricultural plants (Enyedi 1994). In state-owned industry, downsizing was most evident in uncompetitive sectors with outdated technology, such as mining, steel and textiles. The first wave of lay-offs particularly affected those who commuted from the villages because they were relatively unskilled and travel expenses were a burden to employers. In addition there were closures of industrial plants in rural areas. Thus, while unemployment was moderate in the industrial regions, it became a serious problem in agricultural areas that had been a major source of commuting labour. Figure 6.1 (bottom) shows that, at the beginning of the 1990s, about a thousand settlements (a third of all settlements in the country) were defined as being economically underdeveloped and received state subsidy (Fazekas 1994).

As noted above, the cooperative agricultural sector was in difficulties by the late 1980s, a situation that became more serious with the withdrawal of state support. In the underdeveloped regions the situation was particularly difficult, as unemployed industrial workers returned to villages where agricultural work was also being reduced in line with the recession and the removal of the cooperative farms' obligations to provide employment. The crisis could not easily be resolved by the survival strategies previously adopted by individuals and families to supply basic needs. Even where they survived, cooperatives were forced to abandon some of their social welfare functions which had previously maximized employment in agriculture and supported a large number of pensioners (often making up a high proportion of the local populations). Removal or reduction in discounts given to pensioners to buy food from the cooperative had implications for small-scale production which had previously played a major role in satisfying local food needs. Creating new social welfare institutions is essential in this environment so that the resource base can be broadened to support pensioners, as inflation has resulted in a severe decline in their incomes (ibid.). At the same time, households that previously gained incomes from several sources (industrial, commuting, agricultural cooperative, private plot-based activities, or a combination of these) now had to consider other possibilities.

The basic question for the development of new survival strategies is the acquisition of sufficient capital and expertise to start a business. But few households in the underdeveloped regions can manage this because of a shortage of money and educational qualifications below the national average. The poor rural infrastructure is also a constraint. Therefore, most people require external assistance over finance, retraining and the supply of information. The transition years have demonstrated the importance of these considerations (Fazekas 1993) which underpin the growing polarization between the dynamic Greater Budapest area (also northern Transdanubia and the larger cities of southern Hungary) and the peripheral regions of the country. Regions in central Transdanubia and the southeastern part of the Great Plain, with relatively small administrative centres, are in an intermediate situation because there is scope for restructuring despite the scale of the recession.

Regarding the underdeveloped areas of the 1980s, the situation has changed for the better in some cases. The formerly underdeveloped and underpopulated western parts of Transdanubia have been transformed by the development of enterprise links across the border, particularly with Austria where there are close economic and political links. But there are crisis zones in the industrially depressed north, the northeastern border areas and much of the Great Plain (Enyedi 1994). In examining these areas, the AKII found that although the quality of the agricultural land was generally poor, there were considerable local variations. Thus, large enterprises could undertake intensive production of field crops or fruit in selected areas. In particular, the production of berries, vegetables and seed corn could be increased on the private farming principle, given cooperation from the large enterprises on a scale that has been noted elsewhere (Dorgai 1992; Tóth and Varga 1993). Such intensive use of land can be vertically integrated with processing and other supporting industries, thereby increasing the scope for improving employment locally.

The expansion of services provided by the transformed agricultural cooperative (especially in food processing) is important in ensuring local supplies of perishable commodities such as meat, milk and vegetables. This is particularly important where there are towns and holiday resorts providing potential markets. In the case of mountainous areas, wood-based industries provide development potential, as in Zala county which has the best natural conditions for silviculture and investment per unit of forest is twice the national average (Buzás 1993). Such an approach offers a solution where cropping is no longer viable; all the more because conversion to woodland or grassland provides environmental protection. There is much potential for such work in the agriculturally marginal Zemplén hills (Konkolyné Gyuró 1989). A larger forest area could enhance the potential for tourism, particularly in connection with hunting which is now subject to new legislation to ensure sustainable management. Land should under no circumstances be left unused, as has often happened during recent years.

In Transdanubia, agriculture could be more closely integrated with the tourist industry of Lake Balaton. Enterprising farmers from the village of Tab in Somogy county are already supplying fresh fruit to holiday homes in the area and it is well known that other opportunities for competition exist, given the quality and price of food supplied under present arrangements during the summer months (Halász 1989). Meanwhile, farmers in the north and northeast could benefit from increased patronage by people from Budapest and the towns of the northern part of the Great Plain, because there are interesting monuments and buildings that could be renovated, to say nothing of the Eger and Tokaj vineyards. Agrotourism could also emphasize game, fish and honey as elements in the local cuisine. Eventually, a range of services characteristic of foreign tourism could be built up (Dorgai and Varga 1989). Such a growth in tourism would not only benefit farmers but could generate employment in landscaping, crop protection and transportation, as well as commerce.

But improvement of the commercial infrastructure is a precondition for success. Therefore it must be emphasized that agricultural enterprise and other forms of private enterprise, even with local authority involvement, will not be sufficient to develop tourism and light industry without external support. There will have to be an element of direction and therefore government economic policy will be decisive. Capital will tend to gravitate towards economic sectors that offer the prospect of high profits, increased productivity and security, with corresponding neglect of other activities. Economic policy should help the producers in the underdeveloped regions to meet the pressures of the free market, otherwise agriculture will continue to decline. This will have a negative impact on the landscape, requiring appropriate conservation measures, but there will also be more serious social problems in the rural areas affected. In order to avoid higher demands for welfare at a later date, there is an economic case to support farming and forestry, along with processing industries. Production from the land would increase and this would have a positive impact on rural living standards.

CONCLUSION

The Hungarian government faced an array of problems in 1990 and it was unfortunate that there was no overall agricultural strategy to deal with all the difficulties in a consistent manner. The Smallholders' Party was particularly influential in ensuring that agrarian policy was approached through the principle of historical justice. The politicians tried to create the necessary conditions for the return of peasant farming, but most of the people who benefited from restitution were not committed to small-scale agriculture and preferred to operate within a cooperative system to which the government was ideologically opposed. Agriculture could not cope with high inflation in an economic situation complicated by falling demand linked with lower incomes and reduced exports. The price 'scissors' phenomenon has meant that increasing amounts of agricultural produce are needed to pay for manufactured goods. Most of the income generated by privatization of the food-processing industry was collected by the state treasury and not used for the modernization of the sector as a whole. However, the formidable challenge of finding a comprehensive solution persists mainly because the crisis in agriculture is far from being purely an economic issue. As regional, social and environmental issues intersect, it becomes clear that there is a fundamental issue which the whole of society must face. This is because the issue of how rural communities can exploit their natural resources in a sustainable manner will determine the future of society itself. The whole of Hungarian society has an interest in solving the economic problems of the underdeveloped areas where the land resources offer the best prospects for investment and job creation.

REFERENCES

Alvincz, J. and K. Mohácsi (1993), 'Átalakulás és privatizáció az élelmiszeriparban: húsipari tapasztalatok', *Közgazdasági Szemle*, **40** (3), 267-76.
Buzás, Gy. (1993), 'A vállalati és a termelési struktúra változásának tendenciai Nyugat-Dunántúl mezőgazdaságában', *Gazdálkodás*, **37** (7), 23-6.
Domokos, Z. (1992), 'A mezőgazdasági szövetkezetek átalakulásának kérdőjeleiről', *Gazdálkodás*, **36** (3), 53-6.
Dorgai, L. (ed.) (1992), *A jövedelem-differenciálódás a szociális feszültségek és a munkanélküliség ágazati valamint térségi összefuggesei*, Budapest: AKII.
—— and Gy. Varga (1989), 'Az elmaradott térségek fejlesztésének feltételei és tennivalói', *Gazdálkodás*, **33** (6), 48-56.
Enyedi, Gy. (1994), 'Területfejlesztés, regionális átalakulás a posztszocialista Magyarországon', *Társadalmi Szemle*, **40** (8-9), 133-9.
Fazekas, B. (1994), 'A hátrányos helyzetű mezőgazdasági térségek', *Statisztikai Szemle*, **72** (1), 21-35.
Fazekas, K. (1993), 'A munkanélküliség regionális különbségeinek okairól. A foglalkoztatási térségek tipizálása', *Közgazdasági Szemle*, **40** (7-8), 694-712.
Földes, Gy. (1995), *Az eladósodás politikatörténete 1957-1986*, Budapest: Maecenas.
Halász, P. (1989), 'A mezőgazdasági kistermelés szerepe az elmaradott térségek fejlesztésében', *Gazdálkodás*, **33** (10), 34-44.
Harcsa, I. (1993), 'Az átalakuló mezőgazdasági kistermelés', *Gazdálkodás*, **37** (8), 1-10.
Herczeg, I. (1995), 'Az üzletrész problémája a mezőgazdasági szövetkezetekben', *Szövetkezés*, **15** (2), 33-50.

Hoóz, I. (1992), 'A határmenti települések elnéptelenedése', *Statisztikai Szemle*, **70** (12), 1005-18.
Hovanyecz, L. (1996), 'Beszélgetés a magyar mezögazdaság helyzetéről', *Társadalmi Szemle*, **50** (1), 3-10.
Juhász, J. (1991), 'Hungarian agriculture: present situation and future prospects', *European Review of Agricultural Economics*, **18**, 399-416.
Juhász, P. and K. Mohácsi (1993), 'Az élelmiszer-gazdaság átalakításának ellentmondásai', *Közgazdasági Szemle*, **40** (7-8), 614-24.
—— (1994), 'Magyar élelmiszer-gazdaság-tények, problémák, lehetőségek', *Közgazdasági Szemle*, **41** (7-8), 621-32.
—— (1995), 'Az agrárágazat támogatásának néhány összefüggése', *Közgazdasági Szemle*, **42** (5), 471-84.
Karalyos, Zs. (1992), 'Szövetkezeti átalakulás politikai erőtérben', *Gazdálkodás*, **36** (4), 51-4.
Keserű, J. (1993), 'Rendszerváltás az agrárágazatban', *Társadalmi Szemle*, **47** (3), 14-25.
—— (1995), 'Agrárpolitikai útkeresés Magyarországon 1989-1994', *Társadalmi Szemle*, **49** (7), 88-94.
Konkolyné Gyuró, E. (1989), 'A területhasznositás optimalizálása a Zemplénihegység térségében', *Gazdálkodás*, **33** (11), 39-50.
Laczó, F. (1994), 'A tulajdonszerkezet változása a mezőgazdaságban', *Gazdálkodás*, **38** (3), 1-12.
Magda, S. and J. Helgertné Szabó (1993), 'Az átalakuló termelőszövetkezetekről', *Gazdálkodás*, **37** (1), 14-21.
Pető, I. and S. Szakács (1985), *A hazai gazdaság négy évtizedének története 1945-1985*, Budapest: Közgazdasági és Jogi Könyvkiadó.
Prugberger, T. (1992), 'Az új szövetkezeti kárpotlási és földtörvényalkotás kihatása a magyar agrárviszonyokra', *Szövetkezés*, **12** (1-2), 29-57.
—— (1995), 'A szövetkezetek alkotmányjogi szabályozásának kérdéseihez', *Szövetkezés*, **15** (1), 13-24.
Rab, L. (1994), *Mélyszántás*, Budapest: T-Twins Kiadó.
Sipos A. and P. Halmai (1988), *Válaszúton az agrárpolitika*, Budapest: Közgazdasági és Jogi Könyvkiadó.
Swain, Nigel (1985), *Collective Farms Which Work?*, Cambridge: Cambridge University Press.
Szakács, S. (1989), 'A reform kérdése és a a termelés (Meghatározottságok és adottságok a magyar mezőgazdaságban, 1968-1985)', *Agrártörténeti Szemle*, **31** (1-4), 56-117.
Teknős, P. (1987), *A kiegészítő tevékenység szerepe a mezőgazdasági vállalatok gazdálkodásában*, Budapest: AKI.
Tóth, A.E. (1970), *Háztáji gazdaság, foglalkoztatottság és jövedelem*, Budapest: MTA Közgazdaságtudomány Intézet.
Tóth, E., (1989), 'A szervezeti és az érdekeltségi rendszer fejlesztése a gazdaságilag elmaradott térségek nagyüzemeiben', *Gazdálkodás*, **33** (12), 49-57.

—— and Gy. Varga (1993), *A falusi lakosság égető foglalkoztatási gondjai és a megoldást célzó alternatívák*, Budapest: AKII.

—— (1995), *A mezőgazdasági termelőszövetkezetek helyzete és sorsa az átalakítás időszakában*, Budapest: AKII.

Varga, Gy. (1993), 'A mezőgazadaság és a szövetkezetek átalakulása', *Társadalmi Szemle*, **47** (4), 32-41.

Zsarnóczai, S. (1995), 'A különböző üzemformák helyzete a mezőgazdasági privatizáció során', *Szövetkezés*, **15** (1), 37-48.

7. Poland

Bronisław Górz and Włodzimierz Kurek

INTRODUCTION TO THE PHYSICAL SOCIAL AND ECONOMIC CONDITIONS

In the European context, the quality of Poland's natural environment for agriculture can be described as average. The most favourable element is the large, undulating plain which facilitates mechanized farming and makes for the easy transport of produce. Only about 9 per cent of the area is higher than 300 metres, where altitude imposes limitations on the choice of crops. A major constraint, however, is the highly variable and unstable climate, characterized by maritime air masses coming in from the west and continental air masses from the east. Summers may be either hot and dry or cool and wet, while some are very variable with an alternating pattern. Winters are even more variable, with short frosts and thaws and the repeated onset and disappearance of snow cover. The period of plant growth (the number of days with mean temperature above 5 degrees Celsius) varies from about 220 days in the Silesian lowlands and Subcarpathian valleys to less than 190 days in the Carpathians and Sudety Mountains and in the northeast corner of the country. This has a significant influence on the different farming structures used in Poland, restricting to a few areas the cultivation of plants with the greatest heat requirements (wheat, sugar beet, fruit trees and vegetables in the open field). From the point of view of agriculture, the quantity and timetable of precipitation is important. Average rainfall in Poland is not great and it varies from 500 to 700mm a year, with the driest area in the centre. Particularly unhelpful vagaries of climate are the sporadic droughts which affect the whole country, causing considerable losses in harvests of grain, root crops and other plants. The Polish climate also features such hazards as light frosts,

170   *Privatization in Rural Eastern Europe*

hailstorms and floods. Podzol soils (some 55 per cent) and brown earths (about 20 per cent) dominate in Poland, with limited occurrences of marshland, muds, limestone soils, chernozems and black earths. According to qualitative evaluation, very good and good soils (classes I–III) amount to 25.6 per cent of the land cover. Medium (class IV) soils account for 39.8 per cent, while poor and very poor (classes V–VI) soils are found over 34.6 per cent of the country. Medium and poor soils are the most common.

Agrarian Structures and Settlement Patterns

In Polish agriculture there are three forms of ownership: private land accounted for 80.3 per cent of agricultural land area in 1994, the state held 10.0 per cent and cooperatives 3.1 per cent. State farms are found mainly in the west and north of the country (Figure 7.1) where they

Source: Rocznik Statystyczny 1994.

Figure 7.1   Poland: state sector share of agricultural land, 1994

account for 30–60 per cent of the agricultural land, with the highest levels in Szczecin, Koszalin and Slupsk voivodships. Poland is quite different from most other East European countries in retaining a large private sector under communism and, as a result, there is no major problem of agricultural privatization. On the other hand, it is a difficult task to increase the size of excessively small private farms, raise the technological level and increase productivity. In 1994 there were 2.03 million farms (excluding holdings of less than one hectare) with an average area of just 7.6ha. Farms of 1–5ha accounted for 54.5 per cent of the total, farms of 5–10ha for 26.7 per cent and those over 10ha only 18.8 per cent. Small farms, arising from subdivision, were common in pre-communist Poland, but post-war industrial development and the politics of full employment encouraged further splitting of farms to suit people with two jobs. Today's small farms are one of the greatest barriers to agricultural development. In addition, Polish agriculture is characterized by great fragmentation of landholdings, especially in the south. Many farms are formed of a multitude of separate pieces of land dispersed over a wide area. This increases transport costs and makes mechanization more difficult.

Rural population
During the post-war period, the most important factor influencing the social and economic situation of rural Poland was the flow of people from the country to the towns. The proportion of rural dwellers among the population at large fell from 66 per cent in 1946 to 38.1 per cent in 1994. The greatest change was in eastern Poland and the flow of people to the cities would have been even greater if there had not been administrative barriers and housing shortages. Also, a large section of the rural population travelled to work – often over considerable distances – in industry, construction and other branches of the economy. Those who combined farmwork with non-agricultural activity were most numerous in southeastern Poland and in other areas close to the large urban centres. Because of the tradition of pluriactivity, the numbers working in agriculture on each 100ha of utilized farmland fell only marginally from 26.8 in 1950 to 19.7 in 1993. However, the effect of the large rise in numbers employed

outside agriculture meant a decline in the proportion employed in agriculture from 53.6 to 25.5 per cent over the same period, although even this percentage is high by European standards.

Migration to the towns affected the rural demographic (age and sex) structure and produced many social problems. People of post-productive age amount to 15 per cent of the rural population in the country as a whole, but in the east the figure is 20–30 per cent. The rural sex structure is heavily unbalanced, especially for younger age groups: for example, for people aged 20–34, there are 88 women for every hundred men. Hence there are problems in transferring farms to younger people and a shortage of young women who can become a farmer's wife. These difficulties are most evident in areas which are most heavily dependent on agriculture. Another problem is the feminization of farmwork, as women, apart from their normal family duties, are heavily involved in the fields and in tending animals. This is unsatisfactory because women have a heavy workload while, at the same time, it is difficult to introduce modern farming methods. The rural population, and particularly the farming population, is poorly educated compared to the urban population. This is partly due to the weakness of the education system in rural areas and the large distances that children must travel to get to school. As a result, agricultural advancement is constrained.

Dispersed villages, as well as fragmented holdings, characterize the Polish rural settlement structure. At present there are 39,274 villages, or one village for every 375 rural inhabitants. Most villages have between 100 and 500 people. Poor living conditions in the rural areas may be linked with an excessive dispersal of housing and poor infrastructure including a lack of trade and service networks, cultural institutions and health facilities. Increasingly since 1989, Polish villages have assumed a multifunctional character. Farming, forestry, industry and recreation are all common, but it is rare to find a monofunctional village solely dependent on farming except in the east. The most complex village functional structures are found in the south and centre. This is significant for regional development because rural areas with a multifunctional character are at present in a relatively strong economic situation and are less endangered than areas dependent entirely on farming.

PRIVATIZATION SINCE 1989

At the end of 1989, the process of rebuilding Poland's political, social and economic system began. This involved the development of the private sector and the introduction of the capitalist economy, including a liberalization of prices and the opening of the domestic market to foreign goods. At the same time the role of the state declined (although it remained strong in social policy) which the influence of local authorities increased. Privatization proved to be an important stimulus for social and economic change (Jalowiecki 1994), especially in the highly urbanized areas of Warsaw, Łódź and Cracow, with their surrounding voivodships, which account for 62 per cent of the total number of private firms in Poland today. Much of the ownership change has been due to the privatization of state enterprises. Up to the end of 1994, privatization embraced about 4,700 state companies active in industry, agriculture and trade and other (1,400 enterprises in 1992 alone). Privatized enterprises have 1.34 million employees, which is 23.2 per cent of the total number working in the state sector (for industry alone that share rises to 34 per cent). However, the proportion of state enterprises that have been privatized varies considerably across the country. There are high values for the highly-developed voivodships, but also for some of the weaker ones too (Figure 7.2).

By the end of 1994, the private sector already accounted for almost 61 per cent of Poland's total workforce, compared with 44 per cent in 1989. Even under communism there were many private enterprises, particularly in agriculture where three-quarters of land comprised individual private farms. Agricultural workers accounted for nearly 47 per cent of all private sector workers in 1989 but by the end of 1994 this share had declined to 43 per cent (Table 7.1).

Figure 7.3 shows the share of private agriculture and large industrial enterprises such as coal and lignite mines, copper ore mines and metallurgical complexes. The largest numbers working in the private sector as a percentage of the total workforce (more than 75 per cent in some cases) are found in the agricultural voivodships of the eastern part of the country, while the lowest shares are found in heavily industrialized and urbanized voivodships such as Katowice (about 40 per cent) and Legnica (46 per cent). As regards contemporary Polish development, major changes have occurred in ownership in non-agricultural parts of the economy where the percentage of workers in the private sector increased

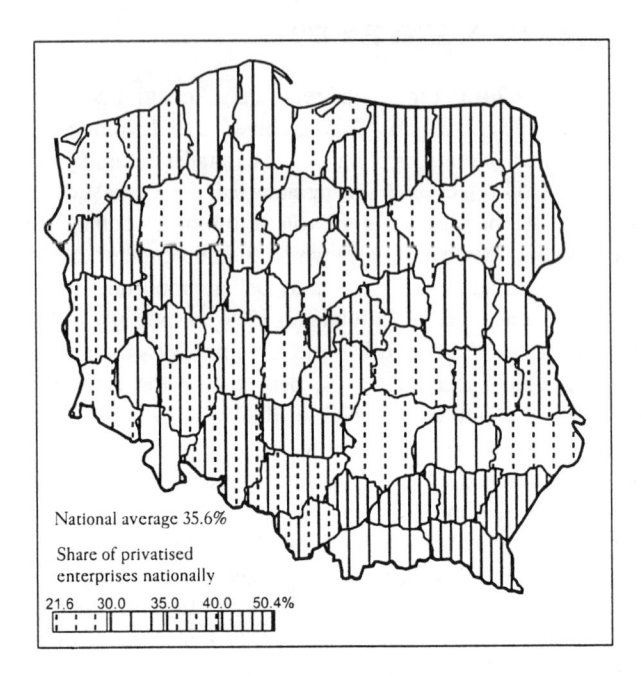

Source: Ministerstwo Przekształceń Własnościowych.

Figure 7.2 Poland: privatization of state enterprises at the end of 1994

from 12.4 per cent in 1989 to 48.1 per cent in 1994 (Table 7.2). The greatest change over the five years was in the privatization of commercial trade. There was also a noticeable rise in the construction industry's level of privatization. Generally, however, change in industry was rather slow. Meanwhile, state ownership remains almost complete in the school system and the health and social services. The slow pace of change in the ownership is due largely to the lack of capital. Before 1989, Poles living in Poland had practically no chance of possessing large amounts of capital and so they are not in a position at present to buy large factories or farms. In such a situation, foreign capital has a major role to play in ownership changes, most clearly by buying larger enterprises.

Hardship is also a key factor in the privatization of state enterprises in

Table 7.1 Poland: private sector workers, 1989–1994

Year	National workforce		Agricultural workforce		
	A	B	A	B	C
1989	17.13	44.3	4.52	78.7	46.9
1990	16.51	45.8	4.42	86.6	50.6
1991	15.60	51.1	4.26	89.3	47.7
1992	14.97	54.6	4.04	91.8	45.3
1993	14.76	58.9	3.92	92.2	41.5
1994	14.99	60.7	4.02	95.3	43.1

Notes: A = Workforce (m.); B = Percentage in the private sector; C = Private sector farmworkers as a percentage of all private sector workers.

Source: Roczniki Statystyczne Polski, 1989, 1993, 1995.

Table 7.2 Poland: private sector employment by economic branches, 1989–1994

Branch	1989		1994	
	A	B	A	B
Farming and forestry	4.67	76.4	4.02	95.9
Other sectors	12.18	12.4	10.91	48.1
Industry	4.89	14.6	3.63	44.8
Construction	1.32	26.8	0.84	79.3
Trade and repair	1.50	7.5	2.22	94.6
Health and social welfare	0.80	0.4	1.00	3.7

Notes: A = Numbers employed (m.); B = Percentage in the private sector. Note that data on the private sector share for 1989 are not completely comparable with 1994, because of difference in the classification criteria.

Source: Roczniki Statystyczne Polski 1990, 1995.

176 Privatization in Rural Eastern Europe

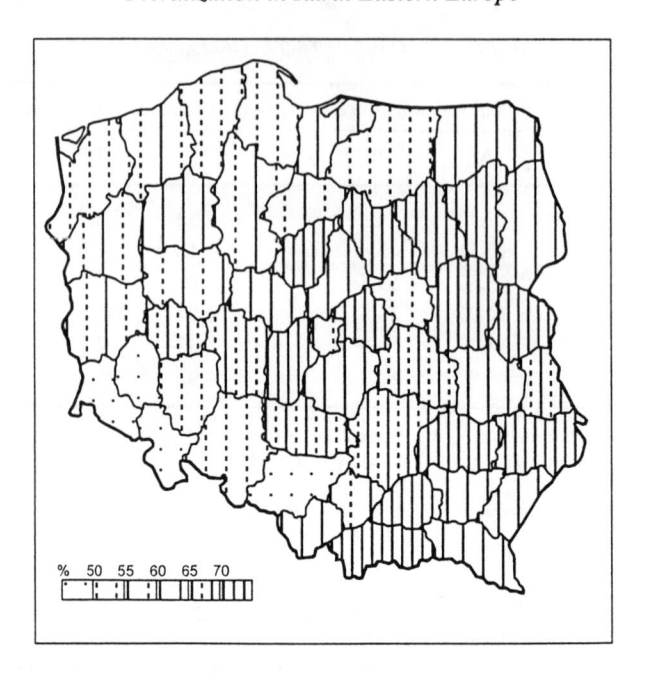

Source: *Rocznik Statystyczny Województw* 1994.

Figure 7.3 Poland: private sector employment, 1993

agriculture. In 1989 the state held some 4.20m.ha of which 3.48m.ha was productive farmland (18.5 per cent of the total area of productive land: 18.80m.ha). In 1994, the state's holding was down to 1.87m.ha or 10 per cent of the total area of farmland (then 18.65m.ha) (*Roczniki Statystyczne* 1989–94). State farms were endowed with high budgets and production costs were much greater than on private farms. In 1989, state farms received 28 per cent of all mineral fertilizers for Polish agriculture and almost 29 per cent of industrially produced fodder, yet they produced only 11.1 per cent of the total production. Cuts in subventions for state farms and the introduction of hard market rules meant many such enterprises lost the ability to produce and were also unable to pay off their debts to banks. By the end of 1991, there were 747 such insolvent farms, that is 51.3 per cent of the total. By March 1993, there were 1,067 or 73.3 per cent of the total (Olko-Bagieńska 1994).

A particularly difficult situation arose on farms with poor soil in regions such as the Sudety Mountains. The privatization of state farms started in the middle of 1991 when many found themselves in a very bad financial state. In some cases, productive assets such as the machinery and breeding stock were run down. Unfortunately, the first results of privatization were inconspicuous, since up to the end of 1991 a mere two farms were privatized. The situation on the remaining farms became still worse and so in January 1992 the National Treasury's Agency for Farm Ownership came into being, vested with responsibility for all state farm assets. The agency was to carry through privatization and deal with all problems arising, such as alternative employment for laid-off agricultural labourers. It currently oversees the running of the state farms and works on programmes for their restructuring. Eventually the selling or leasing of farms to individuals or workers' cooperatives is envisaged. Land may also be used for national parks and in some cases the churches may have a role. However, only 65,300ha (2 per cent) were sold by the end of 1994 and the agency was widely criticized for its costly failures. At that time it was still looking after 3.64m.ha of land formerly belonging to 1,647 liquidated state farms plus 0.44m.ha gained from the State Land Fund (that is, obtained from private owners in return for welfare benefits). In addition there were 833 distilleries, 264 meat plants and slaughterhouses, 1,523 pastures, 2,953 grain stores and 0.33 million dwelling houses.

SOCIAL AND ECONOMIC CONSEQUENCES OF PRIVATIZATION

Rural Unemployment

In the first two years of reform (1990–91) there was a substantial decline in both production and the standard of living. However, as early as 1992 an appreciable economic growth was observed and GDP increased by almost 2.6 per cent. This progress was maintained, and Poland boasts one of the most successful transition economies, developing the most rapidly. However, problems remain, especially in the rural areas of Poland and in agriculture. Some of them, such as high agrarian overpopulation or land fragmentation, go back to the last century when Poland did not have a developed industry and when the economy was based mainly on agriculture. But the inadequate capacity in food processing and the low technical level of Polish agriculture remain, because of neglect in the communist period when the state held a monopoly of economic and service activities. It was the state that organized agricultural production as well as the purchase and processing of agricultural products. These deficiencies have become even more apparent recently through the almost complete disorganization of the agricultural market, aggravating the fall in the income suffered by the farming population on account of the rapid rise in production costs used in comparison with agricultural commodity prices (the so-called price 'scissors').

In November 1994, registered unemployment in rural areas stood at 834,000, or 12.4 per cent of the active population. But this figure does not include the several hundred thousand farmowners who lost their second job (typically in an urban factory) but who cannot draw unemployment benefit. These people are very numerous in the southern and southeastern parts of the country where farms no larger than three or four hectares cannot support a family. Throughout the communist period, industrial areas were created (in Konin, Płock, Pulawy and elsewhere) to supplement rural incomes. In 1988, about 36.3 per cent of the entire active population living on farms had some employment outside agriculture, most frequently in industry, construction and transport. But in the south and west the rate was usually more than 40 per cent and in some regions, such as Bielsko and Katowice voivodships, it exceeded even 50 per cent. However, the reforms have made it more difficult and expensive to commute, while many jobs have been lost. Thus, the efforts of the communist government to relieve overpopulation in small farms by making ancillary employment available (and thereby facilitating the constitutional right to work) has given rise to high 'hidden unemployment' in rural areas today. In the year 1994, only 27.3 per cent of farmers had a second job, although the proportion was still relatively high in Katowice voivodship, at more than 40 per cent. The decline in wage employment for Polish farmers has arisen in part from the dissolution of state-owned agricultural enterprises. In Słupsk voivodship, where such enterprises worked more than 60 per cent of the agricultural land, rural unemployment reached 19 per cent, the highest figure in the country (Figure 7.4). In Koszalin, Legnica and Olsztyn it exceeded 14 per cent. But high rural unemployment was also registered in several voivodships

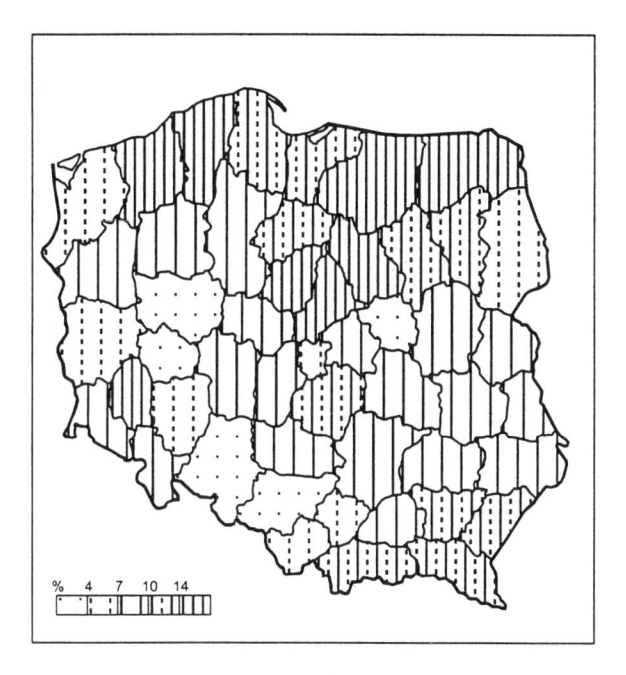

Source: Ministerstwo Rolnictwa i Gospodarki Żywnościowej.

Figure 7.4 Poland: rural unemployment, 1994

with only a small number of state farms and other enterprises if there were many people commuting to work in the town, as was the case in Płock and Włocławek voivodships.

A consequence of job losses has been an increase in the number declaring agriculture as their principal occupation. In the country as a whole, the agricultural workforce grew by more than 13 per cent between 1989 and 1994, but in the regions with the highest number of dismissals the growth reached levels of up to 31.2 per cent (Krosno and Rzeszów), thus reflecting the scale of the hidden unemployment problem, which some experts think is of a scale comparable with the inter-war period. The present rate of employment in agriculture in Poland is 26 per cent, which means more than 20 persons per 100ha of agricultural land, rising to 40–50 in the southern and southeastern parts of the country. According to estimates in the early 1990s, agriculture employed 47 per cent more workers than was necessary: in other words a surplus of more than two million. The highest figures were recorded in the southeast and south, but the centre was also above the average (Table 7.3). There is no way these people can transfer to the urban areas at the present time and so the approach must be to use them more effectively in agriculture or elsewhere in the rural economy. This should be possible because production per hectare of agricultural land – as well as production per worker – is low, while the service sector (in relation to both the rural economy in general and agriculture in particular) is very poorly developed.

Table 7.3 Poland: macroregions with the highest levels of hidden unemployment in agriculture

Macroregion	Employment in agriculture (th.)		'Surplus' (%)
	Actual	'Indispensable'*	
Southeast	1,135	363	68
South	508	203	60
Centre	596	304	49
Northwest	364	251	31
Northeast	419	331	21
North	347	295	15

Note: * Related to agricultural production

Source: Bezrobocie agrarne szansa – zagrozeniem rozwoju wsi (Wydawnictwo Centralnego Urzędu Planowania, 1993).

Rural and Agricultural Services

The problems of Polish agriculture also relate to the collapse of the old systems of technical, commercial and financial support. Until 1990 there were many organizations (often monopolies) which supplied mineral fertilizers, agricultural machines and building materials or engaged in wholesale and retail trade. Many belonged to the state while others were linked with the cooperatives, although the latter were under state control and thus decisively different from their Western European counterparts. Every kind of activity was closely regulated by the government and subject to their norms. Thus, general stores were opened in rural communities with a threshold permanent population (normally) exceeding 300. As a result, in 1978 there were no stores whatsoever in more than 16,000 small villages (mostly those with a population of less than 200 people), although they accommodated 36 per cent of all the rural communities (Kühnemann 1984). At that time, trade was organized mostly by the Peasants' Mutual Aid Agricultural Cooperative Central Office (Centrala Rolniczych Spółdzielni 'Samopomoc Chłopska') which managed three-quarters of all the country stores. Over some 60 per cent of rural Poland the retail trade network was poorly developed and the eastern part of the country was the worst affected. Meanwhile, the purchasing centres for grain, fruit and milk, as well as sales outlets for fertilizers, machines and building materials were also distributed according to a plan drawn up centrally.

However, despite the prevailing 'economy of shortage' these organizations could exert a beneficial effect in areas with a large number of small farms. An example is the creation of a large fruit-growing area in the Carpathians through the encouragement of production and service cooperatives. Another example is the assistance to cattle breeding by creamery cooperatives. Moreover, it was not usually difficult for small farmers to sell their cereals, fruit, milk or potatoes, since the state was obliged to buy even modest quantities through its purchasing centres without any application of market economy rules. However, the network of the agricultural product purchasing centres was largely organized before 1970 when individual farmers had to sell milk, meat, grain and potatoes on a quota basis related to farm size. Thus the distribution of those purchasing centres did not correspond to the needs of farmers when the quota system was abolished and produce could be sold more liberally.

The situation changed after 1989 when market reforms were accompanied by the privatization of agricultural services and the appearance of both foreign and domestic competition. The demand for food fell and it became more difficult to sell agricultural products at a time when the cooperatives born in the communist period were starting to collapse, especially in view of the loss of foreign markets (mainly in the FSU) and significant cuts in food processing. There was considerable chaos and a good deal of overproduction. It seems quite paradoxical that private farmers, who are organizationally best prepared for the transition, find themselves unable to cope with the new situation. They are very reluctant to create institutions that would help them adapt to the new economic conditions and so intervention by the state is necessary in the form of financial and legal assistance.

One of the more problematic phenomena related to agricultural services and restraining their development is the cautious behaviour of the former monopolists, mainly the aforementioned cooperatives as well as the so-called Farmers' Circles (*Kółka Rolnicze*) providing mechanization services to agriculture. Despite the reforms introduced in Poland, these institutions are not changing the forms of their activity. They often survive only because they sell their property or hire out buildings for production or offices.

Rural Incomes

One of the more difficult issues accompanying the transformations of the Polish economy is a very significant decline in farm incomes after 40 years of stable or improving fortunes. The situation was particularly bad in 1990 and 1991, with declines of 51.4 and 26.1 per cent, respectively, over the previous years. By 1992, per capita GDP was very much lower in agricultural voivodships than in those that were more industrialized: only 11,760 new zlotys in Suwałki compared with 4,330 new zlotys in Warsaw. Eastern Poland in general was poor, with incomes less than 85 per cent of the national average, while in Warsaw the average was exceeded by more than 30 per cent. The decline in farm incomes meant that living standards were impaired – all the more in view of the 'price scissors' whereby farm inputs rose more steeply in price than outputs. In 1988, an Ursus 2812 tractor cost the equivalent of 202 quintals of wheat, rising to 371 quintals in 1994. The price of 100 kilograms of mineral fertilizer was equal to the price of 0.41 quintals of wheat in 1988 but 1.1 quintals in 1994 and that of 100 litres of diesel oil equalled 1.75 and 3.6 quintals in the respective years. Data gathered by the Agricultural Economy Institute of the Polish Academy of Sciences (Instytut Ekonomiki Rolnej Polskiej Akademii Nauk') show that in 1991 only 2.3 per cent of all the households examined were capable of accumulating capital. Thus the great majority of farmers had no means of investing in the development and modernization of their holdings. Most farmers were extremely apprehensive about the mechanisms of the market economy: only a third believed that there would be good opportunities for development, and as many as 86 per cent thought that the state should guarantee the purchase of the entire agricultural production (Rosner 1993). Improved farm incomes are clearly crucial for the future of rural areas, for without such progress it will be impossible to restructure agriculture and invest in measures to increase production.

Taking both public and private sectors into account, investment was reduced by 44.3 per cent in 1991 and by 50.2 per cent in 1992 compared with 1990 (Table 7.4). Outlays on mechanization were reduced almost five times and in the case of irrigation almost 2.5 times. During the same period, the number of tractors in use decreased by almost 13,000, and trucks by more than 15,000, or more than half. This was related mainly to the privatization of state-owned agricultural enterprises. Meanwhile, the consumption of mineral fertilizers declined steeply from some 200kg/ha for all agricultural land at the end of the 1980s to only 60kg/ha by 1992. Also, because of low incomes, farmers became less interested in the artificial insemination of cattle.

Table 7.4 Poland: investment in agriculture, 1985–1992

Sector	Investment in Nzlm. (fixed prices)			
	1985	1990	1991	1992
Construction	11.39	548.82	414.93	443.55
Mechanization	12.43	551.76	190.00	117.54
Electrification	0.26	7.08	1.25	1.42
Irrigation	3.43	110.24	55.27	41.07
Veterinary services	0.12	1.61	0.37	0.68
Miscellaneous	1.71	95.13	87.76	66.61
Total	29.34	1314.64	749.58	670.87

Source: Roczniki Statystczne, 1985–1992.

However, these changes did not take place uniformly. The fall in investment was least evident in voivodships with big cities and in those with a well-developed economy was better developed (such as Warsaw, Cracow and Łódź). The steepest fall occurred in the north and west, where farmland was being privatized. Interestingly, in several voivodships where the majority of farms are very small, investment outlays on agriculture were relatively high, as in Bielsko-Biała, Katowice, Kielce and Rzeszów (Figure 7.5).

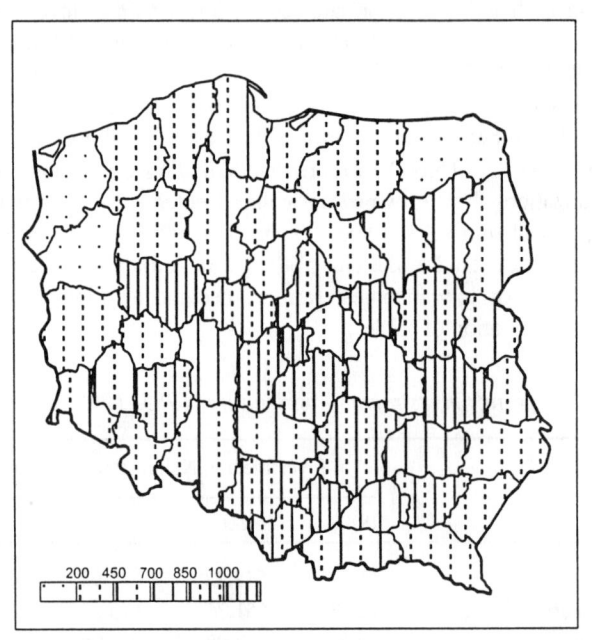

Source: Rocznik Statystyczny Rolnictwa 1993.

Figure 7.5 Poland: investment in agriculture, 1992 (thousand zloty per 100ha of agricultural land)

Technical Infrastructure

One of the most serious obstacles impeding change in Polish agriculture and restraining the improvement in the rural standard of living is the insufficient development of infrastructure, that is of the water supply and sewerage systems, electrification, roads, and so on.

The situation is still poor and constrains the development of agriculture and rural living standards generally. In 1993, almost 73 per cent of the houses had a water supply system, but some 26 per cent were using farm wells, which often supplied only poor quality water. Hence, the construction of collective supply systems is an urgent necessity. Work has been proceeding quite promptly, aided by a good deal of foreign assistance: from 47,000 houses connected each year in the 1980s, the number rose to

Table 7.5   Poland: rural infrastructure, 1980–1994

	Houses connected (thousands) in			Growth 1989–94	Percentage connected 1994
	1980	1989	1994		
Water	402.0	823.7	1,405.4	170.6	36.7
Sewerage	31.5	37.2	58.7	157.8	1.5
Gas	68.9	236.8	545.3	230.5	14.2

Source: Roczniki Statystyczne, 1981, 1990, 1995.

116,000 between 1989 and 1994 (almost 130,000 in 1994 alone) (Table 7.5). An even faster pace of change has occurred in the installation of gas pipe networks, although the use of liquid gas from gas cylinders is still very popular. Between 1989 and 1994 there were 62,000 connections each year on average, compared with only 18,700 during the 1980s. Meanwhile, however, the development of the sewerage system has been very slow. In 1994, nearly 59,000 houses were connected to the communal sewerage system (less than 2 per cent of all rural dwellings in Poland). Some people use their own septic tanks, but this applies to little more than 40 per cent of households (Zawadzki 1993). Hence there are serious deficiencies, especially where the availability of piped water means a high level of effluent that is a pollution threat for the soil as well as both surface and underground water quality. But sewer construction is often very expensive in the view of the dispersal of houses.

Water piping is poorest in eastern Poland where half the houses are not yet connected (Figure 7.6). The west and the north are very well served because more than 90 per cent of households have piped water (95.6 per cent in Koszalin; 94.2 per cent in Slupsk). The gas-pipe system is best developed in the southeast where local natural gas deposits exist: in Krosno almost 63 per cent of rural houses have gas installed, while in Rzeszów the figure is 30 per cent. By contrast, some voivodships (including Konin, Lomza and Płock) have no rural gas supplies at all. But

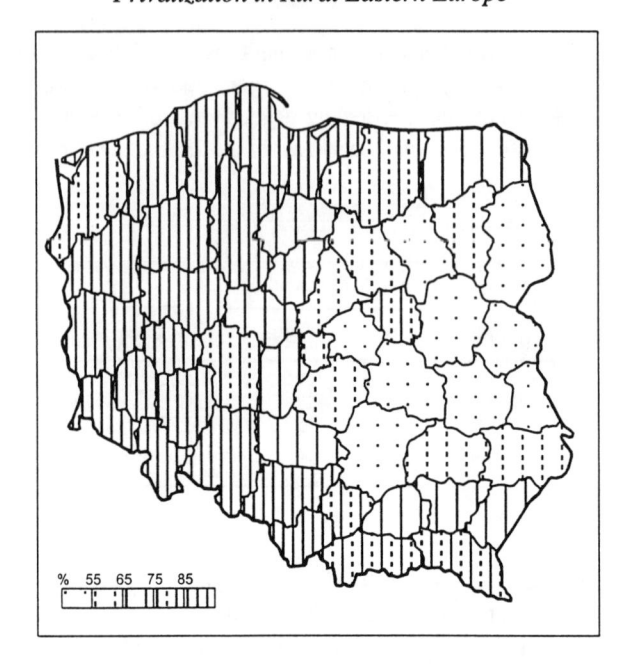

Source: Rocznik Statystyczny Rolnictwa 1993.

Figure 7.6 Poland: rural dwellings with piped water, 1992

the electricity network is widespread after the completion of the rural electrification programme in the mid-1970s. Since then, the main problem has been to increase the use of electricity in agricultural production and to reduce the frequency of power cuts. This requires some modernization of electrical networks and the installation of electrical appliances to dry cereals and hay, and to prepare fodder for animals. Considerable progress has been noted recently. At the same time, however, the rural consumption of electricity has been diminishing because of the rise in price. In 1989 electricity consumption per hectare of agricultural land amounted to 695kWh, falling by 52 per cent to 335kWh in 1993.

The expansion of the telephone network in Poland has also been proceeding very rapidly, with an increase in the number of rural phones by more than 90 per cent from 354,000 in 1989 to 673,000 in 1994 (that is, 64,000 new telephones were installed every year and 92,000 in

1992). However, the ratio of 45.8 phones per thousand of the rural population in 1994 is less than a quarter of the urban equivalent of 181.6. The development of the telephone network over Poland's territory is not uniform. Moreover, the rural provision is only 21 per thousand in Przemysl voivodship compared with 76 in Biała Podlaska. There are sharp variations in the eastern, southern and southeastern voivodships of Poland, whereas differences are relatively slight in the north and west where provision is generally good (Figure 7.7).

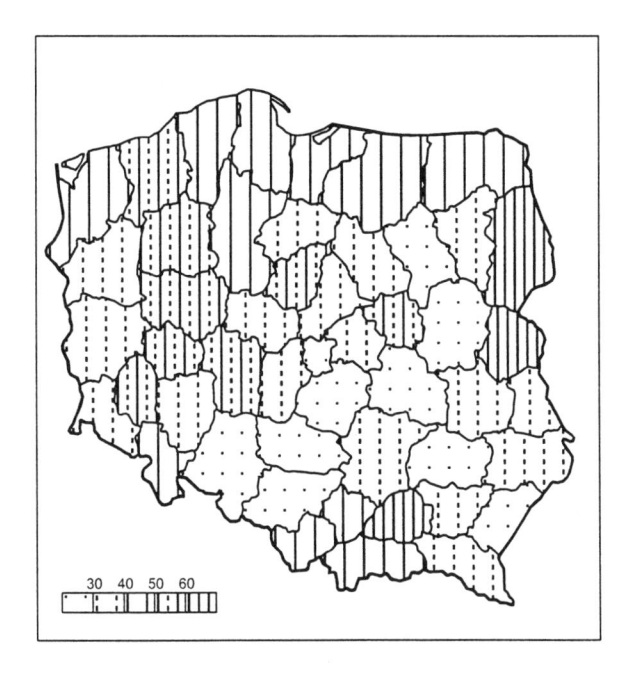

Source: Rocznik Statystyczny Województw 1994.

Figure 7.7 Poland: rural telephones per 1,000 rural inhabitants, 1992

Services

Many of the changes accompanying the Polish economic reforms and privatization concern commercial, financial and machinery services which are developing under very difficult economic conditions,

188 *Privatization in Rural Eastern Europe*

with insufficient capital and inadequate state intervention. Moreover, changes often take place spontaneously and in a manner contrary to public expectations (Urban 1995). However, the number of shops, purchasing centres and service points has increased by some 60 per cent as a result (almost exclusively) of private investments. These private facilities have been highly competitive in comparison with the state-owned enterprises. In 1993, the private sector's share in rural trading exceeded 80 per cent, while its share in services came close to 100 per cent.

In the late 1980s, more than 70,000 shops and kiosks operated in Polish rural areas, selling a variety of goods. By 1993, this number had increased by 31 per cent to almost 92,000 (Figure 7.8). The greatest change occurred in central and southern Poland, with a growth of more

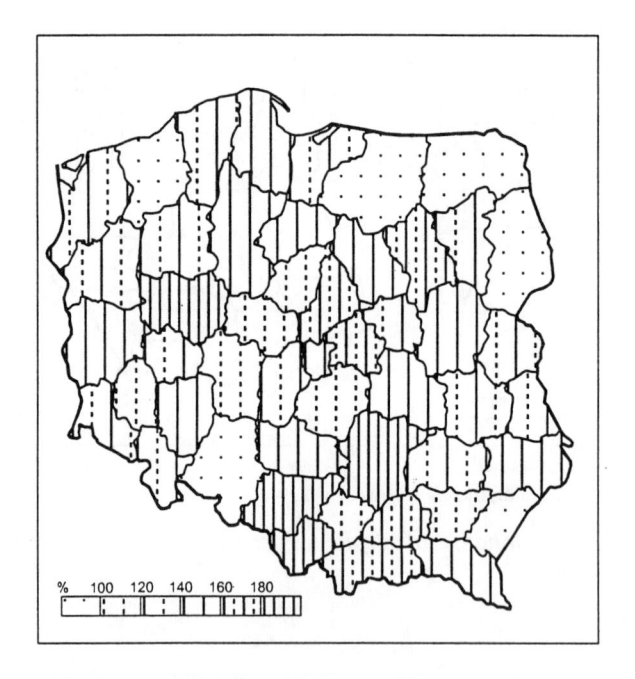

Source: Rocznik Statystyczny Województw 1989 and 1995.

Figure 7.8 Poland: shops in rural areas – percentage change, 1988–1994

than 70 per cent in some voivodships. By contrast, there was hardly any change in eastern Poland and in parts of the north. Indeed, the number of shops actually declined in Białystok, Koszalin, Olsztyn and Suwałki where there is high unemployment and the economy is in deep crisis. In eastern Poland, the rural trade network was already much less developed than in the south and west, with disparities of 50-100 per cent recorded. However, there has been a rapid development of wholesaling in the rural areas, where about 95 per cent of the small warehouses belong to private owners. The great majority are situated in the vicinity of towns.

Research conducted throughout the country by the Agricultural Economy Institute (Instytut Ekonomiki Rolnej) reveals that on average there are about 100 trade points in each local authority area or *gmina* (Kurek and Urban 1995). It is clear that, during the period 1989-93, rural services underwent relatively radical change as the number of service points increased by nearly 36 per cent (Goraj and Drozdz 1995) and expansion continues. The changes are generated almost exclusively by the private sector and state services are now being closed down quite rapidly. Private owners are trying to meet the new demands of the population, and businesses dealing with electronic equipment (including video rentals), household appliances and car repairs are growing very quickly.

A complex situation arises over services related to agriculture, but the decline in farm incomes means that the agricultural population is buying substantially fewer services than are really necessary for agricultural production. It is estimated that these purchases were nearly 50 per cent lower in 1993 than in 1989. Nevertheless, many significant changes in the network, ownership structure and type of the services offered can be observed in rural areas. The number of service points increased by nearly 54 per cent after 1989, with a growth of 160 per cent in private services balanced by a decline of some 50 per cent in state-owned establishments (Goraj and Drozdz 1995). Growth has also occurred in services helping farmers with the means of production and the purchase of agricultural products. In 1989, much agricultural machinery, such as tractors and combine harvesters, ceased being supplied by the government and instead they became widely available (although at much higher prices) through the market system of supply and demand. Contracts which gave farmers guaranteed sales for their produce (at fixed prices) were abolished at the same time. So whereas farm inputs such as fertilizers and machines were provided through the government and cooperative sale centres before 1989, private agents have now become the main suppliers. In 1993, they supplied more than half the mineral fertilizers and about 40 per cent of the agricultural machinery, building materials and fodder. Direct purchasing from the producer was always important in the case of tractors and some other types of machinery. This is still the case, and currently about 80 per cent of all tractors are bought direct from the manufacturer (Kurek and Urban 1995). Meanwhile, trade at open-air markets retains its significance.

After 1989, also, the purchasing of agricultural products became more diverse, although change has been slow and has brought considerable difficulty for small farms selling only small quantities of products. Purchasing used to be controlled by the Peasants' Mutual Aid Cooperatives (Gminne Spółdzielnie 'Samopomoc Chłopska') but private agents now buy almost half the fruit and vegetables, 40 per cent of the meat and a quarter of the grain. Markets have become important for the sale of farm producers as places to sell their produce, although there is a great deal of variation in local conditions across the country. There are differences between suburban areas and places situated a long way from the towns and the food-processing plants. There are also variations according to the farmer's financial situation, although most farmers try to sell at markets in order to get a higher price and make fuller use of their labour resources. By contrast, commodity exchanges, which in the majority of the European countries constitute the most important outlet for agricultural products, have been developing very slowly in Poland. Forty exchanges, located mainly in big towns, were in operation in 1994. The largest one, with a yearly turnover of US$31 billion, is in Poznań. Other major exchanges (with a turnover of US$4–5 billion) are located in the north and east: Białystok, Gdańsk, Lublin, Olsztyn and Szczecin.

NEGATIVE FEATURES ASSOCIATED WITH AGRICULTURE

It is very difficult to gauge the influence of restructuring on agricultural production because these changes are not the only determinants of farm output (Table 7.6). During the years 1960–91, the average output of

Table 7.6 Poland: agricultural production, 1989–1994

	1989	1990	1991	1992	1993	1994
Net production (1981–85 = 100)	111.8	105.7	104.0	92.7	94.6	n. a.
Farmland (m.ha)	18.7	18.7	18.7	18.7	18.6	18.6
Cereals area (th.ha)	8,377	8,531	8,726	8,321	8,506	8,481
Cereals production (m.t)	23.2	24.1	23.7	17.1	19.9	18.5
Cereals yield (qu/ha)	32.7	33.2	31.9	24.0	27.5	25.7
Oil plants (th.ha)	583	525	483	437	363	398
Potatoes production (m.t)	34.4	36.3	29.0	23.4	26.3	23.1
Vegetables production (th.t)	5,436	5,628	6,019	4,774	6,138	5,369
Fruit production (th.t)	1,557	979	1,873	2,386	2,706	2,111
Pasture (th.ha)	2,069	2,005	1,850	1,699	1,599	1,277
Cattle (m.)	10.7	10.0	8.8	8.2	7.6	7.7
Pigs (m.)	18.8	19.5	21.9	22.1	18.9	19.5
Sheep (m.)	4.4	4.1	3.2	1.8	1.3	0.9
Milk production (bn litres)	15.9	15.4	14.0	12.8	12.3	11.8

Source: Roczniki Statystyczne 1989, 1994, 1995.

grain, potatoes and sugar beet varied by an average of 20 per cent from the mean, while for certain special and orchard crops, this average variation reached about 70 per cent. Specialists attribute these fluctuations mainly to the weather, but also to the weak development of infrastructure (such as managed irrigation systems to cope with droughts) and the limited use of industrially produced fodder mixes. The past few years have again seen major variations in production but there appears to be a regressive trend because output was several percentage points less in each successive year from 1991 to 1994. Difficult weather conditions had a decisive role to play in this, but agricultural restructuring was probably of equal importance. A reduction in the area sown with crops was evident in the first year of privatization on former state farms. During 1989–94, the area under crops decreased by 1.4m.ha or about 10 per cent. Large areas of fallow and setaside land are now found throughout Poland, mostly on state lands where cultivation has been discontinued. However, some of the land belongs to private farmers who have ceased cultivation because of low returns.

The appearance of large areas of unused agricultural land is a new feature in the Polish landscape because in 1989 only 150th.ha were so affected. Figure 7.9 shows the correlation with state ownership, for the

Source: Jakubowicz and Ciok 1995.

Figure 7.9 Poland: fallow and temporary setaside – share of total arable land, 1994

two voivodships with the highest proportion of lands belonging to the state – Koszalin (62 per cent) and Zielona Góra (51 per cent) – also have the highest proportion of unused arable land (more than 30 per cent, which means that one hectare in three is setaside of one kind or another). In other voivodships in the north and west, the share of unused land frequently exceeds 20 per cent. But there are also areas of fallow and setaside land in some heavily-industrialized and urbanized voivodships such as Katowice and Warsaw. The problem of uncultivated land has become controversial because specialists argue that on the state lands, nearly 30 per cent of which (about 1m.ha) belong to the poorest-quality classes V and VI, it is economically irrational to contemplate farming. At a time of sluggish demand, the primary aim should be to minimize production costs. Yet, most of the uncultivated land lies in areas of high unemployment caused by laying-off the former state farm workers. They receive benefits which cost almost twice as much money as was previously paid in budget allocations to the state farms. The social costs of untilled land are thus very high, while the economic rationale is debatable.

Another problem in Polish agriculture which is caused by the transformation process is the decline in the harvest of basic crops, further reducing the cultivated area of some industrial and fodder plants and accelerating the decline in cattle and sheep numbers. To understand why, we must take into consideration regional variations linked with levels of economic development that are, in turn, rooted in history and exacerbated by poor education and major variations in agriculture's service infrastructure. Observing the changes that have occurred so far, it is evident that in the more advanced areas with a diversified economic structure, the process of agricultural restructuring has proceeded more harmoniously than in areas with a monolithic economic structure. This fact of regional development will have a particularly negative effect on the development of eastern regions of the country. According to Gorzelak (1994), some voivodships lying on Poland's eastern 'wall' (Biała-Podlaska, Chełm, Suwałki and Zamość) are locked in a backward state, so that the new economic conditions may even reinforce the process of regression and instigate other negative economic processes.

Depressed rural regions are not a new phenomenon. The voivodships of eastern Poland lack adequate resources of population and capital to ensure the development of agriculture. The rural people are badly educated and the level of infrastructure is very low. Moreover, for the last 20 years there has been substantial emigration of young people to the towns and a decline of interest by country people in agricultural development. During the present period of change (1988-94) grain yields in the north fell by as much as 40 per cent, while the national output declined by only 18 per cent (Figure 7.10). This cannot be linked simply with drought because the difference is so great.

194   *Privatization in Rural Eastern Europe*

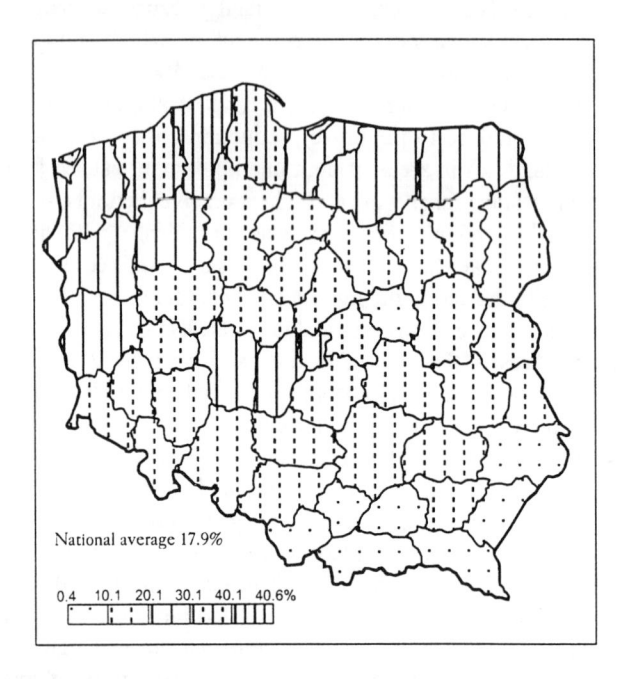

Source: Jakubowicz and Ciok 1995.

Figure 7.10   Poland: decline in cereal yields between 1988–1990 and 1992–1994

Instead, an almost fourfold reduction in the use of mineral fertilizers and a large decline in the application of pesticides had an immense influence on the change. Again, while the number of cattle per 100ha fell 24.1 per cent in 1990–94, the decline was greater in the west and exceeded 50 per cent in some voivodships (Figure 7.11). The decline in sheep numbers was evident immediately the communist era ended and the rate has accelerated as reform has proceeded. By 1994 the numbers had fallen below a million, barely a fifth of the 1989 level. The decline in cattle and sheep is reflected in the contraction of pasture from 2.0m.ha in 1990 to less than 1.3m.ha in 1994.

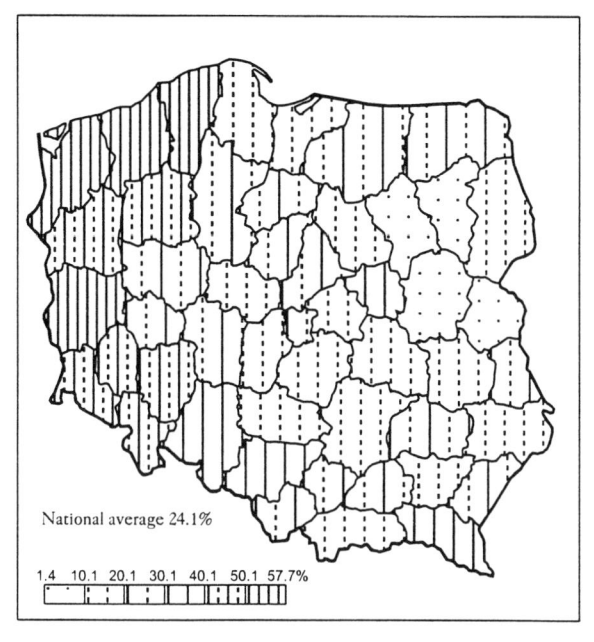

Source: Jakubowicz and Ciok 1995.

Figure 7.11 Poland: decline in cattle, 1992–1994

PROSPECTS FOR FURTHER REFORM

Since the Second World War there have been several attempts at economic reform in Poland, but they have not produced the expected results. They were carried out under the communist system and aimed at convergence between Poland and the highly-developed economies of Western Europe. There was also a desire to reduce the gap in living standards between city and country. But, because reforms were not linked with political changes it was not possible to make fundamental economic change and raise living standards. It was only with the reforms starting in 1989, following the demise of the communist system, that there has been a degree of success. It is possible to accelerate economic development and bring about improvements in rural areas.

Most Poles not only approve of these changes but are actively participating in bringing them about. Today's reforms seek an end to land fragmentation, a rise in farm productivity and an end to hidden unemployment. Polish politics should not focus on farming in isolation so much as the countryside as a whole. The government's policy document 'Strategy for Poland' says that structural reform and high farm output will be realized through developing multifunctional economies in the villages, including farming enterprises, services (for both families and enterprises), agrotourism and other activities related to rural population as a whole.

Among the most important reasons for this approach is the unemployment (both visible and invisible) of about two million people in agriculture. Agriculture is presently too inefficient, producing only 7 per cent of GNP while employing 27 per cent of the total workforce, so there must be consolidation which will displace even more farmworkers. But today, unlike the situation before 1989, there are no chances of employment in state enterprises in the towns, nor is there any real possibility of migration from the villages to the towns. The unemployed living on farms must create new types of employment for themselves in the country. The development of new businesses in rural areas may start with a rise in demand for high-quality food. Polish agriculture today has a big problem selling its produce, not only because of low demand, but also because of low trading and production standards. Therefore new farming organizations are needed to look after the inputs (fertilizers, machinery and seed) and the sale of agricultural commodities on the domestic and export markets. Improvements in infrastructure, food processing and light manufacturing could create more jobs and call for a greater range of skills. This could go some way towards relieving stagnation in the small villages (with about 200 inhabitants) whose number increased by about 600 (or 4 per cent) between 1980 and 1989 as a result of heavy out-migration by people seeking improved living conditions in the towns.

Development is linked with the idea of joining the EU; the rural areas are already involved in various programmes to adjust the Polish economy to European standards, for there is certainly a great disparity in conditions that will need a heavy investment to overcome. Above all, the government wants to attract investment aimed at the development of rural infrastructure job creation. A starting loan of US$200 million has been received from the World Bank for various programmes including roads and waterways, sewerage and telephones. Part of that loan (about US$50 million) is earmarked for the development of small business, which should provide some opportunity for the unemployed. Apart from investment-induced development, the Polish government budget allows for some modest financial aids to ameliorate unemployment and encourage an increase in farm size.

To continue reforms in agriculture, 150,000 new jobs must be created every year. If this happens, then some 750,000 very small farms of 1-3ha – 35 per cent of the total – might be eliminated in a few years. But such a programme is a non-starter in view of Poland's present economic difficulties. Thus it seems that there will be no significant reduction in the number of farms before 2010. Therefore, the immediate task should be more effective use of labour (especially the heavy work) in order to improve the financial returns. However, most farms (1.2-1.3 million) are constrained in their development by the advanced age of the owner, the total lack of capital or poor soil. These farms will obviously disappear over the longer term. The remaining one million farms are in a better situation, although scarcely more than half (some 550,000, although some economists say only 400,000), have a chance of sustained development. These enterprises already account for a large share of production. They are mechanized and would repay investment.

But one of the hardest problems of the Polish reform process lies in the massive regional variations in development levels. It is much easier to reconstruct the rural economies of more highly-developed regions than those of lagging regions. This is particularly true for the eastern regions mentioned earlier, which have very poor technical and service infrastructures and low-tech agricultural production. The government has funded several regional programmes for rural areas, taking into account their background history and the potential for development. A particular problem exists in the south and southeast with small farms of 2-3ha. Here there is high rural population density, high unemployment and low farm earnings. Reform will be very difficult. The price of land is the highest in the country at about US$2,400 per hectare compared with only $250 per hectare in the north. Pluriactivity will be important, especially agro-tourism in the Carpathian Mountains. It may also be possible to increase the area sown with higher-value crops such as vegetables and fruit.

Local government (commune and village councils) could play a significant role in rural reform. They receive a budget from central government and have shown that they can use their resources very efficiently. Very rapid growth has taken place over the last few years in border regions close to the German frontier, where new border crossings have been used by Germans coming to shop in Poland where prices are lower. On a smaller scale, there has also been an influx from the Czech Republic and Slovakia. This border cooperation is largely concerned with the sale of farm produce, which has led to the opening of additional shops and wholesale establishments, and hotels, motels and restaurants. The system of Euroregions is very effective in encouraging greater activity in border areas. Such regions have been created through agreements with the Czech Republic, Germany, Slovakia and Ukraine. However, the Tatra region was established as a result of an agreement between local authorities without central government input.

REFERENCES

Adamowicz, M. (1994), 'Strukturalne zmiany obszarów wiejskich w krajach wspólnoty europejskiej', *Człowiek i środowisko* (Warsaw: Wydawnictwo Instytutu Gospodarki Przestrzennej i Komunalnej), **18** (1), 5-21.

Goraj, L. and J. Drozdz (1995), 'Przeksztalcenia w sferze usług produkcyjnych i bytowych na wsi', *Zagadnienia Ekonomiki Rolnej*, No. 1, pp.80-89.

Herer, W. and W. Sadowski (1993), 'Zmiany struktury agrarnej na tle struktury i wielkości zatrudnienia w calej gospodarce', *Studia i Materiały Zakładu Badań Statystyczno-Ekonomicznych GUS i PAN* (Warsaw: Główny Urząd Statystyczny, Polska Akademia Nauk), **42**, 73.

Jakubowicz, E. and S. Ciok (1995), *Regionalne zroznicowanie procesów transformacji w Polsce* (Referat na Konferencji w Szklarskiej Porębie), Warsaw: Uniwersytet Warszawski, Instytut Geografii.

Kühnemann, A. (1984), *Warunki i strategia konsumpcyjnej obsługi ludności wiejskiej: na przykładzie woj. opolskiego*, Opole: Instytut Sląski.

Kurek, E. and R. Urban (1995), 'Procesy dostosowawcze kanałów rynku wiejskiego. Zagadnienia', *Ekonomiki Rolnej*, **1**, 33-43.

Olko-Bagieńska, T. (1994), 'Procesy restrukturyzacji rolnictwa państwowego w Polsce', *Człowiek i Środowisko*, **18** (1), 81-97.

Polish-European Community (1990), *An Agricultural Strategy for Poland*, Washington, DC: World Task Force.

Rosner, A. (ed.) (1993), *Rolnicy 92: rolnicy wobec zmian systemowych*, Warsaw: Wydawnictwo 'Krag'.

Szemberg, A. (1992), 'Przemiany agrarne w latach 1988-1992', *Zagadnienia Ekonomiki Rolnej*, No. 1-2, 3-21.

Urban, R. (1995), 'Procesy dostosowawcze otoczenia rolnictwa do warunków gospodarki rynkowej', *Zagadnienia Ekonomiki Rolnej*, No. 1, 24-33.

Zawadzki, W. (1993), 'Infrastruktura a zróznicowanie obszarów wiejskich', *Zagadnienia Ekonomiki Rolnej*, No. 3, 30-42.

8. Romania

David Turnock

Throughout the modern period, Romania has been known as an agrarian country generating substantial surpluses of cereals and livestock. Although food exports were less important during the communist period, priority was given to intensification in the main arable regions. However, agrarian structures have seen quite dramatic change over the last 150 years. Emancipation from serfdom was achieved in 1864 but without sufficient land for viable peasant farms. The settlement was obstructed by landlords who evaded their obligations to make two-thirds of their estates available for peasant holdings. In view of the limited opportunities in the towns, the increase in population resulted in progressive subdivision of holdings. Dependence on labour contracts with the estates led to abuses that culminated in the peasant revolt of 1907 and land reform after the First World War. There was progress towards viable family farms and cooperative systems were encouraged, especially during the Second World War. Further land reform after 1945 accentuated the problems of minifundia and helped to create the conditions for communist collectivization. This latter system was highly centralized and there were persistent attempts to marginalize any tendencies towards the development of a 'second economy', despite the problems that the central planning system was encountering (Brezinski and Petersen 1990; Sampson 1983).

It was especially in Romania that pragmatism in agricultural policy in the interest of higher output and productivity was circumscribed by lingering ideological sensitivities among the communist authorities. Households valued the private plot, which could be secured through 120 'labour-days' for the cooperative (Cernea 1974). There was a scheme to encourage piecework through the sharecropping logic of the *accord global* which provided a means of securing access to fodder to boost household livestock rearing: cash income was less desirable because money could be more easily earned in industry and hence there were many resignations when cooperatives started paying in cash. However, the 'extremism' of the later years of the Ceauşescu presidency prevented any significant reform (Fischer 1989; Pecsi 1989). Indeed, the socialist model was firmly upheld through the 1980s with the prospect of tighter state coordination and further specialization (Gilberg 1980). The Romanian system remained 'one of exploiting agriculture far more than the rest of the economy and society [thus accentuating the] social abyss between most of the urban and rural population segments' (Wädekin 1990, p.324). Cheap food and cheap labour were extracted under a system of 'oppressive and inefficient command farming' while capital inputs per hectare and per worker remained 'lower than in other East European countries with collectivized agriculture except for Albania' (ibid.).

Socialist agriculture comprised cooperative and state farms with various forms of coordination including the Agro-Industrial Councils for State and Cooperative Farms ('Consiliul Unic Agroindustrial de Stat şi Cooperatist': CUASC) and a number of trusts, some involving industrial units (Giosan 1964). There was a link with the draconian rural resettlement programme of *sistematizare* in the sense that the proposed new towns were the CUASC centres while the need for labour by each council helped to determine the viability of villages in each area (Turnock 1986, 1991a). Some mountain districts were not collectivized, because of a 'lack of infrastructure and administrative control capacity' (Wädekin 1990, p.324). Mountain households gave produce to kin or friends in the city (in the interest of social contact and exchange), while selling for cash on the open market and contracting with the state, through a production plan (*Plan de Producţie*), to deliver animals and other commodities in return for low-cost fodder with which more livestock could be reared (Ronnas 1987, 1989). By letting peasants dispose of their surpluses through the second economy, the state reasoned that more would be extracted than would be possible under collectivization. But of course the state tried to get more by introducing new regulations (such as registration of livestock), propagandist appeals for good citizenship, stimulative acquisition prices, reduced transport costs, collecting state-contracted milk at the farm gate, and premiums for high-quality stock.

The tendency for production plan quotas to increase and for prices to weaken left peasants with little surplus to sell on the open markets, where prices were in any case controlled by the regime of maximum prices adopted in the later years of the Ceauşescu presidency. Restrictions on the use of non-family labour and the lack of an effective land market prevented any amalgamation of holdings. Hence, young people were encouraged to take advantage of any possibilities for daily commuting to factory work in the towns, to the same extent as in other areas where cooperatives were formed (Beck 1976). Those who could not get factory work because they were too old or because their farm was too remote had to regard agriculture (whether cooperative or individual farm) as a resource to be exploited in the short term. Proposals were made for development in remoter rural areas by creating small livestock-rearing associations (Dobrovici 1972; Dumitru 1972) and by more comprehensive schemes of rural diversification (Rey 1979). But the peasants were suspicious of any state proposals for new forms of cooperation while the authorities were inhibited by ideological objections from supporting private farm businesses.

AGRARIAN REFORM

Since the revolution, the situation has been transformed by several measures (Bordanc et al. 1994). First, the government decided in 1990 to provide smallholdings for every cooperative farm member (0.5ha) and for all other rural dwellers including state farm employees answerable to shareholders (0.25ha). Meanwhile, the state farms have remained intact, but they have been converted into commercial companies with subdivision to allow for separate management of crop and livestock enterprises. Families who were expropriated in order to create the state farms in the first place (or whose land subsequently passed to such farms through land exchanges) have become shareholders in the appropriate company, but without restitution of the land itself – 164,000 people now hold shares in a total of approximately 561 companies responsible for some 2m.ha (15 per cent of the country's agricultural land). The future of the cooperatives was initially uncertain. When the government wrote off the debts of bankrupt agricultural organizations and established a free market in agricultural commodities (Gheorghe 1992), it was expected that the cooperatives would carry on. But there were many cases of spontaneous liquidation in the hill and mountain areas, although the police and those with vested interests tried to check the process of disintegration (Kideckel 1993a, 1993b). The government recognized the revolutionary nature of the action and framed their restitution programme in order to bring almost all the land seizures within the law – a shrewd political move because it ensured overwhelming support for the Salvation Front government in the rural areas over an opposition which championed restitution in the first place, but on a scale that might have provided for larger estate holdings in conflict with the peasant ethos (Lazar 1996a).

The Land Law ('Legea Fondului Funciar') of February 1991 is fundamental to the present privatization phase in Romanian agriculture (Pop 1994). It provided for the allocation of former cooperative farmland and the free distribution of the animals (or the proceeds realized from the sale of animals) formerly held by the 3,588 cooperative farms and 132 economic associations of cooperative farms ('Asociaţie Economică Intercooperatistă' or AEI). Families with a valid claim on the basis of previous ownership could receive holdings of up to 10ha (arable equivalent), although some elderly people settled for small plots, because their capacity for work was limited, while younger people with families wanted as much land as possible. State-owned forest land was also subject to redistribution, but only up to a maximum of one hectare in the case of each valid claim (and with the proviso that the total holding, covering farmland and forest, should not exceed 10ha). Such a limit was critical in 'giving land to as many people as possible' including cooperative workers who had not previously owned land, while precluding 'the recreation of a viable propertied middle class in agriculture ... that might exert certain kinds of pressure on the state' (Verdery 1994, p.1076).

Some 5.06 million people are potential beneficiaries in respect of a total of 9.11m.ha (covering almost two-thirds of the country's cropland). Thus, the cooperative farms, which held 63 per cent of the cropland land in 1985, have disappeared, while individual landed properties increased their share of the land from 9 per cent in 1985 to 76 per cent of the property (and 84 per cent of the number of farm units in 1995). The remaining land falls to companies with a majority of state-owned capital (that is, the former state farms), with 11 per cent, and plots managed by municipalities and research stations, with 13 per cent. By August 1993, almost 90 per cent of the available land had been distributed to roughly four-fifths of those eligible, providing holdings with an average size of approximately 2ha. The grant of a provisional title (*titlul de posesie*) was followed up by cadastral action (involving location, measurement and delimitation) and the issue of the definitive titles (*titlul de proprietate*). Many people have successfully insisted on the return of family land at its former site or *vechile amplasamente*, although in many cases this is not possible because old landmarks have disappeared while much former farmland has been either afforested or built up. However, it is clear that if all potential owners are to be satisfied, the average area will decline. Given all the practical problems, the restitution process has been slow, not least because of the need for cadastral and credit laws. However, whereas 22 per cent of the titles were issued by April 1994, the proportion almost doubled, to 42 per cent, by May 1995. Progress was well above average (50 per cent or more) in the 14 counties of Argeş, Bacău, Bistriţa-Năsăud, Buzău, Constanţa, Dâmboviţa, Dolj, Galaţi, Sălaj, Sibiu, Suceava, Timiş, Tulcea and Vrancea. These counties are scattered across Transylvania and Banat, but they also fall into a discontinuous belt along the Sub-carpathians of Muntenia and Moldavia (from Argeş through Dâmboviţa, Buzău, Vrancea and Bacău) and a block in the southeast (Constanţa, Galaţi and Tulcea). On the other hand, progress was relatively slow (25-30 per cent) in a group of Transylvanian counties: Braşov, Covasna, Harghita, Maramureş and Mureş.

These differences reflect the considerable spatial variations in the relationships between the people claiming land and the land available, and further variations when the balance between arable land and pasture is taken into account (Bordanc 1995, 1996). In the hill country there is a balance of pasture (on the higher ground) and arable land (on the lower ground), but population pressure is high with 50–60 persons per 100ha of cropland. In the plains there is a much better supply of land in relation to demand, with a substantial amount of cultivated ground per active person (4–5ha) and a low density (20–30 active persons per 100ha). In individual counties, the amount of cropland available for redistribution varies from about 10th.ha in the mountains (where most of the land consists of pastures and hayfields) to more than 400th.ha in the plains. When the population is considered in relation to the land available it is evident that there is relatively heavy demand in Argeş, Bacău, Bihor, Buzău, Prahova and Vâlcea. These are areas of rapid urbanization and industrial development, leading to loss of farmland and a growth in the number of people with the right to ownership (a number which reaches 270,000 in the case of Bucharest and the Ilfov Agricultural Sector). It should be noted, however, that some counties in the lowlands (such as Brăilă, Călăraşi, Giurgiu and Ialomiţa) have only about 220th.ha of cropland for redistribution (the national average) because of a relatively small territory and a prominence of state farms.

Much delay in settling claims has arisen through shortcomings in the work of local and county commissions, a lack of surveyors and, in some areas, a lack of adequate documentation. The main problem has been the stiff competition for land from people who have valid claims which cannot all be met, because there is no mechanism whereby restitution vouchers have a certain value which will buy more or less land depending on the price, which in turn will be influenced by the level of demand. Since there is no clear 'pecking order' claimants must be suitably assertive in dealing with the local land commissions. Verdery (1994) mentions the Germans in Aurel Vlaicu commune (Hunedoaraă) who regained the 70ha they lost through expropriation in favour of poor Romanian peasants in 1945. The latter helped form the cooperative, but the Germans refused to accept shares in state farmland as compensation and won their case. The same author suggests that the chief losers in the competition are widows, people in cities (who are easily deceived), immigrants and some elements of the former village poor. Those who tend to succeed are local politicians, officials responsible for implementing the restitution law and some elements of the old village élite (ibid., p.1104). However, half the 534.4 thousand farm workers (that is, people working for salaries on the still-intact state farms and elsewhere) have either no land or a plot of less than one hectare (Henry 1994). Out-migration has also affected people who cannot claim land under the restitution law but who previously worked for the cooperative farms; many Gypsies have been forced to move from villages to the edge of towns in the hope of finding work.

However, the private sector is now in place and its role in agricultural production has gradually increased from 56.1 per cent in 1990 to 86.5 per cent in 1995 (Table 8.1). But only 30 per cent of the families receiving former cooperative farmland were both members of

Table 8.1 Romania: role of the private sector in agriculture, 1990–1995

		Value of production (m.lei current prices)					
		1990	1991	1992	1993	1994	1995
Agriculture	Total production	266	751	2,104	7,371	16,589	23,679
	Private sector	149	595	1,699	6,228	14,336	20,492
	Percentage	56.1	79.3	80.8	84.5	86.4	86.5
Crops	Total production	141	495	1,219	4,637	10,092	14,324
	Private sector	79	404	987	4,026	8,820	12,634
	Percentage	56.0	81.6	80.9	86.8	87.4	88.2
Livestock	Total production	125	256	885	2,734	6,497	9,355
	Private sector	70	191	712	2,202	5,516	7,858
	Percentage	56.3	74.8	80.5	80.6	84.9	84.0

Source: A. Radoca, 'Evoluţia sectorului privat in economia României', *Revista Română de Statistică* **45** (1), 1996, 5.

cooperative farms and former farmowners. One-fifth of the population consists of former cooperative members whose families did not contribute land when the cooperatives were formed (and who therefore qualify for holdings no larger than 0.5ha), and half the new owners are from the towns, often having only limited experience of agriculture (Bulgaru et al. 1992; Ianos et al. 1992a). The new farmers also have to decide whether to work their land independently or join an association. In 1994, land worked by individual families totalled 5.2m.ha made up of 2.89 million separate units with an average size of holding of 1.8ha (Table 8.2). Meanwhile, some 16,555 associations, involving 746,800 families, worked a total area of 1.87m.ha (160ha each), while 4,054 formally constituted (*juridic*) associations involving 750,300 families worked 1.81m.ha (450ha each). Overall, some 40 per cent of the privatized farmland is being worked by associations, strongly encouraged by the state in the early days (Parpală 1993b), and 60 per cent by individual families. By 1996, individual farms were somewhat more prominent with the completion of restitution but forecasts for 2000 suggest a substantial consolidation in favour of associations while the average size of individual farm may increase only slightly.

Table 8.2 Romania: individual farms and associations 1994–2000

	1994				1996				2000			
	A	B	C	D	A	B	C	D	A	B	C	D
Individual	2.89	2.9	5.20	1.8	3.6	3.6	8.1	2.3	1.9	1.9	6.0	3.1
Family Association	0.75	16.6	1.89	160.0	n.a.	15.0	1.65	110.0	n.a.	18.6	3.93	210.0
Formal Association	0.75	4.0	1.81	450.0	n.a.	4.0	1.63	415.0	n.a.	3.7	1.45	385.0

Notes: A Households (m.); B Organizations (th., but m. for individual farms); C Total area (m.ha); D Average holding (ha).

Source: *Romanian Business Journal*, 1996.

Individual farming tends to involve the larger families and a relatively high proportion do not have any regular salary (Table 8.3), although the differences are too accentuated on account of the element of consensus in the two main environmental areas. However, whereas in the hill and mountain areas virtually all the land is worked by individual families, the associations are prominent in the lowlands. Moreover, many holdings in the lowlands are split between the two modes and small family plots form a buffer (*tampon*) between the village itself and the principal agricultural surfaces, following the tradition of *bun de familia* which continued under communism through private plots. Today, many families entrusting their land to an association will usually retain a small piece to be worked casually by their own labour. Some families with plenty of labour opt to work their own holding intensively, maximizing income by using animal power for ploughing and distributing locally generated organic manure rather than chemical fertilizers. Households planning to farm privately had significantly more family members involved in farming (and more members in total) than households intending to join associations; they were also 'slightly but significantly younger' (Meurs 1996, p.173). Meanwhile, there are also distinctions between formally constituted associations (which often incorporate elements of the former communist cooperatives) and loose family associations with a fluctuating membership.

Table 8.3 Romania: analysis of households, 1992

Household category		Total households	Number of active members/salary earners (th)					
			One	Two	Three	Four	Five	No salary
All households								
	Active	7,288.7	1,835.2	2,687.0	614.5	225.4	68.5	1,858.2*
	Salaried	7,288.7	1,985.9	2,240.2	335.6	86.4	18.0	2,622.6
Pensioner								
	Active	2,679.1	566.0	303.6	92.9	22.7	5.1	1,687.7*
	Salaried	2,679.1	482.3	230.8	45.3	8.8	1.6	1,910.3
Other inactive								
	Active	277.0	66.5	28.8	8.2	2.3	0.7	170.5*
	Salaried	277.0	56.6	18.5	3.5	0.7	0.1	197.5
Other non-agricultural								
	Active	3,759.4	1,029.3	2,125.9	410.2	150.2	45.3	
	Salaried	3,759.4	1,345.5	1,962.0	282.4	76.2	16.2	274.8
Individual farming								
	Active	490.0	149.2	193.9	87.5	43.8	15.3	
	Salaried	490.0	85.1	24.1	3.7	0.6	†	376.2
Association member								
	Active	83.2	24.2	34.8	15.7	6.4	2.1	
	Salaried	83.2	16.4	4.8	0.7	0.1	†	61.3

Notes: * Refers to pensioners and other inactive persons with the status of head of household; † = less than 0.1.

Source: Revista Română de Statistică 43 (4–5), 1994.

However, despite the scope for large-scale working provided through the associations, agriculture is not nearly so highly consolidated in the business sense as was formerly the case. Where individual small farms are worked as such, they are frequently split into four or five separate plots through fragmentation. This reduces the chances of getting all land ploughed and slows the autumn campaign. During the spring 1996 campaign, fragmentation cost an estimated 15th.t of fuel and 4 million hours of time: a total cost of 115 billion lei. Costs have been estimated at 350 billion lei over a full year (Lazar 1996b). Farmers lack capital because the modest incomes secured from the former cooperatives were insufficient to generate stocks of capital for use under privatization; after taking care of basic necessities, cash was usually spent on building materials for the construction or renovation of houses. Meanwhile, bank loans attract exorbitant rates of interest which virtually no peasants can contemplate. In any case, banks prefer to lend to large processors who in turn deal with large producers through forward purchase contracts. Yet, failure to use proper rotation methods results in low yields and the loss of 3m.t of cereals each year (valued at 1,000 billion lei according to 1996 prices).

Private households seem to respond better to market stimuli through increased output of fodder, vegetables and grapes, while reducing the production of sugar beet, barley and sunflowers, that is, market vegetables rather than 'planners' crops'; associations initially sought overall increases in output and employment, despite excess labour, falling GDP and poor export opportunities. Hence, 'under these conditions associations' willingness to expand appears to continue the behaviour of output maximizing, centrally planned firms' (Meurs 1996, p.175). Although pay is linked to farm performance, management is not evidently adjusting production to the conditions prevailing. However, association members are keenly watching the results and competition exists between associations in particular villages. Ianos (1995) has discussed the case of Semlac commune in Arad county which has six agricultural societies and two associated groups, with changes constantly taking place in the membership of these organizations. Three of the societies lost a high proportion of their members (35–80 per cent) because of poor results, and people tried to join one of the three other societies which were perceived as being more successful (especially the '1 Decembrie' company that was reconstituted on the former CAP structure). Initially the members of the latter were elderly residents owning little land but the present leadership has decided to restrict local membership in favour of outside residents (who accounted for a fifth of the members in 1993 compared with only three per cent in 1992). Meanwhile, more local families have been starting to farm individually and the area involved increased from 356ha in 1992 to 1,016ha in 1993 (although the 1993 wheat yields on the individual farms were much lower than those achieved by the '1 Decembrie' company, because of lack of fertilizer and technical knowledge and the difficulty of gaining access to machinery at the preferred moment). Another strategy is for members of a company to work some of their land individually and 248 members of '1 Decembrie' were working 0.25–0.40ha in this way in 1993 (compared with 170 members in 1992). There is also competition for machine services and farmers are prepared to store their crops if the prices are not acceptable.

The signs are that the redeployment of labour will result in a growth of interest in individual farms without the involvement of agricultural societies or associated groups (Gavrilescu 1996; Mateescu 1996). Once people have received their definitive ownership certificates it will be possible for a land market to develop, with the more successful farmers having the possibility of enlarging their holdings and generating more income. There is now a flow of capital into the villages, from pensioners returning to the countryside and building or repairing houses, and also from younger people wanting to come back to their home village eventually, and who therefore improve property inherited from their parents. The villagers themselves are investing the profits derived from farming in home improvements. Capital is also flowing into a privatized service sector nourished by the growth of purchasing power now that farmers have given up stockpiling their produce. Food shops, bars and small manufacturing units have been established in increasing numbers between 1991 and the middle of 1993 and now total 51 in all. There is also a growth in the number of commercial agents as farmers make arrangements with intermediaries to get produce sold at markets as advantageously as possible (rather than use the state institutions or the local urban market).

LAND USE

Although there were some interim difficulties when uncertainty over ownership led to neglect, and administrative shortcomings separated livestock from fodder and interrupted supplies of irrigation water (especially serious under drought conditions), agricultural effort has been maintained and restitution has been almost universally welcomed. But the levels of intensification achieved in the context of central planning have not been maintained. An immediate response to the abandonment of controls after the revolution was a greater emphasis on self-sufficiency on peasant farms to generate the inputs for livestock production and family subsistence. The cropping programme became even more dominated by cereals (especially maize) which are always

Table 8.4 Romania: land-use change (th.ha), 1989–1994

	1989	1994	Change Absolute	Change Percentage
Arable	9,458.4	9,338.0	−120.4	−1.3
Pastures	3,256.9	3,378.4	+121.5	+3.7
Hayfields	1,448.3	1,493.7	+45.4	+3.1
Vineyards	277.5	298.4	+20.9	+7.5
Orchards/ vegetable gardens	318.0	289.0	−29.0	−9.1
Agricultural land	14,759.0	14,797.5	+38.5	+2.6
Forest	6,678.5	6,680.1	+1.6	*
Other	2,401.6	2,361.4	−40.2	−1.7
Total	23,839.1	23,839.1	0.0	0.0

Note: * = less than 0.1.

in deficit in the mountain regions and which naturally attract priority when there are market uncertainties. There are clear changes in land use (Table 8.4). Agricultural land has increased by 2.6 per cent but this is due to larger areas of pasture (conventionally divided between hill pasture and the more valuable hay meadows). Arable land has declined by just over 120ha while an increase in the area of vineyards is balanced by a reduction in orchards and vegetable gardens. There are spatial variations in the picture because 62,700ha of arable land have been lost in Transylvania (a decline of 2.7 per cent) while the nine counties in the southeast have experienced a reduction of only 2,900ha (0.1 per cent). This could indicate a trend towards specialization, which is born out to some extent by information on the value of production, discriminating between crops and livestock.

There has been a sharp decline in production and especially in livestock, which seems paradoxical in view of the increase in pasture. However, this change in land use really has negative consequences as far as livestock are concerned because the crucial factor is the supply of cereals and fodder crops. There is an increased share of the total value of production falling to crops: 54.4 per cent in 1989, rising to 65.9 per cent in 1991 before falling slightly to 62.9 per cent in 1993 and 60.8

Table 8.5 Romania: agricultural production by regions (bn.lei),1989–1992

Year	Region	Crops Value	%	Livestock Value	%	Total Value	%
1989	Romania	107.2	54.4	89.8	45.6	196.9	100.0
	Southeast*	42.9	62.0	26.6	38.0	69.5	100.0
	Transylvania	72.4	50.9	36.8	49.1	109.2	100.0
	(West Transylvania†)	14.3	53.9	12.2	46.1	26.5	100.0
1992	Romania	1,219.3	58.0	884.5	42.0	2,103.9	100.0
	Southeast*	321.4	65.0	172.8	35.0	494.2	100.0
	Transylvania	395.1	53.6	342.4	46.4	737.5	100.0
	(West Transylvania†)	132.6	52.0	122.2	48.0	254.8	100.0
1994	Romania	10,091.8	60.8	6,497.3	39.2	10,741.1	100.0
	Southeast*	2,200.0	64.4	1,215.8	35.6	3,415.8	100.0
	Transylvania	3,622.7	58.8	2,539.4	41.2	6,162.1	100.0
	(West Transylvania†)	1,338.0	60.7	865.9	39.3	2,203.9	100.0

Notes: * Counties of Brăilă, Călăraşi, Constanţa, Galaţi, Giurgiu, Ialomiţa, Ilfov, Tulcea and Vrancea.
† Counties of Arad, Bihor, Caras-Severin and Timiş.

Source: Anuarul Statistic.

per cent in 1994 (against a historic trend in Romania which has seen cropping reduce its share from 69.7 per cent in 1938 to 65.1 per cent in 1950, 62.3 per cent in 1970 and 55.4 per cent in 1980) (Table 8.5). Provisional figures suggest a rise again to 62.7 per cent in 1995 and 66.5 per cent in 1996 as a result of good cereal harvests (19.3m.t in 1996 compared with an average of 16.5m.t for 1990–94). Transylvania was 3.5 percentage points below the national level in 1989 (showing a significant bias to the livestock sector) but 4.4 per cent in 1992 and 2.0 per cent in 1994; while figures for the southeast (7.6 percentage points above the national average in 1989, 7 in 1992 and 3.8 in 1994) show a strong bias towards crops.

Broadly speaking, the arable emphasis in the southeast is maintained in spite of reduced intensification through the problems experienced with the large fattening units for livestock, whose numbers have declined in the southeast by more than the national average. Between 1989 and 1992 cattle numbers in the southeast fell by 50.6 per cent (41.5 per cent nationally), although the decline in sheep and goats was only 22.5 per cent (21.7 per cent nationally) and pigs did slightly better than the national average: a decline of 12.7 per cent against 15.6 per cent nationally. Between 1992 and 1994 there was a further fall in cattle numbers by 11.7 per cent (5.5 per cent nationally) and also in sheep and goats at 14.2 per cent (9.6 per cent nationally) while pigs again did slightly better (a decline of 19.7 per cent compared with 21.3 per cent nationally). Thus, any increase in specialization in the southeast is occurring in the context of a major decrease in total output arising in part from inadequate technical support. In addition to deficiencies in irrigation systems, there has been a decline in the machinery available and the number of tractors declined from 151.7 thousand in 1989 to 146.8 thousand in 1992 (a reduction of 3.3 per cent). Seasonal conditions can introduce short-term distortions, however. In the four counties in West Transylvania (taking in the eastern fringe of Pannonia), the deviation below the national average for crops increased sharply to 6 percentage points in 1992 from only 0.5 in 1989, but the situation was restored in 1996 when the difference was only 0.1 of a percentage point. This reflects a bad year for crops in the west in 1994, with the bias towards animal production occurring in the context of above-average rates of decrease for livestock during 1989–92: marginally for cattle at –41.7 per cent, but more significant for pigs (–31.6 per cent); sheep and goats (–30 per cent); and poultry (–29.8 per cent compared with –23 per cent nationally). West Transylvania's contribution to total national agricultural production fell from 13.5 per cent in 1989 to 12.1 per cent in 1992, but returned to 13.3 per cent in 1994.

The reduction in the level of intensification, which has affected both cropping and livestock (Table 8.6), is primarily due to the reduced demand for farm produce, given the reduction in subsidies and the competition with imported food (Parpală 1992b). Market prices do not justify applying fertilizer dressings conducive to maximum production, especially since subsidies were removed in 1992. Thus, whereas the industry turned out 553.5th.t active substance in 1992 and 602th.t in

Table 8.6 Romania: agricultural activity, 1985–1994

Criteria	1994	1993	1992	1991	1990	1989	1987	1985
Crop area[a]	9.22	9.17	8.91	9.20	9.40	9.70	9.65	9.89
Crop area[b]	71.22	69.77	64.8	65.8	60.7	61.2	62.0	63.6
Crop area[c]	7.72	7.55	7.01	7.16	6.77	7.32	7.30	7.61
Advisory staff (th.)	n.a.	n.a.	n.a.	50.38	66.55	65.58	62.09	59.36
Fertilizer[d]	0.48	0.54	0.42	0.46	1.10	1.16	1.20	1.20
Fertilizer[e]	16.94	17.12	15.79	16.91	24.79	41.60	39.43	34.10
Tractors (th.)	161.2	158.1	146.8	132.8	127.1	151.7	183.8	184.4
Irrigated land (th.ha)	3,104	n.a.	3,202	3,197	3,216	3,168	3,366	2,956
Forest estate (th.ha)	6,369	6,367	6,368	6,367	6,371	6,372	6,353	6,339
Afforested (th.ha)	14.7	10.3	12.6	15.8	25.5	41.4	38.3	42.4
Crop production (absolute m.t)								
Maize	9.34	7.99	6.83	10.50	6.81	6.76	7.53	11.90
Wheat	6.19	5.35	3.23	5.56	7.38	7.94	6.71	5.60
Other cereals	2.65	2.15	2.23	3.25	2.98	3.68	2.65	2.00
Sugar beet	2.76	1.78	2.90	4.70	3.28	6.77	5.22	6.14
Sunflowers	0.76	0.70	0.77	0.61	0.56	0.66	0.75	0.70
Potatoes	2.95	3.71	2.60	1.87	3.19	4.42	4.14	6.63
Vegetables	2.57	2.87	2.63	2.21	2.36	3.73	3.74	5.35
Fruit	0.98	2.18	1.17	1.16	1.45	1.58	1.48	1.96

Crop production (kg per capita)							
Cereals	800.0	680.9	540.2	832.7	738.3	793.9	736.2	858.2
Sugar beet	121.6	78.1	127.3	202.8	140.9	292.5	227.4	270.4
Sunflowers	33.6	30.6	34.0	26.4	23.9	28.3	32.5	30.6
Potatoes	129.6	163.0	114.4	80.8	137.0	190.9	180.5	291.8
Vegetables	113.0	126.2	115.7	95.8	101.3	161.0	162.9	235.6
Fruit	43.1	95.9	51.3	50.2	62.5	68.3	64.5	86.2
Livestock numbers (th. except where otherwise stated)							
Cattle	3,481	3,597	3,683	4,355	5,321	6,291	6,559	6,692
Pigs	7,758	9,262	9,852	10,954	12,003	11,671	14,328	13,651
Sheep and goats	11,642	12,275	12,884	14,827	15,067	16,452	17,829	18,170
Poultry (m.)	70	77	88	106	121	114	127	120
Livestock products							
Meat (m.t)	1.85	1.93	1.89	2.02	2.33	1.91	2.45	2.40
Milk (m.hl)	53.6	47.3	44.9	46.1	44.2	45.3	50.1	52.5
Wool (th.t)	25.1	26.0	28.0	32.5	38.2	35.4	38.9	40.7
Eggs (bn)	5.41	5.63	6.14	7.18	8.08	7.04	7.32	7.24
Livestock products (kg per capita except where otherwise stated)							
Meat	81.5	85.0	83.3	87.3	95.9	95.9	99.6	105.5
Milk (litre)	235.6	208.1	197.5	198.8	190.1	195.5	218.3	230.9
Wool	1.1	1.1	1.2	1.4	1.6	1.5	1.7	1.8
Eggs (units)	238	248	270	310	317	304	319	319

Notes: [a] Total area (m.ha) for main crops; [b] Percentage used for cereals; [c] Crop area under cereals, sugar beet, sunflowers, potatoes and vegetables; [d] Chemical fertilizer (m.t) active substance; [e] Natural fertilizer (m.t); n.a. not available.

Source: *Anuarul Statistic*.

1993, the level was down to 363.7th.t in 1993 and 383.2 in 1994. The Archim (Arad) fertilizer works was forced to close temporarily, as was the Curtea de Argeş bioprotein plant. But a slackening of effort also arises for a number of reasons, some of them specific to the Romanian situation. Romanian farmers have also been compromised by imports at dumping prices, while their inefficiency (through lack of machines and economies of scale) means that there are few possibilities for exports. Domestic food producers are rarely able to offer stimulative prices because of their own cash-flow problems and lack of competitiveness against imported food. Therefore, some lowland farmers have been reluctant to grow sugar beet and sunflowers, for which there is no demand within the household. Cereals can be used on the farm and in addition there is a state cereal buyer (National Agency for Agricultural Products (NAAP), formerly 'Romcereal') to take all the available production except at times of oversupply as in 1995. Meanwhile, in the hilly regions, some farmers have destroyed orchards in order to secure more land for maize, which is valuable for fodder and family subsistence (Iordan and Velcea 1984; Velcea 1996). They concentrate their marketing activity on livestock rearing and the supply of fodder and, given the scarcity of capital, this means maximizing maize cultivation and the production of hay (assisted by scrub clearance on marginal land where the labour is available). Local outlets for small surpluses (such as milk for cheese production) are improving and some communities with a relatively young population with income from non-agricultural employment are hoping to make small investments and restore the status of enterprises such as fruit growing and viticulture (Hirschhausen-Leclerc 1994).

Some crops have been particularly badly hit. A desperate situation is reported for rice growing because of lack of capital, rising costs and expensive loans. There were 70th.ha of rice plantations by the end of the 1980s, but the area has fallen sharply, while money is spent on importing rice of inferior quality; yet pedoclimatic conditions are good by European standards and Romania is a potential exporter. The wine industry has been badly hit by privatization, coupled with the loss of former markets and competition on the home market from cheap imported drinks. The Land Law has resulted in the fragmentation of the vineyards (creating small units which cannot operate efficiently on their own) and the loss of some access roads. A particular cause for regret is the fact that hybrid vineyards are increasing while the planting of 'noble' vines is falling: hence the ageing of the vineyards and falling demand for viticultural planting material. Viticulture areas increased in 1990–95 by 5 per cent, but hybrid vineyards with low yields almost doubled, while high-yielding noble vineyards declined by a fifth (and in many cases completely cleared). Annual planting is less than 2th.ha (previously 7,000) and there is reduced demand for replanting material. The industry wants to see greater state support through subsidized loans for producers to establish or restore plantations on compact surfaces of at least one hectare. In Vrancea, which is a traditional wine-producing region, the period 1990–95 saw a net reduction of 1,300ha in pure-bred vines (with only 275ha replanted) while 960ha were planted with hybrid vines. Hence the region's capacity to produce quality seedlings at Costeşti and Odobeşti is threatened without state support. Vinification plants offer only low prices for grapes, so they run at a quarter capacity or less. There is a need for subsidized interest rates and rescheduled debts. The aim is to size vineyards in line with the domestic market and export potential; provide adequate finance; stop proliferation of hybrids; consolidate vinestocks in their traditional areas; and apply modern technology. Vinegrowers are to have a fifth share in Vinalcool companies through land ownership deeds and nominal privatization coupons, which will make it possible for vinegrowers to form 'wine-cellar cooperatives' and achieve a production of seven tonnes of wine grapes and ten tonnes of table grapes per hectare over a national area of vineyards of 275th.ha by 2010 (Cliza 1995).

In the case of livestock, falling numbers were first recorded in 1987 when the cattle herd began to decline (also poultry, marginally) while livestock overall (measured by conventional units) showed a decline in 1988, continuing (sharply) through both 1989 and 1990. These early declines were the result of a poor fodder supply combined with pressure to export meat; they certainly did not reflect an increase in peasant consumption. However, despite a succession of dry years, the fodder situation is now improving in the peasant sector, as individual farmers are gathering fodder from less accessible areas previously marginalized by the cooperatives because of high labour costs. The number of pigs increased in 1990, although there were falls in the cases of both cattle and sheep. Expansion of the cattle herds will be achieved only slowly because many of the animals inherited from the cooperative farms are of poor quality and are unsuitable for breeding – a situation which arises from poor management in the past and unsuitable buildings. An intelligence report in 1995 revealed a serious decline in national patrimony in the animal breeding sector. Out of approximately 250 animal and poultry breeding farms that existed in 1990, only 20 are now working efficiently, while most are at 15–40 per cent of production capacity, and some have been liquidated. Only nine of the 49 best pig breeding and fattening units have survived and of the 85 most profitable poultry farms, 70 were totally dismantled after 1989. Cattle and sheep breeding centres were reported close to extinction in several cases. The Ciulniţa farm in the Baragan is typical. It was fattening 6,000 cattle in 1992, but only 100 in 1996, plus 200 milk cows and 100 young cattle. Thirty-six of the 40 sheds are empty because fodder prices are equivalent to a cost of 4,869 lei per kilo of meat which can sell at only 2,200 lei because of the price controls then in force. Additional information has revealed that 43 state poultry farms encountered great difficulty in the second half of 1996, because of the rise in the price of feed, cereals (especially barley) and protein supplements. Twelve units were bankrupt by September and were in a state of conservation. Only a third of total capacity (0.30m.t chicken and 3 billion eggs) was in use, as the number of egg-laying hens dropped by a quarter in two months. While prevailing prices were 450 lei/kg for wheat and 500 lei/kg for barley, poultry farms could only break even at a price level of 375 lei/kg, because their output prices were controlled. Short-term support over fodder has been necessary to stave off complete collapse, but in the longer term there must be either price liberalization or higher subsidies (perhaps combined with tax concessions in respect of imported fodder). The new government elected in November 1996 has opted for the former, following World Bank advice that subvention and price maintenance regimes benefit well-to-do consumers and do little to help producers. Price control will end on pigs and pork, poultry and poultry meat, and milk, bread and chemical fertilizers.

THE DRIVE FOR INCREASED EFFICIENCY

Of course, Romanian agriculture is exposed to the uncertainties of the weather, but because of inefficiency resulting from a poor infrastructure (Surd 1994) it is not possible to gain maximum benefit from good conditions or to adequately mitigate adverse situations. As already noted, 1995 was almost a record year for cereals, thanks to good conditions for sowing in both autumn 1994 and spring 1995. But the ministry calculated that the industry could exploit only two-thirds of the potential arising from these favourable circumstances. There were then problems with autumn ploughing in 1995, with freezing temperatures in November and the longest period of snow cover for half a century was experienced: 3.3m.ha could not be ploughed until after the winter. Meanwhile, the 1997 harvest will be adversely affected by a very thin snow cover in the southeast, so that cereals could not be fertilized with tractors because the tyres would damage the crops (aviation methods were not financially viable). Crops will lack nitrogen and phosphorous and yields will be reduced. In these situations, a larger stock of machines would enable critical operations to be fitted more easily into the windows of opportunity.

Underpinning the agricultural situation is a lack of capital investment arising from modest government credits combined with the high cost of bank loans and slender farm profits. Farmers lack financial reserves and so any price increases are immediately disruptive. The 1995 harvest was upset by the rising price of diesel oil, and likewise winter wheat sowing, which had a negative impact on the 1996 harvest, despite a World Bank US$150 billion credit for Romanian private farmers in that year. The state makes some credit available to help farmers with their initial outlays on ploughing, seeds and fertilizer, but difficulties at the National Bank have led to delays and some of the credit provision is never delivered: in the case of the autumn ploughing in 1995, only 324 of the 800 billion lei allocated was actually provided. This meant that farmers cut down on fertilizer dressings, yet low fertilizer application in 1995 kept the average yield for sunflowers to 1,400kg/ha although some farms have potential for 10–12th.kg. Delayed credits in autumn again upset fertilizer operations. Government support to food processors has also encountered delays which again have an impact on peasant farmers who cannot receive immediate payment for deliveries to fodder factories and animal breeding farms (Tabara 1996). There is some relief from high commercial interest rates – as in 1996, when the National Bank was able to advance 60 per cent subsidies on the interest incurred through loans taken out to cover crop production and storage. Some capital is occasionally forthcoming from the State Ownership Fund (SOF) to support 'strategic units' such as the Craiova greenhouse complex which could not keep pace with rising power charges by the local Işalnita power station (100 lei to 30,000 in five years). When young plants were killed off for lack of heat and the enterprise collapsed in 1994, the SOF helped with the installation of boilers to supply hot water more economically and the new business hoped to regain lost markets with a simplified programme producing cucumbers (previously tomatoes, beans and peppers were also produced). The business is now back in profit with a 30th.t annual production capacity and exports to Austria, Germany and Switzerland. However, this is an isolated case and shows what is possible when capital is more freely available.

Contract farming offers a way forward, since peasants look to efficient acquisition schemes with realistic prices and prompt payment. Improved contract prices offered by the National Tobacco Corporation for 1996 proved to be more advantageous for farmers. However, the concept has been most widely applied to cereal growing by NAAP, which deals with the acquisition, stockpiling and marketing of cereals and other products. The government-authorized chemical fertilizer allowances (24–120kg/ha active substance depending on the crop) are available to all producers who contract more than 40 per cent of their production to economic operators authorized by the state (although the system is a difficult one for small farmers to use) and minimum fertilization was built into NAAP contracts for cereals, with respect to 60kg/ha of nitrogen and phosphorous (optimum dressings could be as high as 120–130kg of nitrogen alone, but farmers lack the capital to contemplate intensifying at this level). However, under contract the grower is committed to sell at the NAAP price and in 1996 the average acquisition price was 340 lei/kg for wheat (it actually varied between 220 and 380 lei/kg according to zonal conditions) while the free market price reached 600 lei/kg. Allowing 65 lei/kg for fertilizer and seed and another 100 lei for subsidized interest charges, there is still a difference of 100 lei. On the other hand, farmers who do not take out contracts cannot be sure that the authorized operators will buy their crop, which was a problem with the record cereal harvest of 1995 when low market prices forced peasants to store cereals in their homes in the hope that prices would rise. Because of this experience, the wheat situation in 1996 was difficult. The area sown went down from 2.50 to 1.78m.ha (-28.8 per cent) and a reduced yield of 36.2 per cent (2,961 to 1,888kg/ha) brought the harvest down from 7.41 to 3.30m.t (-55.5 per cent) which is not enough to provide for the bread needed on the home market. The reduced production was greatest on private farms: down from 5.69m.t in 1995 to 2.33m.t in 1996 (-59.1 per cent) The yield was down from 2,831kg/ha to 1,687 (-40.4 per cent) and the area sown from 2.01 to 1.41m.ha (-29.9 per cent). The failure was aggravated by a lack of funding for fertilizer and seed and some bad winter weather. Cereals are of course also crucial for livestock: more barley is needed, partly for brewing and partly for cattle feed. The credits mechanism is bureaucratic and most peasants never get financial help despite laws being passed to help them. The new government wants credit to be more readily available through the banking system and it is to create a special regime for credit cooperatives, as distinct from consumption cooperatives, to strengthen their role in rural areas. It will also abolish agriculture taxes until 2000, and make more help available for ploughing campaigns, for which EU PHARE and other external support schemes will also be available to expedite agricultural adjustment.

Mechanization

Mechanization is very poorly developed, especially in the hill country, with no more than an estimated 37,000 tractors available for mountain farmers. Lack of adequate capacity extends the harvesting period: because of the shortage of harvesters, the 1995 harvesting period for sunflowers was 40 days instead of the optimum of 20 and yields were significantly affected. The total stock is not increasing sufficiently and the pace of modernizing machinery (replacing old tractors) is too slow – only 10,000 in 1995 instead of 20,000. Better maintenance standards are needed by the Agromecs (now undergoing privatization) which are the successors of the machine-tractor stations of the communist period. However, the Agromecs have their own problems of profitability in a situation where mechanized agricultural work is running at only 60-70 per cent of the 1989 level. More than 600 separate Agromecs maintain 4,000 mechanization stations occupying 5th.ha of non-agricultural land, but these enterprises are not allowed to lease land and farm on their own account. Although privatization is going ahead, gross overvaluation of their assets makes for slow progress because share costs are out of line with potential profits; the people keen to invest their vouchers in Agromecs are mainly employees, who are eager to keep their jobs.

However, progress is being made and more machinery is being deployed on private farms when the owners have a close vested interest in good maintenance standards. While the number of tractors in service increased from 160,499 in 1994 to 169,587 in 1995 (5.7 per cent), the stock owned by private farmers increased from 60,417 to 78,175 (29.4 per cent) the therefore the share falling to private farms increased from 37.6 to 46.1 per cent. The total stock of ploughs increased by 7.3 per cent to 106,486 while those on private farms went up by 35.8 per cent to 53,077 (and the share of the total stock from 39.4 to 49.8 per cent). The number of harvesters declined from 42,571 to 36,519 (−14.2 per cent) but the stock on private farms increased from 2,750 to 6,321 (+129.9 per cent) and the share falling to private farms increased from 6.5 to 17.3 per cent. The EU PHARE programme is facilitating the assembly of Western tractors at the Braşov Tractorul plant and there are also a number of trading companies importing foreign machinery. Loans from the United States are helping Romanian farmers obtain machines to work 150th.ha of agricultural land and irrigation systems with reduced water consumption of 40–60 per cent. American suppliers will also set up a distribution network for agricultural equipment spare parts and arrange training courses, with a period of grace of 18 months before the first repayments are due.

The German firm Claas is prominent in Romania through importers in Constanţa (Agroservice) and Timişoara (Agrocomert), while New Holland of the Fiat Group is producing machines in Romania (mainly combines) through a joint venture with the Bucharest manufacturer Semănătoarea. Thanks to a modernization and diversification programme financed by the Romanian State Ownership Fund, this firm is producing its own C110 harvester (incorporating Iveco engines, belts and other components) and also motorized cultivators and hay harvesters for the domestic market – but the workforce has been halved to 3,000 in the process (mostly through natural attrition) (Ciontu 1996).

Romania

Furthermore, several heavy engineering enterprises scattered around the country are diversifying their activities to cater for mountain farmers: Mecanica Ceahlău of Piatra Neamţ, Hart of Miercurea Ciuc, Medro of Drobeta-Turnu Severin, Multim of Timişoara and Tehnic of Oradea. Legmaş of Năvodari is becoming one of the main Romanian producers of small agricultural tractors following a successful restructuring exercise, and production is working up from 500 ecological tractors per annum. The design incorporates Fiat engines and a fibreglass body. The machines are suitable for use in orchards, vineyards and vegetable gardens.

Markets

Prices have gone up with inflation despite government controls on many items until 1997 (Table 8.7). Potatoes went up from 8.6 lei/kg in 1990 to 277.8 lei/kg in 1994, a 32.3-fold increase, while pork went up from 66.2 to 3,639.1 lei/kg (a 55-fold increase) and the cost of a single egg from 2.6 to 135.8 lei (a 52.2-fold increase). However, the domestic market is not too buoyant and farmers have found that inputs have risen more quickly than product prices (Fulea 1993; Gavrilescu 1994). More than double the quantity of produce is needed today for a tractor compared with 1989. There is also the problem of price variations between markets: official marketing statistics show prices for staple commodities ranging up to 30 per cent above and below the average for 41 administrative centres. There is much variation over time and only 11 towns had prices consistently above or below the average for all five months covered by the analysis: the towns, with the average percentage deviations, were Alexandria −13.7, Bacău −6.5, Cluj-Napoca +11.5, Constanţa +6.7, Deva +14.7, Iaşi −6.7, Miercurea Ciuc +6.0, Râmnicu Vâlcea −8.7, Sfântu Gheorghe +8.8, Vaşlui −7.4 and Zalău +6.7. However, most towns in Oltenia and Moldavia had prices below the average while most in Transylvania were above.

Hence it is necessary to increase efficiency of production and marketing so as to boost returns to the farmer, to the point where investment is worthwhile, and provide steadier prices for the consumer (Iordache et al. 1995). The quality of domestic markets is being improved. A big step forward will be the opening of Bucharest Wholesale Market in the southern part of the city. At present producers have to sell under non-hygienic conditions and under the pressure of

Table 8.7 Romania: market prices for agricultural produce in county centres

Month	A	B		C	D	E	F	G	H	I	J	K	L	M
6/93	3.12	73.9	Satu Mare	125.5	17	9	8	4	1	4	0	2	8	5
9/93	4.83	82.0	Slatina	130.2	18	15	6	2	1	3	3	1	7	5
12/93	8.82	80.0	Alexandria	111.7	19	17	3	2	0	5	3	2	7	6
3/94	12.27	80.4	Sf.Gheorghe	119.0	17	13	7	4	1	4	4	0	7	4
6/94	9.18	80.5	Sf.Gheorghe	115.0	16	17	7	1	1	7	1	2	6	4

Notes:

A Average price of a basket of 10 commodities appropriate for the season (th.lei).
B Centre with the lowest price shown as a percentage of the average.
C Centre with the highest price shown as a percentage of the average.
D Number of centres with prices within 5 per cent of the average.
E Additional centres within 10 per cent of the average.
F Additional centres within 15 per cent of the average.
G Additional centres within more than 15 per cent of the average.
H Number of cities with above-average prices: Bucharest (1).
I Number of cities with above-average prices in Muntenia and Dobrogea (11: Alexandria, Braila, Buzău, Calărași, Constanța, iurgiu, Pitești, Ploiești, Slobozia, Târgoviște and Tulcea).
J Number of cities with above-average prices in Oltenia (5: Craiova, Drobeta–Turnu Severin, Râmnicu Vâlcea, Slatina and Târgu Jiu).
K Number of cities with above-average prices in Moldavia (8: Bacău, Botoșani, Focșani, Galați, Iași, Piatra Neamț, Suceava and Vaslui).
L Number of cities with above-average prices in Transylvania (9: Alba Iulia, Bistrița, Brașov, Cluj-Napoca, Deva, Miercurea Ciuc, Târgu Mureș, Sfântu Gheorghe and Sibiu).
M Number of cities with above-average prices in Banat-Crișana-Maramureș (7: Arad, Baia Mare, Oradea, Reșița, Satu Mare, Timișoară and Zalău).

Source: Comisia Națională pentru Statistică, *Buletin Statistic de Prețuri* (Bucharest), Issues 32, 35, 38, 41 and 44.

speculators and middlemen. The aim is to set up a modern distribution system for fruit, vegetables and flowers, bringing together producers, wholesale traders and service providers on the same site. A unitary system will achieve steady supply throughout the year. The market will support collection centres in the surrounding counties: Brezoaiele (Dâmbovița); Ciolpani (Ilfov); Cuza Vodă (Călărași); Giurgiu (Giurgiu); Izvoarele, Alexandria (Teleorman); Mihaiești (Argeș); Movilița (Ialomița); and Vidra (Ilfov). The scheme will include a market proper and agrofood retail markets. The project arises from an association of producers and includes sorting and packaging according to European standards.

Processing

The need to improve food processing involves both farm and factory efficiency so that Romanian products can be competitive against imports and, it is hoped, generate exports in some fields. The milling and baking industry has made progress through some cases of privatization by Employee-Management Buyout after 1989, prior to the mass privatization of 1995. There is increased productivity and lower energy consumption, thanks in part to some new equipment (from Buchler of Switzerland and Pavan of Italy) installed at Bacău, Cluj and Craiova to replace Italian pasta machines of late 1960s vintage (subsequently built in Romania under licence in the 1980s). Breweries are making good progress in modernization. Bere Ciuc of Miercurea Ciuc has put into operation the most up-to-date beer bottling line in Romania (at a cost of DM4 million) through the company's own efforts, and plans to export its product to Moldova. Meanwhile, foreign companies are investing, for example, Tuborg, which has a brewery under construction in Pantelimon near Bucharest with an annual capacity of 500 th.hl, with the same modern production system used by the company in Denmark. Modern bottling lines are being installed in the wine industry, although some production will have to be reorientated towards other drinks and liquors, given the increased emphasis on bulk wine exports (in any case Vinalcool does not have the funds to acquire large quantities of grapes). Finally there are some new projects which demonstrate interesting linkages between fodder factories, flourmills, livestock units and slaughterhouses. In collaboration with Italian companies, Nutrimur (the former state farm of Iernut in Mureș county) has opened a factory for *zooferts* (basic components of concentrated fodder) and a white-flour factory, while building up a pig farm (100,000 head) and a slaughterhouse. By completing work on a fodder factory and a modern slaughterhouse, Avicola Buzău (producer of poultry meat) has cut production costs and entered the export market (in addition to supplies to Bucharest, Buzău, Craiova, Galaţi and Ploieşti). The process started with technological redevelopment of the hen farm using Belgian equipment – automation and computerization were applied to feeding, watering and heating.

The sugar industry has been a problem since 1989, and low factory prices have discouraged farmers from growing sugar beet. The collapse of sugar-beet growing followed the decision to set an acquisition price of 4 lei/kg in 1991 (on top of the producer's obligation to cart beets to the factory). The peasants stopped signing contracts and the area under sugar beet, which had already fallen from 240.3th.ha in 1989 to 195.9th.ha in 1991, declined further to 173.4th.ha in 1992 and 140.6th.ha in 1995. This boosted imports and the area fell in 1994 to 94th.ha. The sugar factories then had to process raw imported sugar, but this could not prevent a deficit on the home market which resulted in sugar imports at competitive prices, sustained in part by subventions in the countries of origin. Meanwhile, sugar content has fallen because of lack of use of fertilizers and insecticides as well as natural calamities: 27.3t/ha in 1989 but 17.3t/ha in 1995. Factories found themselves in an impossible situation, with only a third of capacity being used (partly through supplies of raw sugar at prices higher than those necessary to secure domestically grown sugar beet), yet needing to find resources for modernization after years of neglect after 1989. A French–Romanian programme was launched in 1991 to improve the quality of both sugar-beet cultivation and industrialization at the Năvodari, Roman, Tăndărei and Urziceni factories in 1991 (with Bod, Buzău, Luduş, Târgu Mureş, Oradea and Timişoara in 1992). The French company supplied seeds, equipment and technical assistance. However, the scheme collapsed because of inadequate financing of the sugar factories: their credits were stopped when they were unable to meet the costs of raw sugar imports (a situation aggravated by unfavourable exchange rates and customs taxes) although their efficiency level was above the average for the industry. A special economic–financial supervision was placed over 13 sugar factories in 1996. Thus the area of sugar beet declined 41.5 per cent between 1989 and 1995, but because the net yield fell from 23.6 to 13.9t/ha while the sugar content increased only marginally from 13.6 to 13.9 per cent, the sugar yield fell from 506,600 to 210,400t (down 58.5 per cent). Romania's sugar quota is 450-500th.t which under normal yield conditions should require an area of 150th.ha. However, new regimes are being introduced and the Nectar sugar factory at Paşcani is stimulating growers with 50kg of sugar per tonne of beet delivered and free seed as well. The area is now increasing in Bacău, Botoşani, Neamţ and Suceava counties, and also in Iaşi (Anon 1997b).

Romania also has the capacity to be self-sufficient in dairy produce, but the Association of Private Producers of Milk and Dairy Products sees a problem in state control over acquisition prices for milk and retail prices for produce which has resulted in falling output by state-owned processors. Private-sector involvement is contingent on state invention on the EU model which would involve price liberalization. Dairy equipment produced by Tehnofrig of Cluj has supplied about 20 factories with capacity for 2-3 thousand litres per day as new milk-processing centres have been opened in various parts of the country. Although an efficient collection and processing system throughout the mountain region is still a long way off, this development opens the way for the marketing of local cheeses (including the use of local trade marks). Similar progress is needed with respect to other animal products as well as fruit and vegetables. Mureş Dairy Industry in Târgu Mureş has been upgraded with US$2 million EBRD credit; new facilities include: an ice-cream factory in Reghin; ice-cream vehicles and stands; and packaging machines for butter, powdered milk and fluid products (ending glass packaging and increasing the guarantee period).

Exports

There is a need to improve export performance, which has been outstanding in the past but which, as already noted, has been disappointing since 1989 because of lack of competitiveness and a system of export licences designed to protect the home market and discourage speculators from buying large quantities of wheat from farmers at low prices, when it would be prudent for farmers to store their crop. However, the much improved cereal harvests of 1994 and 1995 generated exports of 2m.t of wheat and 1m.t of maize. This revealed storage difficulties at Constanţa which have resulted in a new 100th.t capacity warehouse (18th.t daily) compared with current capacity of 33th.t (6th.t daily). Moreover, the new facility will be in the free zone with access for 33 thousand deadweight ships compared with 10 thousand deadweight ships for the current facility. There is also scope for growth in the transit business, with 442th.t cereals coming from Hungary and Ukraine in 1995. A two-year EU-supported programme for agriculture in 1996–97 will provide a forecasting system for crops; will deal with constraints inhibiting agricultural exports (quality standards including sanitary and veterinary conditions); will have better information and consultancy services for private farmers; and will provide direct funding and democratically formed agricultural and agroindustrial organizations. According to the EU and the US Department of Agriculture there are now good prospects for agricultural exports over the next ten years. By 2005, Romania should be exporting 2.5–2.8m.t of wheat and 2–2.7m.t of maize annually, and also quantities of sunflower seed. Hungary and Bulgaria should also be in surplus. Livestock are being exported for slaughter in the Middle East, and there is trade in breeding stock with Western Europe. Wine exports are depressed, at only 40 per cent the average for the 1980s, but with potential for growth. Export controls will now be withdrawn (although a temporary tax on wheat exports can be applied until the 1997 harvest). Some vegetable growers are doing well: the Galaţi greenhouse enterprise Seromgal sells a wide variety of vegetables through their own chain of 20 shops (selling vegetables, fruit and canned goods) and exports to Austria, the Czech Republic and Moldova. It is also reported that a German delegation from Deggendorf in Bavaria is interested in financing the growing of thousands of hectares of hemp in the Sânnicolaul Mare area of Banat, which is considered to have optimum climate and soil conditions. Local processing, using appropriate technology, will generate parts for BMW and Audi cars and the whole investment could create 200–300 new jobs in an area where several businesses have been lost through bankruptcy.

Professionalism in Farming

Professional farmers are needed with the business skills and financial resources to cope with the 'grain mafia', which picked up wheat cheaply in 1995 by intimidating farmers into selling quickly and cheaply (Tabară 1996). Yet most Romanian farmers have experienced 'intense pauperization' for lack of logistic and information assistance, while a prosperous group of middlemen have emerged. Agriculture is potentially a dynamic sector, yet young people are reluctant to take up farming and there are smaller numbers passing through the agricultural schools. Farming standards are often low and many new farmers ignore elementary environmental protection norms, applying fertilizer incorrectly, reducing biodiversity, and using inappropriate methods of woodland clearance. There is already soil impoverishment after the intensive farming of the communist period and chaos of transition. But 769th.ha of land has been degraded since 1989 and turned to pasture, while orchards have decreased by 42,875ha and the expansion of vineyards has involved only hybrid vines (noble vines have decreased). However, the government is keen to encourage progressive farmers and intends to create a land market and privatize commercial companies. There will be a transfer of ownership rights on the former state farms to private individuals who will be able to obtain the land to which they are entitled. In this way the restitution process will be completed. Moreover, shares in at least 25 large pig and poultry farms will be sold by tender at market price and some 900 service companies will be privatized or liquidated; this list includes many of the companies into which the massive NAAP concern was subdivided (initially into county-based *Comcereal* distribution companies). There is a desire to develop a middle class in the villages by encouraging enterprising farmers as well as the owners of small and medium-sized enterprises geared to agricultural services and the food industry.

There is considerable external help. Experts from Aveyron in France have established collaboration with Romanian farmers in Tulcea, where a pilot farm has been established (at Baia) with five French families to provide training. Another demonstration farm was set up at Cincșor in 1995: a mixed farm of 50ha producing vegetables, fodder and so on. It was provided by PHARE, which also maintains units in Bulgaria and Hungary with the help of Dutch organizations. The Netherlands have provided US$1.5 million to set up and equip associations of primary producers in the Bucharest area: Descalu, Dobroiești, Domnești, Nuci, Periș and Vidra, with Gruiu in prospect. Shareholding farmers will be responsible for management which will invest a tenth of the profit reinvested and distribute the rest. The associations at Descalu, Domnești, Peris and Nuci will concentrate on milk (vegetables, too, at

Nuci) and will acquire refrigerated tanks. Vidra will deal in vegetables and Dobroieşti in fodder. The project was meant to run from 1993 to 1995, but could continue for two more years, given good results. Cooperation in milk processing could extend nationwide on the basis of a single network, but for the moment the Dutch have also moved on to Iaşi county where further multifunctional cooperatives are being set up, with help for institutions supporting private agriculture.

Romanian agribusiness is attracting foreign direct investment: Canadian capital to the tune of 44.5 million Canadian dollars is being invested in Borcea Agro-Holdings which runs seven commercial companies (with state capital) in Călăraşi county. Such enterprise is the basis of more optimistic forecasts for Romanian agriculture, which points to significant growth by the end of the century, with increased cropping, a big growth of soya to provide protein for animal feed and turn around the livestock sector which is already showing recovery for cattle and pigs, although not for sheep and goats (Anon 1997a).

RURAL DIVERSIFICATION

Rural development is identified as a priority for Romania's integration into European structures, and agriculture lies at the base (Teodoroiu 1996). But with the completion of the restitution process and the development of a land market, it is likely that there will be a consolidation of farm businesses which could result in 20–40ha farms with capital-intensive production technologies. Larger farms could also emerge through kinship or neighbourhood groupings, or else outside capitalists might build up large *nomenklatura* farms through the purchase or renting of peasant plots. The Federation of Associated Privatized Farmers in Romania is looking to farms of 1,000–1,500ha for cereals (250–500ha in hills), 200–250ha for fruit, 100–200ha for viticulture and 50–100ha for vegetables. But it also sees a role for family farms of 30ha, although such farms would be ten times the size of the average individual farm today. Such a structure would therefore create a serious unemployment problem affecting some 2.5 million people within 5–10 years. Hence the need for the growth of non-agricultural business in rural areas to stabilize village communities (Cernescu 1996; Florian and Sârbu 1993). Much of the present farming population would therefore transfer to the secondary and tertiary sectors, as the younger members of peasant households are seeking to do at present. On this basis, the future lies in the further decline of the rural population and an acceleration of rural–urban migration. This would provide more 'gateway cities' to support regional development in Romania (Ianoş et al. 1992b) but would destroy rural communities and threaten local services. The political situation in the rural areas has been reviewed pessimistically because an early renaissance in grass-roots activity was neutralized by the emerging hierarchy of the National Salvation Front (now the Party of Social Democracy) (Kideckel 1992). But the establishment of a new government based on the philosophy of the National Peasant Christian Democrat Party signals a significant change of direction. Romanian concepts of modernity certainly give the village a central role (Rain 1996) and there is a widespread desire to reduce migration and achieve greater demographic equilibrium (Fulea 1996). Non-agricultural work, especially in workplaces outside the village, is crucial (Antal and Kovacs 1996), especially to mobilize the young people who are adaptable but not, so far, committed to work hard in agriculture (Pascaru 1996). Non-agricultural work in the shape of rural tourism would be useful for bringing women into decision-making and management (Fulea and Sima 1996).

However, the situation in the Carpathians is distinct. While small-scale low-intensity stock-rearing in the Romanian Carpathians is traditional, farmers are carefully considering their options in the light of indifferent marketing conditions and food-processing capacities (Iacob 1991; Iosif 1992). Capital investment is not attractive, apart from the purchase of small items of equipment such as circular saws and milling machines powered by electricity. The peasant requires some cash commodities to buy essential items, but there is at the same time a powerful logic in using the farm to support the family (or extended family). Given the very low level of social security guaranteed by the state, this view could be broadened into a wider political philosophy of ambivalence towards its capitalist market economy, preferring the security of small farms which guarantee subsistence and an outlet for most of the family labour. Hence, Carpathian farmers tend to restrict their dealings with the market primarily to the sale of livestock, for which a state-operated marketing system (sometimes stimulated by competition by local food processors) is relatively dependable, and to use part of their land as a means of subsistence. However, while the traditional mixed farm of the Carpathians is certainly capable of offering modest rewards, it does not offer an attractive prospect to school leavers, who show a strong preference for work in industry and the tertiary sector (especially government service in one form or another). The mountain farms could be modernized to achieve greater efficiency for both meat and dairy produce. A big improvement in distribution is needed, including better links with the food processors and an improved technical base for an ecologically sustainable agriculture (Parpală 1993a). Yet there is an independently-minded peasantry in the mountains which quickly demonstrated its opposition to the communist collectives. The old cooperative farm buildings now lie abandoned, with some cases of imaginative demolition to salvage building materials for new construction. In 1991, at Suciu de Sus in the northern county of Maramureş, demolition occurred so that the materials could be used to build a monastery nearby. There can be no doubt about the enthusiasm of many peasants experiencing the euphoria of retrieving their land.

In such regions there is tacit support for the 'Bavarian approach' of family farming linked with pluriactivity (Turnock 1995), for, even though occupational specialization may seem the ultimate ideal, it is clear that there are economic and cultural reasons why this may not be attainable in the short term. In the Carpathians, the small farm base is socially fundamental, so diversification may offer a way forward in Romania and in other mountain regions of post-communist Eastern Europe (Mesei 1996). Yet a rural social policy is needed to safeguard the infrastructure: improve housing standards, extend electricity supplies and extend motor vehicle access to the small villages. A better agricultural advisory service is needed and also measures to encourage small businesses in rural areas. At a time when village communities are becoming less cohesive as a result of tensions between the 'winners' and 'losers' of the transition years, it is important that there should be encouragement for informal cooperation and for the emulation of farming families which have successfully diversified (Vinzce 1995).

Large-scale industry (notably mining) is prominent in some rural areas (Talangă 1995) but it is unevenly distributed. The indigenous development of local industries and handicrafts has been significant where there are few capital demands – for example, the refurbishment of small water-powered mills, which can be undertaken by local craftsmen. In these respects there is a degree of continuity arising through the flexibility shown by some local authorities prior to the revolution. Those who continued to operate small workshops in the communist period often found penal levels of taxation insupportable, although it must be conceded that the local authorities in some areas adopted a more supportive attitude (Turnock 1992). However, the tradition remains and there is a now spontaneous revival of many ancillary activities (Muică and Turnock 1993). The indigenous development of local industries and handicrafts is particularly significant where there are few capital demands. Craftsmen fairs are now taking place to support traditional skills, for example, in 1996 in Târgovişte, where there were sections for fabrics and clothing, ceramics, wood, painted eggs, musical instruments, furs, wickerwork, naive painting and icons. Diversification has also been suggested through small woodcutting enterprises (Micu 1992), appropriate in the context of both the state-owned forests and the small unit of woodland units returned to former owners. Here it is significant that Apuseni inhabitants have been given back rights predating the Second World War that were annulled by the communists. Using identity cards issued by Romsilva, people deriving income from wood processing will receive 10cu.m of wood per person (a minimum of 15cu.m per family). They will also be exempt from tax when the wood products are sold; and will qualify for a 50 per cent reduction on the railway when transporting products. In addition, newly-weds may buy 25cu.m of timber for construction at half the normal price. Finally, there might also be more foreign investment in rural industry, perhaps through light engineering linked with the semi-derelict machine–tractor stations.

These avenues are being explored by the Romanian Agriculture Ministry's 'Commission for Mountainous Regions', set up in 1990 (and restructured two years later as the National Agency for Mountainous Regions) to disseminate the principles of 'mountainology' through education and publicity (Figure 8.1) (Turnock 1993a). This follows the thinking of Rey (1979, 1985), outlined during the communist era as an alternative to the more uncompromising consolidation envisaged under the *sistematizare* policy being adopted at the time (Turnock 1991a). The advocacy of more informal 'micro-cooperatives' in areas of dispersed mountain settlement, such as Vrancea (Dobrovici 1972), was ignored at the time, but the Agency is now producing some imaginative rural plans for specific areas. The Agency's efforts are being

Source: Turnock, 1993a.

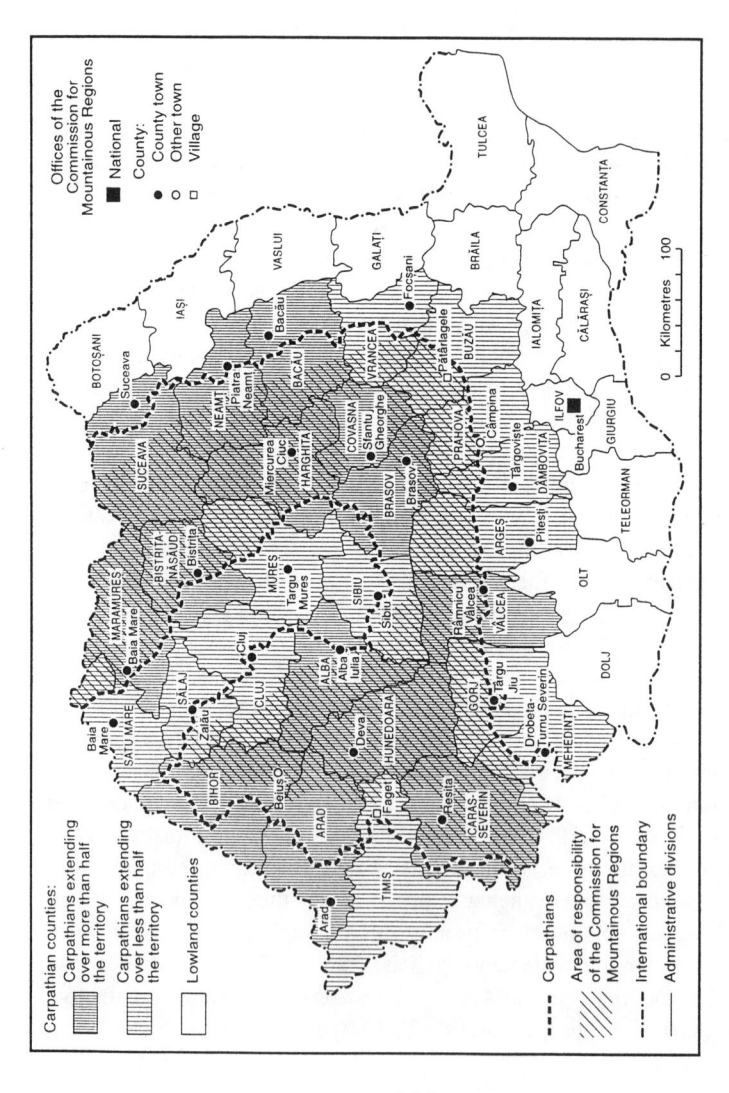

Figure 8.1 Romania: the Carpathians and Agency/Commission for Mountainous Regions

complemented by the planning profession in Bucharest which is looking at physical planning for rural areas underpinned by agricultural development, expansion of the market system, improved land management (including measures to control erosion) and pluriactivity. Although resources are still very limited, the elements of a strategy are being discussed and agricultural experts continue to advocate support for less-favoured areas, including mountain districts (Otiman 1994, p.256). There are also some links with international projects concerned with rural development and sustainability (Derounian 1995).

The Agency's area of responsibility is deemed to cover 773 communes in 27 counties and parts of some additional communes where individual villages satisfy the criteria: high altitude (over 300–350 metres) with slopes generally in excess of 15 per cent and poor accessibility; in addition, land should be used overwhelmingly for pastures, hayfields and forest (with at least 70 per cent of the value of agricultural production consisting of animals, predominantly cattle and sheep). First and foremost, the Agency is trying to reverse the downward spiral of agricultural activity, brought about by low prices which do not stimulate higher inputs. It is also necessary to improve agricultural practices by fertilizing pastures to correct soil acidity, by planting fruit trees and by improved breeding based on the Pinzgau breed. There is also an emphasis on machinery suitable for small mountain farms at local agricultural shows: for example, various tractors and accessories in the 18–45 horsepower range and very small machines for *motorcultoare* (8-12 horsepower) are also available for very small hill farms (Parpală 1992a, 1992b).

The Agency is also concerned with the improvement of rural services, including the extension of electricity supplies. It recognizes all too clearly that a tremendous effort in education will be necessary to develop both awareness and skills among the mass of the peasantry. There is a Mountainology Institute at Cristian near Sibiu with plans for research centres in several small towns (Abrud, Câmpulung Moldovenesc and Gurahonț) and also in the villages of Runcu, Şarul Dornei and Stănești. In addition to provision in agronomic institutes and five university centres (Bucharest, Cluj, Craiova, Iași and Timișoara) there is a Faculty of Mountainology in the town of Vălenii de Munte and classes in some schools (for example, Beiuș in Bihor), and training in mountainology, especially agriculture and agrotourism, will be available in centres in each of the 27 counties with which the Agency is concerned. Forty-seven schools provided facilities for 1992-93 and while these are usually to be found in the towns a number of communes are also involved: Beceni, Borca, Bozovici, Dorna Candrenilor, Gurghiu, Vidra and Voineşti. International cooperation is increasing. The Balkan countries (including Greece and Turkey) cooperate in a new organization, Balkanmontana, which is based at Cristian Mountainology Institute, and there are close links between the Agency and the equivalent organization in France, which has led to the setting up of an innovation centre at Vatra Dornei. The Euromontana organization extends governmental contacts to Austria (collaborating over the improvement of the Pinzgau herd), Germany, Italy and Switzerland. But *ad hoc* arrangements have also been encouraged, for example, the organization Opération Villages Roumains set up in Bruxelles in 1989 to support Romanian villages threatened under the *sistematizare* programme has created many useful contacts. A village in Switzerland (St. Legier) was paired with Morăreni in the Ruşii-Munţi commune of Mureş county in Transylvania and there is now an experiment under way (supported by the Agency) in technology transfer in order to intensify agriculture and improve incomes. Activity has extended into stock breeding, home industries with the marketing association Promorareni, a particularly interesting development.

In Valea Doftanei, the Agency is involved in a pilot project for integrated local development covering local industry (including food processing), improved fodder supply and educational and technical back-up. Several county plans have been founded on 'baseline' surveys and include proposals to revive traditional crafts, improve farm roads and encourage agricultural societies. In the Apuseni Mountains a regional programme is seeking to coordinate activity among the six counties involved. Unfortunately, the Agency's programmes are not yet adequately capitalized, but efforts are being made to improve communication with the farming community through the journal *Viaţa Muntilor*. The economic press has made much of the potential for farm-based community tourism (Ciangă 1991; Popescu 1994), capitalizing on the charm of Romanian villages (Stoica 1990). Various localities have been described (Istrate and Buhu 1990; Roată 1991) with particular attention to the Eastern Carpathians and several constituent areas (Talabă 1991). Model farm buildings have been designed and architectural studies have been made in several areas to see how modern buildings can harmonize with traditional styles. Farm accommodation is now being inspected and classified under the stimulus of simplified planning procedures and tax concessions to encourage rural tourism in the mountains as well as on the Black Sea coast and in the Danube Delta (Mitrache et al. 1996). Local associations are undertaking promotional work and stimulating community initiatives: at Plopis the local company Agromontana, which took over the assets of the former CAP, has diversified into tourism with a small boarding house and campsite at Baile Iaz. National organizations such as ANTREC (National Association of Rural Ecological and Cultural Tourism) are helping to lay down good practice. Supported by improved road access and electrification, tourism could make a big impact in mountain regions such as the Apuseni, where the traditional lifestyle has been undermined by poor services (linked with an extremely dispersed settlement pattern) and a shortage of raw materials to maintain local industries.

Uncoordinated tourism has created problems in mountain areas such as the Bucegi, where more effective controls are needed (Velcea et al. 1993). Without more careful regulation, a growth of rural tourism could undermine the resources on which it depends. Hence the importance of combining the growth of tourism with enhanced regimes of protection such as have been discussed by writers in sensitive areas such as the Apuseni Mountains (Abrudan et al. 1995) and the Cozia and Parâng Mountains in Vâlcea county (Ploaie 1995). With suitable safeguards, however, rural tourism could be a positive benefit in allowing for some further reduction in levels of farm intensification, especially in unstable hill country prone to landslides (Figure 8.2) (Muică and Turnock 1994; Muică and Zăvoianu 1996). Planners have advocated sustainable development and have outlined the implications in terms of a 'green' agriculture (Iosif 1993b), so a future conservation programme to reduce erosion could be tilted in favour of forestry and tourism, with cropping and stocking maintained at today's reduced levels of intensification (Kovacs 1991).

Some of the most serious problems arise in the lowlands, where more education is needed over the use of chemicals. Furthermore, irrigation systems have broken down and are in great need of improvement (Zotta 1993). The former systems of coordination have collapsed with the break-up of the cooperative farms. Water costs are too high for individual farmers to contemplate (but if canals run close to villages, as at Galicia Mare in Oltenia or Ştefan cel Mare in Bărăgan,

238　*Privatization in Rural Eastern Europe*

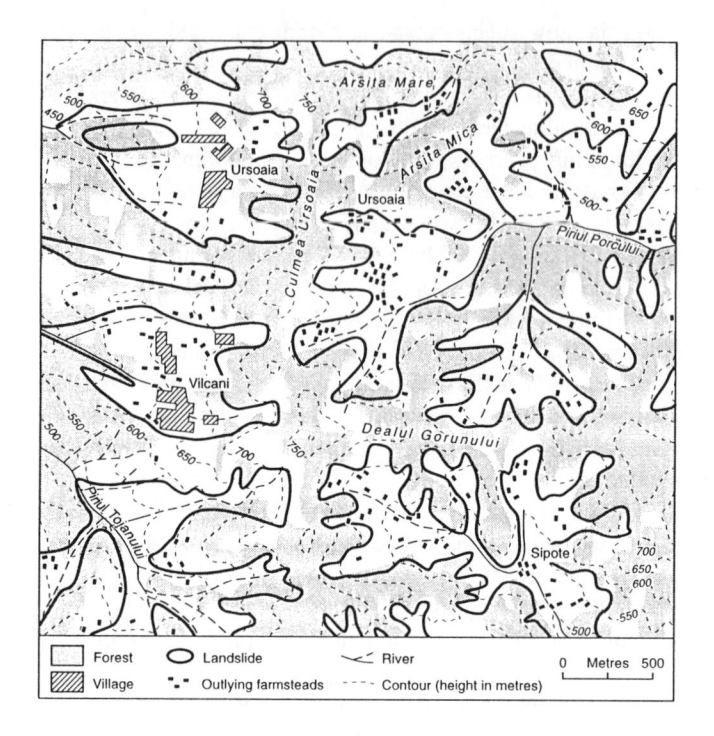

Source: Muică and Turnock 1994.

Figure 8.2　Romania: landslides in Vrancea

water can easily be abstracted illegally and produce good crops on the smallholdings). The shortcomings have been particularly unfortunate in view of the intense drought experienced on the plains in 1993, which meant disappointing results for summer crops (barley and wheat) and even greater problems for the autumn crops (maize, sunflowers and vegetables such as tomatoes). Erosion has occurred through forest cutting, causing serious problems on the Oltenian sands. By contrast, the emphasis on livestock in the hill and mountain country is ecologically desirable because it generates organic fertilizer and the cultivation of some leguminous plants for fodder (an efficient way of increasing soil fertility and controlling the spread of weed), which in turn allows a reduction in the use of pesticides). But while mountainous areas are suitable for pastoralism, there is a danger of overgrazing, which will result in the invasion of low-productive herbaceous associations. On deforested land there may be dwarf bushes which represent disclimax associations with less ecological value. Overgrazing and suppression of this vegetation can lead to erosion (especially where there is scree and rock outcrops) and once the soil is destroyed it takes a long time to recover because pedogenetic processes work much more slowly than in the lowlands. Thus, the removal of 'catina' scrub has reactivated erosion in some areas of hill country while a proliferation of cart tracks and paths for the droving of livestock can aggravate the problem. Simple but efficient methods of preventing erosion are being used (for example, the fencing of plots with scrub hedges can be very beneficial). Programmes of intervention are needed to cover both the short and long term in the context of the local ecosystems (Figure 8.3) (Constantinescu-Galicani 1996).

Local conditions vary and it is importance to apply the sociological research methods of Dimitrie Gusti to recognize the nature of the links between land and community which must be fundamental for any local development plan (Ghinoiu 1996). Yet, a fundamental issue is the proximity of small towns to act as centres around which non-agricultural activity can cluster. A contrast has been drawn between the two adjacent communes in Harghita where the population is overwhelmingly Hungarian. While the people in the lowland area of Sânmartin (with its twin communities of Csikszentmarton and Czekefalva) are heavily involved in non-agricultural activities and use associations to farm the land, the villagers of Kaszon (Plaieşii de Jos commune) work their own fragmented holdings (Nemenyi and Nemenyi 1995). However, even with intensive use of all available labour, such farms cannot support a household without ancillary activities, and where there are insufficient opportunities in local factories and services the possibility arises of creating new farm-based activities such as handicrafts or small manufacturing activities using electricity or water power (Henry 1994). Thus, while the existing market towns may expand on the strength of the labour resources available, such as in Negreşti (Surd and Nicoară 1990) and Târgu Lăpus (Pop and Maier 1990), the question arises as to the best form of support for remoter communities. In this context, certain aspects of the late President Ceauşescu's *sistematizare* may still be appropriate (Turnock 1991a, 1991b), for in addition to the proposed bulldozing

Source: Muică and Zavoianu 1996.

Figure 8.3 Romania: natural potential of the environment in the Pătârlagele area of the Buzău Subcarpathians

of outlying villages it was envisaged that 300–400 rural settlements would be promoted to urban status. The centres of districts comprising groups of cooperative and state farms would acquire functions in administration, services and local industry, including food processing. Little progress was made with the implementation of this programme and the urban network still remains deficient in many areas because there are some historic 'lands' which still lack an urban centre (Ianoş and Talangă 1994; Surd 1991). Indeed, the latest generation of county plans reflect these possibilities, with additional local centres (currently villages) proposed for Bihor county at Popeşti, Sâmbăta, Tinca and Vadu Crişului to strengthen the base of urban hierarchy (Figure 8.4). Of course, these new towns would be backed by the traditional rural settlement system rather than the greatly attenuated structure envisaged under communist planning.

Successful diversification will certainly require an improved network of local centres providing information and trade. Remoteness through distance from dynamic cities is being overcome by modern telecommunications and the Internet. Hence, there is the possibility that the emptying of the countryside could be avoided through more effective local development based on service and information networks rooted on small towns. Local centres could help to improve agriculture and foster closer contact between former state farms and the private restitution holdings which could, in some areas, intensify into fruit growing if appropriate marketing systems were in force. These centres could also coordinate tourist activity with cottages and farm accommodation in the outlying villages, especially if local roads were improved to ensure vehicle access, including public transport. These could support a range of small industries: food processing (possibility of turning out quality products from organic farming through an enlarged processing sector covering dairy products, meat products, preserves and brandy); textiles (with export potential if new equipment can achieve quality at a competitive price); furniture (again, with the need for modern equipment to provide a good finish). Romania has many rural settlements which have traditionally discharged central place functions in their role as district centres (the *plasă* system in force before 1945 and the communist *raion* thereafter). Many such villages provided headquarters for a Consiliul Unic Agroinduistrial de Stat şi Cooperatist (CUASC) in the later Ceauşescu period, and were earmarked for promotion to urban status under the *sistematizare* of the

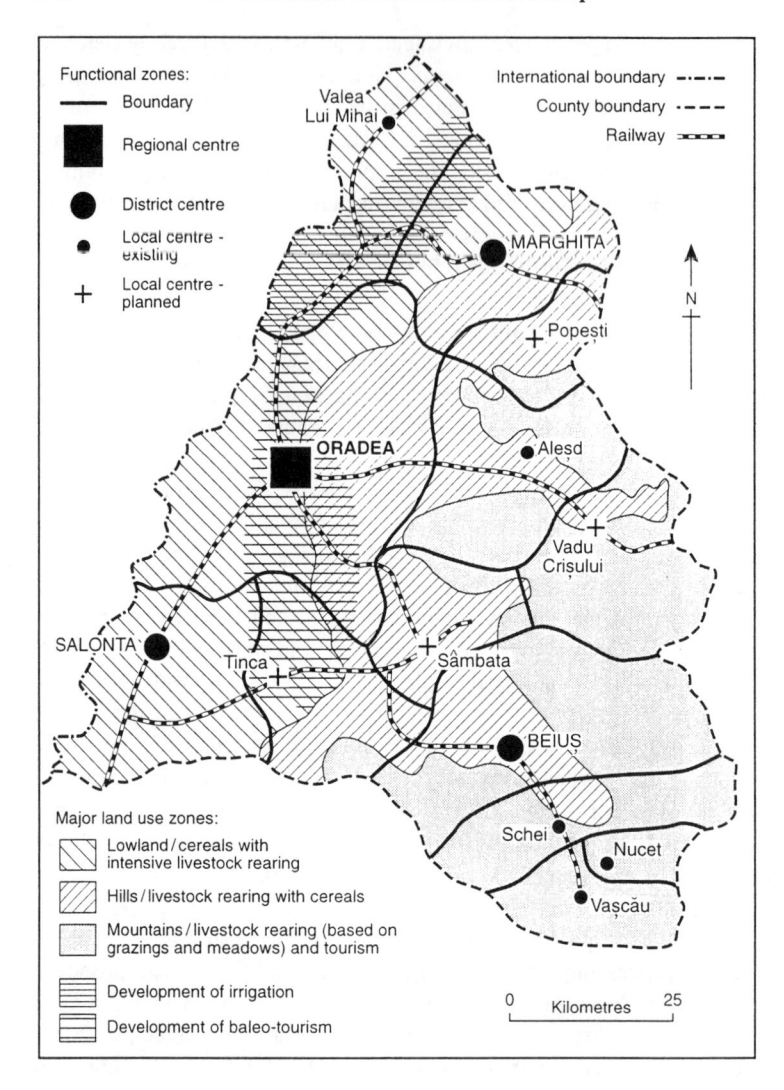

Figure 8.4 Romania: economic and settlement planning for Bihor county

Source: Urbanproiect, Bucharest.

1980s. Some were given experience of 'self-financing', using locally generated income to manage their medical and education services. These places are now following the national political trends towards a more entrepreneurial approach being spearheaded by the new Ciorbea government based on a centre-right parliamentary coalition and the Constantinescu presidency. EU PHARE programmes are again making an important contribution through a 'Fund for Development of the Carpathian Regions' which supports local democracy and civil society through greater citizen participation and cross-border activity. Cooperation is being encouraged between non-governmental organizations (NGOs), business communities and local government through progressive models of regional development. Romania is benefiting from this programme (along with Poland, Slovakia, Hungary and Ukraine) and projects are being supported in such mountain districts as Sighet, Satu Mare, Oradea, Miercurea Ciuc, Piatra Neamţ and Sfântu Gheorghe. There is a specific project for small towns and rural mountain areas (linked with rural mountain tourism in Baia Mare, Braşov and Suceava) encouraging efficiency and innovation.

CONCLUSION

Romanian agriculture has experienced massive structural change as a result of restitution which took place under the Iliescu presidency and will be followed by privatization of state farms under the Ciorbea government and the presidency of Emil Constantinescu. However, production has fallen and although the excellent cereal harvest of 1995 marks a revival in the arable sector, the downward trend in livestock still continues. Production and marketing must become more efficient if returns to farmers are to stimulate investment. Price controls imposed in the interest of consumers created some massive distortions and these have now been removed (although socialists still argue for selective subventions for the benefit of the disadvantaged sections of the community). Membership of the EU will require 20 billion lei for agriculture alone over 10 years (60 per cent in 5 years) because it must close the gap between its own and the European agricultural level; covering domestic needs and creating an export surplus in cereals, edible oil, vegetables, fruit, wine, meat and dairy produce. It is calculated that agriculture could generate 40–44 per cent of the capital needed from its own resources. But agriculture cannot modernize on its own and government will need to find a supportive package that will be stimulative without contributing to the inflation and currency depreciation of recent years. The growth of the food industry is of prime importance for the EU and it must be rehabilitated with a better system of collection and transport, as well as stimulative acquisition prices.

At the same time, it is inevitable that there will be a massive shake-out of labour from agriculture, and this raises the question of the future of the rural population. The present government is aware of the need to improve the quality of life in rural areas with more modern villages (paved streets and improved schooling) if people are going to be motivated to seek non-agricultural employment in the countryside. The way forward for large rural populations might best be seen in terms of further rural–urban migration, with a choice between the reinforcement of large cities and the stimulation of local centres provided by the existing small towns and a selection of the best-placed rural settlements. But at the same time, developing agricultural skills in the countryside and presenting agriculture as a worthwhile career for young people would seem to be an economic necessity which is difficult to reconcile with the ambivalence of prevailing policies. In view of the social importance of small farms there may be relevance in the 'Bavarian approach' through family farms linked with rewarding ancillary employment. A large rural population is a resource which entrepreneurially-minded local authorities may exploit, in anticipation of spontaneous counterurbanizing trends which may be reinforced in the years ahead. In this context, local culture could be a particular asset in the context of community tourism. There are mammoth problems in rebuilding rural enterprise with a modern infrastructure but there are signs that change is on the way.

REFERENCES

Abrudan, I.V. et al. (1995), 'Woodland management and conservation in the Bihor Mountains', in D. Turnock (ed.), *Rural Change in Romania*, Leicester: Leicester University Geography Department Occasional Paper 33, pp.67–70.

Anon (1996), 'An urgent need: sugar industry modernization', *Romanian Business Journal*, **3** (32-3), 13.

—— (1997a), 'Romanian agriculture looks to the year 2000', *Romanian Business Journal*, **4** (1-2), 12.

—— (1997b). 'The food industry in fierce competition with importers', *Romanian Business Journal*, **4** (7), 13.

Antal, A. and L. Kovacs (1996), 'Comparative study of mentality characteristics in a village from Szeklers' land and from the zone of Calata', in A. Barbic et al., *Rural Potentials for a Global Tomorrow*, Bucharest: International Rural Sociology Association with Bucharest University and the Romanian Academy, p.69.

Beck, S. (1976), 'The emergence of the peasant worker in an upland Transylvanian mountain community', *Dialectical Anthropology*, **1**, 365-75.

Bordanc, F. (1995), 'Spatial variations in the process of agricultural land privatization', in D. Turnock (ed.), *Rural Change in Romania*, Leicester: Leicester University Geography Department Occasional Paper 33, pp.39-47.

—— (1996), 'Spatial variations in the progress of land reform in Romania', *GeoJournal*, **38**, 161-5.

—— et al. (1994), 'Consideraţii geografice privind sistemul agricol românesc în perioada de tranziţie', in I. Zavoianu (ed.), *Lucrările sesiuni ştiinţifice anuale*, Bucharest: Academia Română, Institut de Geografie, pp.249-56.

Brezinski, H. and P. Petersen (1990), 'The second economy in Romania', in N. Clos (ed.), *The Second Economy in Marxist States*, London: Macmillan, pp.69-84.

Bulgaru, M. et al. (1992), *Probleme de bază ale agriculturii României*, Bucharest: Institut de Economia Agrară.

Cernea, M. (1974), *Sociologia cooperativei agricole*, Bucharest: Academia de Stiinţe Sociale şi Politice.

Cernescu, T. (1996), 'Aspecte specifice ale evoluţiei satului românesc', in M. Fulea (ed.), *Satul românesc contemporan*, Bucharest: Editura Academiei Române, pp.90-100.

Ciangă, N. (1991), 'Un model de cuantificare a potenţialului şi bazei materiale turistice din regiunea montană', *Studia Universitatis Babeş-Bolyai: Geographia*, **36** (1), 105-8.

Ciontu, G. (1996), 'Romanian harvesters back in competition', *Romanian Business Journal*, **3** (16), 4.

Cliza, D. (1995), 'Romanian vineyards in danger', *Romanian Business Journal*, **2** (38), 9.

Constantinescu-Galicani, V. (1996), 'Habitat rural şi strategii de stabilitaţii lui demografice cu privire specială la sate din Delta Dunării', in M. Fulea (ed.), *Satul Românesc contemporan*, Bucharest: Editura Academiei Române, pp.101-22.

Derounian, J. (1995), 'Rural regeneration in Romania', *Report for the Natural and Built Environment Professions*, No. 5, pp.4-6.

Dobrovici, C. (1972), 'Cercetarea complexă a zonei montane Vrancea: realitaţi perspective şi optimizarea proceselor sociale', *Viitorul Social*, **1**, 825-946.

Dumitru, N.S. (1972), 'Ponderea şi implicaţiile factorului natural în optimizarea sistemului socio-economic al unui zone depresionare', in T. Herseni et al., *Sociologie militans: sociologie geografică*, Bucharest: Editura Ştiinţifică, pp.115-200.

Fischer, M.E. (1989), *Nicolae Ceauşescu: A Study in Political Leadership*, London: Lynne Rienner.

Florian, V. and A. Sârbu (eds) (1993), *Satul Românesc contemporan*, Bucharest: Institut de Economia Agrară.

Fulea, M. (1993), 'Specificul tranziţiei în economia de piaţă în agricultură României', *Sociologie Românească*, **4**, 149-58.

—— (1996), 'Structura socio-economică a populaţiei rurale în perioadă de tranziţie la economia de piaţă', in M. Fulea (ed.), *Satul Românesc contemporan*, Bucharest: Editura Academiei Române, pp.159-70.

—— and E. Sima (1996), 'Women's socioeconomic condition in rural communities', in A. Barbic et al., *Rural Potentials for a Global Tomorrow*, Bucharest: International Rural Sociology Association with Bucharest University and the Romanian Academy, p.81.

Gavrilescu, D. (1994), 'Agricultural reform in Romania: between market priority and strategies for food security', in J.F.M. Swinnen (ed.), *Policy and Institutional Reform in Central Europe*, Aldershot: Avebury, pp.169-209.

—— (1996), 'Şansa fermei familiale în România', in M. Fulea (ed.), *Satul Românesc contemporan*, Bucharest: Editura Academiei Române, pp.39-49.

Gheorghe, S. (1992), *Economia de piaţă: legitaţi şi mecanisme*, Bucharest: Editure Inter-Media.

Ghinoiu, I. (1996), 'Dinamica peisajelor şi zonelor etnografice din România', in M. Fulea (ed.), *Satul Românesc contemporan*, Bucharest: Editura Academiei Române, pp.226-31.

Gilberg, T. (1980), 'Romanian agricultural policy in the quest for the "multilaterally developed socialist society"', in R.A. Francisco et al. (eds.), *Agricultural Policies in the USSR and Eastern Europe*, Boulder, CO: Westview, pp.137-64.

Giosan, N. (ed.) (1964), *Agricultura României 1944-1964*, Bucharest: Editura Agro-Silvică.

Henry, D.C. (1994), 'Reviving Romania's rural economy', *Radio Free Europe/Radio Liberty Research*, **3** (7), pp.18-23.

Hirschhausen-Leclerc, B. (1994), 'L'invention de nouvelles campagnes en Roumanie', *L'Espace Géographique*, **23**, 318-28.

Iacob, G. (1991), 'Consideraţii geografice privind valorificarea fondului funciar şi creşterea animalelor în depresiunea Sibiului', *Terra*, **23** (1), 32-6.

Ianoş, I. (1995), 'The Romanian village advances towards a new state of equilibrium', in D. Turnock (ed.), *Rural Change in Romania*, Leicester: University of Leicester Department of Geography Occasional Paper 33, pp.12-18.

—— and C. Talangă (1994), *Oraşul şi sistemul urban Românesc în condiţiile economiei de piaţă*, Bucharest: Academia Română, Institut de Geografie.

—— et al. (1992a), 'Changements récents dans l'agriculture roumaine', *Revue Roumaine: Géographie*, **36**, 23–30.

—— (1992b), 'Analiza geografică a fostelor resedințe de județ din România', *Studii și Cercetări: Geografie*, **36**, 23–30.

Iordache, A. et al. (1995), 'A new chance for Romanian agriculture', *Romanian Business Journal*, **2** (50), 6.

Iordan, I. and I. Velcea (1984), 'Geografia utilizării terenurilor', in V. Cucu et al. (eds), *Geografia României: geografia umană și economică*, Bucharest: Editura Academiei RSR, pp.313–417.

Iosif, G.N. (1992), 'Perpetuarea unor situații anacronice în industria alimentară', *Tribuna Economică*, **3** (47), 14–15.

—— (1993a), 'Resursele furajere: între opțiune și realitate'. *Tribuna Economică*, **4** (35), 11.

—— (1993b), 'De la agricultura așa-zișa "biologică" la o agricultura modernă', *Tribuna Economică*, **4** (38), 2–3; (39), 3.

Istrate, I. and I. Buhu (1990), 'Dezvoltarea turismului în profil teritorial', *Tribuna Economică*, **1** (22), 13–15.

Kideckel, D.A. (1992), 'Peasants and authority in the new Romania', in Daniel N. Nelson (ed.), *Romania after Tyranny*, Boulder, CO, Westview, pp.67–81.

—— (1993a), *The Solitude of Collectivism: Romanian Villagers to Revolution and Beyond*, Ithaca, NY: Cornell University Press.

—— (1993b), 'Once again the land: decollectivization and social conflict in rural Romania', in H.G. de Soto and D.G. Anderson (eds), *The Curtain Rises: Rethinking Culture, Ideology and the State in Eastern Europe*, Atlantic Highlands, NJ: Humanities Press, pp.62–75.

Kovacs, C. (1991), 'Mecanismes d'action mutuelle dans le système agriculture-environnement', *Studia Universitatis Babeș-Bolyai: Geographia*, **36**, 92–5.

Lazar, T. (1996a), 'Schiță privind strategia reformei în agricultură', in M. Fulea (ed.), *Satul Românesc contemporan*, Bucharest: Editura Academiei Române, pp.11–20.

—— (1996b), 'The upgrading of Romanian agriculture: a must!', *Romanian Business Journal*, **3** (37), 9.

Mateescu, L.M. (1996), 'Strategii microeconomice: opțiuni ale gospodariilor și menajelor rurale', in M. Fulea (ed.), *Satul Românesc contemporan*, Bucharest: Editura Academiei Române, pp.50–55.

Mesei, E. (1996), 'Part-time farms in Romanian villages in the 1990s', in A. Barbic et al., *Rural Potentials for a Global Tomorrow*, Bucharest: International Rural Sociology Association with Bucharest University and the Romanian Academy, p.99.

Meurs, M. (1996), 'The persistence of collectivism: responses to land restitution in Romania', in D. Hall and D. Danta (eds), *Reconstructing the Balkans: A Geography of the New Southeastern Europe*, Chichester: Wiley, pp.169–77.

Micu, R.R. (1992), 'Ecologia exploatorilor forestiere', *Tribuna Econimică*, **3** (51–2), 15–16.

Mitrache, S. et al. (1996), *Agroturism şi turism rural*, Bucharest: Federaţia Româna pentru Dezvoltare Montană.

Muică, C. and I. Zăvoianu (1996), 'The ecological consequences of privatization in Romanian agriculture', *GeoJournal*, **38**, 207-12.

Muică, M. and D. Turnock (1993), 'Prospects for Vrancea: a traditional mountain community in Romania', *GeoJournal*, **29**, 69-82.

—— (1994), 'Living on landslides: the Subcarpathian districts of Buzau and Vrancea', Leicester: Leicester University Geography Department Occasional Paper 29.

Nemenyi, A. and J.N. Nemenyi (1995), *Some Characteristics of Privatization in Rural Areas*, Prague, 16th Congress of the European Society for Rural Sociology.

Otiman, P.I. (1994), *Agricultura România la cumpană dintre mileniile II şi III*, Timişoara: Editura Helicom.

Parpală, O. (1992a), 'Crearea de ferme agricole private viabile', *Tribuna Economică*, **3** (3-4), 25.

—— (1992b), 'Criza generală a agriculturii Româneşti postdecembriste', *Tribuna Economică*, **3** (27), 6; (29), 6; (31), 7; (32), 7; (33), 6-7.

—— (1993a), 'Sistemul de creditare a producatorilor agricoli', *Tribuna Economică*, **4** (12), 11.

—— (1993b), 'Politica structurilor forme asociative în agricultura', *Tribuna Economică*, **4** (30), 9-10.

Pascaru, A. (1996), 'Rural youth at present and in the future', in A. Barbic et al., *Rural Potentials for a Global Tomorrow*, Bucharest: International Rural Sociology Association with Bucharest University and the Romanian Academy, p.49.

Pecsi, K. (1989), 'The extremist path of economic development in Eastern Europe', *Communist Economics*, **1**, 97-109.

Ploaie, G. (1995), 'Tourism and conservation in the mountains of Vâlcea County', in D. Turnock (ed.), *Rural Change in Romania*, Leicester: Leicester University Geography Department Occasional Paper 33, pp.54-60.

Pop, G.P. (1994), 'Evoluţia structurilor agricole în România în perioada 1945-1994', *Studia Universitatis Babeş-Bolyai: Geographia*, **39** (1), 3-17.

—— and A. Maier (1990), 'Potential et structures géodemographiques dans le pays de Lapus', *Studia Universitatis Babeş-Bolyai: Geographia*, **35** (1), 60-68.

Popescu, M. (1994), 'Imens potential de afaceri în zonale de deal şi montane', *Tribuna Economică*, **5** (10), 13-14; (12), 10-12.

Rain, L. (1996), 'Traiectorii ale modernizarii satului românesc contemporan', in M. Fulea (ed.), *Satul Românesc contemporan*, Bucharest: Editura Academiei Române, pp.186-94.

Rey, R. (1979), *Viitor în Carpaţi: progres economic, civilizaţie, socialism*, Craiova: Scrisul Românesc.

—— (1985), *Civilizaţie montană*, Bucharest: Editura Ştiinţifică şi Enciclopedică.

Roată, S. (1991), 'Asupra potenţialului turistic al arealelor carstice din Carpaţii Meridionali şi Podişul Mehedinţi', *Studii şi Cercetări: Geografie*, **38**, 81-8.

Ronnas, P. (1987), 'Agrarian change and economic development in rural Romania: a case study of the Oaş region', *Geografiska Annaler*, **69B**, 51-63.

—— (1989), 'Turning the Romanian peasant into a new socialist man: an assessment of rural development policy in Romania', *Soviet Studies*, **41**, 543-59.

Sampson, S.L. (1983), 'Rich families and poor collectives: an anthropological approach to Romania's "second economy"', *Bidrag til Oststatsforskning*, **2**, 44-77.

Surd, V. (1991), 'Traditional forms of organizing geographical space in Transylvania: "The Lands"', *Studia Universitatis Babeş-Bolyai: Geographia*, **36** (2), 74-80.

—— (1994), 'Critical status of rural Romania', in F. Greif (ed.), *Die Zukunft der ländlichen Infrastruktur in Ostmitteleuropa*, Vienna: Schriftenreihe der Bundesanstalt für Agrarwirtschaft **75**, pp.61-7.

—— and L. Nicoara (1990), 'The socio-professional structure of the active population of the rural settlements in Ţara Oaşului', *Studii Universitatis Babeş-Bolyai: Geographia*, **35** (1), 55-9.

Tabară, V. (1996), 'Belated funding is as harmful as a drought', *Romanian Business Journal*, **3** (4), 6.

Talabă, I. (1991), *Turism în Carpaţii Orientali*, Bucharest: Editura pentru Turism.

Talangă, C. (1995), 'The restructuring of industrial activities in Romanian villages', in D. Turnock (ed), *Rural Change in Romania*, Leicester: Leicester University Geography Department Occasional Paper 33, pp.50-53.

Toderoiu, F. (1996), 'Forţa economică a agriculturii: componenta suport a dezvoltarii rurale', in M. Fulea (ed.), *Satul Românesc contemporan*, Bucharest: Editura Academiei Române, pp.56-69.

Turnock, D. (1986), 'The Rural Development Programme in Romania', Leicester: Leicester University Geography Department Occasional Paper 13.

—— (1991a), 'The planning of rural settlement in Romania', *Geographical Journal*, **157**, 251-64.

—— (1991b), 'The changing Romanian countryside: the Ceauşescu epoch and prospects for change following the revolution', *Environment and Planning, C: Government and Policy*, **9**, 319-40.

—— (1992), 'The Romanian Countryside at the End of State Socialism', Leicester University Geography Department Occasional Paper 22.

—— (1993a), 'Agricultural Change in the Romanian Carpathians', Leicester: Leicester University Faculty of Social Sciences Discussion Papers in Geography 93/2.

—— (1993b), 'Romania', in F.W. Carter and D. Turnock (eds), *Environmental Problems in Eastern Europe*, London: Routledge, pp.135-63.

—— (1995), 'Rural transition in Eastern Europe', *GeoJournal*, **36**, 420–26.

Velcea, I. (1996), 'The rural model in the Romanian Carpathians', in G. Erdeli and W.J. Chambers (eds), *The First Romanian–British Geographic Seminar*, Bucharest: Editura Universității din Bucuresști, pp.59–64.

—— et al. (1993), 'Geographic elements regarding the environmental recovery in the Bucegi Mountains', in C. Muică and D. Turnock (eds), *Geography and Conservation*, Bucharest: Institutul de Geografie, pp.119–21.

Verdery, K. (1994), 'The elasticity of land: problems of property restitution in Transylvania', *Slavic Review*, **53**, 1071–1109.

Vincze, M. (1995), *Changes in the Romanian Villages in the 1990s*, Prague: 16th Congress of the European Society for Rural Sociology.

Wädekin, K.-W, (1990), 'Determinants and trends of reform in communist agriculture: a concluding essay', in K.-W. Wädekin (ed.), *Communist Agriculture: Farming in the Soviet Union and Eastern Europe*, London: Routledge, pp.321–31.

Zotta, B. (1993), 'Contribuții geografice la studiul zonelor irigabile din sud-estul României', *Geographica Timisensis*, **2**, 183–7.

9. Slovakia

Vladimír Drgoňa, Alena Dubcová and Hilda Kramáreková

This chapter seeks to examine the privatization process and its impact on the country's agricultural system. Restructuring of industry has attracted much discussion (Dubcová 1995; Mládek 1995) but the changes in the rural areas have been discussed previously only in very general terms (Blažík 1994; Brabec and Dubcová 1991; Žigrai 1994). We also consider other aspects of rural change in the context of transition towards a market economy; in addition there is an international dimension because changes in agricultural management will have implications for trade with neighbouring countries. Austria has a key position in the transport system with regard to roads, railways and airports as well as the River Danube. Trends in the newly privatized agriculture are difficult to identify with precision because of the short period of transition, along with the additional uncertainly arising from the break-up of the former Czechoslovakia and the consequent need to proceed with a separate legislative programme in Bratislava. Moreover, models of economic change drawn from the developed countries of the world seem to have little relevance in the Slovak case (Ivanička 1994).

The rural areas are extremely important for Slovakia because they account for 90 per cent of a total national area of 4,904m.ha and 43.3 per cent of a total population of 5,324 thousand (1993) (Figure 9.1). Agriculture is very important for the national economy as a whole and the rural areas in particular: 49.9 per cent of the land is used for agriculture (2.45m.ha in 1993, of which 1.48m.ha - 60.4 per cent - is arable). There is 0.46ha of agricultural land per capita and 0.28ha of arable land. Good soils, notably chernozems and Orthic to Albic luvisols (after the FAO classification), occur in zones of

252   *Privatization in Rural Eastern Europe*

(a)   Administrative regions (see page 254)

(b)   Percentage of land in agriculture

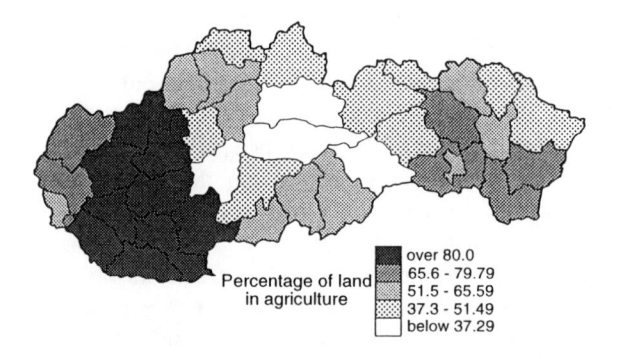

(c)   Market price for agricultural land, by district

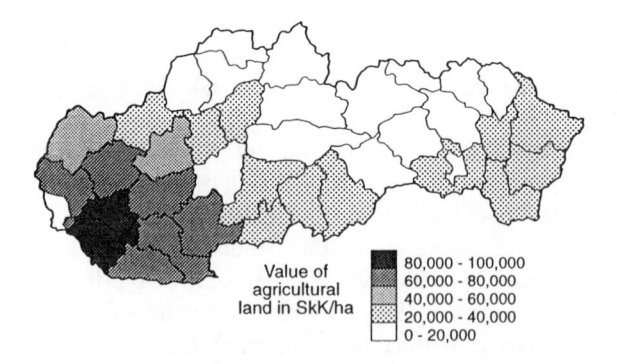

Sources: Kárász et al. 1995 (f); Šabo 1996 (c); Spišiak 1995 (b, d and e).

Slovakia 253

(d) Agricultural production

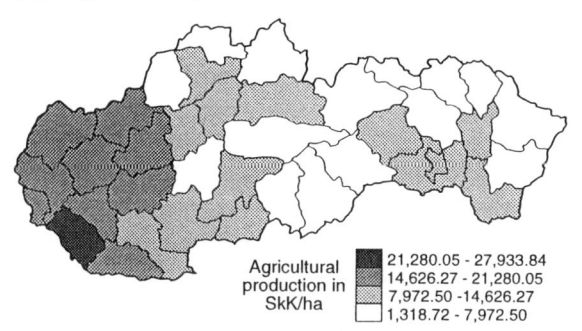

Agricultural production in SkK/ha
- 21,280.05 - 27,933.84
- 14,626.27 - 21,280.05
- 7,972.50 - 14,626.27
- 1,318.72 - 7,972.50

(e) State financial assistance

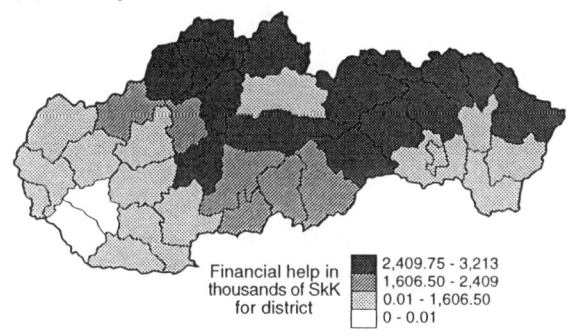

Financial help in thousands of SkK for district
- 2,409.75 - 3,213
- 1,606.50 - 2,409
- 0.01 - 1,606.50
- 0 - 0.01

(f) Employment

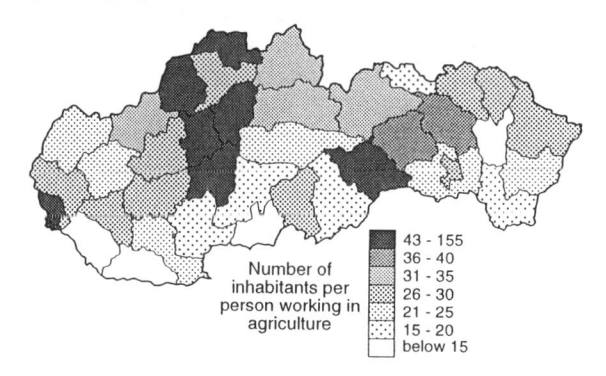

Number of inhabitants per person working in agriculture
- 43 - 155
- 36 - 40
- 31 - 35
- 26 - 30
- 21 - 25
- 15 - 20
- below 15

Figure 9.1 Slovakia: aspects of agriculture, 1994

particularly favourable climatic conditions in the Danube Lowlands. Here, in Slovakia's most productive agricultural region, cereals are found on the flat land while sugar beet is common on the loess hills. Seventy-five per cent of the farmland is arable, a proportion which is almost matched by the figure of 70 per cent for the smaller East Slovakian Lowland (Figure 9.1b). In both these areas there is very little woodland cover. However, conditions vary very significantly across the country. Low-quality soils predominate and these are often partially forested. In the hill and mountain regions, farming is relatively extensive. There are large areas of grassland, while oats and potatoes are prominent in a reduced arable sector. Arable land comprises less than 37 per cent of the agricultural land in Banská Bystrica and adjacent districts.

With a general altitude of 150–180 metres, the Nitra district is typical of conditions on the edge of the Danube Lowland where loess hills are separated by the alluvial floodplains of the Nitra and Žitava rivers which provide a valuable source of irrigation water. Farmed since Neolithic times, the climatic conditions are highly conducive to agriculture, with warm summers and mild winters: an annual average temperature of 9.9 degrees Celsius and annual sunshine of some 2,000 hours. The annual precipitation changes with the elevation which ranks between 550 and 800mm. In terms of texture, the middle-heavy soil is the most prevalent type. Conditions for mechanization are very good because three-quarters of the farmland has a slope of less than five degrees and only 3 per cent is steeper than ten degrees. There are small areas of oak and oak and hornbeam woodland interrupting the continuity of the agricultural land, and the fauna includes some small game. The towns have developed a considerable capacity in food processing and the city of Nitra (population 46.7 thousand in 1961 rising to 87.1 thousand in 1994) is home to Slovakia's only agricultural university, to Agroinstitut (the

---

Figure 9.1: Key to administrative regions (page 252) Ba Banská Bystrica; Bar Bardejov; Br Bratislava; Ca Čadca; Do Dolný Kubín; Du Dunajská Streda; Ga Galanta; Hu Humenné; Ko Komárno; Kos Košice; Le Levice; Li Liptovský Milukáš; Lu Lučenec; Ma Martin; Mi Michalovce; Ni Nitra; No Nové Zámky; Po Poprad; Pov Považská Bystrica; Pr Prešov; Pri Prievidza; Ri Rimavská Sobota; Ro Rožňava; Se Senica; Sp Spišská Nová Ves; St Stará Ľubovňa; Sv Svidník; To Topoľčany; Tr Trebišov; Tre Trenčin; Trn Trnava; Ve Veľký Krtíš; Vr Vranov nad Topľou; Zi Žiar nad Hronom; Zil Žilina; Zv Zvolen.

Centre for Continuing Education), and to the Institute of Livestock Production. The city also hosts international agricultural exhibitions and congresses which are very important for innovation in agriculture and light industry in the district and the country generally (Drgoňa et al. 1996; Ivanička 1994).

THE DEVELOPMENT OF SLOVAK AGRICULTURE

Slovakia remained essentially agricultural until the Second World War. Some farmers did well but there were pronounced regional variations and there was overpopulation in rural areas with poor soil, which led to heavy out-migration. After 1918, the opportunities for emigration were reduced and, at the same time, the new Czechoslovak state introduced land reform by transforming estates of more than 150ha into farms of up to 30ha for a total of 187,423 families. The medium-sized farms generated considerable rural prosperity and accelerated the transition towards a capitalist economy. However, the disappearance of large estates was sometimes injurious to food-processing industries, while some areas that remained overpopulated in relation to the agricultural potential suffered from a lack of capital investment (especially during the crisis years of the 1930s) and stimulative market prices. Most farms were very small and minifundia was even more evident in 1949 than in 1930: 65.4 per cent of holdings were no larger than 5ha in 1930 (71 per cent in 1949), while 20.8 per cent were of 5-10ha in size (19.5ha in 1949). Only 13.8 per cent were larger than 10ha in 1930 (9.5ha in 1949) (Kováč et al. 1989). The farms of up to 5ha accounted for 20.9 per cent of the land in 1930, a much smaller share than the 28.7 per cent accounted for by the 1.1 per cent of farms larger than 50ha. These farms gave Slovakia an agricultural surplus that was absorbed in the Czech Lands.

As a result of an intensive industrialization process after 1945, Slovakia was transformed into an industrial-agricultural country. There were further changes on the land as the property of wartime collaborators and rich farmers (amounting to 1.25m.ha) was reallocated to smallholders and landless peasants by 1947. Then a system of cooperation was announced in 1949 to combine together, with varying degrees of coercion, the land, animals and equipment in each area with the labour of both former smallholders and landless peasants. In general, farmers with holdings smaller than 10ha were, like the landless farmworkers, happy to join cooperatives because they gained secure employment and an equal stake in the community. On the other hand, farmers with holdings of 10–20ha were generally less enthusiastic because their holdings were large enough to offer a degree of prosperity. Therefore such farmers frequently had to be forced into cooperative membership (Spišiak 1995). There were few farms larger than 20ha at this time because most of the farmers in this category had already been condemned as collaborators and expropriated.

From 484 in 1950, the number of united farming enterprises (*Jednotné rol'nícke družstvo* or JRD) increased to 2,683 in 1960 with the total area up from 0.23 to 1.80m.ha while the average size increased from 469 to 672ha. The process was complete, apart from some mountain areas where individual farms persisted for logistical reasons on a total area of 0.53m.ha (0.46m.ha in 1971) compared with 2.06m.ha in 1950. However, there was subsequent consolidation to create larger cooperatives appropriate for specialized production: from 2,109 units in 1971 with an average size of 751ha, the number fell sharply to 638 in 1989 with an average size of 2,330ha. Meanwhile the state farms (*Štátne majetky* or SM) increased their stake from 145th.ha in 1950 to 271 in 1960 and 389 in 1971. Furthermore, the state sector (cooperatives and state farms together) made further inroads during the 1970s and 1980s, controlling 99.3 per cent of the agricultural land in 1989, compared with percentages of 93 in 1977, 82.7 in 1970, 73.5 in 1960 and 14.8 in 1948. This process operated in parallel with a reduction in farmworkers through transfer to industry. As agriculture was brought into the system of centralized decision-making, it was possible to forge closer links with the food industry. A system of mandatory taxation of agriculture, levied on each hectare of farmland with reference to soil quality and farm size, was replaced by arrangements involving the agricultural enterprises and manufacturers which generated taxation revenue for the state. However, despite the fact that ownership rights were nominally safeguarded, people lost the right to manage the land and democratic principles were often violated.

The process may be followed in detail in the case of the Nitra district (Figure 9.2a, see p.270). There were just two cooperatives in 1948 with an average area of 126ha (Kováč et al. 1989), arising largely through the confiscation of large private farms. By 1955 the number reached 83 (average size of 481ha) because of the combination of small farms (mainly of 5-15ha). There was a significant increase in mechanization, while an improved supply of fertilizers and seeds resulted in higher yields. There was also a greater commitment to livestock in the lowland area and improvements in management were accomplished. Further progress in land consolidation in the villages over the next three years brought the number of cooperatives to 110 in 1959, with an average size of 658ha. There was now a cooperative in every village in the district and improvements in rural living standards were very evident, including opportunities for leisure and cultural development. Major organization changes then followed with the consolidation of the cooperatives to reduce the number to 97 in 1970 (average area 715ha) and only 18 in 1989 (ranging in size from 2,315 to 6,862ha and averaging 4,213ha – a much higher figure than the national average of 2,330ha – of which 3,766ha was arable). This was done in the context of 15 cooperative districts and four agrichemical centres which assisted with the application of fertilizers and chemical protection.

PRIVATIZATION IN SLOVAK AGRICULTURE

Privatization of land, animals and buildings has taken place under Czechoslovak Law 42 of 1992 (now recognized as Slovak Law 264/1995) which empowered the cooperatives to return land to the original owners or their heirs, thereby laying the basis for the restoration of the private sector and the creation of new, genuine cooperatives. Therefore the land and buildings as well as the stock of machines have been subject to division. But, while most of the owners are now individuals (apart from the Church, which regained many of its former properties), the cooperatives are still prominent. They were of course unacceptable in their old form because the former owners were treated as employees and insufficient attention was given to local food processing. However, cooperatives can still harness advanced technology more easily than a family farm can, and make more efficient use of machinery. By January 1990, every cooperative had to draw up a transformation programme including a list of members with their share of the property. The approval of more than half the members was required, otherwise the cooperative would be auctioned. In fact, every cooperative was transformed into a united farming cooperative (*Podielnické družstvo*, or PD).

Forty-two per cent of the cooperative property on average (including 71.6 per cent of the agricultural land) belongs to the children of former cooperative members. A percentage of 71.6 of the agricultural land belongs to non-members, although 6 per cent is state-owned and in the case of another 19.7 per cent the owner has not been identified. By contrast, the members own only 28.4 per cent of the economically-used land on average, although the precise figure varies from district to district. Every lawful member could exercise the right up to the end of February 1996 to take their property out of the cooperative and manage it separately. A significant private sector is arising out of the activities of self-employed farmers (*Súkromne hospodáriaci roľníci* or SHR). They may also sell their shares, although their value has often fallen because of poor management. Some cooperatives have been transformed into limited companies (*Spoločnosti s ručením obmedzeným* or SRO) or joint-stock companies (*Akciové spoločnosti*); in the latter case, members receive dividend payments. A very small number of cooperatives opted for transformation into small trading companies or small joint-stock companies. Meanwhile, the government remains much involved in agriculture because the state farms have not yet been privatized. However, it has now been decided that state farms will be decentralized through the formation of trading companies and then privatized quickly through the sale of shares to selected owners. The state farms usually have a specialized production profile whereas the coperatives do not. Some state farms have been excluded from privatization because of their special functions; for example, the Topoľčianky horse-breeding enterprise near Nitra is a major genetic resource.

Thus several types of new private business are emerging out of these changes and it is likely that private farms will slowly increase while cooperatives will decline. There is considerable flexibility, for a land market now exists and even private individuals interested in gardening may rent a small piece of land from a cooperative. The value of land varies considerably, exceeding SkK90,000 per hectare in the Danube Lowlands but falling below SkK8,500 per hectare in the mountains (Figure 9.1c). Predictably, the balance between arable and pastureland (including meadows) changes with progress through the value bands. Only 26.2 per cent of the land in the lowest value band is arable, but the proportions rise progressively to 80.9, 93.5, 95.4 and 98.4 per cent in the higher bands (Table 9.1). Only 15.6 per cent of the arable land is in the lowest value band (SkK5,000–20,000 per hectare) compared with 78.1 per cent of the pasture and meadowland. By contrast, the figures for the highest band (more than SkK91,000 per hectare) are 21.8 and 0.6 per cent respectively. The cooperatives tend to be most prominent on the better land with a preponderance of arable land where working can be mechanized most advantageously on large holdings. They are particularly prominent in the lowlands of western and eastern Slovakia. According to Table 9.2, most cooperatives are in the size groups between 500 and 3,000ha, with an average size of 1,600–1,700ha.

Table 9.1 Slovakia: value of agricultural land, 1994

Value SkK/ha	Agricultural Land (th.ha) and percentage distribution					
	Total		Arable		Pasture/meadow	
5,000–20,000	902.5	38.0	237.3	15.6	665.3	78.1
21,000–50,000	875.7	36.8	708.5	46.5	167.3	19.6
51,000–70,000	133.1	5.6	124.5	8.2	8.5	1.0
71,000–90,000	126.9	5.3	121.0	7.9	5.9	0.7
91,000+	338.3	14.2	333.0	21.8	5.2	0.6
Total	2,376.5	100.0	1,524.3	100.0	852.2	100.0

Source: Spišiak 1995.

However, the growth of private farms is slow (Table 9.3). The inherited structure of large farms with corresponding field systems and mechanization levels makes it difficult to create a small-farm system. Prospective private farmers do not have significant capital stocks and, as former state and cooperative farm workers, they lack knowledge of small farms and management experience of any kind. There is a preference for cooperative working conditions, especially in view of the difficult market situation in agriculture today and the high prices for seeds, fertilizers and other inputs. Under the circumstances the cooperatives offer better living standards as well as good working conditions through regular hours and paid leave. Generally speaking, private farms in the Nitra area have less than 5ha of land and are managed by

Table 9.2 Slovakia: regional distribution of agricultural enterprises, 1994

	Enterprises according to agricultural land (ha) in size bands with an upper limit of								
	1.0	10	50	100	500	1,000	2,000	3,000	3,000+	Total
State farms	–	3	15	7	45	25	20	13	47	175
West	–	2	10	2	17	7	6	5	5	54
Centre	–	–	2	2	16	7	6	4	19	56
East	–	1	3	3	12	11	8	4	23	65
Cooperatives	1	3	3	6	69	223	392	168	96	961
West	–	1	1	4	26	93	184	50	38	397
Centre	–	1	2	1	22	52	82	51	37	248
East	1	1	–	1	21	78	126	67	21	316
Shareholding	2	5	2	2	4	1	7	2	4	29
West	2	3	2	1	2	1	5	–	3	19
Centre	–	–	–	1	1	–	1	2	–	5
East	–	2	–	–	1	–	1	–	1	5
Individual	1,674	4,106	1,439	193	145	18	6	–	–	7,581
West	1,195	1,786	676	108	81	10	2	–	–	3,858
Centre	326	1,547	512	58	42	8	4	–	–	2,497
East	153	774	250	27	22	–	–	–	–	1,226
Limited Co.	2	12	8	4	33	16	17	6	1	99
West	2	7	6	2	18	8	11	5	–	59
Centre	–	5	1	2	12	6	6	1	1	34
East	–	–	1	–	3	2	–	–	–	6

Note: The regions reflect well-established divisions of the country, shown in Figure 9.1a.

Source: Poľnohospodársky cenzus, ŠÚSR, 1994.

men aged 45–55 years who previously worked for cooperative or state farms. Most are concerned with cereal farming, which is more attractive in market terms than livestock farming. Those starting their farms in 1992–94 were successful in getting access to machinery, but in 1996 small private farms received no state support. There is a trend towards private fruit farming in the Cabaj-Čapor, Lefantovce and Veľká Dolina

Table 9.3: Slovakia: organizational structure of agriculture 1992–1994

Sector	Enterprises		Land (th.ha)					
			Total			Arable		
	A	B	A	B	C	A	B	C
End of 1992:								
State farms (SM)	486	0.2	581.9	24.0	1,197.3	362.7	24.1	746.2
Cooperatives (PD)	884	0.3	1,722.3	71.1	1,948.3	1,100.7	73.1	1,245.1
Public companies (SRO)	11,472	3.7	20.9	0.9	1.8	6.0	0.4	0.5
Private farms (SHR)	295,746	95.8	96.7	4.0	0.3	35.0	2.3	0.1
Total	308,588	100.0	2,421.9	100.0	7.8	1,504.4	100.0	4.9
End of 1994:								
State farms (SM)	626	0.2	545.8	22.6	871.9	n.a.	n.a.	n.a.
Cooperatives (PD)	1,086	0.3	1,724.5	71.3	1,588.0	n.a.	n.a.	n.a.
Public companies (SRO)	14,614	4.5	37.2	1.5	2.5	n.a.	n.a.	n.a.
Private farms (SHR)	305,303	94.9	111.1	4.6	0.4	n.a.	n.a.	n.a.
Total	321,626	100.0	2,418.6	100.0	7.5	n.a.	n.a.	n.a.

Notes: A Number; B Percentage distribution; C Hectares per enterprise.

Sources: Michaeli (1995); Spišiak (1996).

areas of Nitra. It is possible that interest in private farming will increase in the future. The Netherlands Ministry of Agriculture is supporting a demonstration farm with 75ha of arable land and 50 head of cattle. This should provide a useful stimulus to agricultural students in the Nitra area.

AGRICULTURE TODAY

Agriculture supplies the population with food and industry with commodities such as leather and textile materials. It employs 12.1 per cent of the working population and is responsible for 12.5 per cent of the entire economic society product. Agriculture accounts for 8.5 per cent of the national income, 6.6 per cent of the gross national product and

5.5 per cent of the gross economic turnover of the Slovak economy in 1994. Per capita values for gross economic turnover in agriculture vary greatly across the regions from SkK1,388 in Košice to SkK24,494 in Dunajská Streda. There is also much variation in production per hectare of agricultural land, with the upper quartile value (exceeding SkK21.2 thousand) attaching to Dunajska Streda in Western Slovakia, while the intermediate values of SkK14.6–21.3 thousand are clustered in the same region (Figure 9.1d).

There are signs of improvement in agriculture with an increased value of production and reduced losses in 1994 compared with 1993 (Table 9.4). This results from the application of new policies to rejuvenate agriculture, but results over a longer period must be considered before clear trends are likely to emerge. However, privatization has been accompanied by a reduction in state support for cooperative farms. Nevertheless, in 1994 government support was SkK6.85 billion and in 1995 it increased to SkK7.6 billion. Most mountain districts attracted more than SkK2.4m., while assistance to the South Slovakian basins and the East Slovakian Lowland was relatively moderate (less than SkK1.6 million) and the most productive districts of the Danube region (Dunajská Streda and Galanta) received virtually nothing (Figure 9.1e).

Table 9.4   Slovakia: profitability of agricultural enterprises, 1993–1994

	Production value and costs (SkKm.)							
	Cooperatives		State farms		Trading Co.		Total	
	1993	1994	1993	1994	1993	1994	1993	1994
Production	33.0	34.7	8.3	8.4	1.3	1.6	42.6	44.6
Costs	35.4	36.4	9.5	9.4	1.2	1.5	46.2	47.3
Profit	–2.4	–1.7	–1.2	–1.0	0.1	0.1	–3.6	–2.7

Source: Institute of Economy, Bratislava.

Under the market system the areas sown to cereals and oil plants have increased while potato production (in which private farmers are now very active) has declined (Table 9.5). The decline of interest in potatoes by cooperative and state farms occurred quite dramatically

Table 9.5 Slovakia: agricultural production, 1991-1994

	1992			1993			1994		
	Area (th.ha)	Prodn (th.t)	Yield (t/ha)	Area (th.ha)	Prodn (th.t)	Yield (t/ha)	Area (th.ha)	Prodn (th.t)	Yield (t/ha)
Agriculture	2,447.0	n.a.	n.a.	2,446.0	n.a.	n.a.	2,446.0	n.a.	n.a.
Arable	1,486.0	n.a.	n.a.	1,483.0	n.a.	n.a.	1,483.9	n.a.	n.a.
Cereals	808.9	3.55	4.42	845.1	3.15	3.78	873.7	3.70	4.30
Potatoes	51.3	0.66	12.86	47.1	0.86	18.15	41.4	0.40	9.67
Sugar beet	45.4	1.33	29.36	32.9	1.11	34.31	33.4	1.11	34.57
Oil plants	70.5	0.13	1.90	74.7	0.13	1.70	87.6	0.16	1.78
Legumes	65.5	0.16	2.42	66.3	0.12	1.88	52.7	0.16	2.87
Fodder	229.5	1.21	5.29	201.3	1.00	4.95	187.7	0.75	3.99

Source: Štatistické ročenky Slovenskej republiky.

between 1992 and 1994 through reduced lending to farmers by the banks and the loss of many agricultural specialists. The dominance of cereals is reduced only in the vicinity of the larger cities, where vegetables and orchards are prominent. Cereal production of some 3.7m.t of grain is derived from 57 per cent of the entire arable land of Slovakia. Winter wheat is prominent on the Danube and East Slovakian lowlands. Barley is grown in the lowlands for malt and in the mountains for livestock feed. Potatoes remain a major source of food for humans and animals, and are also a raw material for light industry and important fodder for agricultural animals. The best-quality potatoes are found in the hill and mountain regions such as Liptov, Orava and Spiš, where they take up a fifth of the arable land. Early potatoes are usually found in the main maize and sugar-beet areas. Lucerne and fodder for silage (with high temperature requirements) remain prominent in lowland areas, while fodder root crops are more closely linked with the hill and mountain areas.

The long-term picture for land-use change shows decreases in agriculture during 1950-70, while forest land increased (although arable increased under collectivization until 1960) (Table 9.6). There was higher priority for ecology during the 1980s, but the area of meadows and pastures continued to decline because of losses to urban areas. Altogether, there has been a decrease of 13.5 per cent in the agricultural area (and 14.4 per cent in the arable land) since 1950, which has arisen through the

Table 9.6 Slovakia: land use, 1950–1993 (th.ha)

	1950	1960	1970	1980	1985	1989	1990	1993
Agricultural land	2,827	2,754	2,628	2,477	2,467	2,453	2,448	2,446
Arable	1,734	1,761	1,683	1,516	1,517	1,506	1,509	1,483
Hop gardens and vineyards	13	17	24	33	34	33	33	31
Meadows and pastures	1,009	901	831	931	818	813	808	835
Forests	1,711	1,793	1,848	1,954	1,955	1,986	1,989	1,911
Water surfaces and urban	398	354	422	468	478	464	466	466

Source: Štatistické ročenky Slovenskej republiky.

increase in forests, water surfaces (related to hydropower projects) and urban zones. Since privatization, the less fertile lands in the hill and mountain areas have been converted to grassland, so reversing the downward trend since 1990. Between 1990 and 1993, the area of permanent grassland has increased by 27th.ha while arable land has decreased by 36th.ha. However, although the mountain grassland is the foundation for livestock rearing (cattle and sheep), the highest cattle densities occur in the Danubean Lowland where pigs are also prominent. However, the high level of intensification based on state investments during the communist period has not been maintained and the numbers of animals – especially cattle – have fallen in response to reduced purchasing power and problems with fodder over higher costs and poorer quality. While there are signs of recovery in crop production, the complexity of the breeding process means that longer time will be needed for livestock numbers to recover.

The structure of agricultural production in the Nitra district is summarized in Table 9.7. Cereals are the leading crop: 11.6 per cent of the 1994 production came from state farms, 71.7 per cent from cooperatives and 16.7 per cent from other farms. The most widely grown grain is wheat (142.7th.t in 1994 from 27.7th.ha), followed by rye (65.5th.t from 16.4th.ha) and maize (33.5th.t from 8.7th.ha). There is also a substantial production of vegetables, oil plants and sugar beet. A high fodder production supports the livestock sector, which is very much geared to pig rearing, based on the production of maize, rye and sugar beet. Numbers

Table 9.7 Slovakia: agricultural production in the Nitra district, 1991–1994

	1991			1992			1993			1994		
	Area	Prodn	Yield	Area	Prodn	Yield	Area	Prodn	Yield	Area	Prodn	Yield
	(th.ha)	(th.t)	(t/ha)	(th.ha)	(th.t)	(t/ha)	(th.ha)	(th.t)	(t/ha)	(th.ha)	(th.t)	(t/ha)
Agriculture	100.4	n.a.	n.a.	100.4	n.a.	n.a.	100.3	n.a.	n.a.	n.a.	n.a.	n.a.
Arable	87.1	n.a.	n.a.	86.4	n.a.	n.a.	86.5	n.a.	n.a.	n.a.	n.a.	n.a.
Cereals	45.7*	253.0	5.5	48.1*	230.0	4.8	51.6	184.7	3.6	53.7	244.7	4.6
Potatoes	0.6*	7.9	12.9	0.8*	12.1	15.2	0.8	9.5	11.8	0.9	n.a.	n.a.
Sugar beet	5.0*	133.7	26.9	4.2*	112.1	26.5	2.1*	67.1	31.6	2.4*	87.3	36.9
Oil plants	n.a.	n.a.	n.a.	n.a.	n.a	n.a.	6.6	n.a.	n.a.	8.0	15.0	n.a.
Legumes	n.a.	n.a.	n.a.	n.a.	n.a.	n.a.	6.3	n.a.	n.a.	5.1	15.5	n.a.
Fodder	9.6*	105.2	10.9	10.4*	74.7	7.2	17.6	50.6	6.0	15.6	57.1	3.6

Note: * Estimate.

Source: Štatistická ročenka Slovenskej republiky, 1995.

have fallen from 136.5 thousand in 1991 to 107.9 thousand in 1994 in line with general trends. Meanwhile, cattle numbers have declined from 55.7 to 31.3 thousand and poultry from 1.41 to 1.07 million (*Štatistická ročenka okresu Nitra*, 1994). Sheep are largely restricted to the foothills of the Tribeč and Pohronský Inovec Mountains.

Organic Agriculture

Ecological factors are playing a more significant role in agriculture (Adamovič 1993; Bedrna 1993; Drgoňa 1996). In 1993, the production of healthier biofoods (using less than 15 per cent of 'allowed chemicals') amounted to 27th.t of grains, 18th.t of tuber crops, 2,500t of vegetables, 1,600t of oil plants and 33th.t of fodder (Štefánek 1993). Ecological principles are also being extended to meat, milk and cheese production. Ecological farming projects were started in 1990 on 15,140ha, of which 12,804ha were arable. Thirty-six agricultural enterprises, spread across 15 districts of Slovakia, set aside part of their land for organic agriculture. The programme was assisted by the Ministry of Agriculture and Nutrition which published its *Rules of Organic Agriculture* in 1992. In 1994, 44 enterprises (36 cooperatives, five private farms and three state farms) were active in bioproduction over a total area of 15,556ha. Although this represents only 0.64 per cent of the total agricultural area, the level is compatible with France, Germany and Switzerland, where organic agriculture is longer established. According to the UN statistics (Department of Agriculture and Nutrition, FAO), Slovakia is producing high-quality organic food in terms of the chemicals used. However, the distribution of activity within Slovakia has been uneven, with more than three-quarters of the land involved in 1994 (approximately 10th.ha) being in Western Slovakia. Although it is expected that each year an additional 5–10th.ha will be included in the programme, resulting in a total area of some 150th.ha by 2010, there are some constraints. Not all regions are suitable, and organic agriculture is not possible around such polluted areas as Bratislava, Jelšava, Košice, Sereď, Šaľa and Vranov nad Topľou, nor in some larger areas such as the upper Nitra Basin, the lower Orava and the central part of the Spiš region. Moreover, given the higher market prices needed to make ecological farming viable, there is only limited demand within Slovakia due to low purchasing power and much organic food is being exported to Austria and Germany. Furthermore, government support, to counter the lower yields arising from reduced use of chemicals, has been reduced by budgetary pressures from SkK90 million in 1991 (4,000 per hectare) to SkK50 million in 1992 (2,500 per hectare), SkK35 million in 1993 (2,000 per hectare) and nil in 1994 (Janku 1993).

AGRICULTURE AND THE RURAL AREA

Agriculture once dominated the rural economy, for three-fifths of the working population was active on the land at the beginning of the century. But this was hardly sustainable and in response to overpopulation in the foothills and mountains, more than 650,000 people emigrated (more than 500,000 to the United States) between 1871 and 1914. Even after the land reform carried out by the Czechoslovak state after 1918, there was considerable rural poverty. In the communist era the formation and rationalization of cooperatives went ahead in parallel with a reduction in farmworkers through transfer to industry: 918,000 in 1948 but 562,000 in 1960 and 360,000 in 1989 (Buchta 1995). Hence, there has been much hidden unemployment in agriculture under communism when the cooperatives, to a large extent, replaced the social functions of the state. But the situation changed dramatically after 1989, when a sharp decrease in employment in agriculture began to take place: from 361,000 in 1989 to 341,000 in 1990, 265,000 in 1991, 218,000 in 1992, 174,000 in 1994 and 158,000 in 1994 (*Štatistická ročenka 1995*). Labour was reduced from 13.28 per 100ha in 1989 to 6.34 per 100ha in 1994. Part of the reason for the rapid decline has related to the closure of many non-agricultural enterprises previously managed by the cooperatives. Now, industrial production is more heavily concentrated in the towns.

However, agriculture is still very important for the rural population because 71.5 per cent of those economically active work primarily in agriculture, forestry and water management (Spišiak 1994). Agricultural companies are building themselves their own places for slaughter of cattle, milking factories and so on. They are also buying stocks and are privatizing the food-producing industry, and in cooperation with other industries they produce many other small items. This sector is even more important in the less-developed regions and among social groups which have not found much employment in local industry. The cooperatives today employ 114,200 workers, 78 per cent of all those engaged in agriculture (146,400) (Košťálová- Mošková 1995). The number of inhabitants per one employee in agriculture is shown in Figure 9.1f, which deals with all employment in agriculture. Agricultural work is most important for the local economy on the Danube Lowlands (Dunajská Streda, Komárno and Veľký Krtíš) and least important in a block of districts in the north, including Čadca, Martin, Považská Bystrica, Prievidza and Žiar nad Hronom.

The agricultural sector is now the second highest (after industry) in terms of unemployment generated: 26,400 people, or 8.2 per cent of all unemployed people at the end of 1994. There are serious social problems because there are few alternatives, especially in the less-industrialized regions of the east and south, with a poor infrastructure: Bardejov, Galanta, Komárno, Levice, Michalovce, Svidník, Veľký Krtíš and Vranov nad Topľou. There is severe depression in the small villages (41.5 per cent of all villages, housing 5 per cent of the total population) with a predominance of older people reflecting low mobility, low purchasing power and poor educational standards, which is not stimulating private business. According to Buchta (1995), rural poverty is not simply related to high unemployment in particular areas and a consequent dependence on welfare. It may have a very severe impact on problem families (with large numbers of children) and specific ethnic-cultural groups such as the the Gypsy population which is heavily dependent on social support. In response to these problems, emergency 'self-support' programmes are being introduced, especially among the older people in the poorer regions of the country. Efforts are being made to improve rural services, including education, and to protect both the landscape and rural culture. Renewed interest in family farming on a part-time basis can have a significant effect on rural regeneration. There is also potential for agrotourism in Slovakia at the present time. It may be possible to revive production by small artisans, much reduced in numbers through the concentration of industry in towns.

A rural development agency has been set up in Slovakia. It is based in Nitra and has branches in Banská Bystrica, Bratislava, Košice, Liptovský Mikuláš, Lučenec, Michalovce, Poprad, Prešov, Rimavská Sobota, Trnava and Žilina. The organization provides advice, education and information with regard to agricultural marketing and the development of such farm enterprises as fruit and grapes, medicinal and technical plants and vegetables. The agency is also encouraging handicrafts, small industries and rural tourism. It is trying to promote small and medium-sized enterprises generally and is supporting a programme of village restoration in collaboration with local inhabitants.

At the district level of Nitra, which has a rural population of 100.4 thousand (1994), compared with 118.2 thousand in 1961, 47.6 per cent of the working rural population of the Nitra district is employed in agriculture. However, 52.8 per cent of the population (112.5 thousand, compared with 62.7 thousand in 1961) lives in the urban areas and so for the total working population agriculture's share is much lower – 14.4 per cent – although this is higher than the national figure of 12.1 per cent. Employment in agriculture in the Nitra district has fallen sharply from 10,841 in 1991 to 7,056 in 1994. In the latter year, 2,463 workers (34.9 per cent) were females. However, the feminization level rises from the cooperatives (where women account for 35.9 per cent of a total labour force of 4,607) and state farms (28.1 per cent of a total employment of 804) to individual and other farms (40.5 per cent of 1,645) (Štatistická ročenka okresu Nitra 1995).

Regarding the future for rural settlement patterns, Spišiak (1995) has produced a series of diagrams (Figure 9.2b) which summarize recent trends. Before 1948 there was relative stability in all villages, but with the formation of the cooperatives after 1948, consolidation began. As the number of cooperatives declined and their average size increased, selective migration was drawn to the villages selected as administrative centres for the larger farms. This took place in two phases and led to the growth of Stage 1 key villages (or 'temporary main rural settlements') and then a smaller number of Stage 2 key villages ('settlements of local importance'). Movement during the first phase was mainly to switch residence but in the second phase there was generally a change in employment linked with the development of non-agricultural functions by the cooperatives. Strangely, however, the identification of key villages did not always harmonize with the territorial organization of cooperatives in the Nitra district, and although most of the cooperatives in existence in 1989 were also Stage 2 key villages, there were exceptions: Alekšince, Hosťovce, Ivánka and Volkovce were centres for cooperatives but were only Stage 1 key villages; conversely, Lapáš, Lefantovce and Zbehy were Stage 2 key villages without cooperatives

270   *Privatization in Rural Eastern Europe*

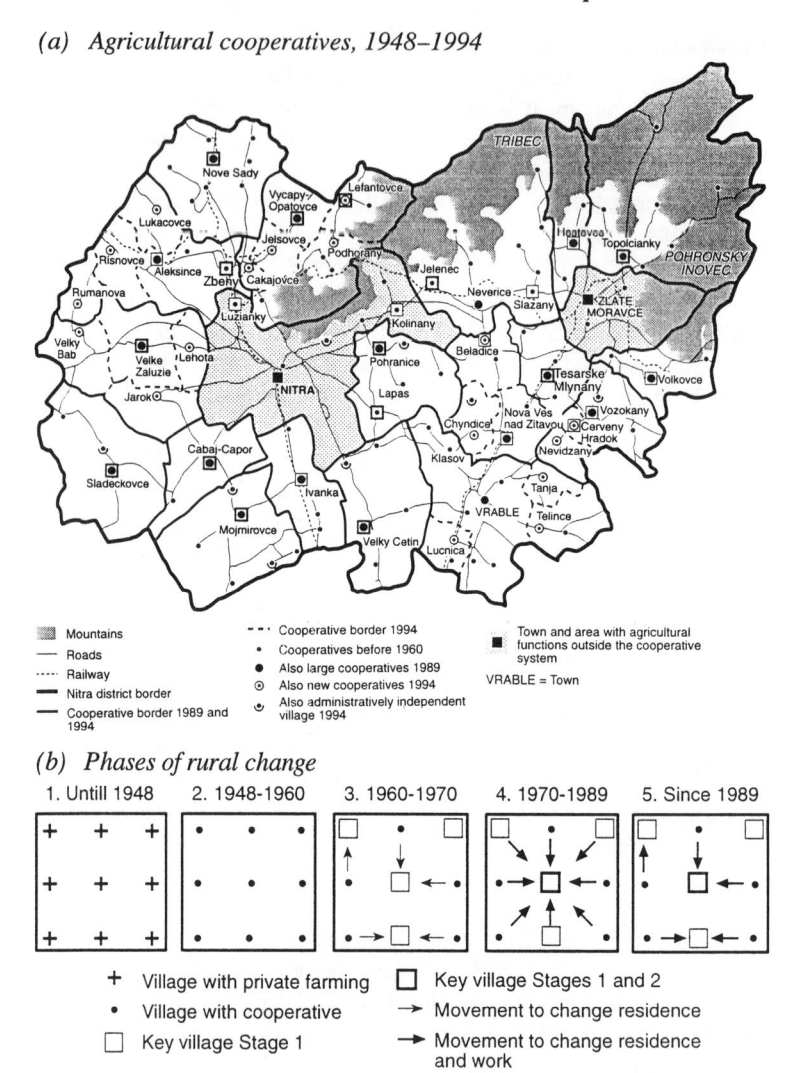

(a) Agricultural cooperatives, 1948–1994

Mountains
Roads
Railway
Nitra district border
Cooperative border 1989 and 1994

– – – Cooperative border 1994
• Cooperatives before 1960
● Also large cooperatives 1989
⊙ Also new cooperatives 1994
◎ Also administratively independent village 1994

■ Town and area with agricultural functions outside the cooperative system
VRABLE = Town

(b) Phases of rural change

1. Untill 1948   2. 1948-1960   3. 1960-1970   4. 1970-1989   5. Since 1989

+ Village with private farming
• Village with cooperative
☐ Key village Stage 1
☐ Key village Stages 1 and 2
→ Movement to change residence
➝ Movement to change residence and work

Sources: Administrative maps (a); Spišiak 1995 (b).

Figure 9.2 Slovakia: cooperatives and rural settlement in the Nitra area

Slovakia 271

(Figure 9.2a). Special situations arose around the towns of Nitra and Zlaté Moravce, where the university and high school (both with a specialized agricultural profile) were respectively in control of business. Since 1989, villages have been able to opt for administrative independence, and this has happened in many cases, especially where the economic potential is high. Not only have the cooperative centres of 1989 taken this decision, but so have many others in the lowland zone, where local cooperatives are now being set up. Several independent villages have not yet taken this step but are expected to do so in the future.

CONCLUSION

Slovak agriculture has seen quite radical change through the reorganization of the cooperatives and the scope for members to take up farming on their own land. Several types of new agricultural business are emerging and it is likely that the private sector will gradually become more important. The changes in agriculture are an important part of the restructuring of the economy as a whole, for privatization is essential to ensure the necessary motivation for successful operations within the market economy. It is a complicated task to establish exactly who owns what, and considerable conflict has arisen. However, it is clear that the prospects vary considerably between the regions because government subsidies are much reduced and the profitability of farming must be seen primarily in terms of land value: 38 per cent of the agricultural land was worth less than SkK20,000 per hectare in 1994 while 14.2 per cent commanded prices in excess of SkK90,000 per hectare. Meanwhile, per capita values for gross economic turnover in agriculture varied from SkK1,388 in Košice to SkK24,494 in Dunajská Streda. These differences may increase if credit becomes more widely available and the full potential of the better land can be realized. There were signs of improvement in 1994 through reduced financial losses compared with 1993, although results over the longer term must be considered before clear trends can be reliably identified. However, the long-term picture for land-use change is likely to be a reversal of the trend noted under communism when arable land increased steadily during the 1950s. Instead, the more marginal arable land will be turned into permanent pasture and the poorest farmland will become forest, especially on steep slopes. Conversion could be rapid in the poorer regions unless there is adequate support in terms of information and education as well as financial help through bank credits and state subventions. Support could be directed towards the encouragement of organic farming and various other forms of diversification. The scale and nature of rural poverty is becoming better understood and the rural development agency is active in encouraging handicrafts, light industry and tourism as well as the more labour-intensive agricultural enterprises.

REFERENCES

Adamovič, J. (1993), 'Organické poľnohospodárstvo', *Životné prostredie*, **27** (5), 270-71.
Bedrna, Z. (1993), 'Vplyv privatizácie na agroekologické systémy v krajine', *Životné prostredie*, **27** (6), 285-6.
Blažík, T. (1994), 'Privatization in the Slovak republic during its independent existence', in J. Kára (ed.), *Regional Conference on 'Environment and Quality of Life in Central Europe – Problems of Transition'*, Prague: International Geographical Union (CD ROM).
Brabec, F. and A. Dubcová (1991), *Kapitoly z geografie poľnohospodárstva*, Nitra: Vysoká škola pedagogická, Pedagogická fakulta.
Buchta, S. (1995), 'Vidiek v sociálnej sieti', *Hospodárske noviny zo dňa*, 22 June.
Drgoňa V. (1996), 'Ecological problems arising from intensive agriculture in Western Slovakia', *GeoJournal*, **38**, 213-18.
—— et al. (1996), 'Transformationsveränderungen und ihre Wiederspiegelung in der Regionalstruktur am Beispiel der Region Nitra', in P. Jordan (ed.), *Wandel der regionalen Strukturen in der Slowakie und im österreichisch-slowakischen grenzgebiet*, Wiener Osteuropa Studien, Vienna: Verlag Peter Lang (in press).
Dubcová, A. (1995), 'Vybrané formy transformácie priemyslu na území Ponitria' in E. Hofmann (ed.), *Postavenie regionálnej geografie Českej republiky a Slovenskej republiky v kontexte nových podmienok rozvoja*, Brno: Pedagogická fakulta Masarykovej univerzity, pp.61-8.
Ivanička, K. (1994), 'Poznatkovo orientovaná spoločnosť a poznatkovo orientovaná ekonomika – základné podmienky tvorby prosperity Slovenska', in K. Ivanička (ed.), *Vývoj ekonomiky na rozhraní tisícročia*, Bratislava: NEZES, pp.3-29.
Janku, J. (1993), 'Alternatívne poľnohospodárstvo', *Trend zo dňa*, 1 September.

Kárász, P. et al. (1995), 'Ekonomický potenciál regiónov Slovenska z aspektu ich rozvojových možností', *Trend zo dňa*, 22 November.
Klinko, L. (1995), 'Bolesti rozvojovej stratégie a transformácie poľnohospodárstva', *Hospodárske noviny zo dňa*, 15 March.
Koštálová-Mošková, M. (1995), 'Družstvá v procese ekonomickej transformácie', *Hospodárske noviny zo dňa*, 1 March.
Kováč, K. et al. (1989), *40 rokov socialistického poľnohospodárstva v okrese Nitra*, Bratislava: Príroda.
Michaeli, E. (1995), *Vybrané kapitoly z regionálnej geografie Slovenska: priemysel, poľnohospodárstvo*, Prešov: Metodické centrum.
Mládek, J. (1995), 'Die Industrie im wirtschaftlichen Transformationsprozess der Slowakei', *Europa Regional*, **3** (1), 28-34.
Sabo, P. (ed.) (1996), *Aspekty implementácie národnej ekologickej siete v SR*, Bratislava: Nadácia IUCN.
Škoríková, D. (1995), *Poľnohospodárstvo okresu Nitra*, Nitra: Fakulta prírodných vied, Vysoká škola pedagogická, Katedra geografie, diplomová.
Spišiak, P. (1994), 'Transformácia poľnohospodárstva na Slovensku', *Geografia v škole*, **2** (1), 11-13.
—— (1995), 'Agrosystém na Slovensku po r.1989', in A. Kowalczyk (ed.), *Zmiany w przestrzeni geograficznej w warunkach transformacji społeczno-ekonomicznej na przykładzie obszarów wiejskich*, Warsaw: Uniwersytet Warszawski - Wydział Geografii i Studiów Regionalnych, pp.176-81.
—— (1996), 'The current rural landscape and agriculture in Slovakia', *Acta Facultatis Rerum Naturalium Universitatis Comenianae*, **37**, 214-21.
Štefánek, M. (1993), 'Organické poľnohospodárstvo má budúcnost', *Hospodárske noviny zo dňa*, 14 July.
Žigrai, F. (1994), 'Niekoľko poznámok k úlohe regionálnej geografie v nových spoločensko-ekonomických podmienkach Slovenska', in V. Drgoňa (ed.), *Postavenie regionálnej geografie Slovenskej republiky a Českej republiký v kontexte nových podmienok rozvoja*, Nitra: Fakulta prírodných vied, Vysoká škola pedagogická, Katedra geografie, pp.42-3.

10. Slovenia

Igor Vrišer

Socio-geographical conditions in the agriculture of Central and East European countries differ in many respects from those in Western Europe and there are also considerable regional variations. The reasons for these contrasts may be sought in the socialist period after the Second World War when agriculture was collectivized by the communist authorities, but also in the development process occurring in the more distant past. This point applies particularly to Slovenia, a new state that was formed in 1991 in the northwestern part of the former Yugoslavia (Pak and Adamič 1992).

THE DEVELOPMENT OF PRIVATE FARMING

A class of private farmers emerged out of the abolition of the feudal social order in the Habsburg Monarchy in 1849–50, following the 'March Revolution' of 1848. But as the former villeins became landowners, one-third of each estate (by value) remained in the hands of the lords, because feudal landed property was preserved by law in cases where the lords had been farming land themselves. Moreover, the law assigned most of the woodland to the lords as compensation for the loss of the feudal services they had previously enjoyed (Grafenauer 1979, pp.461–2). Thus, two social classes arose out of the reforms: a class of landed proprietors and a class of small peasant farmers. The latter group was further differentiated in the second half of the nineteenth century by the distinction between those who owned a farm, as one consolidated unit or as fragmented parcels (*grunt* or *huba*), and largely landless crofters or *kajžarji* (Blaznik et al. 1970, pp.168–70). Many small farms failed because of the high cost of land purchase, along with taxation burdens and competition with the producers from the regions with more favourable natural conditions (such as Hungary and the United States) (Grafenauer, 1979, pp.176-7). The former owners often emigrated, mostly to America, because the economy was too poorly developed to provide jobs for a large agrarian proletariat. The farmland vacated was often purchased by Austrian or Italian burghers and land proprietors from such places as Graz, Trieste, Udine, Venice and Vienna, so that agrarian social problems were assuming an ethnic character at the end of the century.

The crofters and agrarian proletariat sought reforms that would divide big estates for their benefit. Such demands intensified with the collapse of the Habsburg Empire after the First World War. Slovenian territory now lay within the borders of Yugoslavia (apart from a portion in the adjacent provinces of Carinthia and Venezia Giulia) and the new authorities adopted a special Agrarian Reform Act (Blaznik et al., 1970, pp.179-83). Unfortunately, the act was only partially implemented and the 'agrarian question' remained a fundamental social problem between the two world wars. Efforts were made to divide the remaining village common property (pastures and forests), increase cooperation, and improve the financial situation for peasants by establishing local saving banks and granting moratoria on debts. Then, after the Second World War it fell to the new communist authorities to solve the agrarian problem in a revolutionary way. One of their first actions (1945–46) was the nationalization of land owned by foreigners, especially by Germans, Austrians, Hungarians and Italians, who had been the aggressors during the Second World War. However, expropriation also befell all landed proprietors with estates of more than 45ha as well as properties of more than 10ha owned by the Church and other lands owned by other non-farmers that exceeded 3ha. Some 303th.ha was divided among the agrarian proletariat, while the bulk of the expropriated land became state property (Grafenauer 1979, p.889). After the break with the Soviet Union in 1948, the authorities tried to prove their loyalty to the communist idea and started to collectivize private farming in 1949 using the *kolkhoz* model. They received support with the Land Maximum Act of 1953 which restricted private farmers to 10ha of arable land.

However, collectivization on the *kolkhoz* model failed because farmers were strongly attached to their small farms and the policy was abandoned in 1955, when the majority of farming cooperatives were disbanded. The policy of socialization now focused on state farms and the few remaining cooperatives. The confiscated and state-owned lands were given to these enterprises and they were given the option of consolidating their lands at the expense of private farms by expropriation, compulsory purchase or land exchanges. At the same time, the authorities tried to associate private farms with these state enterprises and cooperatives for the purposes of buying their products, granting loans and offering various services. Socialization continued into the 1960s through the transfer of private forests to the control of the state Forest Management Offices as an intermediate step to complete nationalization. But a more constructive policy towards private farming in the 1970s and 1980s enabled considerable investment to take place in the context of a 'cohabitation' of private and socialized farming, with the former comprising about 83.2 per cent of all agricultural lands: 719,200ha or 69 per cent of the entire Slovenian territory (Zavod Republike Slovenije za Statistiko 1994a). However, this process of stabilization went hand in hand with a decline in the agrarian population and a substantial change in farm structure.

Agrarian Population and Farm Structure

Census data show that nineteenth-century Slovenia had a pronounced agrarian character with agriculture accounting for 83.5 per cent of the population in 1857 and 66.6 per cent in 1910, according to Šifrer (1963) who has used Austro-Hungarian statistics as a basis for calculations for Slovenian territory. Data for 1931, taken from Yugoslav and Italian statistics (the latter relating to that part of Venezia Giulia – Slovensko Primorje – which was tranferred to Yugoslavia after the Second World War) show the situation changing only slowly and, according to the official data of the Statistical Office of Slovenia, 41.1 per cent of the population was still farm based in 1953. Communist industrialization then brought the proportion of the agrarian population to 31.6 per cent in 1961 and 7.6 per cent (145,422) in 1991, thereby eliminating the persistent problem of rural overpopulation. A class of peasant-workers arose, with regular work in industry or some other non-agricultural occupation combined with spare-time activity in farming, mainly to supply their own households. In 1991, the number of active persons working full-time in agriculture was only 109,139, of whom 99,990 constituted the economically active agricultural population working on their own agricultural holdings.

At the same time, there have been changes in farm structure. Holdings have always been relatively small, a situation that must be related in part to a land shortage: in 1996 only 614,692ha (30.3 per cent of the country) consisted of agricultural land in the form of arable land, gardens, meadows, orchards and vineyards, although such 'utilized land', with the addition of rough grazings, yielded a total agricultural area of 785,499ha (38.7 per cent of the total land) (Zavod Republike Slovenije za Statistiko 1997, p.16). Agrarian overpopulation was exacerbated by subdivision but eventually, in the socialist period, the decline in the agrarian population resulted in many small parcels coming into the ownership of non-farmers, with only spasmodic agricultural use. For this reason, the Statistical Office started to discriminate between farm households based solely on income from agriculture, those with income based on a mixture of farming and non-agricultural activity, others with no agricultural income whatsoever and a fourth category of farms with no income (that is, without a labour force) (Table 10.1). The number of farms in the first two categories has decreased rapidly over the past 20 years, while the number of farms with purely non-agricultural income sources has increased. The transition (accompanied by further fragmentation) became so intense that even the communist authorities were forced to pass an act to protect 'prospective private farms'. These were identified by village communities and communal assemblies in 1973 with the aim of ensuring that the owners would be active farmers and further partitioning of the holdings would be prevented.

Table 10.1 Slovenia: number and types of farms by source of income, 1960–1991

Farm type (by income source)	Number of farms in							
	1960		1969		1981		1991	
	N	%	N	%	N	%	N	%
Agriculture only	95,918	49.2	80,302	44.5	21,675	11.3	18,585	11.9
Mixed	84,251	43.2	80,043	44.5	52,060	27.1	57,721	36.9
Non-agricultural	11,306	5.8	14,793	8.2	116,533	60.7	79,293	50.6
No income	3,380	1.8	5,289	2.9	1,822	0.9	950	0.6
Total	94,855	100.0	180,228	100.0	192,090	100.0	156,549	100.0

Source: Zavod Republike Slovenije za Statistiko 1994a.

The average private farm size has fallen steadily during the past half century (Table 10.2). It was about 8.3ha before the Second World War, but fell to 6.7ha in 1960, 5.6ha in 1981 (Natek 1987, p.53) and 5.9ha in 1991 (Census 1994). Concurrently, the size structure deteriorated. In 1902, about 35.8 per cent of farms were smaller than 2ha (Melik 1963), compared with 33.2 per cent in 1960 and 31.2 per cent in 1991. The majority of people living on these farms could be regarded as crofters; industrialization and transformation into farms with a mixed source of income was the only possible way forward because they could not increase production or develop a specialized profile. If farm size is considered in relation to income source, it transpires that farms dependent solely on an agricultural income average 7.4ha, compared with 8.36ha for farms with mixed income sources of income and 3.75ha for farms with non-agricultural sources of income. It should be remembered that farms in general consist of only 3.2ha of agricultural land (of which 2.5ha is arable), while the rest of the average 5.87ha holding consists of forest or wastelands (Zavod Republike Slovenije za Statistiko 1994b). By contrast, the average farm in the EU has 13.3ha of agricultural land (Kmetijski Inštitut Slovenije 1992). A further constraint in Slovenia involves the terrain because only 28 per cent of farmland is level; the rest lies in mountainous country (49 per cent) or on karst (13 per cent) or is of rather poor quality in general (10 per cent) (ibid.).

Table 10.2 Slovenia: farm structure, 1902–1991

Size band (ha)	Number of farms and percentage distribution						Total area (ha) and percentage distribution			
	1902		1960		1991		1960		1991	
	N	%	*N*	%	*N*	%	*N*	%	*N*	%
<1	n.a.	20.0	40,657	20.9	44,428	28.4	18,991	1.4	21,097	2.3
1–4	n.a.	16.0	73,417	37.6	56,327	36.0	198,766	15.2	156,436	17.0
5–9	n.a.	18.0	39,130	20.1	28,112	18.0	279,007	21.4	207,466	22.5
10–19	n.a.	15.3	29,167	15.0	19,637	12.5	402,200	30.8	277,288	30.1
20+	n.a.	8.3	12,484	6.4	8,045	5.1	406,585	31.1	257,206	28.1
Total	n.a.	100.0	194,855	100.0	156,549	100.0	1,305,549	100.0	919,892	100.0

Sources: Melik 1963; Natek 1987; Kmetijski Inštitut Slovenije 1992; Zavod Republike Slovenije za Statistiko 1994a.

A further problem for private farms is fragmentation arising out of inheritance (according to the Roman Law) and the functioning of the land market. Typical parcels on private farms range between 0.3 and 0.5ha in size and a single farm comprises 6.9 parcels on average (Belec 1990, p.210). Farmers tend to be distrustful of any attempt by the authorities at consolidations (*commassation*) although such action would reduce the complications of property relations. If anything, the stagnant policy towards private farming which followed the abortive attempt at collectivization helped to preserve the inherited pattern of property relations to a certain extent. However, the introduction of a market economy after 1990 will, sooner or later, raise the key question for the majority of these farms: how to be competitive with the more efficient food producers around the world. A new social classification of farmers can be expected in Slovenia, as in other CEE countries.

AGRICULTURAL PRODUCTION

Private Farming

In 1990, private farms produced about 62.6 per cent of Slovenia's agricultural GDP from 718,900ha of farming land. This share was significantly greater after the Second World War (92.2 per cent in 1955), but preference for manufacturing industry led to an absolute and relative decline that continued through the 1960s. The private farmers were treated as second-class citizens; their better land was expropriated and the management of forests was also taken out of their hands. They lost the prominence they had formerly enjoyed (through ownership and management) in the cooperatives, savings banks and agrarian banks of the pre-communist period, while their agrarian communities were dissolved. State control of the agricultural infrastructure (including the purchasing enterprises, mills, dairies and slaughterhouses) also had a negative impact on private farms. But since the mid-1970s, the authorities have tried to stop this decline by halting expropriation and by introducing a number of positive revitalization measures: credits on favourable terms, expert assistance, marketing arrangements including cooperation with the food industry and minimum social security for farmers.

Nevertheless, the production from private farms continues to fall. In addition to the legacy of discrimination, the marketing system continues to be defective and there are inevitable constraints through small volumes of output, compounded by low yields, poor quality and a conflict between the market and family subsistence, while fragmented holdings make for inefficiency and the elderly workforce registers only a low level of productivity. In 1990, for example, private farming contributed 70.4 per cent of wheat production compared with 94.8 per cent in 1960, 77.7 per cent of maize (97.7), 81.2 per cent of wine (93.6) and 26.5 per cent of hops (94.9 per cent in 1955) (Table 10.3). Clearly, private farming still has a dominant role in the production of many commodities, such as cereals, fodder plants, hay and potatoes, but state (social) farms, financially supported by the authorities, have increased their contribution and are especially prominent in the production of industrial plants (sugar beet and hops), as well as fruits and grapes from newly established orchards and vineyards. A similar division occurs in the livestock sector (Table 10.4) with private farms still dominant in cattle rearing (85.8 per cent in 1990 and 93.9 per cent in 1960) and milk production (92 per cent in 1990 and 87.9 per cent in 1965), while state enterprises and cooperatives are prominent in pigs (1.7 per cent in 1960 but 44.1 per cent in 1990) and poultry (5.2 and 89.7 per cent) reared on modern farms. In this unplanned division of labour it is evident that private farming is dominant in the labour-intensive branches, convenient for small units where much of the production is consumed on the farm, while the larger enterprises take the lead where the market is attractive and where machines can be substituted for manual labour.

Over the past two decades, private farmers have been trying to adapt to market needs. Instead of the traditional mixed farming there is now greater specialization in livestock with a greater production of fodder and larger areas of meadows. Some of the poorer land has been afforested (Vrišer 1987). But private farms are still not sufficiently market orientated and their contribution to the national agricultural output is not entirely satisfactory, leaving aside what is consumed on the farms and marketed through the unregistered 'grey economy'. In 1995, private farms contributed 89.1 per cent of the milk, 81.7 per cent of the cattle and 69.7 per cent of the potatoes, but only 38.3 per cent of the fruit, 35.8 per cent of the cereals, 29.7 per cent of the hops and 13.8 per cent of the pigs. In the case of wine and of poultry, the contribution was

Table 10.3 Slovenia: the role of private farms in crop production, 1955–1996

Total production (th.t) and percentage contribution from private farms

Year	Wheat		Maize		Potatoes		Hay		Wine		Hops	
	N	%	N	%	N	%	N	%	N	%	N	%
1955	72.6	97.1	70.0	98.8	619.9	99.2	1,066.2	97.5	57.1	n.a.	1.8	94.9
1960	119.9	94.8	120.7	97.7	949.7	97.7	1,242.9	n.a.	52.2	93.7	3.1	n.a.
1965	114.5	87.6	124.0	45.3	525.2	97.4	1,263.2	87.3	55.4	76.3	2.8	57.0
1970	133.4	85.4	146.2	78.7	622.1	94.5	1,267.3	73.7	57.8	65.0	3.4	34.5
1975	138.2	87.9	211.5	85.2	468.2	99.0	1,374.5	93.4	78.1	70.3	2.9	33.6
1980	158.7	88.7	214.3	83.9	457.2	99.1	1,315.8	96.1	53.1	74.8	3.1	28.6
1985	161.6	78.0	298.7	87.2	421.7	98.9	1,406.5	96.5	59.9	73.4	4.0	27.7
1990	140.6	70.4	337.6	77.7	413.4	99.2	1,588.0	97.8	56.5	81.2	3.5	26.5
1996	126.7	72.1	271.8	81.6	498.7	98.8	1,546.9	99.2	66.9*	82.8*	1.1	33.2

Note: * 1994.

Source: Zavod Republike Slovenije za Statistiko (1965–94a).

Table 10.4 Slovenia: the role of private farms in pastoral farming, 1955–1997

Year	Animals (th.) or production (m. litres) and percentage contribution of private farms							
	Cattle		Pigs		Horses		Milk	
	N	%	N	%	N	%	N	%
1955	546.8	95.8	424.1	98.3	65.9	95.4	n.a.	n.a.
1960	533.3	93.9	508.9	97.5	58.9	97.8	373.0	n.a.
1965	545.3	86.3	500.1	88.0	51.1	98.5	372.1	87.9
1970	492.9	91.6	449.2	81.7	45.3	99.4	401.5	88.9
1975	557.1	91.8	443.0	77.1	27.0	99.2	465.5	90.8
1980	568.3	88.3	509.1	67.1	18.2	98.7	532.2	90.9
1985	560.9	87.9	565.7	60.4	15.1	97.7	573.9	91.6
1990	532.9	85.8	587.8	54.4	10.4	96.1	578.9	92.0
1997	454.3	93.8	323.7	58.7	8.1	96.5	537.8	93.4

Source: Zavod Republike Slovenije za Statistiko (1965–94a).

insignificant: 0.3 and 0.01 per cent, respectively (Zavod Republike Slovenije za Statistiko 1996).

Notwithstanding the change of social system, private farming is still facing old problems in the new, capitalist conditions. Farms are too small and fragmented to be efficient for modern market-orientated production. In spite of high labour inputs and adequate mechanization, yields remain low, partly because farming is marginalized by the importance of non-agricultural income sources. To illustrate the situation, some data are presented on the yields in Slovenian private farming in 1993 compared with yields in Slovenia as a whole and in the EU: wheat 3.31t/ha (Slovenia 3.84 and EU 4.94); maize 3.50 t/ha (4.02 and 6.68); potatoes 12.51t/ha (12.31 and 28.67); milk 2,613 litres per cow (2,416 and 3,941). These problems cannot be solved simply by the 1991 privatization act, which provides for the return expropriated and confiscated lands to their former owners, the restoration of cooperatives and the introduction of farmers' shareholdings in dairies, slaughterhouses and other plants connected with agriculture.

Social Agricultural Enterprises and Cooperatives

Despite massive support from the communist authorities between 1950 and 1990, these farms have not always produced satisfactory results. Overall, they occupied 7.1 per cent (61,518ha) of farming lands, but 19.6 per cent (397,480ha) of the land in the country. In 1996, they occupied 4.9 per cent of all farmland (38,394ha) (or 6.3 per cent of the entire state, which includes an additional area comprising mainly woodlands). The 1996 situation compares with 6.9 per cent in 1990 (4.3 per cent of all land), 7.6 per cent in 1980 (4.8), 5.2 per cent in 1970 (3.3) and 7.2 per cent in 1950 (5.2). For many years, they were poorly managed and failed to make profits. They were repeatedly reorganized and territorially rearranged on the basis of federal laws (passed in 1952, 1955 and 1965) for the 'rounding-off' of socialist enterprises and cooperatives through compulsory purchase or land exchanges arranged by the local authorities. During the past two decades the technical level has advanced and they have specialized their production under young expert managers with the further support by state credits. But although efficiency and production have improved, they are still high-cost producers by international standards and remain heavily in debt with lands that are often highly fragmented. They are now subject to the privatization programme (Table 10.5) and the total area remaining in state social farming is declining (Vrižer 1996, pp.154–6).

Table 10.5 Slovenia: privatization programme

Laws	Major provisions
Law on Ownership Restructuring	Funds for development, financial compensation and pensions
	Authorized investing companies
	Shareholding corporations
Law on Cooperatives	Cooperatives and/or Shareholding Corporations
Law on Denationalization	Restitution to private owners or their legal successors
Law on the Fund of Agricultural Lands and Forests	Fund of state- or commune-owned agricultural land

Table 10.6 Slovenia: categories of land and land ownership, 1950–1996

Land and farm type (percentage distribution)	Land (th.ha) and percentage distribution in							
	1950	1960	1970	1980	1985	1990	1996	**
All land	2,021	2,025	2,025	2,025	2,025	2,025	2,027	n.a.
Private holdings	72.9	24.5	69.6	69.1	68.7	68.8	70.1	9.5
SOEs and cooperatives	5.2	6.3	5.8	4.8	4.5	4.3	1.9	321.9
Other state lands	21.8	69.1	24.6	26.1	26.8	26.9	23.0	n.a.
Agricultural land	980	875	942	872	867	864	785	n.a.
Percentage of all land								
Private holdings	40.5	17.4	38.5	36.5	35.9	35.5	32.9	3.3
SOEs and cooperatives	3.5	2.0	2.4	3.3	3.1	2.9	3.9	267.0
Other state lands	4.5	23.8	5.6	3.3	3.8	4.2	1.9	n.a.
Percentage of agricultural land								
Private holdings	83.5	40.2	82.7	84.7	84.0	83.1	85.0	
SOEs and cooperatives	7.2	4.7	5.2	7.5	7.1	6.9	4.9	
Other state lands	9.3	55.0	12.1	7.6	8.9	9.9	10.1	

Arable land[a]							
	319	347	331	311	305	305	286	n.a.
Percentage of all land								
Private holdings	13.7	16.0	14.8	13.7	13.2	13.1	12.4	0.4
SOEs and cooperatives	1.4	0.8	1.2	1.6	1.8	1.9	1.7	181.0
Other state lands	0.6	0.3	0.3	0.0	0.0	0.0	0.0	n.a.
Percentage of agricultural land								
Private holdings	87.1	93.4	90.6	89.1	87.9	87.2	87.8	
SOEs and cooperatives	8.9	5.0	7.2	10.8	12.1	12.7	12.1	
Other state lands	4.0	1.6	2.1	0.0	0.0	0.0	0.0	

Notes:

** Average holding (ha) 1994.
[a] Includes gardens, orchards and vineyards.
Agricultural land = arable land plus meadows and pastures.

Source: Zavod Republike Slovenije za Statistiko (1953-54 and 1965-95).

Evaluation of the role and significance of (state/social) agrarian enterprises in Slovenian agriculture is not easy because several diverse factors are intertwined. These include the legally questionable origins of these enterprises, balanced by the economic advantages of production for today's market on large continuous surfaces, high investment levels, expert knowledge and close links with both the food-processing industry and consumer markets orientation (strengths which are not usually matched by private farmers) (Vrižer 1996). This 'socialist sector' has at its disposal a fluctuating area of land: 3–5 per cent of all land, or 5–8 per cent of all agricultural land during the past four decades (Table 10.6). For the most part, the land is of better than average quality and it is generally level. In 1996, arable land and gardens comprised 69.5 per cent, meadows 10.8 per cent, pastures 7.1 per cent, vineyards 7.3 per cent and orchards 5.2 per cent. The structure of the private sector was considerably less favourable: arable land and gardens 30.8 per cent, meadows 45.4 per cent, pastures 16.4 per cent, orchards 4.3 per cent and vineyards 3 per cent (Statistični Urad Republike Slovenije 1996). The socialist enterprises produced 30.9 per cent of the total agricultural production in the country in physical terms (or 31.6 per cent of agriculture's contribution to the social product in 1993 (ibid.).

But in spite of the enormous support offered to the socialized agricultural enterprises and cooperatives by the communist authorities between 1950 and 1990, their role in Slovenian agriculture was not proportionally satisfactory. For many years, they were unprofitable and economically poorly managed. They were repeatedly reorganized and territorially rearranged by the local authorities. Only in the past twenty years, through young experts and favourable credits granted by the state, were they gradually able to consolidate, improve their technical level and both specialize and increase their production. In 1996, there were 191 such enterprises and cooperatives with an average size of 200ha and a workforce of 10,649 (Table 10.7). Fifteen were larger than 1,000ha, 34 fell into the 200–1,000ha bracket and 33 were in the 50–200ha band. However, in spite of some consolidation, many remained fragmented.

Production was mostly specialized in the growing of wheat, maize, sugar beet, hops, fruit and grapes and, in the livestock sector, the rearing of cattle, pigs and poultry. In 1996, 70.1 per cent of the

Table 10.7 Slovenia: production by state social enterprises, 1960–1996

Year	Farms	FarmArea (th.ha)	Production (th.t)				Livestock (th)			**
			Wheat	Maize	Hops	Grapes	Cattle	Pigs	Poultry	
1960	490	154.1	7.59	3.80	n.a.	8.97	32.6	12.4	1,150	10.7
1970	132	116.6	20.22	17.44	2.09	18.38	40.2	82.0	1,970	23.0
1980	247	96.8	17.95	34.42	2.30	21.47	59.6	129.2	8,999	30.0
1990	202	99.0	58.98	75.27	2.58	18.74	86.4	246.6	12,134	39.4
1993	203	62.0	53.10	61.83	2.54	20.40	43.2	240.9	9,385	31.6
1996	191	38.4	44.70	61.30	2.23	18.10	30.0	230.7	8,961	31.6*

Notes:
** Percentage of social production created by agriculture.
*   1993.

Source: Statistični Urad Republike Slovenije 1996.

cropland was used for cereals (43.1 per cent in the private sector), 14 per cent for industrial plants (3.8), 12.7 per cent for fodder (35.2), 2.4 per cent for nurseries (0.9) and 0.7 per cent for vegetables (16.2) (Zavod Republike Slovenije za Statistiko 1996). They achieved output levels similar to those in more developed countries: in 1993 they produced 72.4 per cent of the fruit, 48.7 per cent of the sugar beet, 31.6 per cent of the wheat, 24 per cent of the maize and 20.8 per cent of the wine; also 88.6 per cent of the poultry, 40.6 per cent of the pigs and 9 per cent of the cattle. As the only large farms in the country, they are absolutely essential in supplying the population with food and industry with raw materials, and in generating exports. Although they are high-cost enterprises heavily in debt, they cannot be eliminated in the short term. It would take a long time for the private sector to replace them because after a long period of subordination time is needed to gear up production on a specialized basis. In any case, many of the private farms are small and they serve a primary subsistence function for families deriving their main income outside agriculture.

Agrarian–Geographical Regionalization

In spite of its small territory and the uniformity of its social restructuring, traditional regional differences have been preserved in private farming (Figure 10.1). They derive from the physical resources (climate and terrain) as well as the process of historical and cultural development. Several agrarian systems and agrarian–geographical regions can be noted (Vrižer 1985, 1993).

1. The Alpine, Subalpine and karst region of livestock rearing, including the rearing of dairy cattle and the production of fodder, and associated forestry activities. The area includes the mountainous areas in the centre, south and west of the country. Farms are relatively large and in the Alps there has been a sporadic development of rural tourism.
2. The Pannonian and Subpannonian region concerned with the production of cereals and root crops (especially potatoes), along with cattle rearing (for meat and milk) and pig rearing. These enterprises extend over the lowlands and basins in the centre and east of Slovenia. It is the most important region for production but farms are generally small and highly fragmented (as in Prekmurje), although they are also modern in the agrotechnical sense.
3. In the Subalpine and Subpannonian hill country, the traditional mixed system (combining livestock rearing and cultivation) persists with a high level of self-sufficiency.
4. In some areas with favourable climatic and terrain conditions in the Subpannonian and Mediterranean zones, specialized agriculture has developed: hops in the Savinjska Dolina Valley; vegetables in Slovenian Istria; and both fruit and vines in Slovenske Gorice, Haloze, Slovenian Istria and Goriška Brda. Farms are small and fragmented, but there are profits to be made from intensive cultivation.

THE TRANSFORMATION OF RURAL AREAS

As a result of industrialization and the development of energy and transport infrastructures during this century, there has been a massive change in relationships between urban and rural settlements. Urbanization in Slovenia was delayed, and in 1900 the urban population consisted of only 191,468 people or 15.1 per cent. Meanwhile, the agrarian population accounted for 73.2 per cent, because apart from a few industrial and mining settlements the rural areas were entirely dependent on agriculture. There were few large towns, apart from Trieste, to which the surplus rural population could migrate and so there was much emigration to America and Western Europe at this time.

Source: Vrišer 1993.

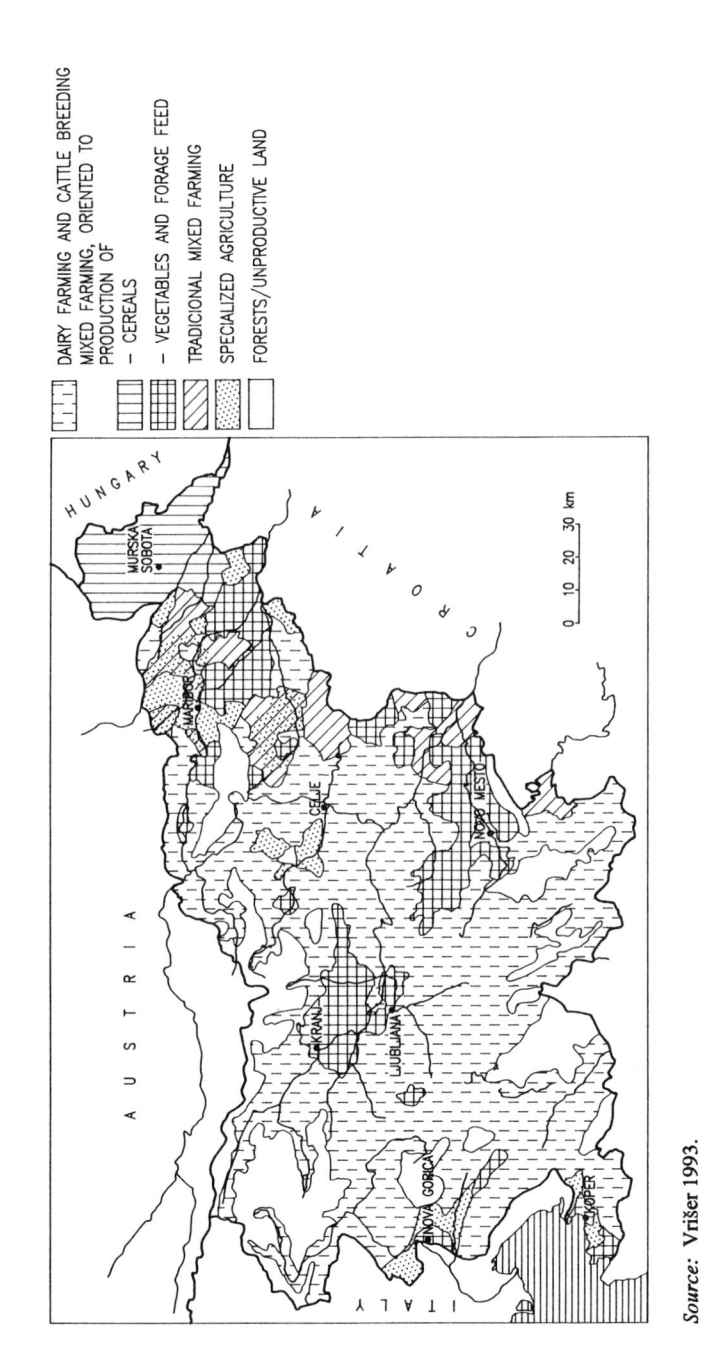

Figure 10.1 Slovenia: systems of agricultural land use, 1985

However, industrialization has triggered powerful rural–urban migration flows and the urban population accounted for 50.5 per cent of Slovenia's total population in 1991. At the same time, the rural population has decreased both absolutely and relatively: from 1,076.6 thousand (84.9 per cent) in 1900 to 1,067.1 thousand (70.9 per cent) in 1953 and 973.9 thousand (49.5 per cent) in 1991 (Zavod Republike Slovenije za Statistiko 1994a). Two sociogeographic types can now bediscerned in the rural areas: 'urbanized' and 'mainly agrarian'. Using several indicators (population growth and density, migration, commuting and the proportion of the agrarian population), Ravbar (1992) calculated that 50.2 per cent of the population was urban (covering 4.4 per cent of the territory), while 30.3 per cent was rural–urbanized (17.4) and 19.5 per cent was rural–agrarian (78.2).

Settlement patterns have also been transformed. In the mid-nineteenth century, nucleated villages in the lowlands contrasted with hamlets and dispersed settlements in the hills and isolated farms in the mountains – a situation largely unchanged from the Medieval period. Central places in the rural areas consisted of parish villages and 'boroughs' (settlements known in Slovenian as *trg*, the equivalent of the German *Marktort* and the Italian *borgata*). Only a few elements of this traditional pattern still remain, mainly in areas of extreme population dispersal. There are now 5,945 settlements in the country with an average population size of 179 (1991), of which 73 are urban and 5,872 rural. But most of the latter are now semi-agrarian, urbanized or industrial in character with agriculture no longer the principal activity. Under the polycentric plan carried out by the communist authorities between 1970 and 1985, many industrial plants were built in rural areas: out of a total of 424 settlements with industrial plants, 226 arose in this way (Vrižer 1987). Furthermore, a network of rural central places emerged during the second half of the twentieth century. In 1900 there were 288 central settlements in Slovenia of which 261 fell into classes I and II, characteristic of rural areas: class I settlement had an administration (municipality office), a four-year elementary school, a post-office and shop; while class II settlements included (additionally) a range of shops and a court and doctor. Higher living standards and an increase in non-agricultural employment have resulted in more rural central places and improved services within these places. In the rural areas in 1994, there were 548 settlements in classes I and II plus another 64 with a higher status which did not exist outside the towns in

1900. Class I settlements now boasted an elementary school catering for the full age range and an inn, in addition to the facilities of 1900, while class II now included a medical centre, pharmacy and bank (Vrižer 1974, 1987).

As part of the communist programme of expanding industry and creating socialist agricultural enterprises, there was an attempt to build cooperative centres in each large village providing a seat for local self-government. These centres of socialization were inspired by the Soviet *agrogorod* and they included shops and a hall which could also be used as a cinema. However, this initiative was abandoned with the collapse of the collectivization drive, although it helped to strengthen the central places at the class I level. Meanwhile, the administrative reorganization of 1958 created large communes with administrative centres offering services above the class II level. Existing class III commune centres were strengthened and some new ones were created. But this damaged the class IV district centres, which lost many traditional functions. The communes had great power in planning the development of the economy, including administrative, social services and spatial policy – so much so that people would refer to 'communal feudalism'. In general, however, the growth of road transport meant that middle-order centres lost out to the larger towns.

At the same time, modern buildings replaced traditional rural houses, while craft workshops and holiday homes also appeared. But while urban influences grew stronger, the 'urban–rural continuum' nevertheless involved a gradual transition (Kokole and Kokole 1969). In recent decades, many urban dwellers have moved into the countryside, and this suburbanizing process is now very strong in the vicinity of the larger towns (Ravbar 1992). The importance of holiday homes continues to increase, with a total of 26,374 recorded by the 1991 census: 19,154 were purpose built while 4,006 are rural houses taken over for recreational use and 3,214 have other origins. The number of vacation dwellings increased in the period 1971–91 from 4,300 to 26,374. Vacation dwellings amount to only 3.85 per cent of the entire housing stock, but the Alps, the Adriatic coast and the Subpannonian grape-growing and fruit-growing hills have influenced the structure and appearance of settlement. In the commune of Radovljica in the Julian Alps, the weight of such dwellings is one-tenth and in the commune of Mozirje in the Savinjske Alpe, it is 5.8 per cent. In the coastal commune of Piran, the proportion is 15.2 per cent and in

Gornja Radgona in the eastern grape-growing region of Slovenske Gorice it is 5.1 per cent. In such areas the holiday homes create problems in the ecological sense because they have often been built in attractive settings without proper permission in the form of an 'urbanistic permit'.

Factory employment accelerated the social restructuring of the rural population through the creation of a class of peasant-workers, many of whom were commuters. The weight of the purely agricultural population in relation to the total population is now less than 10 per cent in much of the country (Figure 10.2). According to the 1991 census, 53.9 per cent of all persons in employment were working away from their place of residence, mostly in the towns and industrial centres. The growth of factory work eliminated the traditional agrarian overpopulation by the 1980s. There was an agrarian population of 120.7/sq.km of agricultural land in 1900, falling to 82.1/sq.km in 1953 (when densities in the east still exceeded 100) and 22.3/sq.km in 1991 (Zavod Republike Slovenije za Statistiko 1994a). Family size was reduced nationally as the birth-rate declined from 34 per thousand in the first decade of the twentieth century to 27.2 per thousand in 1920 and 9.9 per thousand in 1993. Meanwhile, the differences between cities and rural areas diminished. The 1993 birth-rate of 9.9 per thousand nationally ranged from 9.1 Ljubljana to 9.5–10.5 per thousand in typical rural communes of Murska Sobota and Ptuj in eastern Slovenia. Equally, the death-rate of 10 per thousand nationally covered a lower figure in Ljubljana (9.2) and higher figures in the communes of Murska Sobota (12.7) and Ptuj (10.9). The average rural family now comprises 3.7 persons compared with 3.1 in the towns. The rural population has also aged through selective out-migration, and many farms now lack successors: while 11 per cent of Slovenia's population is aged over 65 the proportion in the rural areas is 12.1 per cent, compared with 21.5 per cent for the active population (Zavod Republike Slovenije za Statistiko 1994a). As farms in the mountain and karst regions were abandoned (some during the Second World War), woodland has increased from 838.4th.ha in 1900 (41.3 per cent of the total area) to 1,020.1th.ha in 1993 (50.4 per cent of the total area). In the Alps, the declining use of the high pastures (reflecting the general devaluation of agricultural land under socialism) created an ecological problem, so the local authorities tried to protect the better land from development and

Source: Zavod Republike Slovenije za Statistiko.

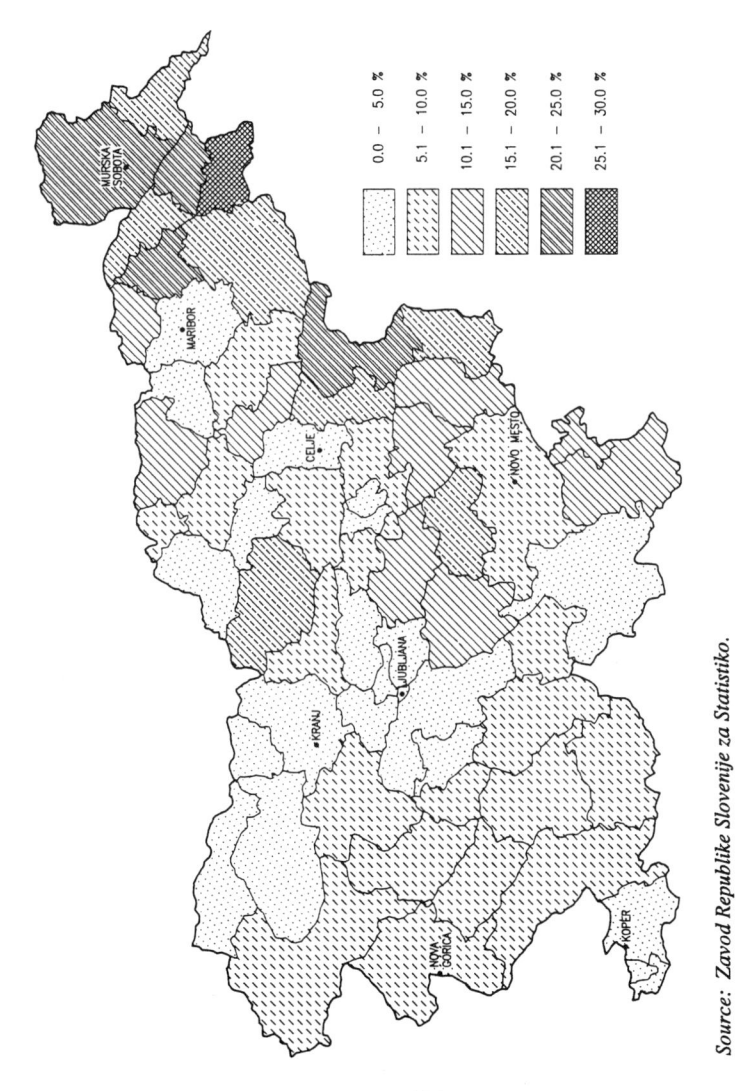

Figure 10.2 Slovenia: agricultural population, 1991

(a) *Polje pri Vodicah*, northwest of Ljubljana with 209 inhabitants. The agrarian population share has fallen from 87.3 per cent in 1953 to 13.8 per cent in 1991, when only two farm households out of 97 had a purely agricultural income. Forty-eight had a mixed-income source and 47 had an entirely non-agricultural income source.

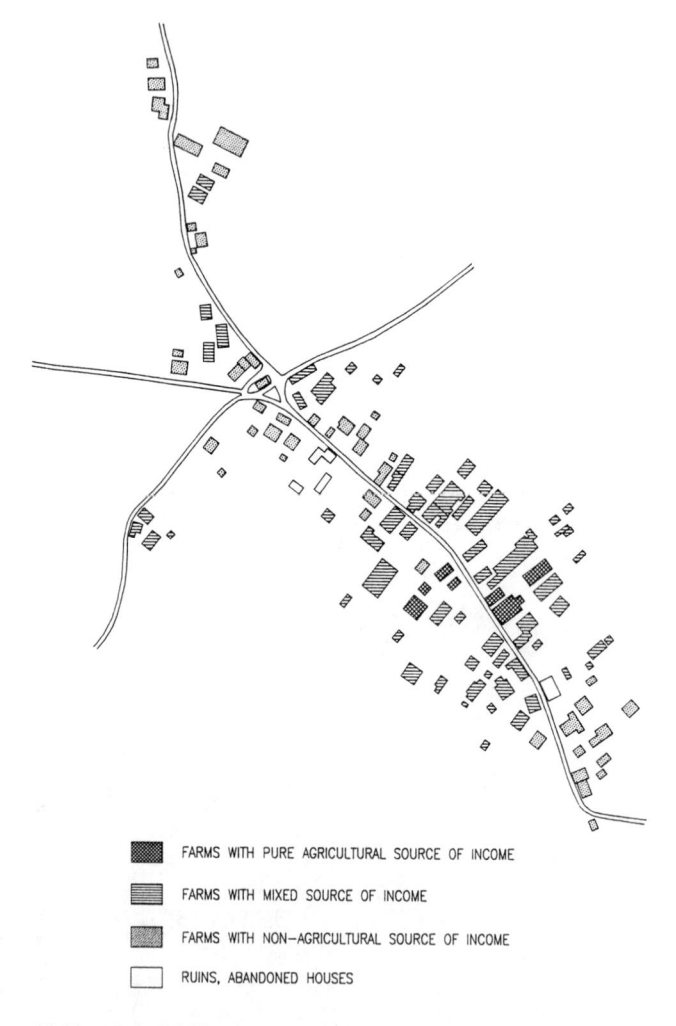

FARMS WITH PURE AGRICULTURAL SOURCE OF INCOME

FARMS WITH MIXED SOURCE OF INCOME

FARMS WITH NON-AGRICULTURAL SOURCE OF INCOME

RUINS, ABANDONED HOUSES

Source: Field study by M. Kezele.

Slovenia 295

(b) Plužna in the Upper Soča Valley with 54 inhabitants. This was once a farming settlement linked with the Italian zinc mine of Care del Predil. In 1991 only one household had a purely agricultural income while the 18 others were all drawing pensions. Twenty houses were being used for vacations and ten were abandoned.

TYPES OF FARMS BY SOURCE OF INCOME

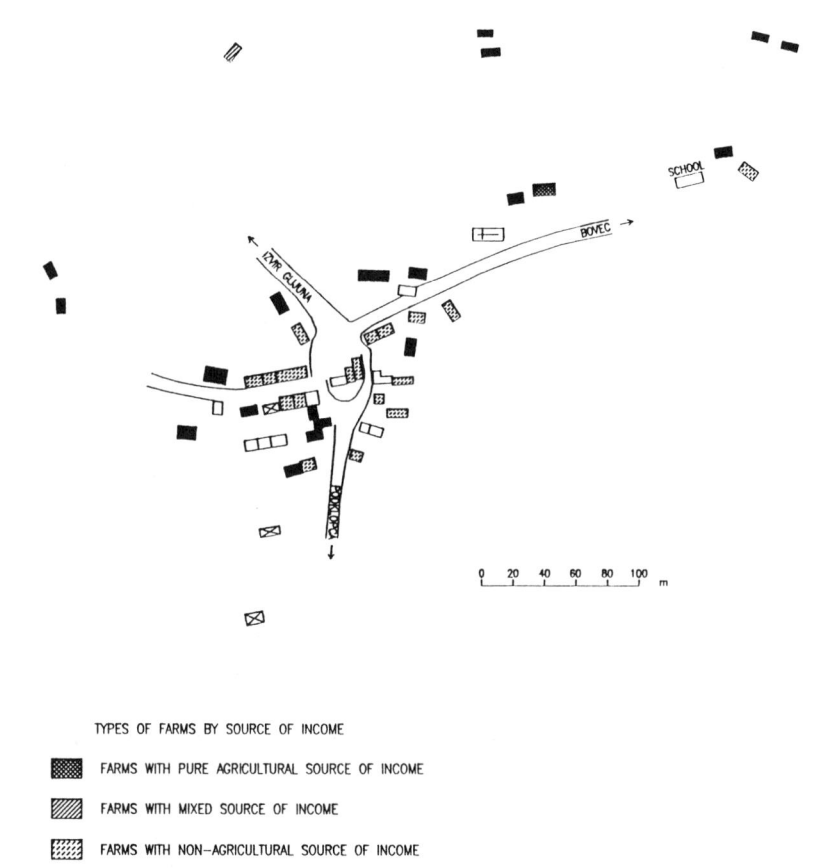

- FARMS WITH PURE AGRICULTURAL SOURCE OF INCOME
- FARMS WITH MIXED SOURCE OF INCOME
- FARMS WITH NON-AGRICULTURAL SOURCE OF INCOME
- SECOND HOMES
- RUINS, ABANDONED HOUSES
- OTHER HOUSES

Figure 10.3 Slovenia: types of farm by income source in the villages of Plužna and Polje pri Vodicah

fragmentation. Land close to the towns was especially vulnerable to 'social fallowing' and a replacement of agricultural uses with recreation and tourism (Klemenčič 1975). Because of a labour shortage, the state/social agricultural enterprises began to hire workers from other parts of former Yugoslavia.

Two demographic situations now occur in rural Slovenia as a result of the transformation of the last half century – areas of transition and areas of depopulation – complementing the urban areas of concentration (Klemenčič 1992) (Figure 10.3). Demographic stagnation and prominence of the urban way of life are typical of the transitional areas which comprise 52.2 per cent of the population and 29.9 per cent of the state territory. Areas of depopulation (characterized by underdevelopment, limited employment possibilities and an ageing population) involve 10.3 per cent of the total population and 32.2 per cent of the territory, mainly border areas with mountain or karst terrain, remote from the main lines of communication and mainly agrarian in character. The communist authorities tried to overcome these differences through a series of 'Consistent Regional Development Acts' (passed between 1971 and 1986) and Slovenia continues the policy of helping the undeveloped and border areas, and especially the demographically endangered areas. The differences between the most-developed (urban–industrial) areas and the least-developed (agrarian) regions narrowed from 1:2.5–3.0 in the 1950s to 1:1.5 in the 1980s. Nine criteria (concerned with the development of productive forces, the effects of the functioning of productive forces and the growth of social standards) were calculated as index points, against the existing republican average of 12 regions and 60 communes for the years 1952, 1961, 1971 and 1982. Urban–rural contrasts narrowed at the same time (Vrižer 1985). But the market economy signals the danger of widening disparities and independent Slovenia is continuing with a regional policy through a 'Development Stimulation of the Demographically Endangered Areas Act' passed in 1990. The state offers financial and expert assistance to the affected areas for various projects to stimulate small private enterprises and improve the local infrastructure. Credits are available under favourable terms along with grants and income tax concessions.

CONCLUSION

It is hard to forecast the future development of Slovenian agrarian economy. Numerous unsolved problems have been inherited from the past period and new problems are emerging as a result of the market economy, the interest in joining the EU, doubts about the liberal land-ownership policy and the search for new markets for agricultural products. But it is certain that the transition will last longer than was initially expected. It is the market that is already affecting the transformation of agrarian economy, much more than the restitution of lands to former owners or their heirs. Many of them abandoned their farms in the past in preference for non-agricultural employment and they remain disinterested in farming today. Meanwhile, the private sector remains in a poor condition after forty years of discrimination. Since there was no market selectiveness between farmers, many unfavourable features from pre-war times have persisted: very small and fragmented holdings and a subsistence approach which inhibits a stronger market orientation and the further introduction of new production methods. Peasants still seek only part-time employment in manufacturing and this increases the number of holdings where farming is only a secondary activity. Conditions in private farming are actually worse than the official statistical data would suggest. Through the abandonment of some farms and the departure of young people from rural areas, the age structure of the active agrarian population has deteriorated. Thus, 21.5 per cent of active people on farms are older than 65 (29.8 per cent on farms worked on a full-time basis and 18.5 per cent on farms worked on a part-time basis where income comes additionally from non-agricultural work (manufacturing and services). Only 5–6 per cent of farmers have secondary or higher education. Some key problems remain unsolved, such as the small size of many farms, the fragmented holdings, and the declining number of farms worked on a full-time basis (which means that the process of 'deagrarization' continues).

Meanwhile, because of denationalization, the former socialist agricultural enterprises and cooperatives are in a critical condition. They have lost their state subsidies and are heavily in debt. They no longer have access to the former Yugoslav market, while their production is often too expensive and insufficiently geared to the world market. But, they are the only large farms in the country with modern technology and management, and until private agricultural production increases, they are essential in supplying the population. Yet the whole of Slovenian agriculture is affected by a serious lack of capital which prevents modernization, specialization and the improvement of the agrarian infrastructure. In any case the great majority of farms are too small and yield insufficient crops to justify investment. Differences become particularly obvious when comparisons are made with EU agriculture, with consequent fears about Slovenia's competitiveness with big international corporations and the threat of a 'total sale' of Slovenian land to rich foreign buyers if EU membership is achieved.

Differences in the standard of living between urban and rural areas were reduced in the 1970s and 1980s. But, with the introduction of a market economy, social and regional differences began to increase again. Therefore, the government has continued with the policy of assistance for the agrarian, mountainous and border regions. But different directions of agricultural policy can also be noticed in the programmes of political parties. Private farmers are supported most by the Slovenian People's Party which originated as the 'peasants' party', and support to private farming is also offered by the Slovenian Christian Democrats and the Socio-Democratic Party. These three parties support privatization and are averse to any remains of the socialist system (for example, through the retention of the former socialist agricultural enterprises). However, while the Slovenian People's Party accepts the goal of EU membership (as do most of the parliamentary parties), it recognizes the vulnerability of agriculture and advocates state protection. Meanwhile, the Liberal Democracy Party of Slovenia is, through its liberal principles, less interested in agricultural problems and believes that many of the current dilemmas will be solved by the market. The left United List of Social Democrats supports agricultural enterprises and the workers employed there.

Notwithstanding the problems of Slovenian agriculture, it is clear that conditions are slowly beginning to change for the better. The interest in farming is increasing and many private farmers are beginning to specialize, especially in viticulture and livestock rearing. Peasant associations are managing dairies, slaughterhouses and mountain pastures. Prices for agricultural products are both protected and relatively favourable, while import is limited in respect of products which are produced in satisfactory quantities by Slovenian farmers.

Partial nationalization of forests has been done away with and peasants are now active on the timber market.

REFERENCES

Belec, B. (1990), 'Razdrobljenost kmetijskih zemljišč kot persistenčni dejavnik inovacijskih procesov v kmetijstvu na primeru Murskega polja', *Znanstvena revija*, **2** (2), 209-21.
Blaznik, P. et al. (eds) (1970), *Zgodovina agrarnih panog: gospodarska in družbena zgodovina Slovencev*, Ljubljana: Džavna Zalžba Slovenije.
Grafenauer, B. (ed.) (1979), *Zgodovina Slovencev*, Ljubljana: Cankarjeva Zalžba.
Klemenčič, M. (1975), 'Sodobni prelog v SR Sloveniji', *Geografski vestnik*, **47**, 75-88.
Klemenčič, V. (1992), 'Settling pattern and demographic structure', in M. Pak and M.O. Adamič (eds), *Slovenia: Geographic Aspects of a New Independent European Nation*, Ljubljana: Association of Geographical Societies of Slovenia, pp.41-50.
Kmetijski Inštitut Slovenije (1992), *Slovensko kmetijstvo v številkah*, Ljubljana: Kmetijski Institut Slovenije.
Kokole, V. and V. Kokole (1969), 'Urbanizacija podeželja v Sloveniji', *Geografski vestnik*, **41**, 3-23.
Melik, A. (1963), *Slovenija*, Ljubljana: Slovenska Matica.
Natek, M. (1987), 'Osnovni tipi zemljiškoposestne strukture v SR Sloveniji leta 1981', *Geografski vestnik*, **59**, 51-65.
Pak, M. and M.O. Adamič (eds) (1992), *Slovenia: Geographic Aspects of a New Independent European Nation*, Ljubljana: Association of Geographical Societies of Slovenia.
Ravbar, M. (1992), *Suburbanizacija v Sloveniji*, Ljubljana: Univerza v Ljubljani, Oddelek za geografijo.
Šifrer, Ž. (1963), 'Razvitak stanovništva Slovenije u poslednjih sto godina', *Stanovništvo*, **1** (1), 339-66.
Statistični Urad Republike Slovenije (1996), *Letni pregled kmetijstva 1994: rezultati raziskovanj 656*, Ljubljana: Statistični Urad Republike Slovenije, p.16.
Vrišer, I. (1974), 'Mesta in urbano omrežje v SR Sloveniji', *Geografski Zbornik: Acta Geographica*, **14** (3), 181-330.
—— (1985), 'Regionalni razvoj v S.R. Sloveniji', *Ekonomska Revija*, **36** (4), 271-88 (also available as 'Regionale Entwicklung in der Sozialistischen Republik Slovenien (Jugoslawien)', *Dela*, **5**, 13-25.
—— (1987), 'Spremembe v zemljiških kategorijah v Sloveniji', *Geografski vestnik*, **59**, 37-49.
—— (1988), 'Centralna naselja v SR Sloveniji', *Geografski vestnik*, **59**, 37-49.
—— (1993), 'Agrarian economy in Slovenia'. *GeoJournal*, **31**, 373-7.
—— (1996), 'The development, present significance and future prospects of socialist agricultural enterprises in Slovenia', *GeoJournal*, **38**, 151-6.
Zavod Republike Slovenije za Statistiko (1953-54/1965-97), *Statistični letopis*

(Socialistične) Republike Slovenije, Ljubljana: Zavod Republike Slovenije za Statistiko/Urad Republike Slovenije za Statistiko.

—— (1994b), *Popis prebivalstva: gospodinjstevi stanovanj in kmečkih gospodarstev v Republiki Sloveniji v letu 1991: reszultati po občinah 617*, Ljubljana: Zavod Republike Slovenije za Statistiko.

11. Aspects of Farm Diversification

Floarea Bordanc, Stanisław Grykień, Nicolae Muică and David Turnock

The country studies have all, in their various ways, pointed out that, while farming is critically important for the wellbeing of the rural areas it is not the only consideration. As labour in agriculture is reduced, as all commentators expect, then the stability of communities will depend very heavily on non-agricultural activities and enterprises outside conventional farming. The range of possibilities is very wide and certainly includes the growth of the service sector, which was much neglected during the communist era, and also an expansion of light industry beyond the modest levels associated with cooperative farm ancillary enterprises. Privatization of the businesses inherited from communism is now widespread and many new ventures have taken root. It has been suggested that former collective farm buildings and redundant machine stations could be transformed into small industrial estates – something which is happening to a limited extent. But growth is spatially much more diverse as small wholesaling businesses appear on small farms on the edge of Polish cities and small shops are opened within dwelling houses or placed in kiosks in private gardens. Small businesses are also developing through the appearance of traders and handicraft-workers previously organized under the umbrella of local consumer cooperatives. Along with the slow growth of private investment in transport they represent a significant element in the privatization of the countryside. However, in this chapter attention is restricted to four topics: organic farming; large-scale food processing; farm-based processing (with reference to distilling); and rural tourism. Each study makes a valid case for diversification.

ECOFARMING, WITH PARTICULAR REFERENCE TO POLAND

Stanisław Grykień

Several chapters in this book have referred to the potential for organic farming, which has been highlighted as part of the wider issues of sustainability and maintenance of biodiversity. These concepts are well established in Western Europe but are now being embraced throughout Eastern Europe (Popescu and Balteanu 1996). In 1996, the Romanians set up a working group on 'Sustainable Agriculture and Biodiversity' with the help of the Heinrich Böll Foundation in Germany (Barboi 1996). The group want to encourage NGOs throughout the country as a means of building expertise among the farming community to produce good-quality food for the market and also for local consumption through agrotourism, which will depend to no small degree on food supply and catering standards. In the case of Albania, Western 'niche' markets should be addressed as a means of stimulating cash crop production and boosting exports. However, such development does require technical assistance and training and injections of capital. According to the OECD (1995), Albania should reinforce its long-held position as one of the world's leading producers and exporters of medicinal and aromatic plants. In Slovakia too, ecological factors are playing a more significant role in agriculture (Bedrna 1993; Drgona 1996). In 1993, the production of healthier biofoods (using less than 15 per cent of 'allowed chemicals') amounted to 33th.t of fodder, 27th.t of cereals, 2,500t of vegetables and 1,600t of oil plants (Štefánek 1993). Ecological principles are also being extended to meat, milk and cheese production. Ecological farming projects were started in 1990 on 15,140ha, of which 12,804ha were arable. Thirty-six agricultural enterprises spread across 15 districts of Slovakia set aside part of their land for organic agriculture. In 1994, 44 enterprises (36 cooperatives, five private farms and three state farms) were active in bioproduction over a total area of 15,556ha. Although this represents only 0.64 per cent of the total agricultural area, the level is comparable with France, Germany and Switzerland where organic agriculture is longer established. It is expected that an additional 5–10th.ha will be included in the programme each year, resulting in a total area of some 150th.ha by 2010. But not all regions are suitable, and organic agriculture is not possible around the more heavily polluted areas. Moreover, given the higher market prices needed to make ecological farming viable, there is only limited demand on the domestic market, and producers must think in terms of export to Austria and Germany. Furthermore, government support has been reduced by budgetary pressures from SkK90 million in 1991 to nothing at all in 1994.

The Polish Case

Ecofarming has become a significant element in Polish farming and could play a part in the development of multifunctional rural economies in the future (Grykień 1995). Poland has favourable conditions for the development of both ecoagriculture and ecotourism. Mineral fertilization of the soil has declined sharply in recent years from the high level of 193kg/ha in 1980 to 175kg/ha in 1985, 95kg/ha in 1990 and 62kg/ha in 1992. These figures compare with dressings well in excess of 200kg/ha in various West European countries and 350kg/ha in Japan in the early 1990s (Główny Urząd Statystyczny 1993). Ecological farming in Poland dates back to the 1930s, when Count Stanisław Karłowski was active on a 1,716ha estate. But after the Second World War, the communists forced farmers to use chemical fertilizers (and fined them if they did not), so until 1989, organic farmers operated unofficially, meeting socially, perhaps under the cover of religious gatherings.

The Polish Association of Food Producers by Ecological Methods (EKOLAND) was set up in 1989 with a base at Przysieka near Toruń. This organization, which is a member of the International Federation of Organic Agricultural Movements (IFOAM), brings together farmers, gardeners, food processors and distributors. EKOLAND is now a serious organization which issues certificates to approved producers. Members must meet the various conditions laid down in order to qualify for ecological production. Thus IFOAM regulations exclude the use of pesticides and call for the use of organic fertilizers and ecological fodder produced on ecofarms. They also cover breeding methods, measures to prevent soil erosion and the additives that may be used by food processors.

In 1989, when association was registered, 27 certificate holders worked a total of 300ha; now the total is 7th.ha and some farms are as

304   *Privatization in Rural Eastern Europe*

large as 400ha. A questionnaire survey was conducted among all the 174 farms existing in 1993 when 2,170ha of arable land was under cultivation (Figure 11.1). Replies were obtained from 120 farms (69 per cent) with a total area of 1,488ha. Thus the average size was 12.4ha, more than twice the national average of 6ha for all private farms in the country. Thirty-eight per cent of the ecofarms are larger than 10ha and only a tenth are smaller than 2ha. Nevertheless, more than a third of the ecofarmers would like to acquire more land by purchase. Farm size is not correlated with soil quality, for more than half the ecofarm area consists of soils in the lowest fertility categories (V–VI) and more than

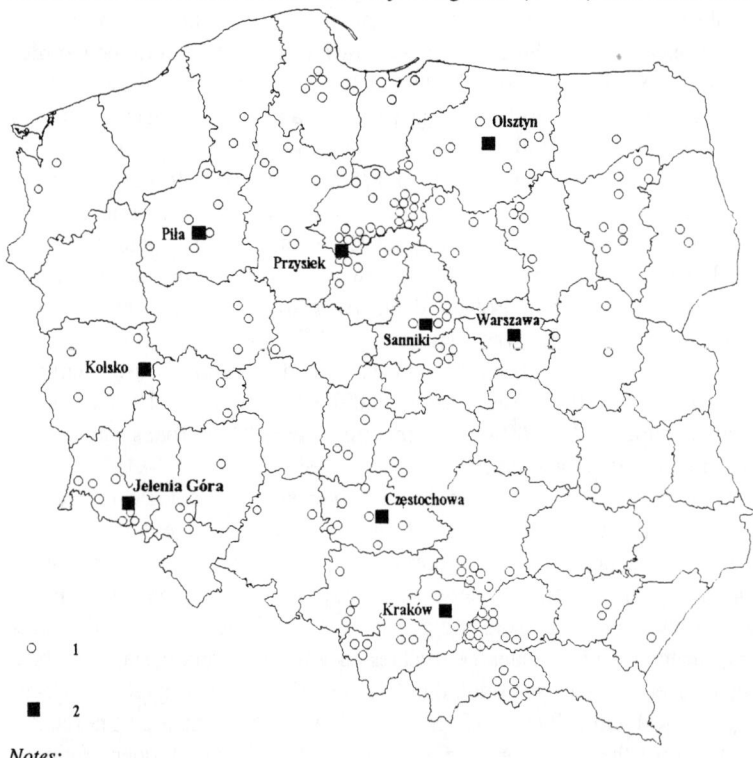

Notes:
1. Ecofarm.
2. EKOLAND information centre.

Source: EKOLAND.

Figure 11.1 Ecofarms in Poland

four-fifths of the land falls into classes IV–VI. But ecofarms are relatively well consolidated, for 38 per cent consist of a single consolidated plot while 22 per cent have two plots and only 29 per cent have more than three.

In view of the poor soil, ecofarms tend to have a larger proportion of pastureland than do farms in general. The prominence of orchards is very much in line with the whole agricultural sector, but fruit bushes (producing berries) are more prominent on ecofarms. Industrial crops are generally absent, apart from small areas of rape, sugar beet and turnips, whereas cereals (including buckwheat and millet) and potatoes are very much in line with the national average. Fodder crops are more prominent because of the need to guarantee the quality of all animal feed used on ecofarms. Fruit and vegetables are also very prominent because of heavy market demand. Traditional crops such as beetroot, cabbage, carrots, celery, parsley and onions are complemented by others which are less well known: amaranths, Jerusalem artichokes, facelia and soya (Figure 11.2; see pp.306–7).

Ecological farming includes the livestock sector. One 22ha farm (run by a former town-based shopkeeper) specializes in goats, fruit and herbs. The communists saw the goat as a symbol of poverty and numbers declined, but now goats are more popular and there is a thriving herd of 50 animals supplying cheese, milk and yoghurt to customers in Gdańsk and Gdynia. Another ecological farmer at Głębock (Jelenia Góra) breeds cattle and grows vegetables. When stocking levels are related to arable land, the ecofarms have higher rates for cattle and goats, but lower levels for horses, pigs and sheep. This is because horses have been replaced by machines to a greater extent than on private farms in general, while pigs would require supplementary fodder that could not be obtained from the necessary sources, and mutton is not in great demand in Poland. Poultry are prominent, and some ecofarms breed rabbits as well. A few farms are concerned with fish-farming and the production of herbs and seeds. There is a total of 17.4ha of herbs on the farms returning questionnaires, including melissa, milk thistle, mint and St. John's Wort. There are good prospects for further expansion.

A model ecological farm near Kamienna Góra is managed by the Krishna Awareness Society, but most members are traditional farmers managing without chemicals. Ecofarmers are relatively young. Eighty-seven per cent are under 50 years of age and 42 per cent are aged between 30 and 40 (for private farms in general the majority are over 50). They

(a) Sowing structure

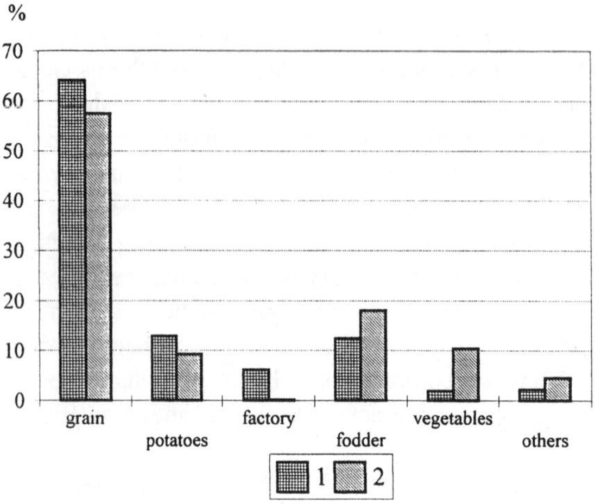
%
70
60
50
40
30
20
10
0
grain
potatoes
factory
fodder
vegetables
others
1
2

(b) Stock production

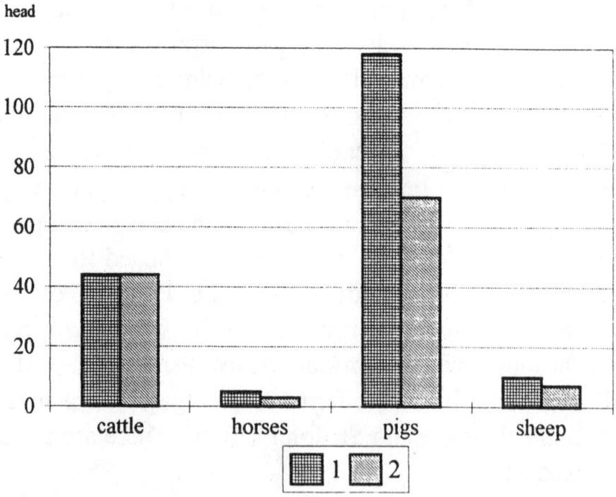
head
120
100
80
60
40
20
0
cattle
horses
pigs
sheep
1
2

Notes:
1. All farms
2. Ecofarms

Sources: *Główny Urząd Statystyczny* and fieldwork.

Aspects of Farm Diversification 307

(c) Age structure of farmers, 1993

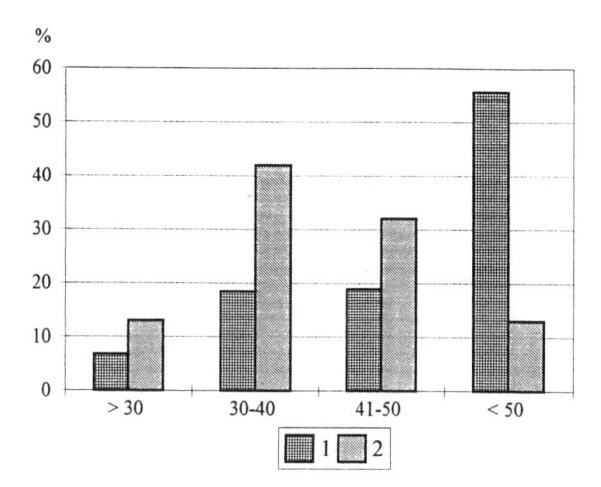

(d) Education of farmers, 1993

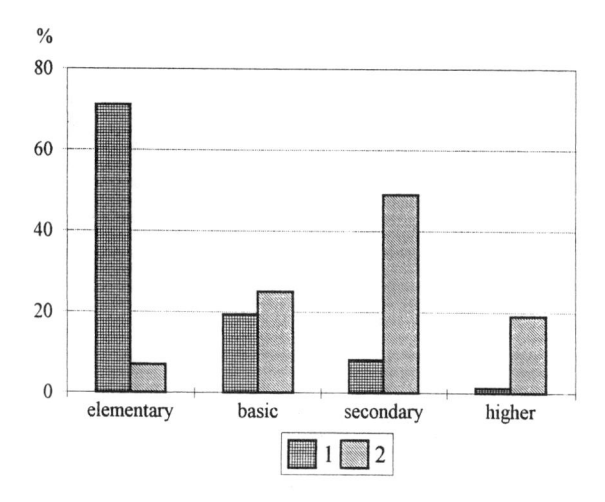

Figure 11.2 Aspects of organic farming in Poland

(a) Ecofarms and the main selling points

Source: Field studies.

are also relatively well educated: 68 per cent have secondary schooling and a fifth are university graduates. However, education correlates with age and Pearson's analysis of correlation produces results of $r = 0.686$ for women and $r = 0.351$ for men. Generally, the younger farmers are better educated, but among those who have decided to take up ecofarming the older farmers have the better qualifications. Almost a third of all ecofarmers surveyed were not born in villages – their decision to enter the business was part of a desire to adopt a radically new lifestyle. However, the remaining two-thirds were already active in

Aspects of Farm Diversification 309

(b)   Shops selling ecofarm produce

Figure 11.3   Markets for ecofarms in Poland

---

farming and more than half the farmers in this group previously ran their farms on conventional lines.

Thirty-five per cent of respondents complained about difficulties with sales (Figure 11.3a). There is a regional component here because those experiencing difficulty are situated in Kielce and Tarnów voivodships and a group extending from Bydgoszcz through Toruń, Włocławek, Olsztyn, Łomża to Białystok. By contrast, ecofarmers from Elbląg and Gdańsk, along with central Poland, Upper Silesia and Wielkopolska had no difficulties. However, there are differences among ecofarmers in the same area, suggesting that ability to make arrangements with individual salespeople and shopkeepers is a critical matter. Some ecofarmers are also in a better position because they have their own transport or run a shop or stall of their own. The questionnaire results show clearly that perceived marketing difficulties increase with the age of the farmer: only 8 per cent of ecofarmers under 30 had problems in selling their produce compared with 52 per cent of those over 50. The young farmers show greater initiative and adapt more easily to the challenging conditions than the older farmers, who often claim that EKOLAND should buy their produce. However, it is surprising that ecofarmers with the best educational qualifications have the greatest problems (a quarter of those with university degrees but only 14 per cent of those with no more than primary education). But the differences are not too great, and age may again be critical because the older farmers are apparently the best educated.

The market for ecological food is still developing, but the large towns are the main consumers: Warsaw, along with Bydgoszcz, Cracow, Łódź, Toruń and the 'Tri-City' of Gdańsk–Gdynia–Sopot (Figure 11.3b). Here there are relatively large numbers of sophisticated customers, including young vegetarians, who have both ecological awareness and relatively high incomes to afford prices 50–100 per cent above the normal market prices (Łuczka-Bakuła 1993). Meanwhile, ecofarms in Nowy Sącz supply health resorts (such as Krynica and Uście Gorlickie) and members of the 'Nowina' cooperative of ecological farmers in Łomża sell part of their produce to the Centre for Children's Health. A kindergarten in Bielsko-Biała and a nursery in Żary buy food from ecofarms in Wieprz and Bieniów – arrangements which arise from marketing initiatives taken by the farmers themselves. Naturally, hospitals and nurseries are likely to be especially interested in ecofood (Soltysiak 1993). It is well known that growing children are in particular danger of suffering from food products tarnished with insecticides. Of course, if ecofarmers cannot find such outlets they can still make the most of the conventional marketing system where the standard regulations are in force. However, most consumers are looking for cheap food and cannot afford the premium required for ecological produce on account of relatively high labour inputs and the cost of the production methods that must be used. It is difficult to convince shopkeepers who have worked in state shops that ecological produce is worth selling. A legal framework is lacking and there is no special help from the authorities beyond the acceptance of a niche in the export market.

Some food is also taken by visitors taking advantage of facilities for agrotourism. Such trade is very important in the lake district of the northeast and the mountains in the south. The significance of this market may increase, since rural tourism has considerable potential for growth. There is already an international dimension through visitors from Western Europe (including members of the international ecological project Eko-Agro-Tourism) and there is an office of the European Centre for Ecological Agriculture and Tourism in Jelenia Góra which is promoting ecotourism through its 'Holiday on Ecofarm' leaflets. Finally, there is also the possibility of local processing of ecofood, and 39 per cent of the respondents were involved in processing related to dairying, cereals, fruit and vegetables and a group of products including herbs, seeds and fish. Thus herb growers process most of their produce, although there is also a sale to the main Polish processor of herbs ('Herbapol'). Most of the ecofarms involved are active in just one category, with milk processing the most prominent (68 per cent). A quarter of the ecofarms process cereals and 15 per cent of them produce fruit and vegetable products. Meat processing is a possibility, but no ecofarms are involved at present.

Most of the farms currently processing have intentions to increase output, including all those processing fruit and vegetables and the majority of those using cereals. There is less enthusiasm in milk processing, where only half those active wish to increase output. This may be linked with complaints about the legal requirements in the milk-processing industry and in the marketing of the produce. Moreover, more ecofarmers expressed an intention to start processing by the end of 1995, so that more than 60 per cent of ecofarmers were probably processing at that time. This is an obvious solution to the problem of loss of value when produce is sold to processors operating on a conventional basis. This is because there are few ecofood processors apart from the farmers themselves. These initiatives over processing are all the more significant because unemployment rates are relatively high in the rural area while capacity in food processing (and industries serving agriculture in general) is low. Many ecofarms which have diversified into food processing have installed sewage systems of the biological-reed type. Bio, a food-processing company certified by EKOLAND, won second prize with its organic gherkins at the First Organic World Exhibition held at Copenhagen in 1996.

Poland therefore has potential for ecofarming and it is an option for a significant number of private farmers. Some farmers think organic farming is primitive and contrary to common sense. Yet, such activity is particularly appropriate where environmental conservation is a priority, as it is in the vicinity of national parks. Ecofarming and related processing installations are good for multifunctional rural development, including rural tourism. However, ecological farming is unlikely to become a dominant force in Polish agriculture and even optimistic forecasts suggest that the proportion of ecofarms will not exceed 2 per cent. An organized marketing system for ecoproducts is lacking, for the economic situation in Poland will not support a network of ecofoodshops (charging relatively high prices) outside the main cities. About 30 per cent of ecofarmers already have problems selling their produce, although it has to be said that the younger farmers are more competent and better understand the market economy. In addition to the limited market there are barriers imposed because many private farmers lack the adaptability and also the educational experience that would give them an adequate understanding of ecological issues. However, the idea of ecological agriculture is popular among young farmers and many have responded to EKOLAND's recruitment programme.

LARGE-SCALE FOOD PROCESSING

David Turnock

Eastern Europe has substantial food-processing capacity, but it is in great need of modernization to improve quality and rationalization to relate capacity to the needs of a market economy. There has been some progress in privatizing the food-processing industry and there is foreign interest in factories producing standardized and branded goods – industries concerned with tobacco, soft drinks, sugar, spirits, and confectionery production, together with brewing and vegetable oils. Such enterprises usually have a relatively favourable financial and marketing position. However, there has not generally been a comprehensive privatization strategy for the food-processing sector and the situation is therefore patchy. But where there is progress it is often because of transformation driven by foreign capital introducing new technology in dairying, sugar refining, meat processing, drinks and confectionery. There is US interest in Polish potatoes, with perceived opportunities in commodities as disparate as apples and oilseeds. Danone of France is manufacturing dairy products in Bulgaria while Danish firms are interested in the country's meat processing, a Dutch firm is producing baby foods and Australians are investing in turkey farms. Unilever has purchased the Baja deepfreezing plant; it will improve technology and develop the facilities to sell Hungarian produce. However, small processing units may well appear through domestic initiatives. Farm income can be boosted through non-farm activities and Polish farmers are setting up wholesale and retail trading businesses and food processing units. One case concerns a meat-processing business near Cracow: an abattoir for pigs had been built and the farmholding extended so as be self-sufficient in fodder (Morgan 1992, p.146). Additional pigs are brought from neighbouring farms in order to operate the abattoir and processing plant at capacity. It may also be possible for enterprises to modernize on their own – banks seem happier to lend to food processors than to farmers, because ownership and security are generally clearer. There will be a need to catch up with the West by offering a wider range of good-quality products which can compete against foreign imports and also penetrate Western markets. East European exports are not yet able to compete on quality and packaging; often they require state subsidy to a level of as much as a half (an example being Polish potatoes and potato products). However, in some countries, such as Hungary, the process is well under way. Finally, there is room for state intervention to eliminate excess capacity on a coordinated basis.

Dairy Products

Rationalization is taking place in Czech dairying because too many plants are now in competition where previously they had their own assured markets. The number of dairies has been reduced by 40 per cent from 170 in 1989 to 102 in 1995, while milk production has declined by the same extent from 4.5 to 2.7 million litres through reduced per capita consumption from 2,50l to 180 million litres (and 9 to 5 kilograms in the case of butter). Although these levels could increase, it is considered necessary for dairies to rationalize at 60 per cent of capacity. The result could be still fewer plants, but they would be modern units capable of exporting. Modern dairies are turning out liquid milk and dairy products including yoghurt and ice cream, with direct delivery to shops. Weaker producers are being weeded out. Slovakia's Milex dairy company in Bratislava has entered into a joint venture with Schardinger of Austria which now has a two-thirds stake. The quality of milk received from producer cooperatives and state farms has been improved to EU standards, although the quantity is still inadequate to fully utilize the production capacity of 200 million litres. Milk production throughout Slovakia has fallen from 1.6 to 0.9 billion litres. The problem is one of profitable operation at prices the public can afford. Most companies will not be able to invest in improved technology and a major rationalization is expected within five years which will greatly reduce the number of plants in favour of the large modern installations that will be able to run at capacity. This could be done by takeovers with a view to closure, but with retention of the suppliers and customers. However, the domestic markets should improve, with additional opportunity for the sale of dairy products in Austria and FSU. Danone, the French yoghurt maker, has acquired the Warsaw-based Wola dairy, adding to its stake in the Mildes dairy in the south of the country. A Dutch food group Nutricia has acquired a 22.5 per cent stake in Hajdutej Tejipari, Hungary's largest regional dairy.

But there is a need for higher standards across the region, where milk often fails to meet EU standards. Many producers in Poland do not respect hygiene regulations. Farms were not encouraged in the past to make improvements because cooperatives purchased large amounts regardless of quality. Only a small proportion of milk is supplied to dairies in trucks guaranteeing a proper temperature. Meanwhile, only a quarter of Poland's 700 processing plants meet international standards. The International Finance Corporation (IFC) has approved a loan for the development of Poland's dairy industry, aiming at the production of natural yoghurt comparable with high-quality imports. Ultra-heat-treated milk is available but accounts for less than 5 per cent of the market. There is also a problem in the dairy industry in Romania: many underfed neglected dairy cows had to be slaughtered, following the collapse of cooperatives. Milk from private farms rarely reaches the market, since peasants prefer to sell cream and cheese which attracts higher prices. It is calculated that Bucharest is supplied with 200 thousand litres of milk daily whereas the demand is 250 thousand litres (Henry 1994, p.21).

There is a need for better dairy equipment, hence the significance of the UK engineering firm APV in setting up APV Polska in 1994 to supply drying equipment for baby food and powdered milk production, and equipment for liquid milk processing, yoghurt, cheese and whey products, butter and low fat spreads, and evaporated and condensed products. Equipment is also available for ice cream, frozen desserts, soups, jams – and ready meals using the high-tech Ohmic heating system.

Sugar

Western penetration of the East European sugar industry is evident through the stake of Eastern Sugar (a joint venture between UK's Tate & Lyle and Générale Sucrière of France) in Hungarian and Slovakian beet sugar refining. Zucker of Uelzen (Braunschweig) in Germany have taken a one-third stake in the Czech refiner Rafinirie Cukru Dobrovice from EBRD. There has also been UK (British Sugar) penetration in Poland through the acquisition of state sugar factories. Polish sugar producers are likely to decrease from 80 to 20–30. But in 1995, Poland's 47 state-run sugar mills were transformed into four state-controlled holding companies which will carry out a revamping exercise – this is attractive to the weaker producers although the holding companies will not necessarily be umbrellas against bankruptcy. Meanwhile, the stronger companies are looking for foreign partners to supply capital and if they succeed, their time in the holding company will be relatively short; some mills such as Nakło have strong worker loyalty with out-of-hours work to carry out developments. It is part of a strategy of consolidation in the face of Western competition. The industry is overproducing and cannot afford to export the surplus at prevailing world prices. Sugar beet is a popular crop for farmers and yields well. The holding companies will enter into contracts with growers and set milling quotas; they will aim at 1.5m.t of production for the home market and 0.3m.t for export and prevent oversupply hitting domestic prices. Romanian sugar-beet processing is not yet competitive despite some state support (Gavrilescu 1994). Much sugar is imported, while the prices offered to domestic sugar-beet producers are too low to be stimulative.

Wine

The wine trade is switching emphasis from the relatively undemanding FSU market of the 1980s to the more discerning West European consumer. East European demand is being served by cheap wine from France and Italy; therefore the East European producers must go upmarket. The Slovenian wine producer Slovenijavino has acquired a US distributor, Laureate Imports, for its 'Avia' wine and 'Atlantic' mineral water. But Czech wine, which is having difficulty competing against imported wine, also needs modernization with the launch of new products with improved presentation. Meanwhile, Romanian wine producers came together in 1990 to form Vinexport Trading, breaking away from the former state exporting company, Prodexport. They formed a joint venture with interests from Denmark, Germany, the Netherlands and the UK. Exports are now running at some 15 million litres per year, of bottled wine and wine in bulk for blending. State wineries have had to reduce capacity in view of privatization of vineyards (resulting in more small-scale production) but some retain their own vineyards (Murfatlar, Târnave/Jidvei and Valea Calugărească) and have modernized by importing new bottling lines.

The Hungarian wine industry is recovering from a depression linked with the anti-alcohol campaign launched in the USSR in 1985 and, much more significantly, with the unification of Germany and the break-up of FSU. The 1992 export volume was only 30 per cent of 1989. The Russian market revived in 1992 and the turnaround started in 1993 and 1994, when exports of 0.94m.hl approached half the 1989 figure of 2.27m.hl, and dollar earnings also showed an increase. There has been an improvement in the quality of wine by using foreign wine-making expertise (reflected by investment in technical improvements and marketing) and restricting yield per vine to 2kg instead of the previous 4.5kg. French and Spanish involvement is restoring the reputation of the Tokaj region, in contrast to the 'Bull's Blood' of Eger (marketed in competition by Egervin and Hungarovin) and the products of Győngyős and Kecskemét promoted by local companies – for instead of the obligation to sell to state wineries, Hungarovin producers can now promote their own wine. Vinarium has also emerged as a marketing consortium of small, high-quality producers in various regions. It now has its own vineyard (along with wine production, bottling and storage equipment) near Balatonboglar. Balaton Boglar, is 53 per cent owned by the German company Henkel which adopted a marketing strategy in 1992 to focus on Germany, Scandinavia and the UK. Reference should also be made to small businesses which have been returned to private ownership. The Unicum distillery in Budapest has teamed up with an Italian wine maker to build a new wine plant near Lake Balaton producing a quality 'Kastely' (estate) brand which will be sold through the Unicum organization at affordably high prices. There are many small producers emerging from the break-up of state farms in 1992 and the refashioning of the cooperatives (although many of these also broke up), such as the Matravolgye cooperative from Markaz on the slopes of the Mátra. The cooperatives take some 4th.t from the 500 members and produce some 30th.hl of wine. As with other small producers, there have been successes in Far Eastern markets and contributions to local tourism through winetasting in the Eger area. Meanwhile, the state wineries have been privatized and Hungarovin, controlled by the German Henkel organization, is investing in upmarket brands ('François' and 'Hungaria') as well as its own 'Egri Bikaver' (Bull's Blood) already noted. However, the state retains control of part of the Tokaj business in order to prevent total disruption – necessary because the privatization of agricultural land has led to much fallowing of land previously used for vineyards. The local Tokaj trading organization buys grapes from individual farmers but has used French and Spanish expertise to produce a quality 'Aszu' wine which, it is hoped, will establish a reputation of the local product after a three-year maturation period. Indeed, the Spanish organization Bodegas Oremos has acquired the best vineyards in the region. There is resentment in Tokaj that assets are sold to foreigners because local vintners lack capital, yet international connections mean that the product is better known.

Despite some quality trade by Vinexport (already mentioned), Romania's vineyards have not yet made the same recovery and until recently the emphasis has been on the clearance of vineyards falling under private ownership, along with neglect or destruction of access roads, water pipelines and plants producing pesticides. Almost 1,000ha of orchards and vineyards have been affected in Vrancea alone. Viticulture has been embarrassed by higher costs through interest payments (hence the need for the rescheduled debts and subsidized interest rates) and a lack of effective marketing, while duties on imported drinks have been lowered. The very small units of vineyard ownership (averaging 0.29ha) prevents rational management using machinery. The selling price for grapes is very low and so vinification centres work at barely a quarter of their capacity; some have been forced to close and there is no incentive for new private plants to open. Many farmers prefer to make their own wine and if the quality is indifferent or the business is not profitable they will switch to something else. Some recovery was evident in 1994 when there were 247th.ha of vineyards (225th.ha producing grapes for winemaking) compared with 224th.ha in 1990. The state wineries are clearly in the best position when they retain their own vineyards, as at Murfatlar, Jidvei and other places already noted.

Beer and Other Beverages

Once again, Western companies are moving into Eastern Europe. There is much activity in Poland, where Heineken of the Netherlands and the German companies Anlagenplanung and Braun und Brunnen are making large investments. Heineken have also entered into a joint venture with the Żywiec brewery as their sole Polish partner. Eventually, Heineken brands will be produced by Żywiec, which is already producing Pepsi Cola. UK's Allied Lyons is retailing British beer through its 'John Bull' establishments in the larger Polish cities. Spirits are also seeing changes, with the domestic vodka producers in Poland now facing competition from Smirnoff vodka (produced under licence from International Distillers and Vintners by IDV Poland. Elsewhere, Pepsi-Cola hope to be Eastern Europe's leading soft drinks producer by the end of the century. A large investment will take place in the Czech Republic and Slovakia, following successful programmes in Hungary and Poland. In Prague, a manufacturing and bottling plant (in a former munitions factory) is being modernized and a distribution network will follow. In Slovakia there will be six regional distribution centres. The scale of the investment will be similar to K-Mart, and the two will comprise the largest investments in the country since 1989.

The brewing industry of the Czech Republic makes an interesting study. Here the 72 breweries were formerly protected through fixed marketing areas for each producer, although Budvar Budweiser and Urquell were exported through the Koospol foreign trade company. Czech brewers are now seeking foreign partners and the leading breweries such as Budejovicky Budvar, Jihočeske Pivovary (also based in České Budějovice), Plzeňsky Prazdroj, Pivovary Radegast, StaroBrno and Staropramen (Prague) are coming to the fore. BrauUnion of Austria has taken a stake in the Brno-based brewery StaroBrno while the UK brewer Bass, in addition to a one-third stake in Stceopramen, is bidding for Jihočeske Pivovary (South Bohemia Breweries) against American and Danish competition. Meanwhile, the world's largest brewer, Anheuser-Busch, wants an ownership stake in Česke Budejovice's Budvar brewery (licensed holder of the 'Budweiser' trade name in Europe which Anheuser-Busch wishes to use for its product). Jihočeske Pivovary has cooperated with Wolverhampton and Dudley Breweries in the UK so that 'Zamek' (Castle) lager from Samson Brewery in Česke Budejovice can be marketed through the UK. A merger of Jihočeske Pivovary with the neighbouring brewery, Budejovicky Budvar, is also thought to be a possibility, bringing together the two major breweries in the city of Česke Budějovice. Meanwhile, Ostrava Brewery has expanded its market through the purchase of a brewery in Poland where beer is making inroads into a market where spirits were previously dominant.

These moves threaten the small independent breweries which fear a further decline in their market share as competition increases. Total beer output in the Czech Republic fell from 2 billion litres in 1992 to 1.8 billion litres in 1993 (blamed on the increase in taxation) but exports by the leading firms remained steady at 100 million litres. Thus, while many smaller breweries have lost ground, the leading brewers have increased output with the benefit of foreign investment and experienced marketing staff attracted from the Koospol company. They hope to increase their exports to counter intense competition at home, made worse by the loss of the market in Slovakia where protectionist policies are now in force. Foreign investment can pose a threat to traditional beers, which is why the Anheuser-Busch initiative has not yet succeeded. But the smaller breweries may face severe difficulties unless they can develop niche products (such as Pardubice Porter) with export possibilities. Privatization has brought freedom to compete, but success depends on capital investment, which is difficult without foreign partners.

Throughout Eastern Europe local breweries are being acquired for modernization and capacity increases to sustained current production plus output of beers for which the new owners are already famous. An alternative strategy is to build up new breweries from scratch as a means of marketing established brands. Stella Artois of Belgium has acquired a stake in Zagreb brewery which is being privatized (with half the shares for employees and a proportion of the balance reserved for pension funds). Belgium's Interbrew has taken a stake in Zagrebacka Pivovara,

Croatia's largest brewing concern. Belgium's 'Brewinvest' has a 67 per cent share in Burgasko Pivo for US$5 million and Germany's Braun und Brunnen company has acquired the Kamenitsa Brewery of Plovdiv so that the Bulgarian brewery can be reprofiled (using German technology) and Schulteis beer exported to Greece and Turkey. At the same time BrewInvest (representing two Greek subsidiaries of major beverage bottlers) has acquired a majority holding in Bulgaria's Stara Zagora brewery. There will be a large investment, and production will remain under the Stara Zagora label. Efes Brewery, a subsidiary of the Turkish Anadolu Group, is to invest US$40 million to build Romania's largest brewery in Ploieşti (with an annual production of 300 million litres.

Other Products

Unilever has penetrated Eastern Europe to avoid import duties as high as 40 per cent for margarine entering Hungary. Investment is also a way of building up market share quickly and it is good for image building to be seen to be assisting in the transition process. In Hungary, Unilever has acquired the leading ice-cream manufacturer VMTV and they have joined the Italian company Ferruzzi in acquiring NMV (a producer of oilseed, margarine and detergent). McVitie's (a subsidiary of United Biscuits) has acquired 80 per cent of Poland's state-owned biscuit factory, San of Jarosław. The aim is to build on the company's present market share of one-fifth, to diversify with a possible salty snacks plant and to expand into Belarus and Ukraine. Nestlé of Switzerland has purchased a 45 per cent stake in Winiary, Poland's largest producer of powdered soups and desserts. The firm has also expressed interest in a joint venture with Poland's state-owned chocolate manufacturer Goplana, in order to secure a production base. By contrast, Cadbury Schweppes of the UK has opened a new factory near Wrocław. Philip Morris has taken a stake in the Cracow cigarette factory for US$227 million, with an investment programme of US$145 million to follow. The French Seita Group have invested US$64 million in a 33 per cent stake in the Radom cigarette manufacturer, while Germany's Reemtsma Cigarettenfabriken have offered US$130 million for the Poznań factory. US Schooner Capital Group is acquiring a majority stake in the edible oil producer NZT Brzeg.

There has been much foreign interest in modernizing Bulgaria's food-processing industry. The maize products plant at Razgrad has been sold to Amylum, while a Greek food manufacturer has invested in the ice-cream factory at Varna and the French dairy concern Bongrain has purchased a majority shareholding in the Repcelaki Sajygar cheese factory, following its 36 per cent stake in the Veszpremtej ice-cream maker. The Swiss firms Kraft Jacobs Suchard (KJS) and Nestlé have acquired stakes in chocolate and confectionery enterprises in Sofia – the KJS majority holding 'Republika' is resulting in the modernization of the factory and continued production of established lines alongside innovations from Switzerland. Here, as elsewhere, foreign involvement is having a positive effect on food distribution, which is the subject of much public concern over both quality and cost. People do appreciate that food is available but 'the low status given to retailing, together with the centralized process for distribution prevented competition and innovation in agro-food sectors', especially in the context of declining investment (Mueller and Mueller 1996, p.172). Despite the influx of Western producers, Bulgarian food firms could pay more attention to processing as well as to quality and cost.

FARM-BASED FOOD PROCESSING IN RURAL AREAS: PLUM BRANDY (ŢUICĂ) DISTILLING IN THE ROMANIAN SUBCARPATHIANS

Nicolae Muică and David Turnock

The previous discussion of food processing concerned relatively highly capitalized businesses. But it is also possible for enterprise to develop more widely across rural areas with relatively modest investment on farms or in small premises in the villages. In Romania, as in other East European countries, modern marketing systems have been slow to penetrate the rural areas and challenge the subsistence farming tradition (Lamarche 1991; Maurel 1994). Today, Romania's small mixed farms provide food for the family and a limited amount of produce for the market – mainly livestock in the hill and mountain regions. Maximizing the value of farm produce for domestic consumption has required diverse procedures for processing and storage, which remained prominent until collectivization. Although much of this traditional activity has disappeared through competition from large-scale urban-based producers, there is no reason why it should not be resurrected. Of course, it will be necessary to satisfy regulations concerned with quality and hygiene, but where the necessary skills are still available, there is the possibility of development through bank loans combined with the assistance of organizations concerned with small and medium-size enterprises in rural areas. More thought will have to be given to an ecological agriculture appropriate to local physical conditions and the demand for high-quality food. Possibilities could include cheese, salami and preserved fruits, although the main thrust of this section concerns the distillation of brandy, another traditional product of Carpathian agriculture.

In the Subcarpathian region of Romania, fruit constitutes an important part of agricultural production and this branch has suffered severely as a result of the revolution. In the absence of efficient marketing and stimulating prices, large areas of orchards and vineyards have been neglected or deliberately cleared to make way for other enterprises, such as maize cultivation. Intervention to stabilize the situation is desperately needed, especially the vineyards. However, in the case of plum trees, the trend is operating in the reverse direction because new plantings are being made in many areas. This is because the plum is especially useful for the peasant. It is an important source of sugar and the fruit can be conserved in various ways – perhaps most significantly through the production of the spirit known as *țuică* or plum brandy. Distilling has therefore become traditional in Romania not so much through the use of cereals (although German and Polish influence to this effect is of some significance in Transylvania), but through the processing of plums (and some related fruits) which are prominent in the hill country and the mountain fringes (Figure 11.4) (Stefănescu 1972). Despite the discouragement of distilling in rural areas under communism (especially in areas that were collectivized) there are good opportunities today in the context of farm diversification and pluriactivity, which is crucial for the survival of small farms in the hill regions of the country.

Although large distilleries were built in the towns, using a range of raw materials (Zane 1970), but many country people have traditionally produced plum brandy for their own use, including small amounts used for presents or barter. In the earlier part of this century a production of

Source: Stefănescu 1972.

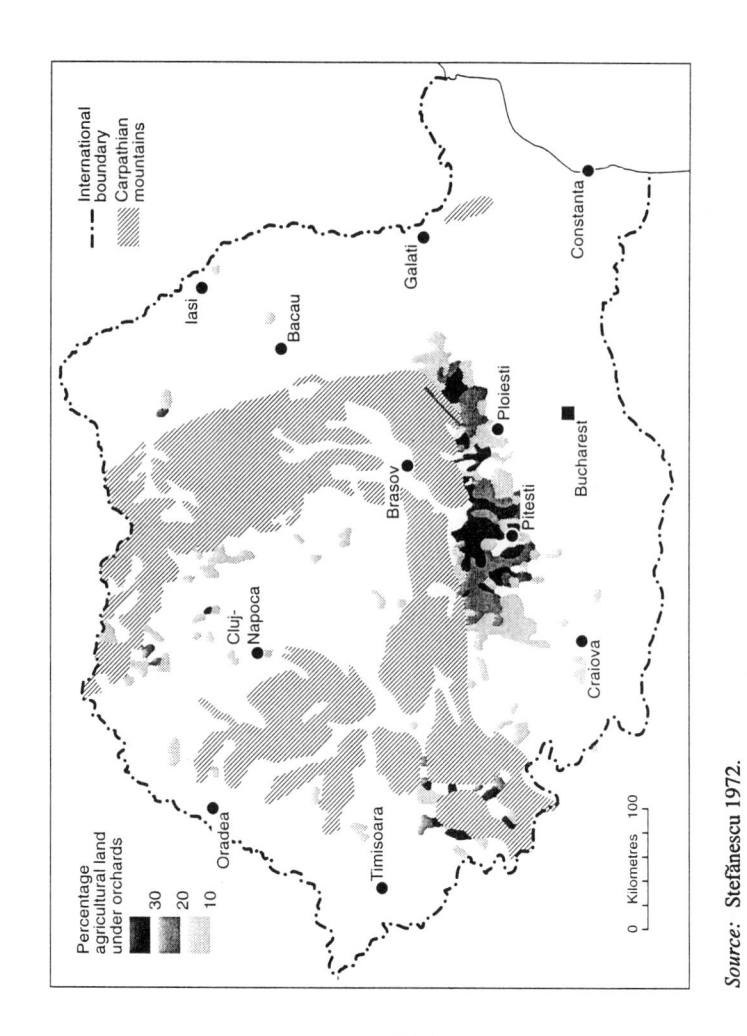

Figure 11.4 Fruit-growing areas of Romania

200–300 litres might well be obtained in a good year (from approximately half a hectare of plum trees within a holding of some 5ha in all). Typically, stocks would be large enough to cope with poor years when plums might be scarce, perhaps due to severe weather at the time the trees were in blossom. There would not normally be large surpluses, but people with an inclination for business and sufficient self-discipline not to drink all their stocks could enjoy a significant income from selling brandy. A thrifty farmer with plum trees in his garden and an additional orchard in the hills (perhaps in a small sheltered depression or *padină*, making up a hectare of ground altogether out of a total holding of some 10ha) might well produce 1,000 litres of spirit and farmers with good orchard soils, well developed by landsliding, might realize up to 3,000 litres in a good year. In the past, estate owners would have had even larger stocks.

Thus there would always be some people in the villages with *ţuică* for sale to neighbours who might find themselves short at the time of important ceremonies. Some peasants might even run informal drinking houses, taking *ţuică* from the cask (*butoi*) in a small measure (*toi*) of 50 or 100 grams suitable for individual glasses. The proceeds from such business were not inconsiderable, especially in poor years when prices might rise considerably. Exchanges were also made between *ţuică* from the Subcarpathians and cereals from the plains: peasants from the plains might take their cereals to the hills for barter or else the hill people would arrive in the lowlands with potatoes, fruit and plum brandy. In this way, plum brandy distilling was a form of *industria sătească pentru schimb* (Vulcănescu and Simionescu 1974, p.94) and involved the use of much-frequented trading roads: *drumuri meşteşugărilor* (ibid. p.69). Traditionally, much of the marketing was carried out at the *nedei* fairs on the high ground as peasants from the mountain valleys congregated on the watersheds. But the colonization of the plains and the gradual introduction of modern communications increased the importance of trading centres on the lower ground and especially *la hotarul dintre dealuri şi câmpie* (the hill–plain contact) (ibid. p.111). Townspeople without relatives in the villages could always get *ţuică* by placing an order with a peasant coming regularly to their market with diverse produce: quantity, quality and price would normally be agreed in advance. It was rare for shops to sell plum brandy before the Second World War and it is still uncommon, although some retail outlets are now appearing.

Țuică production was adversely affected by collectivization because stills were usually confiscated, not least because any peasant owning a still was persecuted as a *chiabur* (rich peasant) or exploiter against whom the class war was waged. The logic behind this discrimination derived from the custom whereby peasants without a still would borrow from a neighbour and pay a tax (or *vamă*) amounting to about a tenth of the production, so possession of a still was a significant indicator of wealth. At the same time, state control of fruit and alcohol stocks allowed prices to rise steeply in what was a monopoly situation. Cooperatives would normally see to it that at least one still was retained under their control, so that local fruit could be distilled for trade purposes. Rather than merely retain a traditional still, the authorities might centralize plum brandy production in a small factory, as at Pătârlagele (Buzău) and Stoenești (Vâlcea), although not to the complete exclusion of smaller stills that might continue to be used by the cooperatives in the remoter valleys. From the technical point of view they were reasonably efficient, although the practice of fermenting the plums brought from cooperative property in concrete pits sunk into the ground was not particularly successful as alcohol was lost because of the lower temperature and slower fermentation. There was also a suggestion that a chemical reaction involving the concrete adversely affected the bouquet of the brandy.

In some areas, peasants were forbidden to indulge in any part of the brandy distillation process. At Balcești (Vâlcea), peasants were not even allowed to ferment their plums and produce *borhot*, which is the basis of the distillation process. Their fermenting vessels were confiscated (along with the still and storage vessel). They would have to buy their *țuică* from the cooperative distillery or curry favour with those who worked in the still house in order to obtain stocks of brandy by barter. However, in areas with a more liberal management regime, such as Pătârlagele (Buzău), peasants could quite legally ferment the plums from their own gardens (plus any fruit stolen from the cooperative orchards) provided that they arranged with the factory for further processing. In the autumn, therefore, the peasant would arrive at the factory with a cartload of fermented plums contained in a specially-constructed cask or *cărator*, whereupon the *borhot* would be checked for strength and volume. The factory would take about two-thirds of the fermented fruit and give the peasant the *țuică* equivalent of the other third. Thus a peasant supplying 100 litres of *borhot* (from which 20 litres of *țuică* would normally be obtained) would receive 5 litres of brandy plus some cash.

Private operations by collectivized peasants might be tolerated where their houses and plots were more than 15-20km from a distillery owned by CAP or the local authority. But in any case, many peasants found ways of distilling illicitly in the home or elsewhere, although in much smaller quantities than before. Where the authorities were moderate in their seizures of equipment and took only the wooden cap (or *capac*) of the still as a simple means of stopping production, a new lid might be acquired in the course of time so that activity could recommence when it was considered safe enough to do so – typically at night, without light, although there was always the danger that smoke or smell might alert the authorities or their informers. Alternatively, small copper, enamelled or earthenware stills with as little as 8-10 litres capacity might be used. It was even possible to dispense with the still altogether and use a large enamelled kitchen pot (*oală mare*) of 20-30 litres within which a smaller vessel (*cratiţă*) of one or two litres was placed on a stand above the *borhot*. The top of the pot would then be covered by another vessel containing cold water and the contact sealed with *mămăligă* (maize pudding) in order to contain the vapours. Heating the *borhot* would then lead to the condensation of alcohol and its collection in the *cratiţă* (Figure 11.5). In villages where peasants were forbidden even to make *borhot* it would have been necessary to carry out all the operations in a clandestine manner with increased risk of detection. But there were many ways of getting by and the most reliable methods involved understandings with accommodating officials. Where the communist authorities were reasonable, many stills of 40-60 litres might operate legally for individual use, especially in areas with plenty of fruit, such as Muscel and the Drajna-Chiojd depression. Traditional skills were therefore retained, despite the challenging environment.

Meanwhile, *ţuică* production continued under licence in non-collectivized areas and although the taxes were generally higher under communism it was usually possible to produce larger quantities than the authority stipulated. Peasants in such areas were often able to purchase equipment outlawed in collectivized villages. Exchanges were still made with farming people on the plains who thought that the hill peasants, retaining their own farms, must indeed be rich. They would exclaim ironically '*venira Americanii!*' ('here come the Americans!') when the distillers arrived with their surpluses. In the formerly collectivized villages, *ţuică* production is now increasing, although the capacity will be limited until additional trees are planted and begin to bear fruit. In some

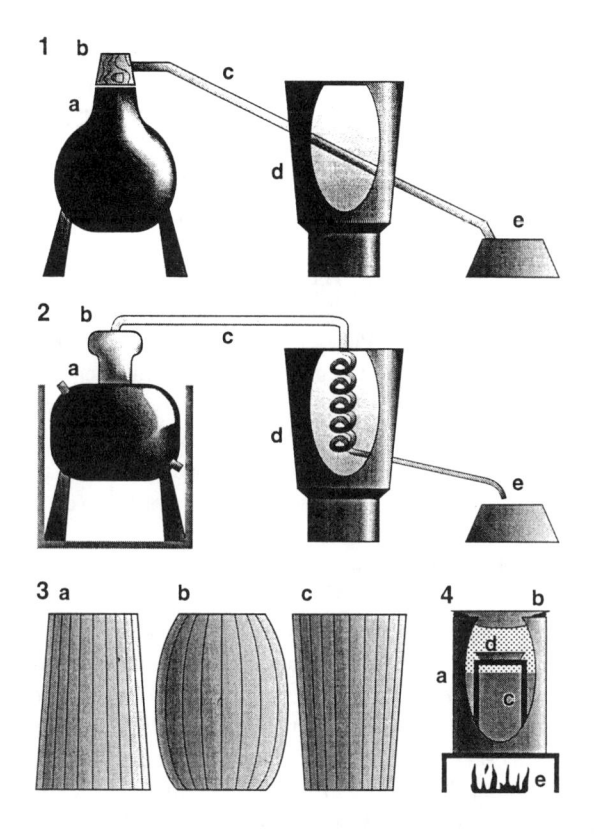

Notes:
1. Old-style distilling equipment: (a) copper still (*cazan*) on trivet (*pirostrii*); (b) wooden lid (*capac*); (c) wooden connector (*buba*) and copper pipe (*ţeava*); (d) cooling vat (*putină*) on a wooden stand (*scaun*); (e) spirit receiver (*botă*).
2. New-style distilling equipment: (a) copper still and trivet bricked into a *corlon*, with openings for filling (*gura de golire*); (b) copper lid (*capac* or *comanac*) permanently attached to the still; (c) horizontal copper pipe(s) (*cumpănă*) leading to a coil (*spiral*) or condensing cylinder; (d) and (e) as above.
3. Fermenting vats: (a) *streadz* (Mehedinţi); (b) *zăcătoare* (Wallachia); (c) *cadă* (Banaţ and Transylvania).
4. Equipment suitable for distilling in the domestic kitchen and widely used during the communist period: (a) enamelled pot of 30–40 litres (*oală mare*); (b) metal basin containing cold water, sealed to the pot by wheat meal paste (*cocă*); (c) stand (*scaun*); (d) vessel to collect the condensed vapours (*cratiţă*); (e) fire or burner.

Source: Muică and Turnock 1996.

Figure 11.5 The distilling process for the production of plum brandy

areas, the draconian rural planning of the communist period took some families further away from their plum trees (Muică and Turnock 1994, p.19), so more use is made of apples and pears. Another constraint arises from the loss of much of the equipment stock under communism. But now that production is starting again, modern equivalents are being adopted, while some traditional equipment is being repaired for further use. Distilling operations vary greatly in size. As a result of experience under communism, a large number of small stills are now in use, some of them made of earthenware. They can be operated in farmhouses and courtyards and make good sense in areas with only limited amounts of fruit, such as the Mehedinţi Plateau. The coexistence of large and small producers seems likely to remain because the tradition of hiring out stills has become less common: not only do many families possess their own small stills, but the larger operators wish to avoid the risk of damage to their equipment which in any case is usually permanently installed within a metal, brick or stone *corlon* in order to conserve heat.

Buildings and Their Location

Ţuică production often takes place in the house or courtyard but a special distillery building, or still-house, may be erected using wooden beams. The name *căzanie* (plural *căzanii*) is normally used but there are many local variants: *povarna* in Gorj and Vâlcea, whereas in the Siriu Mountains of Buzău and in Vrancea the name *velniţa* is used. In Transylvania names like *horincărie* and *palincărie* are clearly related to the local names for *ţuică*. Construction of such buildings might be undertaken in the open country, where a water supply could most easily be arranged, and distilleries might well be located away from dwelling houses because of the risk of fire breaking out (Giurescu 1974, p.198). Such dispersed distilleries could then be used as a refuge in the event of rain while working in the fields or travelling between the house and the holding. It could also be used for sheltering animals. In Gorj it is common for storeyed houses to include a *pivniţa* at ground level (Stanculescu et al. 1973, pp.36-43), and in the Gura Văii area of the Danube Defile it is usual for peasants to maintain a secondary farmstead or *pimniţa* where there are fruit trees and a store for the wine and *ţuică* produced (Apolzan 1987, pp.312-13). In the Platforma Luncanilor a *casa de bârne* in Cioclovina is described as providing storage for food and fodder as well as a *voz* for fermenting plums (ibid., p.96).

Still-houses tended to disappear under communism because of security considerations, but many of the locations are still remembered by the peasants and given names such as 'La Căzanii' or 'La Căzanie'. Some buildings were acquired for display in open-air ethnographical museums. At Dumbrava Park in Sibiu there is an exhibit from Sirbești (Gorj). The premises were constructed in 1935 and transferred to Sibiu in 1966. According to the guidebook (Bucur et al. 1986, p.69) the still-house is

> a rectangular building with oak-beam framework and a porch at the front. The high walls are lined with two rows of alder-boards, the second row covering the joints of the first row. The high roof is in four slopes, covered with shingles, with a chimney above the ridge. The entrance is over two metres wide, allowing the passage of large casks and vats.

There are two stills, one with a wooden *capac* and another (with a capacity of 500 litres) with a copper lid. A steady flow of water is supplied to the cooling vat by a water wheel with scoops which pour water into a flume. The same museum also houses a specially constructed press-house for fermenting plums and storing casks of brandy. It was built at Polovragi (Gorj) in 1883 and taken to Sibiu in 1967. The two-storey *pimniţa* stands on a slope.

> It is made up of a cellar (built of stone masonry and quick-lime mortar) and the press-house proper which forms the first floor of the building. The press-house is built of square horizontal fir-beams joined in end-to-end joints. The roof is in four slopes and is covered with shingles. There is a small room facing the first floor of the press-house, decorated with sculptured poles and closed in with a railing made of boards joined together by grooves. The entrance is a wide double door allowing the passage of large casks. The access is by a massive ladder, carved out of a tree-trunk. The stone cellar is used for housing the fermenting vats and for storing food. The first floor is used for keeping the casks of plum brandy, placed in a row opposite to the door, various other [items] used for plum-picking as well as kegs made by the village cooper. (ibid., pp.71-2)

However, the practice of erecting still-houses is being revived to a modest degree. One example was noted at Brâncovenești north of Reghin (Mureș) in 1993 and another at Carasova, south of Reșița (Caras-Severin) in 1994. In both cases a small building was erected by the stream and a small waterwheel (with tin cans for scoops) provided a steady supply of cooling water. The cans emptied water into a flume which ran into the distillery building. However, in such circumstances it would not be usual to leave the equipment unattended throughout the year. Constantin Butuca has built a still-house beside the Muscel stream in Pătârlagele, which measures 4 × 4.8 metres and has piping to pump water from the river into a roof tank and also to evacuate warm water and *boască* (the residue left in the still after distillation) back into it. Butuca was the local bakery manager under communism but is now a private businessman with a flourmill and plum brandy distillery. The still capacity is only 145 litres (modest in comparison with the situation before communism) and yields 35 litres of brandy with a good *borhot*; for the ratio of still capacity to spirit distilled in one batch varies from 5:1 to 8:1, depending on the quality of the fruit. In the case of relatively poor *borhot*, the later part of the distillation may be thrown away. These new distilleries often display interesting innovations. The priest at Panatău (Buzău) has constructed a still-house and plans to erect a copper vessel above the still so that the *țeava* (the copper pipe which transfers the vapours from the still to the condensing vessel) can pass through it and preheat a quantity of *borhot* in preparation for the next batch. The still is quite small (140 litres) and efficiency is therefore to be sought through minimizing the delays between successive batches.

In 1996, three new private distilleries were noted higher up the Muscel Valley between the villages of Muscel and Fundăturile. Each consists of a shed standing by the stream and housing a still of 100–200 litres, served by a steady water supply using a leat, for it is widely believed that a continuous supply of cold water is needed for a good *țuică* (the cold water sinks in the condensing vessel while warm water rises). These new still-houses also have a gravity system to evacuate *boască* into the stream (in one case a tank has been sunk into the river bank so the residue can be stored and carried back to the farm for use as low-grade pig fodder). The stills are hired by peasants for a *vamă* of several litres of brandy. There has to be a well-organized family unit to cart the *borhot* and wood for the fire: the fermented fruit is carried by cart and ladled out by wooden bucket with a long handle into plastic bins from which it can be ladled in smaller quantities into the still. It is also necessary to attend to the fire very carefully and, during distillation, to wind the handle (*tijă*) which agitates the *borhot* and prevents any burning on the bottom of the still. However, the occasion is usually a convivial one with food, nuts and mamaliga available for the family group and passers-by who demand a drink as the first spirit emanates from the condensing vessel and into the receptacle (*botă*) in which it accumulates. Quality may be checked through the use of a small bottle, while quantity in the *botă* can be measured using a dip-stick. Of course, even a small 40-litre still in a courtyard may be hired out, although the smaller scale of the operation usually lends itself to transport in plastic buckets and drums without the need for horses or a *cărator*. Peasants who used to take their *borhot* to the factory are now using their own small still or else are hiring along the lines described. Only the local state farm continues to make use of the central distillery which was once such a conspicuous symbol of socialist agriculture in the Pătârlagele community. Peasants with surplus fruit may deliver to the factory and receive 4 litres of brandy for 100kg of fruit, but under normal conditions the peasant would not consider this good business.

Future Prospects

Plums have long been important for Romanian peasants and they remain an important part of the harvest routine in the Subcarpathians. Traditional preserving methods are still used and new orchards are being planted to increase the output of plum brandy, which arguably has a good future in commerce. Making full use of the fruit resources has been advocated by several experts on mountain agriculture (Giurcăneanu 1988, p.84; Rey 1979, p.273). Under the conditions of the transition it offers a way forward towards sustainable development (Pascariu 1993) and agricultural experts have recommended support for the food industry in general (Otiman 1994, p.256). Some smallholders are already planting more plum trees and recent research suggests that young families in the Subcarpathians are keen to invest to rebuild both orchards and vineyards (Hirschhausen-Leclerc 1994, p.322). Farm diversification could therefore include non-agricultural farm-based activities covering the distilling of *ţuică* and its marketing partly to farm visitors (through agrotourism) but mainly to the urban consumers or even for export. However, under the present conditions of private farming with a very strong necessity for diversification there would seem to be scope for peasants to produce brandy by working to agreed standards and for the production to be marketed more widely. It will obviously be difficult for *ţuică* to build up a significant world market share given the investments that have been made by the competition. But Scotch whisky started off in a roughly comparable situation and there is no reason why plum brandy should go on being treated with such reverence as Romania's best-kept secret. The cachet of a rural industry operating in an ecologically sustainable environment, with a still largely unwritten folk-history behind it, provides further enhancement of the potential for the continued valorization of agriculture in the Romanian Carpathians.

RURAL TOURISM WITH PARTICULAR REFERENCE TO ROMANIA

Floarea Bordanc and David Turnock

Rural tourism is a long-established interest in the northern countries, although much of it involved second homes rather than income for farmers. Second homes and weekend excursions were common in Prague's southern environs in the 1920s and 1930s when many simple timber chalets (sometimes in joint ownership) were built close to railway stations in areas of environmental and scenic interest. Hence the appearance of cottage settlements, a new element of the rural landscape, in forests as well as some of the more marginal (that is, steeply sloping) agricultural land. Such settlements expanded while traditional rural communities were stagnating and under communism, when certain activities generally available to free societies were constrained, there was an unprecedented boom in the construction of cottages around Prague and the provincial cities. By the end of the 1980s, this trend was also characteristic of small towns even where there were no major environmental problems in the urban cores. However, tourist villages in the Polish Carpathians (especially those close to the Tatra and Babia Góra) have maintained higher rates of population growth than other villages in the Polish Carpathians. They show a reduced level of out-migration by women, and support more people of productive age. They also have a better infrastructure in terms of commercial and cultural facilities, and above all they show abundant evidence of new housebuilding, including houses of large capacity which can offer rooms to tourists as well as family accommodation for three generations. Tourism integrates closely with agriculture in that catering for visitors can provide an additional outlet for farm produce, although we are also reminded that 'population growth and the uncontrolled expansion of the buildings reduce the tourist attractiveness of some areas' (Kurek 1996, p.196). In FGDR, all the new *Länder* encourage the growth of 'green' tourism and recreation through preserving and improving the landscape and providing good amenities and facilities (for example, accommodation but also walking, cycling and horse-riding routes). They also offer subsidies to farmers to diversify into farm tourism and help in marketing rural tourism enterprises.

A larger forest area in Hungary could enhance the potential for tourism, particularly in connection with hunting which is now subject to new legislation to ensure sustainable management. In Transdanubia, agriculture could be more closely integrated with the tourist industry of Lake Balaton. Enterprising farmers from the village of Tab in Somogy county are already supplying fresh fruit to holiday homes in the area and it is well known that other opportunities for competition exist, given the quality and price of food supplied under present arrangements during the summer months. Meanwhile, farmers in the north and northeast could benefit from increased patronage by people from Budapest and the towns of the northern part of the Great Plain, for there are interesting monuments and buildings that could be renovated, to say nothing of the Eger and Tokaj vineyards. Agrotourism could also emphasize game, fish and honey as elements in the local cuisine. Eventually, a range of services characteristic of foreign tourism could be built up. Such a growth in tourism would not only benefit farmers but could generate employment in landscaping, crop protection and transportation, as well as commerce. But improvement of the commercial infrastructure is a precondition for success, so it must be emphasized that agricultural enterprise and other forms of private enterprise, even with local authority involvement, will not be sufficient to develop tourism and light industry without external support.

In Yugoslavia, rural developments could link with fishing, including new housing (sometimes on stilts) in the alluvial zone; also hostels, restaurants and camping – especially in alluvial areas close to the towns of Apatin, Novi Sad and Sombor. There is also some hunting tourism (Curcić and Kicosev 1996). In the Iron Gates area, where agriculture has been hit by a loss of land, tourism could provide some compensation, especially an ecologically acceptable rural tourism respecting the national park status of the area (Tosics 1996). In a situation where many villages are in decline, with negative rates of natural increase, growth may be dependent on tourism and new industrial technologies (Djurdjev 1996). In Albania, as part of a somewhat faltering four-year tourism development plan, which has attracted US$150 million of investment, Italian and Kuwaiti interests are involved in developing a number of projects along the hitherto largely untouched Ionian coast. Tourist villages could provide useful markets for Albanian farmers, although there is scope for a genuine rural tourism more firmly rooted in cultural and environmental considerations (Misha 1996). Economists stress the limitations of tourism as a source of agricultural diversification of agriculture. There is certainly benefit in providing accommodation and increasing local demand for food. However, 'while tourism may increase local demand for food, particularly for some regions and some products, total tourist-generated demand is limited' (Tanic n.d., p.23).

Ecotourism and the Small Family Farms of the Romanian Carpathians

Romania has long been an important tourist destination, but under the communist system there was little scope for private enterprise and the rural areas were generally neglected – although some authors were aware of the opportunities in the mountain regions where provision was largely restricted to chains of chalets, most prominent in the Bucegi and Făgăraş Mountains (Rey 1985). Now the benefits of ecotourism are becoming better understood (Cater and Lowman 1994), especially in rural areas where employment opportunities must be linked with the concept of sustainability (Bramwell and Lane 1994). The consensus view is that modern agriculture should be developed only as far as the ecological limits (Dent and McGregor 1994), with additional inputs into household budgets from 'pluriactivity' as farmers become involved in the most appropriate ancillary activities. The experience of East European countries is significant because land restitution has been prominent in the transition to a market economy. Many small family farms have emerged, in addition to those that survived communist programmes of collectivization, but it is essential that other sources of income are exploited because few of the farms are larger than 10ha and many are much smaller (Cochrane 1991). Even though occupational specialization may seem the ultimate ideal, there are economic and cultural reasons why this may not be attainable, at least in the short

Aspects of Farm Diversification 335

term (Marsden 1990). Agrotourism is one such possibility (Misiak 1993) and this section explores the scope for development in Romania, where the authors have carried out a joint research project in recent years (Turnock 1995).

Restitution has created some 5 million small farms. In the lowlands, systems of cooperation through 'associations' are in force in many areas (Bordanc 1995; Ianoş et al. 1992). By contrast, in the Carpathian Mountains (Figure 11.6), where there is little cropping to necessitate coordinated use of machinery, it is more usual for each holding to be worked independently with informal subletting arrangements where necessary (Bordanc 1996). Where villages are situated close to the towns, commuting to urban-based employment is possible, but in the remoter areas more opportunity must be sought within the rural environment. A comparison has been made between the two adjacent communes in Harghita where the population is overwhelmingly Hungarian. While the people in the lowland area of Sânmartin (with its twin communities of Csikszentmarton and Czekefalva) are heavily involved in non-agricultural activities and use associations to farm the land, the villagers of Kaszon (Plaieşii de Jos commune) work their own fragmented holdings (Nemenyi and Nemenyi 1995). However, even with intensive use of all available labour, such farms cannot support a household without ancillary activities (Antal and Kovács 1996). Where there are insufficient opportunities in local factories and services, the possibility arises of creating new farm-based activities such as handicrafts or small manufacturing activities using electricity or water power (Parpală 1992). What is clear is that, for the moment, the small family farm must be the base for rural planning (Silvas 1995).

The potential for tourism in Romania's Carpathian Mountains is much discussed (Erdeli and Istrate 1996), with recreation and second-home ownership seen as important departures from the *sistematizare* model of rural planning during the communist period (Misiak 1993). It is not only a question of fine scenery, made accessible by an excellent transport system which has been necessary to link the lowlands of Moldavia and Wallachia with Transylvania, but also attractive cultural landscapes with both historical monuments and a live display of rural activity which is remarkable by general European standards today for the diversity of customs, festivals, handicrafts and occupations (Ghinoiu 1996). There is also potential for winter sports and for medical treatment linked with

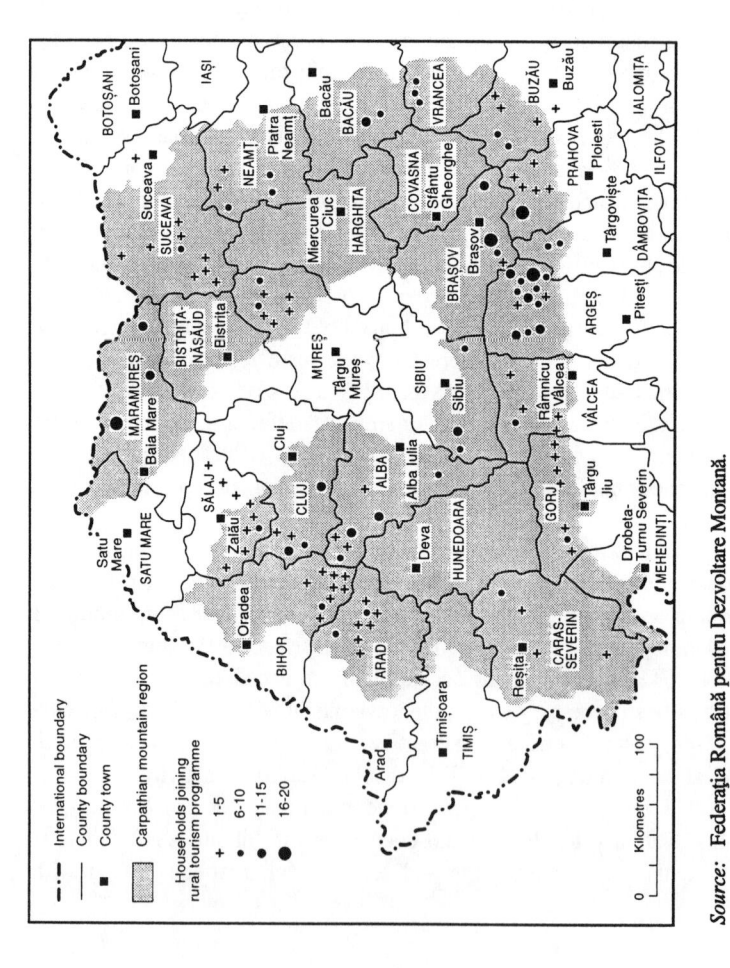

Source: Federaţia Română pentru Dezvoltare Montană.

Figure 11.6 Rural tourism in the Romanian Carpathians

mineral waters and climatic stations (Cianga 1994) (Table 11.1). Thus, while some villages are outstanding for folklore or handicrafts, others may be attractive for their scenic pastoral landscapes, hunting and sporting facilities and choice of fruits and wines (Istrate and Bran 1995b). The potential has been acknowledged by foreign consultants: 'family orientated tourists, nature lovers, excitement and adventure seekers, outdoor enthusiasts and those interested in farming or forestry based holidays can all gain from visiting Romania' (Walker et al. 1995, p.52). To people coming from abroad, Romanian rural houses appear attractive and traditional: 'to such persons a stay in a traditional Romanian home would be an added attraction as long as standards are reasonable' (ibid., p.43). There is particular opportunity among 'those seeking to experience a different and unusual culture who would be willing and have a desire to stay in good basic accommodation in a house or farm set in attractive countryside and prepared to undertake their own exploration of their surroundings' (ibid., p.48). Houses in villages might also be attractive to tour operators seeking overnight accommodation, and there are opportunities for small shops and other retail outlets near developing tourist locations.

Table 11.1 Typology of tourist villages in Romania

Function	Examples
Ethnography and folklore	Bodgan Vodă (Maramureş); Lereşti (Argeş), Sibiel (Sibiu), Vaideeni (Vâlcea), Vamă (Suceava)
Art and handicrafts	Izvorul Crişului and Marga (Cluj); Tismana (Gorj)
Climate and scenery	Bran, Fundata and Sîrnea (Braşov)
Hunting and fishing	Bistriţa, Gurghiu and Vişeu Valleys; Danube Delta
Fruit and wine	Agapia and Vânători Neamţ (Neamţ); Recaş (Timiş)
Pastoral farming	Jina (Sibiu); Vaideeni (Valcea)
Sport	Fundata, Moeciu and Sîrnea (Braşov)

Source: Istrate and Bran 1995b.

The underlying rationale is that in contrast to holiday activities specific to classical tourism, such as sun-bathing and swimming, winter sports, urban tours and conferences, rural holidays can best cater for a different range of activities: walking and mountain climbing; the study of nature, culture and ancestral values; hunting and fishing; and sports such as canoeing and horse riding. The approach is seen as a progressive one, offering income and employment while remaining firmly rooted in the Rio de Janeiro declaration on sustainability. Romanian academics contemplating the rural future (Popescu and Bălteanu 1996) see agrotourism as a possible trigger for development, which could extend from farming and food processing to handicrafts and infrastructure (Olaru et al. 1994). Such a view is vindicated by experience in the Bran-Rucar corridor, close to the tourist centre of Braşov, where out-migration is relatively low (Fulea 1996) because there is considerable opportunity for young people (Pascaru 1996). According to the Director of the Tourism Research Institute, V. Glavan (1995), rural tourism is of great potential importance under the plan to increase the number of foreign tourists from 5.9 million in 1994 to 7.2 million in 2000. It is intended that there will be facilities in 8,500 rural households by 2000, which could provide Romania with a 'niche' in the market and spread the benefits of tourism more widely throughout the country without the need for heavy investment. Because costs are relatively low, agrotourism is accessible to a large section of the travelling public, both domestic and foreign.

Satisfying the Preconditions

However, while the opportunity exists it cannot be exploited immediately by people who have little capital and virtually no experience of private enterprise after half a century of central planning. Individual households will need some aptitude for running a business, which could depend on current non-agricultural activities or family experiences going back to the pre-communist period. The stimulus of finding extra work to keep younger members of the family at home may be a critical spur for action, and awareness of the potential may be strengthened by proximity to a main highway and a situation in a relatively developed region. A small capital stock (perhaps delivered by a relative living abroad) may be crucial; likewise a level of confidence in making professional contacts (advisory services and banks) and dealing with local élites. But the motivation of individual families will need to be reinforced by local courses to teach the basic skills of looking after visitors and carrying out domestic improvements.

Aspects of Farm Diversification 339

There is a need for both community and individual effort to identify resources and evolve diversification plans (Ion-Tudor 1996a). Visitors will be attracted by the notion of an 'escape' to rural civilization and therefore a total ethnological and folklore approach is needed, as well as individual family effort. It is important to balance economic, social, cultural and religious values so that sustainable development is achieved. The interests of tourists have to be balanced with those of local communities whose active participation is needed, along the with input from the business community, local government and the mass media. Publicity may also be handled by local organizations with which individual households can register. Coordination is also needed to ensure the availability of good-quality souvenirs. Older people should be motivated to pass on their skills so as to safeguard the quality of production and diversify into new craft products. 'There is an urgent need to establish a link between the excellent archaeological and folk museum service as visitors to these attractions are clearly willing to purchase quality handicrafts and folk products from the area' (Walker et al. 1995, p.49). In other words, not only is training necessary but marketing and 'network cooperation' as well, perhaps through a local craft association. At the moment, it is often difficult to get information about festivals concerned with folk song and dance although there is scope for development of such events, which could be of international importance if they were held in small resorts with both hotel and farm accommodation available. The Internet will doubtless be a major source in the future, but publicity is important nationally and also at the local level, 'where the commune mayors must get involved in developing the infrastructure required for rural tourism' (ibid.).

Financial help from domestic or external sources is another precondition. It could take the form of grants, loans, tax concessions, or all three. 'As long as there is no assistance such as low interest rates on long-term credits necessary for accommodating tourists, especially foreign tourists, rural tourism will remain a rare flower' (Rautu 1996, p.13). Growth will be slow, with the domestic sector principally in mind. Investment is needed to improve the infrastructure which is still very poor in some areas (Surd 1994). While excessive sophistication would be counter-productive, it is also true that visitors are increasingly discerning and good standards are required. There comes a point where low standards will discourage all but the most intrepid, especially in the case of international tourism because foreign visitors with cars that require surfaced roads and lead-free petrol will be loath to deviate from the main routes. Alongside a good standard of accommodation, 'a verification and grading system will be needed to ensure the product is of an adequate standard before it is widely marketed' (Walker et al. 1995, p.45). In addition to improved communications (including telecommunications) and shopping facilities, local sightseeing opportunities (rambles on waymarked paths and visits to historic buildings, festivals and local industries) need to be marketed through attractive and up-to-date brochures.

Considerations fundamental to the successful development of rural tourism extend to nature conservation to ensure the retention of scenic resources. It is clear that rapid and uncoordinated development of tourism has created problems in mountain areas such as the Bucegi, where more effective controls are needed (Velcea et al. 1993). Without more careful regulation, a growth of rural tourism could undermine the resources on which it depends. 'Protection of rare species and representative vegetation types is essential at a time of increasing anthropic pressure: such action must be combined with measures to maintain landscape diversity and safeguard wildlife habitats' (Muică and Popova-Cucu 1993, p.15). The largest protected area at present is the Retezat National Park, created in 1935. It now covers 54,400ha, including a nature reserve of 18,400ha where no economic activity is permitted. Similar regimes should be provided for the Bucegi and other sensitive areas such as the Apuseni Mountains and the Cozia and Parâng Mountains in Vâlcea county (Ploaie 1996; Rusenescu 1980). The former includes the Padeş-Cetatile Ponorului-Scarisoara karst complex and the gorges of the Criş Repede and Cheia Turzii, while the latter would safeguard a cluster of existing nature reserves including Călcescu: a geomorphological and vegetation reserve embracing the picturesque Călcescu-Păsăru glacial *cirque* with the three lakes of Călcescu, Păsăru and Vidal. Management should impose grazing restrictions (backed by measures to restore the alpine grassland and scrub vegetation), control motor traffic in critical areas and reduce poaching. Several new parks have been scheduled but the necessary legislation is still awaited (Istrate and Bran 1995a; Olaru 1994). As well as environmental protection to ensure an unpolluted environment, ecofarming has a significant bearing on rural tourism through assurances to tourists about the quality of food produced. Sustainable agriculture has very good prospects in the hills and mountains, whereas only gradual change towards this idea can be expected in the plains.

Aspects of Farm Diversification   341

Fundamental to any initiatives in tourism is an appropriate legislative framework. If Romanian tourism is to be profitable, a modern legal framework should be put in place, preferably in harmony with EU legislation, so that the Ministry of Tourism can regulate the industry and exercise control through subordinate organizations. There should be more attention to protecting the tourist as the consumer, and guarantees may have to be deposited by authorized operators. Professional associations would be valuable in this respect and the Ministry now consults with such bodies. Promotional work is also needed at the national level to stimulate more international tourism and, in particular, to achieve higher levels of tourist spending – quoted at only US$68 per visitor in Romania, compared with US$265 in Poland, US$600 in the Czech Republic and US$4,000 in Sweden (Pais 1997). Finance is also a crucial issue given the present climate of high inflation, high interest and liquidity difficulties which makes banks cautious in advancing loans. There are not sufficient parameters for evaluating financial risk. Of course, in rural tourism individual developments tend to be small and partnerships with foreign enterprises may not be appropriate, but it would be useful for a Romanian tourist bank to support investment activity with inexpensive credits.

Action Taken Since the Revolution

Immediately after the revolution, the government set up a Commission for the Mountainous Regions within the Agriculture Ministry to disseminate the principles of 'mountainology' through education and publicity (Turnock 1993). This was inspired by the thinking of Rey (1979), elaborated during the communist era as an alternative to the more uncompromising consolidation of rural settlement envisaged under the rural planning (*sistematizare*) policy then in force (Turnock 1991). The Commission's area of responsibility was deemed to cover 773 communes in 27 counties and parts of some additional communes where individual villages satisfy the relevant criteria: high altitude (over 300–350 metres) with slopes generally in excess of 15 per cent and poor accessibility; in addition land should be used overwhelmingly for pastures, hayfields and forest (with at least 70 per cent of the value of agricultural production consisting of animals, predominantly cattle and sheep). In addition to a national headquarters in Bucharest, the Commission operated in each of the relevant counties with offices in the county town or, occasionally in a smaller settlement within the mountain territory (Figure 11.6).

First and foremost, the Commission tried to reverse the downward spiral of agricultural activity, brought about by low prices which could not stimulate higher inputs. They sought to improve agricultural practices by fertilizing pastures to correct soil acidity, by planting fruit trees and by improved breeding based on the Pinzgau breed. Importance was attached to providing machinery suitable for small mountain farms and the Commission was also concerned with the improvement of rural services, including the extension of electricity supplies. Research was encouraged through the Mountainology Research Institute at Cristian near Sibiu, with its several branches and model farms scattered throughout the mountain regions. Education in mountainology was provided in various schools and universities, including a special Mountainology Faculty at Vălenii de Munte. Foreign exchanges gave some farmers useful experience and model buildings were publicized. In Valea Doftanei, the Commission became involved in a pilot project for integrated local development covering local industry (including food processing), improved fodder supply and educational and technical back-up. Several county plans were founded on 'baseline' surveys and included proposals to revive traditional crafts, improve farm roads and encourage agricultural societies. Efforts are being made to improve communication with the farming community through the journal *Viaţa Munţilor*.

The Commission was reorganized at the end of 1992 as part of a streamlining of the bureaucracy to achieve substantial economies. Instead there is a National Agency for the Mountainous Regions with 28 county services as before. But the new organization is much smaller and the loss of many staff members, with valuable expertise and experience, has been strongly deplored (Rey 1994). Moreover, the new organization is less well endowed, lacking its own means of transport at the county level where it became part of a larger organization concerned with all aspects of agricultural administration. However, the work started in 1990 is still continuing (Ion-Tudor 1996b). Although resources are still very limited, the elements of a strategy are being discussed and agricultural experts continue to advocate support for less-favoured areas, including mountain districts (Otiman 1994, p.256). In addition to the Research Institute, there is a Foundation for Agriculture and Food Economics at Reghin and a Centre for Training and Innovation for Development in the Carpathians (the latter established in 1996 at Vatra Dornei). The Agency has

Aspects of Farm Diversification 343

developed the international links established by its predecessor, which became a member of the 'Euromontana' organization in 1991. Since 1994, it has been represented on the Board of Directors and it has participated in drafting the European Charter of Mountain Regions through the Council of Europe. Romania is now connected with international projects concerned with rural development and sustainability (Dcrounian 1995). France is assisting with a training programme, while Germany and Switzerland have established pilot stations for integrated mountain development (the Swiss at Măgureni in Prahova county and Ruşi Munţii in Mureş county).

The Agency has encouraged the development of handicrafts in the interest of farm diversification and workshops are now on the increase. Products such as the ceramics of Horezu command rewarding prices, and it is reported that foreign visitors will pay DM300–500 for 'cloche' hats made from peacock feathers in the Salva area of Bistriţa-Năsăud. By no means the least significant aspect of the Agency's achievements has been its work in supporting NGOs such as the Mountain Farmers' Association in the Dorna area near Suceava. There is also a Romanian Working Group on Sustainable Agriculture and Biodiversity which has attracted support from the Heinrich Böll Foundation in Germany since 1995, with a view to promoting sustainable agriculture and produce in which visitors will have confidence (Barboi 1996). However, most important here is the Federation for Mountain Development, which has taken much effective action in the field of agrotourism. This organization has been working with the government to make it easier for farmers to diversify into agrotourism. Designs for farmhouses which could include rooms for tourists have been circulated. These drawings include three-storey houses similar to those commonly found in the Polish Carpathians (Rusu-Grigore 1993b). On the international front, expertise is being obtained from Gîtes de France (France's national federation of rural tourism), which has 40 years' experience. In addition, Eurogîtes (European Federation of Rural Economic and Cultural Tourism) has 22 national and regional member associations, including Romania. The Romanian entries in the Eurogîtes catalogue are increasing, although the total number remains small.

Moreover, fiscal concessions are being negotiated, for it is a daunting prospect in a country where rural houses often lack bathrooms and interior toilets for small farmers to contemplate the major works of modernization needed for entry into the tourism business. Bureaucratic planning procedures could well prove a deterrent. It used to be necessary for farmers with only two or three rooms to obtain permits from the water, electrical and sanitation authorities before going into the tourist business. But now, as a result of legislation enacted in 1994 for the mountain zone, the Danube Delta and the Black Sea coast, these approvals are no longer needed. Moreover, approved farms and guesthouses (the latter having 3-20 rooms) providing quality services can gain exemption of taxes for 10 years. A grading system is also provided and costs fluctuate according to standards within the range of 15-25 thousand lei per night (£3-5 sterling) for a twin-bedded room, plus a further 20 thousand lei (about £4 sterling) if meals are required (Mitrache et al. 1996). So far, just over a thousand households have been invited to apply for classification as units of agrotourism. These are spread somewhat unevenly over 20 of the counties with mountain territory within their limits. In the other counties, progress has yet to be made. Just over 60 per cent of households accepted, but with a substantial difference between the Curvature and Eastern Carpathians (above the average) and Banat-Oltenia and Western Carpathians where the response was much poorer (Table 11.2 and Figure 11.2). It is not clear why there should be such a clear contrast, although there is a strong tourist tradition in parts of the high-scoring regions which may result in a particularly positive attitude. The work of the local authority may be very important for a big growth of interest was reported in Vama (Suceava) in response to encouragement by local officials.

Table 11.2 Households joining the agrotourism project in Romania

Cluster	Counties	Households invited to register (A)	Households accepting (B)	B as percentage of A
Western Carpathians	5	327	180	55.0
Eastern Carpathians	5	270	175	64.8
Banat-Oltenia	4	185	99	53.5
Curvature Carpathians	6	397	271	68.3
Total	20	1,179	725	61.5

Source: Romanian Federation for Mountain Area Development.

New Organizations and the PHARE Programmes

Other specialist organizations have come to the fore to stimulate agrotourism. A National Association of Rural Ecological and Cultural Tourism (Asociaţia Naţionale pentru Turism Rural Ecologic şi Cultural din România: ANTREC) has branches in 23 counties covering such areas as the Apuseni Mountains (Alba, Cluj and Bihor), Banat Mountains (Caras-Severin), Bran-Rucăr Corridor (Braşov), Bucovina (Suceava), Central Moldavia (Bacău and Neamt), Crişana (Bihor), Danube Delta (Tulcea), Litoral (Constanţa), Maramureş, Marginimea Sibiului (Sibiu), Northern Oltenia (Gorj and Vâlcea), the Subcarpathian Hills (Argeş and Dâmboviţa), the Transylvanian Hills (Harghita and Mureş) and Vrancea. Constituted in 1994 at Bran, near Braşov, ANTREC has 2,000 accommodation places on its books, ranging from boarding houses to peasant households and sheepfolds. It is affiliated to Eurogîtes and collaborates with the Ministry of Tourism and the Ministry of Agriculture over ecotourism in the Carpathians. The aim is to organize all those willing to practise or support rural tourism: householders, tour organizers and environmental organizations. ANTREC is also encouraging progress on the gastronomic side of the business. It organized two events in 1996 and attracted an international entry thanks to its protocol of cooperation with Hungary's National Association for Rural Tourism. A competition for *sarmale* (a New Year delicacy consisting of cabbage rolls or vine leaves stuffed with meat and cornflour and eaten with horseradish) was held at Praid (Harghita) in September, reciprocating Hungarian hospitality in 1995, and a pie competition was held in Bacău later in the year.

In several areas there are commercial organizations within which groups of private householders operate, such as 'Branimex' near Braşov and 'Montana Borşa' which is active in the area round the Maramureş town of that name. Local tourist associations are growing up, such as 'Agromontana', 'Agro-Tur' and 'Botiza' in Maramureş (Rusu-Grigore 1993a). The 'Tourist Coop' agency in Valcea county has produced a guide book (*Ghid Agroturistic Montan*) listing addresses in the villages of Malaia, Vaideeni and Voineasa where accommodation can be found. A pilot project might well be undertaken in this area, to develop interest among the monasteries as well as among the small farms. Meanwhile, there is an important external stimulus through 'Opération Villages Roumains' (OVR), set up by a group based in Belgium and supported by the EU under its 'PHARE' programme. OVR has developed a strategy for tourism based on eight pilot zones covering 40 selected villages in the north of the country. Each village has produced an information pack to describe the local facilities and opportunities (including visits to monasteries, folk festivals and craft workshops). In each case there is a link with a village in Belgium (or another West European country) to help with external marketing: for example, Vadu Izci is paired with the Belgian village of Brain le Compe. About a thousand bed-nights were secured during the first year of operations (1994) and the scheme may be extended to other parts of the country.

ANTREC and OVR together provide a viable base for cooperation with the EU's aid programme for Eastern Europe (Plop 1996). This is known as PHARE, although its scope now goes way beyond the countries of Hungary and Poland for which the name of the organization was first devised. PHARE works with OVR in respect of infrastructure and training and with ANTREC for promotion and implementation. Under the Village Tourism Pilot Project (VTPP), undertaken in collaboration with OVR, the four villages of Arieşeni (Alba), Bran (Braşov), Vadu Izei (Maramureş) and Vama (Suceava) should finish up with a standard of rural tourism coordination (covering information, product development and infrastructure and customer service, provided through a Local Tourism Infrastructure Fund) appropriate for a demonstration role with respect to the local development of tourism activity. This project will also demonstrate the complementarity of local activity and Ministry of Tourism plans. Meanwhile, PHARE also works with ANTREC on the Promotion of Rural Tourism Programme. While having strong links with the VTPP, this is primarily intended to promote Romanian rural tourism at exhibitions and fairs of both local and international importance. It will also establish an effective rural tourism reservation network sustainable in the medium term; design brochures and signposts; print materials; and organize symposia and workshops. The work is being concentrated on another group of villages in Transylvania, bringing the total involved in the ECU0.9-million infrastructure project to ten. At the same time, PHARE tries to encourage the right ethos for an 'alternative' rural tourism restricted to a small scale so as not to swamp the community, because success depends on exposure to specific rural values. Standards of service are important but there is always a time when the training stops and the natural way takes over. Genuine local handicrafts are always popular and a varied range of local produce (including local drinks, foodstuffs and mineral waters) is preferable to excessive duplication.

PHARE is also supporting integrated development in the Apuseni Mountains, where inhabitants are being given back rights predating the Second World War which were annulled by the communists. Using identity cards issued by the state silvicultural authority Romsilva, people deriving income from wood processing will receive 10cu.m of wood per person; exemption from tax when wood products are sold; and 50 per cent reduction on the railway when the goods are transported. Newly-weds can buy 25cu.m of timber for construction at half the normal price (Pervain 1996). In addition, PHARE is supporting a Resource Centre for Tourism in Braşov to encourage local initiatives through help on a consultancy basis for marketing and management. There is also a financial assistance component which depends on location of the project in a priority zone mentioned in the Basic Plan for tourism (such as the Prahova Valley) and help from local authorities. This initiative complements the ventures with ANTREC and OVR which lie exclusively in the field of rural tourism. Finally, PHARE is supporting enterprise more generally through a local development fund concerned with small- and medium-scale enterprises developing in partnership with local institutions and organizations. A wider Fund for the Development of European Carpathian Regions supports projects to bolster local democracy and civil society through cross-border cooperation among the states of Hungary, Poland, Romania, Slovakia and Ukraine.

Tourist Regions

Predictably, the possibilities for agrotourism are uneven, even within the mountain region and it is not surprising that clusters in Figure 11.6 endorse the regions with the greatest potential (Istrate and Buhu 1990). Agrotourism is well established in the Curvature Carpathian and the Braşov area in particular (Olteanu et al. 1994). Traditional rural functions in the Bran-Rucar corridor (pastoralism and transhumance, with forests and woodworking) have been diversified by commuting and tourism. Tourist villages such as Bran, Moeciu de Sus, Podul Dâmboviţei and Rucar 'have a natural picturesque setting with farms spread among the karst forms, alternating with shelters and sheepfolds, lacking stress-inducing factors, with a favourable climate and wonderful landscapes' (Velcea 1996, p.63). It is a zone of particular opportunity, lying close to the metropolitan region with good communications and opportunities for winter sports. The local organization 'Branimex' manages accommodation in some 60 households. Many houses have been improved and the company's services extend to transporting visitors from Bucharest and providing local excursions. The area is well known for its enterprise in tourism, aided by the Dracula connection at Bran Castle and proximity of a large urban population to take advantage of special events (such as a Lovers' Weekend organized for St. Valentine's Day). There is now a proposal to create a regional Balkan centre for rural and ecological tourism at Bran. Meanwhile, nearby in the Prahova Valley, potential growth areas for rural tourism have been identified in such areas as Câmpina/Cheia, Slănic/Vălenii de Munte and Valea Doftanei (Curelea 1993).

Another cluster picks out the Apuseni or Western Mountains where there are skills in handicrafts (wood carving, leather processing, milling, wool processing) and a significant gastronomic aspect to rural tourism. EU assistance is helping to build up the industry in the Apuseni, particularly around Poieni, which is a centre for the Drăgan Valley, and the massif of Vlădeasa, with its rich flora and fauna (Ion-Tudor 1995). There are several lakes associated with the hydropower projects, including Fantănele with its tourist complex at Beliş, and Lake Drăgan close to the mountain resort of Stână de Vale. A range of accommodation is now available: farms as well as hotels, with pensions and tourist hostels on the mountains (Cocean 1992). The PHARE programme for mountain agriculture and integrated development was worth ECU950 thousand in 1996. As already noted, it is combined with government measures to boost employment (Pervain 1996). As noted above, a government programme now encourages people to settle in the area if they have specialized education (or higher training) and to work for public institutions or in a religious capacity. In addition to the free allowances of wood for building and repairs, there are reduced taxes as well as concessionary prices for energy and water. A major infrastructural programme is under way and local handicrafts and festivals are being encouraged (Ion-Tudor 1996c). Where the settlement pattern is extremely dispersed it is possible that, with improved access, small hamlets could find a future as holiday villages (Cocean and Surd 1984; Surd 1992).

In the far north there is a great opportunity in the Suceava region which could be promoted as 'Little Switzerland'. International tourism may be linked with modernized hotels in the main centres, complemented by agrotourism in the Dorna-Rarău Mountains (Uscatu 1992). Besides the mineral waters and the diverse flora of such protected areas as the Tarnovul Mare nature reserve, the pastoral traditions of the Dorna Depression are of great touristical interest with fresh dairy products readily available in such villages as Dorna Arini, Dorna Candreni, Poiana Stampei and Şaru Dornei. Mushrooms and forest fruits are also prominent in the local dict where the savoury dishes traditionally prepared over the Christmas and New Year period are outstanding. Other resources for rural tourism are the monasteries of Northwestern Moldavia, which extend across Neamt and Suceava counties, and notable churches such as Durău. Accommodation provided in the Trotuş Valley of Bacău (including Berzunţi, Oituz and Târgu Ocna) is convenient for the Dărmăneşti Depression, the Tarcău Mountains and the waters of Slanic Moldova, while the limestone scenery of the Bicaz Gorges and the artificial lake in the Bistriţa Valley lie close to facilities at Bicaz Chei, Ceahlău and Viişoară. The Vrancea network, including Neguleşti, Tulnici and Vidra and also the small resort of Soveja, ties in with the Tişiţa Gorges and the 'fires' of Andreiaşu (based on a hydrocarbon seepage), with the Vrancea vineyards and First World War mausoleums a little further afield.

Maramureş is outstanding for its rich ethnography, especially apparent in villages such as Bistra, Leordina, Moisei and Petrova. The wooden church of Ieud dates from 1364, and shows the quality of the woodcarving tradition, which is demonstrated today by the 'small timber mansions' which are characteristic of new house building by shepherds and woodcutters in the Iza Valley (Iacob 1995). These 'heritage' resources, enhanced by the ceramics of Săcel, and the tradition of wood exploitation by narrow-gauge railways (in the Vaser Valley) and rafting on the Viseu, a tributary of the Tisa, are highlighted in the informal rural plan for the area by Iacob, who advocates (1994) small hydropower schemes and a growth of rural tourism. The scenically attractive Rodna Mountains offer potential for winter sports and, apart from remoteness, which could be overcome by better regional airports, roads and telecommunications, the only drawback is the pollution associated with non-ferrous metallurgical industry.

Meanwhile, in Northern Oltenia there are links with the spas as well as much rich folk art: folklore events in Bărbăteşti and Vaideeni, with much traditional architecture; ceramics and wood carvings at Horezu (including 'Cock of Horezu' ceramics) and carpet weaving at Tismana, a village famous for its monastery. In the Olt defile stands the Cozia monastery, complementing the mountain and proposed national park of that name, and the Bujoreni ethnographical museum. The spas of the Râmnicu Vâlcea area are outstanding, while the historic Loviştea Depression has a base for winter sports in Voineasa with excellent opportunities for hill walking and nature study in the Lotru Mountains and the glaciated Parâng Mountains (Oprea 1969; Ploaie 1995). National park status is envisaged for parts of this region but although a total of 12 new parks were created in 1990, legislation providing resources for their management is not yet realized. Immediately adjacent to this area in the upper Olt region is the attractive south Transylvanian district of Sibiu, with the possibility of snow in some areas for up to six months of the year. The outstanding Făgăraş Mountains can be explored from a base in a range of villages as well as from the small resort and climatic station of Păltiniş (1,450 metres). Pastoral traditions blend with traditional Romanian architecture in Mărginimea Sibiului (a cluster of villages at the foot of the Cibin Mountains) and fortified churches are to be found in villages such as Biertan, in the hill country north of Sibiu.

Conclusion

Since the revolution, Romania has started to rebuild its tourist industry. In keeping with the principle of sustainability, there will be a stronger rural component to take advantage of the opportunities and also to meet an important social need for pluriactivity on the small family holdings which have arisen through land restitution. Romania's 'Strategy for Development of the Mountain Zone' seeks agricultural modernization combined with support for a range of ancillary activity including agrotourism. However, there are important preconditions that must be satisfied, not only to ensure the necessary transport, communications and information but also to stimulate enterprise in the villages at both the community and individual household level. In turn, all this depends on substantial support from government and international agencies. While Romania is setting up a National Fund for Mountain Support as a pillar for durable development, it is also significant that the country is looking ahead to the enlargement of the EU because links with Western Europe have generated considerable funding under the PHARE programme as well as a framework of principles to underpin the sustainable development of mountain regions in general. A draft Mountain Law ensures compensation for natural handicaps in order to stabilize the population (especially young families), improve infrastructure and make better use of agricultural, touristic and other resources within ecological limits. Even so, progress will be gradual, dependent on the success of pilot projects in the more promising regions.

REFERENCES

Antal, A. and L. Kovacs (1996), 'Comparative study of mentality characteristics in a village from Szeklers' land and from the zone of Calata', in A. Barbic et al., *Rural Potentials for a Global Tomorrow*, Bucharest: International Rural Sociology Association with Bucharest University and the Romanian Academy, p.69.

Apolzan, L. (1987), *Carpaţii: tezaur de istorie*, Bucharest: Editura Ştiinţifică şi Enciclopedică.

Barboi, D.C. (1996), 'Concept of sustainable agriculture penetrating Romania', *Romanian Business Journal*, **3** (50), 7.

Bedrna, Z. (1993), 'Vplyv privatizácie na agroekologické systémy v krajine', *Životné prostredie*, **27** (6), 285–6.

Bordanc, F. (1995), 'Spatial variations in the process of agricultural land privatization', in D. Turnock (ed.), *Rural Change in Romania*, Leicester: Leicester University Geography Department Occasional Paper 33, pp.39–47.

—— (1996), 'Spatial variations in the progress of land reform in Romania', *GeoJournal*, **38**, pp.161–5.

Bramwell, B. and B. Lane (eds) (1994), *Rural Tourism and Sustainable Rural Development*, Clevedon: Channel View Publications.

Bran, F. (1995), 'Ecoturismul în România', *Tribuna Economică*, **6** (22), 16.

Bucur, C. et al. (eds) (1986), *Museum of Folk Technology Guidebook*, Sibiu: Museums' Complex of Sibiu.

Cater, E. and G. Lowman (1994), *Ecotourism: A Sustainable Option*, London: Wiley.

Cianga, N. (1994), 'The setting up of the balneotouristic system in the Romanian Carpathians', *Studia Universitatis Babeş-Bolyai: Geographia*, **39**, 101–9.

Cocean, P. (1992), 'Modele de amenajare turistică a unor regiuni muntoase din România', *Studia Universitatis Babeş-Bolyai: Geographia*, **37**, 121–5.

—— and V. Surd (1984), 'Probleme ale asezărilor din carstul Muntilor Apuseni', *Buletinul SSG din RSR*, **7**, 111–15.

Cochrane, N.J. (1991), 'Prospects for Eastern Europe's private agriculture in the nineties', in J.R. Lampe (ed.), *Private Agriculture in Eastern Europe*, Washington, DC: Woodrow Wilson International Center, East European Studies Program, pp.81–102.

Curcić, S. and S. Kicosev (1996), 'Tourist potential of the alluvial plain of Yugoslavia', in C. Vert et al. (eds), *Proceedings of the Second Regional Geography Conference: Geographical Researches in the Carpathian-Danube Space*, Timişoara: Universitatea de Vest din Timişoara, Departamentul de Geografie, Vol.1, pp.468-78.

Curelea, C. (1993), 'Agroturism montan: magnetul peisajului prahovean', *Viaţa Munţilor*, **3** (9), 6.

Dent, J.B. and M.J. McGregor (1994), *Rural and Farming System Analysis: European Perspectives*, Wallingford: CAB International.

Derounian, J. (1995), 'Rural regeneration in Romania', *Report for the Natural and Built Environment Professions*, No. 5, 4-6.

Djurdjev, B.S. (1996), 'Rural population decline along the Danube bank in the Bačka region', in C. Vert et al. (eds), *Proceedings of the Second Regional Geography Conference: Geographical Researches in the Carpathian-Danube Space*, Timişoara, Universitatea de Vest din Timişoara, Departamentul de Geografie, Vol.1, pp.319-27.

Drgona, V. (1996), 'Ecological problems arising from intensive agriculture in Western Slovakia', *GeoJournal*, **38**, 213-18.

Erdeli, G. and I. Istrate (1996), *Amenajari turistice*, Bucharest: Editura Universităţii din Bucureşti.

Fulea, M. (1996), 'Structura socio-economică a populaţiei rurale în perioadă de tranziţie la economia de piaţa', in M. Fulea (ed.), *Satul românesc contemporan*, Bucharest: Editura Academiei Române, pp.159-70.

Ghinoiu, I. (1996), 'Dinamica peisajelor şi zonelor etnografice din România', in M. Fulea (ed.), *Satul românesc contemporan*, Bucharest: Editura Academiei Române, pp. 226-31.

Giurcăneanu, C. (1988), *Populaţia şi aşezările din Carpaţi româneşti*, Bucharest: Editura Ştiinţifică şi Enciclopedică.

Giurescu, C.C. (1974), *Contributions to the History of Romanian Science and Technique from the Fifteenth to the Nineteenth Century*, Bucharest: Editura Academiei RSR.

Glavan, V. (1995), 'Rural ecological and cultural tourism', *Romanian Business Journal*, **2** (44), 16; **2** (45), 16; **2** (46), 16.

Główny Urząd Statystyczny (1993), *Rocznik Statystycny 1993*, Warsaw: GUS.

Grykień, S. (1995), 'Ekologiczne gospodarstwa rolne w Polsce', *Czasopismo Geograficzne*, **66** (2), 175-89.

Henry, D.C. (1994), 'Reviving Romania's rural economy', *Radio Free Europe/Radio Liberty Research*, **3** (7), 18-23.

Hirschhausen-Leclerc, B. von (1994), 'L'invention de nouvelles campagnes en Roumanie', *L'Espace géographique*, **23**, 318-28.

Iacob, G. (1994), 'Repere geografice privind revitalizarea economiei maramureşului', *Studii şi cercetări: geografie*, **41**, 85-9.

—— (1995), 'Ţara Maramureşului: straveche vatră românească de locuire cultură şi civilizaţie', *Lucrările Seminarului Dimitrie Cantemir, Iaşi*, **11-12**, 185-97.

Ianos, I. et al. (1992), 'Changements récents dans l'agriculture roumaine', *Revue Roumaine: Géographie*, **36**, 23-30.

Ion-Tudor, C. (1995), 'Romania: Transylvania Poieni', *Romanian Business Journal*, **2** (50), 16.
—— (1996a), 'Rural tourism: alternative of a lasting development', *Romanian Business Journal*, **3** (22), 16.
—— (1996b), 'Durable development in Romania's Carpathians', *Romanian Business Journal*, **3** (29), 16.
—— (1996c), 'Growth of development rate of traditional zones', *Romanian Business Journal*, **3** (31), 8.
Istrate. I. and F. Bran (1995), 'Perspectiva dezvoltării durabile a turismului românesc', *Tribuna Economică*, **6** (20), 28; **6** (21), 30.
—— (1995b), 'Agroturismul în România', *Tribuna Economică*, **6** (32), 26; **6** (33), 26; **6** (34), 26.
Istrate, I. and I. Buhu (1990), 'Dezvoltarea turismului în profil teritorial', *Tribuna Economică*, **1** (22), 13–15.
Kurek, W. (1996), 'Agriculture versus tourism in rural areas of the Polish Carpathians', *GeoJournal*, **38**, 191–6.
Lamarche, H. (ed.) (1991), *L'agriculture familiale: une réalité polymorphe: comparison internationale*, Paris: L'Harmattan.
Luczka-Bakula, W. (1995), *Uwarunkowania produkcji i konsumpcji żywności ekologicznej*, Poznań: Akademia Ekonomiczna.
Marsden, T. (1990), 'Towards a political economy of pluriactivity', *Journal of Rural Studies*, **6**, 375–82.
Maurel, M.-C. (1994), *La transition post-collectiviste: mutations agraires en Europe Centrale*, Paris: L'Harmattan Collection 'Pays de l'Est'.
Misha, G. (1996), 'Albania: on the beach', *Business Eastern Europe*, **25** (14), 6.
Misiak, W. (1993), 'The rural areas of Romania after the sistematization experiment', *East European Countryside*, **1**, 57–64.
Mitrache, S. et al. (1996), *Agrotourism şi turism rural*, Bucharest: Federaţia Română pentru Dezvoltare Montană.
Mueller, R. and J. Mueller (1996), 'Policy concerns in Bulgarian food distribution', *GeoJournal*, **38**, 167–74.
Muică, C. and A. Popova-Cucu (1993), 'The composition and conservation of Romania's plant cover', *GeoJournal*, **29**, 9–18.
—— and I. Zăvoianu (1996), 'The ecological consequences of privatization in Romanian agriculture', *GeoJournal*, **38**, 207–12.
Muica, N. and D. Turnock (1994), *Living on Landslides: The Subcarpathian Districts of Buzău and Vrancea*, Leicester University Geography Department Occasional Paper 29.
—— (1996), 'The potential for traditional food and drink products in Eastern Europe: fruit processing – especially brandy (*ḫuică*) distilling – in Romania', *GeoJournal*, **38**, 197–206.
Nemenyi, A. and J.N. Nemenyi (1995), 'Some characteristics of privatization in rural areas', Prague: Paper delivered at the 16th Congress of the European Society for Rural Sociology.
OECD (1995), *The Albanian Agro-food System in Economic Transition*, Paris: OECD.

Olaru. I. (1994), 'Ecoturism și dezvoltare durabilă', *Carpații României*, **1** (2), 3.

—— et al. (1994), 'Turismul rural: date argumente soluții', *Carpații României*, **1** (1), 3–6.

Olteanu, I. et al. (1994), 'Moeciu-Bran: cultura-economie-ecologie în Carpații României', *Carpații României*, **1** (1), 17–19.

Oprea, A. (1969), 'Ansamblul turistic Lotru', in V. Tufescu et al. (eds), *Lucrarile colocviului național al geografie turismului*, Bucharest: Institut de Geologie–Geografie, pp.164–7.

Otiman, P.I. (1994), *Agricultură României la cumpăna dintre mileniile II și III*, Timișoara: Editura Helicon.

Pais, A. (1997), 'Tourism: an industry that might be very profitable for Romanians', *Romanian Business Journal*, **4** (6), 16.

Parpală, O. (1992), 'Crearea de ferme agricole private viabile', *Tribuna Economică*, **3** (3–4), 25.

Pascaru, A. (1996), 'Rural youth at present and in the future', in A. Barbic et al., *Rural Potentials for a Global Tomorrow*, Bucharest: International Rural Sociology Association with Bucharest University and the Romanian Academy, p.49.

Pervain, A. (1996), 'Aspects of unemployment in rural space', in A. Barbic et al., *Rural Potentials for a Global Tomorrow*, Bucharest: International Rural Sociology Association with Bucharest University and the Romanian Academy, p.66.

Ploaie, G. (1995), 'Tourism and conservation in the mountains of Valcea County', in D. Turnock (ed.), *Rural Change in Romania*, Leicester: Leicester University Geography Department Occasional Paper 33, pp.54–60.

—— (1996), 'The impact of tourism and conservation on agriculture in the mountains of Vâlcea County', *GeoJournal*, **38**, 219–27.

Plop, L. (1996), 'Phare programme support for rural tourism', *Romanian Business Journal*, **3** (22), 16.

Popescu, C. and D. Bălteanu (1996), 'Transition and sustainable development: some geographical paradigms in Romania', *Eureg: European Journal of Regional Development*, **3**, 61–4.

Rautu, C. (1996), 'Middle class important for agriculture', *Romanian Business Journal*, **3** (18), 13.

Rey, R. (1979), *Viitor în Carpați: progres economic civilizație socialism*, Craiova: Scrisul Românesc.

—— (1985), *Civilizație montană*, Bucharest: Editura Științifică și Enciclopedică.

—— (1994), 'Bine va fi pentru Munții Carpați bine va fi și pentru România', *Carpații României*, **1** (3), 4–5.

Rusenescu, C. (1980), 'Dezvoltarea zonei turistice Lotru și protecția mediului inconjurator', in L. Badea and S. Dragomirescu (eds), *Lucrarile celui de-al IV lea colocviu de geografia turismului*, Bucharest: Institut de Geografie.

Rusu-Grigore, M. (1993a), 'Perspectivele agroturismului montan', *Viața Munților*, **3** (5), 7.

—— (1993b), 'Agroturism montan: locuință pentru primirea oaspeților', *Viața*

Muțiilor, **3** (7), 6.
Silvas, E. (1995), 'Gospodaria țărănească: obstacol sau șansă de relansare a agriculturii?', *Tribuna Economică*, **7** (25), 17-18; **7** (26), 15.
Soltysiak, U. (1993), *Rolnictwo ekologiczne od teorii do praktyki*, Warsaw: EKOLAND Leben and Umwelt.
Stanculescu, F. et al. (1973), *Tezaur de arhitectura populară din Gorj*, Bucharest: Editura Scrisul Românesc.
Štefánek, M. (1993), 'Organické polnohospodárstvo má budúcnost', *Hospodarske noviny zo dna*, 14 July.
Stefanescu, I. (1972), 'Fruit growing in Romania', *Revue Roumaine de Géographie*, **16**, 125-32.
Surd, V. (1992), 'Sistemele de așezări din Munții Apuseni', *Studia Universitatis Babeș-Bolyai: Geographia*, **37**, 91-100.
—— (1994), 'Critical status of rural Romania', in F. Greif (ed.), *Die Zukunft der ländlichen Infrastruktur in Ostmitteleuropa*, Vienna: Schriftenreihe der Bundesanstalt fur Agrarwirtschaft 75, pp.61-7.
Tanić, S. (ed.) (n.d.), *Agriculture in Croatia: A Strategy for Development*, Zagreb: Ministry of Agriculture and Forestry.
Tosics, B. (1996), 'The Djerdep settlements in Yugoslavia', in C. Vert et al. (eds), *Proceedings of the Second Regional Geography Conference: Geographical Researches in the Carpathian-Danube Space*, Timișoara: Universitatea de Vest din Timișoara, Departamentul de Geografie, Vol.1, pp.335-40.
Turnock, D. (1991), 'The planning of rural settlement in Romania', *Geographical Journal*, **157**, 251-64.
—— (1993), *Agricultural change in the Romanian Carpathians*, Leicester: University of Leicester Faculty of Social Sciences Discussion Papers in Geography 93/2.
—— (1995), 'Rural transition in Eastern Europe', *GeoJournal*, **36**, 420–26.
Uscatu, T. (1992), 'Strategia dezvoltarii turismului in profil teritorial: zona montană a Bocovinei', *Terra*, **24** (3-4), 101-5.
Velcea, I. (1996), 'The rural model in the Romanian Carpathians', in G. Erdeli and W.J. Chambers (eds), *The First Romanian–British Geographic Seminar*, Bucharest: Editura Universitatii din București, pp.59-64.
Velcea, V. et al. (1993), 'Geographic elements regarding the environmental recovery in the Bucegi Mountains', in C. Muică and D. Turnock (eds), *Geography and Conservation*, Bucharest: Geographical International Seminars, pp.119-21.
Vulcănescu, R. and P. Simionescu (1974), *Drumuri și popașuri străvechi*, Bucharest: Editura Albatros.
Walker, S. et al. (1995), *Integrated Development Strategy in Valcea County Romania: Report to the UK Environmental Know-How Fund*, Oxford: Brookes University, School of Planning.
Zane, G. (1970), *Industrie din România in a două jumătate a secolului al XIX-lea*, Bucharest: Editura Academiei RSR.

12. Conclusion

David Turnock

The East European agrarian situation has become highly complex, with substantial variations in the thrust of agrarian legislation, investment and community response among the 13 countries of the region, including Germany (Braverman et al. 1993; Swinnen 1994). Economic efficiency goals pointed to retention of cooperatives with only limited opting-out, coupled with indirect restitution as far as possible. On the other hand, advocates of 'natural justice' called for full and direct restitution and the demise of the cooperatives, although in practice a compromise has provided for partial restitution (combining the direct and indirect options) which allows the cooperatives to continue on a reduced scale where the membership so desires. Much greater structural change has occurred in agriculture than in any other sector, thanks to the widespread adoption of policies of land 'restitution' to former owners and 'distribution' to the farm workers and the rural population in general (Brooks and Lerman 1994). Both measures were politically necessary, although to differing degrees across the region. Conceptually the restoration of ownership rights enhances the social status of many rural dwellers through a process of 'reagrarization' and *embourgeoisement* (Szelenyi 1988; Szelenyi and Manchin 1986) and it thereby rejects the Stalinist revolutionary ethos (reacting to the aberrations of capitalism) as the conventional road for Eastern Europe. Instead of 'collectivization' to neutralize the rich peasants (*kulaks*) and simplify the command structure, the evolutionary process towards a democracy based on property ownership is being resumed after a traumatic interruption (Gabor 1991; Gorlach 1993).

STRUCTURAL CHANGE

Structural change has been very disruptive (Csaki 1990). In parts of Romania peasants unilaterally took over their land, and cooperatives therefore collapsed. Despite some attempt at restraint by the police, the government recognized the revolutionary nature of the action and framed their restitution programme in order to bring almost all the land seizures within the law – a shrewd political move because it ensured overwhelming support for the government in the rural areas over an opposition which championed restitution in the first place, but on a scale that might have provided for larger estate holdings in conflict with peasant ethos. Where the peasants have waited for the state to act, redistribution has often been slow, with long delays in the issue of definitive titles. Uncertainty has resulted in some land not being worked at all during the year of policy implementation. Moreover, coordination which previously operated over quite large areas has collapsed and in Romania irrigation schemes which formerly depended on joint management by cooperative and state farms have broken down. In Bulgaria, although liquidation committees have tried to retain equipment in the local area, there have been disputes over its ownership due to transfers of tractors and lorries from socialist farms to specialist agencies. There have also been complications over disputed boundaries in Bulgaria through changes in local authority boundaries, and amalgamation of farms into agroindustrial complexes and subsequent disbandment without proper documentation: some claimants do not know in which commune they should file claims. Land commissions have an incentive to delay because they will be disbanded when the job is finished (Monk 1996).

The net result is that land has been transferred to people who are often too old to farm it, or to heirs in the towns who cannot use the land efficiently. One expert has said that 'there is something perverse' in arrangements that devolve ownership 'to those that are not in a position to farm and for whom the realities of agricultural production are alien' (Swain 1992, p.17). But there is a strong moral argument in favour of restitution, and there is no reason why land allocated to town dwellers should not be worked on a sharecropping basis by people permanently resident in the countryside. Ethical fine-tuning was needed to balance the injustice of expropriation under communism with the unfairness of leaving people employed by the cooperatives (including many Gypsies in Romania and Turks in Bulgaria) without a significant stake in the land on account of compensation to people living in the towns with little aptitude for farming. Some governments were clearly ideologically committed to private farming, but sometimes for good reasons – as in Bulgaria, where the Union of Democratic Forces government of 1991 opposed pooled claims for land in cereal-growing areas because of suspicion that cooperatives behind such tactics were 'old guard' strongholds.

State Farms

For the state farms, one viable solution is to transfer the land to large private farming companies: for example, *Agrargesellschaften* in the FGDR, where some are now doing well where they have good soils suitable for high-quality production (such as cereals for brewing) and management has been skilled enough to carry out reorganization. Many of Albania's state farms have been reorganized into joint-stock companies with joint participation of workers, managers and the state. In the latter case, the lowland district of Kavajë became a model. The fruit-growing farms of Kavajë and Rrogozhinë, with a total land area of 864ha, established joint ventures with an Italian–Romanian group. The same group subsequently took a similar initiative with a Durrës agricultural enterprise, with the intention of improving agricultural processing (with 300ha of heated glasshouses) and stimulating tourism. State farms are also being retained in Romania, even where former owners were expropriated by decree. In such cases the interested parties will receive only shares in a farming company and not a land allocation. Moreover, Romanians have found that one way to solve the problem of insufficient land to satisfy restitution claims is to transfer the claim to state farms where it is not necessary for local land commissions to allocate a holding but merely to provide a share of the production, making the financial share-out increasingly fragmented. Between 1991 and 1994, Romanian state farms 'became veritable rubber sacks, their capacities stretched in some cases well beyond those implied by the farms' actual surfaces' (Verdery 1994, p.1081). Retention of large farms has encouraged some foreign capital, as in Hungary which has some particularly fertile land and a tradition of progressive farming with a relatively favourable structure. However, while 90-year leases are available on large holdings of some 20th.ha (with irrigation facilities and the potential for high-quality dairy and vegetable production), there is also the possibility of obtaining land in smaller blocks (ideally in the range of 800–1,500ha) which will provide viable holdings for individual private farmers with scope for further job creation.

The problem with retaining large farms is financial. In Croatia, state farms have been converted into joint-stock companies, but their mode of operation has not changed significantly: their objective is to keep the enterprise together, and this pleases the workers who hold up to half the stock and wish to protect their employment. There is also a political problem where there is strong feeling that the land should be available to enlarge small private farms or to meet outstanding restitution claims. In Poland, there is a policy of piecemeal transfer of state farms to the private sector. Solidarity governments showed a strong interest in privatization and hence the decision that a State Agricultural Property Agency, operating from 15 regional offices, should administer the State Land Fund, comprising the state farms and also the private holdings of elderly farmers in return for old-age pensions. Ideally, leasing or selling units of about 600ha would make a useful contribution to the structure of Polish farming. In Romania the new Centre-Right government is to privatize the state-owned companies which have taken over the former state farms. In the Czech Republic, state farms have been privatized through the 'coupon method', which results in highly dispersed ownership in the first instance, but the great majority have been sold to individual persons or groups of up to eight people, often technicians drawn from the middle and upper echelons of the communist management who have good knowledge of the land and sufficient skills to draw up sound privatization plans. In Slovakia, it has now been decided that state farms will be decentralized through the formation of trading companies and then privatized quickly by the sale of shares to selected owners. In Slovenia, the state agricultural enterprises and cooperatives became crucial for supplying the population with food. Production from large, continuous surfaces makes for an explicit market orientation. Privatization is now envisaged, but excessive fragmentation would be dangerous because the private farmers are not yet in a position to supply the market adequately.

The New Farm Structure

'It is naive to expect people who have worked for up to 30 years as operatives in a large production organization to suddenly become entrepreneurs' (Swain 1992, p.9). This point is all the more evident in view of limited finance which has been allocated to structural change. Thus, there is considerable interest in retaining the cooperative system with new 'friendly' structures to replace the highly centralized cooperatives which emerged under communism and with some reduction in labour. In FGDR there is a strong desire to retain the principle of cooperation despite the Bavarian attitude of government that favoured family farms. 'Thus the survival and dominance of large scale cooperatives and farm companies can be said to be despite rather than because of federal government policy' (Wilson 1996, p.160). Alternatively, land could be taken over by partnerships, farming companies or family farms and there is no doubt that interest in private farming is increasing (Young 1993).

Private farming survived under communism on the high ground in Moravia, and also in Czech Silesia where the holdings were small and the owners could not be intimidated as *kulaks*. On the fertile plains, private farms were marginalized under communism, but some have made a comeback since 1989. Meanwhile, the cooperative strategy remains attractive on poorer land where agriculture was formerly protected by subsidies and where the prospects are particularly uncertain at the present time (Hudečková and Lošták 1992, 1993). Yet the revamped cooperatives no longer have the guarantee of state support and there is always the possibility of bankruptcy if the business is not efficiently run. Embarrassed by debts, cooperatives may have to shed labour and they may eventually collapse altogether. Where they succeed, there is uncertainty over non-agricultural enterprises that may have to close or be transferred to private management. Nevertheless, Swain (1993b, p.12) argues that cooperatives should still be actively promoted: 'they have the potential to initiate a cycle of economic growth which might develop more quickly than waiting for the rich farmer to buy out the poor farmer; and the dispossessed poor farmer to migrate to the town and swell the urban homeless unemployed'. In 1995, more than 400 of Hungary's 1,300 cooperatives were still functioning, many of them still managed by people who had been in charge through much of the communist period (not just highly qualified people who had moved in during the 1980s).

On the other hand, Elek (1991) asserts that part-time farming in Hungary is more specialized, modernized and market orientated than in other parts of Eastern Europe. This is because the last two decades of agricultural policy have given the peasants more market experience and trading skills which will be advantageous in the rebuilding of family farming (Harcsa 1993; Kovach 1991). In Romania, small farms may not be a good basis for future efficiency, so perhaps there could be kinship or neighbourhood arrangements to cope with groups of small, scattered holdings where it is necessary to make long journeys on foot, carrying simple tools to carry out routine tasks. In the mountains, peasants also have also to cope with the depredations of wild animals which they are forbidden to hunt. In Bulgaria, only 6 per cent of landholders are thinking of setting up in farming on their own account, because holdings are small and there is an element of inertia deriving from the availability of a cooperative system which 'deprives owners from more long term thinking' about future land markets (Davidova 1994, p.48). Younger farmers are more forward looking, but there is still a widespread fear of the future and a reluctance to make decisions (Dobreva 1994). New cooperatives are taking shape, as at Souhindol in central Bulgaria where a cooperative was first created in 1909; the new owners have revamped an organization that now includes a bakery, a meat-processing plant and vineyards. Similar considerations apply in FGDR where many owners prefer to remain within a farm cooperative or limited company as they lack necessary experience to farm alone, and prefer the security and social benefits of working in a large farm business (Bergmann 1992). Family farming is mainly becoming reestablished in areas with a tradition of family farming such as Sachsen-Anhalt (full-time farms) and Thüringen (part-time farming), although this is dependent on the presence of non-farm employment. Within the Hungarian cooperatives, agricultural work became so specialized that the average worker is only a specialist in his or her own particular part of the production process, and this is to say nothing of the problems of marketing, taxation and bookkeeping. There is also an overriding uncertainty that is compounded by the lack of a real processing industry.

Rationalizing landholding structures is a complex task when there is so much variation. There are clearly ideological positions to consider and some political parties have stated clear preferences. Some shades of opinion would emphasize the motivation of private property to generate the hard work needed to secure efficient farm production in the context of liberalized prices and free trade where farmers must also make rational decisions if they are to survive (Monk 1996). Such opinion would reject the paternalism of socialism and seek to build society on the basis of SMEs in all sectors of the economy (Giordano, 1993). On the other hand, socialists would tend towards ambivalence over the work ethic and would emphasize cooperation and security in keeping with the 'entitlement mentality'. However, farmers are generally practical and it is their preferences that are crucial. First of all, at the level of ownership, land is property, a means of production (income and wealth) and a means of subsistence and survival. The overriding values, which will affect attitudes to selling, leasing and entry into cooperatives, will vary between different places and they will also change through time with widening economic knowledge, higher education standards and an increased role for women (Dobreva 1996). Hence, it is necessary to look at interest groups within the farming community. Under the conditions existing in Hungary today, it is possible to recognize different groups of landowners according to their agricultural interests and aspirations (Meszaros 1994).

The first group, consisting of the beneficiaries of restitution and including many pensioners and urban dwellers, will offer their land for rent and thereby gain a source of income. The second group, which is made up of former cooperative members and employees, will exercise their ownership rights through a continuation of the cooperative system. On a part of their property they may wish to continue private plot farming, while leaving the rest with the cooperative in order to secure a job and the services needed to support private agricultural activity. Many will wish to maintain small-scale production as a supplementary source of work, existing in symbiosis with the large enterprise with which they associate simply as labourers. The third group are those cooperative members and employees who simply wish to maintain secure employment for themselves through land ownership, so they place the whole of their land into a cooperative which, they hope, will guarantee them a job. The fourth group of newly independent agronomists or traders create a private farm-based economy, although this 'middle peasant' system of private farming is only possible if larger areas of land can be acquired through either renting or purchase to justify long-term investment and a viable production plan. At the same time, there are different shareholder interests within the cooperatives (Kovacs 1993; Sebestyen 1993). It is important to recognize the interests of these different shareholder categories, although all of them are looking to worthwhile dividends on their business shares. First, there are the cooperative members whose ownership is based on their work within the cooperative. They have a primary interest in maintaining this activity and maximizing income from this source. Meanwhile, the retired cooperative members are interested in the welfare functions of the cooperative, although these obligations complicate the management of the cooperatives because, with reduced government support, they can only administer their social programmes with great difficulty. Finally, the external business shareholders are interested only in dividends and they will tend to oppose higher wages for the workers and support for other members.

In an attempt to generalize, it may be suggested that there is a distinction between very small 'subsistence' or 'hobby' farms and larger units that aim at economic viability and production for the market. Csaki and Lerman (1993) therefore distinguish between small subsistence farms and large diversified agribusinesses. The first situation involves small pieces of land (although the areas are cumulatively large) and has been regarded as being peripheral enough to be described as 'deagrarization' (Pavlin 1991). Many small landowners can enjoy spare-time farming by working a section of their land themselves and handing over the rest to a reformed cooperative that can use labour efficiently and leave most of the owners free to work full time in non-agricultural activities. For such people there is neither an instinct nor an economic stimulus to take up private farming on a larger scale. In Poland and parts of the Balkans (especially Poland and FFRY where collectivization was never forced through to completion) peasant farms are very small and it has become traditional to work these farms intensively while taking up non-agricultural employment as available. However, the scale and reliability of such employment has not been sufficient to break the link with the land and erode the value of a subsistence holding as a 'way of life'. Despite some reduction from the figure of 653,374 in 1960, there were still 534,266 family farms in Croatia in 1991, consisting on average of 2.7ha divided into 5.4 parcels of 0.5ha each (ranging from 0.40 to 1.24ha) (Zimbrek and Zutinic 1996). Consolidation has been discouraged by the lack of a formal land market, partly because transactions were forbidden and partly because of high capital transfer taxes (recently reduced). There has also been a strong desire to hold on to land as a security and to avoid any impression of 'failure' that the disposal of land might imply within the community: 'selling the land, the patrimony, in some parts of our country the rural community considers as a sign of personal business failure' (Tanic n.d., p.12). In addition, the land is an economic security for elderly farmers, and the number of farms in Croatia has not declined in line with depopulation (Stambuk 1991).

Selective rediscovery of entrepreneurship in Hungary (Juhasz 1991) also leaves open the question whether land should continue to be worked in large units by reformed cooperatives as opposed to small family farms. Where there are good non-agricultural opportunities and where there are perceived benefits through shared use of machinery, cooperation is more likely. Market uncertainties may also stimulate loose forms of cooperation. Cooperative associations in Albania helped to develop market awareness, an increase in productivity and a greater use of machinery, and assisted a move away from the subsistence agriculture and use of female and child labour which was characterizing the new family farms (Civici 1996). Cooperative farms in East Germany have also been credited with significant innovations (Niehues-Jeuffroy 1994). Support for cooperatives is reinforced by negative perceptions of farming independently. In FGDR, as in other countries, many of the reestablished properties are too small to form viable farmholdings without renting additional land, and the owners lack capital to undertake necessary investment. Furthermore, attitudes to family farming are ambivalent after 40 years of collective farming. Discussion in the Albanian context has revealed other constraints, including uncertainty over input supplies, the intensity of the competition and the financial risk; also concern over the primitive marketing system, poor access to information and technical assistance, high rates of interest for credit and unpredictable rates of inflation, and an inadequate legal system to permit the buying and selling of land (Leiby and Marra 1993). On the other hand, where there are fewer opportunities for non-agricultural employment and labour-intensive agriculture is the main option, then individual operation may be preferred, especially when experiences with communist cooperatives were 'off-putting' and peasants appreciate the freedom to make their own decisions (Nemenyi 1996a, 1996b; Abraham 1996).

It is reasonable to argue that initial decisions by farmers have been heavily influenced by sentiments relating to the 'comfort' (meant in the broadest sense) enjoyed under communism, measured against the perceived uncertainties of the transition. As time goes on, decisions may be reconsidered. Small farms may be consolidated while some cooperative members may decide to go independent. Either way, Eastern Europe may see a growth of private farming. Indeed, even where cooperatives remain, there is much leasing of land and buildings to businesses which are now run separately (often by companies or by private farmers previously prominent in the cooperative organization who have decided to opt out).

Farming companies rent 97.1 per cent of their land, while other private farms larger than 100ha rent 85 per cent (with a proportion of two-thirds for all non-company private farms). Altogether, farming companies now occupy 17.1 per cent of the farmland in the Czech Republic, and other private farms 18.2 per cent. It is also possible to lease land from state farms which have seen their share of land worked fall from 25.3 to 15.3 per cent. Thus, while some ideologists may deplore the demise of cooperatives, there is a clear trend towards private farming. Yet there are no overwhelming economic advantages in favour of really large holdings (Kovach 1994a), and there is an effective choice between farming companies running estates and viable family farms which can employ people full-time and justify ownership of machinery. 'It seems reasonable to expect the emergence of private farms of 50-100ha in Romania, Bulgaria and Poland' (Cochrane 1994, p.335).

Private farming companies may work as much as 900ha (with owning and leasing) while others may fall into the 50-100ha range, with the smallest less than 5ha. Farms larger than 100ha (some comprising small estates recovered through restitution in FCS) are particularly rational for the use machines, but 30-70ha farms can also be viable, specializing in grain and sunflowers. However, mixed 'nostalgia farming' on 15-30ha restitution holdings is satisfactory in the long term although it may be most suitable for middle-aged people with income from other jobs and access to basic machines. Holdings of 10ha can be rewarding where machinery can be acquired cheaply (second-hand from Germany with loans obtained through local contacts) and where crops such as hops can be grown. Machinery and fertilizers are critical areas in view of the high cost of credit but some private farmers have been able to lease land and machinery from the state farms. Strategies seem to vary with age but all peasant households are trying to make rational decisions. However, at present the majority of private farms are even smaller than 10ha. Of the 52,003 private farms in the Czech Republic in 1993, 53.6 per cent were smaller than one hectare and 28.5 per cent were between one and 10ha, while 9.8 per cent were between 10 and 30ha; with 8.1 per cent larger than 30ha. Old people and the unemployed are often active on 1-5ha holdings. They produce their own food, although the small plots are not suitable for livestock. At the same time, increasing areas are being taken over by people who want to use rural land for non-agricultural purposes as part of a suburbanizing trend: including gardening and hobby farming by the owners of weekend cottages and by younger people from the towns who seek an escape from unemployment in small-scale farming. Pavlin (1991) describes this activity as 'post-deagrarization' (rather than 'reagrarization') because it lies outside conventional farming. However, hobby farming should not be despised: not only can there be a useful combination of agriculture and other activities, but farming may recruit talented young people from the towns who may be able to take over holdings owned by their father or even by their grandfather.

Most people who leave the cooperatives try to take up entrepreneurial activities in the service sector, dealing in agricultural machinery or commerce. It is common for partnerships to emerge because this way it is easier to raise the finance to secure former cooperative properties, such as mills, workshops and commercial premises in general. Some of those inclined towards entrepreneurship may well have been independent farmers in the past, but it will be impossible to build a new private agricultural system on the basis of this elderly group. Others are economically active and wish to farm their restituted land as a hedge against unemployment and impoverishment, or they may already be unemployed and seek to maintain a small amount of land that can provide their food and generate a little income. But because of capital shortage and limited knowledge and business experience, the future of these small farms is highly problematic. Much will depend on agricultural policy and the ability of these groups to represent their interests through the political process. Of course, where the cooperative has become bankrupt or has been dissolved, there is little alternative for the members but to take up private farming. But the future is highly uncertain because they are forced into small-scale production on just two or three hectares of land with the benefit of whatever equipment they have been able to salvage from the former cooperative. When groups of people break away from the cooperatives with entrepreneurial intentions, they may well combine with non-cooperative members and use external land and business contacts to establish some kind of private company, but if more businesspeople are going to enter farming there will have to be a better credit system and incentives to provide good prospects for profitability. At present it seems that of the million people currently employed in agriculture and food processing, only about 10,000 can be expected to become entrepreneurs. The number directly employed will almost certainly fall, while the number of those with supplementary income from agriculture will increase. There is insufficient 'attachment to the land' to achieve a renaissance in the absence of all the economic preconditions already referred to. Yet the social aspects are important, because many rural dwellers are existing on very low incomes since the social functions of the cooperatives have been eroded. It is important that local or national government, or both, should accept responsibility for these welfare functions, which in many cases are no longer being discharged adequately. Even if industry can eventually absorb the unemployed, further rural depopulation will leave the villages impoverished. Hence the need for a conscious programme of job creation in rural areas. Such attempts will be discussed in the concluding part of this chapter.

A critical issue for the future is the emergence of skilled full-time farmers working viable holdings. The new private farmers may be professional people who played a leading role on the cooperatives and now take full advantage of their skills and contacts. Former managers are well placed to become 'nomenklatura farmers' in the event of cooperatives becoming bankrupt. While trying to get good returns for shareholders, they are often ready to acquire property in the event of collapse. There are also cases of partnerships between peasants with complementary skills, to lease state-farm land in Poland, with the possibility of buying it at a later stage when restitution issues have been resolved (Harcsa 1993). They may also rent machines (with the intention to buy later if they can) or may purchase outright through down payments of one-fifth and instalments for the rest over seven years. Good relations between local peasant families will accelerate the process of putting together small units of land ownership in larger functional units with a pooling of machines and labour. This may happen irrespective of whether the units of ownership derive from existing farms, restitution holdings, land taken out of cooperatives or acquisitions arising through vouchers.

Several factors seem likely to tip the scales in favour of the professionals or alternatively the peasantry (Rose and Tikhomirov 1993). Cooperative leaders are in a strong position when farms are declared bankrupt because of superior knowledge about markets and other aspects of the farming business (Pryor 1992). They can exploit their monopoly of power and information to obtain the best property to launch their own private farm, and some may even hasten the bankruptcy scenario. Where cooperatives are very large (including several village communities) the leaders have great informational advantages over the dispersed membership. On the other hand, family solidarity can strengthen the peasants' position, and result in farms based on kinship ties or informal networks. Skilled rural workers may have connections through workshop industries which can be beneficial in joint farming and encourage group withdrawal from the cooperative, taking with them an appropriate mix of assets. Tractor drivers can work together on a private farm with the skills to drive and maintain machines. Expertise in agricultural engineering (coping with FSU machines, making spare parts and handling fertilizers and pesticides) may be complemented by wives' knowledge in finance and accounting. People who did well in farming under the communist reforms (in poultry rearing, for example) may have capital to buy land. All these scenarios are more likely to emerge in a well-integrated village community.

Thus far the changes seem to have heightened tensions within rural society where there is much disillusionment over the progress of the transition. The symbiosis between private and cooperative farms achieved under communism is being replaced by competition. Labour-intensive activities left to cooperative members and workers are now becoming independent. Conflict between private and cooperative farmers may be heightened by allegations of theft from the cooperative fields, but even the remaining cooperative farmers seem to have lost some of the solidarity and mutual support previously evident. The increase in private farming brings the prospect of increasing amounts of land being farmed by people who have no links with the village concerned. Incomers will have little idea about the village as a community and may unwittingly upset the local lifestyles. Tensions may be aggravated by 'historical resentments' (linked with pre-communist landholding) which complicate thinking about the most desirable arrangements for the future. Yet, rather than community stress, family farms need a supportive environment of institutions concerned with information and training as well as cooperation and marketing (Cochrane 1991). Governments have little money to finance structural change, although there have been some limited programmes to help farmers acquire machinery. In any case, it has been argued that state intervention should be resisted, despite the temptations arising from the recent history of central planning and the elaborate arrangements for agriculture in the EU (Karp and Stefanou 1994). But at least a system of planning control must be provided and local organizations should evaluate their resources, establish priorities and try and attract capital investment.

PRODUCTION AND MARKETING

Agriculture has adapted more readily to the transition than industry, through decline in output in the early 1990s (Table 12.1) and a more simplified enterprise pattern, because fundamentally it 'had no possibility to avoid pressures from reform' (Kraus et al. 1994, p.125). Instead of a closed socialist system, there is now a wider global context, with domestic farmers and food processors struggling to control the agro-food complex and assert their own interests (Hudečková and Lošták 1996). Throughout the region there has been a decline in production through the removal of food subsidies and consequent reduction in demand which, in turn, has discouraged investment. There has also been competition from imports, difficulties in former export markets, and inadequate domestic marketing systems. Uncertainty has increased because of privatization and the need to adjust to a market economy with a weak institutional set-up and tension between liberal agricultural policies and protection of consumers. There is no clear strategy for producers (Vincze 1996).

Table 12.1   Percentage change in agricultural production in Eastern Europe, at constant prices, 1990–1996

Country	1990	1991	1992	1993	1994	1995*	1996*
Bulgaria	–6.0	–0.3	–12.0	–18.1	–1.0	3.0	3.8
Czech Republic	–2.3	–8.9	–12.1	–0.8	–2.5	3.0	3.0
Hungary	–4.7	–6.2	–18.0	–14.7	3.0	2.0	3.0
Poland	–2.2	–1.6	–12.8	2.4	–10.0	2.0	2.0
Romania	–2.9	–3.7	–9.2	12.4	4.0	2.0	3.0
Slovakia	–10.3	–8.5	–26.0	–12.0	–3.0	3.0	2.0

Note: * Estimate

Sources: (1990–1992) T. Vuics, 'The agricultural change and its social effect in Mid-Eastern Europe', Conference Paper, 1995; (1993–1996) Economist Intelligence Unit.

The reduced level of intensification throughout Eastern Europe can be seen in terms of increased cereal deficits through a dip in output, linked with some increased trade dependence (Table 12.2). Falling output is clearly a function of lower yields which, in the case of cereals,

Table 12.2 Cereal production and trade in Eastern Europe, 1980–1993

Country	Domestic production (m.t) (A) and net trade (B) in											
	1980		1985		1990		1991		1992		1993	
	A	B	A	B	A	B	A	B	A	B	A	B
Albania	0.87	−0.01	1.05	–	1.04	+0.15	0.49	+0.24	0.42	+0.54	0.61	+0.65
Bosnia-Hercegovina									1.36*	–	1.26*	–
Bulgaria	8.68	+0.04	7.13	+0.45	7.89	+0.27	8.97	+0.51	6.67	−0.54	5.75	+0.14
Croatia									2.36	−0.04	2.73	−0.04
FCS	10.74	+2.05	11.77	+0.39	12.49	+0.05	11.94	−0.17	10.20	−0.12		
Czech Republic											6.47	+0.27
FGDR	9.64	+4.01	11.64	+1.72	12.33	+1.27						
Germany							39.27	−3.01	34.76	−6.81	36.22	−4.12
Hungary	13.61	+0.06	14.78	−2.14	12.51	−0.85	15.80	−1.25	9.98	−4.19	9.04	−2.06
Macedonia									0.62	+0.12	0.50	+0.10
Poland	18.34	+7.77	23.79	+2.32	28.01	+1.48	27.81	−0.35	19.96	−0.44	23.42	+2.89
Romania	20.23	+1.09	23.05	−0.12	17.19	+1.14	19.31	+1.69	12.29	+1.69	15.49	+2.64
Slovakia											3.20	–
Slovenia									0.43	+0.54	0.40	–
FFRY	15.27	+1.11	15.84	−0.77	13.66	+0.79	19.18	−0.85				
Yugoslavia									6.85	–	7.66	–

Notes: + net import; − net export; * Estimate.   Source: FAO Yearbooks.

potatoes and sugar beet for example, have fallen during the years 1991-93 after the gains of the communist period (Table 12.3). Livestock breeding has also suffered a setback – in Hungary, for example, a reduction in consumption of meat and dairy products of 30-40 per cent has been reported, with bread becoming a more prominent element in the diet. The number of pigs has halved because of reduced home consumption and exports, while the cattle population has declined from 1.25 to 0.78 million. Farm incomes can only be maintained by reduced investment, inputs (fertilizer, irrigation water and machinery) and labour (Juhasz 1991). Fertilizer use in Poland has decreased from 200 to 70kg/ha and there has been a tenfold decrease in agrochemicals, reinforcing 'a tendency for the extensification of farming operations in the face of declining profitability and market uncertainty' (Morgan 1992, p.147). Such has been the severity of the 'price scissors', with prices rising faster for manufactures than for agricultural commodities at farm gate prices.

For Hungarian farmers, the increases in their cash income have been much smaller than the rising cost of farm inputs – by between a half and a third if tractors and fertilizers are considered. In FCS, intensive farming was encouraged under communism, even in the less-attractive foothill zones where higher subsidies ('differential bonuses') were paid to cooperatives and state farms, although not to the remaining private farmers. Subsidies are now less generous and so between 1989 and 1994, agricultural output decreased by about a quarter and intensity is now about 20-30 per cent less than the most advanced European countries. A further factor has been some uncertainty arising from delay in implementing restitution measures. Structural change has been particularly disruptive for agricultural production, leaving specialized stock-rearing units divorced from their fodder supplies and undermining irrigation schemes which formerly depended on joint management by cooperative and state farms (Vrišer 1993). Cuts in stocking levels have arisen through the abandonment of buildings inconveniently situated in relation to the restructured farmholdings. Demand has been reduced in part by the withdrawal of the Red Army, which generated a substantial market in several countries, especially FCS, FGDR and Poland. The textile industry, which used to be a very heavy consumer of agricultural raw materials, has been slimmed down. Finally, natural hazards, such as drought in Hungary

Table 12.3 Yield and production of major crops in Eastern Europe, 1961–1993

	Average yield (qu/ha) and production (m.t)							
	1961-65		1981-85		1986-90		1991-93	
Country/Crop	Yield	Prod.	Yield	Prod.	Yield	Prod.	Yield	Prod.
Cereals								
Albania	10.6	0.29	28.6	1.02	29.1	1.01	20.3	0.51
Bosnia*							36.6	1.31
Bulgaria	19.0	4.86	41.4	8.55	39.5	8.20	33.2	7.13
Croatia*							41.2	2.54
FCS	21.8	5.66	43.2	10.90	47.7	11.81	43.7	10.60
FGDR	25.3	5.97	41.4	10.37	45.5	11.16		
Hungary	20.3	6.90	49.5	14.41	48.5	13.78	41.2	11.61
Macedonia*							25.0	0.56
Poland	17.0	15.43	27.4	22.23	31.1	26.11	27.9	23.73
Romania	15.9	11.10	34.4	21.70	39.3	23.39	25.9	15.70
Slovenia*							35.2	0.41
FFRY	17.3	3.80	39.0	16.77	37.4	15.65	36.8	14.45
Yugoslavia*							29.0	7.26
Total	23.7	54.01	36.5	105.95		111.11		
Potatoes								
Albania	73.1	0.03	83.9	0.13	88.4	0.11	85.0	0.07
Bosnia*							51.1	0.03
Bulgaria	86.0	0.40	106.3	0.42	120.0	0.43	115.0	0.52
Croatia*							78.3	0.49
FCS	114.0	5.63	185.7	3.59	183.1	3.19	172.2	2.76
FGDR	166.0	12.07	205.9	9.95	240.0	10.37		
Hungary	79.0	2.00	182.1	1.44	176.9	1.26	146.8	1.18
Macedonia*							91.2	0.11
Poland	154.0	43.68	167.0	36.59	190.2	36.14	168.9	29.57
Romania	85.0	2.60	192.3	5.75	163.6	5.51	116.4	2.73
FFRY	87.0	2.71	92.5	2.57	79.9	2.27	76.9	2.07
Yugoslavia*							62.0	0.65
Total	139.6	69.12	166.9	60.44	182.4	59.28		

Table 12.3 – continued

Sugar beet								
Albania	172.1	0.08	371.2	0.32	347.8	0.32	91.9	0.06
Bosnia							503.3	0.08
Bulgaria	205.0	1.44	220.9	1.11	157.9	0.63	191.0	0.43
Croatia*							331.9	0.53
FCS	270.0	6.28	244.6	7.30	345.6	6.26	349.5	5.57
FGDR	243.0	5.37	287.1	7.09	303.4	6.47		
Hungary	246.0	3.09	382.2	4.45	393.4	4.50	303.1	3.70
Macedonia*							346.7	0.05
Poland	268.0	11.44	330.3	15.61	345.9	14.67	335.3	12.69
Romania	149.0	2.64	217.1	6.07	210.0	5.83	195.7	3.13
Slovenia*							304.0	0.08
FFRY	279.0	2.34	426.6	6.12	406.0	5.82	359.7	3.96
Yugoslavia*							280.1	2.02
Total	244.3	32.68	324.6	48.07	316.5	44.51		

Note: * Countries of Former Yugoslavia whose figures have been added together to produce the totals for FFRY for 1991–93.

Source: FAO Yearbooks

and Romania in 1993, have been compounded by the breakdown of irrigation systems.

In addition to a fall in yield there has been some conversion of arable land to pasture or forestry. The largest decrease in FCS has occurred in the regions bordering Germany because of the disintegration of state farms, some of which were working whole districts such as Cheb and Tachov. Another factor has been the very small scale of land restitution in these regions. Meanwhile, the area of meadows and pastures has increased significantly over 1990–95, by about one-sixth, mostly as a result of the transfer of arable land. Large areas of fallow and setaside land are now found throughout Poland, mostly on state lands where cultivation has been discontinued. However, some of the land belongs to private farmers who have ceased cultivation because of low returns. This is economically rational because at a time of sluggish demand the primary aim should be to minimize production costs. Similar changes are evident in other countries: for example, whole areas of Albanian upland agriculture, particularly the hillside terracing which had received substantial investment of financial and labour resources in the 1960s and 1970s, have been abandoned. Land-use changes have also been highlighted through the 'deagrarization' reported from the Slovenian littoral (Pavlin 1991, pp.116–17). In Romania, not only have maize and potatoes been given greater emphasis at the expense of sugar beet and fruit growing, but some farmers have cut down fruit trees because they give top priority to self-sufficiency in maize, which provides both human food and animal fodder; this policy ensures ample provision of food for peasant households (with surpluses which pass to family members through private deals) but reduces supplies to the open market. But the underlying rationale for change is the same in all cases: if there is no clear economic stimulus through efficient marketing at rewarding prices, peasants who are free to plan their own activities will tend to concentrate on self-sufficiency and restrict their marketing to livestock, which are relatively easy to dispose of.

In Poland, the network of the agricultural product purchasing centres was largely organized before 1970, when individual farmers had to sell milk, meat, grain and potatoes on a quota basis related to farm size. The situation changed after 1989 when market reforms were accompanied by the privatization of agricultural services and the appearance of both foreign and domestic competition. The local markets have become more important for the sale of farm producers as places to sell their produce, although there is a great deal of variation in local conditions across the country. There are differences between suburban areas and places situated a long way from the towns and the food-processing plants. By contrast, commodity exchanges, which in the majority of the European countries constitute the most important outlet for agricultural products, have been developing very slowly in Poland. Forty exchanges, located mainly in big towns, were in operation in 1994. The largest one, with a yearly turnover of US$31 billion, is in Poznań. Other major exchanges (with a turnover of US$4–5 billion) are located in the north and east: Białystok, Gdańsk, Lublin, Olsztyn and Szczecin. There are few experienced market managers and consequently prices vary quite sharply through both space and time (Morgan 1992). An increasing number of private dealers offer a localized service, but have not yet got the expertise to operate through wider networks so that surpluses and deficits can be balanced out. They may prefer a small turnover with prices as high as possible, which may result in farmers being left with produce that is nevertheless in short supply in areas just beyond the immediate locality.

There are now some signs of change. While mixed farming on the Slovenian coast has declined, there is specialization in fruit growing, olive growing and viticulture, with the intensively cultivated surfaces coexisting with physically similar ground when farmers are working along traditional lines with low levels of intensification and considerable neglect in the case holdings worked by older people. In Albania, agriculture has been prominent in the economic recovery which began in 1993 (Pata and Osmani 1994). There is less emphasis now on cotton, soya beans and tobacco, but more fodder is being produced and food markets are well stocked with dairy products, meat, fruit and vegetables which earn profits to rejuvenate private agriculture. Albania should once again become a net exporter (Zanga 1994). However, there is still a long way to go to restore supplies of fertilizers and pesticides and renovate irrigation projects that were destroyed or neglected during the transition. In Romania, many of the large livestock-rearing and -fattening complexes inherited from communism remain inefficient, with dwindling herds and persistent fodder shortages. But some have attracted investment and have not only mechanized the feeding system but have integrated with business with a fodder factory, slaughterhouse and meat packing plant.

THE RURAL SITUATION

There is the challenge of investment and modernization to create commercial farmers 'out of a cushioned quasi-subsistence agricultural system' at a time of rising prices and high interest rates (Swain 1992, p.10). Currently (1995) state farms in Poland average 2,800ha, compared with 6ha for the private sector, which employs 25 persons per 100ha compared with 13 persons in the state sector. The bigger farms will certainly succeed where there is good management in regions like the Poznań area of Poland, with its successful orchards and greenhouses linked with processing plants (with leasing and cooperative arrangements). Here there are family farms running intensive pig-rearing systems based on farm-grown potatoes, whey and vitamin supplements. One million Polish farms approach viability, although scarcely more than half (some 550,000, although some economists say only 400,000), have a chance of sustained development. However, it is difficult to be categorical about the minimum size of a viable holding, especially in the context of vegetable growing and viticulture, while the pluriactivity option widens the range of possible scenarios still further. The people most likely to succeed in private farming may be the 'green barons' with modest stocks of capital, managerial experience and, as already noted, agribusiness contacts (Kovacs 1993). But private farms of 50-100ha may well prove viable in countries where there is a rural labour surplus (Cochrane 1994, p.335). If marketing remains difficult and cooperatives are bankrupted, many more private farmers will be 'created by poverty, by the bankruptcy of the collective farms, by unemployment in industry and by the withdrawal of unemployment benefits from those who, after all, have their land to fall back on' (Swain 1993a, p.18). The scenario of rural overpopulation and subsistence agriculture would involve an extension of the situation evident in Poland, Romania and FFRY today where the rural infrastructure is often very poor (Surd 1994). Farm units in Croatia have declined more slowly than production, reflecting increased diversification and feminization. Land is valued on the grounds of sentiment and security (Stambuk 1991).

The most likely scenario is that many fewer people will be needed on the land (Table 12.4). Agricultural employment in Eastern Europe is rapidly declining from about one-fifth in 1990 to a tenth in 1995 and an anticipated 5 per cent at the turn of the century. In Poland the decline in the farming population has been estimated at 400,000 to 500,000 people between 1988 and 1993 and even so a further 333,000 are considered to be surplus (Wecławowicz 1996, p.145). In the former GDR, labour is down from 884,000 to 208,000 but still needs a further reduction by as much as one half (Bergmann 1992). Regional programmes could accelerate the pace where a lot of manual work could easily be replaced by machinery (Staziak 1989). Not all these losses apply to conventional farming jobs: in the Czech Republic about half the decrease in agricultural employment since 1989 has arisen from the loss of work in non-agricultural enterprises (mainly in industry and construction) associated with cooperatives and state farms and enumerated under agriculture for this reason. The consequences are even more serious when it is considered that in Albania, collectivized agriculture previously absorbed up to 70,000 young people entering the national job market each year. Plainly,

Table 12.4 Agricultural population, 1985–1994

Country	Population active in agriculture (th.) and percentage of the total active population) in											
	1985		1990		1991		1992		1993		1994	
	N	%	N	%	N	%	N	%	N	%	N	%
Albania	715	52.0	762	48.5	756	47.7	764	47.1	762	46.4	758	45.7
Bulgaria	670	14.9	539	12.2	519	11.8	504	11.4	486	11.0	464	0.6
FCS	906	11.1	772	9.3	747	9.0	727	8.7	–	–	–	–
FGDR	873	9.3	758	8.1	736	7.9	–	–	–	–	–	–
Hungary	752	14.5	590	11.5	565	11.0	541	10.5	517	10.0	496	9.5
Poland	4,676	24.4	4,030	20.8	3,914	20.1	3,806	19.5	3,713	18.9	3,613	18.2
Romania	2,839	25.0	2,356	20.2	2,265	19.4	2,154	18.6	2,078	17.9	1,997	17.1
FFRY	2,679	26.7	2,254	21.7	2,237	20.8	–	–	–	–	–	–

Source: FAO Yearbooks.

farming can no longer be regarded as a first-choice 'career' for a large number of people wishing to start work.

Since 1989, most rural areas have experienced some degree of impoverishment which has undermined the relatively comfortable lifestyles of even the village-based élites (Toth 1992). There is severe depression in the small villages of Slovakia (41.5 per cent of all villages, housing 5 per cent of total population), with a predominance of older people reflecting low mobility, low purchasing power and poor educational standards, which is not stimulating private business. Rural poverty impinges very severely on problem families (with large numbers of children) and specific ethno-cultural groups such as the Gypsy population, which is heavily dependent on social support.

In response to these problems, emergency 'self-support' programmes are being introduced, especially among the older people in the poorer regions of Slovakia. Meanwhile, there are serious social problems when, as in Poland, much of the 'setaside' land falls into areas of high unemployment, caused by the laying off of the former state-farm workers. They receive benefits which cost almost twice as much money as was previously paid in budget allocations to the state farms. Thus the social costs of untilled land are very high, and the economic rationale overall is debatable in the short term. Unemployment undermines the work ethic and aggravates problems of crime, alcoholism and drug addiction although, to some extent, the problem may be 'hidden' on small private farms which seek – albeit inefficiently – to absorb the additional labour. Fear of pauperism leads to higher involvement in small-scale farming to ensure self-sufficiency although, at the same time, it leads to higher consumption of animal fats which are not good for public health. People may also be forced into activities on the margins of legality, such as smuggling cigarettes across Poland's borders with Belarus and Lithuania.

Rural–urban migration has been very significant in Albania, where strict controls were in force during the communist period (Hall 1996; Sjoberg 1991). Migrants, notably from the country's harsh northeastern districts of Kukës and Dibër, have moved southwards in search of better land, access to major urban areas, or both, preferring the middle coastal lowlands and access to the commercial centres of Tirana and Durrës. Some 350,000 have migrated in this way in just three or four years. The other side of the coin has been rapid growth in the towns, much of it unregulated. The spontaneous settlement of Bathore, near Kamëz, is of particular concern. Attracting some 30,000 settlers, the 'town' has little by way of infrastructure: no drinkable water or sewerage system, electricity or roads. The large numbers of people involved and the buildings being erected pose health problems within the sites themselves and present potential threats to neighbouring settlements. Third, the unplanned increase in population poses a serious physical planning problem and spontaneous movement to relatively fertile areas has hampered redistribution of agrarian land.

But there are opportunities in the countryside for non-agricultural activity. In the Czech Republic in 1991, a total of 1.76 million residents commuted to work in a location lying outside their place of residence. In 1980 the figure was 1.7 million, so there has been an absolute increase and a growth in proportion (relating to the economically active population) as well. But now a section of the rural population is able to pursue business at home in areas that were effectively closed in the past: small farms and workshops, shops, public houses and boarding houses. This trend has been reinforced by the loss of many urban jobs and the transfer of several thousand town dwellers to new homes and occupations in the countryside where houses have been purchased (or obtained through restitution). Both old and new houses provide space for such new functions at relatively low cost (to both owners and tenants) compared with the urban situation. There are also new jobs connected with wholesale trade and cottage industry; environmental protection; landscape and water management; and agrotourism. Meanwhile, the remaining rural population in Bulgaria perceives the city less as a place of prosperity, offering good prospects for the young, and more as a difficult and dangerous environment. As a result, villagers are reappraising their own situation *vis-à-vis* their urban counterparts and raising their own sense of esteem after years of self-condemnation. The lifestyle has improved, while living costs remain relatively low. Country people have more opportunity to satisfy their elementary needs and have immediate access to good-quality foodstuffs. The lower crime rate is appreciated, as is the greater sense of security, familiarity and warmth in personal relations. Bulgaria has great natural resource potential for agriculture and tourism where analysts expect to see faster economic growth in the future. Hence Bulgaria's countryside may well flourish, given the country's agricultural traditions and a willingness on the part of the new landowners to rise to the demands of independent farm work.

But to retain viable communities and satisfy the young people, rural services must be improved. Water is critically short in parts of the Balkans, as studies of Bulgaria have recently highlighted (Knight 1995). In Albania, a shortage of good-quality water has continued to pose problems for a number of rural areas. Some farmers are able to water their crops from wells, but ground water is often saline, notably along the coastal plain. Many distant villages are still only accessible by foot or mule and farmers may travel, with difficulty, three kilometres to their fields and 20 kilometres to the nearest market. Local rural public transport has deteriorated with the loss of the availability of cooperative and state-farm buses. The country's overall telephone provision, at 16 lines per thousand population, is the lowest in the region, going down to a figure of only seven per thousand in the rural areas. A reliable power supply is needed in the countryside and only in the late 1990s should there be some benefit from an EBRD and World Bank aid programme to improve electricity distribution. The situation is better in Poland and almost 73 per cent of the houses had a water supply system in 1993, although the remainder were using farm wells, which often supplied only poor-quality water. Hence, the construction of collective supply systems is an urgent necessity. Work has been proceeding quite promptly, aided by a good deal of foreign assistance: from 47,000 houses connected each year in the 1980s, the number rose to 116,000 between 1989 and 1994.

An even faster pace of change has occurred in the installation of gas-pipe networks, although the use of liquid gas from gas cylinders is still very popular. Meanwhile, however, the development of the sewerage system has been very slow. But sewer construction is often very expensive in the view of the dispersal of houses. The expansion of the telephone network in Poland has also been proceeding very rapidly, with an increase in the number of rural phones of more than 90 per cent from 354,000 in 1989 to 673,000 in 1994.

In Poland in the late 1980s, more than 70,000 shops and kiosks were operating in rural areas, selling a variety of goods. By 1993, this number had increased by 31 per cent to almost 92,000. It is clear that during the period 1989–93, rural services underwent relatively radical change as the number of service points increased by nearly 36 per cent and expansion continues. The changes are generated almost exclusively by the private sector, because state services are now being closed down quite rapidly. There is also change in the provision of agricultural services because the number of service points increased by nearly 54 per cent after 1989, with a growth of 160 per cent in private services balanced by a decline of some 50 per cent in state-owned establishments. Direct purchasing of machinery from manufacturers remains important and currently about 80 per cent of all tractors are bought direct. Open-air markets also retain their significance.

In terms of human resources, the situation is not wholly problematic. Rural people tend to be poorly qualified: 11.7 per cent of the active population are university graduates in towns, but the proportion is only 1.9 per cent in villages; for high school graduates the proportions are 36.4 and 16.3 per cent, respectively (Lup 1996). Communities have become stressful and may need mediation to resolve conflicts arising from land reform in Romanian villages; there is a growing need for social welfare to monitor and diagnose the new social situation, to cope with poverty and unemployment and help with regeneration (Sobczak 1996). However, on the whole, villages are in a relatively strong position when it comes to reaching collective decisions. Even when there is a division in language there may be solidarity (claimed in Romania) and acceptance of other cultures (Poledna 1996). Many are politically ambivalent, but they manifest considerable interest in NGOs, including community associations (Abraham 1996). 'The majority of Bulgarian rural areas have potential both in natural and human resources for non-agricultural activities, especially for small industry, rural tourism and craft production' (Draganova 1996). The fertility of rural women in Bulgaria is higher than in the towns, while the average number of children per family is the same (1.8) and the rural birth-rate is lower by only 0.5 percentage points (Kozhunarova 1996). Communities have viewpoints to express and they should be included in the planning process; for example, in the Danube Delta, they should be encouraged to take an interest in local sustainable developments and stop depopulation (Constantinescu-Galiceni 1996). Local leadership should be stimulated in backward areas such as Hungary's Cserehat (Fekete and Swain 1996) and the important role for women in farm diversification and the rebuilding of the countryside should be recognized (Verbole 1996). Women have been less well educated in the past and they are frequently the main victims of poverty and unemployment. Many have lost jobs on state farms or have lost control on the family farms when unemployed husbands have returned from the factories to take charge at home. Yet a fifth of Poland's two million farms are still managed by women, who are also prominent in food processing, education, health, commerce and social assistance, although not enough in management and science (Sawicka 1996). 'It is therefore imperative that steps be taken for the systematic promotion of women in managerial and decision-making positions according to their education status and professional accomplishments' (Fulea and Sima 1996, p.81).

But generalization can be misleading and it is worth noting the regional contrasts referred to for East Germany. There are development areas experiencing pressures for non-agricultural development: these are the urban fringes of Berlin, Magdeburg, Halle, Leipzig, Dresden and Erfurt, and also rural areas bordering key transport corridors. There are also agricultural development areas with fertile soils (notably the loess soils stretching from Magdeburg in Sachsen-Anhalt to Dresden in Sachsen) and, finally, remoter rural areas isolated from urban centres and with marginal soil quality (hence designated 'less-favoured areas'), such as southern Thüringen, southwest Sachsen and southern Brandenburg, where unemployment may be high. A roughly parallel situation can be seen in the Czech Republic, which has the fastest growth occurring in and around Prague, where there is a low unemployment rate of less than one per cent and an intensive rhythm of construction activity. Many second homes are being converted into permanent homes, especially in the hinterland of large cities. On the other hand, the country has problems with its 'inner borderland', manifest through a declining and ageing population, and a dilapidated housing stock with only limited opportunities for recreational use.

Contrasts have been alluded to in Poland between areas with optimal conditions for agricultural development, with significant flows of capital investment and an increasing average size of holding (although with increasing pollution by agrochemicals and soil erosion) and poorer regions with a fallowing of plots and a growth of afforestation, combined with inadequate opportunities in manufacturing and tourism which leads to depopulation. There may also be some conflict with protected areas (Wojciechowski 1996). In dynamic areas, land values would prevent extreme inefficiency. In the more advanced areas of Poland, where there is a diversified economic structure, the process of agricultural restructuring has proceeded more harmoniously than in areas with a monolithic economic structure, such as comprise the voivodships lying on Poland's eastern 'wall' which are locked in a backward state, so that the new economic conditions may even reinforce the process of regression and instigate other negative economic processes (Gorzelak 1996). Since the rural people are badly educated and the level of infrastructure is very low, the voivodships of eastern Poland lack adequate resources for agricultural development. Moreover, for the last 20 years there has been substantial emigration of young people to the towns and a decline of interest in the land. During the years 1988–94, grain yields in the north fell by as much as 40 per cent although the national output declined by only 18 per cent. This cannot be linked simply with drought because the difference is so great. Instead, an almost fourfold reduction in the use of mineral fertilizers and a large decline in the application of pesticides had an immense influence on the change.

In the Balkans, there are many areas with poverty problems, resulting in falling reproduction. This can be seen in the case of people who do not possess land, and in the Turkish community in particular (Vladimirova and Rangelova 1996). Croatia's population is highly fragmented, with more than half the settlements inhabited by fewer than 200 people compared with about a third in 1948 (Table 12.5). Agricultural effort is flagging: 55.3 per cent of the 569,000 private farms in 1981 had no active full-time labour; the proportion reached 86.3 per cent for the smallest farms (less than one hectare) but was still 15.9 per cent for holdings of eight hectares or more. A survey of rural youth born in Croatia between 1943 and 1952 showed that 16.7 per

Table 12.5 Distribution of settlements in Croatia, 1948–1991

Settlement size (persons)	1948		1991	
	Settlements	%	Settlements	%
Below 200	2,278	34.4	3,430	51.2
200–499	2,416	36.4	1,829	27.3
500–999	1,277	19.2	831	12.5
1,000–1,999	511	7.7	369	5.5
2,000–9,999	142	2.1	196	2.9
10,000–99,999	14	0.2	35	0.5
100,000+	1	–	4	0.1

Source: Brkic and Zutinic 1993, p.168.

cent started work in farming (1968) but only 2.3 per cent remained (Brkic and Zutinic 1993, p.172). Of 522,000 working-age youth (aged 15-27) in 1987, only 7.4 per cent were farmers; out of 31,000 marriages in 1987, only 4.6 per cent of husbands were farmers.

Meanwhile, non-agricultural employment in the villages is limited and Croatian communities are struggling to find an identity with poor perspectives that are deeply discouraging for rural youth. There is a great need for new forms of enterprise, and for demographic stabilization and revitalization (ibid., p.173). On balance, it will be encouraging if rising incomes can increase demand for food and make agriculture more profitable, with a more buoyant land market revealing the optimum farm size and stimulating farmers to invest and intensify (Cochrane 1994, p.335). But in much of Eastern Europe, country people are encountering a worst-case scenario: private farms are being 'created by poverty', with subsistence agriculture signalling a drift back to rural overpopulation which will be difficult to sustain with equanimity in the late twentieth century with greater movement and effective information flows (Swain 1992b, p.10).

It is these latter cases that constitute the main problem regions in Eastern Europe. It is here that a welfare agenda is most critical, reflecting the ideological inclination of socialist governments that would try and maintain high levels of employment through labour-intensive cultivation (including rabbit breeding, fruit growing and the cultivation of mushrooms and vegetables) to support continuing part-time work in agriculture. Such opinion would also cite the great scope for small businesses in agriculture to take care of crop spraying, combine harvesting or butter production using local milk surpluses (Kovach 1994b). While remote rural areas have common problems, they also have their own unique community characteristics, as the Romanian sociologist Dimitrie Gusti argued in the 1930s (Wierzbicki 1996). Kaleta has echoed his sentiments in remarking (1993, p.91) that 'the countryside as a social environment creates quite unique structure' requiring procedures different from general sociology. Such sentiments are echoed by Doppler's (1994) concept of 'farming systems' specific to each area through the structure of farms and enterprises inherited from the communist past and the nature of the transition process in each area: the opportunities and the way they are perceived by farming people.

An important question is how far Eastern Europe will identify with the Swiss–Bavarian model of relatively small farms combined with a significant rural industry. Families involved in pluriactivity (where farm occupancy is supported by a range of activities with the flexibility of family labour as the critical issue) have been seen as 'social anomalies' in a world dominated by capital. The economic factors of uneven development and constrained choice may be complemented by a web of social relations supporting an ideological commitment to family-based farming (Marsden 1990). South Moravia shows the tendency towards a dispersal of employment in manufacturing, reinforced by workshops on the former state and cooperative farms. Although pluriactivity is often dictated by poverty, it may remain part of the community ethos, especially in mountain regions where there are opportunities for diversification in commerce and agrotourism (Barbic 1993). In countries where the private sector is relatively well established much progress is being made in combining small-scale agriculture with woodcutting, handicrafts and tourism, as in the Polish Carpathians (Pine 1992, 1993, 1994). Improved education is seen as a base for rural development in Albania. In other areas, pluriactivity may be an appropriate focus for government support (Ferruni 1995).

Environmental Issues

Communist successes in agriculture are based on the exploitation of past investments in rural infrastructure, without adequate renewal, and what can only be described as plundering of the natural resources. In Bulgaria there has been a loss of soil fertility because maximum output was maintained by the application of chemical fertilizers, which encouraged soil compaction and erosion leading to a loss of biodiversity and other long-term factors detrimental for cultivation. The countryside also suffered from the effects of industrialization through air and water pollution. The Bulgarian ecological movement 'Ekoglasnost' warned the public in 1989 that all fruit and vegetables were contaminated by both chemicals and atmospheric pollutants. In 1990, it was disclosed that some 54th.ha of farmland were polluted with heavy metals and cultivation on the 900ha worst affected had to be prohibited. Recent research in the Burgas region has revealed serious problems with soil erosion, calculated at 43.1t/ha each year (twice the national average and the highest rate recorded anywhere in the country). Much of this is due to excessive application of fertilizer during the communist period, together with poor animal waste disposal methods. This resulted in inadmissibly high nutrient levels in the water supply, which suffered further contamination from unsafe levels of agricultural pesticides. In the 1980s, the waste material generated by large-scale breeding farms for pigs, poultry and cattle in the then Czechoslovakia equalled the sewage output of a town of 40–80 thousand inhabitants, but there was little interest in building cesspools or purification facilities. Undesirable ecological changes are also occurring through privatization (Bettram 1992) because new private farmers generally lack the financial means, the technical knowledge and the inducement to embrace environmentally friendly practices.

The farming future may well require permanently reduced production levels, for the rural areas of Eastern Europe cannot be divorced from trends occurring in the continent as a whole (Black et al. 1995). Surpluses in the EU threaten domestic markets and although PHARE funding for Eastern Europe is still linked with classic production philosophy of CAP, this may not be realistic over the longer term. Therefore, agricultural production should now be stabilized at a lower level, not only to reflect the fall in demand but also to facilitate a measure of environmental recovery.

In the Czech Republic it is considered important to ensure the continued use of pastureland where landscape quality would be damaged by further neglect. In addition, the enhancement of landscape quality is to be sought through changes in agricultural production. The aim should be to encourage the transfer of further arable land and to convert arable land to forestry on steeply sloping land. More generally, agricultural programmes should identify sample farms that are using alternative agricultural practices and identify physical and biological indicators for sustainable agriculture, with a view to developing improved criteria for the assessment of food safety and water and soil quality. But while some reduction of intensification may be ecologically desirable, too steep a decline in production may complicate the restoration of self-sufficiency and the desired switching of aid away from food and towards structural change throughout the economy. Sustainability should therefore be the rationale for state intervention through conservation programmes (Bettram 1992). Vogler (1996) looks at changing field patterns in the Dedelow area of FGDR (close to the border with Szczecin) and correlates new boundaries with the subdivision of former cooperative farms into three or four units. Here, as in Slovakia, it is intended that agricultural land should become more highly compartmentalized through the restoration of some of the 'biolines' removed during the communist period. But greater ecological consciousness (Dobreva and Koleva 1996) will require reeducation for all users of the landscape as well as more adequate land-use documentation to ensure that business intentions are properly harmonized with landscape potentials.

In the FGDR today, all the new *Länder* are encouraging the growth of 'green' tourism and recreation through preserving and improving the landscape and improving provision of amenities and facilities, including walking, cycling and horse-riding routes. But the potential for rural tourism must be linked with the careful management of the mountains, to prevent erosion by both overgrazing and excessive visitor pressure, as demonstrated in the Parâng Mountains where national park designations may provide the necessary protection in an area opened up to visitors by the expansion of wood processing and the development of hydro-electricity (Ploaie 1996). Spatial discrimination is necessary to identify the worst problems. In the Czech Republic, disruption through environmental problems is worst in North Bohemia and the border areas: Bruntál, Česka Lípa, České Krumlov, Chomutov, Jablonec nad Nisou, Karlovy Vary, Louny, Most, Tachov, Teplice, Ústi nad Labem and Vsetín. Equally, remedial action has to be focused on specific areas, hence the protective measures which are being taken in the glaciated Tatra Mountains National Park (1954), where erosion requires the closure of some routes and the establishment of additional areas of mixed woodlands (Wiska and Hindson 1991). There is also scope for conservation in those rural settlements where the buildings and cultural manifestations offer resources for community-based ecotourism, yet where there is much dereliction (Pozes 1991). There is an important role for local government, whose power has been increased by decentralization. Village councils in Albania could take useful environmental initiatives in critical areas, although it has been pointed out that many local government units are too small to marshal the resources to undertake major projects in conservation or employment creation (Swain 1996).

GOVERNMENT INTERVENTION

There is an instinct for government intervention in the rural sphere, given the tight regulation of agriculture through central planning. Croatia has come up with a comprehensive agenda which includes promotion of producer associations (including specialist organizations for milk, olive oil, fish and oil crops) and viable credit institutions, including a Fund for Agricultural Development. Reference is made to rehabilitation and resettlement in war areas and the redistribution of the remaining state-owned land (much of it currently leased to private farmers). Fertilizers are a problem, because while the average application is less than the European average, there is a wide gulf between 310kg/ha in the former state–social sector and only 69kg/ha in the private sector. Neither situation is optimal: the high level should be reduced for ecological reasons and to increase profitability and the low level on private farms should be increased to obtain better credit arrangements and lower fertilizer prices. Attention is also to be given to the reorganization of food processing, which still needs financial support and import protection as the price for continued production of vegetable oils, sugar, animal feed and milk (Stebelsky 1995). Similar attention is also needed for the producers of farm inputs such as the fertilizer and machinery enterprises. Inefficiency in these inherited state industries is seen as a major factor in the significant decline in the terms of trade for agriculture (Tanic n.d., p.50). Processing units are technically competent in their respective fields but they 'lack skills in financial management' and are not yet 'sufficiently profit-oriented' (ibid., p.34). In the case of dairies, milk collection costs are very high because of the small average herd size, while rape seed and sunflower extraction capacities are inadequate for domestic needs and technology is obsolete. Croatia also seeks a regionalization of agricultural policy to deal with the Adriatic and mountain areas, as previously attempted under communism during the years 1970–90 (ibid., pp.52–3). The government wishes to review the economic feasibility of expanding high-value crop production in coastal areas in the light of prevailing microclimates, to support the rehabilitation of olive growing and to explore the scope for lowering production costs for marine and freshwater aquaculture.

However, while there is much restructuring outstanding in some countries, there is little enthusiasm in government circles for a protective farm policy which currently provides an effective social safety net for small producers in Western Europe. Such a programme would be too expensive and, indeed, it is becoming clear that any further enlargement of the EU (possibly affecting Visegrád countries by 2000 and Balkan countries early in the next century) will involve reform of the EU's CAP. Support for agriculture as a percentage of total government expenditure has fallen steadily between 1990 and 1994: from 9.1 to 3.7 per cent in Hungary, from 4.7 to 2.4 per cent in Poland and from 18.4 to 5.7 per cent in Slovakia. Limited action is being taken to protect farmers from low-cost imports, with Slovenia offering protection through minimum import prices (Bojnec 1994). But there is significant intervention in marketing to help both producers and consumers. In the Czech Republic, there is a market fund for the buying and selling of beef, cereals and milk. There is also limited market intervention through Hungary's Agricultural Market Office in respect of five commodities: maize, wheat, beef, pigmeat and milk. Slovakia's Agriculture and Food Chamber brings together producers (state farms, cooperatives and private farmers alike) and processors in a bid to coordinate supply and demand, while there have been some commodity schemes to stop the decline in production arising from the removal of subsidies and price controls and the problems encountered in export markets. Poland has an Agricultural Market Agency to stabilize the farm produce market and protect farmers' incomes. In Slovenia the government must implement the laws on privatization, which will break up the large ('state' and 'social') farms. However, it is also aware that these large enterprises are important food producers and if the new farmowners are unable to maintain production the domestic market will suffer (Vrišer 1993).

Conclusion 389

There is also some support to farmers in the more difficult areas. Payments were still made in Slovakia in 1994 to support mountain agriculture, although total outlays were much reduced. Meanwhile, the most productive districts of the Danube region (Dunajská Streda and Galanta) received virtually no financial assistance. Likewise in the Czech Republic, there is still a regime of subsidies over what is approximately the poorest quarter of regions of the total agricultural land. In Romania, an Agency for the Mountainous Regions uses agronomists displaced by the collapse of the old cooperatives to work as agricultural advisers in each commune, to encourage farm improvement through better stock breeding (many of the animals reared on the old cooperatives were of very poor quality), improved local food processing and diversification into activities where investment in the past has been very low. High-quality agricultural produce could include cheese and preserved fruits, which are traditional products of Carpathian agriculture. However, budgetary pressures limit such help, and Western experts have argued that historic precedents in both Eastern and Western Europe should be set aside (Karp and Stefanou 1994). The problems of agriculture are not unique to this sector of the economy and financial assistance should arguably be arranged through banks with governments kept at arm's length. Management of agriculture through production support would certainly consume resources and reduce government flexibility.

There is also some help for exporters because a favourable trade balance in agricultural commodities is highly desirable, but Albania and Bulgaria have become net importers, and Poland and Romania increasingly so (Table 12.6). The Hungarian government is keen to maintain the ability to export (seen as crucial for the balance of payments) and has some money for export subsidies. But over the long term, Hungary believes that competitiveness should not be stimulated by subsidies but should arise by exploiting comparative advantages (good arable land and skilled farmers). Meanwhile, in Poland 'soft loans' are available for traditional priority sectors: dairying, livestock and wool. These are considered necessary to prevent excessive food imports (forecast at US$400 million net for 1995). At the same time, the growth of food exports has been stimulated by income tax exemptions for export-orientated investments. However, the Czech Republic considers it is uneconomic to try and produce more for export, because of the need to compete with subsidized exports from other countries including the EU. Poland also has a sugar surplus, but export is possible only with subsidies. In Hungary,

Table 12.6 Net trade in agricultural products in Eastern Europe, 1988–1994

	Trade balance* (US$bn) in						
	1988	1989	1990	1991	1992	1993	1994
Albania	−0.07	−1.07	+0.02	+0.13	+0.25	+0.31	+0.21
Bulgaria	−0.63	−0.67	−1.18	−0.45	−0.58	−0.30	−0.40
Croatia	–	–	–	–	–	*	+0.17
FCS	+1.48	+0.99	+0.62	+0.22	+0.22	–	–
Czech Republic	–	–	–	–	–	−0.03	+0.36
FGDR	+1.76	+1.73	+0.92	–	–	–	–
Germany	+16.17	+151.0	+18.28	+19.44	+20.72	+14.47	+16.11
Hungary	−1.30	−1.45	−1.59	−1.97	−1.96	−1.15	−1.21
Macedonia	–	–	–	–	−0.09	+0.01	+0.02
Poland	+0.54.	+0.61	−0.64	−0.50	+0.11	+0.66	+0.55
Romania	−0.21	+0.07	+1.28	+0.69	+0.82	+0.70	+0.30
Slovenia	–	–	–	–	–	+0.18	+0.20
FFRY	+0.16	+0.30	+1.54	+0.49	–	–	–

Note: * + denotes net import; − denotes net export.

Source: FAO Yearbooks.

despite good trade relations with FSU and much export of pigmeat, trade was adversely affected by EU-subsidized exports, with deferred payment with which Hungary cannot compete.

However, there is certainly a need for a rural social policy to ensure welfare for the farming population (Kapitanski and Anastasova 1994) and to encourage diversification, although it should be clearly separated from agriculture policy. It is calculated that to maintain structural change and farm consolidation, eliminating 750,000 very small farms of 1–3ha, 150,000 new jobs must be created in Poland every year. In 1992 therefore, Poland launched an 'Opportunities for Rural Areas and Agriculture' programme to provide preferential credits and subsidies. But broadly similar action is needed in the other countries and in FGDR, financial support for job creation is provided through a joint Federal-*Land* regional economic structure programme which aims at improving industrial infrastructure and enabling the establishment and expansion of firms. SMEs are thought to be most suited to rural locations and all the *Länder* offer subsidies to farmers to diversify into farm tourism and help in marketing rural tourism enterprises. In the Czech Republic there are regional programmes to restructure agricultural production, create new jobs in the service sector and renew energy sources. There has been support of small businesses and Swain (1994) has noted the potential for revamping former machine stations as light industrial centres.

Infrastructure is another important concern, and for rural areas of the FGDR situated close to large urban centres, an improvement in transport links to encourage commuting is considered a priority. Improvements in village housing, infrastructure, environment and social and cultural amenities are important to maintain the present population, particularly young people, and to attract new people into rural areas. Villages participating in the *Dorferneuerung* scheme receive subsidies to cover 80 per cent of costs of community works (such as replanning a village centre) and up to half the cost of private works (such as housing renovation). The scheme has been effective for physical regeneration, but less successful in creating new jobs or safeguarding services. Meanwhile, in the Czech Republic, measures have been taken to cope with high unemployment, low incomes and a lack of opportunity outside agriculture, and to stabilize settlements suffering heavy out-migration through improvement in the housing stock. Local authorities have only modest resources but infrastructure, education and health are widely seen as priorities. It is difficult to see how there can be adequate resourcing for employment creation to bring about the desired rate of structural change in East European agriculture and there may be no significant reduction in the number of farms in Poland before the year 2010. On agricultural grounds, there is a good case for intervention that will facilitate the creation and smooth operation of a land market dealing with selling and leasing (Henry 1994) but such action needs to be balanced by social policies to improve social security and non-agricultural job creation.

International projects could make a difference, but apart from humanitarian aid the scale of assistance has been modest. To help with rural infrastructure, Poland has received a starting loan of US$200 million from the World Bank for roads and waterways, sewerage and telephones. About a quarter of the loan is earmarked for the development of SMEs, which should provide some opportunity for the unemployed. Albania has received gifts of farm machinery from Germany, and loans from China have facilitated the import of Chinese farm machinery. Agricultural joint ventures reflect foreign interest in Balkan agriculture, which make all the difference between cash-starved enterprises on the verge of bankruptcy and farms where investment has boosted efficiency and created export opportunities. Fiatagri has been involved in pilot projects in northern Albania for mechanizing the sowing and harvesting of maize and rice, employing machinery previously untried within the country. Provision of laser technology to help with soil levelling has also been beneficial in improving yields. Finally, the International Development Agency established a rural development fund to grant loans that will enable small farmers to buy implements, processing equipment and livestock in order to help establish small rural businesses. Initiatives of this kind are multiplying throughout the region with EU PHARE and EBRD as prominent agents where important innovations are involved. It is also worth adding that the concept of 'Euroregions' is significant for the regeneration of previously isolated border regions. A Carpathian region has been created through agreements by Hungary, Poland, Slovakia and Ukraine (with some Romanian participation) and in Hungary, the formerly underdeveloped and underpopulated western parts of Transdanubia have been transformed by the development of enterprise links across the border, particularly with Austria, where there are close economic and political links (Turnock 1996). Deric et al. (1996) refer to the need for new planning systems in marginal areas, which will overcome national frontiers: for example, a unified approach to the Drina Valley on the Bosnian–Serbian border. There are implications here for the development of local democracy and decentralization in favour of local administration.

As a final point in a survey which has ranged widely and, it is hoped, brought the issues of the countryside into the heart of the transition debate, it is appropriate to mention the importance of Western experience in regional development and the enterprise culture. There can be no guarantee that the peripherality of much of Eastern Europe can be overcome, but just as modern information flows make it politically impossible for rural poverty to coexist with urban prosperity, so it may be argued that the Internet and modern telecommunications in general will help the development of small rural centres so that they can become viable growth areas for small enterprises in the secondary and tertiary sectors in rural areas (Kłodziński 1992). Foreign investment may not filter all the way down the central place hierarchy but indigenous enterprise could find good uses for former cooperative farm and machine stations as recently suggested (Swain 1994, p.9). Derei and Djordevici (1996) have clearly differentiated between three growth scenarios for northern Serbia. A high-growth scenario means expansion in two complementary zones along the Danube, both upstream and downstream of Belgrade, avoiding too much pressure on the capital and the Iron Gates and inducing some return migration to the countryside. Moderate growth will mean further emigration by young people and increasing pressure on the district towns, while low growth will mean much emigration to Belgrade and Novi Sad, with little investment in rural infrastructure and little new housing outside the larger towns. The towns will be 'regional niches' without any of the growth in adjacent rural areas anticipated under the moderate growth and especially the rapid growth scenarios (ibid.). It is important that not only should the potential for growth be maximized, but that technology and 'know-how' should be available to ensure the stability of rural areas through a paradigm that will combine economic rationality (small food processing based on family farming), cultural values (identity linked with the traditions of the peasant class) and sound ecological practice (Kaleta 1996). Rural regeneration thus becomes a critical theme for research which needs greater attention by grant-awarding bodies in Western Europe (Helasiewicz 1996).

REFERENCES

Abraham, D. (1996), 'Cultural changes in rural communities in Romania', in R. Abrahams (ed.), *After Socialism: Land Reform and Rural Social Change in Eastern Europe*, Oxford: Berghahn Books.

Barbic, A. (1993), 'Rural development in the time of deconstructing the one-party political system and centrally planned economics', *Eastern European Countryside*, **3**, 41-7.

Bergmann, T. (1992), 'The reprivatization of farming in eastern Germany', *Sociologia Ruralis*, **32**, 305-16.

Bettram, G. (1992), 'Nature conservation and agricultural practices in Slovenia', in A. Gilg et al. (eds), *Progress in Rural Planning*, Vol. 2, London: Belhaven, pp.167-75.

Black, R. et al. (1995), *Rural Europe: Identity and Change*, London: Arnold.

Bojnec, S. (1994), 'Agricultural reform in Slovenia', in J.F.M. Swinnen (ed.), *Policy and Institutional Reform in Central European Agriculture*, Aldershot: Avebury, pp.135-68.

Braverman, A. et al. (eds) (1993), *The Agricultural Transition in Central and Eastern Europe and Former USSR*, Washington, DC: World Bank.

Brkic, S. and D. Zutinic 1993, 'The Croatian village and family farm under pressure of change', *Poljoprivedna znanstvena smotra*, No. 58, 165-76.

Brooks, K.M. and Z. Lerman (1994), 'Farm reform in the transition economies', *Finance and Development: A Quarterly Publication of the International Monetary Fund and the World Bank*, **31** (4), 25-8.

Civici, A. (1996), 'From subsistence to mixed farming: the model for agricultural development in Albania', in A. Barbic et al., *Rural Potentials for a Global Tomorrow*, Bucharest: International Rural Sociology Association with Bucharest University and the Romanian Academy, pp.99-100.

Cochrane, N.J. (1991), 'Prospects for Eastern Europe's private agriculture in the nineties', in J.R. Lampe (ed.), *Private Agriculture in Eastern Europe: Prospects for the 1990s and Lessons of the Pre-war Cooperatives and Land Reforms*, Washington, DC: Woodrow Wilson International Center, East European Studies Program, pp.81-102.

—— (1994), 'Farm restructuring in Central and Eastern Europe', *Soviet and Post-Soviet Review*, **21**, 319-35.

Constantinescu-Galiceni, V. (1996), 'Rural habitat and strategies of development in an area with ecological domination', in A. Barbic et al., *Rural Potentials for a Global Tomorrow*, Bucharest: International Rural Sociology Association with Bucharest University and the Romanian Academy, pp.83-4.

Csaki, C. (1990), 'Agricultural change in Eastern Europe at the beginning of the 1990s', *American Journal of Agricultural Economics*, **72**, 1733-42.

—— and Z. Lerman (1993), 'Land reform and the future role of cooperatives in agriculture in the former socialist countries of Europe', in C. Csaki and Y. Kislev (eds), *Agricultural Cooperatives in Transition*, Boulder, CO: Westview, pp.143-59.

Davidova, S. (1994), 'Changes in agricultural policies and restructuring of Bulgarian agriculture: an overview', in J.F.M. Swinnen (ed.), *Policy and Institutional Reform in Central European Agriculture*, Aldershot: Avebury, pp.31-76.

Derei, B. and D. Djordevici (1996), 'The future land use pattern in the Danube region of Serbia: a scenario approach', in C. Vert et al. (eds), *Proceedings of the Second Regional Geography Conference: Geographical Researches in the Carpathian-Danube Space*, Timişoară, Universitatea de Vest din Timişoară, Departamentul de Geografie, Vol. 1, pp.537-43.

Deric, B. et al. (1996), 'Sustainable development of marginal regions in FR Yugoslavia', in I.B. Bowler (ed.), *Research on the sustainability of rural systems*, Leicester: Leicester University Geography Department Occasional Paper 34, pp.99-100.

Dobreva, S. (1994), 'The family farm in Bulgaria: tradition and change', *Sociologia Ruralis*, **24**, 340-53.

—— (1996), 'Is land a fortune to the Bulgarian peasants?', in A. Barbic et al., *Rural Potentials for a Global Tomorrow*, Bucharest: International Rural Sociology Association with Bucharest University and the Romanian Academy, p.92.

—— and G. Koleva (1996), 'The ecological instability of the Bulgarian countryside today', in A. Barbic et al., *Rural Potentials for a Global Tomorrow* Bucharest: International Rural Sociology Association with Bucharest University and the Romanian Academy, p.89.

Doppler, W. (1994), 'Farming systems approach and its relevance for agricultural development in Central and Eastern Europe', in J.B. Dent and M.J. MacGregor (eds), *Rural and Farming Systems Analysis: European Perspectives*, Wallingford: CAB International, pp.65-77.

Draganova, M. (1996), 'Bulgarian countryside set in motion after standstill', in A. Barbic et al., *Rural Potentials for a Global Tomorrow*, Bucharest: International Rural Sociology Association with Bucharest University and the Romanian Academy, pp.94-5.

Elek, P.S. (1991), 'Part-time farming in Hungary: an instrument of tacit decollectivization?' *Sociologia Ruralis*, **31**, 82-8.

Enyedi, G. (1990), 'Private economic activity and regional development in Hungary', *Geographia Polonica*, **56**, 53-62.

Fekete, E.G. and L. Swain (1996), 'Preparation for a global tomorrow: local leadership development in an underdeveloped rural region of Hungary', in A. Barbic et al., *Rural Potentials for a Global Tomorrow*, Bucharest: International Rural Sociology Association with Bucharest University and the Romanian Academy p.93.

Ferruni, L. (1995), 'Opportunities for sustainable rural development in Albania', Paper presented at the 16th Congress of the European Society for Rural Sociology, Prague.

Fulea, M. and E. Sima (1996), 'Women's socio-economic condition in rural communities', in A. Barbic et al., *Rural Potentials for a Global Tomorrow*, Bucharest: International Rural Sociology Association with Bucharest University and the Romanian Academy, p.81.

Gabor, I. (1991), 'Private entrepreneurship and re-embourgoisement in Hungary', *Society and Economy*, **13**, 122-33.

Giordano, C. (1993), 'Not all roads lead to Rome', *Eastern European Countryside*, **1**, 5-16.

Gorlach, K. (1993), 'The embourgeoisement trajectory: how it works in Polish society', in J. Szmatka et al. (eds), *Eastern European Societies on the Threshold of Change*, Lampeter: Edwin Mellen Press, pp.161-74.

Gorzelak, G. (1996), *The Regional Dimension of Transformation in Central Europe*, London: Jessica Kingsley.

Hall, D.R. (1996), 'Albania: rural development migration and uncertainty', *GeoJournal*, **38**, 185-9.

Harcsa, I. (1993), 'Small scale farming, informal cooperation and the household economy in Hungary', *Sociologia Ruralis*, **33**, 105-8.

Helasiewicz, A. (1996), 'Rurality and the postmodern time', in A. Barbic et al., *Rural Potentials for a Global Tomorrow*, Bucharest: International Rural Sociology Association with Bucharest University and the Romanian Academy, p.96.

Henry, D.C. (1994), 'Reviving Romania's rural economy', *Radio Free Europe/Radio Liberty Research*, **3** (7), 18-23.

Hudečková, H. and M. Lošták (1992), 'Privatization of Czechoslovak agriculture: results of a 1990 sociological survey', *Sociologia Ruralis*, **32**, 287–304.
—— (1993), 'Privatization in the Czech agriculture', *Eastern European Countryside*, **3**, 47–56.
—— (1996), 'Relations to the globalisation challenge in the Czech agro-food complex', in A. Barbic et al., *Rural Potentials for a Global Tomorrow*, Bucharest: International Rural Sociology Association with Bucharest University and the Romanian Academy, pp.98–9.
Juhasz, J. (1991), 'Hungarian agriculture: present situation and future prospects', *European Review of Agricultural Economics*, **18**, 399–416.
Kaleta, A. (1993), 'In the search of new paradigms of rural development', *Eastern European Countryside*, **3**, 85–94.
—— (1996), 'Revitalisation of the CEE countryside', in A. Barbic et al., *Rural Potentials for a Global Tomorrow*, Bucharest: International Rural Sociology Association with Bucharest University and the Romanian Academy, pp.92–3.
Kapitanski, Y. and M. Anastasova (1994), 'Problems of social insurance in the agricultural sector during the transition to a market economy', in F. Grief (ed.), *Die Zukunft der ländlichen Infrastruktur in Ostmitteleuropa*, Vienna: Schriftenreihe der Bundesanstalt für Agrarwirtschaft 75, pp.33–8.
Karp, L. and S. Stefanou (1994), 'Domestic and trade policy for Central and East European agriculture', *Economics of Transition*, **2**, 345–71.
Kideckel, D.A. (1992), 'Peasants and authority in the new Romania', in D.N. Nelson (ed.), *Romania After Tyranny*, Boulder, CO: Westview, pp.67–81.
Klodzinski, M. (1992), 'Processes of agricultural change in Eastern Europe: the example of Poland', in R.M. Auty and R.B. Potter (eds), *Agricultural Change, Environment and Economy*, London: Mansell, pp.123–37.
Knight, G.C. (1995), 'The emerging water crisis in Bulgaria', *GeoJournal*, **35**, 415–23.
Kovach, I. (1991), 'Rediscovering small scale enterprise in rural Hungary', in S. Whatmore et al. (eds), *Rural Enterprise: Shifting Perspectives on Small Scale Production*, London: Fulton, pp.78–96.
—— (1994a), 'Privatization and family farms in Central and Eastern Europe', *Sociologia Ruralis*, **34**, 369–82.
—— (1994b), 'Part-time small-scale farming or a major form of economic pluriactivity in Hungary', in J. Szmatka et al. (eds), *Eastern European Societies on the Threshold of Change*, Lampeter: Edwin Mellen Press, pp.175–91.
Kovacs, D. (1993), 'Political change and the generation effect among agricultural cooperative managers in Hungary', *Sociologia Ruralis*, **33**, 100–104.
Kovacs, K. (1993), 'The slow transition of Hungarian agriculture', *Anthropological Journal of European Cultures*, **2**, 105–27.
Kozhunarova, V. (1996), 'The demographic potential and the future of the Bulgarian village', in A. Barbic et al., *Rural Potentials for a Global Tomorrow*, Bucharest: International Rural Sociology Association with Bucharest University and the Romanian Academy, pp.89–90.

Kraus, J. et al. (1994), 'Agricultural reform and transformation in the Czech Republic', in J.F.M. Swinnen (ed.), *Policy and Institutional Reform in Central European Agriculture*, Aldershot: Avebury, pp.107-34.

Leiby, J.D. and M.C. Marra (1993), 'Albanian agriculture: perspectives on the future', *Albanian Economic Tribune*, **1** (13), 24-5.

Lup, A. (1996), 'The evolution of the socio-economic structure of the Dobrogea village', in A. Barbic et al., *Rural Potentials for a Global Tomorrow*, Bucharest: International Rural Sociology Association with Bucharest University and the Romanian Academy, p.46.

Marsden, T. (1990), 'Towards the political economy of pluriactivity', *Journal of Rural Studies*, **6**, 375-82.

Meszaros, S. (1994), 'The reform process in Hungarian agriculture: an overview', in J.F.M. Swinnen (ed.), *Policy and Institutional Reform in Central European Agriculture*, Aldershot: Avebury, pp.77-106.

Monk, S. (1996), 'Problems of Bulgarian land reform', in D. Hall and D. Danta (eds), *Reconstructing the Balkans: A Geography of the New Southeastern Europe*, Chichester: Wiley, pp.179-86.

Morgan, W.B. (1992), 'Economic reform the free market and agriculture in Poland', *Geographical Journal*, **158**, 145-56.

Nemenyi, A. (1996a), 'New associations as modalities of modernisation in agriculture', in A. Barbic et al., *Rural Potentials for a Global Tomorrow*, Bucharest: International Rural Sociology Association with Bucharest University and the Romanian Academy, pp.68-9.

—— (1996b), 'New strategies of farming in Romania', in A. Barbic et al., *Rural Potentials for a Global Tomorrow*, Bucharest: International Rural Sociology Association with Bucharest University and the Romanian Academy, p.101.

Niehues-Jeuffroy, J. (1994), 'Les innovations dans les coopératives agricoles dans les nouveaux Länder', in M.-C. Maurel (ed.), *Les décollectivizations en Europe Centrale: itinéraires de privatisation*, Paris: Espace Rural 33, pp.41-50.

Pata, K. and M. Osmani (1994), 'Albanian agriculture: a painful transition from communism to free market challenges', *Sociologia Ruralis*, **24**, 71-83.

Pavlin, B. (1991), 'Contemporary changes in the agricultural use of land in the border landscape units of the Slovene littoral', *Geografica Slovenica*, **22**, 1-119.

Pine, F. (1992), 'Uneven burdens: women in rural Poland', in S. Rai et al. (eds), *Women in the Face of Change: The Soviet Union, Eastern Europe and China*, London: Routledge, pp.57-75.

—— (1993), '"The cows and pigs are his, the eggs are mine": women's domestic economy and entrepreneurial activity in rural Poland', in C.M. Hann (ed.), *Socialism: Ideals, Ideologies and Local Practice*, London: Routledge, pp.227-42.

—— (1994), 'Privatisation in post-socialist Poland: peasant women work and restructuring of the public sphere', *Cambridge Anthropology*, **17** (3), 19-42.

Ploaie, G. (1996), 'The impact of tourism and conservation on agriculture in the mountains of Valcea County, Romania', *GeoJournal*, **38**, 219-28.
Poledna, S. (1996), 'Conflict mediation in rural areas', in A. Barbic et al., *Rural Potentials for a Global Tomorrow*, Bucharest: International Rural Sociology Association with Bucharest University and the Romanian Academy, p.68.
Pozes, M. (1991), 'Development of rural settlements in the commune of Koper', *Geographica Slovenica*, **22**, 114 (in Slovenian with an English summary).
Pryor, F.L. (1992), *The Red and the Green: The Rise and Fall of Collectivised Agriculture in Marxist Regimes*, Princeton, NJ: Princeton University Press.
Repassy, H. and D. Symes (1993), 'Perspectives on agrarian reform in East Central Europe', *Sociologia Ruralis*, **33**, 81-91.
Rose, R. and E. Tikhomirov (1993), 'Who grows food in Russia and Eastern Europe?', *Post-Soviet Geography*, **34**, 111-26.
Sawicka, J. (1996), 'Changes in the socio-economic position of rural women in Poland', in A. Barbic et al., *Rural Potentials for a Global Tomorrow*, Bucharest: International Rural Sociology Association with Bucharest University and the Romanian Academy, pp.3-4.
Sebestyen, K. (1993), 'Transformation of cooperatives in Hungarian agriculture', in C. Csaki and Y. Kislev (eds), *Agricultural Cooperatives in Transition*, Boulder, CO: Westview, pp.301-9.
Sjöberg, O. (1991), *Rural Change and Development in Albania*, Boulder, CO: Westview.
Sobczak, M. (1996), 'Social welfare in the countryside in the transformation period toward market economy', in A. Barbic et al., *Rural Potentials for a Global Tomorrow*, Bucharest: International Rural Sociology Association with Bucharest University and the Romanian Academy, p.98.
Stambuk, M. (1991), 'Agricultural depopulation in Croatia', *Sociologia Ruralis*, **31**, 281-9.
Staziak, A. (1989), 'Changes in rural settlement in Poland up to 2000', *Geographia Polonica*, **56**, 109-14.
Stebelsky, I. (1995), *The Food System in the Post-Soviet Era*, Boulder, CO: Westview.
Surd, V. (1994), 'Critical status of rural Romania', in F. Grief (ed.), *Die Zukunft der ländlichen Infrastruktur in Ostmitteleuropa*, Vienna: Schriftenreihe der Bundesanstalt für Agrarwirtschaft 75, pp.61-7.
Swain, N. (1992), 'Transitions from collective to family farming in Post-Socialist Central Europe: Background and Strategies for Change', Liverpool: University of Liverpool Centre for Central and East European Studies Working Papers Rural Transition Series 5.
—— (1993a), *Transitions to Family Farming in Post-socialist Central Europe*, Liverpool: University of Liverpool Centre for Central and Eastern European Studies.
—— (1993b), *From Kolkhoz to Genuine Cooperative: Transition Problems in Central European Agriculture*, Liverpool: University of Liverpool Centre for Central and Eastern European Studies.

—— (1994), *Agricultural Development Policy in the Czech Republic: Is One Really Necessary?*, Liverpool: University of Liverpool Centre for Central and East European Studies Working Papers Rural Transition Series 34.

—— (1996), 'Rural employment and rural unemployment in the post-socialist countryside', *East European Countryside*, **2**, 5-16.

Swinnen, J.F.M. (ed.) (1994), *Overview of Policy and Institutional Reform in Central European Agriculture*, Aldershot: Avebury.

Szelenyi, I. (1988), *Socialist Entrepreneurs: Embourgeoisement in Rural Hungary*, Madison, WI: University of Wisconsin Press.

—— and R. Manchin (1986), *Peasants, Proletarians, Entrepreneurs: Transformation of Rural Social Structures Under State Socialism*, Madison, WI: University of Wisconsin Press.

Tanic, S. (ed.) (n.d.), *Agriculture in Croatia: A Strategy for Development*, Zagreb: Ministry of Agriculture and Forestry.

Toth, A. (1992), 'The social impact of restructuring in rural areas of Hungary: disruption of security or an end to the rural socialist middle class?', *Soviet Studies*, **44**, 1039-43.

Turnock, D. (1996), 'Cross-border cooperation as a factor in the development of transport in Eastern Europe', in A. Dingsdale (ed.), *Transport in Transition: Issues in the New Central and Eastern Europe*, Nottingham: Nottingham Trent University Trent Geographical Papers 1, pp.5-29.

Verbole, A. (1996), 'Making women visible: Slovenia's national action plans to promote the status of rural women in sustainable rural development', in A. Barbic et al., *Rural Potentials for a Global Tomorrow*, Bucharest: International Rural Sociology Association with Bucharest University and the Romanian Academy, p.3.

Verdery, K. (1994), 'The elasticity of land: problems of property restitution in Transylvania', *Slavic Review*, **53**, 1071-1109.

Vincze, M. (1996), 'Uncertainty about Romanian agricultural development', in A. Barbic et al., *Rural Potentials for a Global Tomorrow*, Bucharest: International Rural Sociology Association with Bucharest University and the Romanian Academy, p.101.

Vladimirova, K. and R. Rangelova (1996), 'Welfare and employment of village populations in Bulgaria', in A. Barbic et al., *Rural Potentials for a Global Tomorrow*, Bucharest: International Rural Sociology Association with Bucharest University and the Romanian Academy, pp.97-8.

Vogler, I. (1996), 'Privatisation of agriculture in Eastern Germany: geographical consequences', in I.R. Bowler (ed.), *Research on the Sustainability of Rural Systems*, Leicester: Leicester University Geography Department Occasional Paper 34, pp.61-3.

Vrišer, I. (1993), 'Agrarian economy in Slovenia', *GeoJournal*, **31**, 373-7.

Wecławowicz, G. (1996), *Contemporary Poland: Space and Society*, London: UCL Press.

Wierzbicki, Z.T. (1996), 'Dimitrie Gusti amd his school', *East European Countryside*, **2**, 109-14.

Wilson, O. (1996), 'Emerging patterns of restructured farm businesses in Eastern Germany', *GeoJournal*, **38**, 157-60.

Wiska, A. and J. Hindson (1991), 'Protecting a Polish paradise', *Geographical Magazine*, **63** (6), 1-2.

Wojciechowski, K.H. (1996), 'Dilemmas in the restructuring of rural areas in eastern Poland', in I.R. Bowler (ed.), *Research on the Sustainability of Rural Systems*, Leicester: Leicester University Geography Department Occasional Paper 34, pp.117-18.

Young, C. (1993), 'A bitter harvest?: Problems of restructuring in East Central European agriculture', *Geography*, **78**, 69-72.

Zanga, L. (1994), 'Albania optimistic about economic growth', *Radio Free Europe/Radio Liberty Research*, **3** (7), 14-7.

Zimbrek, T. and D. Zutinic (1996), 'Arrangement renewal and development of rural areas and agricultural resources of the Republic of Croatia', *East European Countryside*, **2**, 59-70.

Index

abandonment 51, 114, 117, 160, 210
  see also farm abandonment
Abrud 235
Academy of Sciences 182
accessibility 26, 52, 58, 70, 114, 216, 217, 235, 241, 341, 378, 382-3
acidification, acid rain 23, 137
acquaculture *see* fishing
active population 5, 28, 88, 93, 105, 110, 115, 154, 158-9, 178, 204, 261, 267, 269, 276, 292, 297, 366, 378, 380
adjustment *see* restructuring
administration, administrative centres 6, 13-14, 16, 21, 30, 33-6, 50, 55, 62, 120, 123, 163, 171, 201, 241, 253, 269, 291, 342
  see also government and local government
Adriatic 14, 60, 291, 388
advanced regions *see* growth areas
advice *see* information
aesthetic quality *see* landscape quality
affluence 6-7, 25, 27, 78, 113, 146, 162, 252, 325-6, 360, 362, 379, 393
afforestation 76, 214
  see also woodlands
Africa 87
ageing 15, 28, 31, 52, 79, 110, 118, 296, 382
Agency for Farm Ownership (Poland) 177
Agrargesellchaften (East Germany) 358
Agrarian Reform Act (FFRY) 275
agrarian *see* agricultural
agribusiness 87-8, 230
  see also agricultural-industrial complex
agricultural-industrial complexes (Bulgaria) 17, 19
agricultural adjustment, development 27, 30, 138, 140, 172, 182, 193, 197, 221, 232, 235, 243-4, 350, 382
  see also modernization

agricultural advisory service 232, 233, 252, 262
  see also agronomist and professionals
agricultural chemicals *see* chemicals, fertilizer etc.
agricultural college, institute, university 16, 57, 235, 252, 271
agricultural depots *see* food storage
agricultural education 57
agricultural employment, population, workforce 5, 14-17, 26, 51, 72-4, 78, 84, 95, 103, 105-10, 122-6, 130, 134-7, 141, 146, 153, 158, 160, 171-2, 175, 177, 179, 189, 196, 206, 207, 230-31, 251, 253-6, 267-8, 276-7, 286, 292, 356, 358-9, 363, 380, 383, 390
agricultural enterprise, structure 145-6, 149, 151, 171, 193, 196, 202, 253, 266, 269, 357-68
  see also farm business
agricultural equipment 8, 56-7, 84, 98, 117, 140, 158-9, 162, 221, 229, 231, 252, 325-6, 357, 361, 366, 392
agricultural exports *see* exports
agricultural imports *see* imports
Agricultural Land Ownership and Land Use Law (Bulgaria) 69
agricultural machinery 8, 10, 14-15, 19, 21-2, 25, 51-2, 55-7, 76, 81, 84, 88, 95, 123-4, 128, 145-7, 157, 159-60, 169, 171, 177, 180-84, 190-91, 196-8, 210, 213-15, 219, 221-2, 235, 252, 257, 260, 280-82, 305, 317, 335, 342, 364-8, 371, 375, 380, 388, 392
  see also machine-tractor stations
Agricultural Marketing Agency (Poland) 389
Agricultural Marketing Office (Hungary) 388
agricultural missions 55-6
agricultural policy 14, 124-5, 128, 131,

401

135-6, 138, 141, 148, 159, 165, 262, 298
  see also government and Ministry of Agriculture
agricultural production, regions 8-10, 13-15, 18-19, 21, 23, 26, 37, 50-52, 55-7, 74-7, 79-85, 89, 93-104, 116-17, 123, 130, 138, 145-50, 153, 155-6, 158, 162, 163-7, 169, 171, 174-5, 180-81, 186, 190-91, 196-8, 200, 206, 209, 220-21, 225-6, 229-30, 233, 243, 252, 251, 261-4, 271, 275-8, 279-96, 302, 307, 310-11, 316-17, 321-2, 333, 341, 358, 361, 369-75, 382, 386-91
agricultural quota *see* quota
agricultural reform *see* land reform
agricultural school 31, 229, 271
agricultural society 236, 343
Agricultural Structure and Coastal Protection Programme (East Germany) 128
agricultural subsidies *see* subsidies
Agriculture Adjustment Act (East Germany) 125
Agriculture Credit Programme (East Germany) 130
agriculture, agricultural land 49-57, 69-85, 94-113, 123, 145-58, 163-97
  see also under individual land uses
Agrifoods 57
agrogorod 30, 32
Agroindustrial Councils for State and Cooperative Farms (Romania) 22, 201, 241
agroindustrial town (Romania) 32
agroindustry 56, 357, 363, 376
  see also agribusiness
Agrokompleks Sudety 16
Agromecs (Romania) 221
agronomist 83, 156, 362, 389
agrotechnology *see* technology
agrotourism 116-17, 136, 164, 196, 197, 230, 236-9, 288, 298, 311-12, 331-51, 379, 384
  see also tourism
air pollution 23, 85-7, 385
airport, air transport 251, 352
Alba, Alba Iulia 224, 234, 345-6
Albania, Albanians 1-6, 9, 11-13, 27-9, 49-68, 201, 301, 334, 358, 364, 370, 372-5, 377-8, 385, 387, 389-90, 392
Albitalia 57

alcohol, alcoholism 83, 316, 325-6, 378
Alexandria 224-6
Alps 13, 26, 59, 288, 291, 292
Alps-Adria Working Community 37
amalgamation 16, 20, 31, 34, 36, 123, 202, 357
amenities *see* rural services and services
America 30, 275, 288
  see also Canada and USA
anarchy 51
animal feed *see* fodder
animal husbandry, animals *see* cattle, livestock etc.
apartment blocks 25, 114
apples 313, 328
Apuseni 233, 236-9, 340, 347-8
arable farming *see* cropping
Arad 210, 212-14, 224, 234
archaeology 59, 339
architecture 59-60, 62, 78, 136, 236-7, 333, 335, 340, 342, 350
Argeş 204-5, 225, 234, 345
aromatic plants 57, 65, 301
artisans 60, 268
  see also handicrafts and workshops
assets 146, 177, 222, 244, 368
associated municipalities (FCS) 34
association (Romania) 207-10, 229, 237, 241
Association of Food Producers by Ecological Methods (Poland) 303-4, 306, 311
Athens 62
attar of roses *see* roses
Australia 313
Austria-Hungary *see* Habsburg Empire
Austria 18, 60, 118, 163, 220, 228, 236, 267, 275, 303, 314, 318, 392
automomy 18, 34-5, 124
autumn 219-21, 238, 325
Aveyron 229

Babia Góra 332
baby food 313, 315
Bacău 204-5, 224-6, 227, 234, 345, 352
backward area 13, 18, 26, 31, 35-6, 56, 74, 110, 118, 134-5, 140, 142, 160-63, 173, 193, 197, 268, 275, 296, 342-3, 381-2, 384, 392
Baia Mare 224, 243
Baja 161
bakery, baking 84, 331, 361

Index

balance of payments 146, 389
Balaton Lake 164, 316-17, 333
Balkans 1, 6, 8, 37-8, 236, 348, 363, 382, 392
Baltic 6
Banat 204, 228, 344
bankruptcy 145, 159, 176, 203, 218, 228, 315, 360, 366-7, 376, 392
banks 88-9, 176, 209, 219-22, 262, 272, 275, 279, 291, 313, 322, 338, 341, 389
Banská Bystrica 252-5, 268
Bărăgan 3, 10, 218, 237
Bardejov 253-5, 268
barley 71, 75-7, 79, 102, 209, 218, 221, 238, 263
barter 324-5
Bass 319
Bathore 63
Bavaria 232, 244, 360, 384
beaches 59
beans 220
beef, beef cattle 120, 130
bees 77
Beius 235
Békés, Békéscsaba 160-61
Belgium 84, 226, 319, 345-6
Beliş 348
Benešov 97-8, 100-101, 106-7
Bengrain 321
Berisha, S. 63
Berlin, Berlin Wall 27, 36, 121, 132-3, 138, 381
Beroun 97-8, 100-101, 106-7
Beskids 94
Bezirke 120
Biała Podlaska 170, 174, 176, 179, 184, 186-8, 193, 193-6
Białystok 170, 174, 176, 179, 184, 186-8, 189, 190, 193, 195-6, 306, 374
Bielsko-Biała 35, 178, 184, 309
Bihor 204, 212, 234, 241-4, 345
biocorridor, bioline 16, 23
biodiversity 85, 112, 229, 343, 385
biofood, bioproduction *see* organic farming
biogas 116
biosphere reserves 137
birds 87
birth control, birth rate 62, 79, 134, 292
Bistriţa, Bistriţa-Năsăud 204, 224, 234, 343
black earth 170

Black Sea 6, 38, 74, 87, 237, 344
Blansko 97-8, 100-101, 106-7
blending 316
boarding house 115, 348, 378
Bod 226
bogs 137
Bohemia 33, 36
see also Central Bohemia, East Bohemia etc.
Bohemian-Moravian Uplands 103-4, 108
bonds 54
border *see* frontier
Borsod-Abrauj-Zemplen 153, 160
Bosnia-Hercegovina 2, 29, 49, 370, 392
Botevgrad 85
Botoşani 224, 227, 234
bottling 316, 319
Boubin 112
boundaries 70, 74
see also frontier
Braila 6, 205, 212, 224, 234
Bran 338, 345, 347-8
Brandenburg 121-2, 129, 132-3, 381
Braşov 204, 222, 224, 234, 243, 338, 345-6
Bratislava 251, 253-5, 266, 268, 314
Braun und Brunnen 318, 320
BrauUnion 319
bread 56, 77, 218, 221
bread grains *see* cereals
Břeclav 97-8, 100-101, 106-7
breeds 10
see also crop breeding
brewing 151, 221, 225, 312, 318-20, 358
BrewInvest 320
brigade 50
British Sugar 315
Brno 9, 97-8, 100-101, 106-7, 318-19
brown earth 170
Bruntál 97-8, 100-101, 106-7, 387
Brzeg 320
Bucegi 237, 334, 340
Bucharest 222, 225, 229, 235-8, 314, 341
Budapest 18, 37, 161, 163, 317, 333
buffalo 77
building materials 117, 137, 180-81, 190, 209, 232
buildings *see* factories, farm buildings, housing etc.
Bulgaria 1-5, 9-10, 12-13, 17, 19, 28-9, 32, 34, 69-92, 228, 314, 320-21, 357-8, 361, 365, 369-70, 372-3, 377,

381, 385, 389-90
Bulgarians 70, 72, 78
bureaucracy *see* administration
Burgas 71, 73-4, 79-80, 86, 320, 385
bus 58, 115, 118, 379
business shares (Hungary) 152-5, 158, 160
business, business culture 11, 17, 34, 99, 136, 147-50, 152, 155-7, 159-61, 163-5, 229, 243, 244, 321, 324, 333-7, 350, 360, 363-4, 366-7, 378, 386, 393
see also private enterprise, small- and medium-sized businesses etc.
butter 227, 315, 384
buying *see* market
Buzău 204-5, 224, 226-8, 234, 240, 328, 330
Bydgoszcz 170, 174, 176, 179, 184, 186-8, 193, 195-6, 306

Cadbury Schweppes 320
Čadca 253-5, 268
cadmium 86
Călărasi 205, 212, 224-6, 230, 234
camping, campsite 26, 113, 333
Câmpulung Moldovenesc 235
canning 151, 228
capital, capitalism 7, 12, 37, 51-2, 57, 62, 65, 74, 131, 145-6, 152, 155, 157, 159-60, 163, 165, 173-4, 182, 188, 193, 197, 201, 210, 216, 219-21, 230-32, 244, 252, 259, 282, 297, 301, 302, 317, 321, 338, 356, 363, 366, 368, 376, 382, 384
see also investment
Caras-Severin 212, 234, 329, 345
career 11, 15, 51, 244
Carinthia 275
Carpathians 21, 24, 35, 193, 232-4, 332-50, 384, 389, 392
carpets 350
carrots 305
cars 113, 134, 228
cash crops 53, 65, 302
see also industrial crops
catering 26, 65, 164, 198, 332-3, 344-5, 348-9
cattle 8, 17-18, 50, 52-3, 76-7, 79, 81-2, 86, 108, 181, 183, 191, 194, 195, 212-14, 215-19, 230, 235, 264, 266, 282, 287, 288, 341, 389
see also beef cattle and dairy cattle

Ceauşescu, N. 32, 201-2, 239
Central Bohemia 98, 104, 118
Central Europe, Central and Eastern Europe 1, 102, 274, 279
central planning *see* planning
Central, Non-Central Settlements (FCS) 109
centralization 17, 138, 325, 364
see also planning
Centrally Guided Enterprises (FCS) 94
ceramics 343
cereals 8-9, 14-15, 19, 50, 53, 71, 77, 79-80, 86, 147, 151, 181, 186, 191-2, 193-5, 200, 209, 211, 216-17, 218-22, 228, 230, 252, 260, 262-3, 265-6, 280, 287, 288, 305, 311, 324, 358, 370-72, 374, 382, 388
Česká Lípa 97-8, 100-101, 106-7, 387
České Budějovice 97-8, 100-101, 106-7, 318-19
Česky Krumlov 97-8, 100-101, 106-7, 387
cesspools 108, 385
see also slurry
chalets 113, 332, 334
charities 52
Cheb 99-100, 100-101, 104, 106-7, 373
cheese 216, 227, 266, 301, 305, 314-15, 321-2
Chelm 170, 174, 176, 179, 184, 186-8, 193-6
chemical industry 10, 58, 85, 213, 237, 266-7
chemicals 18, 58, 88, 108, 257, 302, 371, 382, 385
see also fertilizer and pesticides
Chernobyl 85
chernozem 1, 251
children 11, 53, 57, 63, 136, 258, 268, 364, 381
see also infant mortality
China 392
chocolate *see* confectionery
Chomutov 97-8, 100-101, 106-7
Christian Democratic Party (Slovenia) 298
Chrudim 97-8, 100-101, 106-7
church 25, 78, 123, 257, 275, 302, 352-3
see also religion
Ciechanów 170, 174, 176, 179, 184, 186-8, 193, 195-6
cigarettes *see* tobacco
cinema 30, 291

Ciorbea, V. 243
Ciulnița 218
civil society *see* democracy and social change
climatic station, climate 1, 15, 59, 83, 87, 160, 163, 169, 190–91, 219, 221, 228, 252, 288, 290, 324, 337, 350
closure 18, 95, 105, 131, 134, 203, 218, 267, 314, 318, 388
see also abandonment
Cluj, Cluj-Napoca 224–6, 227, 234, 235, 345
coach *see* bus
coal 99, 111, 140
coalition 148, 150
coast 10, 14, 35, 50, 54, 58, 60, 62, 79, 237, 291, 334, 374–5, 378–9
coercion 5, 8, 11, 21, 69
collaboration *see* cooperation
collectivisation 7, 8, 11–12, 14, 30, 36, 49–51, 69–70, 74, 78, 83–4, 122–3, 131, 134, 160, 200–202, 232, 274–9, 279, 291, 322, 324–6, 334, 356, 363, 377
see also cooperative farms
Comecon 14, 18, 74, 82, 102
command economy *see* communism and planning
commassation *see* consolidation
commerce, commercial centres 6, 25, 159, 165, 333, 339, 341, 366, 378, 381, 384
see also markets and trade
Commission for Mountainous Regions (Romania) 233, 341–3, 389
commodity exchanges 190
Common Agricultural Policy (CAP) 388
commonland 75–6, 275
communications *see* telecommunications and transport
communist party, power 8, 11, 20, 69, 72, 74, 78, 84–5, 87–8, 93, 95, 102, 109–10, 114, 145, 148–9, 151, 160, 171, 178, 181, 195, 200, 201, 207, 223, 229, 230, 232–5, 267, 271, 275–80, 286, 291, 296, 301, 303, 305, 326, 328–30, 332, 334–5, 347, 359–60, 362, 364, 371, 375, 377–9, 384–5, 388
see also coercion, state socialism etc.
community facilities *see* rural services
community *see* rural community
commuter, commuting 15, 26–7, 35, 115–16, 136, 160, 163–4, 171, 179, 202, 290, 292, 347, 391
companies *see* farm companies and individual foreign companies
Comparative Research Institute (Hungary) 153
compensation 8, 54–5, 122, 128, 205, 274, 333, 358
Compensation and Indemnity Act (East Germany) 126
competition 18, 52, 55, 117, 125, 134, 136, 142, 151, 163, 164, 181, 205–6, 209, 225, 227, 231, 241, 275, 279, 298, 313, 315–16, 318–19, 333, 374, 390
compulsory purchase *see* expropriation
computing *see* technology
confectionery 151, 312–13, 321
confiscation *see* expropriation
conservation 22–3, 60, 108–12, 135, 165, 218, 237, 312, 340, 386–7
consolidation 7–8, 31–3, 51, 58, 70, 81, 196, 207, 208, 217, 230, 233, 257, 269, 275–9, 286, 305, 315, 341, 363, 391
Constanța 6, 204, 212, 224–6, 228, 234, 345
construction 16, 27, 34, 65, 80, 105, 109, 113, 116, 118, 123, 146, 171, 174–5, 178, 183, 209–10, 232–5, 328, 332, 347–8, 382
consumer, consumer goods, consumption 14, 55, 98, 138, 164, 223–6, 301, 306, 367, 371, 377–8, 383, 386, 388–9
see also market
contamination 23, 85–7, 124, 137, 385
see also pollution
contract farming 220–21, 226, 318
conurbation *see* urban settlement
conversion 103–4, 109, 113, 117–18, 135, 164, 228, 272, 280, 373, 386
convertible currency *see* foreign exchange
cooperation, cooperative 8, 10, 18, 37, 230, 236, 252–3, 267, 275, 279, 314, 339, 346
see also cooperative farm
Cooperative Associations (East Germany) 123
cooperative farm members 16, 50, 54, 108, 146, 152–4, 156–60, 163–5, 202–3, 205, 209–10, 257–8, 271, 362, 368
cooperative farms 9, 11, 15–16, 18–19, 25–6, 30–31, 50–52, 54, 58, 80–81, 87–8, 94–5, 98–9, 102–3, 105, 117, 123–5,

130-31, 136, 141, 145-65, 170-71, 200-201, 217-19, 232-3, 237, 239, 241, 252-9, 264, 266-71, 275-6, 279, 283-7, 297, 301, 317, 356-8, 360-68, 371, 375-76, 379, 387, 393
  see also LPG
coordination *see* cooperation
copper 33, 326, 330
core-periphery *see* backward areas, growth areas and regional variations
Corfu 60
Costantinescu, E. 241-6
Costeşti 217
costs 15, 55, 78, 85, 87, 115, 128, 130, 134, 141, 146-7, 155-6, 160, 163, 176, 178, 193, 201, 205, 208, 216, 217, 219, 226-8, 237, 262, 264, 275, 283, 287, 297, 310, 317, 321, 338, 371, 374, 378-9, 388
cottage, cottage industry *see* housing, second homes and rural industry
Cottbus 23
cotton 9, 50, 52-3, 75-6, 375
Council for Mutual Economic Assistance *see* Comecon
Council of Europe 112, 343
countryside *see under* land use and rural issues
coupon method (privatization) 95, 160, 359, 367
courthouse 290
Covasna 204, 234
Cozia 237, 340
Cracow 170, 173-4, 176, 179, 183-4, 186-8, 193, 195-6, 306, 313, 320
crafts, craft skills *see* handicrafts
Craiova 220, 224-7, 235
credit, credit cooperative 19, 31, 52, 56-8, 84, 88, 148, 153, 158, 160, 219-22, 227-8, 271-2, 279, 283, 286, 296, 339, 341, 364-66, 387, 391
crime 79, 378
crisis 7, 14, 83, 145, 147, 163-4, 165, 252
Croatia 1-2, 21, 29, 37, 359, 363, 370, 372-3, 376, 382-3, 387
crofter *see* smallholder
crop breeding *see* plant breeding
crop specialization *see* specialization
crop spraying *see* chemicals
crop varieties *see* plant breeding
crop zonation *see* agricultural regions

crops, cropping 3, 7, 9-10, 13-16, 19, 24, 50, 52, 55-6, 74-5, 82, 84-6, 94, 102, 104, 109, 123, 130, 147, 156, 160, 163, 169-70, 191, 200, 202, 205-6, 209, 211-20, 230, 243, 251-2, 258-9, 263-6, 271, 277, 286-7, 288, 304, 307, 325-6, 333, 335, 365, 373, 386, 388, 390
  see also cereals, industrial crops etc.
crown domains 8
Cserehat 381
cucumber 220
cuisine *see* catering
cultural facitilies, heritage 25, 59-60, 112, 123, 136, 138, 172, 244, 257, 337, 350, 381
  see also folklore
Curtea de Argeş 216
customs, customs-free zones 37, 226, 320
cycling 58, 135, 333
Czech Lands, Czech Republic 93-119, 134, 198, 228, 252, 341, 347, 365, 369-70, 376, 378, 382, 386-91
Czechoslovakia (FCS) 1-5, 7, 9, 11-16, 23, 28-9, 33-4, 251, 252, 257, 267, 313, 315-16, 318, 365, 370-71, 377, 385, 390
Częstochowa 170, 174, 176, 179, 184, 186-8, 193, 195-6

dairy cattle, dairying 52, 64, 130-31, 151, 181, 217-19, 232, 241-6, 267-8, 279, 280, 282, 288, 298, 311, 313-15, 321, 332, 334-5, 337-9, 350, 359, 371, 375, 388, 390
  see also cheese, milk etc.
Dalmatia 17
Dâmboviţa 204, 225, 234, 345
dams 23, 55
  see also hydroelectricity
Danube 6, 10, 71, 74, 77, 79, 237, 251-2, 262-4, 268, 328, 344-5, 381, 389
Dark Ages 6
Dayton Accord 49
Debrecen 161
debt 15, 22, 95, 98, 128, 145, 176, 203, 217, 275, 283, 287, 297, 317, 360
decentralization 50, 258, 359, 387
Děčín 97-8, 100-101, 106-7
decision-making 8, 19, 59, 148, 231, 361, 364-5, 381
decollectivization 69, 75, 98

decree *see* law
deficit *see* shortage
deforestation 238
demand *see* consumer *and* market
democracy, democratic society 93, 95, 241, 321, 338, 347, 392, 356
Democratic Party (Albania) 51, 63
demography *see* population
demonstration farm 8, 229, 261, 342, 358
  see also pilot project
Denmark 84, 313, 316
depopulation 27, 30–31, 36, 61, 78, 89, 160, 231, 292, 363, 367, 371, 381–2
deportation 11, 105
depressed area, depression 145, 163, 267
  see also backward area
dereliction, derelict land 137, 140
desalination 10, 50
detergent 320
Deva 224–6
devaluation *see* land value
development area, zone *see* growth area
development *see* agricultural development, industrial development, planning etc.
Development Stimulation and Demographically Endangered Areas Act (Slovenia) 296
Devnja 87
diaspora *see* émigré
Dibër 63, 378
differential bonuses (FCS) 102
Dimitrovgrad 32
disease *see* medical services
dissolution *see* abandonment
distilling 177, 217, 301, 317, 321–32
diversification 8, 26, 50, 57, 136, 140–41, 193, 196, 202, 222, 231–45, 267–72, 303, 311–12, 320, 322, 331, 333–5, 338–9, 343–51, 360–62, 376, 378, 381–4, 389–92
  see also pluriactivity
dividends 153–4, 158
Dobrogea 3, 10
documentation *see* information
Dolj 204, 234
dollar *see* foreign exchange
Dolný Kubín 253–5
Domažlice 97–8, 100–101, 106–7
domestic tourism *see* tourism
Dorferneuerung (East Germany) 136–7, 141, 391
Drăgan 348

drainage 10, 50, 160
  see also sewerage
Dresden 27, 120, 138, 140, 381
Drin 55, 392
drink 64, 151, 225, 312–13, 317–18, 347
drinking water 24, 63, 184–5
Drobeta-Turnu Severin 223–5
drought 23, 51, 83, 169, 191, 193, 210, 217, 238, 373, 382
drug addiction 378
Ducros 55
dumping 216
Dunajská Streda 253–5, 262, 268, 271, 389
Durrës 9, 50, 55, 57, 60, 63, 358, 378

earnings *see* income
East Berlin *see* Berlin
East Bohemia 98, 103–4, 105–8
East Germany (FGDR) 1–5, 12–17, 23, 27–9, 31, 33–4, 36, 120–44, 333, 364, 370–73, 377, 381, 386, 391
East Slovakia 252, 259, 262–3
ecoagriculture, ecofarming *see* organic farming
ecological issues *see* environmental awareness and environmental damage
economy, economic growth, economic restructuring 58, 69, 74, 93, 110, 134, 145–6, 148–50, 160–61, 171–2, 177, 182, 198, 231, 261, 279, 296, 298, 312, 360, 369
  see also restructuring
ecotourism *see* tourism and sustainability
edible oil *see* oil plants
education 15, 25–7, 32, 108, 113, 163, 172, 193, 233, 235–8, 237, 252, 268, 297, 306, 308, 313, 342, 348, 362, 377, 381–2, 384
  see also schools
efficiency 8, 15, 17–18, 60, 155–6, 197, 216, 219–32, 239, 244, 279, 283, 325, 330, 356–7, 360–61, 363, 374, 392
Eger 161, 164, 316–17, 333
eggs 75–6, 98, 215, 218, 223
Egypt 57, 65
Eighteenth Century 6
Eisenhüttenstadt 32
Ekoglasnost 85–6, 385
Elbląg 71, 174, 176, 179, 184, 186–8, 193, 195–6, 306
elderly people 134, 142, 153, 159, 172,

203, 209, 280, 359, 363, 365–6, 377
electrical equipment, electricity 58, 63, 137, 183–4, 185–6, 189, 225, 231–4, 235–8, 288, 335, 342, 344, 348, 379
Elena 85
elite 25, 205, 377
embourgeoisement 18, 356
emigration 30, 60–61, 66, 252, 267, 288, 382, 393
émigré 57, 61
emissions *see* air pollution
employee–management buyout 225
employment 6, 13–14, 16, 31–2, 36–7, 56–7, 59, 63, 65, 146, 154–6, 160, 163, 166, 171, 173, 176–7, 196, 202, 229, 267, 269, 292, 296, 319, 333–5, 338, 362, 365, 376–7, 379, 384, 387, 391
energy *see* electricity and renewable energy
engineering 223, 233, 368
   see also agricultural machinery
enlargement *see* expansion
enterprise, entrepreneur *see* business culture
environmental awareness, management, policy 24, 62, 85, 87, 102, 108, 110–13, 116–17, 125, 135–6, 141, 145, 164, 238, 266, 302, 306, 312, 332, 334, 345, 385–7, 393
environmental damage, problems 17, 22–4, 35, 60, 78, 84–8, 99, 108–9, 111, 124, 137, 142, 166, 229, 237, 263, 292, 294, 332, 385–7
environmental inspectorate 87
environmentally friendly *see* sustainable
equality, equalization 33, 35, 135, 195
Erfurt 138, 381
erosion 10, 22, 24, 85–6, 103, 108, 239–40, 303, 382, 384, 387
estates 6–7, 70, 122, 126, 200, 203
ethnic minorities *see* minorities
ethnography *see* folklore
Eurasia 87
Eurogîtes 343
Euromontana 343
Europe 83, 196, 216, 335, 374
European Bank for Reconstruction and Development (EBRD) 58, 383, 392
European Commission (EC) 124, 141
European Strategy of Biological and Landscape Diversity 112

European Union (EU) 58, 82, 102, 117, 120, 136, 138, 141–2, 196, 221, 228, 243, 278, 282, 297–8, 314, 341, 346, 348, 350, 368, 385, 388, 390, 392
   see also PHARE
European Union Structural Fund 136
Euroregions 197, 392
eviction *see* expropriation
expansion 31, 36, 54, 146, 196
expenses *see* costs
experience, expertise 17, 111, 131, 158–9, 163, 206, 221, 302, 312, 316, 319, 328, 331, 342, 360–61, 364, 366, 374–6, 393
experimental farms *see* demonstration farms and research
exports 10, 15, 18, 22, 37, 61, 65, 81, 83, 102, 145–6, 165, 196, 200, 209, 216, 217, 243, 267, 287, 296, 302–3, 311, 313–16, 319–20, 357, 369–71, 375, 389–90, 392
expropriation 7, 51, 54, 63, 94–5, 122–3, 126, 148, 202, 205, 256, 275–9, 279, 283, 325–6, 357–8
expulsion 13, 114, 160
extensification 120, 135, 371
   see also conversion and non-chemical systems
external aid *see* foreign aid

factories 15, 25–6, 57, 174, 204, 220, 225–8, 239, 291, 292, 315–21, 325, 331, 335, 375, 380
Făgăraş 334, 350
fairs 324
Fakijska 86
fallow 191–2, 373, 377, 382
   see also social fallow
family farm 14, 19, 51, 53, 95, 124, 130–31, 136, 138, 141, 156, 200, 231, 333–50, 360–61, 363–4, 368, 375, 393
family *see* household
Far East 317
farm abandonment 13–14, 51, 56, 122–3, 178, 275–6, 279, 292, 297, 317, 357, 360, 366, 373, 375
farm amalgamation *see* amalgamation
farm association (Albania) 53, 56, 58
farm buildings 9, 16, 19, 22, 95, 98, 117, 123–4, 128, 136–7, 140, 146–8, 159, 218, 232, 236, 257, 301, 328–31, 371
farm business, enterprise 5, 98, 122, 125,

Index

128-33, 138, 142, 230-31, 276-9, 357-68, 371
  see also cooperative farm, small farm, state farm etc.
farm companies, partnerships 95, 99, 130, 157, 159-60, 202-4, 258, 260, 267, 358-60, 364-77
farm debts *see* indebtedness
farm diversification *see* diversification
farm income *see* incomes
farm machinery *see* agricultural machinery
farm management 6, 23, 108, 111, 116, 123, 134, 157-8, 209, 218, 251, 256-9, 267, 279, 283, 286, 317, 357-60, 363, 367, 371, 374, 376, 381, 389
farm profits *see* profits
farm quota *see* quota
farm structure *see* farm business
farm subsidies *see* subsidies
farm tourism *see* agrotourism
farm workers *see* agricultural employment
Farmers' Circles (Poland) 21, 182
farms *see* cooperative farms, small farms
fattening *see* livestock fattening
fauna 348
Federal government, federation 1, 120, 124, 130-31, 135-6, 138, 141
Federation of Associated Privatized Farms (Romania) 230
feminization 15, 30, 53, 172, 269, 376
fertility *see* soil fertility
fertilizer 1, 10, 15-16, 19, 23, 59, 87-8, 108, 117, 124, 176, 180-81, 190, 194, 196, 207, 214, 220, 221, 226, 229, 235, 239, 257, 259, 303, 342, 365, 371, 375, 382, 385, 387-8
festival *see* fair
feudal lords 6-7, 78, 274
feudalism, feudal services 6-7, 37, 274
  see also feudal lords and serfs
Fiat 222
Fiatagri 55, 392
fields, field system 14, 16, 20, 30, 52, 74, 85, 108, 169, 172, 259, 328, 350, 379
Fier 9, 50
finance 34, 51, 84, 87, 95, 102, 128, 135, 140-42, 151, 154, 158-9, 163, 177, 180, 182, 190, 217, 219, 220, 226, 228, 241, 254, 271-2, 275, 279, 296, 339, 341-2, 347, 350, 360, 364, 366, 368, 374, 385, 388-9
  see also capital

First World War 160, 200, 275, 352
fish, fish farming, fisheries 15, 59, 77, 81, 164, 305, 311, 333, 337-8, 387-9
flax 9
floodplain 10, 252
flora *see* flowers
flour, flourmill 81, 225, 330
flowers 9, 20, 225, 338-9
Flurneuordnung (East Germany) 125
Focşani 224
fodder 9-10, 14, 17, 53, 77, 81, 86, 102, 176, 186, 190-91, 193, 201, 209, 211, 216, 217-19, 220-21, 225, 229-2, 236, 238, 263-6, 280, 283, 287, 303, 305, 313, 328, 342,
folklore 335, 337, 339-40, 346, 352-3
  see also cultural heritage
food aid *see* foreign aid
Food and Agriculture Organization (FAO) 251
food distribution 8, 21
food exports *see* exports
food imports *see* imports
food market, food marketing *see* markets
food prices *see* pricing
food processing 7-8, 10, 17, 38, 52, 56-7, 64, 84, 95, 99, 102, 117, 131, 145, 149-51, 157-8, 160, 164-6, 178, 181, 190, 196, 209, 217, 219, 225-8, 229, 231-4, 236, 241, 243, 252, 255-7, 279, 282, 287, 301, 303, 312-32, 338, 342, 358, 361, 369, 375-6, 381, 388-9, 393
food storage 8, 51, 177, 210-11, 220, 228
food supply *see* agricultural production
food, food chain, food distribution 8, 21, 50-51, 79, 117, 131, 146, 163-4, 196, 200-201, 210, 213-15, 261, 279, 287, 302-3, 311, 318, 321-2, 328, 330, 333-4, 340, 359, 365-6, 374, 379, 386
foreign aid, assistance, cooperation 51, 55-7, 61, 66, 116, 118, 185, 229, 315, 317-18, 333, 380, 386
foreign capital, enterprise, investment 49, 150-51, 155, 230, 233, 251, 275, 298, 312, 319-21, 337, 339, 341, 358, 392-3
foreign exchange 22, 59, 88, 146, 316, 318, 374
  see also trade
foreign tourism *see* tourism
forest, forestry *see* woodcutting and woodland

Former Czechoslovakia *see* Czechoslovakia
Former German Democratic Republic (FGDR) *see* East Germany
Former Soviet Union (FSU) *see* Soviet Union
fragmentation 31, 52–3, 65, 70, 78, 153, 171, 196, 208, 216, 239, 275, 277, 279, 283, 288, 297, 335, 358–9, 361
France 55, 84, 105, 120, 236, 313–17, 321
free market 18, 22, 81, 165, 201
fringe areas *see* backward areas and urban fringe
frontier 23, 35–7, 55, 61–2, 71, 85, 94–5, 98, 104, 111, 114, 134, 160, 163, 197, 243, 296, 298, 373, 378, 392
frontier regions 11, 36, 102, 118
frost 23, 83, 169
fruit 20, 57, 64–5, 79–80, 85–6, 156, 164, 169, 181, 190–91, 197, 216–17, 225, 228–30, 235, 269, 280, 287, 288, 291, 305, 311, 322–5, 328, 331, 333, 337, 342, 348, 358, 374–5, 384, 389
Frýdek Mistek 196–8, 100–101, 106–7
Fund for Agricultural Development (Croatia) 387
Fund for Development of the Carpathian Regions 243
funding institutions 56–8, 136, 221
see also capital, World Bank etc.
furniture 241

Gabrovo 84
Galanta 253–5, 262, 268, 389
Galaţi 6, 204, 224, 226, 228, 234
game *see* hunting
garden 18, 103, 114, 147, 258, 277, 286, 301, 303, 324–5, 365
see also private plot
gas 185, 380
gastronomy *see* catering
Gdańsk 170, 174, 176, 179, 184, 186–8, 190, 193, 195–6, 305–6, 374
Gdynia 305–6
gender 28, 172
see also women
Generale Sucrière 315
German Democratic Republic *see* East Germany
Germans 13–25, 56, 105, 114, 198, 205, 220, 222, 228

Germany 7, 103–5, 118, 198, 236, 302–3, 315–18, 320, 343, 356, 358, 360–61, 365, 370, 373, 390, 392
see also East Germany and West Germany
Gh. Gheorghiu-Dej *see* Oneşti
gherkins 311
Giant Mountains 114
Gîtes de France 339
Giurgiu 205, 212, 224, 234
glasshouses 9, 19, 57, 147, 220, 358
Głogów 21, 33
Gniezno 35
goats 53, 213, 215, 230, 305
Golem 60
Góra Pulawska 25
Gorbachev, M. 83
Goriska brda 288
Gorj 234, 328–9, 345
Gorlice 35
Gorna Or'ahovitsa 85
Gornja Radgona 292
Gorzów Wielkopolski 170, 174, 176, 179, 184, 186–8, 193, 195–6
Gotse Delchev 78
government agencies 140, 177
see also individual agencies
government policy, regulation: agriculture 14–24, 50–52, 54–5, 69–72, 77, 84, 94–9, 108–9, 116, 125–6, 135–6, 165, 202–11, 218, 225–30, 233–46, 257–62, 267, 275–91, 298, 303, 313, 357–9, 361, 363, 366, 368, 387–93
see also Ministry of Agriculture
government policy, regulation: economy and privatization 80–81, 89, 165, 196–8, 227, 348
government policy, regulation: environment *see* environmental policy
government policy, regulation: general 22, 120, 124, 130–31, 138, 141, 148–9, 154, 160, 165, 178, 196, 222, 258
government policy, regulation: population and rural social policy 62–4, 118, 173, 232, 268–71, 297, 367
government policy, regulation: tourism and services 60–61, 232
grants 31, 296, 339
see also loans
grapes 18, 71, 75–6, 209, 217, 225, 269, 280, 287, 291, 318

Graz 275
grazings 1, 9, 13, 71, 75-6, 80-81, 83, 86, 103-4, 116-17, 135, 137, 164, 177, 191, 194, 211, 228, 235, 239, 252, 258, 263-4, 275, 275, 286, 292, 298, 305, 341, 373, 386
  see also mountains
Great Plain of Hungary 3, 31-2, 163, 333
Greece 56-8, 61-2, 71, 81, 84, 320-21
Greeks 61-2
green issues see environmental awareness and sustainability
Green Report on the State of Czech Agriculture 98
gross domestic product see economy
growing season 3, 169
growth area 26, 54, 138, 140, 173, 196, 296, 338, 382, 392
Gurahont 235
Gyöngyös 316
Györ 161
Gypsies 205, 268, 358, 377

Habsburg Empire 6, 35, 274-9, 292, 324
hall 30, 291
Halle 138, 381
Haloze 288
Haná 98, 104, 108
handicrafts 26, 59-60, 232-5, 236, 239, 269, 275, 291, 301, 335, 337-9, 342-3, 346-8, 381, 384
hard currency see foreign exchange
Harghita 204, 234, 239, 335, 345
harvest, harvester 10, 15, 18, 55, 211, 219, 221-3, 228-30, 331, 384, 392
Harz 36, 137
Haskovo 71, 73-4, 79-80, 85
Havlíčkův Brod 97-8, 100-101, 106-7
hay, hayfield see fodder and grazing
hazardous waste see waste
health 15, 26, 63-4, 113, 381
  see also medical services
heathland 137
heavy industry 93, 193
  see also metallurgy
heavy metals 85-6
hedges see biolines
Heineken 318
hemp 9, 228
herbs 305, 311
herds see livestock
heritage 352

  see also cultural heritage and natural heritage
high ground, highlands see hills, mountains and uplands
hills, hillslopes 10, 50-51, 61-2, 71, 102, 108, 117, 160, 203, 204, 207, 210-11, 216, 230, 252, 263-4, 267, 291, 321, 324, 326, 374, 371
hinterland 36, 86, 103, 118
hiring 325, 328, 330
  see also land leasing
historic buildings see architecture
hobby farm 363, 366-7
  see also small farm
Hodonin 97-8, 100-101, 106-7
holiday home, resort 26, 164, 291-2, 295, 309, 339
honey 64, 76, 164
hops 102
hornbeam 252
horses, horseriding 258, 282, 305, 334, 338
horticulture 87, 123
hospitals see medical services
hostel, hotel 60, 198, 350
hot water 57, 220
household 7-8, 37, 50, 52, 78, 118, 134, 148, 154, 163, 200, 202, 204, 205, 207-9, 216, 231, 239, 276, 280, 287, 296, 321, 328, 330, 335, 338-9, 344-5, 350, 365, 374, 384
  see also family farm
household plot see private plot
housing 25, 27, 37, 55, 78, 109-10, 114-16, 118, 124, 136-7, 141, 146, 171, 177, 185, 209-11, 232, 291-2, 301, 326, 328, 332-3, 337, 343, 348-9, 379-80, 382, 391, 393
  see also second homes
Hradec Krákové 97-8, 100-101, 106-7
human resources see population
Humenné 253-5
Hunedoara 205, 234
Hungarians 239, 275
Hungary 1-5, 10, 12-13, 17-19, 22-6, 28-9, 31-4, 36-7, 145-68, 229, 243, 275, 313, 315-16, 318, 320, 345-7, 358, 360, 362-4, 369-73, 377, 381, 388-90, 392
hunting 164, 333, 337-8, 361
hydroelectricity 10, 26, 35, 55, 77, 263, 348, 387

Ialomița 205, 212, 225, 234
Iași 224–6, 234, 235
ice cream 314–15, 321
ideology 12, 15, 21, 32, 124, 131, 141, 149, 165, 200, 358, 361, 365, 384
Ilfov 205, 225, 234
imports 15, 51, 57, 64–5, 77, 102, 173, 213–15, 222, 226–8, 298, 313–16, 369–70, 388–90
Improvement of Regional Economic Structure Programme (East Germany) 135
in-migration *see* migration
incentives 9, 14–15, 160
incomes 15, 18, 36, 50, 59, 61, 74, 89, 116, 128, 146, 149, 152, 154–5, 158–9, 160, 163, 165, 178, 182–4, 189, 201, 209–10, 233, 277, 282, 287, 294, 297, 306, 324, 332, 334, 338, 362–3, 365–7, 371, 374, 383, 389
indebtedness *see* debt
individual farm *see* private farm
industrial-agricultural complexes (Bulgaria) 17
industrial crops 8–9, 14, 50, 52, 72, 76, 193, 269, 280, 286, 305
industrial development, industrialization 6, 8, 15–16, 24, 27, 30, 32, 35, 72, 74, 79, 85–7, 93, 99, 105, 108, 111, 116, 126, 135, 146, 149, 160, 163–5, 171–2, 175, 182, 201, 205, 230–31, 232, 251, 261, 267–8, 275, 276, 278–9, 287, 290, 292, 297, 315, 367–9, 371, 379, 382
see also under sectors
inefficiency 9, 15, 20, 75, 108, 196, 201, 216, 280, 375, 378, 382, 388
inflation 52, 89, 149, 163, 165, 222, 244, 341
information 51–2, 55, 87–8, 95, 135, 147, 152–3, 157, 159, 163, 205
infrastructure 8, 13, 21, 26, 31, 49, 56–61, 63, 66, 108, 116, 124, 135–6, 138, 163–4, 165, 184–7, 190, 193, 196–8, 201, 219, 232, 244, 268, 280, 288, 297, 332–3, 338–9, 346, 351, 376, 378, 382, 385, 391, 393
see also transport, water management
initiative *see* business culture
Inner Borderland (Czech Republic) *see* backward area
innovation 6, 11, 18, 60, 236, 243, 252, 321, 364, 392

insecticides, insects 23, 226, 310
insecurity, instability *see* uncertainty
Insufficiently-Developed Areas (FFRY) 36
integration 17, 136, 146, 151, 163, 164, 230, 348
intensification 1, 10, 16, 19, 23, 31, 38, 102–4, 114, 123, 138, 156, 160, 164, 200, 207, 212 13, 220, 226, 230, 236, 288, 363, 369, 371, 375–6, 383, 386
Interbrew 319
interest 52, 89, 209, 217, 220–21, 317, 339, 341, 364
international aid, assistance *see* foreign aid
International Development Agency 56
International Distillers and Vintners 318
International Finance Corporation 314
international investment *see* foreign investment
international sanctions *see* sanctions
international tourism *see* tourism
international trade *see* trade
Internet 241, 339, 393
investment 7–8, 10–11, 13, 15, 17–18, 25–6, 36–8, 51, 54, 56–9, 65, 74, 80, 128, 130–31, 134, 140, 145–6, 150–51, 156, 160, 164, 166, 182–4, 188, 197, 210, 216, 219, 222, 223, 230, 276, 286, 298, 316, 318, 320–21, 356, 366, 368–9, 371, 374–5, 382–3, 385, 389–90, 392–3
Iron Curtain 11, 111, 114
Iron Gates 333, 393
irrigation 1, 10, 22–3, 50, 56, 58, 66, 82, 183, 191, 210, 213, 214, 223, 228, 237, 252, 357–8, 371, 373, 375
Islam 78
Istanbul 6
Italian-Romanian Adventure East Service 57
Italy 55–8, 60–61, 81, 225, 236, 275–9, 295, 316–17, 334, 358
Iveco 222

Jablonec nad Nisou 3, 97–8, 100–101, 106–7, 387
Jablonna 9
Jambol 85
Jantra 85
Japan 103, 303
Jaruzelski, W. 19
Jaslo 35

Index

Jelenia Góra 3, 170, 174, 176, 179, 184, 186–8, 193, 195–6, 305, 311
Jelšava 266
Jesenice 26
Jičín 97–8, 100–101, 106–7
Jidvei 316, 318
Jihlava 97–8, 100–101, 106–7
Jindřichův Hradec 97–8, 100–101, 106–7
job creation *see* employment and labour
job losses *see* labour shakeout and unemployment
joint venture 56–7, 150, 222, 314, 316, 358, 392
Julian Alps 291
Junker 122

Kalisz 170, 174, 176, 179, 184, 186–8, 193, 195–6
Kamëz 57, 63, 378
Kamienna Góra 305
Kanina 78
Kaplicko 116
Kaposvár 161
Karlovy Vary 97–8, 100–101, 106–7, 387
karst 13, 31, 278, 288, 292, 296, 347
Karviná 97–8, 100–101, 106–7
Kato Aromatik 57, 65
Katowice 170, 173–4, 176, 178–9, 184, 186–8, 192, 195–6
Kavajë 57, 358
Kazanlik 9
Kecskemet 316
key village 31–2, 69
Kielce 170, 174, 176, 179, 184, 186–8, 193, 195–6, 306
kindergarten 32, 309
kiosks 65, 188, 301, 380
Kladno 97–8, 100–101, 106–7
Klatovy 97–8, 100–101, 106–7
K-Mart 318
know-how, knowledge *see* information
Kolín 97–8, 100–101, 106–7
kolkhozy 94, 146, 149, 275–9
  see also collective farms
Komárno 253–5, 268
Konin 35, 170, 174, 176, 178–9, 184–8, 193, 195–6
Korçë 9, 50
Košice 253–5, 262, 266, 268, 271
Kosovo 49, 62
Koszalin 170–71, 174, 176, 178–9, 184–9, 192, 195–6

Kouklen 86
Kovachevitsa 78
Kraft Jabobs Suchard 321
Kraków *see* Cracow
K'rdzhali 72
Kroměříž 97–8, 100–101, 106–7
Krosno 35, 170, 174, 176, 179, 184–8, 193, 195–6
Krynice 309
Kukës 63, 378
Kutná Hora 97–8, 100–101, 104, 106–7
Kuwait 60, 334
Kyustendil 77

Labe 103, 108
labour 5, 8, 11–13, 18–19, 21–2, 31, 51, 53, 57, 93, 135–7, 147–8, 155, 190, 197, 202, 209–10, 216, 217, 222, 231, 239, 256, 280, 335, 360, 364, 367, 372, 374, 378, 384
labour contracts 7, 200
labour intensification 7, 76, 280–82, 301, 364, 368, 384
labour productivity 16, 105, 108, 165, 180, 196, 200–201, 209, 225, 280, 364
labour shakeout 5, 38, 120, 163, 222, 244, 360
labour shortage 13, 26, 296
labour surplus *see* overpopulation
lagging region *see* backward area
lagoons 10, 50
lakes 10, 50, 59, 70, 117, 348–9
  see also Balaton Lake, hydroelectricity and Masurian Lakes
Land Commission (Romania) 205–6, 357–8
land distribution, redistribution 51–2, 54, 56, 64, 122–3, 152–3, 155, 203–4, 255, 275, 356, 358, 378, 387
land drainage *see* drainage
land exchange, market 51–2, 54, 58, 64, 84, 117, 128, 177, 202, 210, 230, 258, 275–6, 279, 283, 297, 304, 359, 361–4, 367–8, 392
Land Law (Romania) 203, 216
land leasing 84, 126–8, 131, 147, 177, 222, 230, 335, 358–9, 362, 364–5, 375, 387, 392
land reclamation *see* reclamation
land reform, settlement 6–7, 14–20, 33, 37, 51–5, 70, 81, 99, 134, 198, 200, 202–11, 255, 267, 274–8, 380

land restitution, rights 37-8, 53-5, 81-2, 84, 95-9, 104, 124-33, 148-50, 203-11, 230, 232, 243, 257-61, 297
land seizure *see* expropriation
Land Settlement and Administrative Company (East Germany) 126, 140
land tax 102, 256
see also differential bonus
land use 3, 109, 111-13, 116, 155, 160, 211-18, 263-4, 271, 288
see also conversion, grazing, woodland etc.
land value 13, 138-40, 160, 197, 253, 258-9, 262, 271, 292
see also pricing
Länder 120, 124, 128, 130, 135-6, 138, 141, 333
landlessness 7, 122, 255-6, 275, 360, 382
landowners, landownership 6-7, 15, 51, 54, 69-70, 74, 78, 81, 84, 89, 95-9, 122, 126, 137-8, 145, 148-50, 155-6, 170-71, 203, 206, 210-11, 217, 256-58, 274-8, 279, 282, 284-9, 297, 313, 356, 358-9, 361-4, 377, 379
landscape management, quality 85-9, 108, 110-12, 116, 135, 165, 268, 333, 335, 337, 340, 386
Landwirtschaftliche Produktionsgenossenschaften (FGDR) 16, 122-3, 125-6, 128, 137, 140
large farm 12, 17-19, 31, 37, 80, 85, 88, 146-7, 155-9, 160, 163, 164, 174, 209, 230, 259, 269, 280, 287, 297, 358-65, 389
see also cooperative farm, state farm etc.
latifundia *see* estates
law, legal system, legislation 6-7, 10, 52, 69, 88, 95, 141, 148-9, 151-5, 157-9, 164, 182, 251, 333, 340-41, 344, 350-51, 356-7, 378
lead 72, 86
leather 261, 348
legal title 54, 56, 70, 81, 204, 210, 274, 310, 357
Legnica 170, 174, 176, 178-9, 184, 186-8, 193, 195-6
legumes *see* vegetables
Leipzig 138, 381
leisure facilities 25, 123, 257
Leninváros *see* Tiszaujváros
Less Favoured Areas 130, 140, 233-4

Levice 253-5
Lezno 170, 174, 176, 179, 184, 186-8, 193, 195-6
Liberal Democratic Party (Slovenia) 298
Liberec 23, 97-8, 100-101, 106-7
lifestyle *see* living standards
light engineering 26, 31, 165, 196
light industry 21, 26, 252, 263, 301, 333, 391
lignite 33
limestone 170
linkage 17, 225, 256
Liptov, Liptovský Mikuláš 253-5, 263, 268
liquid sewage *see* sewage
liquidation *see* closure
Lithuania 378
Litoměřice 97-8, 100-101, 106-7
littoral *see* coast
livestock 6, 8-9, 11, 15, 16-17, 19, 22-3, 26, 30, 49-51, 55-6, 74, 76, 80-81, 84, 95, 102, 108, 111, 123, 128, 130, 140, 146-7, 159, 172, 200-201, 205, 207, 211-16, 217-19, 221, 225, 228-30, 230-31, 235, 238, 243, 252, 255, 257, 263-4, 280-82, 287, 298, 305-7, 341, 365, 374, 388, 391, 392
livestock breeding, rearing 8, 50, 78, 81-2, 84, 177, 202, 217-18, 220, 228, 235, 258, 264, 303, 342, 371, 375-6, 385
livestock fattening 8-9, 213, 218
livestock feed *see* fodder
living standards 21, 56, 78, 108, 125, 135-6, 141, 160, 165, 172, 182, 184, 195, 244, 257, 259, 298, 306, 368, 377, 379
Ljubljana 292
loans 56, 66, 88-9, 153, 196, 209, 216, 217, 219, 276, 314, 322, 339, 341, 365, 390, 392
see also foreign aid
local authority, local government 17, 22, 26, 30, 33, 36, 114, 165, 173, 198, 204, 233, 243, 280, 283, 286, 291, 325-6, 333, 339, 344, 347, 357, 366-7, 387, 391-2
Łódź 170, 173-4, 176, 179, 183-4, 186-8, 193, 195-6, 306
loess 71, 120, 140, 252
Łomża 170, 174, 176, 179, 184-8, 193, 195-6, 306, 309
lorries 357

Louny 97-8, 100-101, 106-7, 387
Lovech 71, 73-4, 79-80
low ground, lowlands 9, 51, 54, 57, 62, 103, 109, 117, 205, 207, 216, 237, 252, 257, 268, 271, 288-4, 324, 335, 358, 378
Lublin 170, 174, 176, 179, 184, 186-8, 190, 193, 195-6, 374
Lučcncc 253-5, 268
lucerne 263
Ludogorsko Plateau 86
Luduş 226
Lusatian Mountains 114
Lushnje 9, 50

Macedonia 2, 29, 370, 372-3
machine-tractor stations 15-16, 57, 221, 233, 391, 393
  see also agricultural machinery
machinery parks *see* machine-tractor stations
Magdeburg 120, 138, 140, 381
maintenance 16, 123-4, 221
maize 9, 23, 55, 75-7, 79-80, 102, 210, 216, 228-30, 238, 263-4, 280, 282, 287, 320, 326, 330, 374, 388, 392
malt 263
malting barley *see* barley
mămăligă (Romania) *see* maize
management 17, 19, 25, 57, 87, 89, 95, 102-3, 110-12, 117, 148-50, 154, 158, 160, 164, 231, 279, 298, 333, 347, 350, 381, 386, 388
manufacturing *see* industry
manure 9, 23, 59, 87, 207
Maramureş 204, 232, 234, 345-6, 352
margarine 320
marginal areas *see* backward areas
Maritsa 74, 85-6
market demand, market functions, marketing, market share 7-9, 17-18, 20, 32, 50, 52, 56, 59, 65, 82, 88, 98, 108, 116-17, 126, 131, 135-6, 146, 149, 151, 158, 163, 176, 178, 181, 189-91, 193, 196, 204, 209, 210, 213-15, 217, 220-21, 223-6, 229, 231, 235, 241, 251, 255, 259, 262, 266-7, 269, 271, 279, 280, 286, 297-9, 300-303, 305-6, 309-11, 314, 316-22, 326, 331, 333-4, 339-40, 346-7, 359, 361, 364, 368-75, 379, 383, 389
  see also free market

market economy *see* economy and private enterprise
market gardening 71, 82, 138
  see also vegetables
market reform *see* privatization, reform and restructuring
marshland 170
Martin 253-5, 268
mass media 61, 339
Masurian Lakeland 16, 311
Mátra 317
maximum prices 22, 202
meadow 17, 75, 103-4, 258, 263-4, 277, 280, 286, 373
meat, meat processing, meat products 14, 20, 53, 75-6, 79, 84, 117, 151, 164, 177, 181, 190, 215-19, 225, 228, 232, 241, 266-7, 280, 283, 288, 298, 297, 311, 313, 345, 374-5
mechanization *see* agricultural machinery
Mecklenburg-Vorpommern 120-21, 129, 132-7, 140
medical services 15, 30, 56, 58, 63, 243, 291, 309, 335
medicinal plants 65, 269, 302
Medieval 6, 113
Mediterranean 38, 59, 288
medium-size farm 7, 255
Mehedinţi 234, 328
Mělník 97-8, 100-101, 106-7
melons 52-3, 79
metallurgy 72, 86, 163, 352
Michalovce 253-5, 268
middle class 203-4, 229
Middle East 38, 99
Miercurea Ciuc 223-7, 243
migration 5-6, 11, 27-8, 30, 32, 34, 35-6, 58, 60-62, 66, 78, 116, 134, 162, 163, 172, 193, 196, 205, 231-2, 244, 269, 290, 296, 332, 338, 378, 391
military bases, zones 23, 124, 137
military farms (FCS) 94, 99
milk 75-6, 86, 98, 117, 120, 164, 181, 191, 215, 216, 227, 229, 266-7, 282, 288, 302, 305, 314-15, 374, 384, 387-8
milling, mills 231-4, 279, 315, 348, 366
  see also flourmilling
mineral water 316, 337, 347
minerals, mining 24, 30, 38, 72, 86, 111, 124, 137, 140, 163
  see also under individual minerals
minifundia *see* small farms

Ministry of Agriculture 56, 64, 77, 81, 84, 94, 98, 103, 116–17, 153, 219, 233, 266, 341, 345
minorities 61–2, 72, 275
  see also by cultural, ethnic group
Miskolc 161
Mladá Boleslav 97–8, 100–101, 106–7
mobility *see* migration
model farm *see* demonstration farm
modernization 6, 8, 16, 147, 158, 226–30, 231, 291, 298, 312–14, 316, 318–19, 321, 323, 352, 359, 375
Moldavia 3, 6, 204, 223, 335, 345, 352
Moldova 225
monastery 232, 346, 352–3
Monfredonia 57
monoculture 8, 23, 50
monopoly 55, 83, 151, 178, 180, 182, 325, 367
Montana 71–3, 79–80
Montenegro 62
Moravia 95, 98, 103–8
mortality 62, 79
Most 97–8, 100–101, 106–7, 360, 384
motel 26, 198
Mountain Farmers' Association (Romania) 343
mountain farmers, mountains 1, 3, 8–9, 13, 20–21, 28, 31–2, 50, 54, 58–60, 78, 85, 103, 109, 160, 164, 201, 203, 207, 210–11, 223, 227, 232, 233, 237, 238, 243, 252, 256, 258, 262–4, 267, 278, 290, 292, 296, 311, 321, 324, 331, 340–48, 361, 386–9
mountainology 233–8
Mountainology Research Institute (Romania) 235, 342
Mozirje 291
multifunctional *see* diversification
municipalities *see* local authorities
munitions 318
Muntenia 204
Mureş 204, 226–9, 234, 236, 329, 345
Murfatlar 318
Murska Sobota 292
museums 60, 339
musical instruments 233
mutton 305

Náchod 97–8, 100–101, 106–7, 387
Nakło 315

National Agency for Agricultural Products (Romania) 216, 220, 229
National Agency for Mountainous Regions (Romania) 233–8
National Association for Rural Ecological and Cultural Tourism (Romania) 237, 345–7
national park 24, 112, 137, 177, 312, 333, 350, 386
National Peasant Christian Democrat Party (Romania) 231
National Salvation Front (Romania) 203, 231
natural decrease, increase 62–3, 160, 334
natural heritage 59, 112
natural resources *see* physical conditions
nature reserves *see* protected areas
navigation 10
Năvodari 223, 226
Neamţ 227, 234, 345, 352
Negreşti (Satu Mare) 239
Nestlé 320–21
Netherlands 55, 84, 230, 260–61, 313, 316, 318
New Economic Mechanism (Hungary) 18
New Holland 222
New *Länder see* East Germany
new towns 32, 241, 243
niche market 59, 65, 302, 311, 338
nickel 86
Nineteenth Century 6, 78, 113, 274–8
Nitra 16, 252–5, 259–60, 264–5
nitrates 87, 219–21
Nógrád 18, 153, 161
nomenklatura see communist
non-agricultural activities *see* diversification, pluriactivity and individual activites
non-chemical systems 56, 58
non-governmental organization (NGO) 243, 381
non-viable village (Romania) 32–3
North Bohemia 98–9, 104, 111, 114, 387
Nové Zámky 253–5
Novi Sad 333, 393
Nový Jičín 97–8, 100–101, 106–7
Novy Targ 21
Nowy Sącz 35, 170, 174, 176, 179, 184, 186–8, 193, 195–6, 309
nursery *see* kindergarten
nutrient levels 87

Index 417

Nyírhegyháza, Nyírség 160, 161
Nymburk 97-8, 100-101, 106-7

oak 252
oats 252
occupation 78
Ócsa 14
Odobeşti 217
Ogosta 85
oil, oil plants 191, 219, 243, 262-6, 312-13, 320, 387-8
old people *see* retirement
oleaginous crops 9, 55
olive, olive oil 375, 387
  see also oil plants
Olomouc 97-8, 100-101, 104, 106-7
Olsztyn 170, 174, 176, 178-9, 184, 186-9, 190, 193, 195-6, 306, 374
Olt, Oltenia 223, 234, 238, 344-5, 352-3
Oneşti 32
onions 156
Opava 97-8, 100-101, 106-7
open market *see* free market
opencast *see* quarry
Opération Villages Roumains 236, 345-7
Opole 170, 174, 176, 179, 184, 186-8, 193, 195-6
Oradea 223-5, 226, 242, 243
Orava 263, 266
orchards 9-10, 18-19, 24, 147, 211, 216, 223, 229
organic farming 59, 65, 109
organization 15, 95, 147-9, 152, 157, 180-81, 209-10, 257, 317
Organization for Economic Cooperation and Development (OECD) 65, 302
Orikum 60
Ostrava 97-8, 100-101, 106-7, 319
Ostroleka 170, 174, 176, 179, 184, 186-8, 193, 195-6
Ottoman Empire 6, 78
out-migration *see* migration
overpopulation, overstaffing 7, 18, 117
owner occupation *see* private farm
Ownership and Use of Farmland Act (Bulgaria) 69-72
ownership certificate *see* legal title

packaging 313, 316
painting 233

Pannonia 288, 291
  see also Great Plain of Hungary
paprika 156
Parâng 237, 340, 350, 386
Pardubice 97-8, 100-101, 106-7
parliament 69, 149
part-time farming *see* pluriactivity
partition *see* subdivision
Paşcani 227
pastoral farming *see* livestock
pastoral landscape *see* landscape
pasture *see* grazing
Pătârlagele 325, 330-31
patriarchal system 78
Pazardjik 77
pears 328
peasant-worker *see* commuter
peasant, peasant farm, peasantry 6-8, 11, 17-19, 21, 25, 31, 51-2, 69, 71, 81, 146, 148-9, 151, 156, 165, 200, 202-3, 205, 209, 217, 220, 226, 231, 232, 255-6, 274-8, 298, 324-6, 356-7, 361, 363, 367, 374, 393
Peasants' Mutual Aid Cooperatives (Poland) 181, 190
Pécs 161
Pelhřimov 97-8, 100-101, 106-7
pension *see* boarding house
pensioners, pension funds *see* retired people
People's Party (Slovenia) 298
pepper 220
perfume 9
peripheral areas *see* backward areas
pesticides 22, 87-8, 124, 194, 238, 317, 375, 382, 385
pharmaceuticals 57, 65
pharmacy *see* rural services
Philip Morris 320
phosphates 87, 219-21
physical conditions, resources 50-51, 84-8, 102-3, 108, 145, 160, 163, 166, 169-70, 216, 227, 252, 275, 278, 288, 322, 373, 379, 381
  see also climate, soil etc.
Piatra Neamţ 223-5, 243
pigs 8, 17, 76-7, 79, 81-2, 108, 130, 191, 213, 215-19, 226, 230, 264, 282, 287, 288, 305, 330, 359, 371, 376, 385, 388, 390
Piła 35, 170, 174, 176, 179, 184, 186-8,

193, 195-6
pilot projects 55, 229, 236, 342-3, 345
  see also demonstration farms
pine 23
Piotrków Tryb. 170, 174, 176, 179, 184, 186-8, 193, 195-6
Piran 291
Písek 97-8, 100-101, 106-7
Piteşti 224
plains 3, 58, 71, 74, 79, 169, 324, 326, 340
planning 8, 11-12, 17, 33-8, 52, 64, 83, 87, 99, 109, 111, 115, 136, 200, 209-11, 233, 256, 291-2, 338, 361, 368, 379, 381, 387
plant breeding 10, 15
Płock 35, 170, 174, 176, 178-9, 184-8, 193, 195-6
Ploieşti 224, 226, 320
Plovdiv 71, 73-4, 77, 79-80, 86, 320
plums 321-32
pluriactivity 27, 131, 140, 146, 153, 155-6, 159-60, 163, 164, 171-2, 178, 197, 216
Plužna 295
Plzeň 97-8, 100-101, 106-7, 318
Podhale 35
podzol 1, 170
Pohronský Inovec 266
Poland 1-5, 9, 11-13, 16-17, 19-25, 27-9, 31-5, 37, 94, 105, 134, 169-99, 301-13, 318-20, 332, 341, 343, 346-7, 359, 363, 365, 367, 369-82, 384, 388-92
Poles 25
political clout, political parties 17, 72, 89
  see also government and individual parties
political stability see stability
Polje pri Vidocah 294
pollution 22-4, 26, 35, 72, 85-9, 185, 266, 303, 352, 382
  see also environmental damage
'pollutor pays' principle 87
Pologne Hongrie Actions pour la Reconversion Economique (PHARE) 56-7, 66, 116, 221, 229, 243, 345-8, 351, 385, 392
Pomerania 31
ponds see lakes
poor see poverty
Poprad 253-5, 268
population 3, 38, 50, 56, 62, 72, 74, 77, 99, 111, 135, 138, 160, 172, 175-6, 178, 181, 193, 205-6, 251, 268, 276, 287, 288, 290, 292, 296-7, 333, 356-7, 380-81
  see also active population, depopulation, gender, migration etc.
population surplus see overpopulation
pork 120, 218, 223
Porto Palermo 60
ports 6, 74
post office 30, 290
Pošumavi 116
potatoes 17, 52, 75-6, 79, 102, 130, 181, 191, 214-17, 223, 252, 262-3, 265, 280, 282, 288, 305, 313, 324, 371-2, 374, 376
poultry, poultry houses 18-19, 53, 65, 76-7, 79, 81-2, 108, 117, 130, 147, 151, 213, 215-19, 226, 229, 266, 280, 287, 368, 385
Považská Bystrica 268
poverty 25, 49, 54, 56, 62, 159-60, 205-6, 229, 267-8, 275, 305, 338, 360, 366-7, 376-8, 380-81, 383-4, 389, 393
  see also backward regions
power see electricity, government, state socialism etc.
power station 23, 220
  see also hydroelectricity
Poznań 35, 170, 174, 176, 179, 184, 186-8, 190, 193, 195-6, 320, 374-5
Prachatice 97-8, 100-101, 106-7
Prague 95, 97-8, 100-101, 103, 106-7, 109, 113, 115, 118, 318, 332, 382
Prahova, Prahova Valley 205, 234, 347-8
Prehistory 6, 252
Prekmurje 288
Přerov 97-8, 100-101, 106-7
Prešov 253-5, 268
Příbram 97-8, 100-101, 106-7
price-fixing, price liberalization, pricing 7-8, 14, 18-19, 21-2, 53, 64, 84, 98, 103, 108-9, 146, 148-50, 164, 166, 173, 178, 182, 186, 189-91, 198, 201-3, 210-11, 213-15, 218-21, 223-31, 233, 235, 243, 255, 259, 266, 271, 298, 303, 306, 309, 312, 314-15, 317, 322, 324-5, 342, 348, 361, 371, 374-5, 387-8
  see also maximum prices
Prievidza 253-5
primary schools see schools

private enterprise, sector 31, 64, 149, 165, 173, 189, 205, 227, 258, 268, 317–18, 325, 334, 359, 380
  see also small- and medium-sized enterprises, private farm etc.
private farm, property 5–6, 9, 12, 17, 20, 25, 28, 53–4, 57, 94, 98–9, 117, 124, 130, 155–9, 164, 171, 173, 181, 191, 200, 204–11, 217, 221, 227, 230, 241, 256–61, 266, 268–9, 271, 274–80, 279–82, 284–91, 298, 304–5, 312, 314, 331, 333–50, 358–60, 362–8, 374, 376, 378, 383, 385, 387, 389
  see also peasant farm
private plot 8, 11, 14, 17, 18, 20, 49–50, 75, 78, 81, 83, 94, 146, 155, 158, 163, 200–201, 207, 326, 362, 365–6, 368, 382
privatization 50, 54, 56–8, 75, 80–81, 83–4, 87–9, 95–8, 117, 124–8, 138–42, 149–57, 171, 173–91, 203–11, 216, 217, 222, 225, 229, 243, 251, 257–61, 264, 271, 283, 298, 301–3, 316–17, 319, 359, 369, 374, 385, 389
Producer Association (Croatia) 387
production plan (Romania) 201–2
production *see* agricultural production
profitability, profits 15, 18, 22, 27, 52, 65, 83, 88–9, 102, 123, 153, 160, 165, 210, 219–21, 222, 262, 283, 286, 288, 318, 361, 366, 371, 375, 382, 388
Property with Justice National Association (Albania) 54
property, property relations, property rights 18, 70, 98, 114, 123–4, 142, 147, 152–3, 155–7, 159, 255, 257–8, 275, 279, 362, 364
  see also legal title and by type of ownership
proprietors *see* landowners
Prostěov 97–8, 100–101, 106–7
protected areas, protection 23–4, 36, 111–12, 137, 319, 340, 369, 382, 386, 388
  see also biosphere reserves, national parks etc.
protein 17, 216, 218, 230
Prussian Empire 6
Przemysl 170, 174, 176, 179, 184–8, 193, 195–6
Ptuj 292
public houses 115, 290, 378
Pulawy 178

pulses 52
purchasing centres (Poland) 181, 188
purchasing, purchasing power *see* consumption

qualifications, quality 11, 15, 65, 102, 124, 146, 152, 163, 184, 196, 216, 226, 243, 252, 256, 263–4, 266, 279–80, 286, 302, 305, 312–14, 316–17, 321–2, 324, 331, 333, 339–40, 358–9, 379–80, 386, 389
quarrying 33, 99, 111, 124, 137
  see also mining
quota 12, 22, 181, 201–2, 374

rabbits 305, 384
radiation 85
Radom 35, 170, 174, 176, 179, 184, 186–8, 193, 195–6, 320
Radovljica 291
railway 6, 21, 58, 113, 233, 251, 332, 347, 352
rain, rainfall 10, 58, 169, 328
  see also acid rain
Rakovník 97–8, 100–101, 106–7
Râmnicu Vâlcea 224–6, 350
rape 120, 305, 388
rationalization *see* restructuring
raw materials 8, 10, 108, 287, 322
  see also under individual commodities
Razgrad 79, 84, 321
rearing *see* livestock rearing
recession 89, 163
reclamation 10, 50, 70, 111
reconstruction 38, 80, 116, 209, 333
Recovered Territories 25
recreation 13, 108–9, 113–15, 118, 135, 138, 172, 291–2, 382
  see also leisure and tourism
recycling 24
redundancy *see* unemployment
reform 7, 61, 88, 178, 181–3, 187, 195–8, 201, 369, 374
  see also land reform
refugees 122
refurbishment *see* regeneration
regeneration 62, 118, 136–7, 209, 279, 380, 391, 393
Reghin 227, 329, 342
region, regional development, regional planning 26, 33–7, 59, 71–3, 79–80, 93, 95, 110–11, 116, 118, 145, 231,

243, 255, 271, 318
regional inequality, variation 35, 134, 138, 141, 160–63, 187, 193, 274, 288, 296, 298, 393
   see also backward areas
regional specialization 38, 50
   see also agricultural regions
religion 6, 95, 339, 348
   see also church
remissions, remittances 61, 65
remoteness, remote area 140, 142, 241, 335
   see also accessibility
renewable energy 116, 135
renovation *see* reconstruction
rent 102, 147, 155–6, 158, 231, 258
reorganization *see* restructuring
repair, repair centres 25, 57, 65, 78, 81, 105, 123, 136, 175, 190, 210, 348
   see also maintenance
Research and Information Institute for Agricultural Economics (Hungary) 153, 163
research, research station 87, 93, 109, 153, 163, 189, 204, 228, 235, 239, 331, 335, 342, 347
reserves *see* protected areas
reservoirs *see* hydroelectricity and lakes
resettlement *see* land settlement
Reşiţa 224, 329, 342
resort, resort village *see* holiday resort and individual resort
resources, resource base *see* labour, finance, physical conditions and population
restaurant *see* catering
restitution 54, 84, 115, 142, 148, 151, 153–6, 165, 229, 335, 350, 356–9, 362, 365–7, 371, 373, 379
   see also land restitution
restoration *see* reclamation and reconstruction
restructuring 8, 11, 66, 120, 124–42, 145, 222, 251, 271, 286, 291, 312–13, 358, 372, 388, 391
   see also economic growth, restructuring and rural planning, development
retailing *see* shopping
Retezat 340
retirement 134, 152–5, 158, 163, 207, 210, 268, 292, 295, 319, 339, 359, 361–2, 365

retraining *see* training
revitalization *see* regeneration
revolution 8, 18–19, 202–3, 210, 233, 275, 322, 341, 350, 356–7
Rhodope 78, 85
rice 55, 216, 392
rich *see* affluent
Rimavská Sobota 253–5, 268
risk 52, 117, 157, 341, 364
rivers 10, 70
   see also under individual rivers
roads 26, 63–4, 66, 70, 116, 124, 184, 216, 232, 236–9, 241, 251, 291, 317, 324, 338–9, 352
Rodna 352
Rokycany 97–8, 100–101, 106–7
Roman 236
Romania 1–6, 9–10, 12–13, 15, 22, 25, 28–9, 32–3, 200–250, 316–17, 321–51, 357–8, 361, 365, 369–70, 372–4, 376–7, 381, 383, 390–91, 392
Romanian Principalities 6
roses 9
Rostock 27
Rožňava 253–5
Rrogozhinë 57, 358
rubbish *see* waste
rural amenities, facilities *see* rural services
rural business *see* small- and medium-sized enterprises
rural communities, settlement 7, 21, 25–33, 77, 87, 111, 113, 136, 138, 141–2, 160, 163, 166, 181, 216, 230–40, 256, 269, 277, 279, 301, 332, 335, 338–9, 342, 350, 356, 362–3, 367, 379–81, 384
   see also villages
rural credit *see* credit
Rural Development Agency (Slovakia) 268–9, 271
rural development, planning, transformation 5, 22, 49, 51–66, 80–90, 94–118, 124–33, 135–8, 235–7, 251, 267–71, 288–96, 326, 333, 335, 341, 352, 357, 376–7, 385, 387–93
rural economy *see* under sector
rural housing *see* housing
rural industry 26, 113, 116, 162, 233, 237, 239, 241, 268–9, 291, 332, 335, 341, 342, 368, 379, 381, 391–2
   see also industrialization
rural infrastructure, services 25–6, 31–2, 78, 116–18, 123, 134–7, 141, 164, 172,

Index 421

180–81, 187–90, 193–8, 230–40, 268, 301, 333, 342, 379–80, 386, 391–3
see also post office, schools, shopping etc.
rural migrants *see* migration
rural population 146–7, 160–61, 171–2, 195–8, 230–40, 267–1, 288–92, 375–92
see also agricultural population, rural communities, villages etc.
rural regions 34–5, 145, 160–63, 193, 290
rural restructuring *see* rural development, planning
rural settlement *see* villages
rural society *see* rural communities
rural tourism *see* agrotourism and tourism
Ruse 17, 71–2, 79–80
Rychnov nad Kněžnou 97–8, 100–101, 106–7
rye 9, 71, 264
Rzeszów 170, 174, 176, 179, 184–8, 193, 195–6

Sachsen 120–21, 129, 132–3, 135–7, 140, 381
Sachsen-Anhalt 120–21, 129, 131–3, 140, 136–7, 361. 381
Sächsische Schweiz 137
Saľa 266
Sălaj 204, 234
salami 322
salaries *see* wages
Salgótarján 161
sanctions 62
sands 238
sanitation 23, 344
Sânnicolaul Mare 228
Sanok 35
Satu Mare 224, 234, 243
savings bank *see* bank
Savinjske Alpe 291
Scandinavia 317
scenery 24, 113, 118, 335, 337, 340
Schierke 36
school farms 94, 99
schools 27, 30, 51, 63, 78, 134, 163, 174, 235, 290–91, 306, 342
see also education and kindergarten
Schooner Capital Group 320
science *see* research and technology
scrub 14, 216, 239
second economy 200–201
secondhand vehicles 58, 64

second homes 26, 113–15, 117–18, 332–3, 335, 365, 381
Second World War 13–14, 50, 77, 122, 196, 200, 233, 255, 274–80, 279, 292, 303, 324, 347
security 11, 25, 36, 79
see also frontiers
seeds 94, 164, 196, 217, 220, 227, 257, 259, 305, 311
Seita Group 320
self-sufficiency *see* subsistence
selling *see* market
Semily 97–8, 100–101, 106–7
Semlac 209
Senica 253–5
Serbia 62, 392–3
Serbs 62
Sereď 266
serfdom, serfs 6, 200, 274
see also feudalism
services 93, 109, 116, 136, 155, 158–9, 180, 187–90, 231, 232, 276, 291, 297, 335, 338, 348, 366, 368, 374, 380, 393
see also rural services, transport etc.
setaside *see* fallow
settlement pattern *see* urban, village and individual settlements by name
sewage, sewerage 23–4, 26, 63, 108, 116, 124, 184–6, 197, 311, 380, 382
Sfântu Gheorghe 224–6, 243
sharecropping 7, 200–201, 357
shareholder, shares 153–4, 157, 160, 202–3, 205, 222, 229, 258, 260, 282, 319, 358–9, 362–3, 367
sheep, sheep pens 8, 10, 19, 52–3, 76–7, 79, 81–2, 130, 147, 191, 194, 213, 215, 218, 235, 264, 266, 301, 341, 345, 347
shipping 6
Shkodër 9, 50
shopping, shops 26, 30, 115, 123, 134, 180–81, 188–9, 198, 210, 225, 228, 230, 290–91, 306, 310–11, 313, 318, 321, 324, 337–40, 343, 380
shortage 60, 115, 118, 171, 181, 221, 226, 366
Sibiu 204, 224, 234–7, 345, 350
Siedlce 35, 170, 174, 176, 179, 184, 186–8, 193, 195–6
Sieradz 170, 174, 176, 179, 184, 186–8, 193, 195–6
Sighet 243
Silesia 21, 169, 360

Silistra 77
sistematizare (Romania) 33, 201, 233, 239, 242–3, 335, 341
Skierniewice 170, 174, 176, 179, 184, 186–8, 193, 195–6
skill 51, 95, 134, 147, 196, 229, 233, 235, 244, 322, 326, 348–9, 361, 367–8, 388, 390, 392
Sklarska Poręba 23
Slănic 348
Slatina 224
slaughterhouse *see* meat packing
Slivnica 85
Slobozia 224
Slovenske Gorice 288, 292
Slovakia 2, 7, 16, 198, 243, 251–73, 302, 314–15, 318–19, 347, 359, 369–70, 378, 388–9, 392
Slovenia 1–2, 6, 13, 21, 26, 28–31, 274–300, 359, 370, 372–3, 375, 390
Słupsk 170–71, 174, 176, 178–9, 184–8, 193, 195–6
slurry 18, 124
small- and medium-sized enterprises (SMEs) 25, 32, 56, 59, 65, 105, 110, 115, 118, 135, 146, 160, 197, 210, 229, 232–5, 236–9, 239, 241, 268–9, 296, 301, 317, 322, 335, 347, 361, 384, 391
see also kiosks, shops and small farms
small border traffic 18
small business *see* small- and medium-sized enterprises
small farm 7, 10–11, 17–19, 51–3, 56, 58, 76, 84, 87–8, 98, 124, 128, 146–9, 155–6, 163–6, 178, 181, 183, 197, 200, 202, 220, 231–4, 235, 255, 257, 274, 278–9, 279, 282, 287, 288, 298, 301, 316, 324, 335, 350, 360–62, 378, 383–4
Smallholders' Party (Hungary) 148, 165
smallholders, small scale production 7, 18, 20, 117, 122, 156, 202, 238, 256, 274, 331
see also peasant farm and small farm
Smolyan 77
smuggling 55, 378
snow 10, 169, 219
Soča 295
social amenities, benefits *see* welfare
social change, system 5, 25, 93, 136, 148–50, 166, 171, 241, 282, 292
social classes, relations 7–8, 16, 113, 123, 146, 268, 274, 279

Social Democratic Party (Slovenia) 298
social fallowing 13, 296
social issues, problems, unrest 50, 145, 165, 172, 193, 268, 275
social services *see* welfare
socialist agricultural enterprise, socialist agriculture 22, 25, 30–31, 74, 76, 80, 83, 94–105, 117, 123, 163, 170, 178, 183, 191, 201, 256, 275, 280, 280–85, 291, 292, 298, 331, 357, 359
see also cooperatives
socialist sector and socialist economy, socialist organization 16–17, 20, 145–6, 201, 274, 292, 298
Sofia 71, 73–4, 79–81, 85–6
soft drinks *see* drinks
soil compaction, pollution 85–7, 124, 303–5, 324, 342
soil, soil fertility 1, 3, 16, 22–3, 55, 62, 64, 71, 85–6, 98, 102–4, 111, 120, 123, 138–40, 160, 170, 177, 185, 216, 228, 239, 251–2, 255, 378, 382, 385–6, 392–3
Sokolov 97–8, 100–101, 106–7
Sombor 333
Somogy 160, 163–4, 333
Sopot 306
Sopron 18, 37, 161
Souhindol 84, 362
South Bohemia 98, 104
Soviet Occupation Zone *see* East Germany
Soviet Union 10, 14, 30, 32, 35, 83, 94, 99, 181, 275, 291, 314, 316, 390
see also Belarus, Ukraine etc.
sowing 55, 219, 221, 307, 392
soya beans 53, 230, 305, 375
Spain 120, 316–17
specialists *see* professionals
specialization 9, 14, 16, 50, 201, 211, 213, 258, 283, 287, 298, 334, 357, 360–61, 365, 371, 375
spirits 157, 312, 318
Spiš, Spišská Nová Ves 253–5, 263, 266
splitting *see* subdivision
spoil heaps 111
spontaneous settlements (Albania) 63, 66
sport 114, 337
see also winter sports
spruce 23
Sredna Góra 85
stability 18, 49, 109, 112–13, 116–17, 140, 151, 269, 276, 322, 386, 391

Stalinism, Stalin, J. 15, 20, 356
Stâna de Vale 348
Stará Lubovňa 253-5
Stara Planina 85
Stara Zagora 320
State Agricultural Property Agency (Poland) 359
state agriculture *see* socialist agricultural enterprises, state farms etc.
state farms 7-9, 11-14, 16, 18, 25, 31, 49, 54, 56-8, 78, 94-5, 98-9, 102, 105, 117, 150, 170-71, 177-9, 191-2, 201-3, 205, 218, 229, 241, 243, 256, 258-61, 264, 266, 269, 275, 314, 317, 357-9, 365, 371, 373, 376-9, 389
  see also Volkseigene Güter
State Land Fund (Poland) 177, 359
state-owned enterprises, state socialism 7-38, 49-51, 55, 150-51, 173-4, 180, 187-90, 196, 201, 233, 275, 316-17, 320
  see also nationalization and planning
State Ownership Fund (Romania) 220, 222
Stella Artois 319
steppe 1, 6, 10
stock, stock exchange *see* shares
stockpiling *see* food storage
Stoeneşti 325
storage 10, 15
  see also food storage
Strakonice 97-8, 100-101, 106-7
structural adjustment, change *see* restructuring
students 115, 261
Subcarpathians 204, 240, 321-32
subcontracting 26
subdivision 117, 171, 200, 78
subletting *see* land leasing
subsidies 14, 17-19, 21-2, 89, 102-3, 109, 117, 128, 135-7, 146, 148-9, 163, 176, 217-19, 213, 220-21, 226, 243, 297, 317, 333, 361, 369, 371, 389-91
subsistence 6, 8-9, 15, 17-18, 31, 53, 94, 210, 216, 231, 262, 271, 280, 282, 287, 288, 298, 313, 321, 362-4, 374-6, 378, 383, 386
subventions *see* subsidies
Suceava 204, 224, 227, 234, 243, 343-6, 348-9
Sudetanland, Sudeten Mountains, Sudety 16, 21, 23, 169, 177

sugar beet 9, 53, 71, 75-6, 79, 102, 169, 191, 209, 216-17, 226-8, 263-5, 280, 287, 305, 315, 371, 373-4
sugar, sugar refining 17, 151, 226-8, 312-13, 388, 390
summer 164, 238, 252, 333
Šumperk 97-8, 100-101, 106-7
sunflowers 9, 53, 75-6, 79-80, 86, 209, 216-17, 219, 221, 228, 238, 358, 365
supplementary establishments (Hungary) 146
supplementary income *see* pluriactivity
surplus 6, 8, 17, 50, 116, 201-2, 209, 216, 228, 243, 255, 288, 324, 326, 331, 374, 376, 384-5, 390
sustainability 59, 108, 135-6, 141, 145, 164, 232, 237, 302, 331, 333-4, 350-51, 381, 386
Suwałki 170, 174, 176, 179, 182, 184, 186-9, 193-6
Svidnik 253-5, 268
Svitavy 97-8, 100-101, 106-7
Switzerland 84, 103, 220, 225, 236, 343, 384
Szabolcs-Szatmár-Bereg 18
Szczecin 170-71, 174, 176, 179, 184, 186-8, 190, 193, 195-6, 374, 386
Szeged 36, 161, 333
Szolnok 161
Szombathely 161

Tab 164
Tábor 97-8, 100-101, 106-7
Tachov 97-8, 100-101, 104, 106-7, 373, 387
Tăndărei 236
Tanne 36
tanya (Hungary) 31-2, 156, 159
Târgovişte 224, 233
Târgu Jiu 224
Târgu Lăpuş 239
Târgu Mureş 224, 227
tariffs 149
Tarnobrzeg 170, 174, 176, 179, 184, 186-8, 193, 195-6
Tarnów 170, 174, 176, 179, 184, 186-8, 193, 195-6, 306
Tate & Lyle 315
Tatra 198, 332, 387
taxation, tax-raising 31, 34, 55, 72, 146, 149, 153, 158, 221, 226, 228, 233, 237, 256, 275, 296, 319, 326, 339, 344, 347,

361, 363, 390
technical crops *see* industrial crops
technological assistance, technology 6, 10, 51-2, 55, 65, 87, 95, 149, 158, 163, 171, 178, 180, 184-7, 197, 213, 217, 226-8, 228, 230, 232, 236, 257, 283, 286, 288, 297, 302, 313, 316, 320, 334, 359, 385, 388
telecommunications, telephones 27, 58, 137, 186-8, 197, 241, 340, 352, 379-80, 392-3
Teleorman 225, 234
television *see* mass media
temperature 3, 102, 169, 219
tenants, tenure 54, 98, 115
Teplice 377
terracing 10, 14, 50-51, 61, 374
terrain *see* hill, mountain, topography etc.
tertiary sector *see* services and rural services
textiles 26, 31, 163, 233, 241, 261
Thuringen 26, 120-21, 124, 129, 131-3, 140, 361, 381
Timiş, Timişoara 204, 212, 222-5, 226, 234, 235
Tirana 9, 50, 56-7, 62-3, 378
Tisa, Tisza 23, 352
Tiszaújváros 32
title *see* legal title
tobacco 9, 64, 71, 75-6, 79-80, 82-3, 151, 156, 312, 375, 378
Tokaj 164, 333
tomatoes 75-6, 86, 220, 238
tools *see* agricultural equipment
topography 51, 278, 288, 290
Topoľčanky 258
Topoľčiany 253-5
Topolnica 85
Topolovgrad 85
Toruń 303, 306
totalitarian *see* communist
Tourism Research Institute (Romania) 338
tourism, tourists 13, 26, 35, 38, 54, 57, 59-61, 74, 89, 113-16, 118, 135, 138, 140, 164-5, 236-7, 241, 271, 296, 311, 317, 331-51, 358, 379, 381-2, 384, 386
see also agrotourism and holiday resort
tourist accommodation *see* boarding house, hotel, holiday resort etc.
towns *see* new towns and urban centres

toxic gases *see* air pollution
tractors 56-7, 76, 182-4, 190, 213, 214, 219, 221-4, 235
trade 9, 35, 82, 172-6, 222, 251, 258, 301, 311, 316-17, 324-6, 331, 359, 361-2, 388-90
see also commerce, distribution, exports and imports
trade centre 53
trading companies *see* farming companies
training 53, 56-8, 65, 117, 134-6, 163, 229, 302, 339, 343, 346
Transdanubia 163-4, 333, 392
transfer *see* conversion
transformation 8, 11, 30, 56, 69, 95, 98, 109, 152-3, 156, 163, 164, 182, 255, 257-8, 279, 296, 297
transhumance 347
transition 7, 49, 65, 69, 80, 117-18, 163-4, 175, 228, 232, 251, 255, 291, 296, 297, 331, 364, 369-9, 375, 384, 392
transport 14, 17, 26, 31, 38, 56, 58, 64-5, 70, 105, 109, 115, 118, 136, 138, 163, 178, 201, 226, 241, 288, 291, 301, 306, 324, 333, 335, 342, 347-8, 350
Transylvania 204, 212-14, 223, 236, 320, 328, 335, 345, 350
Třebíč 196-8, 100-101, 106-7
Trebišov 253-5
Trenčín 253-5
Treuhandanstalt (East Germany) 126, 139
trg (Slovenia) 290
Tribeč 266
Trieste 30, 275, 288
Trnava 253-5
Trotuş 352
Tuborg 225
ţuică (Romania) 321-32
Tulcea 204, 212, 224, 229, 234, 345
turkey 313
Turkey, Turks 72, 85-6, 236, 316-17, 320, 358, 382
see also Ottoman Empire
turnips 305
Turoszów 23
Tychy 32

Uherské Hradiště 97-8, 100-101, 106-7
UK 84, 315-19
Ukraine 198, 243, 320, 347, 392
uncertainty 52, 54, 61, 117, 142, 153,

158-9, 210, 219, 251, 360, 364, 366, 371
undevelopment, underdevelopment *see* backward areas
unemployment 5, 64-5, 88, 108, 110, 116, 118, 134-5, 138, 140, 145, 154, 159-60, 163, 177-9, 189, 197, 230, 267-8, 311
unification 120-22, 124, 126, 128, 130, 134, 137-9, 316, 360, 365-7, 378-80, 382, 391-2
Unilever 313, 320
Union of Democratic Forces (Bulgaria) 358
United Biscuits 320
United Farming Enterprises (Slovakia) 256, 258
United Nations 62, 266
university 306, 380
unskilled 17
uplands 50-51, 56, 62, 102, 374
Upper Silesia 306
uranium 140
urban areas, centres, dwellers 9, 11, 13, 24, 26-7, 30, 32, 34, 37, 50-51, 61, 63, 65, 73-4, 80, 84, 108, 110-11, 115, 117, 136, 140, 147, 155, 164, 171, 173, 180, 186, 190, 196, 201-2, 205-7, 230, 239, 239, 241, 243-4, 263-4, 268-9, 271, 290-91, 292, 296, 301, 312, 318, 357-8, 360, 362, 365-6, 374, 379-80, 381-2, 391, 392
urban fringe 13, 19, 24, 103, 113, 116, 134, 138, 142, 190, 205, 263, 291-2, 322, 324, 331-2, 335,
Urziceni 236
USA 21, 60, 84, 105, 267, 275, 319
Ústi nad Labem 97-8, 100-101, 106-7, 387
Ústi nad Orlicí 97-8, 100-101, 106-7
utilities, utility services *see* electricity, gas, water etc.

vacation home *see* holiday home and second home
Valassko 116
Valcea 234, 238, 328, 340, 345, 352
Valea Calugărească 316, 318
Valea Doftanei 236, 342, 348
Vălenii de Munte 235, 342, 348
value *see* land value
Varna 71, 73, 79-80, 82, 86-7, 321

Vas 160
Vaslui 224-6, 234
Vatra Dornei 235, 343
veal 120
vegetable oil *see* oil plants
vegetables 9, 19-20, 52-3, 64-5, 71, 79-80, 82, 85-6, 147, 156, 164, 169, 190-91, 197, 209, 211, 223, 225, 227-32, 238, 243, 263-6, 287, 288, 305, 311, 375-6, 384
see also individual types
vegetation *see* phyiscal conditions and woodland etc
Veliko Turnovo 77, 85
Veľký Krtíš 253-5, 268
Venezia Giulia, Venice 275-9
vernacular architecture *see* architecture
Veszprém 161
veterinary services 19, 183, 228
viable holdings 58, 81, 122, 124-5, 128-33, 135, 200, 266, 359, 364-5, 367, 376
Vienna 275
villages 7, 17-18, 20, 22, 24, 30-31, 34, 36, 58, 61-2, 65, 114-15, 136-7, 147, 156, 160, 172, 181, 196-8, 201, 209, 230-40, 257, 268, 275, 277, 290-91, 301, 306, 321, 324, 326, 333, 335, 337, 341, 352-3, 367, 377, 391
see also key village and tourist village
vineyards, viticulture 9-10, 14, 18-19, 79, 83-4, 147, 164, 211, 216, 217, 223, 229, 277, 280, 286, 288, 298, 316-19, 322, 331, 333, 361, 375-6
Visegrád 388
visitors *see* tourists
Vlorë 9, 50
vodka 318
voivodship (Poland) 34, 169-98
Volkseigene Güter – VEG (East Germany) 16, 123, 125-6
Vorë 57
voucher privatization *see* coupon privatization
Vrancea 204-5, 212, 217, 234-7, 317, 328, 345
Vranov nad Topľou 253-5, 266, 268
Vsetín 97-8, 100-101, 106-7, 387
Vyškov 97-8, 100-101, 106-7

wages 7, 12, 15, 19, 65, 134, 154, 178, 207, 363
Wałbrzych 170, 174, 176, 179, 184,

186–8, 193, 195–6
walking 135, 333, 350, 361, 379
Wallachia 335
war, war damage 25, 49, 255
warehouse 179, 189
see also food storage
Warsaw, Warszawa 9, 17, 35, 170, 173–4, 176, 179, 182–5, 186–8, 192, 195–6, 306, 314
waste 24, 58, 108, 111, 114
water pollution 85, 124
water power *see* hydroelectricity
water, water management 9–10, 15, 22–4, 26, 58, 87, 108, 110, 112, 116, 124, 137, 184–6, 210, 223, 226, 232, 237, 252, 263–4, 267, 317, 328–30, 335, 344, 348, 371, 378–80, 385
see also drinking water and wells
waterlogging 23
wealth *see* affluence
weather *see* climate
weekend cottage *see* holiday home and second home
welfare 15, 25, 123, 131, 136, 154, 158, 160, 163, 165, 174–5, 177, 231, 268, 279, 361, 363, 367, 378–80, 381–82, 384, 388, 390
wells 58, 184, 379–80
West 37, 59, 65, 81, 84, 125, 313, 315, 318, 321, 389, 390
West Bohemia 98, 103–4
West Germany 27, 36, 120, 123–4, 126, 131, 134, 136, 141
West Slovakia 259, 262, 266
Western Europe 6, 9, 30, 62, 93, 120, 180, 228, 274, 288, 302–3, 311, 316, 346, 350–51, 388–9, 393
see also European Union
wheat 23, 75–7, 169, 182, 214, 219, 220, 228, 238, 263–4, 280, 282, 287, 388
wholesaling 65, 180, 189, 197, 223, 301, 313, 379
Wielkopolska 306
wildlife 59, 87, 252, 340, 361
see also hunting
wind 23
see also erosion
wine 83, 225, 228, 243, 280, 283, 287, 316, 318, 328, 337
see also vineyards
winter 77, 169, 219, 263
winter sports 335, 337

Wolverhampton & Dudley Breweries 319
women 134, 136, 142, 160, 163, 172, 205, 231, 269, 332, 362, 364, 381
woodcutting, wood processing 25, 38, 164–5, 229, 233, 239, 288, 347–9, 384
woodland 7, 9, 13, 22–4, 56, 59, 70, 76, 87, 103, 109–13, 125, 135–7, 164–5, 172, 203, 211, 214, 233, 235, 237, 252, 263–4, 267, 271, 274–9, 278, 279, 283, 292, 299, 332–3, 337, 341, 347–9, 373, 386–7
wool 53, 76, 215. 390
workers, working population *see* active population and labour
working conditions *see* living standards
workshops 60, 81, 115, 159, 233, 291, 343, 366, 367, 378, 384
World Bank 15, 56, 58, 66, 84, 196, 218–20
World Conservation Union 112
world market *see* market
World War One, Two *see* First World War *and* Second World War
Wrocław 170, 174, 176, 179, 184, 186–8, 193, 195–6, 320
Wrocławek 170, 174, 176, 179, 184, 186–8, 193, 195–6, 306

yield 1, 15, 55, 72, 85–6, 102, 130, 193–5, 209, 219, 221, 227, 257, 280, 282, 298, 316, 371–2, 381, 392
yoghurt 314–15
young people, youth 15, 28, 51, 62, 78, 87
Yugoslavia 1–5, 7, 11–13, 15, 21, 24, 28, 35–6, 274–9, 296, 297, 314–15, 318–19, 333, 347, 359, 363, 369–70, 372–3, 376–80, 388–90, 392

Zagreb 319
Zala, Zalaegerszeg 161, 164
Zalău 224–6
Zamość 170, 174, 176, 179, 184, 186–8, 193, 193–6
Žďar nad Sázavou 97–8, 100–101, 106–7
Zemplén 164
Zhivkov, T. 69
Žiar nad Hronom 253–5
Zielona Góra 170, 174, 176, 179, 184, 186–8, 192–3, 195–6
Žilina 253–5
zinc 72, 86, 295

Žitava 252
Zlaté Moravce 270–71
Zlín 97–8, 100–101, 106–7
Znojmo 97–8, 100–101, 106–7
Zofin 111

zoning *see* agricultural regions and specialization
Zucker 315
Zvolen 253–5
Żywiec 318